DANIEL
A COMMENTARY AND SURVEY SERIES

THE TIMES OF THE GENTILES
&
THE TIMES OF JERUSALEM

Premillennial

Dispensational

King James Version

Based on sound and Influential Bible Institute Material from a Past Generation

By

Dr. Jack Moorman

> **Disclaimer**
>
> The author of this work has quoted the writers of many articles and books. This does not mean that the author endorses or recommends the works of others. If the author quotes someone, it does not mean that he agrees with all of the author's tenets, statements, concepts, or words, whether in the work quoted or any other work of the author. There has been no attempt to alter the meaning of the quotes; and therefore, some of the quotes are long in order to give the entire

Copyright © 2017 by Jack Moorman
All Rights Reserved
Printed in the United States of America

ISBN 978-0-9985452-3-3

All Scripture quotes are from the King James Bible.

No part of this work may be reproduced without the expressed consent of the publisher, except for brief quotes, whether by electronic, photocopying, recording, or information storage and retrieval systems.

Address All Inquiries To:
THE OLD PATHS PUBLICATIONS, INC.
142 Gold Flume Way
Cleveland, Georgia, U.S.A.
Web: www.theoldpathspublications.com
E-mail: TOP@theoldpathspublications.com

DEDICATION

To the dear people of Bethel Baptist Church in Wimbledon, London, who love the *Blessed Hope*.

TABLE OF CONTENTS

- DEDICATION 3
- TABLE OF CONTENTS 4
  - The Temple Mount and Eastern/Golden Gate viewed from above the Mount of Olives 10
- INTRODUCTION 10
  - DANIEL, THE PROPHET 10
  - Daniel 10
  - The Apostle John 11
    - THE TWOFOLD MESSAGE AND CHANGE OF LANGUAGE IN THE BOOK OF DANIEL 11
    - THE TWO MAIN DIVISIONS OF DANIEL 11
    - DANIEL 2 AND 7: THE SPAN AND END OF THE TIMES OF THE GENTILES 12
    - DANIEL 3 TO 6: THE CHARACTER OF THE TIMES OF THE GENTILES 12
    - DANIEL 9: TWO ATTEMPTS TO DISLODGE THE CORNERSTONE OF CHRONOLOGY AND PROPHECY 13
    - ONE: A GENTILE CHRONOLOGER PUSHED DANIEL BACK IN TIME BY ADDING NEARLY A CENTURY TO THE PERSIAN PERIOD 13
    - TWO: A JEWISH CHRONOLOGER BROUGHT DANIEL FORWARD BY CUTTING MORE THAN A CENTURY FROM THE PERSIAN PERIOD 14
    - DANIEL IS MOVED TO A "BACK ROOM" IN THE HEBREW BIBLE 14
    - EIGHT BAISIC FACTS THAT SHOW THE CURRENTLY USED PTOLEMAIC CHRONOLOGY IS RIDDLED WITH CONTRADICTIONS 16
    - CURRENT PTOLEMAIC CHRONOLOGY: LIVING ON BOTH SIDES OF A LONG GAP .. 17
      - There are "many sprightly 130-year-olds" 17
    - BIBLICAL CHRONOLOGY: FOUNDED ON THE CORNERSTONE. 18
- COMMENTARY 20
- THE TIMES OF THE GENTILES 1- 7 20
  - A. THE BEGINNINGS OF THE TIMES OF THE GENTILES 1 20
  - DANIEL 1. DANIEL AND HIS THREE COMPANIONS IN BABYLON 20
    - The First Deportation 1:1,2. 20
    - The Attempt to Indoctrinate and Assimilate 1:3-7. 21
    - The Steadfastness of Daniel 1:8-16. 23
    - Four Shining Lights in Babylon 1:17-21. 25
- THE TIMES OF THE GENTILES 1-7 27
  - B. THE OVERVIEW OF THE TIMES OF THE GENTILES 27
  - (Aramaic Language Begins) 2 27
  - DANIEL 2. THE METALLIC COLOSSUS 27
    - The "Forgotten" Dream 2:1-13. 27
    - The Request and Prayer of Daniel 2:14-23. 30
    - Daniel is Brought before Nebuchadnezzar 2:24-30. 33
    - Daniel Reveals the Dream 2:31-35. 35
    - The Metallic Colossus: Five Empires During The Times of the Gentiles 35
    - Daniel Interprets the Dream 2:36-45. 37
    - The Gold of Babylon. 38
    - The Silver of Media-Persia. 39
    - The Brass of Greece. 39
    - Brass or Bronze! 40
    - Alexander the Great is Shown the Book of Daniel! 41
    - The Iron of Rome. 43
    - The Roman Empire at the Height of its Power and Extent 43
    - The Roman Empire as Divided by Diocletian 44
    - The Iron Chunks of the Roman Empire Continue unto the Time of the End 44
    - The Iron and Clay of Revived Rome. 45
    - What is the Clay? 46
    - The Ten Toes Become Ten Horns! 47
    - GDP of Ten Leading Nations 49
    - The Stone Mountain of The Messiah's Kingdom. 49
    - This is a Corner and Foundation Stone 51
    - This is a Mountain Stone 51

A COMMENTARY AND SURVEY SERIES: DANIEL

- This is a Stumbling Stone 52
- Daniel and His Friends are Promoted 2:46-49 52

THE TIMES OF THE GENTILES 1-7 55
C. THE CHARACTERISTICS OF THE TIMES OF THE GENTILES 3-6 55
1. A TIME OF ENFORCED FALSE RELIGION: NEBUCHADNEZZAR'S IMAGE 3 55
DANIEL 3. THE GOLDEN IMAGE ON THE PLAINS OF DURA 55
- The Setting Up of The Great Image 3:1-7 55
- Nebuchadnezzar's 666 Image on the Plain of Dura 57
- "Worship" Gatherings During the Times of the Gentiles 59
- Whatever Happened to the Blood? 60
- It may be called "worship," but it is far removed from the worship of the Bible! 63
- The Deliverance of The Hebrews 3:19-27 66
- The Son of God or "a son of the gods" 70
- The Proclamation of Nebuchadnezzar 3:28-30 71

THE TIMES OF THE GENTILES 1-7 74
C. THE CHARACTERISTICS OF THE TIMES OF THE GENTILES 3-6 74
2. A TIME OF EXPANSION AND INSTABILITY: 74
NEBUCHADNEZZAR'S MADNESS 4 74
DANIEL 4. THE TREE AND THE BEAST VISION 74
- Nebuchadnezzar's Proclamation 4:1-3 74
- Nebuchadnezzar's Dream: The Circumstances 4:4-9 75
- Nebuchadnezzar's Dream: The Description of Babylon 4:10-18 77
- Dubai: A Middle Eastern Illustration of Latter Day Babylon? 78
- Burj Khalifa 78
- Buildings Above 1000 Feet (the Height of London's Shard) in Five Skyscraper Cities 79
- (The Skyscraper Center, May 2015. Including buildings under construction.) 79
- New York: A Western Illustration of Latter Day Babylon? 80
- What City is Like This Great City? 80
- The Woman in the Basket Prophecy 81
- Babylon – Kabbalah – Freemasonary Link! 82
- Is the Roman Goddess Libertas the Woman in the Basket ? 83
- Libertas 84
- The Rays of the Sun Signifying Illumination 84
- The Masonic Cornerstone of the Statue of Liberty 85
- Libertas in Paris to be disassembled, packed into 214 cases and shipped to New York 86
- Parallels with the Zechariah Prophecy 87
- Libertas Lifted to Her Pedestal and Base 88
- "Is not this great Babylon that I have built" (Daniel 4:30)? 88
- The Times of the Gentiles Begin and End with a Beast 90
- Nebuchadnezzar's Dream: The Interpretation 4:19-27 93
- Nebuchadnezzar's Dream: The Fulfilment 4:28-33 96
- Nebuchadnezzar's Great Babylon 97

THE TIMES OF THE GENTILES 1-7 102
C. THE CHARACTERISTICS OF THE TIMES OF THE GENTILES 3-6 102
3. A TIME OF SACRILEGE: BELSHAZZAR'S FEAST 5 102
DANIEL 5. BABYLON'S LAST NIGHT, THE HANDWRITING ON THE WALL 102
- Kings of Babylon During the Seventy Years 103
- The Feast of the King 5:1-4 103
- The Word of the LORD 5:5-9 104
- The Handwriting on the Wall 106
- The Counsel of the Queen 5:10-12 107
- The Appearance of the Prophet 5:13-16 109
- The Reprimand of the King 5:17-24 110
- The Meaning of the Words 5:25-31 112

THE TIMES OF THE GENTILES 1-7 115
C. THE CHARACTERISTICS OF THE TIMES OF THE GENTILES 3-6 115
4. A TIME OF ENSHRINING BAD LAWS: 115
DARIUS' LIONS DEN 6 115
DANIEL 6. DANIEL IN THE LION'S DEN 115
- The Persian Empire 115

TABLE OF CONTENTS

    Daniel's Elevation by Darius 6:1-3. 116
    Daniel's Entrapment by a Bad Law 6:4-10. 117
    Daniel's Descent into the Lion's Den 6:11-17. 119
    Daniel's Deliverance from the Lion's Den 6:18-24. 121
    The King's Decree and Daniel's Prosperity 6:25-28. 123

THE TIMES OF THE GENTILES 1-7 127
D. The End of the Times of the Gentiles: Gentile Perspective 7 127
DANIEL 7. FOUR ENDTIME BEASTS AND THE ADVENT OF THE MESSIAH 127
    The Interpretive Key to Chapter 7 127
    The Great Sea and the Four Beasts 7:1-8. 129
    The Key Characteristics of the Four Beasts 132
    The Four Beasts of Daniel Seven 133

THE LION AND EAGLES WINGS. 134
    The Britain View 134
    The Britain and America View 135
    The Eagle has Fallen ! 136
    THE BEAR 136
    THE LEOPARD 137
    Is it a German Leopard? 138
    Is it an Islamic (Arab/African) Leopard? 140
    The Four Wings on the Back of the Leopard Egypt: Syria, Jordan, Iraq and Saudi Arabia 141
    The Leopard Nations and Psalm 83 142
    The Psalm 83 Coalition 144
    The "Pricking Briers" Around Israel 145
    The Gog and Magog Coalition 145
    The Rapidly Approaching War 146
    Israel's Borders Expand 148
    Prisoners of War are Taken 148
    The Nations are Astonished 149
    The Setting of the Stage for the Antichrist 149
    A Signal to Christians 150
    Islamic State 151
    ISIL, not just ISIS, The Plot Thickens! 151
    How is Islamic State Supplied ? 152
    Just How Extensive Are ISIS' Supply Lines? 153

THE FOURTH BEAST, THE TEN HORNS AND THE LITTLE HORN 154
    The Beast Itself 155
    Religious Unity and the Fourth Beast 156
    The Ten Horns 158
    The Little Horn 159
    The People of the Prince that Shall Come and The Recent Muslim Antichrist View 160
    Do Early Sources Show Arabic Romans Destroying Jerusalem in AD 70? 160
    Distinguishing Between the Legions and Auxiliaries in the Roman Army 162
    The Roman General Titus 162
    Before AD 70, Titus Served in Germania (southern) and Britannia 163
    The Roman Advance on Jerusalem 163
    The Roman Legions that Attacked Jerusalem 164
    V Macedonian Legion (European) 164
    XII Fulminata Legion (Eastern) 165
    Inscription in Boyukdash, (near Baku) Azerbaijan left by XII Fulminata 165
    XV Apollinaris Legion (European) 165
    X Fretensis Legion (Judaea, Syria) 165
    The Theory that the AD 70 Conquerors of Jeruasalem were Arabic, and that the Future Antichrist will be Muslim is Not Sustained by the Evidence 166
    The Destruction of Jerusalem in 70 AD 167
    Catapulta, by Edward Poynter (1868) 168
    Relief of the Sack of the Temple on the Arch of Titus in Rome 169
    The Daniel Chapters 7/8/9/11 Link to the Origin of the Coming Antichrist 169
    The Four Divisions of Alexander's Empire 170
    The Ancient of Days and the Son of Man 7:9-14 172

The Four Recountings of Daniels Vision in Chapter 7	180
The First Inquiry and Answer: The Four Beasts Generally 7:15-18.	181
The Second Inquiry: The Fourth Beast and Little Horn 7:19-22.	182
The Answer: The Extent of the Fourth Beast, the Little Horn and the Kingdom of the Messiah 7:23-28.	184
II THE TIMES OF THE GENTILES REGARDING JERUSALEM 8-12	**189**
A. THE END OF THE TIMES OF THE GENTILES:	**189**
JEWISH PERSPECTIVE (Hebrew Resumes) 8	**189**
DANIEL 8. THE VISION OF THE RAM, GOAT AND LITTLE HORN	**189**
IF I FORGET THEE O JERUSALEM !	190
An Overview of Biblical Jerusalem	**190**
The Jebusites	190
Mount Moriah	190
Geography	191
Jerusalem's Four Mountains	191
Two Other Mountains	192
Jerusalem's Deep Valleys	192
The Walls and Gates of Jerusalem	193
The Walls and Gates During Nehemiah's Time Superimposed upon the Current Walls	193
Jerusalem at the Time of Christ	194
The Gates and Walls of Old Jerusalem Today	195
LION'S GATE	195
HEROD'S GATE	196
DAMASCUS GATE	196
NEW GATE	196
JAFFA GATE	197
ZION GATE	197
DUNG GATE	198
GOLDEN / EASTERN GATE	198
THE TEMPLE MOUNT, THE WORLD'S FLASHPOINT !	199
The Temple Mount and Eastern/Golden Gate	199
Viewed from the East Above the Mount of Olives	199
The Eastern Gate and the Ancient Holy of Holies	199
Tradition	200
The Sealed Gate	200
The East Gate and the Return of the Messiah	200
The Research of Asher Kaufman	200
TheTemple Mount looking west from above the Golden Gate, showing the alignment of the Dome of the Tablets	201
Detail of the Dome of the Tablets	202
(A) The Dome of the Tablets, (B) The Dome of the Rock, (C) The El Asqa Mosque	203
A Possible "Compromise Temple" Location	203
The Foundations of the Earlier Eastern Gate	204
The Vision Given To Daniel 8:1-14.	**205**
The Introduction to the Vision	**206**
The Persian Empire	207
Shushan Today	207
The Vision of the Ram with Two Horns.	208
The Ram and Goat Vision	208
The Vision of the Goat.	209
Alexander's Death After Attempting to Rebuild Babylon	210
Alexander's Empire Divided Among His Four Generals	211
Is the Little Horn Antiochus Epiphanes?	211
The Vision of the Little Horn.	212
The Threefold Origin of Antichrist as Given in Daniel	212
Are Both Good and Evil Angels Cast Down During the Tribulation?	213
Three Common But UntenableViews of the 2300 Days	215
A Look At The Numbers	216
Will the Antichrist and False Prophet Make an Evening and Morning Telecast from the Temple Mount for 2300 Days?	216

TABLE OF CONTENTS

As Titus Did in 70AD, Antichrist Will Terminate Israel's Christ-less Sacrifices: 217
The Three Accounts of the Olivet Discourse Compared..217
Both 70 AD and the End Time Tribulation are Described in Luke; But no Description is Given of the Temple Desecrations..218
Only the Tribulation (and with the Tribulation Temple Descration) is Described in Matthew and Mark 218

II THE TIMES OF THE GENTILES REGARDING JERUSALEM 8-12 229
A. THE END OF THE TIMES OF THE GENTILES: JEWISH PERSPECTIVE (Hebrew Resumes) 8 229
B. THE SEVENTY WEEKS OF YEARS UPON JERUSALEM AND THE JEWISH PEOPLE 9..229
DANIEL 9. THE PROPHECY OF THE SEVENTY WEEKS..229
Israel and Her Seventy Weeks is the Clock by Which God Marks Prophetic Time 229
The Time and the Occasion of the Seventy Weeks Prophecy 9:1,2................................230
The Intrusion of Ptolmy's 93 Years into Daniel's Prophecy 232
Daniels Prayer: His Confession 9:3-15...233
Daniels Prayer: His Petition 9:16-19..238
Daniel Prayed for Jerusalem Itself to be Rebuilt Immediately (Not Only the Temple)..........239
About the Time of the Evening Oblation 240
Consider The Vision ! 242

The Seventy Week Prophecy 243
The Seventy Weeks: Its Overview..243
The Millennial Temple of Ezekiel 40-48 248
Three Events Between the End of the Sixty-Ninth Week and the Beginning of the Seventieth Week..248
The Decree of Cyrus is the Commandment that Launches the Seventy Weeks 249
CURRENT PTOLEMAIC CHRONOLOGY: LIVING ON BOTH SIDES OF A LONG GAP. 252
Sir Robert Anderson's "Solution" for the Overlap..252
BIBLICAL CHRONOLOGY: BASED ON THE CORNERSTONE. 253
The Seventy Weeks: Seven Weeks followed by Sixty-Two Weeks. 255
The Seventy Weeks: After Sixty-Nine Weeks, (1) The Messiah is Cut Off, (2) Jerusalem is Destroyed, (3) Desolations Unto the Time of the End..255
AND UNTO THE END OF THE WAR DESOLATIONS ARE DETERMINED 259
Auschwitz-Birkenau...259
The Jewish Holocaust Country by Country: The National WWII Museum, New Orleans..........259
Dresden..260
The Seventy Weeks: The Last and Seventieth Week 9:27...261
Zion Square Jerusalem circa 1939, To be Renamed Tolerance Square..........................264
The Annual Jerusalem Gay Pride Parade..264
The Antichrist Will Be All That His Names Say He Is!..265
The End and Objective of the Seventy Week Prophecy is Very Good 266

II THE TIMES OF THE GENTILES REGARDING JERUSALEM 8-12 267
C. The Desolations and Final Blessing of Jerusalem 10-12..267
1. Desolations and The Glory of Christ 10 267
2. Desolations: Future to Daniel 11:1-35..267
3. Desolations and Final Blessing 11:36-12:13..267
4. Desolations and The Glory of Christ 10 267
DANIEL 10. INTRODUCTION TO THE LAST PROPHECY OF DANIEL 267
The Time of the Prophecy and the State of the Prophet 10:1-3.......................................267
The Vision of Christ 10:4-9. 269
The Appearance of Christ in Revelation 1:13-16...270
The Appearance of Christ in Revelation 19:11-16..270
The Appearance of Christ in Daniel 10:5,6..270
The Threefold Ministry to Daniel 10:10-21..272
Daniels Strengthening in Chapter 10 273

II THE TIMES OF THE GENTILES REGARDING JERUSALEM 8-12 278
C. The Desolations and Final Blessing of Jerusalem 10-12..278
1. Desolations and The Glory of Christ 10 278
2. Desolations: Future to Daniel 11:1-35..278
3. Desolations and Glory: Future to Us 11:36-12:13..278
DANIEL 11. JERUSALEM'S CONFLICT: ANCIENT DAYS AND LAST DAYS 278

Where in Daniel 11 is the Beginning Point of the Tribulation?......278
Two Precursor Desolations: Antiochus (175-164 BC) and Titus (70 AD)......280
The Primary Desolation: Antichrist During the Tribulation......280
Five Kings of Persia followed by a Mighty King of Greece 11:1-4......280
Darius the Mede (and Cyrus)......281
The First King After Daniel: Cambyses......282
Persian Seal of Cambyses Capturing Pharaoh Psamtik III......283
The Second King After Daniel: Pseudo Smerdis......283
Behistun Inscription of Darius Hystaspe Placing Foot on Pseudo Smerdis......284
The Third King After Daniel: Darius Hystaspes......284
Relief of Darius Hystaspes in Persepolis......284
The Fourth King After Daniel: Xerxes......288
Relief of Xerxes at Persepolis......288
The Persepolis Complex Built Mainly by Xerxes......289
Compare the Palaces of Darius and Xerxes......289
Xerxes Land and Sea Invasion of Greece......290
The Lashing of the Hellespont (Dardanelles)......291
Not the Time nor the King of Esther's Marriage!......292
How Many Years from Xerxes to Alexander the Great?......293
The Brevity of the Persian Evidence......293
The "Shortness" of the Jewish Evidence......295
The Inherent Weakness in the Greek Evidence......296

The Mighty Grecian King: Alexander the Great......**298**
Coin of Alexander the Great, British Museum......298
Note Again: Josephus' Account of Alexander the Great Meeting the Jewish High Priest and Being Shown the Book of Daniel......299
Alexander Meeting the Jewish High Priest at the Gates of Jerusalem......300
Alexander's Empire Divided Among His Four Generals......301
The Seleucid and Ptolemaic Wars From Alexander to Antiochus Epiphanes 11:5-20......301
The Seleucid Dynasty; Seleucus I to Antiochus Epiphanes......302
Coin of Antiochus III the Great, British Museum......303
Antiochus Epiphanes: A Forerunner to the Antichrist 11:21-35......305
A Summary of the Vile Person......306
Antiochus Epiphanes: His Early Reign 11:21-23......307
Antiochus Epiphanes: His Expanding Power 11:24-28......308
Antiochus Epiphanes: His Waning Power and Persecution of the Jews. 11:29-31......310
Antiochus Epiphanes: Israel in the Storm From That Day to the Last Days 11:32-35......311
The Maccabean Revolt......312
Antiochus Epiphanes, A Biblical Foreview of the Coming Antichrist......315
Several Examples of the Age Spanning Gaps in the Bible......317
The Willful King, the Antichrist of the Last Days 11:36-45......318
The Willful King is Not the King of the North......318
The Religion of the Willful King 11:36-39......319
Does "Not Regard the God of His Fathers" Refer to the Greek Orthodox Church ??......321
Will the Huge Homosexual Agenda of Barak Obama Prepare the Way for the Antichrist?......323
The God of Forces at the Beginning of the Times of the Gentiles......326
The Warfare of the Willful King 11:40-45......327

Warfare in the Middle of the Tribulation: Daniel 11:40-45 and Ezekiel 38, 39.......**328**
THE INVASION OF RUSSIA & HER ALLIES......328
II. THE INVASION BY THE ARMIES OF THE WILLFUL KING......331
Six Steps of Antichrist to World Dominion and Utter Dissolution......332

II THE TIMES OF THE GENTILES REGARDING JERUSALEM   8-12......**336**
C. The Desolations and Final Blessing of Jerusalem 10-12......**336**
1. Desolations and The Glory of Christ 10......**336**
2. Desolations: Future to Daniel 11:1-35......**336**
3. Desolations and Glory: Future to Us 11:36-12:13......**336**
DANIEL 12. THE CHARACTER AND TIMES OF THE GREAT TRIBULATION......**336**
ABOUT THE AUTHOR......**346**

DANIEL
THE TIMES OF THE GENTILES *AND* THE TIMES OF JERUSALEM

The Temple Mount and Eastern/Golden Gate viewed from above the Mount of Olives

INTRODUCTION

DANIEL, THE PROPHET

Daniel, like Ezekiel was a Jewish captive in Babylon. He was of royal or princely descent (Dan 1:3). For his rank and personal qualities he was trained for palace service. In the polluted atmosphere of an oriental court he lived a life of singular holiness and usefulness. His long life extended from Nebuchadnezzar to Cyrus. He was a contemporary of Jeremiah, Ezekiel (Ezek 14:20), Joshua, the high priest of the restoration, Ezra, and Zerubbabel.

Daniel's name means *God is Judge*. This accords with the subject of the book: judgement upon the Gentile world kingdoms, and particularly the judgement that will fall upon the earth in the days of Christ's Return. Note in connection with this the *Jehovah/Elohim* contractions in the four Major Prophets. The first two, Isaiah and Jeremiah, prophesied *in the Land*; while Ezekiel and Daniel prophesied *outside the Land* in Babylon during the captivity. It is providentially significant that *Jah* is compounded with Isai**ah** and Jeremi**ah**; but *El* is compounded with Ezeki**el** and Dani**el**. In the Abrahamic Covenant, Jehovah pledged the Land to Israel (cp. Gen 13:14-16). Thus, *in the Land*, Isaiah and Jeremiah bear the specific Covenant Name; but *outside the Land*, Ezekiel and Daniel bear the more general Name.

Daniel was *greatly beloved*, and with this unique statement he is the Old Testament counterpart to the Apostle John, *the disciple whom Jesus loved*. This is Heaven's singular honour for the men through whom the books composing the two primary pillars of Bible Prophecy were written (Daniel and Revelation).

Daniel

- *I am come to shew thee; for thou art **greatly beloved** (Dan 9:23).*
- *O Daniel, a man **greatly beloved** (Dan 10:11).*
- *O man **greatly beloved** (Dan 10:19).*

The Apostle John

- one of his disciples, **whom Jesus loved** *(Jhn 13:23).*
- the other disciple, **whom Jesus loved** *(Jhn 20:2).*
- that disciple **whom Jesus loved** *(Jhn 21:7).*
- the disciple **whom Jesus loved** *(Jhn 21:20).*

Daniel was esteemed for his spiritual wisdom and prayer life. When the king of Tyre was upbraided for his arrogant claim of wisdom, he is rebuked with the scornful: *Thou art wiser then Daniel* (Ezek 28:3). And, with Jerusalem on the brink of destruction: *Though these three men, Noah, Daniel, and Job, were in it, they should deliver but their own souls by their righteousness, saith the Lord GOD* (Ezek 14:14).

THE TWOFOLD MESSAGE AND CHANGE OF LANGUAGE IN THE BOOK OF DANIEL

Daniel is the indispensable introduction to New Testament prophecy, the themes of which are: the apostasy of the Church, the manifestation of the Antichrist, the Great Tribulation, the Return of Christ, the Resurrections and the Judgments, the Millennial Reign of Christ and the Eternal Ages. These, except the first, are Daniel's themes also.

But Daniel is distinctively the Book of the *Times of the Gentiles* (Lk 21:24). God had made Israel the centre of a system of nations, peoples and languages that arose in consequence of the judgment on Babel. God had committed the sceptre of the world to Israel's hand (Deut 32:8). In consequence of her persistent idolatry, He took that sceptre from Israel and placed it in the hands of Nebuchadnezzar and his successors. Daniel's vision sweeps the course of Gentile world-rule from Nebuchadnezzar's accession to the Anti-Christ's destruction and the setting up of Christ's Millennial Reign when Jerusalem will again be at the center of the world's nations (Isa 2:2).

Daniel is also is the Book of the *Times of Jerusalem* relative to the great world empires and especially Gentile rule in the last days (9:24-27). There is a remarkable feature in Daniel which gives the *key* to its basic structure. After the Introduction in Chapter 1 where Daniel is brought into Nebuchadnezzar's palace, a surprising change takes place near the beginning of Chapter 2. From verse 4 onwards to the end of Chapter 7, the book rather than being written in Hebrew is written in *Aramaic*, a Gentile language. While there are several other brief usages of Aramaic in the Old Testament, what we have here in Daniel is completely unique. Therefore, here in Daniel when the focus is on Gentile world power, a Gentile language is used. When the focus shifts more to Israel (Dan 8-12) the Book returns to the Hebrew language. This device by the Holy Spirit gives a startling and unique emphasis to the Book of Daniel.

THE TWO MAIN DIVISIONS OF DANIEL

I THE TIMES OF THE GENTILES 1-7

A. The Beginnings of the Times of the Gentiles 1

B. The Overview of the Times of the Gentiles (*Aramaic* Begins) 2

C. The Characteristics of the Times of the Gentiles 3-6

    1. A Time of Enforced False Religion: Nebuchadnezzar's Image 3

    2. A Time of Expansion and Instability: Nebuchadnezzar's Madness 4

    3. A Time of Sacrilege: Belshazzar's Feast 5

INTRODUCTION

    4. A Time of Enshrining Bad Laws: Darius' Lion's Den 6

   D. The End of the Times of the Gentiles: Gentile Perspective 7

II THE TIMES THE GENTILES REGARDING JERUSALEM 8-12

   A. The End of the Times of the Gentiles: Jewish Perspective (*Hebrew* Resumes) 8

   B. The Seventy Weeks of Years upon Jerusalem and the Jewish People 9

   C. The Desolations and Final Blessing of Jerusalem 10-12

    1. Desolations and The Glory of Christ 10

    2. Desolations: Future to Daniel 11:1-35

    3. Desolations and Glory: Future to Us 11:36-12:13

DANIEL 2 AND 7: THE SPAN AND END OF THE TIMES OF THE GENTILES

It is commonly taught that Chapter 7 presents the same world empires as given in Chapter 2 (Babylon, Persia, Greece and Rome; and in both cases picture the entire span of the *Times of the Gentiles*). It is believed that the *beasts* of Chapter 7 present God's view of these empires, while the *metals* of the great statue in Chapter 2 are how they appear to man. There is a parallel between the fourth *metal* and the fourth *beast* (the Roman Empire), but in Chapter 7 the vision is of four dominant powers <u>*near the end*</u> of the Times of the Gentiles.

> *These great beasts, which are four, are four kings, <u>which shall arise out of the earth</u>. But the saints of the most High shall take the kingdom, and possess the kingdom for ever, even for ever and ever (Dan 7:17,18).*

When Daniel wrote these words, Greece had *already risen* as a strong and influential nation. Persia had *already risen* and was preparing to conquer Babylon. And, Babylon had not only *already risen*, but was under its last feeble king, Belshazzar, and in its final death throes as an empire. For this and other reasons, Daniel 7 cannot be a mere repetition of Chapter 2. It instead presents four dominant powers that will arise and exercise influence in the Mediterranean region during the last days. Note how this is shown in the above Outline.

DANIEL 3 TO 6: THE CHARACTER OF THE TIMES OF THE GENTILES

It is common to present the events of Chapters 3-6 (Nebuchadnezzar's image and madness, Belshazzar's feast, the lion's den) in an entirely historical context. These events certainly are historical and give important lessons for facing trial in all ages. However, as they directly follow the *Metallic Colossus* picturing the entire span of the *Times of the Gentiles*, it is reasonable to see them as also **a prophecy of the characteristics** of the long Age from Nebuchadnezzar to the Return of Christ. For example, Nebuchadnezzar's madness is shown to illustrate the instability of the world's leaders throughout (i.e. *seven times*) the Times of the Gentiles.

> *Let his heart be changed from man's, and let a beast's heart be given unto him; and let <u>seven times pass over him</u>. This matter is by the decree of the watchers, and the demand by the word of the holy ones: to the intent that the living may know that the most High ruleth in the kingdom of men, and giveth it to whomsoever he will, and setteth up over it the basest of men….<u>seven times shall pass over thee</u>, till thou know that the most High ruleth in the kingdom of men, and giveth it to whomsoever he will (4:16,17,25).*

DANIEL 9: TWO ATTEMPTS TO DISLODGE THE *CORNERSTONE* OF CHRONOLOGY AND PROPHECY

One of Scripture's foundational prophecies is that of the *Seventy Weeks* in Daniel 9. It has been called *God's Clock for Israel*. It is also rightly viewed as the Bible's prophetic and chronological *cornerstone*. It foretells the time of the death of Christ after which it leaps forward to the last seven terrible years before the Millennial Reign, *the time of Jacob's Trouble* (Jer 30:7). Any attempt to alter the time this *clock* begins to tick, or to dislodge it from its place as a chronological cornerstone will result in the greatest confusion.

There are two fundamental and yet little known ways that the crucial prophecy of Daniel 9 has been mishandled. The standard Gentile chronology has added years and pushed the dates of Daniel back by nearly a century. The traditional Jewish chronology has removed years and brought Daniel and his prophecy of the Weeks forward by more than a century. The first was due to disbelief and ignorance of Daniel 9, and reliance instead upon the notoriously unreliable records of the Persian period. The second came about *precisely because the Jewish leaders knew only too well to Whom the Weeks of Daniel 9 pointed and needed to have the prophecy point to someone else!* I have compiled substantial documentation for this in *Bible Chronology: The Two Great Divides*.

ONE: A GENTILE CHRONOLOGER PUSHED DANIEL BACK IN TIME BY *ADDING* NEARLY A CENTURY TO THE PERSIAN PERIOD

Few are aware that the well-known dates given for the times in which Daniel lived have 93 years added from a secular source. For a start this is at variance with the fact that **the Bible itself** (without any addition or subtraction from secular sources) **gives a complete chronology from Adam to the crucifixion of Christ**. For example, from among the Bible's many chronological statements, Luke 3 gives an unbroken genealogy from Adam to Christ; and the Seventy Week prophecy of Daniel 9 gives the years from the Cyrus Decree to rebuild Jerusalem (at the end of the captivities in Babylon) to the Crucifixion of Christ.

When one reads Daniel 9 in conjunction with the passages dealing with the Cyrus Decree, it is clear that the **counting** of the Seventy Week prophecy was to begin **shortly after** Daniel received the prophecy (Dan 9:1,2; 18-27). It is also clear that the Cyrus Decree not only allowed the Jews to return and rebuild the Temple, **but also rebuild Jerusalem** (Isa 44:28; 45:13). This latter point is denied because it completely refutes any idea of adding 93 further years from secular history before Jerusalem is rebuilt!

According to the prophecy, there will be 69 weeks of years (483 year) *from the going forth of the command to restore and to build Jerusalem* (9:25) until the Messiah is *cut off* (9:27). This *command* can only be the Cyrus Decree to which Scripture gives substantial emphasis (later Persian kings also gave permission, but this was not a new decree but based on the Cyrus Decree). With our Lord crucified in 33 AD it should be a simple matter to subtract 483 years and arrive at a date of about 450 BC for the Cyrus Decree and the beginning of the count of the *weeks*. Daniel then would have received the prophecy a short time before 450 BC.

With such a direct and Biblical computation, why then do we have the intrusion of this 93 year addition? If at the beginning of Daniel 9 (at about the 70th year of Daniel's captivity) it is stated that there would be a *total* of *seventy years in the desolations of Jerusalem* (9:2); WHY then **at the end of Daniel's 70 years in Babylon will Jerusalem still not be built for another 93 years**! The answer is *depressingly simple!* Some 600 or more years after Daniel, the esteemed astronomer, *astrologer*, mathematician and geographer Ptolemy (died c168 AD) compiled his *Canon of Kings*. This is considered the primary source for dating the reigns of rulers in the ancient world. On the basis of what Ptolemy considered were the length of Persian, Greek and Roman king-reigns, he pushed back Persia's capture of Babylon by nearly a century earlier than what the Book of Daniel shows. The scholarly world (with a few exceptions) has chosen to follow Ptolemy rather than the Bible with the result that the "standard dates" commonly accepted and often printed in our Bibles have been inflated by these 93 years.

The decision to follow Ptolemy turns a blind eye to the well-known fact that while the length of Roman reigns is accurate; that of Greek reigns (mainly before Alexander) is much less so, and that of Persian reigns is so unreliable that what Ptolemy listed for Persian kings is not much more than an educated guess. History has been shown to give a reasonably accurate length of time from Alexander's defeat of Persia (331 BC) unto Christ; but with the Persian period before Alexander, there is not only great uncertainty as to the length of the reigns but also to the number of Persian kings.

TWO: A JEWISH CHRONOLOGER BROUGHT DANIEL FORWARD BY *CUTTING* MORE THAN A CENTURY FROM THE PERSIAN PERIOD

If it comes as a surprise that Ptolemy **expanded** the Persian period by 93 years (probably by simple error without ulterior motive), it will come as a shock that the traditional Jewish Chronology (*The Sedar Olam Rabbah*, 2nd Century AD) **cuts radically** the length of the Persian Empire, from Cyrus to Alexander, to only 53 years; and this *with a very special motive*!

In the decades after the Crucifixion, Jewish leaders were faced with the unbearable dilemma that their own Prophet Daniel so emphatically gave the exact time of the Crucifixion of Christ. Something therefore had to be done to show that the *Week*s could point to someone else. The solution was to **compress** their national history so that Daniel's Weeks would shoot well beyond the Crucifixion of AD 33. The history of Persia from the fall of Babylon to its defeat by Alexander was the logical place to apply the editorial knife.

The compiler of the new chronology was the influential Akiva ben Joseph (known as Rabbi Akiva), a greatly loved, and leading contributor to the Talmud. His *The Sedar Olam Rabbah* ("The Great Order of the World") adapted Israel's national chronology in such a way that the *Weeks* of Daniel could point tolerably close to one of Israel's national heroes. That man was Bar Kokhba, who died fighting the Romans in 135 AD.

In the estimation of Rabbi Akiva, Simon Bar Kosiba was virtually the Messiah!

The Jewish sage Rabbi Akiva indulged the possibility that Simon Bar Kosiba (Bar Kokhba) could be the Jewish messiah, and gave him the surname "Bar Kokhba" meaning "Son of a Star" in the Aramaic language, from the Star Prophecy verse from Numbers 24:17: "There shall come a star out of Jacob". (http://en.wikipedia.org/wiki/Bar_Kokhba_revolt)

Jewish editorial work regarding Daniel did not only extend to this *adapted* chronology of Israel's history, it extended to the Bible itself. The text and wording of Daniel were not affected. The Jewish scribes remained as diligent as ever in copying of the inspired words of Daniel. It did however affect its *place* in the Hebrew Bible.

DANIEL IS MOVED TO A "BACK ROOM" IN THE HEBREW BIBLE

In our Bible Daniel is found in its rightful place among the four Major Prophets. This however is not the case with the Hebrew Scriptures. The Hebrew *Tanakh* has a threefold division: the Law (*Torah*), the Prophets (*Nebhiim*) and the Writings (*Kethubhim*). Daniel is not found in the second division (the Prophets) but in the third division (the Writings).Therefore in the Hebrew Bible Daniel is not included among the Major Prophets – Isaiah, Jeremiah, Ezekiel, or among the twelve so-called Minor Prophets – Hosea to Malachi. Different explanations are given for this, but we think Matthew Henry in his day *zeroed in* on true reason.

> Some of the Jewish rabbin are loth to acknowledge him to be a prophet of the higher form, and therefore rank his book among the *Hagiographa* [Greek name for the Writings], not among the prophecies, and would not have their disciples pay much regard to it. One reason they pretend is because he did not live such a mean mortified life as Jeremiah and some other of the prophets did, but lived like a prince, and was a prime-minister of state; whereas we find him persecuted as other prophets were (ch. 6), and mortifying himself as other prophets did, when he *ate no pleasant bread* (10:3), and fainting sick when he was under the power of the Spirit of prophecy (8:27).
>
> Another reason they pretend is because he wrote his book in a heathen country, and *there* had his visions, and not in the land of Israel; but, for the same reason, Ezekiel also must be expunged out of the roll of prophets. But the true reason is that he speaks so plainly of the time of the Messiah's coming that the Jews cannot avoid the conviction of it and therefore do not care to hear of it. But Josephus calls him one of the *greatest* of *the prophets*, nay, the angel Gabriel calls him a *man greatly beloved.*

Thankfully, as noted above, this did not affect the Words of the Book of Daniel. The Masoretic Text (from Hebrew *masoreth*, "tradition") is the sound text of the *Tanakh* (Old Testament) upon which the King James Bible is based. The Jewish scribes copied faithfully and meticulously the inspired Words of the Old Testament. However prior to Rabbi Akiva's "solution" for the fact that Daniel 9 pointed to the time of Christ's Crucifixion, an interim measure was taken by moving Daniel from the second division (the Prophets) to the third "less conspicuous" division (the Writings). That this happened can be seen from the fact that Josephus, writing toward the end of the First Century indicates that Daniel belonged to the Prophets and not the Writings. From his statements on the Hebrew Canon (Contra Apion I, 38-39 [8]), Gleason Archer concludes:

> There is no possibility that Josephus could have regarded Daniel as belonging to the *Writings*. Very clearly he included it among the *Prophets* (*The Expositors Bible Commentary*, pp. 7,8).

Shortly after, in AD 90, there is an account of Daniel being officially placed in the Writings of the Jewish Canon. And there it remains unto this day.

> But what happened to the writing called the scroll of Daniel? From what we can ascertain, sometime between AD. 70-110. probably 90 AD., (perhaps the Sanhedrin itself) the Rabbis determined at the Council of Jamnia that the book of Daniel would be placed in and fixed in the third section of the TANAKH / or Kethuvim (Writings)…
> The formation of the Writings/Kethuvim was developed between 105 BC and 16 BC…It was the Patriarch Gamaliel II who presided over the Sanhedrin during the council of Jamnia in which a scroll of Daniel was officially placed in the Kethuvim Writings (Charles Eisenberg, *The Book of Daniel-A Well Kept Secret*, p.21).

The scribes of Israel may not have placed Daniel in the same company as the rest of the Prophets, but in Matthew 24:15 our Lord esteemed Daniel as one of the Prophets.

> *When ye therefore shall see the abomination of desolation, spoken of by **Daniel the prophet**, stand in the holy place, (whoso readeth, let him understand).*

Therefore in order to hide the truth that after 483 years *Messiah would be cut off* (Dan 9:25,26), and that this can only refer to the Messiah they placed on the Cross, the Jewish rabbis moved the Book of Daniel to *a back room* of their Bible, and *rewrote the years* of the history of their nation. Yet one day soon that same nation will *look upon him whom they have pierced* (Zech 12:10).

Note: The current Jewish Date for 2014/15 is **5775**. This is their Biblical computation from Adam. In fact a count of the years from the Bible (KJV or Tanakh) will come to a figure

INTRODUCTION

of just above 6000 years; this with the Creation of Adam at about 4000 BC. The primary reason for the fewer years in Israel's date is the *Sedar Olam*.

We return now to the Current Chronology followed by nearly everyone.

EIGHT BAISIC FACTS THAT SHOW THE CURRENTLY USED *PTOLEMAIC* CHRONOLOGY IS <u>RIDDLED WITH CONTRADICTIONS</u>

1. There will be 69 Weeks or 483 years (Dan 9:23-26) from the decree to rebuild Jerusalem unto the Crucifixion of Christ. This means the decree was issued in about 450 BC. **The current chronology** puts the decree in 445 BC during the reign of a different king than Cyrus (from Ptolemy's king list). Adding 483 years to 445 BC places the Crucifixion well beyond the usual 30-33 AD date.

2. The: (1) Fall of Babylon to Persia, (2) Daniel receiving the 70 Week Prophecy, (3) The Cyrus Decree to rebuild Jerusalem (when the counting of the Weeks begins) – all took place in a short time (three years at most, probably a lot less). That *this is a short time* is clear from reading Daniel 9, and it is exactly what Daniel prayed for (9:19). **The current chronology** agrees that Daniel received the prophecy of the Weeks shortly after the fall of Babylon, but then says the decree and the count of the Weeks cannot begin for another 93 years. Why? They believe Ptolemy's Persian king list rather than the Bible!

3. The Jerusalem destroyed by Nebuchadnezzar is limited to a desolation of 70 years (Dan 9:2). This simple fact is completely ignored and contradicted by **current chronology** that says Jerusalem was destroyed in 586 and permission to rebuild the city did not come until 445.

4. The Cyrus Decree is the primary decree. The subsequent permissions given to Ezra and Nehemiah were based entirely upon what Cyrus commanded. This Decree is the only one to which the words of Daniel 9:25 could apply: <u>Know therefore and understand, that from the going forth of the commandment to restore and to build Jerusalem unto the Messiah the Prince shall be seven weeks, and threescore and two weeks: the street shall be built again, and the wall, even in troublous times.</u>

    This was something Daniel could *know* then and there! Daniel is an old man now, he would not *know* it if the command did not come until long afterwards (he would be in Heaven!). Yet **current chronology** places *the going forth of* this *command* in the time of a much later king on Ptolemy's list; makes the date 445 BC and then pushes Daniel's reception of the prophecy back to 538 BC.

    Scripture gives a great deal of prominence to the Cyrus Decree; yet **current chronology** ignores that it was a command to rebuild the city (Isa 44:28; 45:13) and concentrates instead on its command to rebuild the Temple.

5. The Biblical Chronology for these times is composed of *one cohesive unit*. The **current chronology** is made up of *two units* separated by a long gap. The gap is "filled in" by nothing more than Ptolemy's lengthy list of Persian kings. This presents a major problem: *a substantial number of Jewish leaders are found on both sides of the gap.* As a result we are introduced to some *very spritely 130-year-olds*!

6. Daniel 11:1-3 presents a very limited number of Persian Kings from the joint reign of Cyrus and Darius down to Alexander the Great. This passage clearly shows the extent to which Ptolemy's list has been expanded.

7. The *multiple* titles given to Persian Kings are a chief source of confusion. Whereas an Egyptian or Roman king generally had a single title, i.e. *Pharaoh* or *Caesar*; there is evidence to show that the same Persian king (as a promotion) could bear additional titles. In the earlier part of his reign he might be called *Ahasuerus* (*Aha* = Mighty; *Suerus* = King). Later he could be called *Artaxerxes* (*Arta* = Great; *Xerxes* = King or Shah). It is especially important to recognize this when reading Ezra, Nehemiah and Esther and Esther. The regnal years of the Persian King to which Esther, Ezra and Nehemiah are linked is the prominent Darius Hystaspes who began his 36 year reign 8/9 years after the death of Cyrus. In these three books he is identified by his titles (Darius Hystaspes =*Ahasuerus, Artaxerxes*).

8. The 69 weeks to the Crucifixion are divided into two groups: *7 weeks* and *62 weeks* (49 years and 434 years). The Biblical Chronology shows them to be *a very busy time* and clearly linked to Persian kings. They cover the time from the Cyrus Decree down to the reforms and wall building undertaken by Nehemiah.

*(Nehemiah 9:25) Know therefore and understand, that from the going forth of the commandment to restore and to build Jerusalem unto the Messiah the Prince shall be **seven weeks**, and threescore and two weeks: **the street shall be built again, and the wall**, even in troublous times. (9:26) And after threescore and two weeks shall Messiah be cut off....*

Nehemiah's work is *at the end* of these 49 years and draws to a conclusion the events of the Old Testament. The **current chronology** puts Nehemiah *at the beginning* the 49 years and *the rest is an empty gap*! There is nothing of significance during the years; nor is there anything to mark their end. What the Bible sets out as a key segment in chronology is left hanging.

CURRENT PTOLEMAIC CHRONOLOGY: LIVING ON BOTH SIDES OF A LONG GAP.

There are "many sprightly 130-year-olds"

It may come as a surprise that the famous scientist Issac Newton studied the prophecies and chronology of the Book of Daniel. As far back as 1728 he wrestled with the fact that the Ptolemaic reckoning faced a very big problem when its dates are compared with the lists of names in Nehemiah 10 and 12 (And that is only the start!). Others have seen the same thing. A brief outline of these **traditional dates** will show what the problem is.

605   1st Deportation to Babylon.
Daniel taken. *Time of Gentiles begins*.

597   2nd Deportation: Ezekiel taken with King Jehoiachin.

586   3rd Deportation: Jerusalem destroyed. ***Ezra's father Seraiah, slain*** (2 Kg 25:18; Ezra 7:1-5).

539   Persia (Darius the Mede, Dan 5:31) conquers Babylon.

538   Daniel is given 70 Week prophecy: 1st year of Darius (Dan 9:1).

536   Cyrus Decree (1st year of reign, Ezra 1:1):70 years after 1st Deportation.
- Jews allowed to build Temple.
- **Zerubbabel brings back first exiles.** *Many leaders among exiles "still active" 91 years later in time of Nehemiah.*

535   Temple begun, but work stopped.

520-15 Ministries of Haggai and Zechariah.

INTRODUCTION

515   Temple completed. (Note: The times between the events down to this point are accurate, but because they are pushed back, the dates are inaccurate).

515-458 GAP: NOTHING BUT PTOLEMY'S KING LIST

458   <u>**Ezra brings back second group of exiles**</u>.

- Institutes reforms.
- *Even if Ezra was not born until his father died (586), he is now at least 128!!*

445   Nehemiah weeps over report of fallen walls of Jerusalem *141 years after they were destroyed* (Neh 1)! He returns to rebuild wall of Jerusalem.

- **Count of the Weeks begin**: *93 years after given to Daniel! Overrun Crucifixion!*
- 17 Priests/Levites return with Zerubbabel (Neh 12) and aid Nehemiah's reforms (Neh. 10). To be leaders in 536, they were *likely 130 years old in 445*!
- For further examples of *leaders that are too old* see *Bible Chronology: The Two Great Divides.*

BIBLICAL CHRONOLOGY: FOUNDED ON THE <u>CORNERSTONE</u>.

There are Sixty-Nine Weeks (483 years) from the Cyrus Decree permitting Jerusalem to be rebuilt until the Crucifixion of Christ. <u>*The First Week*</u> *(49 years) gives the events and dates for the closing period of Old Testament History.*

520   <u>1st Deportation to Babylon</u>.

- 3rd year of Johoiakim's 11 year reign (Dan 1:1).
- Daniel taken.
- Beginning of *Times of the Gentiles* (cp. Lk 21:24).

511   <u>2nd Deportation to Babylon</u>.

- 11th year of Johoiakim's reign and 3rd months of Jehoiachin's reign (2 Kng 24:6-8).
- Ezekiel and Jehoiachin taken.

500   <u>3rd Deportation to Babylon and Jerusalem destroyed</u>.

- 11th year of Zedekiah's reign (2 Kng 25:1-10).
- Ezra's father Seraiah, is slain (2 Kg 25:18; Ezra 7:1-5).

484   Last dated prophecy in Ezekiel: 27th year of Jehoichin's captivity (Ezek 29:17).

474   Last dated event in the captivity: Jehoiachin released from prison.

- 37th year of Jehoiachin's captivity (Jer 52:31), and 1st year of Evil-merodach, King of Babylon's reign (Jer 52:31).
- After Evil-merodach, Daniel gives the 1st year (7:1), 3rd year (8:1) and death (ch. 5) of Belshazzar the last king of Babylon. It does not give the years connecting them.

453   Persia (Darius the Mede, Dan 5:31) conquers Babylon.

452   **Daniel is given the 70 Week prophecy**: 1st year of Darius the Mede (Dan 9:1).

- Daniel has been in Babylon for nearly 70 years.
- Daniel (9:2) had been reading Jeremiah 25:11,12:

*And this whole land shall be desolation, and an astonishment; and these nations shall serve the king of Babylon **seventy years**. And it shall come to pass, **when seventy years are accomplished**, that I will punish the king of Babylon…*

- Daniel had also been reading 2 Chronicles 36:19-23:

*And they **burnt the house of God, and brake down the wall of Jerusalem**, and burnt all the palaces thereof with fire, and destroyed all the goodly vessels thereof. (36:20) And them that had escaped from the sword **carried he away to Babylon**; where they were servants to him and his sons **until the reign of the kingdom of Persia**: (36:21) **To fulfil the word of the LORD by the mouth of Jeremiah, until the land had enjoyed her sabbaths**: for as long as she lay desolate she kept sabbath, to fulfil **threescore and ten years**. (36:22) Now **in the first year of Cyrus king of Persia**, that the word of the LORD spoken **by the mouth of Jeremiah** might be accomplished, the LORD stirred up the spirit of Cyrus king of Persia, that he made a proclamation throughout all his kingdom, and put it also in writing, saying, (36:23) Thus saith Cyrus king of Persia, All the kingdoms of the earth hath the LORD God of heaven given me; and **he hath charged me to build him an house in Jerusalem**, which is in Judah. Who is there among you of all his people? The LORD his God be with him, and **let him go up**.*

450 **Cyrus Decree (1ˢᵗ year of reign, Ezra 1:1): 70 years after 1ˢᵗ Deportation.**

- **Count of the Weeks begin: 483 years to the Crucifixion of Christ.**
- **Seven Weeks begin: 49 Years to 402/1 and conclusion of Nehemiah's reforms.**
- **Jews allowed to rebuild Jerusalem and Temple.**
- **Zerubbabel brings back the first exiles.**

434 1ˢᵗ year of Darius Hystapes King of Persia. The remainder of the First Week (33 years) is dated to Darius' reign.

- He is the *third king* of Daniel 11:1-3; following Cyrus and Cambyses.
- He is also known in Scripture as *Ahasuerus* and *Artaxerxes* (an additional honour).

432 2nd year of reign: After stoppage, work on Temple/ City resumes (Ezra 4:24).

- Ministry of Haggai during 2ⁿᵈ year of reign (Hag 1:1).
- Ministry of Zechariah during 2ⁿᵈ and 4ᵗʰ year of reign (Zech 1:1; 7:1).

431 3ʳᵈ year of reign: Vashti in Book of Esther deposed (Est 1:1).

428 6ᵗʰ year of reign: Temple finished (Ezra 6:15). A little over 70 years since destruction.

427 7ᵗʰ year of reign: **Ezra brings back second group of exiles** (Ezra 7:7).

422 12ᵗʰ year of reign: Haman's plot foiled (Est 3:7).

414 20ᵗʰ year of reign: **Nehemiah's trip to rebuild walls of Jerusalem** (Neh 2:1).

402/1 32ⁿᵈ year of reign: Nehemiah's 2ⁿᵈ trip to Jerusalem (Neh 13:6).

- Further reforms concluded.
- Malachi's ministry occurs here or shortly after.
- **Conclusion of 7 Weeks, 62 Weeks remaining to Crucifixion of Christ.**

331 Persia falls to Alexander the Great.

COMMENTARY

THE TIMES OF THE GENTILES 1- 7

A. THE BEGINNINGS OF THE TIMES OF THE GENTILES 1
DANIEL 1. DANIEL AND HIS THREE COMPANIONS IN BABYLON
The First Deportation 1:1,2.

In the third year of the reign of Jehoiakim king of Judah came Nebuchadnezzar king of Babylon unto Jerusalem, and besieged it. (1:2) And the Lord gave Jehoiakim king of Judah into his hand, with part of the vessels of the house of God: which he carried into the land of Shinar to the house of his god; and he brought the vessels into the treasure house of his god.

This first chapter gives us a much fuller account of Daniel than of any of the other Old Testament prophets from Isaiah to Malachi. Isaiah, Jeremiah, Ezekiel with the others began almost immediately with their divine pronouncements, but with Daniel there is a much fuller account of his beginnings. Here, along with the Apostle John in setting up one of the two great pillars of Bible Prophecy is *a man greatly beloved* of Heaven (Dan 9:23; 10:11; 10:19; cp. Jhn 13:23; 20:2; 21:7; 21:20).

We read now of the first of the three invasions Nebuchadnezzar would launch against Jerusalem. These would extend over a period of 20 years with the last resulting in the destruction of Jerusalem. As the executioner of God's purposes against His disobedient people, Nebuchadnezzar began immediately, shortly before the 1st year of his *sole* which did not begin until the *fourth year of Jehoiakim* (Jer 25:1). This besieging of Jerusalem marks the beginning of Gentile dominion over Jerusalem, the *Times of the Gentiles*. It is a dominion that will extend unto the Second Coming of Christ (Lk 21:24). Little however did the king of Babylon realize that while this would mark the beginning of the 70 year Captivity for Judah, it was also *the 70 year countdown* to Babylon's own doom (Jer 25:11,12).

Nebuchadnezzar became master of Jerusalem. He **besieged Jerusalem**. About a century before the king of Assyria *besieged* Jerusalem (2 Kng 18:9), but he did not become its master, for then Judah had *a king who prayed* (Hezekiah) and God answered his prayer (Isa 37:36). Now there is no praying king on the throne. The last king who *prayed* was Josiah, and has been dead for about three or four years. The revival and reforms he so fervently worked for (2 Chron 34,35) died with him. The traditional date for this invasion is 605. The Biblical date as shown above is 520.

Nebuchadnezzar became the master of Jerusalem's King. Nebuchadnezzar came **in the third year of the reign of Jehoiakim king of Judah… and the Lord gave Jehoiakim king of Judah into his hand**. This wicked and idolatrous king squandered state funds on a new palace (Jer 23:13-19). He is best known for cutting up Jeremiahs prophecies of this very judgement (Jer 36). But the judgement came nevertheless, and despite attempts at resistance, Johoiakim is left as nothing more than a tributary to Nebuchadnezzar for about eight years. He then rebelled and that was his ruin (Jer 22:18,19).

Note: Jeremiah wrote about this shortly after in the 4th year of Jehoiakim (Jer 25:1). This was the 1st year of Nebuchadnezzar's *sole* reign. See Daniel 2:1 for his 2nd year.

Nebuchadnezzar became the master of Jerusalem's Temple. **And the Lord gave…part of the vessels of the house of God: which he carried into the land of Shinar to the house of** *his god; and he brought the vessels into the treasure house of his god* (1:2). Nebuchadnezzar did not then destroy the city but he did begin to deplete it. And here is *a judgement that began at the House of God* – a house which so soon after the death of Josiah had fallen into deep apostasy (1 Pet 4:17). Isaiah prophesied that because Hezekiah showed the Temple treasures to the king of Babylon's ambassadors (Isa. 39:6, 7), that the Babylonians would return to carry away the treasures. Many of the holy vessels are now taken as trophies of victory to the ***house of his god***.

Here is the righteous judgement of God: Judah had brought the images of other gods into His Temple, and now He gives the vessels of the Temple to be carried into the treasuries of their gods. But note, It was only *part of them* that went now; some were left them to see if they would take the right course to prevent the carrying away of the remainder.

See Jer. 27:18.

The Attempt to Indoctrinate and Assimilate 1:3-7.

And the king spake unto Ashpenaz the master of his eunuchs, that he should bring certain of the children of Israel, and of the king's seed, and of the princes; (1:4) Children in whom was no blemish, but well favoured, and skilful in all wisdom, and cunning in knowledge, and understanding science, and such as had ability in them to stand in the king's palace, and whom they might teach the learning and the tongue of the Chaldeans. (1:5) And the king appointed them a daily provision of the king's meat, and of the wine which he drank: so nourishing them three years, that at the end thereof they might stand before the king. (1:6) Now among these were of the children of Judah, Daniel, Hananiah, Mishael, and Azariah: (1:7) Unto whom the prince of the eunuchs gave names: for he gave unto Daniel the name of Belteshazzar; and to Hananiah, of Shadrach; and to Mishael, of Meshach; and to Azariah, of Abednego.

A general account of those to be indoctrinated. Though more was to be taken later, in his first incursion Nebuchadnezzar took the best: the best of the Temple treasures and the best of Judah's young men; especially those with a connection to royalty and nobility. These were the trophies of his success and after a thorough indoctrination (brainwashing) would serve him to the betterment of Babylon.

The tutor of this enterprise. ***And the king spake unto Ashpenaz the master of his eunuchs*** (1:3). This immediately causes a shock and gives an insight into how bad the environment was into which the best of Judah's young men have now been brought. Eunuchs oversaw the king's harems and Ashpenaz oversaw them. Does this mean that Daniel was made a eunuch? The naming of Ashpenaz and the following prophecy may imply that he was. However, Ezekiel 14:20 may imply that he was not. While this is considered an open question, in the 27 places in the Bible where the word *eunuch* is found, and unlike the *Ethiopian eunuch* (Acts 8:27), the term is never directly applied to Daniel.

• *Behold, the days come, that all that is in thine house, and that which thy fathers have laid up in store unto this day, shall be carried into Babylon: nothing shall be left, saith the LORD. And of thy sons that shall issue from thee, which thou shalt beget, shall they take away; and <u>they shall be eunuchs in the palace of the king of Babylon</u> (2 Kng 20:17,18).*

• *Though Noah, <u>Daniel</u>, and Job were in it, as I live, saith the Lord GOD, they shall <u>deliver neither son nor daughter</u>; they shall but deliver their own souls by their righteousness (Ezek 14:20).*

The students of this enterprise: ***certain of the children of Israel, and of the king's seed, and of the princes; Children in whom was no blemish, but well favoured, and skilful in all wisdom, and cunning in knowledge, and understanding science, and such as had ability in them to stand in the king's palace*** (1:3,4).

DANIEL 1: DANIEL AND HIS THREE COMPANIONS IN BABYLON

Young men, ***children***, were to be chosen. It was hoped that they would be pliable and compliant; they would forget Jehovah, forget Jerusalem, and forget their own people. They would be completely moulded and incorporated into Chaldean way of life. And so today young men and women and all of God's people are warned:

> • *I beseech you therefore, brethren, by the mercies of God, that ye present your bodies a living sacrifice, holy, acceptable unto God, which is your reasonable service. And <u>be not conformed to this world</u>: but be ye transformed by the renewing of your mind, that ye may prove what is that good, and acceptable, and perfect, will of God (Rom 12:1,2).*

> • <u>*Love not the world*</u>, *neither the things that are in the world. If any man love the world, the love of the Father is not in him. For all that is in the world, the lust of the flesh, and the lust of the eyes, and the pride of life, is not of the Father, but is of the world. And the world passeth away, and the lust thereof: but he that doeth the will of God abideth for ever (1 Jhn 2:15-17).*

Gifted men were to be chosen. Not only were they to have lineage, royalty and nobility, but on the surface they must look the part. They must have a presence about them that was difficult to be found among the young men of Babylon. They must also have an uncommon genius. It was not to be a limited genius either. They must be ***skilful in all wisdom, and cunning in knowledge, and understanding science***. As such they would be able to ***stand*** and not be intimidated in the court of Nebuchadnezzar. Not only to attend his royal person, but to preside over his affairs of state.

But *what a waste* is this if it is only done for self and Babylon and not done unto the glory of God. The apostle Paul had many natural attributes, but when recounting them said:

> *But what things were gain to me, those I counted loss for Christ. Yea doubtless, and I count all things but loss for the excellency of the knowledge of Christ Jesus my Lord: for whom I have suffered the loss of all things, and do count them but dung, that I may win Christ, And be found in him, not having mine own righteousness, which is of the law, but that which is through the faith of Christ, the righteousness which is of God by faith (Phil 3:7-9).*

The goal of this enterprise: ***whom they might teach the learning and the tongue of the Chaldeans*** (1:4). *Give instructions to a wise man and he will be yet wiser* (Prov 9:9). This does not likely mean the magical arts, divination and religion of the Babylonians. If it did, Daniel and his companions, as with the kings meat and wine, *would not defile themselves* with it (1:8). This would include agriculture, general science, mathematics and especially astronomy. From the days of the first Babylon and its tower *whose top may reach unto heaven* (Gen 11:4), the Babylonians were the great astronomers of the ancient world. They sent to Hezekiah *to inquire of the wonder that was done in the land* (2 Chron 32:21) when the *sun returned ten degrees* (Isa 38:8). This was the kind of learning that *the wise men from the east* had (Matt 2:1).

The maintenance of this enterprise. ***And the king appointed them a daily provision of the king's meat, and of the wine which he drank: so nourishing them three years, that at the end thereof they might stand before the king*** (1:5). This was an instance of Nebuchadnezzar's generosity and kindness. If they did not as Mephibosheth *eat continually at the kings table* (2 Sam 9:13), they were offered the same food and drink that *continually* came to his table. They were given a liberal education and with it a liberal maintenance. But it was all godless and the latter had a special taint to it. This godlessness in the *university of Babylon* is now about to be pressed further.

Note: Babylon, like the world with the Christian, is using *the carrot and stick* approach. It has learned from past conquests that ***three years*** are usually needed to indoctrinate and assimilate. For some it takes longer, other shorter, *a few never*!

A particular account of Daniel and his companions. Nebuchadnezzar took the best from Judah and now we are introduced to *the best of the best*.

Note their Hebrew names given by their parents. There is something of Jehovah or Elohim in these names (1:6). ***Now among these were of the children of Judah, Daniel*** (*Elohim is my Judge*)***, Hananiah*** (*The grace of Jehovah*)***, Mishael*** (*He that is the strong Elohim*)***, and Azariah*** (*Jehovah is help*).

Note their Babylonian names given by their captors (1:7): *Unto whom the prince of the eunuchs gave names: for he gave unto Daniel the name of Belteshazzar; and to Hananiah, of Shadrach; and to Mishael, of Meshach; and to Azariah, of Abed-nego.*

Ashpenaz, the *prince of the eunuchs,* changed their names, partly to show his authority over them and their subjection to him, and partly in token of their being naturalized and made Chaldeans. But it went further! It was designed to make them forget *the God of their fathers* (Deut 26:7), and the *guide of their youth* (Jer 3:4). They gave them names connected with Chaldean idolatry. **Belteshazzar** signifies the *keeper of the hidden treasures of Bel;* **Shadrach**—The *inspiration of the sun,* which the Chaldeans worshipped; **Meshach**—*Of the goddess Shach,* under which name Venus was worshipped; **Abed-nego**, The *servant of the shining fire,* which they worshipped also. Thus, though Babylon would not force them from the faith of their fathers to the idols of their conquerors, yet by major steps, as here, or by giving them the comforts of Babylon, they did what they could to gradually draw them into the religion of Babylon.

The Steadfastness of Daniel 1:8-16.

But Daniel purposed in his heart that he would not defile himself with the portion of the king's meat, nor with the wine which he drank: therefore he requested of the prince of the eunuchs that he might not defile himself. (1:9) Now God had brought Daniel into favour and tender love with the prince of the eunuchs. (1:10) And the prince of the eunuchs said unto Daniel, I fear my lord the king, who hath appointed your meat and your drink: for why should he see your faces worse liking than the children which are of your sort? then shall ye make me endanger my head to the king. (1:11) Then said Daniel to Melzar, whom the prince of the eunuchs had set over Daniel, Hananiah, Mishael, and Azariah, (1:12) Prove thy servants, I beseech thee, ten days; and let them give us pulse to eat, and water to drink. (1:13) Then let our countenances be looked upon before thee, and the countenance of the children that eat of the portion of the king's meat: and as thou seest, deal with thy servants. (1:14) So he consented to them in this matter, and proved them ten days. (1:15) And at the end of ten days their countenances appeared fairer and fatter in flesh than all the children which did eat the portion of the king's meat. (1:16) Thus Melzar took away the portion of their meat, and the wine that they should drink; and gave them pulse.

The resolve of Daniel. ***But Daniel purposed in his heart that he would not defile himself with the portion of the king's meat, nor with the wine which he drank.*** (1:8).

They had changed Daniel's name, but they could not change his faith and principles. Whatever they wanted to call him, he still retained his convictions of *an Israelite indeed* (Jhn 1:47). Whatever studies they gave him in the syllabus of the *learning and tongue of the Chaldeans* (1:4), he would apply his mind diligently. BUT he was resolved that *he would not defile himself with the portion of the king's meat,* he would not meddle with it, nor *with the wine which he drank*, Daniel knew how to be *in* the world but not of the world; *in* Babylon but not of Babylon. The classroom did not pose too great of a problem but Nebuchadnezzar's dining hall did.

Meat from the royal table was doubtlessly slain and prepared according to pagan ritual and offered to a god (Exod 34:15; 1 Cor 10:21). Much like *halal* meat is today! The same

DANIEL 1: DANIEL AND HIS THREE COMPANIONS IN BABYLON

general principles apply to the wine. The best of God's people did not drink it at all (Lev 11:45,46; Num 6:2-4; Deut 29:6; Prov 23:31; 1 Cor 10:21). When the wine starts flowing a lot of things *come unhinged*. If the Bible does not completely forbid its use, it does *everywhere* warn against it. When God's people are in a *Babylon* they have need to take special care that they *partake not in her sins* (Rev 18:4).

The appeal of Daniel. It was an appeal God had already prepared for. ***Therefore he requested of the prince of the eunuchs that he might not defile himself. Now God had brought Daniel into favour and tender love with the prince of the eunuchs*** (1:8,9). Herein was an ongoing work. *He made them to be pitied of all those that carried them captives* (Ps. 106:46). It does not say that *all* who carried them away pitied, but *among the all* there will always be some to show pity and mercy. When a believer sets out to take a stand, he may be surprised where some help will come from.

The fear of the prince. ***And the prince of the eunuchs said unto Daniel, I fear my lord the king, who hath appointed your meat and your drink: for why should he see your faces worse liking than the children which are of your sort? then shall ye make me endanger my head to the king*** (1:10). Ashpenaz was responsible for Daniel and his companion's well-being, and he was very happy to pursue this (1:9); but it is also true that his own well-being depended upon it.

The proposal of a test. ***Then said Daniel to Melzar, whom the prince of the eunuchs had set over Daniel, Hananiah, Mishael, and Azariah, Prove thy servants, I beseech thee, ten days; and let them give us pulse to eat, and water to drink. Then let our countenances be looked upon before thee, and the countenance of the children that eat of the portion of the king's meat: and as thou seest, deal with thy servants. So he consented to them in this matter, and proved them ten days*** (1:11-14). Daniel makes this proposal to the under-officer, the steward, ***Melzar***. Nothing but ***pulse*** and ***water*** for ***ten days***. The word *pulse* is derived from a word which means "to sow"; denoting things grown from seeds sown in the ground. Thus a wide variety of vegetables. If this was not as succulent and tasty as what the king was serving, it was every bit as healthy and likely more so. Pulse would include dates and nuts which provided the protein in this meatless diet. Further, this diet probably kept them away from the dining hall. *Better is a dinner of herbs where love is, than a stalled ox and hatred therewith* (Prov 15:17). By this we see that, *Man shall not live by bread alone, but by every word that proceedeth out of the mouth of God* (Matt 4:4). If God gave these instructions to Daniel (which He did), then pulse and water shall be the most nourishing food and drink. It was *health to the navel and marrow to the bones* (Prov 3:8), while the pleasures of sin in the dining hall were *rottenness to the bones* (Hab 3:16).

The outcome of the trial. ***And at the end of ten days their countenances appeared fairer and fatter in flesh than all the children which did eat the portion of the king's meat. Thus Melzar took away the portion of their meat, and the wine that they should drink; and gave them pulse*** (1:15,16). They put on weight and had a healthier look than all the rest. Their countenance also told of a clearer mind, spiritually and mentally. There was a lot of *excess* in the dining hall. Therefore to the believer: *Let your moderation be known unto all men, the Lord is at hand* (Phil 4:5).

Had Daniel not passed this *first dining hall test*, this would have been the last we hear of Daniel or his Book. This will not be the last test. For both him and his three companions others will follow, including a *fiery furnace* and a *lion's den*. Nor do the *ten days* of this trial indicate that the others will be of short duration. His entire tenure in Babylon will be a trial, and that for seventy and more years.

Here is the first lesson and illustration of the *Times of the Gentiles*; it will be a time of indoctrination and assimilation.

Four Shining Lights in Babylon 1:17-21.

As for these four children, God gave them knowledge and skill in all learning and wisdom: and Daniel had understanding in all visions and dreams. (1:18) *Now at the end of the days that the king had said he should bring them in, then the prince of the eunuchs brought them in before Nebuchadnezzar.* (1:19) *And the king communed with them; and among them all was found none like Daniel, Hananiah, Mishael, and Azariah: therefore stood they before the king.* (1:20) *And in all matters of wisdom and understanding, that the king enquired of them, he found them ten times better than all the magicians and astrologers that were in all his realm.* (1:21) **And Daniel continued even unto the first year of king Cyrus.**

Their great attainments in learning. *As for these four children, God gave them knowledge and skill in all learning and wisdom* (1:17). They took their course work seriously, were very diligent, and studied hard. We may suppose their tutors, finding them of an uncommon capacity to learn, spent a lot of time with them. That being said, their wisdom was from above. It was God and God alone who gave them such an abundance of **knowledge and skill in all learning and wisdom**. Note the three passages from James and one from Ecclesiastes:

- *If any of you lack wisdom, let him ask of God, that giveth to all men liberally, and upbraideth not; and it shall be given him (Jms 1:5).*

- *Every good gift and every perfect gift is from above, and cometh down from the Father of lights, with whom is no variableness, neither shadow of turning (Jms 1:17).*

- *But the wisdom that is from above is first pure, then peaceable, gentle, and easy to be intreated, full of mercy and good fruits, without partiality, and without hypocrisy (Jms 3:17).*

- *For God giveth to a man that is good in his sight wisdom, and knowledge, and joy: but to the sinner he giveth travail (Eccl 2:26).*

The *double portion* given to Daniel: *and Daniel had understanding in all visions and dreams*. He was given a gift which went far beyond that which comes from diligent study. As our Lord said, he is *Daniel the prophet* (Matt 24:15). Through him *the Spirit of Christ which was in him did signify* (1 Pet 1:11). Like Joseph, Daniel could interpret divinely given dreams (Gen 41:12). Shortly he would deal with dreams given to Nebuchadnezzar (Dan 2,4). He will by this gift be like Moses:

If there be a prophet among you, I the LORD will make myself known unto him in a vision, and will speak unto him in a dream (Num 12:6).

Their great acceptance with the king. Nebuchadnezzar is a pagan king who had been used as a chastening rod against Israel. He is king of the world. He is also from a worldly standpoint one of the wisest men on earth. He is now about to be introduced to a far higher kind of knowledge.

Note their examination. *Now at the end of the days that the king had said he should bring them in, then the prince of the eunuchs brought them in before Nebuchadnezzar. And the king communed with them* (1:18,19). After *three years* spent in class rooms of Babylon (indicating that they were at least in their later teens when they began), they are now presented to the king with the other graduates. Nebuchadnezzar himself examined and *communed with them*. He could do it, being a man not just of rank but also of learning. He will see for himself what the progress has been with these students.

Note their superiority: *and among them all was found none like Daniel, Hananiah, Mishael, and Azariah: therefore stood they before the king. And in all matters of wisdom and understanding, that the king enquired of them, he found them ten times better than all the magicians and astrologers that were in all his realm* (1:19, 20). The examination was not narrow or restricted; it was *in all matters of wisdom and understanding.* They had learned their lessons well both in depth and breadth.

They excelled well above the other Hebrews. Perhaps these had been dismissive of the four men in their *dining hall decision*. Now it can be known that something deeper was at stake. They greatly excelled above all the other so-called sages in the land. In fact *ten times* better. Of them it could be said as the Psalmist wrote:

> *O how I love thy law! it is my meditation all the day. Thou through thy commandments hast made me wiser than mine enemies: for they are ever with me. I have more understanding than all my teachers: for thy testimonies are my meditation. I understand more than the ancients, because I keep thy precepts (Psa 119:97-100).*

Nebuchadnezzar was soon aware of something extraordinary in these young men; and he was soon aware that they possessed something far beyond what he had been used to getting from *the magicians and astrologers that were in all his realm*. *What is the chaff to the wheat* (Jer 23:28)? What are the magicians' rods to Aaron's (Exod 7:12)? There was no comparison with anything he had seen before. This examination has shown that his own advisers are *weighed in the balance and found wanting* (Dan 5:27). And so it is also with the world's knowledge when compared with a spiritual knowledge of the Bible.

> *That their hearts might be comforted, being knit together in love, and unto all riches of the full assurance of understanding, to the acknowledgement of the mystery of God, and of the Father, and of Christ; In whom are hid all the treasures of wisdom and knowledge (Col 2:2,3).*

Note their elevation: *therefore stood they before the king.* A spiritual knowledge of the Living and Written Word brings the believer into the presence of the King.

> • *Seest thou a man diligent in his business? he shall stand before kings; he shall not stand before mean men (Prov 22:29).*

> • *Jesus answered and said unto him, If a man love me, he will keep my words: and my Father will love him, and we will come unto him, and make our abode with him (Jhn 14:23).*

Note Daniel's continuance. **And Daniel continued even unto the first year of king Cyrus** (1:21). though not always in the same favour and reputation. He lived and prophesied for another 70 years until Cyrus of Persia, Babylon's conqueror took the throne. This is mentioned here to intimate that he lived to see the deliverance of his people out of their captivity and their return to their own land. This does not say that Daniel did not live longer, but, that he lived to see this important epoch (cp. 10:1).

In this and the five following chapters which illustrate the *Times of the Gentiles*, we see contrasted the Man of God and the Man of the World.

The Man of God is distinguished by: Purity (ch 1), Prophecy (chs 2,4,5), Bravery (chs 2,6) and Fidelity (chs 1,6).

The Man of the World is marked by: Foolishness (chs 2,4), Idolatry (chs 3,5,6), Vanity (ch 4) and Blasphemy (ch 5).

THE TIMES OF THE GENTILES 1-7

B. THE OVERVIEW OF THE TIMES OF THE GENTILES
(Aramaic Language Begins) 2
DANIEL 2. THE METALLIC COLOSSUS

It was said (1:17) that Daniel had *understanding in dreams*; and here we have an immediate and prominent instance of it. This soon made him famous in the court of Babylon, as Joseph by the same means came to be in the court of Egypt. But this dream extends further than the one Joseph interpreted for Pharaoh. That one was seven years of famine and seven years of plenty. And while this one will also encompass plenty and famine, its extent will be for at least two and a half millennia. It is the *Times of the Gentiles* (that time of Gentile dominion over Jerusalem; Lk 21:24) stretching from Nebuchadnezzar's day down to the Return of Christ. It is not seen in just one nation as Joseph saw for Egypt; but it unfolds in five great world empires, with the fifth being in the immediate time of Christ's Return.

The "Forgotten" Dream 2:1-13.

And in the second year of the reign of Nebuchadnezzar Nebuchadnezzar dreamed dreams, wherewith his spirit was troubled, and his sleep brake from him. (2:2) Then the king commanded to call the magicians, and the astrologers, and the sorcerers, and the Chaldeans, for to shew the king his dreams. So they came and stood before the king. (2:3) And the king said unto them, I have dreamed a dream, and my spirit was troubled to know the dream. (2:4) Then spake the Chaldeans to the king in Syriack, O king, live for ever: tell thy servants the dream, and we will shew the interpretation. (2:5) The king answered and said to the Chaldeans, The thing is gone from me: if ye will not make known unto me the dream, with the interpretation thereof, ye shall be cut in pieces, and your houses shall be made a dunghill. (2:6) But if ye shew the dream, and the interpretation thereof, ye shall receive of me gifts and rewards and great honour: therefore shew me the dream, and the interpretation thereof. **(2:7) They answered again and said, Let the king tell his servants the dream, and we will shew the interpretation of it.** *(2:8)* **The king answered and said, I know of certainty that ye would gain the time, because ye see the thing is gone from me.** *(2:9)* **But if ye will not make known unto me the dream, there is but one decree for you: for ye have prepared lying and corrupt words to speak before me, till the time be changed: therefore tell me the dream, and I shall know that ye can shew me the interpretation thereof.** *(2:10)* **The Chaldeans answered before the king, and said, There is not a man upon the earth that can shew the king's matter: therefore there is no king, lord, nor ruler, that asked such things at any magician, or astrologer, or Chaldean.** *(2:11)* **And it is a rare thing that the king requireth, and there is none other that can shew it before the king, except the gods, whose dwelling is not with flesh.** *(2:12)* **For this cause the king was angry and very furious, and commanded to destroy all the wise men of Babylon.** *(2:13)* **And the decree went forth that the wise men should be slain; and they sought Daniel and his fellows to be slain.**

The date of the dream. ***And in the second year of the reign of Nebuchadnezzar dreamed dreams*** (2:1). A question has been raised about this date. If Daniel was carried to Babylon in Nebuchadnezzar's "1st year" which is assumed to be the ***third year of Jehoiakim*** (Dan 1:1,2), and if he and his companions were presented to the king in the 3rd year (1:5), how then could this dream take place in the 2nd year? The answer is that Daniel 1:1,2 does not say that Nebuchadnezzar invaded Jerusalem in his 1st year, for though he was *Nebuchadnezzar king of Babylon* he was likely still co-regent with his father. According to Jeremiah 25:1 the 1st year of Nebuchadnezzar did not begin until the ***fourth year of Jehoiakim***. Therefore, Nebuchadnezzar received this dream three years after he besieged Jerusalem but in only the

DANIEL 2: THE METALLIC COLOSSUS

2nd year of his sole reign. Compare this further parallel with Joseph: *at the end of two full years Pharaoh dreamed* (Gen 41:1).

Note: In Jerusalem at this time, King Johoiakim in his 5th year (Nebuchadnezzar's 2nd year) burned Jeremiah's scroll. This act by the king marked an official rejection of Jehovah and His Word. Nevertheless the Word of God will continue to go forth, and this time through a Gentile monarch.

The anxiety of the dream: ***Nebuchadnezzar dreamed dreams, wherewith his spirit was troubled, and his sleep brake from him*** (2:1). He ***dreamed dreams***, that is, a dream consisting of many distinct parts and which completely filled his head. Solomon speaks of a *multitude of dreams* (Eccl. 5:7); and when *a dream cometh through the multitude of business* (Eccl 5:3). We read further that *the sleep of the labouring man is sweet* (Eccl 5:12), but because of this dream ***his spirit was troubled, and his sleep brake from him***. He had his guards nearby, but they could not keep out the trouble that had entered the kings head. The troubler of Israel was troubled, and that from God.

It is significant that not to Daniel but to the first representative of the *Times of the Gentiles* this dream was given. Nebuchadnezzar had reason to be troubled, for at the end of the dream is the destruction of all of which he is the head (2:44,45).

The call for help concerning the dream. ***Then the king commanded to call the magicians*** (*hartummin* = engravers, writers of magic spells), ***and the astrologers*** (*ashshapim* = they claimed occult knowledge through star positions), ***and the sorcerers*** (*mekashshepim* = general practitioners of occultism listed in Deut 18:9,10 and practiced by Judah's king, Manasseh, 2 Chron 33:4-6), ***and the Chaldeans*** (*kasdim* = a distinct caste of "superior" occult practitioners), For his solution Nebuchadnezzar is calling on the demonic! He had however listened to them *rattle on* many times in the past. This time it will be different; he calls on them ***to shew the king his dreams*** (2:2,3).

The first appeal for a description of the dream is made in *Syriack*. ***Then spake the Chaldeans to the king in Syriack, O king, live for ever: tell thy servants the dream, and we will shew the interpretation*** (2:4). With this we are introduced to the Aramaic section of Daniel (2:4-7:28), a Gentile language, thus alerting to the fact that on a level not seen before in the Old Testament we are entering *The Times of the Gentiles*. It is highly appropriate that as this section of Daniel outlines the long era of Gentile domination over Israel down to the Return of Christ, and now inaugurated by Nebuchadnezzar, we should have this change from Hebrew to a Gentile language.

Here in this "first verse" of *The Times of the Gentiles* we have an insight into what kind of *times* they will be. There will be a great deal of *DEMONISM* (four classes of occult practitioners), *PRIDE* (*O king live forever*), *INEFFECTIVENESS* (*tell thy servants the dream, and we will shew the interpretation*).

The plea is refused; they are threatened with death. ***The king answered and said to the Chaldeans, The thing is gone from me: if ye will not make known unto me the dream, with the interpretation thereof, ye shall be cut in pieces, and your houses shall be made a dunghill. But if ye shew the dream, and the interpretation thereof, ye shall receive of me gifts and rewards and great honour: therefore shew me the dream, and the interpretation thereof*** (2:5,6). Despite their good wishes and compliments the king insists that they must tell him the dream itself for ***the thing is gone from me***.

Nebuchadnezzar says that he has forgotten. We should ask that if he had so completely forgotten and with no clue at all, then why is he be in such a rage and passion over something that he knows absolutely nothing? These advisors had often come before the king; never before had their lives been put into such a balance and so suddenly. Nebuchadnezzar must have both *the dream, and the interpretation* and it must be NOW!

The second appeal for a description is brief. ***They answered again and said, Let the king tell his servants the dream, and we will shew the interpretation of it*** (2:7).

Certainly that is a reasonable request? For normal advisors; Yes! For advisors who claim supernatural powers; No! With these powers you claim, "if you can do one you should be able to do the other." If your powers enable you to give *the interpretation* then the same powers should be able to *tell the dream*.

Their plea is refused; they are charged with duplicity. ***The king answered and said, I know of certainty that ye would gain the time, because ye see the thing is gone from me. But if ye will not make known unto me the dream, there is but one decree for you: for ye have prepared lying and corrupt words to speak before me, till the time be changed: therefore tell me the dream, and I shall know that ye can shew me the interpretation thereof*** (2:8,9). Nebuchadnezzar accuses them of stalling for time - ***gain the time.*** They hoped he would "cool off and forgets the matter"; or ***till the time be changed***: till the king no longer cares or affairs of state would make the dream, whatever it meant, irrelevant.

Again Nebuchadnezzar thunders out: ***Tell me the dream, and I shall know that ye can shew me the interpretation thereof***. The simple fact that these occultists did not even attempt a description of the dream, even in the face of certain death, strongly indicates that the king *had not forgotten the dream*. They recognized that he was putting them on trial for their *past performances*. This fact is further indicated by the king saying: ***for ye have*** (have in the past) ***prepared lying and corrupt words to speak before me***. They knew that if they now attempted an answer they would be shown as a sham and immediately put to death.

The third appeal becomes highly impassioned. Here, as in the first and likely the second, the elite Chaldeans make the appeal. ***The Chaldeans answered before the king, and said, There is not a man upon the earth that can shew the king's matter: therefore there is no king, lord, nor ruler, that asked such things at any magician, or astrologer, or Chaldean. And it is a rare thing that the king requireth, and there is none other that can shew it before the king, except the gods, whose dwelling is not with flesh*** (2:10,11). God in the background made these pagan occultists confess the utter falsity of their claims of supernatural revelation. He is now going to display in order in sharp focus and bright contrast His omnipotence to reveal through Daniel the knowledge of the future.

Superlatives are heaped into this appeal but it is all in vain: ***not a man upon the earth that can shew the king's matter…. no king, lord, nor ruler, that asked such things….a rare thing…. there is none other…. except the gods***. And, except for expressing it in their pagan way, they are right! They are made to confess that it cannot be done. Nebuchadnezzar is applying a simple test; he is doing what the Bible tells believers of all ages to do. When confronted with those who claim divine revelation apart from the Bible ***direct tests must be applied***. This is especially the case today (as in the charismatic movement) with those who claim to have the gift of tongues and prophecy.

> • *When a prophet speaketh in the name of the LORD, if the thing follow not, nor come to pass, that is the thing which the LORD hath not spoken, but the prophet hath spoken it presumptuously (Deut 18:22).*

> • *Thus saith the LORD of hosts, Hearken not unto the words of the prophets that prophesy unto you: they make you vain: they speak a vision of their own heart, and not out of the mouth of the LORD (Jer 23:16).*

DANIEL 2: THE METALLIC COLOSSUS

• To the law and to the testimony: if they speak not according to this word, it is because there is no light in them (Isa 8:20).

• Beloved, believe not every spirit, but try the spirits whether they are of God: because many false prophets are gone out into the world (1 Jhn 4:1).

• For I testify unto every man that heareth the words of the prophecy of this book, If any man shall add unto these things, God shall add unto him the plagues that are written in this book (Rev 22:18).

Their plea is refused; they are given the sentence of immediate death. In vain do they plead! ***For this cause the king was angry and very furious, and commanded to destroy all the wise men of Babylon. And the decree went forth that the wise men should be slain; and they sought Daniel and his fellows to be slain*** (2:12,13). The doom passed upon ***all the wise men of Babylon***, There is but *one decree for them all* (2:9), and now that ***decree has gone forth***. They all stand condemned, without exception or distinction. The decree extended even to ***Daniel and his fellows*** (though they knew nothing of the matter); the righteous must perish with the wicked. Daniel has now learned that the high place to which one is elevated can be a dangerous place. And that, even though the king was *highly pleased* with him and had found him *ten times better* than the wise men (1:19,20).

The Request and Prayer of Daniel 2:14-23.

Then Daniel answered with counsel and wisdom to Arioch the captain of the king's guard, which was gone forth to slay the wise men of Babylon: (2:15) He answered and said to Arioch the king's captain, Why is the decree so hasty from the king? Then Arioch made the thing known to Daniel. (2:16) Then Daniel went in, and desired of the king that he would give him time, and that he would shew the king the interpretation.

(2:17) Then Daniel went to his house, and made the thing known to Hananiah, Mishael, and Azariah, his companions: (2:18) That they would desire mercies of the God of heaven concerning this secret; that Daniel and his fellows should not perish with the rest of the wise men of Babylon. (2:19) Then was the secret revealed unto Daniel in a night vision. Then Daniel blessed the God of heaven. (2:20) Daniel answered and said, Blessed be the name of God for ever and ever: for wisdom and might are his: (2:21) And he changeth the times and the seasons: he removeth kings, and setteth up kings: he giveth wisdom unto the wise, and knowledge to them that know understanding: (2:22) He revealeth the deep and secret things: he knoweth what is in the darkness, and the light dwelleth with him. (2:23) I thank thee, and praise thee, O thou God of my fathers, who hast given me wisdom and might, and hast made known unto me now what we desired of thee: for thou hast now made known unto us the king's matter.

Given the praise Nebuchadnezzar had heaped upon Daniel and his companions (1:19,20), it may seem strange that he did not call him to interpret the dream. But as Daniel had separated himself from the kings dining hall; God in his providence kept Daniel separate from the kings counsellors. God's Words will not be pooled together with demonic mumblings.

We have seem already in Ezekiel (14:14-18; 28:3), that Daniel was highly thought of for both prudence and prayer. As a prince he had power with God and man; by prayer he had power with God, by prudence he had power with men. In these verses we have a remarkable example of both.

By prudence Daniel dealt with men. ***Then Daniel answered with counsel and wisdom to Arioch the captain of the king's guard, which was gone forth to slay the wise men of Babylon: He answered and said to Arioch the king's captain, Why is the decree so hasty from the king? Then Arioch made the thing known to Daniel*** (2:14,15).

With Arioch. When this captain of the king's forces swept through Babylon apprehending all the wise men, Daniel and his companions were also caught in the net. Like the sword of war which *devoureth one as well as another* (2 Sam 11:25). Daniel, however, remained calm; he **answered with counsel and wisdom**. He did not rage or fret or plead, but simply asked. **Why is the decree so hasty?** *A soft answerer* (in this case a soft question) *turneth away wrath, but grievous words stir up anger* (Prov 15:1). **Then Arioch made the thing known to Daniel**. This reply allows Daniel to take the matter higher.

<u>With Nebuchadnezzar</u>. **Then Daniel went in, and desired of the king that he would give him time, and that he would shew the king the interpretation** (2:16). *Where the word of a king is there is power* (Eccl 8:4), and never more so than with Nebuchadnezzar. Yet it is also true that *the king's heart is in the hand of the LORD, as the rivers of water: he turneth it whithersoever he will* (Prov 21:1). Daniel asks for a stay of execution and an extension is granted.

<u>By prayer Daniel conversed with God</u>. Daniel though still young had long known how to pray, and now in this great crisis he does what he has always done. HE PRAYS.

<u>He makes the matter known</u>. Not to many, only his three companions. **Then Daniel went to his house, and made the thing known to Hananiah, Mishael, and Azariah, his companions** (2:17). He *went to his house,* there to be alone with God but also to engage his three fellow believers to pray. Praying friends are valuable friends. We do not know if or how many outside of that house in Babylon were praying at this crisis hour. Homes where prayer is offered will become less and less as the Return of Christ draws near. *When the Son of man cometh will he find faith on the earth* (Lk 18:1).

Note: This is a *model prayer* (i.e. a prayer for all of us to follow, and often in a metrical form). Daniel 9:3-19 is also a model prayer. Compare also 6:9-11; 10:2-12.

<u>He was specific in his prayer</u>. **That they would desire mercies of the God of heaven concerning this secret; that Daniel and his fellows should not perish with the rest of the wise men of Babylon** (2:18). Prayer is to look up to God as the *God of heaven,* a God above us, and who is Lord over us, to whom we owe our worship and adoration. Our Saviour has taught us to pray, *our Father which art in heaven* (Matt 6:9). And, whatever good we pray for, our dependence must be upon the *mercies of God.* Here the need was revelation and deliverance, but that can only come from the *mercies of God.*

They desired mercy **concerning this secret**. *The secret things belong unto the LORD our God: but those things which are revealed belong unto us and to our children for ever* (Deut 29:29). The Book of Daniel deals with both *secret things* (now about to be revealed), and *sealed things* (though now revealed, not understood until the end of the age. Dan 12:9,10; Rev 22:10).

They desired mercy **that Daniel and his fellows should not perish**. Mercy was needed concerning their imminent peril. They were like Peter in prison, facing death in the morning and yet like him, after praying *they went to sleep!* *He giveth his beloved sleep* (Psa 127:2). Daniel is *greatly beloved* (9:23;10:11,19). Daniel goes to sleep while the rest of the wise men in Babylon have a very anxious night.

<u>He receives the answer</u>. **Then was the secret revealed unto Daniel in a night vision** (2:19). Before the completion of the Scriptures we read that God would on occasion reveal truth in dreams and visions.

> *God speaketh ... in a dream, in a vision of the night, when deep sleep falleth upon men, in slumberings upon the bed; Then he openeth the ears of men, and sealeth their instruction (Job 33:14-16).*

The same vision that had been given to Nebuchadnezzar (who *inaugurated* the Times of the Gentiles) is now given to Daniel who will now *interpret* those long and unfolding times.

DANIEL 2: THE METALLIC COLOSSUS

Daniel and his friends prayed. This was the *knock* that opened the door of heaven. Christ said *knock, and it shall be opened unto you* (Lk 11:9).

He gives God the glory. **Then Daniel blessed the God of heaven** (2:19). Before he tells the king, he worships the *God of heaven*. Immediately Daniel turned his prayers into praises. As he had prayed in full assurance that God would do it, so he gave thanks in full assurance that God has done it. His prayer is not recorded, but his thanksgiving is.

Praise is first given for who God is. **Daniel answered and said, Blessed be the name of God for ever and ever: for wisdom and might are his** (2:20). There is a *forever* in God which is to be blessed and praised; it is unchangeably and eternally in Him. His *Name* is His Person and Personality. His *wisdom and might* are the expressions of His Person. With men *wisdom and might* are separated; but God is *able* to do what He *knows* to do.

Praise is given for what God does. **And he changeth the times and the seasons: he removeth kings, and setteth up kings: he giveth wisdom unto the wise, and knowledge to them that know understanding: He revealeth the deep and secret things: he knoweth what is in the darkness, and the light dwelleth with him** (2:21,22).

Five ongoing acts of God in the affairs of men are here listed.

(1) **He changeth** *the times and the seasons*. He is the absolute Controller of the timing of Gentile dominion over Israel. He controls its rise as here in the time of Nebuchadnezzar. He will bring about its collapse in the days of Antichrist and the Return of Christ. That the term *times and the seasons* relates especially to Israel can be seen in Christ's reply to the Disciples. They would not *know the times and seasons* (experience their conclusion).

When they therefore were come together, they asked of him, saying, Lord, wilt thou at this time restore again the kingdom to Israel? And he said unto them, It is not for you to know the times or the seasons, which the Father hath put in his own power (Acts 1:6,7).

(2) **He removeth** *kings, and setteth up kings*. Are those that were kings removed and deposed? Do they abdicate? Are they laid aside? It is God that *removes kings*. Are the *poor raised out of the dust*, to be *set among princes* (Psa 113:7,8)?

• *That the living may know that the most High ruleth in the kingdom of men, and giveth it to whomsoever he will, and setteth up over it the basest of men (Dan 4:17).*

• *Thus saith the Lord GOD; Remove the diadem, and take off the crown: this shall not be the same: exalt him that is low, and abase him that is high. I will overturn, overturn, overturn, it: and it shall be no more, until he come whose right it is; and I will give it him (Ezek 21:26,27).*

• *Put them in fear, O LORD: that the nations may know themselves [to be but] men. Selah (Psa 9:20).*

(3) **He giveth** *wisdom unto the wise, and knowledge to them that know understanding*. This is Biblical knowledge. This is to those who desire the knowledge of the Lord.: *Then shall we know if we follow on to know the LORD* (Hos 6:3). *Unto you that hear shall more be given* (Mk 4:24). This is especially true of the knowledge of Bible Prophecy. *But none of the wicked shall understand, but the wise shall understand* (Dan 12:10).

(4) **He revealeth** *the deep and secret things*. As He has always done in the Scriptures and particularly in the prophetic Scriptures; He *discovereth deep things out of darkness, and bringeth out to light the shadow of death* (Job 12:22). He will *bring*

into judgment every secret thing, whether it be good, or whether it be evil (Eccl 12:14).

(5) ***He knoweth*** *what is in the darkness, and the light dwelleth with him.* He is *Light*; He is *the Father of lights* (1 Jhn 1:5; 1 Tim 6:16; Jms 1:17).

Praise is given for what God has now done. ***I thank thee, and praise thee, O thou God of my fathers, who hast given me wisdom and might, and hast made known unto me now what we desired of thee: for thou hast now made known unto us the king's matter*** (2:23). All that which God does, He has now done for Daniel. As God did for the *fathers* (1 Kng 8:57), so now He does for him. What was hidden from the celebrated Chaldeans who made the interpreting of dreams their profession, is revealed to Daniel, a captive-Jew, a young man, much their junior. Here in worldly Babylon God will now put honour upon the *Spirit of prophecy* (Rev 19:10) just when he was putting contempt on the *spirit of divination* (Acts 16:16).

Note the respect Daniel gives to his companions in this thanksgiving: *and hast made known unto me now what **we** desired of thee: for thou hast now made known unto **us** the king's matter*. Though the matter was revealed to Daniel yet it was also in answer to *their* prayers.

Daniel is Brought before Nebuchadnezzar 2:24-30.

Therefore Daniel went in unto Arioch, whom the king had ordained to destroy the wise men of Babylon: he went and said thus unto him; Destroy not the wise men of Babylon: bring me in before the king, and I will shew unto the king the interpretation. (2:25) Then Arioch brought in Daniel before the king in haste, and said thus unto him, I have found a man of the captives of Judah, that will make known unto the king the interpretation. (2:26) The king answered and said to Daniel, whose name was Belteshazzar, Art thou able to make known unto me the dream which I have seen, and the interpretation thereof? (2:27) Daniel answered in the presence of the king, and said, The secret which the king hath demanded cannot the wise men, the astrologers, the magicians, the soothsayers, shew unto the king; (2:28) But there is a God in heaven that revealeth secrets, and maketh known to the king Nebuchadnezzar what shall be in the latter days. Thy dream, and the visions of thy head upon thy bed, are these; (2:29) As for thee, O king, thy thoughts came into thy mind upon thy bed, what should come to pass hereafter: and he that revealeth secrets maketh known to thee what shall come to pass. (2:30) But as for me, this secret is not revealed to me for any wisdom that I have more than any living, but for their sakes that shall make known the interpretation to the king, and that thou mightest know the thoughts of thy heart.

Daniel's appeal to Arioch: ***Destroy not the wise men*** (2:24). Daniel brought this message with all speed. The sentence has now been superseded. Though under the Law of God they deserved to die and stood condemned for dealing in demonic arts. Yet now there is a reprieve. To Paul in the ship God gave the souls of all that sailed with him (Acts 27). To Daniel in Babylon God gave the preservation of all the wise men; yet as we will shortly see they will not return this kindness (3:8).

Note: Daniel says three things to Arioch the executioner: ***Destroy not... bring me before the king... I will show the interpretation***. This same threefold appeal could be made by soul winners today. It is like Moses who *stood between the dead and the living; and the plague was stayed* (Num 16:48).

Daniel is brought before Nebuchadnezzar: ***I have found a man*** (2:25). There will always be a man or woman to *stand in the gap* (Ezek 22:30). Sometimes it may be a bit belated as when Mordecai appealed to Esther: *Who knoweth whether thou art come to the kingdom for such a time as this* (Est 4:14). But here there was no delay; it was ***done in haste***.

DANIEL 2: THE METALLIC COLOSSUS

The question is put to Daniel: ***Art thou able*** (2:26). A *captive of Judah*! Such a young man! His surprise is much like that of King Saul with David before the battle with Goliath (1 Sam 17). And like Saul with David, Nebuchadnezzar seems to have forgotten his previous encounter with Daniel. Kings have a lot on their minds. The king's twofold question to Daniel is the same he had put to the wise men: ***Art thou able to make known unto me the dream which I have seen, and the interpretation thereof?***

Note: God makes *able* those whom the world often thinks and speaks less of. This was **Daniel, whose name was Belteshazzar** – a Judean captive who was given a name change by his captors (cp. Acts 11:26; 1 Cor 1:27,28).

<u>Daniel presents the *God of Heaven* to Nebuchadnezzar</u>. As always Daniel gives and will give throughout this Book *all* of the glory to God: ***But there is a God in heaven*** (2:28).

The utter feebleness of Nebuchadnezzar's counsellors. Daniel first displays God's omniscient glory against the background of the foolish incompetence of Babylon's wise men. ***Daniel answered in the presence of the king, and said, The secret which the king hath demanded cannot the wise men, the astrologers, the magicians, the soothsayers, shew unto the king*** (2:27). This is too much for them O King. Therefore let not the king put to death these for not doing what they cannot do. Look upon them as Job did to his "comforters". *Now you are nothing; miserable comforters are you all* (Job 16:2). Cast them off; listen never again to them, but do not put them to death.

The all-sufficiency of Daniels God. ***But there is a God in heaven that revealeth secrets*** (2:28). Though they cannot find out the secret, let not the king despair of having it found out, for *there is a God in heaven that reveals secrets*. The insufficiency of man should drive us to our all-sufficient God. *There is a God in heaven* (and it is well for us there is) for there is certainly none on earth who can meet the deepest needs of our soul. For example people today practically worship at the "altar" of Steve Jobs and Apple Computer. But all of its aura, wealth and influence could not keep its co-founder alive. Steve Jobs was born in 1955 and died 2011. There is nothing out there except the God of Heaven and the Bible from Heaven. *For ever, O LORD, thy word is settled in heaven* (Psa 119:89).

> *Now to him that is of power to stablish you according to my gospel, and the preaching of Jesus Christ, according to the revelation of the mystery, which was kept secret since the world began, But now is made manifest, and by the scriptures of the prophets, according to the commandment of the everlasting God, made known to all nations for the obedience of faith: To God only wise, be glory through Jesus Christ for ever. Amen (Rom 16:25-27).*

<u>Daniel declares the future implications of the dream</u>: ***and maketh known to the king Nebuchadnezzar what shall be <u>in the latter days</u>. Thy dream, and the visions of thy head upon thy bed, are these; As for thee, O king, thy thoughts came into thy mind upon thy bed, what should come to pass hereafter: and he that revealeth secrets maketh known to thee <u>what shall come to pass</u>*** (2:28,29). This is a vision that both spans the ages of Gentile rule (*what shall come to pass*) and also declares the **latter days** when Gentile rule will come to an end and Christ will rule.

> *The kingdoms of this world are become the kingdoms of our Lord, and of his Christ; and he shall reign for ever and ever (Rev 11:15).*

<u>Daniel disclaims all personal merit in revealing the dream</u>. ***But as for me, this secret is not revealed to me for any wisdom that I have more than any living, but for their sakes that shall make known the interpretation to the king, and that thou mightest know the thoughts of thy heart*** (2:30). God alone may have all the praise for what is now to be revealed.

The revelation was not through Daniel's *wisdom*. It is with Daniel as it was with Joseph before Pharaoh:

And Pharaoh said unto Joseph, I have dreamed a dream, and there is none that can interpret it: and I have heard say of thee, that thou canst understand a dream to interpret it. And Joseph answered Pharaoh, saying, It is not in me: God shall give Pharaoh an answer of peace (Gen 41:15,16).

The revelation was not for Daniel's *sake* alone. The phrase **but for their sakes that shall make known the interpretation to the king** raises the question: Who is *their*? It must mean Daniel *with* his three companions. They were under the same sentence of death. They prayed for the same revelation. Now that the revelation is given they must share in the same deliverance (2:17-19,23). They will be the *light* in Babylon that must not be extinguished.

Daniel Reveals the Dream 2:31-35.

Thou, O king, sawest, and behold a great image. This great image, whose brightness was excellent, stood before thee; and the form thereof was terrible. (2:32) This image's head was of fine gold, his breast and his arms of silver, his belly and his thighs of brass, (2:33) His legs of iron, his feet part of iron and part of clay. (2:34) Thou sawest till that a stone was cut out without hands, which smote the image upon his feet that were of iron and clay, and brake them to pieces. (2:35) Then was the iron, the clay, the brass, the silver, and the gold, broken to pieces together, and became like the chaff of the summer threshingfloors; and the wind carried them away, that no place was found for them: and the stone that smote the image became a great mountain, and filled the whole earth.

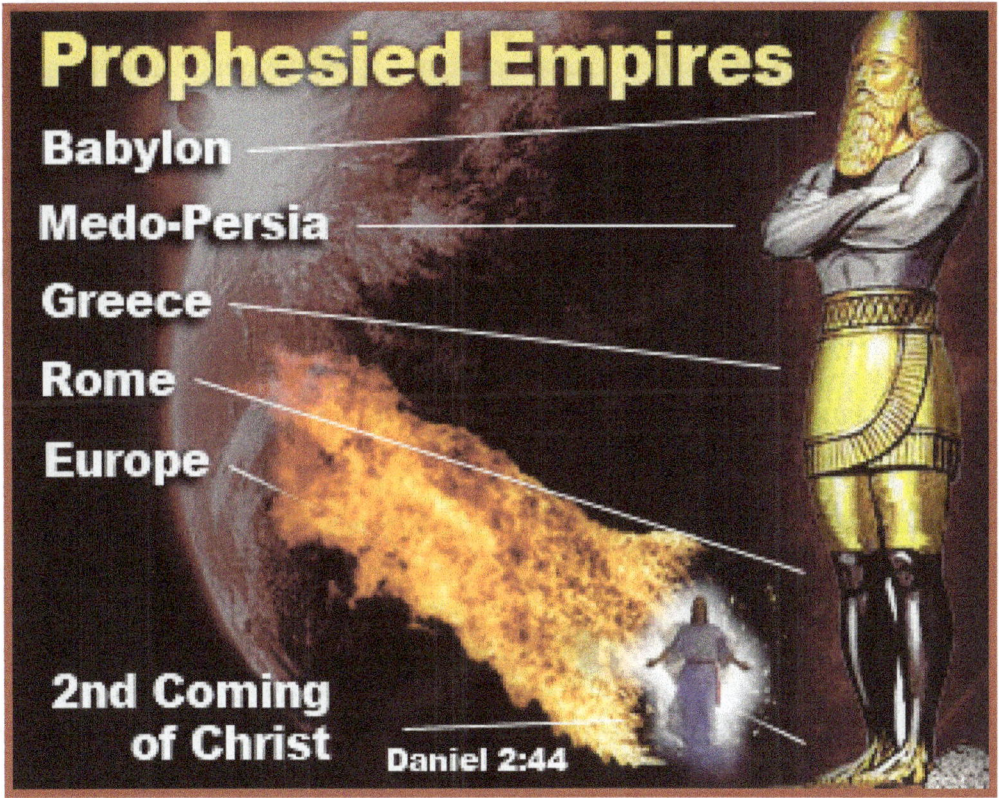

The Metallic Colossus: Five Empires During The Times of the Gentiles
(Image from https://www.worldslastchance.com/end-time-prophecy)

Daniel here gives full satisfaction to Nebuchadnezzar concerning his dream and the interpretation. The great king had been kind to this poor captive in his maintenance and education. He had been brought up at the king's expense and preferred in his court. And now

DANIEL 2: THE METALLIC COLOSSUS

the king is repaid: first with an overview of what he saw, and then with an interpretation of its different parts.

The Image: An Overall View. ***Thou, O king, sawest, and behold a great image. This great image, whose brightness was excellent, stood before thee; and the form thereof was terrible*** (2:31). Nebuchadnezzar likely was an admirer of statues and had his palace and gardens adorned with them; however; he was also a worshipper of images and now in a dream a ***great image*** has been set before him. This might intimate what the real value was of the images he bestowed so much cost upon and paid such respect to. As far as anything of lasting worth they were a mere dream.

The king saw the image of a man; the image of a living man, for ***it <u>stood</u> before him***. Nebuchadnezzar's own statues were of stone, and though they were standing, they were dead. This seemed to have a certain life about it.

This image was admirable in the eyes of its friends: the ***brightness was excellent***. It was terrifying, formidable and dreaded by all its enemies. Its ***form thereof was terrible***; both the features of the face and the postures of the body made it so.

The Image: A View of Its Parts. ***This image's head was of fine gold, his breast and his arms of silver, his belly and his thighs of brass, His legs of iron, his feet part of iron and part of clay*** (2:32,33). That which was most remarkable in this image was the different metals of which it was composed—the ***head of gold*** (the richest and most durable metal), the ***breast and arms of silver*** (the next to it in worth), the ***belly and sides of brass***, the ***legs of iron*** (still baser metals), and lastly the feet ***part of iron and part of clay***. See what the things of this world are; the further we go in them the less valuable they appear. So it is with the life of a man. It may seem to begin with a bright *head of gold*, but it soon degenerates and before long the life is found to be both hard and unstable; feet *part of iron and part of clay*. But this as we will see is not an image of *a* man, but *empires of men*. So it will be with all *the kingdoms of the world and the glory of them* (Matt 4:8).

The Image: A View of Its End and Successor. ***Thou sawest till that a stone was cut out without hands, which smote the image upon his feet that were of iron and clay, and brake them to pieces*** (2:34). ***Then was the iron, the clay, the brass, the silver, and the gold, broken to pieces together, and became like the chaff of the summer threshingfloors; and the wind carried them away, that no place was found for them: and the stone that smote the image became a great mountain, and filled the whole earth*** (2:35). Yes, Nebuchadnezzar was an admirer of the *kingdoms of this world and the glory of them*. To him the sight was very magnificent and impressive. Perhaps as he listened to Daniel, it *more than* occurred to him that he and his great Babylon have a part in this *this great image, whose brightness was excellent*. But what became of this image? The next scene shows that it is not something that the king would want, for it is brought to nothing.

He saw ***a stone cut out*** unseen, ***without hands***; and this stone flew against, struck, smote the image with a lethal blow. But it did not smash against the *golden head* or the *silver chest*; it ***smote the image upon his feet that were of iron and clay, and brake them to pieces***. And with the feet gone, the rest of the image must fall, and it did.

He saw the most complete destruction conceivable of this *metallic colossus*. It was ***broken to pieces***. It was broken in pieces ***together***; none of it was left standing. The *broken pieces* were beaten so small that they ***became like the chaff of the summer threshingfloors***. But not even a pile of dust was left; for ***the wind carried them away***. And even here the destruction does not end, for wherever one looked, ***no place was found for them***. Nothing at all could be found in the smallest patch or corner on the face of the entire earth, no matter how remote or hidden or distant. Nebuchadnezzar saw UTTER DESTUCTION. The image is the world and all its glory. This is the world that the Bible tells us *not to love* (1 Jhn 2:15).

He saw the vastness and extent of what first appeared as a ***stone cut out without hands: and the stone that smote the image became a great mountain, and filled the whole earth***. The Destroying Stone was everywhere and seen everywhere; it *filled the whole earth*. The lofty impressive image was gone and gone completely. *This is what Nebuchadnezzar saw.*

Daniel Interprets the Dream 2:36-45.

This is the dream; and we will tell the interpretation thereof before the king. (2:37) Thou, O king, art a king of kings: for the God of heaven hath given thee a kingdom, power, and strength, and glory. (2:38) And wheresoever the children of men dwell, the beasts of the field and the fowls of the heaven hath he given into thine hand, and hath made thee ruler over them all. Thou art this head of gold. (2:39) And after thee shall arise another kingdom inferior to thee, and another third kingdom of brass, which shall bear rule over all the earth. (2:40) And the fourth kingdom shall be strong as iron: forasmuch as iron breaketh in pieces and subdueth all things: and as iron that breaketh all these, shall it break in pieces and bruise. (2:41) And whereas thou sawest the feet and toes, part of potters' clay, and part of iron, the kingdom shall be divided; but there shall be in it of the strength of the iron, forasmuch as thou sawest the iron mixed with miry clay. (2:42) And as the toes of the feet were part of iron, and part of clay, so the kingdom shall be partly strong, and partly broken. (2:43) And whereas thou sawest iron mixed with miry clay, they shall mingle themselves with the seed of men: but they shall not cleave one to another, even as iron is not mixed with clay. (2:44) And in the days of these kings shall the God of heaven set up a kingdom, which shall never be destroyed: and the kingdom shall not be left to other people, but it shall break in pieces and consume all these kingdoms, and it shall stand for ever. (2:45) Forasmuch as thou sawest that the stone was cut out of the mountain without hands, and that it brake in pieces the iron, the brass, the clay, the silver, and the gold; the great God hath made known to the king what shall come to pass hereafter: and the dream is certain, and the interpretation thereof sure.

The Meaning. Five verses are given to the revelation of the dream, and now ten are given to its interpretation. Concisely repeating the kings dream, Daniel now proceeds to interpret it. The monarchy-vision gives the course and end of *the Times of the Gentiles* (Lk 21:24), that is, of Gentile world-empires and dominion, evidenced especially by their dominion over Jerusalem. The four empires were not represented by four distinct statues, but by one statue with four metals. This is because they were all of one and the same spirit and each was more or less against Jerusalem. The capitals of the two former empires lay eastward of Judea, the two latter westward.

These empires, while if not necessarily possessing the entire inhabited earth, they are *able* to do so (Dan 2:38). These are Babylon, Media-Persia, Greece (under Alexander), and Rome. Rome is seen divided, first into two (the legs), fulfilled in the Eastern and Western Roman empires, and then into ten (the toes), fulfilled during the Tribulation and time of Antichrist. As a whole, the image gives the imposing outward greatness and splendour of the Gentile world-power but as we will now see *it is unstable*.

The Deterioration. From the *head of gold* (2:38) to the *iron of the fourth kingdom* (Rome) there is deterioration in fineness. There is with each metal a lower specific gravity (gold = 19; silver = 11; brass/bronze = 8.5; iron = 7.8). Thus with each metal being lighter, the statue is top-heavy and unstable. There is however with each descending metal an increasing hardness and strength (2:40). But the very quality of the fourth kingdom is its *strength*, that also is undermined, and in a twofold way.

(1) Deterioration by division: The kingdom is divided into two, the legs (Eastern and Western empires), and these are again divided into kingdoms, the number of which when the Stone smites the image will be *ten* toes (2:42; cp 7:23,24).

(2) Deterioration by admixture; the iron of the Roman imperium mixed with the clay of the popular will and democracy. Though of course much more fair and humane, and especially as so many absolute monarchs have ruled for self and not the good of the people; the clay of democratic rule with its system of checks and balances is often unworkable, godless, fickle, changeable, frequently corrupt and often does not result in the common good.

The Catastrophic End. The smiting Stone destroys the Gentile world-system (in its final form) by a sudden and irremediable blow, not by the gradual processes of conversion and assimilation. Then, and not before, does the Stone *become a mountain which fills the whole earth* (cp. Dan 7:27). Such a destruction of the Gentile monarchy-system did not occur at the First Coming of Christ. On the contrary, He was put to death by the sentence of an officer of the fourth empire, which was then at the zenith of its power. Since the Crucifixion the Roman Empire has followed the course marked out in this vision. Gentile world dominion based on the remnants of the Roman Empire still continue and will do so until the crushing blow of the Stone. Immediately following its sudden and catastrophic judgment (*Armageddon*; Rev 16:14-16:14; 19:21), the Kingdom of Heaven is set up on earth (cp. Dan 4:26). Christ will reign upon David's Throne in Jerusalem (Lk 1:32, 33).

Note especially that the *Times of the Gentiles* begins and ends with a ***great image*** (Dan 2:31; Rev13:14,15)!

The Gold of Babylon.

This is the dream; and we will tell the interpretation thereof before the king. Thou, O king, art a king of kings: for the God of heaven hath given thee a kingdom, power, and strength, and glory. And wheresoever the children of men dwell, the beasts of the field and the fowls of the heaven hath he given into thine hand, and hath made thee ruler over them all. Thou art this head of gold (2:36-38).

With Nebuchadnezzar listening in silence and no doubt complete wonder, Daniel now proceeds to the interpretation. Notice again how though he alone is the speaker he brings his three companions into the proceedings. ***This is the dream; and we will tell the interpretation thereof before the king.***

Nebuchadnezzar is ***a king of kings*** (Isa 47:5; Jer. 27:6; Ezek 26:7). He is not ***the*** *King of Kings* (Rev. 19:16), but is *a king par excellence* to whom had been committed the fullest plenitude of power (cp. Dan. 4:30). He more than any other king the prime example of an absolute ruler (both good and bad) until Antichrist (Rev 13:7) and until Christ Himself (Rev 11:15).

His advancement was not of himself. Let not Nebuchadnezzar attribute this elevation to his own politics or fortitude; it is *the God of heaven* that has **given thee a kingdom, power, and strength, and glory**. Not since Solomon has so much been given an earthly king (1 Kng 3,4).

His dominion was vast. ***And wheresoever the children of men dwell, the beasts of the field and the fowls of the heaven hath he given into thine hand, and hath made thee ruler over them all***. This envisions that dominion originally assigned to unfallen man (Gen 1:28; 2:19-20) and lost through the Fall. It is now temporarily delegated to Nebuchadnezzar and the Gentile world powers; but, because of their abuse, it will be *taken*, and *taken finally* by the Son of Man, *the King of Kings* who at His Second Advent will restore to the earth the lost inheritance (Psa 8:4-6).

Nebuchadnezzar with his Babylon is ***the head of gold***. This alludes to the wealth of Babylon (Isa 14:4; Jer 51:7; cp. Rev. 18:16), and the absolute God-derived autocracy of Nebuchadnezzar. There were other powerful world-empires before, most notably Egypt and Assyria, but Babylon vanquished them both. Babylon also unlike these previous empires ruled over Jerusalem. It is therefore Babylon that is ***the head*** and inaugurates the Times of the Gentles. Babylon was a *head*, for its wisdom, eminency and absolute power. It was a head of ***gold*** for its wealth (Isa. 14:4). According to the historian Herodotus (484-425 BC) it was a *city of gold*. Yet it would only last for another 70 years and only three kings of Babylon are mentioned in the Bible. According to Matthew Henry, Nebuchadnezzar reigned 45 years, Evil-merodach, 23 years and Belshazzar, 3 years. According to Herodotus Babylon had a high wall upon which three chariots could ride abreast but this did not prevent the early end to Nebuchadnezzar's empire.

The Silver of Media-Persia.

And after thee shall arise another kingdom inferior to thee (2:39).

Though the next empire would conquer Babylon, Nebuchadnezzar is told no more than this. The Medes and Persians would be not be so rich and opulent (*silver* rather than *gold*). Persia had a much vaster dominion than Babylon but did not have its total control. The central Persian government lacked the absolute autocracy of Babylon (5:18-19). The Persian nobles shared the government with the king (6:14,15), and the provinces gained increased independence.

This kingdom was founded by Darius the Mede and Cyrus the Persian, in alliance with each other, and therefore represented by *two arms, meeting together in the chest*. Nebuchadnezzar saw the figure of the statue of a man and thus it would have *the general proportions of a man*. Therefore with the shoulder, Persia's horizontal size on the statue is much greater than Babylon (the width of the head) and points to the much greater area of the Persian Empire. However *folded arms on the chest* give a vertical distance that is in conformity to what the Bible reveals of the length of Persian rule. If the head can represent 70 years, folded arms on a chest could be close to the 122 years we have calculated. The Bible shows that Persia conquered Babylon at about 453 BC and history accurately records the fall of Persia to Alexander the Great in 331 BC (see pages 9,10). This is not far from the conclusion of Matthew Henry who is his day was not so encumbered by Ptolemaic chronology as teachers are today.

Some reckon that this second monarchy lasted 130 years, others 204 years. The former computation agrees best with the Scripture chronology.

As the Lord dealt with Nebuchadnezzar, so it should be noted that at beginning of the second empire the Lord dealt very convincingly with Cyrus (Isa 44,45) and Darius the Mede (Dan 6). We have also evidence from Jewish history of His dealings with Alexander the Great. Therefore during these long Times of the Gentiles, monarchs have been made to know that while God *in times past suffered all nations to walk in their own ways. Nevertheless he left not himself without witness* (Acts 14:16,17).

The Brass of Greece.

and another third kingdom of brass, which shall bear rule over all the earth (2:39).

The third kingdom showed further deterioration politically. For Babylon it was a God-derived autocracy in Nebuchadnezzar's absolute rule. In the Persian kings it was rule springing from nobility of birth. In Greece, it was individual influence acquired by personal achievement that brought leaders to the throne. This appeared especially in the conquests of Alexander the Great who by the power of the sword *bear rule over all the earth*. For Rome, lowest of all, the emperor was appointed by popular military election, and so the ruling power centered in popular choice.

The "inferior" quality of the second empire in comparison to the first, and so on, was in a political sense, in their departure from God-appointed absolute authority. That sovereignty was abused by Nebuchadnezzar, as *king of kings*, but is to be realized in the Messiah, as the true *Kings of kings* (Rev. 19:16), manifested in *the kingdom, which shall never be destroyed* (2: 44). Accordingly, *inferior* (2:39) means in the quality of government, not necessarily inferior in other respects, such as worldly power and influence, geographical extent, and military strength.

Brass or Bronze!

As Babylon was noted for her gold, so Persia was for her silver. The Persians are known to have introduced a widespread system of silver coinage based on the *Daric*. In their conquest of Persia the Greeks gathered an abundance of silver objects. Babylon and Persia then discovered that gold and silver can *rust*. It was useless as a "hedge" against trouble.

> *Your gold and silver is cankered; and the rust of them shall be a witness against you, and shall eat your flesh as it were fire. Ye have heaped treasure together for the last days (Jms 5:3).*

Coming to Greece, the Brass Kingdom, Ezekiel 27:13 records:

> *Javan [Greece], Tubal, and Meshech, they were thy merchants: they traded the persons of men and **vessels of brass** in thy market.*

Greece was famous as a nation of brass merchants, trading objects of brass throughout the Mediterranean region. This raises a question. Was it brass or was it bronze? Critics of the King James Bible say that the "translators confused brass with bronze. The process for making brass (melting copper with zinc) was unknown in Old Testament times. Whereas bronze smelting (copper with tin) was widespread at a very early age." The AV does not use the word *bronze*; it is always *brass*.

- *Tubal-cain, an instructor of every artificer in **brass** and iron (Gen 4:22).*
- *Thou shalt overlay it with **brass** (Exod 27:2).*
- *Thou shalt also make a laver of **brass** (Exod 30:18).*
- *... out of whose hills thou mayest dig **brass** (Deut 8:9).*
- *he cast two pillars of **brass** (1 Kng 7:15).*
- *he made two chapiters of molten **brass** (1 Kng 7:16).*
- *... and all these vessels which Hiram made to King Solomon for the house of the LORD, were of **bright brass**. In the plain of Jordan did the king cast them, in the clay ground (1 Kng 7:45, 46).*
- *Iron is taken out of the earth, and **brass** is molten out of the stone (Job 28:2).*
- *and another third kingdom of **brass**, which shall bear rule over all the earth. (Dan 2:39)*

ANSWER: The Israelites must have known to mix zinc with their copper, or at least as the following shows, smelted with zinc-rich copper, for how else would they have had *bright brass* (1 Kng 7:45). The following summarizes the common view:

> Copper-zinc alloys were produced as early the 5th millennia BC in China and were widely used in east and central Asia by the 2nd and 3rd century BC. These artefacts,

however, may be best referred to as 'natural alloys', as there is no evidence that their producers consciously alloyed copper and zinc. Instead, it is likely that the alloys were smelted from zinc-rich copper ores, producing crude brass-like metals. (http://metals.about.com/od/properties/a/The-History-Of-Brass.htm)

The fact remains that what we now call *bronze* and not *brass* was the chief alloy of the ancient world. However, formerly in English it was not called *bronze*! Until more recently, "brass" was the general term used for copper-based alloys, whether with zinc or tin. The word "bronze" was first introduced into the English language (from the Italian *bronzo*) during the 16th century, but did not displace the use of "brass" as the term for both until well into the 19th century (see *The Oxford Dictionary of English Etymology, The Etymological Dictionary by W. W. Skeat*, and the *Oxford English Dictionary*, unabridged). Therefore, while the term may need to be explained today, the AV translators were quite correct in their choice of the word which had long-standing usage both before and after 1611.

Alexander the Great is Shown the Book of Daniel!

Greece as a nation existed for many centuries, but it reached empire status (its appearance on the statue) with Alexander the Great and his conquest of Persia. There is historical evidence that as the God of Israel dealt with Nebuchadnezzar, Cyrus and Darius the Mede, He also dealt with Alexander. The Jewish historian *Josephus* gives the following remarkable account of Alexander's conquests when he was about to attack Jerusalem. It should also be noted that Josephus mentions both Sanballat and Jaddua the High Priest (from the book of Nehemiah) in connection with Alexander. This is further confirmation of the relative shortness of the Persian era. See *Bible Chronology: The Two Great Divides*, pp. 106,107.

> About this time it was that Darius heard how Alexander had passed over the Hellespont, and had beaten his lieutenants in the battle of Granicum, and was proceeding farther; whereupon he gathered together an army of horse and foot, and determined that he would meet the Macedonians before they should assault and conquer all Asia.
>
> So he passed over the river Euphrates and came over Taurus, the Cilician mountain; and at Issus of Cilicia he waited for the enemy, as ready there to give him battle. Upon which Sanballat was glad that Darius was come down; and told Manasseh that he would suddenly perform his promises to him and this as soon as ever Darius should come back, after he had beaten his enemies ... but the event proved otherwise than they expected, for the king joined battle with the Macedonians, and was beaten, and lost a great part of his army. His mother also, and his wife and children, were taken captives, and he fled into Persia. So Alexander came into Syria, and took Damascus, and when he had obtained Sidon, he besieged Tyre, when he sent an epistle to the Jewish high priest ... that what presents he formally sent to Darius he would now send to him, and choose the friendship of the Macedonians ... but the high priest answered his messengers, that he had given his oath to Darius not to bear arms against him and he said that he would not transgress this while Darius was in the land of the living. Upon hearing this answer, Alexander was very angry;
>
> But Sanballat thought he had now gotten a proper opportunity to make his attempt, so he renounced Darius, and taking with him seven thousand of his own subjects, he came to Alexander; and finding him beginning the siege of Tyre, he said to him, that he delivered up to him these men who came out of places under his dominion, and did gladly accept of him for their lord instead of Darius. So when Alexander had received him kindly, Sanballat thereupon took courage, and spake to him about his present affair. He told him, that he had a son-in-law, Manasseh, who was brother to the high priest Jaddua; and that there were many others of his own nation now with him, that were desirous to have a temple in the places subject to him; that it would be for the king's advantage to have the strength of the Jews divided into two parts ... Whereupon Alexander gave Sanballat leave so to do; who used the utmost diligence, and built the temple, and made Manasseh the priest, and deemed it a great reward that his

daughter's children should have that dignity; but when the seven months of the siege of Tyre were over, and the two months of the siege of Gaza, Sanballat died. Now Alexander, when he had taken Gaza, made haste to go up to Jerusalem; and Jaddua the high priest, when he heard that, was in an agony, and under terror, as not knowing how he should meet the Macedonians, since the king was displeased at his foregoing disobedience. He therefore ordained that the people should make supplications, and should join with him in offering sacrifices to God ... whereupon God warned him in a dream, which came upon him after he had offered sacrifice, that he should take courage, and adorn the city, and open the gates; that the rest appear in white garments but that he and the priests should meet the king in the habits proper to their order. ... Upon which, when he rose from his sleep, he greatly rejoiced; and declared to all the warning he had received from God.

And when he understood that he was not far from the city, he went out in procession, with the priests and the multitude of the citizens. ... [And] Alexander, when he saw the multitude at a distance, in white garments, while the priests stood clothed with fine linen, and the high priest in purple and scarlet clothing with his mitre on his head having the golden plate on which the name of God was engraved, he approached by himself, and adored that name, and first saluted the high priest. The Jews also did all together, with one voice, salute Alexander, and encompass him about: whereupon the kings of Syria and the rest were surprised at what Alexander had done, and supposed him disordered in his mind. However, Parmenio alone went up to him, and asked him how it came to pass, that when all others adored him, he should adore the high priest of the Jews? To whom he replied, "I did not adore him, but that God who hath honored him with that high priesthood; for I saw this very person in a dream, in this very habit, when I was at Dios, in Macedonia, who, when I was considering with myself how I might obtain the dominion of Asia, exhorted me to make no delay, but boldly to pass over the sea thither, for that he would conduct my army, and would give me the dominion over the Persians ... And when he had said this to Parmenio, and had given the high priest his right hand, the priests ran along by him, and he came into the city; and when he went up into the temple, he offered sacrifice to God, according to the high priest's direction, and magnificently treated both the high priest and the priests. **And when the book of Daniel was showed him, wherein Daniel declared that one of the Greeks should destroy the empire of the Persians**, he supposed that himself was the person intended; and as he was then glad, he dismissed the multitude for the present, but the next day he called them to him, and bade them ask what favors they pleased of him: whereupon the high priest desired that they might enjoy the law of their forefathers and might pay no tribute on the seventh year. He granted all they desired:

So when Alexander had thus settled matters at Jerusalem, he led his army into the neighboring cities; and when all the inhabitants, to whom he came, received him with great kindness, the Samaritans ... desired that he would come to their city, and do honor to their temple also.

Now when Alexander was dead, the government was parted among his successors ... About this time it was that Jaddua the high priest died, and Onias his son took the high priesthood. This was the state of the affairs of the people of Jerusalem at this time. (XI.313-347).

The Grecian Empire was divided into four parts after Alexander's death with Egypt and Syria being the most powerful. Daniel 11 describes the almost constant warfare between these two (the king of the north and the king of the south) and then spans the centuries to the the tumultuous times of Christ's Return. With vast areas becoming *Hellenised* and speaking Greek, Greece even in its divided form outlasted the Babylonian and Persian empires. But after existing in one form or another for another three hundred years, it too began to decline. The Greeks grew tired of looking after the affairs of the world and with another empire further to the west rising in power, Greece showed no inclination to challenge it. This empire was Rome.

The Iron of Rome.

His legs of iron (2:32). And the fourth kingdom shall be strong as iron: forasmuch as iron breaketh in pieces and subdueth all things: and as iron that breaketh all these, shall it break in pieces and bruise (2:40).

The importance of the fourth kingdom in both its historical and final form is obvious from the fact in Daniel 2 more is said about it than that the preceding empires combined. In 30 BC the legions of Rome marched through Egypt on their way to Israel and the Middle East. In a very short time nearly the entire known world lay directly under Rome's power or influence. She quickly filled the vacuum left by a decaying Grecian Empire. Israel and the entire Mediterranean region were under her control.

The Roman Empire is shown in the statues with two iron legs. While many refer this to the division of Rome between east and west after her rise to power, in fact it refers (at least in the first instance) to the vast expanse of the Roman Empire. Far more than the other empires which were to the east (Babylon and Persia) or to the west (Greece), the iron legs of Rome spanned and subdued both. From Mesopotamia in the east to Spain in the west Rome *subdued*, *broke in pieces* and *bruised*.

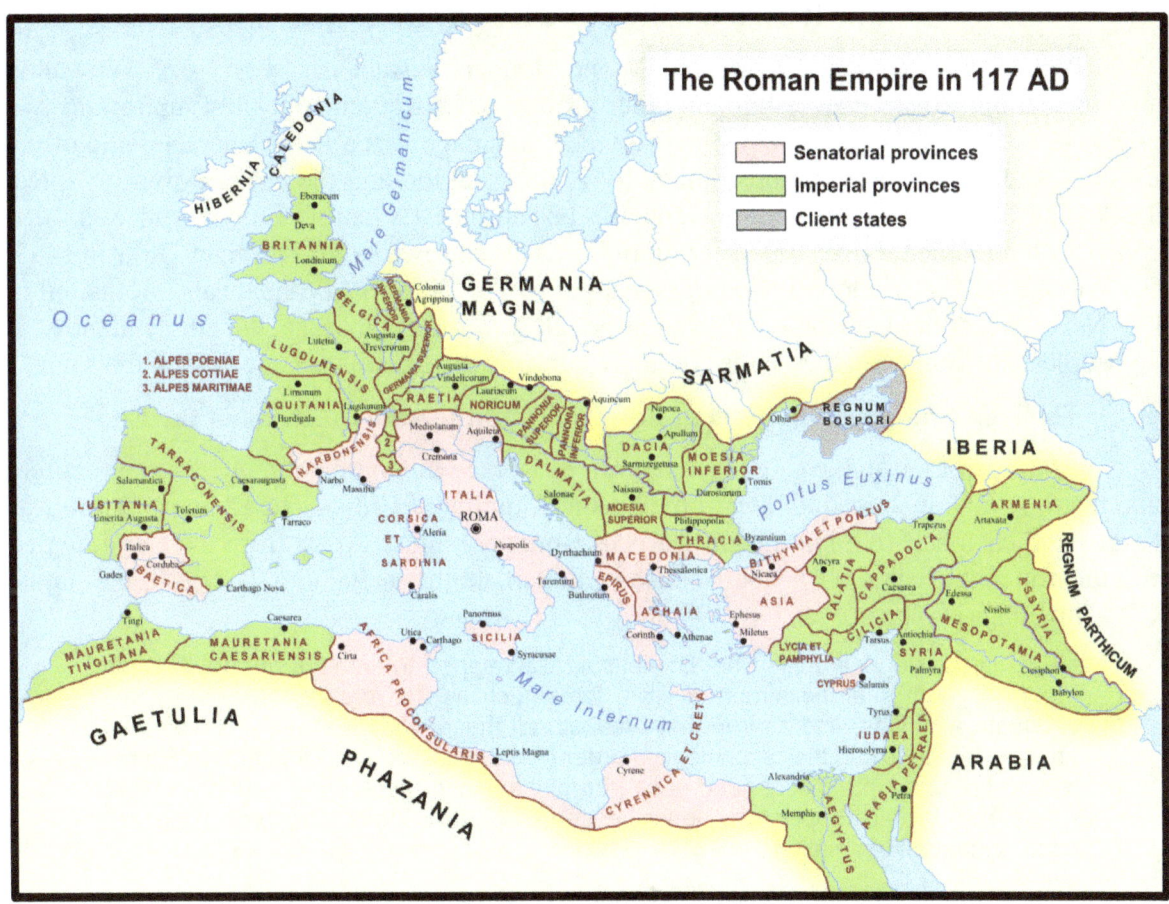

The Roman Empire at the Height of its Power and Extent

The Roman Empire as Divided by Diocletian

When the Roman Empire could no longer sustain its vast size, unwieldy communication, weaker leadership and other problems, Diocletian split the Empire into two halves – Eastern and Western. When first divided, language was a major characteristic of the division. The western leg was predominantly Latin speaking and the eastern division spoke Greek. The Eastern Roman Empire eventually became the Byzantine Empire and was ruled from Constantinople for over 1000 years until it was overthrown by the Ottoman Turks in 1453. The Western half after a long period of onslaught by the Visigoths, Vandals and Goths fell in 476. Nevertheless though Rome fell in an imperial, governmental sense, the ethnic identity of the peoples who inhabited these areas (to a greater or lesser sense) remained much the same.

The Iron *Chunks* of the Roman Empire Continue unto the Time of the End

The legs of the statue show that the *iron* of Rome will continue in one form or another unto the time of Antichrist and then of the Second Coming of Christ. The Roman Empire was divided and each half fell, but integral parts of Rome remained. Apart from the clay mingled with the iron in the feet, there is not the introduction of another metal into the legs of the statue. N.W. Hutchings explains:

> Let us notice very carefully what Daniel said will happen to the legs of iron: And the fourth kingdom shall be strong as iron; forasmuch as iron breaketh in pieces and subdueth all things; and as iron that breaketh all these, shall it break in pieces and bruise (Dan. 2:40). In the chronological order of empires, the iron kingdom, or Rome, was to break up into pieces, and each iron piece would represent a nation. In other words, the Roman Empire has never ceased to exist. It has simply broken up into various independent nations.
>
> The preservation of the Roman dictatorial form of government is evident in the two strongest nations in the eastern leg and the western leg today — Germany and Russia. Germany named its king Kaiser, which is German for "Caesar." Russia named its king czar, which is Russian for "Caesar." The Bolshevik Revolution, which was taken over by the communists, replaced the government of Russian czars with a system of commissars, or communist "Caesars."
>
> Rome began to break up in AD 476 but endured in some form until AD 963 when its dissolution became a historical fact. Even so, as the prophecy of Daniel foretold, Rome continued to rule the world in its broken state. Each chunk of the iron in the legs became

an empire: the Spanish Empire, the British Empire, the Dutch Empire, the Italian Empire, the Belgian Empire, the French Empire, etc.

Also, according to the prophecy of Daniel, the iron chunks from the broken legs would jostle against each other and bruise. History has recorded the literal fulfilment of this part of the prophecy: French-English wars; Spanish-English wars; the Napoleonic wars; and both World War I and World War II were started by European powers that were once integral parts of the old Roman Empire.

Many attempts have been made since AD 963 to put the humpty-dumpty Roman Empire back together again. Napoleon tried time and time again, yet he was never able to conquer England. Hitler tried, but he made the same mistake that Napoleon made — he tried to conquer Russia before taking England. According to the prophecy of Daniel, and related prophecies in Revelation, Rome would not be revived through conquest, but rather by common agreement. This prophecy has been fulfilled in our day through the Common Market Alliance.

It should be noted that according to the prophecy based on Nebuchadnezzar's dream, the iron pieces of Rome would eventually break up. This final disintegration of ancient Rome is represented by the pieces of iron and clay in the feet of the image, indicating that it would occur in the very extremity of the age. This occurred after World War II, and it came about mostly through agreements made by Joseph Stalin of Russia and Franklin Roosevelt. These two world leaders represented the two most powerful nations in the world to emerge from the second world holocaust. Winston Churchill of England protested to President Roosevelt that he could not agree with the extermination of the British Empire, but his protests availed little.

Almost immediately after World War II, the Roman colonial system began to break up. Colony after colony of France, England, Germany, Italy, Holland, Belgium, etc., gained or were granted independence. The only shadows of Rome that were left were a few nations with British commonwealth status like Canada, Australia, and New Zealand. (Exploring the Book of Daniel, pp. 49-51).

The Iron and Clay of Revived Rome.

(2:41) And whereas thou sawest the feet and toes, part of potters' clay, and part of iron, the kingdom shall be divided; but there shall be in it of the strength of the iron, forasmuch as thou sawest the iron mixed with miry clay. (2:42) And as the toes of the feet were part of iron, and part of clay, so the kingdom shall be partly strong, and partly broken. (2:43) And whereas thou sawest iron mixed with miry clay, they shall mingle themselves with the seed of men: but they shall not cleave one to another, even as iron is not mixed with clay.

Here we have the Roman Empire in its last extremity. We know this is so because in the next two verses (2:44,45) it will suddenly be destroyed and replaced by *the Stone, cut out without hands*. The Bible's emphatic summary of Rome's final stage is that it will be *strong and weak*! This is a most fitting description of the European Union. It is indeed clay mixed with iron, strong nations mixed with week nations: strong and weak economically, strong and weak militarily, strong in the north of Europe, weaker in south. They are strong or weak in relation to the Roman Catholic Church. Strongly Catholic countries are often the weaker. Nevertheless as we will show there is *a far more fundamental explanation for the clay*. But first, note again N.A. Hutchings incisive comments:

First, we notice that these ten toes represent a kingdom in the very extremity of the age. We know that they will comprise a kingdom because we are told the kingdom shall be partly strong, and partly broken. But what kingdom is Daniel speaking of here? He mentions the first kingdom, Babylon; the second kingdom, Medo-Persia; the third kingdom, Greece; the fourth kingdom, Rome. But when he gets to the toes, he does not say the fifth kingdom, but simply the kingdom. The reason Daniel did not identify the toes as a fifth kingdom is because he was still referring back to the fourth kingdom, Rome. Even though the kingdom would break up into pieces and never cleave together again, the pieces themselves are still referred to as a kingdom. Even in the toes we find the iron and the clay mixed together. We refer to this ten-nation kingdom in the end of the age as the Revived Roman Empire.

Even after the final breakup of Rome there remained a need for an exchange of manufactured goods and agricultural products. Therefore, except in times of wars or political upheavals, a European fair was held yearly at Versailles, France. At these fairs produce of all kinds was brought by farmers and merchants to be exchanged or sold. Also, trade agreements were made. These fairs were called the common market.

After World War II with the loss of colonies, the nations of Europe could no longer depend upon needed imports from these former territories. Therefore, the need for a revival of the common market concept arose. This need was consummated through a treaty in Rome binding Italy, France, Germany, Holland, Belgium, and Luxembourg to a common market agreement (pp. 52,53).

Today there is a common parliament and a president, a common passport, a common currency, a common wage scale, a common tax structure, a common military force through NATO. Though remaining independent nations, they act politically as a unit in their international dealings; for example with the United States, Russia and Israel.

There are as we are all aware huge stains in the EU. This is precisely in accord with what was long ago prophesied in Daniel 2:41-43; it is an amalgamation of clay and iron. Note especially verse 43: ***And whereas thou sawest iron mixed with miry clay, they shall mingle themselves with the seed of men: but they shall not cleave one to another, even as iron is not mixed with clay.*** "They" must refer to the leadership inherent in the ten toes (2:41). "**Seed of men**" must refer to general populace over which they rule. This points us back to the basic question (that while always there) will become so all pervasive at the end of the age:

What is the *Clay*?

Daniel 2:43 says clay is ***the seed of men***. It is mankind generally. It is fallen human nature: unstable, pliable, fickle, vacillating. It is what we inherit from Adam. It is because *man is clay* that every politician approaching every election can proclaim as if it has never been proclaimed before: WE NEED CHANGE!

• As is the **earthy**, such are they also that are earthy: and as is the heavenly, such are they also that are heavenly. And as we have borne the image of the earthy, we shall also bear the image of the heavenly (1 Cor 15:48,49).

• He brought me up also out of an horrible pit, out of the **miry clay**, and set my feet upon a rock, and established my goings (Psa 40:2).

Both the so-called strong and weak nations of Europe have entire populations of clay. That is what man is! Think how pliable the strongest nation in Europe, Germany, became in the 1930s when tens of millions lined the street to laud Adolf Hitler!

For us in the west it is difficult to imagine living in anything other than a democracy. Yet, the well-intentioned attempt of democratic government - *of the people, by the people, for the people* - does not always work in much of world (though of course, if workable, the checks and balances of democratic government are far better than the abuses that arise in a totalitarian state!).

Apart from God-appointed leadership there will always be failure. In Old Testament Israel God Himself led the people (cp. 1 Sam 8:19) and then later appointed the line of kings from the House of David (*elections were not held every four or five years!*). Only when the Second Psalm is fulfilled and a King arises from this same House of David (Luke 1:32,33) will true and righteous government will be seen on earth. Until then it will be chaotic, *because man is clay*.

> • *Thus saith the Lord GOD; Remove the diadem, and take off the crown: this shall not be the same: exalt him that is low, and abase him that is high. I will overturn, overturn, overturn, it: and it shall be no more, until he come whose right it is; and I will give it him (Ezek 21:26,27).*

> • *Yet have I set my king upon my holy hill of Zion. I will declare the decree: the LORD hath said unto me, Thou art my Son; this day have I begotten thee. Ask of me, and I shall give thee the heathen for thine inheritance, and the uttermost parts of the earth for thy possession. Thou shalt break them with a **rod of iron**; thou shalt dash them in pieces like a potter's vessel. Be wise now therefore, O ye kings: be instructed, ye judges of the earth. Serve the LORD with fear, and rejoice with trembling. Kiss the Son, lest he be angry, and ye perish from the way, when his wrath is kindled but a little. Blessed are all they that put their trust in him (Psa 2:6-12).*

> • *And he shall rule them with a **rod of iron**; as the vessels of a potter shall they be broken to shivers: even as I received of my Father (Rev 2:27).*

> • *And she brought forth a man child, who was to rule all nations with a **rod of iron**: and her child was caught up unto God, and to his throne (Rev 12:5).*

> • *And out of his mouth goeth a sharp sword, that with it he should smite the nations: and he shall rule them with a **rod of iron**: and he treadeth the winepress of the fierceness and wrath of Almighty God (Rev 19:15).*

This **iron rod** will be wielded through a *King* who *shall reign in righteousness, and princes* who *shall rule in judgment* (Isa 32:1). There is currently *iron* in the constitutional and legal instruments of the Europe Union but until (as Scripture reveals) their arises a centralized and totalitarian *rod of iron* government under the Antichrist the EU nations will not **cleave one to another.**

Because *man is clay*, the *clay* was of course *always present* in the previous empires, but the strong centralized governments of these empires *kept it at bay* and it did not manifest itself in the statue of Daniel Two. With the attempts of democratic government in the latter end of the Times of the Gentiles, the *clay* appears.

The Ten Toes Become Ten Horns!

Today (2015) there are 28 member states in the European Union; of these 19 have the Euro as their currency. There has been every attempt to make this union a true union and **cleave one to another** but it has fallen far short of that ideal. Nevertheless a major transformation is coming. In Daniel 2 we read of *toes*, obviously **ten toes**. Hereafter we read of **ten horns** (Dan 7; Rev 13,17). Europe is about to be *thrown together*! This however will last for only a short while (Rev 17:12).

> • *After this I saw in the night visions, and behold a fourth beast, dreadful and terrible, and strong exceedingly; and it had great <u>iron teeth</u>: it devoured and brake in pieces, and stamped the residue with the feet of it: and it was diverse from all the beasts that were before it; and it had **ten horns** (Dan 7:7).*

> • *And of the **ten horns** that were in his head, and of the other which came up, and before whom three fell; even of that horn that had eyes, and a mouth that spake very great things, whose look was more stout than his fellows (Dan 7:20).*

> • *And the **ten horns** out of this kingdom are ten kings that shall arise: and another shall rise after them; and he shall be diverse from the first, and he shall subdue three kings (Dan 7:24).*

> • *And there appeared another wonder in heaven; and behold a great red dragon, having seven heads and **ten horns**, and seven crowns upon his heads (Rev 12:3).*

> • *And I stood upon the sand of the sea, and saw a beast rise up out of the sea, having seven heads and **ten horns**, and upon his horns ten crowns, and upon his heads the name of blasphemy (Rev 13:1).*

> • So he carried me away in the spirit into the wilderness: and I saw a woman sit upon a scarlet coloured beast, full of names of blasphemy, having seven heads and **ten horns** (Rev 17:3).
>
> • And the angel said unto me, Wherefore didst thou marvel? I will tell thee the mystery of the woman, and of the beast that carrieth her, which hath the seven heads and **ten horns** (Rev 17:7).
>
> • And the **ten horns** which thou sawest are ten kings, which have received no kingdom as yet; but <u>receive power as kings one hour with the beast</u> (Rev 17:12).
>
> • And the **ten horns** which thou sawest upon the beast, these shall hate the whore, and shall make her desolate and naked, and shall eat her flesh, and burn her with fire (Rev 17:16).

Daniel's vantage point begins with Babylon; the Apostle John who views the *Seven Heads* observes it from the two preceding empires – Egypt and Assyria. Both viewpoints conclude with Rome and the Ten Horns. Horns speak of power and this power comes from the Antichrist who in turn receives his power from Satan (Rev 13:3). *And the* **ten horns** *which thou sawest are ten kings, which have received no kingdom as yet; but <u>receive power as kings one hour with the beast</u>* (Rev 17:12). These *horns* will coerce not only Europe but the World itself into an iron clad union with the Antichrist. Note how emphatically this is stated in Revelation 13.

> (13:1) And I stood upon the sand of the sea, and saw a beast rise up out of the sea, having seven heads and **ten horns**, and upon his horns ten crowns, and upon his heads the name of blasphemy. (13:2) And the beast which I saw was like unto a leopard, and his feet were as the feet of a bear, and his mouth as the mouth of a lion: and the dragon gave him his power, and his seat, and great authority. (13:3) And I saw one of his heads as it were wounded to death; and his deadly wound was healed: and **all the world** wondered after the beast. (13:4) And they worshipped the dragon which gave power unto the beast: and they worshipped the beast, saying, **Who is like** unto the beast? **who is able** to make war with him? (13:5) And there was given unto him a mouth speaking great things and blasphemies; and power was given unto him to continue forty and two months. (13:6) And he opened his mouth in blasphemy against God, to blaspheme his name, and his tabernacle, and them that dwell in heaven. (13:7) And it was given unto him to make war with the saints, and to overcome them: and **power was given him over all kindreds, and tongues, and nations**. (13:8) And **all that dwell upon the earth** shall worship him, whose names are not written in the book of life of the Lamb slain from the foundation of the world. (13:9) If any man have an ear, let him hear. (13:10) He that leadeth into captivity shall go into captivity: he that killeth with the sword must be killed with the sword. Here is the patience and the faith of the saints. (13:11) And I beheld another beast coming up out of the earth; and he had two horns like a lamb, and he spake as a dragon. (13:12) And he exerciseth all the power of the first beast before him, and **causeth the earth and them which dwell therein** to worship the first beast, whose deadly wound was healed. (13:13) And he doeth great wonders, so that he maketh fire come down from heaven on the earth in the sight of men, (13:14) And deceiveth **them that dwell on the earth** by the means of those miracles which he had power to do in the sight of the beast; saying to **them that dwell on the earth**, that they should make an image to the beast, which had the wound by a sword, and did live. (13:15) And he had power to give life unto the image of the beast, that the image of the beast should both speak, and cause that as many as would not worship the image of the beast should be killed. (13:16) And **he causeth all**, both small and great, rich and poor, free and bond, to receive a mark in their right hand, or in their foreheads: (13:17) And that **no man** might buy or sell, save he that had the mark, or the name of the beast, or the number of his name. (13:18) Here is wisdom. Let him that hath understanding count the number of the beast: for it is the number of a man; and his number is Six hundred threescore and six.

GDP of Ten Leading Nations

The Ten Toes/Horns are seen rising out of the Roman Empire; that is: what it was, what it continued to be in one form or another, and what it will be in the last days. As ancient Rome ruled (or had the power to rule) the entire populated earth, so it will be in its final form under the Antichrist. Therefore though we often think of the horns as being European in origin, it must be remembered that Rome's rule extended to peoples far beyond what is today called European. As the Antichrist will have worldwide control (Rev 13:7), some of the horns may not be European. Nor can we know their identity before the Rapture and before the Antichrist empowers certain nations to become *horns* (Rev 17:12). Currently the following **ten** nations are the most powerful economically and have long been dominant nations

	GDP in billion U.S. dollars
United States	17,416.25
China	10,355.35
Japan	4,769.8
Germany	3,820.46
France	2,902.33
United Kingdom	2,847.6
Brazil	2,244.13
Italy	2,129.28
Russia	2,057.3
India	2,047.81

The Stone Mountain of The Messiah's Kingdom.

Thou sawest till that a stone was cut out without hands, which smote the image upon his feet that were of iron and clay, and brake them to pieces (2:34). Then was the iron, the clay, the brass, the silver, and the gold, broken to pieces together, and became like the chaff of the summer threshingfloors; and the wind carried them away, that no place was found for them: and the stone that smote the image became a great mountain, and filled the whole earth(2:35). And in the days of these kings shall the God of heaven set

DANIEL 2: THE METALLIC COLOSSUS

up a kingdom, which shall never be destroyed: and the kingdom shall not be left to other people, but it shall break in pieces and consume all these kingdoms, and it shall stand for ever (2:44). Forasmuch as thou sawest that the stone was cut out of the mountain without hands, and that it brake in pieces the iron, the brass, the clay, the silver, and the gold; the great God hath made known to the king what shall come to pass hereafter: and the dream is certain, and the interpretation thereof sure (2:45).

The Time of the Coming Kingdom. Believers are taught to pray (the *first* petition of the Lord's Prayer): *They kingdom come, thy will be done on earth as it is in heaven* (Matt 6:10). Yet here we are told *when* that Kingdom will come. It is **in the days of these kings shall the God of heaven set up a kingdom** (2:44). It is in the days after the Rapture, when the *ten horned nations* have done their worst, when the second half of the seven years of the wrath of God is completed (Rev 14:10,11) and when the last *forty-two months* have run their course (Rev 11:2; 13;5). It is then that *the God of heaven* shall *set up a kingdom*. Therefore the Lord's Prayer is a prayer for a *hastening* of the events described here that will culminate in His Return.

The Continuance of the Coming Kingdom. It **shall never be destroyed: and the kingdom shall not be left to other people...it shall stand forever** (2:44). Every previous kingdom had been destroyed. *Change and decay all around I see.* This Kingdom shall be as the *days of heaven* (Deut 11:21; Psa 89:29); its subjects as the *stars of heaven* (Gen 26:4; Exod 32:13), not only innumerable, but gloriously immutable. This kingdom will extend throughout the Millennial Reign and then into the Eternal Ages. *Of the increase of his government and peace* **there shall be no end**, *upon the throne of David, and upon his kingdom, to order it, and to establish it with judgment and with justice from henceforth* **even for ever**. *The zeal of the LORD of hosts will perform this* (Isa 9:7).

The Judgement Inflicted by the Stone: *...a stone...which smote the image upon his feet that were of iron and clay, and brake them to pieces* (2:34). ***Then was the iron, the clay, the brass, the silver, and the gold, broken to pieces together, and became like the chaff of the summer threshingfloors; and the wind carried them away, that no place was found for them*** (2:35). ***It shall break in pieces and consume all these kingdoms... it brake in pieces the iron, the brass, the clay, the silver, and the gold*** (2:44,45). The Stone did not smite the image on the golden head, or silver chest, or brass stomach, or iron legs. It **smote the image upon his feet that were of iron and clay.** This is a climatic end time judgement. It did not take place gradually through the centuries. Yet as it is also true that Rome encompassed the previous empires, so the metals of those empires also appear in the destruction. Rome was not an innovator but an assimilator of the cultures it conquered. Note the three fold listing of these metals. First the original order on the statue, and then two lists giving the order of their destruction.

- Verses 32,33: gold, silver, brass, iron, iron and clay.
- Verse 35:   iron, clay, brass, silver, gold.
- Verse 45:   iron, brass, clay, silver, gold.

Note that *gold* (Babylon), the first on the image, is last in the two destruction lists. This conforms with the fact that while Daniel presents the Times of the Gentiles from a Roman standpoint; Isaiah (13,47); Jeremiah (50,51) and Revelation (17,18) see the final stage of the worldly, godless, arrogant Gentile world as *Babylon*.

But whether it be Rome, Babylon or the other characteristic metals on the statue, when struck on the feet at Christ's Second Coming it will be so utterly destroyed that it is likened to ***the chaff of the summer threshingfloors; and the wind carried them away, that no place was found for them*** (2:35).

<u>The Stone From a Mountain that Becomes a Mountain</u>. ***And the stone that smote the image became a great mountain, and filled the whole earth*** (2:35). This is ***a stone cut out of the mountain without hands*** (2:45). Contrasted with the empires on the image that were *made with the hands* and intellect of man, the Messiah was not created by human agency. His *goings forth have been of old from everlasting* (Micah 5:2). As the Old Testament Temple was a foreshadowing of Christ (Jhn 2:19-21), strict orders were given that *there was neither hammer nor axe nor any tool of iron heard in the house, while it was in building* (1 Kng 6:7). The ***mountain*** is Christ's eternal Godhead, majesty and magnitude (1 Tim 3:16; Heb 1:8). The ***stone*** is His incarnation and humanity. It is His coming into the world – both at His First and Second Comings.

This is a Corner and Foundation Stone

• *From thence is the shepherd,* **the stone** *of Israel (Gen 49:24).*

• **The stone** *which the builders refused is become* **the head stone of the corner**. *This is the LORD's doing; it is marvellous in our eyes (Psa 118:22,23).*

• *Therefore thus saith the Lord GOD, Behold, I lay in Zion for* **a foundation a stone**, *a tried stone,* **a precious corner stone**, **a sure foundation**: *he that believeth shall not make haste (Isa 28:16).*

This is a Mountain Stone

• *And the stone that smote the image became* **a great mountain**, *and filled the whole earth (Dan 2:35).*

• *Great is the LORD, and greatly to be praised in the city of our God,* **in the mountain of his holiness** *(Psa 48:1).*

• *And it shall come to pass in the last days, that the* **mountain of the LORD'S house** *shall be established* **in the top of the mountains**, *and shall be exalted above the hills; and all nations shall flow unto it. And many people shall go and say, Come ye, and let us go up to* **the mountain of the LORD**, *to the house of the God of Jacob; and he will teach us of his ways, and we will walk in his paths: for out of Zion shall go forth the law, and the word of the LORD from Jerusalem (Isa 2:2,3).*

• *They shall not hurt nor destroy in all* **my holy mountain**: *for the earth shall be full of the knowledge of the LORD, as the waters cover the sea (Isa 11:9).*

• *O Zion, that bringest good tidings, get thee up into* **the high mountain**; *O Jerusalem, that bringest good tidings, lift up thy voice with strength; lift it up, be not afraid; say unto the cities of Judah, Behold your God (Isa 40:9)!*

• *In* **the mountain of the height of Israel** *will I plant it: and it shall bring forth boughs, and bear fruit, and be a goodly cedar: and under it shall dwell all fowl of every wing; in the shadow of the branches thereof shall they dwell (Ezek 17:23).*

• *In the visions of God brought he me into the land of Israel, and set me upon* **a very high mountain**, *by which was as the frame of a city on the south (Ezek 40:2).*

• *So shall ye know that I am the LORD your God dwelling in* **Zion, my holy mountain**: *then shall Jerusalem be holy, and there shall no strangers pass through her any more (Joel 3:17).*

• *But in the last days it shall come to pass, that* **the mountain of the house of the LORD** *shall be established* **in the top of the mountains**, *and it shall be exalted above the hills; and people shall flow unto it. And many nations shall come, and say, Come, and let us go up to the mountain of the LORD, and to the house of the God of Jacob; and he will teach us of his ways, and we will walk in his paths: for the law shall go forth of Zion, and the word of the LORD from Jerusalem (Mic 4:1,2).*

DANIEL 2: THE METALLIC COLOSSUS

*• Thus saith the LORD; I am returned unto Zion, and will dwell in the midst of Jerusalem: and Jerusalem shall be called a city of truth; and **the mountain of the LORD of hosts the holy mountain** (Zech 8:3).*

*• And he carried me away in the spirit to **a great and high mountain**, and shewed me that great city, the holy Jerusalem, descending out of heaven from God (Rev 21:10).*

This is a Stumbling Stone

In its relation to Israel, Christ as the Stone has been *a stone of stumbling* on which Israel has been *broken* but not destroyed as the world system will be. Application can be made to all lost sinners; either we fall upon Him in repentance or He falls on us in judgement.

*• Unto you therefore which believe he is precious: but unto them which be disobedient, **the stone** which the builders disallowed, the same is made the head of the corner, And **a stone of stumbling**, and **a rock of offence**, even to them which stumble at the word, being disobedient: whereunto also they were appointed (1 Pet 2:7,8).*

*• And in that day will I make Jerusalem **a burdensome stone** for all people: all that burden themselves with it shall be cut in pieces, though all the people of the earth be gathered together against it (Zech 12:3).*

*• Jesus saith unto them, Did ye never read in the scriptures, **The stone** which the builders rejected, the same is become **the head of the corner**: this is the Lord's doing, and it is marvellous in our eyes? Therefore say I unto you, The kingdom of God shall be taken from you, and given to a nation bringing forth the fruits thereof. And whosoever shall fall on **this stone** shall be broken: but on whomsoever it shall fall, it will grind him to powder (Matt 21:42-44).*

The Certainty of The Vision. ***Forasmuch as thou sawest that the stone was cut out of the mountain without hands, and that it brake in pieces the iron, the brass, the clay, the silver, and the gold; the great God hath made known to the king what shall come to pass hereafter: and the dream is certain, and the interpretation thereof sure*** (2:45). Daniel gave a proof of the certainty of the vision. It is based on the incarnate and glorified Redeemer (***the stone was cut out of the mountain without hands***), the true KING OF KINGS (Rev 19:16) returning to earth to set up His Kingdom upon the basis of His purchased redemption. Therefore ***the dream is certain, and the interpretation thereof sure.***

The utter truthfulness of the Words of Scripture is based on the Person and Work of the Lord Jesus Christ.

Heaven and earth shall pass away, but my words shall not pass away (Matt 24:35).

Daniel and His Friends are Promoted 2:46-49.

Then the king Nebuchadnezzar fell upon his face, and worshipped Daniel, and commanded that they should offer an oblation and sweet odours unto him. (2:47) The king answered unto Daniel, and said, Of a truth it is, that your God is a God of gods, and a Lord of kings, and a revealer of secrets, seeing thou couldest reveal this secret. (2:48) Then the king made Daniel a great man, and gave him many great gifts, and made him ruler over the whole province of Babylon, and chief of the governors over all the wise men of Babylon. (2:49) Then Daniel requested of the king, and he set Shadrach, Meshach, and Abednego, over the affairs of the province of Babylon: but Daniel sat in the gate of the king.

One might have expected that when Nebuchadnezzar was contriving to make his own kingdom everlasting, he would be enraged at Daniel who foretold of its fall, and of the kingdom that would follow and replace it, and that ultimately another kingdom of another nature would be *the* everlasting kingdom. But, instead he received it as an oracle of God.

Nebuchadnezzar was almost ready to look upon Daniel as a little god. ***Then the king Nebuchadnezzar fell upon his face, and worshipped Daniel, and commanded that they***

should offer an oblation and sweet odours unto him (2:46). Though he saw him as a man, a young man, yet recognized that the God to Whom Daniel had already given such a firm testimony, was most certainly with him. Daniel testified in behalf of what God could do in revealing secrets and it most certainly came to pass.

> Daniel answered in the presence of the king, and said, The secret which the king hath demanded cannot the wise men, the astrologers, the magicians, the soothsayers, shew unto the king; But **there is a God in heaven that revealeth secrets**, and maketh known to the king Nebuchadnezzar what shall be in the latter days. Thy dream, and the visions of thy head upon thy bed, are these; As for thee, O king, thy thoughts came into thy mind upon thy bed, what should come to pass hereafter: and **he that revealeth secrets** maketh known to thee what shall come to pass. But as for me, **this secret is not revealed to me for any wisdom that I have** more than any living, but for their sakes that shall make known the interpretation to the king, and that thou mightest know the thoughts of thy heart (2:27-30).

It was the custom of the country by ***falling on the face*** to give honour to kings, because they have something of a divine power in them (cp. *I have said, You are gods*. Psa 82:6); and therefore this king, who had often received such veneration, now paid the same to Daniel who had so clearly shown that he was a bearer of divine revelation. What Nebuchadnezzar did was wrong, yet by this God magnified His Word and extracted from the proud potentate such a veneration even though he had only been given this glimpse of it. So we would like to think that Nebuchadnezzar was worshiping the Word more than the man, but this was probably not the case.

Likely Daniel having already testified so firmly of God would have shown disapproval in the same manner as Peter said to Cornelius, *Stand up, I myself also am a man* (Acts 10:26); or as the angel said twice did to the Apostle John, *See thou do it not* (Rev 19:10; 22:9). Therefore in the next verse the king turns his praise from Daniel to Daniel's God.

Nebuchadnezzar Acknowledged the God of Daniel to be the Great God. ***The king answered unto Daniel, and said, Of a truth it is, that your God is a God of gods, and a Lord of kings, and a revealer of secrets, seeing thou couldest reveal this secret*** (2:47). This is not the same as saying the He is the only God. But the three things he says are a major step in the right direction. Daniel's God is above all gods in dignity and over all gods in dominion. He is a ***Lord of kings***, from whom they derive their power and to whom they are accountable. He is a ***revealer of secrets***; what is most secret He sees and can reveal, and what He has revealed is what was secret and which none but Himself could reveal (1 Cor 2:10). However, as we will see from the next chapter the king still has a good way to go! Later we will hear from Nebuchadnezzar a much higher acknowledgement of his faith.

> • Nebuchadnezzar the king, unto all people, nations, and languages, that dwell in all the earth; Peace be multiplied unto you. I thought it good to shew the signs and wonders that the high God hath wrought toward me. How great are his signs! and how mighty are his wonders! his kingdom is an everlasting kingdom, and his dominion is from generation to generation (4:1-3).

> • Now I Nebuchadnezzar praise and extol and honour the King of heaven, all whose works are truth, and his ways judgment: and those that walk in pride he is able to abase (4:37).

Nebuchadnezzar Promotes Daniel to Great Honour. ***Then the king made Daniel a great man, and gave him many great gifts, and made him ruler over the whole province of Babylon, and chief of the governors over all the wise men of Babylon*** (2:48). Because God had magnified him, therefore the king magnified him.

Does wealth make men great? In this case it added to Daniel's greatness. The king *gave him many great gifts*. It was not for self-enrichment but gave Daniel the greater capacity of doing good to his brethren in captivity.

Does power make a man great? He made him **ruler over the whole province of Babylon**, which no doubt had great influence upon the other provinces; he made him likewise chancellor of the university, *chief of the governors over all the wise men of Babylon*. Since they could not do what the king would have them do, they are now obliged to do what Daniel would have them do. Some no doubt learned their lessons well and continued to learn them well; for at the time of the birth of Christ *there came wise men from the east to Jerusalem, Saying, Where is he that is born King of the Jews? for we have seen his star in the east, and are come to worship him* (Matt 2:1,2).

Joseph, like Daniel, was advanced in the court of the king of Egypt for his interpreting of dreams; and Pharaoh called him *Zaphnath-paaneah—a revealer of secrets*. This same thing the king of Babylon said about Daniel.

<u>Daniel Makes Request for the Promotion of the Three Friends</u>. **Then Daniel requested of the king, and he set Shadrach, Meshach, and Abednego, over the affairs of the province of Babylon: but Daniel sat in the gate of the king** (2:49). Upon entering his high office, this was his first item of business. He procured places in the government for Shadrach, Meshach, and Abednego. Those that helped him with their prayers shall share with him in his honours. Thus the good that Daniel would do for Babylon and especially for his captive Israelites would now be further extended.

So having now seen the beginning of the *Times of the Gentiles* and how those Times span the ages to the Second Coming of Christ, we now see the characteristics of those times. These describe what the believer must often face in this world.

THE TIMES OF THE GENTILES 1-7

C. THE CHARACTERISTICS OF THE TIMES OF THE GENTILES 3-6

1. A TIME OF ENFORCED FALSE RELIGION: NEBUCHADNEZZAR'S IMAGE 3

DANIEL 3. THE GOLDEN IMAGE ON THE PLAINS OF DURA

At the close of Chapter Two we left Daniel's companions, Shadrach, Meshach, and Abednego, in honour and power, princes of the provinces, and preferred for their relation to the God of Israel. But in this lower world during the *Times of the Gentiles*, honour and glory for the believer may often be the exception rather than the rule, and matters may change very suddenly. Here those same three men so greatly esteemed by Nebuchadnezzar are now under his wrath; and that for a matter that will be very common during the Times of the Gentiles: *enforced state religion*. They are prepared to suffer rather than to sin and Hebrews 11:34 gives their memorial: they *quenched the violence of fire*.

Theodotion, a Hellenistic Jewish scholar in Ephesus, made a Greek translation of Daniel in 150 AD. In this he said Nebuchadnezzar erected this statue at the time of his third invasion and destruction of Jerusalem. Some see this as a reason for Daniel's absence from the events of Chapter Three and would place the chapter some eighteen years after Nebuchadnezzar had his vision. This however has not been verified by anyone else and there is no indication at all of it taking place at Jerusalem's destruction. Two such major events occurring concurrently would certainly be linked together by Scriptural and historical record.

The Setting Up of The Great Image 3:1-7.

Nebuchadnezzar the king made an image of gold, whose height was threescore cubits, and the breadth thereof six cubits: he set it up in the plain of Dura, in the province of Babylon. (3:2) Then Nebuchadnezzar the king sent to gather together the princes, the governors, and the captains, the judges, the treasurers, the counsellors, the sheriffs, and all the rulers of the provinces, to come to the dedication of the image which Nebuchadnezzar the king had set up. (3:3) Then the princes, the governors, and captains, the judges, the treasurers, the counsellors, the sheriffs, and all the rulers of the provinces, were gathered together unto the dedication of the image that Nebuchadnezzar the king had set up; and they stood before the image that Nebuchadnezzar had set up. (3:4) Then an herald cried aloud, To you it is commanded, O people, nations, and languages, (3:5) That at what time ye hear the sound of the cornet, flute, harp, sackbut, psaltery, dulcimer, and all kinds of musick, ye fall down and worship the golden image that Nebuchadnezzar the king hath set up: (3:6) And whoso falleth not down and worshippeth shall the same hour be cast into the midst of a burning fiery furnace. (3:7) Therefore at that time, when all the people heard the sound of the cornet, flute, harp, sackbut, psaltery, and all kinds of musick, all the people, the nations, and the languages, fell down and worshipped the golden image that Nebuchadnezzar the king had set up.

As we cannot be certain concerning the date of this account, only that if this image which Nebuchadnezzar dedicated had any relation to that which he dreamed of (and that seems *very* likely) it is probable that it happened not long after; some reckon it to be about the seventh year of Nebuchadnezzar, a year before Jehoiachin's captivity, in which Ezekiel was carried away (*Matthew Henry*).

<u>The Setting Up of the Image</u>. ***Nebuchadnezzar the king made an image of gold, whose height was threescore cubits, and the breadth thereof six cubits: he set it up in the plain of Dura, in the province of Babylon*** (3:1). Babylon was full of idols already, yet now

DANIEL 3. THE GOLDEN IMAGE ON THE PLAINS OF DURA

Nebuchadnezzar must have one more. For those who have forsaken the one only living God, and begin to set up many gods, will find the gods they set up so unsatisfying that they must continue to add to them. It was because of their idolatry that Judah was carried captive into Babylon the capital of idolatry. The following two verses were not said of Babylon but of Judah, and that not long before these present events. Judah as see never before is about to witness the utter hatefulness of this terrible sin.

> • But where are thy gods that thou hast made thee? let them arise, if they can save thee in the time of thy trouble: for according to the number of thy cities are thy gods, O Judah (Jer 2:28).

> • For according to the number of thy cities were thy gods, O Judah; and according to the number of the streets of Jerusalem have ye set up altars to that shameful thing, even altars to burn incense unto Baal (Jer 2:28).

The *Gold* of the Image. It was ***an image of gold***. What most impressed the historian Herodotus of Babylon was its gold. From the empire's vast conquests, gold was gathered. Gold was seen everywhere in the city. But now there will be one special place for it to be seen, not far from the city itself, perhaps about six miles, there will be *an image of gold*.

Much has been written concerning the composition of this image; much about how much gold? In the Tabernacle, The Ark, the Altar of Incense and the Table of Shewbread, the boards and the inner pillars were golden, but it was shittim wood overlaid with gold. Thus though partially made of wood, the Incense Alar was called the *golden altar* (Exod 40:26). In the case of the Mercy Seat and Candlestick which were solid gold they are said to be made of *pure gold* (Exod 25:17,31). This same applied in the Temple:

> And Solomon made all the vessels that pertained unto the house of the LORD: the altar of gold, and the table of gold, whereupon the shewbread was, And the candlesticks of pure gold (1 Kng 7:48,49).

Without telling us otherwise we will simply leave the description of Nebuchadnezzar's image as the Bible does. It was *an image of gold*. Nations have long impoverished their domains as they *lavish gold out of the bag* for fashioning of their idols (Isa. 46:6).

Captive Israelites having just left Egypt did it with a golden calf. Now with Nebuchadnezzar the same is done but on a vastly greater scale. Perhaps the fashioning and utter valuableness of this image draws into clearer understanding what is intended in the description of **the last image** of the *Times of the Gentiles*. The taxes of the empire could have gone for the construction Nebuchadnezzar's image. Note how this may relate to the Scripture comparison of the *golden calf* and *the image of the beast*:

> • And Aaron said unto them, Break off the golden earrings, which are in the ears of your wives, of your sons, and of your daughters, and bring them unto me. And all the people brake off the golden earrings which were in their ears, and brought them unto Aaron. And he received them at their hand, and fashioned it with a graving tool, after he had made it a molten calf: and they said, These be thy gods, O Israel, which brought thee up out of the land of Egypt (Exod 32:2-4).

> • And deceiveth them that dwell on the earth by the means of those miracles which he had power to do in the sight of the beast; **saying to them that dwell on the earth, that they should make an image to the beast**, which had the wound by a sword, and did live (Rev 13:14).

The Size of the Image; ***whose height was threescore cubits, and the breadth thereof six cubits***. It exceeded the ordinary height of a man by fifteen times (for that would only be four cubits, or six feet). On the other hand its proportions at approximately ninety feet by nine feet were far narrower than that of a man. Many therefore have viewed the image as a golden column with the figure of a man at the top. By its measurements and in conjunction with the six kinds of musical instrument used in the call to worship (3:7), the number 666 (Rev 13:18) is stamped upon the image: **60** cubits – **6** cubits – **6** musical instruments.

Nebuchadnezzar's 666 Image on the Plain of Dura

The Location of the Image. Nebuchadnezzar *set it up in the plain of Dura, in the province of Babylon.* It needed to be on a plain where nothing would distract but close enough to Babylon to be easily reached. Such a place has been found, about 6 miles from the ancient city. Hutchings writes:

> We should accept the Scripture for what it says — that it was an image of gold. Of course, such a colossus made of the heaviest metal on earth would have weighed thousands of tons, and of necessity, would have had to be built upon a sturdy foundation. Fausset's Bible Dictionary and Encyclopedia states that Oppert found on the plains of Dura, southeast of Babylon, now called Duair, the pedestal on which a colossal statue once stood. So without doubt, the king of Babylon... did dedicate a monstrous golden image. Either Nebuchadnezzar's heirs who followed him on the throne, or the Medo-Persians, cut the image up for the gold that was in it, leaving only the huge pedestal on which it stood (pp. 62,63).

The Meaning of the Image. Beginning with man's creation on the sixth day, Scripture has shown further that the number SIX is the number of Man, whereas SEVEN is shown to be the number of Divine Completeness. The 666 that characterizes this image is a picture of man's ultimate attempt to reach self-deification. Apart from Christ's Atoning Sacrifice and being received by Him, Seven can never be reached; not SIX, not SIX SIX, not SIX SIX SIX. When the Antichrist comes this ultimate attempt at self-deification will be undertaken. And here at the beginning of the *Times of the Gentiles* Nebuchadnezzar attempts self-deification. Hutchings explains.

> We have every reason to believe that this was the same image which Nebuchadnezzar saw in his dream, with the exception that he made the entire image of gold, not inferior metals. We may indeed wonder if Nebuchadnezzar did not believe the interpretation that Daniel gave, but it is apparent that it was not so much that the king did not want to believe it, he simply did not approve of it. It did not strike his fancy that his kingdom would fall to another. He did not like the idea that his great wealth and power would fall to another. Kings never do. The more they accumulate, they more they become reluctant to face the reality of death. We read the words of Solomon in Ecclesiastes

DANIEL 3. THE GOLDEN IMAGE ON THE PLAINS OF DURA

> 2:18: Yea, I hated all my labour which I had taken under the sun: because I should leave it unto the man that shall be after me.
>
> The Chaldeans tickled Nebuchadnezzar's ears by always giving him their traditional greeting: O king, live forever. This salutation was subsequently altered to: "Long live the king," because it became apparent over the centuries that kings, more or less, live threescore and ten years like everyone else. But Nebuchadnezzar, like so many, was pleased by this deceiving flattery of these spiritists. He preferred fiction to fact. He certainly entertained the idea that he was divine and would live forever; so in his unrealities, he sought to alter God's plan. He would make the entire image of gold, the metal ascribed to himself and his empire; therefore, he would live forever and his kingdom would stand forever. He would prevent the God of Daniel from anointing His own King over the nations, and when the rock struck, his golden image would stand.
>
> There have been many kings, politicians, philosophers, and generals who have tried to prevent the course of history as determined by God from continuing its natural course to its predestined conclusion. But no one to this date has been able to change the history of the world as presented in the image that Nebuchadnezzar saw in a dream. We read in Isaiah 14:24: The Lord of hosts hath sworn, saying, Surely as I have thought, so shall it come to pass: and as I have purposed, so shall it stand (pp. 63,64).

But see here how the good impressions made upon Nebuchadnezzar were lost and probably not after too long of a time. He had acknowledged that the God of Israel *is of a truth* a *God of gods* and a *Lord of kings* (2:47); and yet now, in defiance of the express law of that God, he sets up an image to be worshipped. He not only continues in his former idolatries, but contrives this new one, where he himself may well be part of the object worshipped. Strong convictions often come short of a sound conversion.

<u>The Summons to Leaders of the Entire Empire</u>. ***Then Nebuchadnezzar the king sent to gather together the princes, the governors, and the captains, the judges, the treasurers, the counsellors, the sheriffs, and all the rulers of the provinces, to come to the dedication of the image which Nebuchadnezzar the king had set up. Then the princes, the governors, and captains, the judges, the treasurers, the counsellors, the sheriffs, and all the rulers of the provinces, were gathered together unto the dedication of the image that Nebuchadnezzar the king had set up; and they stood before the image that Nebuchadnezzar had set up (3:2,3).*** Messengers are despatched to all parts of the kingdom to *gather together the princes*, dukes, and lords, all the peers of the realm, with all officers civil and military, *the captains* and commanders of the forces, *the judges, the treasurers or general receivers, the counsellors,* and *the sheriffs, and all the rulers of the provinces;* **they must all come** to the dedication of this image upon pain and peril of what shall fall thereon.

He summons the great men, for the great honour of his idol. It is to the glory of Christ that *kings shall bring presents unto him* (Psa 68:29; 72:10). But until that day, and throughout the *Times of the Gentiles*, the call will go out for great public gatherings to honour someone or something of far less importance and often vain foolishness. If the leaders come, the common people will be bound to follow. Nebuchadnezzar will now have a gathering of the entire world.

In obedience to the king's summons all the magistrates and officers of that vast kingdom leave the services of their particular countries, and come to Babylon, to the dedication of this golden image; long journeys many of them took and expensive ones, and all upon a very foolish errand. As the idols are senseless things, such are the worshippers! But one and all they came ***and they stood before the image that Nebuchadnezzar had set up***. Note the repetition that begins to occur in this chapter. Already ***"the image that Nebuchadnezzar had set up"*** has been stated three times.

<u>The Proclamation to the Gathered Worshippers</u>. ***Then an herald cried aloud, To you it is commanded, O people, nations, and languages, That at what time ye hear the sound of***

the cornet, flute, harp, sackbut, psaltery, dulcimer, and all kinds of musick, ye fall down and worship the golden image that Nebuchadnezzar the king hath set up: (And whoso falleth not down and worshippeth shall the same hour be cast into the midst of a burning fiery furnace (3:4-6). A herald proclaims to the "the order of service" to the vast assembly of grandees. At the signal given, they must fall down prostrate and worship the **golden image which Nebuchadnezzar the king has set up** (4th mention).

All must worship. Regardless of which ***people, nations, and languages*** they were of, they are now seen as *one*: *To you it is commanded*. Whatever other gods they worship at other times, they must worship *the golden image which Nebuchadnezzar the king has set up*.

All must worship together. They must all do this at the same time in order to show forth their communion with each other in this idolatrous service. If the leaders do it *on que* then notice will be taken by the common people to do the same.

All must worship together with the music. The herald gives notice that music will play a major part in the proceedings. A four-fold repetition of the list of instruments used greatly stresses the music aspect of the event (3:5,7,10,15). A vast orchestra with sections containing six special instruments and *all other kinds* of Babylonian music is assembled. It will be the signal to start the "worship" and would likely continue during the "worship." Music is a great mover and persuader. Here it would serve to adorn the solemnity and to sweeten and soften the minds of those that had doubt. Here is fleshly music and fleshly worship bound together in a world gathering. There was also music at the worship of the golden calf (Exod 32:18)! This, and especially in these latter times, is a picture of the *Times of the Gentiles* - huge religious gatherings bound together by the *glue* of *contemporary praise music*.

All must worship together with the music or face the furnace. ***And whoso falleth not down and worshippeth shall the same hour be cast into the midst of a burning fiery furnace*** (3:6). If the kings command does not convince you! If the orchestra's music does not draw you! Then certainly ***a burning fiery furnace*** will terrorize you into submission.

The Compliance of the Vast Assembly (almost!). ***Therefore at that time, when all the people heard the sound of the cornet, flute, harp, sackbut, psaltery, and all kinds of musick, all the people, the nations, and the languages, fell down and worshipped the golden image that Nebuchadnezzar the king had set up*** (3:7). Standing at attention, motionless, silently, the vast throng waited. Then with great musical precision the instruments began to play, both wind-instruments and hand-instruments, *the cornet and flute,* with the *harp, sackbut, psaltery,* and *dulcimer,* the melody of which they thought was entrancing and alluring enough to draw them to the devotion they were now about to pay. Immediately they all, as one man, as soldiers that move to a bugle call, *all the people, nations, and languages, fell down and worshipped the golden image.* Here were the charms of music to allure them comply and the terrors of the fiery furnace to frighten them into compliance. They were *drawn* by the concert and *driven* by the fiery furnace. They all obeyed; they are all prostrated on their faces (but not quite!).

"Worship" Gatherings During the Times of the Gentiles

Throughout the *Times of the Gentiles* these same two methods (the concert and the furnace) have been used to draw multitudes into a false kind of Christian "worship." Today we are especially seeing the *CONCERT*. Contemporary Christian Music (CCM) is the magnet used to draw many into a lowest common denominator kind of faith and then to no Biblical faith at all.

Graham Kendrick has been at the forefront of the modern CCM movement. Back in the late 1970s I checked a chorus book compiled by him for the number of songs that mentioned the *Blood of Christ*. In over 200 pages of choruses I found a very few; as I recall *fewer than ten*. This compared with the traditional hymnals of previous generations is like comparing Abel's sacrificial lamb with Cain's basket of fruit (Gen 4:3-5; Jude 11). *When the Son of Man cometh, shall he find faith on the earth* (Lk 18:8)? Singing *Bloodless* praise music is mark of these last days (2 Pet 2:1). Consider the following from Joyce Fox:

Whatever Happened to the Blood?

- *What can wash away my sin? Nothing but the blood of Jesus*!

- *Would you be free from your burden of sin? There's power in the blood! Power in the blood*!

- *There is a fountain filled with blood, drawn from Emmanuel's veins ...*

- *When I See the Blood, I will pass, I will pass over you.*

- *O, the blood of Jesus ... it washes white as snow*!

Remember those songs? We used to have a lot of hymns about the blood of Jesus. The songs told how the blood of Jesus was the only thing that could make a sinful heart clean, could protect the believer from the snares of the enemy, and was an absolute necessity in the life of every Christian. They were powerful songs with a powerful message. But what happened to them?

It was 'way back in the nineteenth century when the assault on the blood of Jesus first became obvious. Mary Baker Eddy, founder of the cult of Christian Science, wrote: "The material blood of Jesus was no more efficacious [effective, powerful] to cleanse from sin when it was shed upon "the accursed tree" than when it was flowing in his veins." There it was. The opening salvo in a war that has been raging now for more than 125 years!

Jesus Himself declared, ...*For this is my blood of the new testament, which is shed for many for the remission of sins* (Mt. 26:28). So who do you think is telling the truth, here? The blood of Jesus is not simply a clichéd phrase used to invoke the concept of the authority of Christ or the idea of God's saving grace. The blood of Jesus is central to the doctrines of the Church. We could never survive as Christians without the blood of Jesus to wash us, strengthen us, heal us, and sustain us! Without the blood there can be no salvation. Is it any wonder that the enemy of Jesus has fought so hard to remove all mention of the blood from the Church in general? Hebrews 9:22 says clearly, *Without the shedding of blood there is no remission of sins*.

Look in many popular hymnals and you will find not a single mention of the blood of Christ! If a beloved hymn could be salvaged, the references to blood were removed and the hymn was preserved but just as the blood of Christ cannot be ignored if salvation is your goal, songs that sing of the blood lose all meaning when the blood is removed!

I remember when the removal of these songs was first suggested in the 1970's and 80's. There was an uproar of protest from the laity and some churches that suggested such a thing backed down, but some didn't.

It soon became obvious to the enemy that the tactic of labeling the Church as "a bloody religion" just wasn't going to fly. So, he began a more subtle tack. He began taking all hymns out of the church. Pleading the need to appeal to the youth and the "unchurched," music within the church began to move progressively further away from hymnology and closer to the rock, rap, and soul music of the world.

Instead of a piano and/or organ, the platform was redesigned to accommodate guitars, drums, and an electronic keyboard. Instead of a music minister or "song leader" and a choir, the pulpit was moved to one side or removed to make room for anywhere from one or two to eight or ten people standing behind microphones. Instead of a hymnal, words now are flashed on the wall or a screen ... and none of those words are, "The blood of Jesus." And, in many churches, people insert earplugs in their ears when the music starts and sit or stand in silence because they honestly can't learn the melody because of the pounding beat of the snares, traps, and bass drums as well as the rhythm, lead, and bass guitars.

Nowadays it's almost impossible to find a church that sings, "psalms, hymns, and spiritual songs" as Paul said. Instead, we sing "worship songs" or "worship choruses"...Name a contemporary song that talks about the saving power of the blood of Jesus, I challenge you!
(http://www.gracecentered.com/what-happened-to-the-blood.htm)

If Graham Kendrick has been at the forefront of the modern CCM movement then *Hillsong* leads the way today in massive "worship" concerts. Do the gatherings of Christ and His disciples bear any resemblance to the music and lights of a *Hillsong* kind of concert??

"Admist the buzz of their new album and successful U.S. tour of the same name, the acclaimed Sydney, Australian-based church band Hillsong UNITED took some time out to speak to our own Ryan Barbee about their new record....."

DANIEL 3. THE GOLDEN IMAGE ON THE PLAINS OF DURA

If these pictures from the *Hillsong* website impress many, they are hugely surpassed by the following "worship" gatherings to see the Pope!

It may be called "worship," but it is far removed from the worship of the Bible!

• *Fear not, little flock; for it is your Father's good pleasure to give you the kingdom (Lk 12:32).*

• *Enter ye in at the strait gate: for wide is the gate, and broad is the way, that leadeth to destruction, and many there be which go in thereat: Because strait is the gate, and narrow is the way, which leadeth unto life, and few there be that find it. Beware of false prophets, which come to you in sheep's clothing, but inwardly they are ravening wolves (Matt 7:13-15).*

All of this is a "conditioning process" to *the gathering* of Revelation 13:11-18.

DANIEL 3. THE GOLDEN IMAGE ON THE PLAINS OF DURA

The Accusation Against The Hebrews 3:8-15.

Wherefore at that time certain Chaldeans came near, and accused the Jews. (3:9) They spake and said to the king Nebuchadnezzar, O king, live for ever. (3:10) Thou, O king, hast made a decree, that every man that shall hear the sound of the cornet, flute, harp, sackbut, psaltery, and dulcimer, and all kinds of musick, shall fall down and worship the golden image: (3:11) And whoso falleth not down and worshippeth, that he should be cast into the midst of a burning fiery furnace. (3:12) There are certain Jews whom thou hast set over the affairs of the province of Babylon, Shadrach, Meshach, and Abednego; these men, O king, have not regarded thee: they serve not thy gods, nor worship the golden image which thou hast set up. (3:13) Then Nebuchadnezzar in his rage and fury commanded to bring Shadrach, Meshach, and Abednego. Then they brought these men before the king. (3:14) Nebuchadnezzar spake and said unto them, Is it true, O Shadrach, Meshach, and Abednego, do not ye serve my gods, nor worship the golden image which I have set up? (3:15) Now if ye be ready that at what time ye hear the sound of the cornet, flute, harp, sackbut, psaltery, and dulcimer, and all kinds of musick, ye fall down and worship the image which I have made; well: but if ye worship not, ye shall be cast the same hour into the midst of a burning fiery furnace; and who is that God that shall deliver you out of my hands? (3:16) Shadrach, Meshach, and Abednego, answered and said to the king, O Nebuchadnezzar, we are not careful to answer thee in this matter. (3:17) If it be so, our God whom we serve is able to deliver us from the burning fiery furnace, and he will deliver us out of thine hand, O king. (3:18) But if not, be it known unto thee, O king, that we will not serve thy gods, nor worship the golden image which thou hast set up.

Why Daniel was not summoned is not said. Perhaps he was away on a distant imperial mission. Whatever the reason for his absence, the enemies of the Jews found it more *politic* to begin with less powerful and influential targets before attacking the one whom the king regarded as having divine character (2:46).

It may seem strange that Shadrach, Meshach, and Abednego, would be present at this assembly, when as is likely they knew its purpose. Why did they not stay out of the way? Surely it was because they would obey the king's orders as far as they could and would be ready to bear a public testimony against this gross idolatry.

The Allegation of *Certain Chaldeans*. **Wherefore at that time certain Chaldeans came near, and accused the Jews** (3:8). Perhaps these Chaldeans (the *elite* among the wise men. 2:2,4) were among the *magicians* and *astrologers* that bore a grudge to Daniel and his companions because they had so completely eclipsed them revealing the king's dream. They forget how their own lives were spared by these same men, and now this is how they are going to repay them. Thus Jeremiah *stood before God, to speak good for those* who afterwards *dug a pit for his life* (Jer 18:20).

They Appeal to the King's "Immortality." **They spake and said to the king Nebuchadnezzar, O king, live for ever** (3:9). This was the usual greeting but it now bears special connection the image Nebuchadnezzar has set up. They approach him as if it is only his honour and the good of his kingdom that they are concerned about.

They Appeal to the King's Decree. **Thou, O king, hast made a decree, that every man that shall hear the sound of the cornet, flute, harp, sackbut, psaltery, and dulcimer, and all kinds of musick, shall fall down and worship the golden image** (3:10). Note again the emphasis on the music accompanying the decree. Music will be *compelling* during the Times of the Gentiles.

They Appeal to the King's Penalty. **And whoso falleth not down and worshippeth, that he should be cast into the midst of a burning fiery furnace** (3:11). The law has just been made. The punishment for disobedience can allow no exceptions or ambiguity or reconsideration. It is either *worship the image* or *the midst of the fiery furnace*.

They Appeal concerning *Certain* Jews. ***There are certain Jews whom thou hast set over the affairs of the province of Babylon, Shadrach, Meshach, and Abednego; these men, O king, have not regarded thee: they serve not thy gods, nor worship the golden image which thou hast set up*** (3:12). This was no surprise by their accusers. They were waiting and watching while the others were "worshipping."

They press the point by showing that these men were Jews, foreigners, captives, men of a despised nation and religion; yet the king had *set them over the affairs of the province of Babylon*. It was therefore an ungrateful piece of insolence for them to disobey the king's command. Given their high station it was a bad example to see them standing while all the rest of the "worshippers" were obediently on their faces.

They press the point that it was done maliciously and in contempt of the king and his authority. "They have *no regard upon thee*; they *serve not the gods*, **nor worship the golden image which thou hast set up** (4th mention).

The Rage of the King. ***Then Nebuchadnezzar in his rage and fury commanded to bring Shadrach, Meshach, and Abednego. Then they brought these men before the king*** (3:13). Nebuchadnezzar fell into a great passion of rage and fury. How could it be that this mighty king that he had rule over so many nations, had no *rule over his own spirit* (Prov 25:28). How unfit was he to rule reasonable men who could not himself be ruled by reason! It was certainly no surprise to hear that these men did not serve his gods, for he knew very well they never had served them. *The discretion of a man deferreth his anger; and it is his glory to pass over a transgression* (Prov 19:11). But, *the wrath of a king is as the roaring of a lion* (Prov 19:12). So was the wrath of this king. With the king in a heightened state of rage, these three men were *brought before him* and appeared with an undaunted courage and unshaken composure.

The Interrogation. ***Nebuchadnezzar spake and said unto them, Is it true, O Shadrach, Meshach, and Abednego, do not ye serve my gods, nor worship the golden image which I have set up*** (3:14)? The case is laid before them in short. The king asked them whether the report was true. *Ye* have not served *my* gods? *Ye* that I have nourished and brought up, educated and promoted. *Ye* that have such a reputation for wisdom will not **worship the golden image which I have set up** (5th mention). Note: the faithfulness of God's servants has long been a wonder to their persecutors. And to the unconverted generally: *Wherein they think it strange that ye run not with them to the same excess of riot, speaking evil of you* (1 Pet 4:4).

The Ultimatum. ***Now if ye be ready that at what time ye hear the sound of the cornet, flute, harp, sackbut, psaltery, and dulcimer, and all kinds of musick, ye fall down and worship the image which I have made; well: but if ye worship not, ye shall be cast the same hour into the midst of a burning fiery furnace; and who is that God that shall deliver you out of my hands*** (3:15)? Nebuchadnezzar was willing to admit them to a new trial. If they will accept the music and accept what the music is directing them to do: that they **worship the image which I have made** (6th mention), then all will be fine."

If they persist in their refusal they shall immediately be *cast into the fiery furnace*, and shall not have so much as an hour's reprieve. So in a few words it is either —*Turn, or burn.* As the king knew they were buoyed with a confidence in their God, he insolently hurls back at them: ***And who is that God that shall deliver you out of my hands***? "Let him, if he can."

It seems not to be that long since we heard Nebuchadnezzar confess that their God was a *God of gods* and a *Lord of kings* (2:47). Proud men (for a while!) are still ready to say as Pharaoh, *Who is the LORD that I should obey his voice* (Exod 5:2)?

DANIEL 3. THE GOLDEN IMAGE ON THE PLAINS OF DURA

<u>The Answer of the Hebrews</u>. There was no debate, no consideration or counsel. They did not even need to call a prayer meeting. They knew the Mind of God. With exemplary calmness they give their answer. **Shadrach, Meshach, and Abednego, answered and said to the king, O Nebuchadnezzar, we are not careful to answer thee in this matter** (3:16). They are respectful to the king, but there is nothing in their answer that looks like a compliment. They do not begin as their accusers, *O king! live for ever*. There was no attempt to put him into a good humour, An entire range of emotions was open to these three men, but they answer with dignity, respect and got right to the point.

They Were *Not Careful to Answer*. Note the word careful. Here it means simply, *full of care*. Of course one would have to be clear on the facts of the case; but they did not need to prepare an elaborate defence. Here is a good example of our Lord's admonition.

> *And ye shall be brought before governors and kings for my sake, for a testimony against them and the Gentiles. But when they deliver you up, take no thought how or what ye shall speak: for it shall be given you in that same hour what ye shall speak. For it is not ye that speak, but the Spirit of your Father which speaketh in you (Matt 10:18-20).*

They were Dependent upon the Lord. **If it be so, our God whom we serve is able to deliver us from the burning fiery furnace, and he will deliver us out of thine hand, O king** (3:17). It was this that enabled them to look with so much calmness upon death; death in all its terrors; death *the king of terrors* (Job 18:14). Like Moses they *feared not the wrath of the king*, but *endured as seeing him that is invisible* (Heb 11:27). Therefore, *If it be so*, if we are brought to this strait, if we must be thrown into the fiery furnace, we are well assured that our God is both able and willing to deliver us. This is a straight answer to "Nebuchadnezzar's "*who is that God that shall deliver you out of my hands*" (3:15).

They were Resolved to do Right. **But if not, be it known unto thee, O king, that we will not serve thy gods, nor worship the golden image which thou hast set up** (3:18). *But, if not;* if God in His infinite does not do what we know He can and is willing to do, yet *be it known unto thee, O king* we will have nothing at all to do with your gods or **the golden image which thou hast set up** (6th mention). Death is a small thing in comparison to bringing dishonour to the One and True God. Their resolve is like that of the Apostles.

> *And when they had brought them, they set them before the council: and the high priest asked them, Saying, Did not we straitly command you that ye should not teach in this name? and, behold, ye have filled Jerusalem with your doctrine, and intend to bring this man's blood upon us. Then Peter and the other apostles answered and said, We ought to obey God rather than men (Acts 5:27-29).*

It was idolatry that brought Israel to Babylon. At about this time back in Judah, those whom Jeremiah was warning and those of whom Ezekiel prophesied were still worshiping idols. We would not like to know how many Jewish men were in that vast host that lay prostrate before *the golden image Nebuchadnezzar set up*. But for these three men a *line has been drawn in the sand*. There will be no expedients, no rationalization. We will not do it! May a remnant of God's people show this same resolve in these final days of the age.

The Deliverance of The Hebrews 3:19-27.

> *Then was Nebuchadnezzar full of fury, and the form of his visage was changed against Shadrach, Meshach, and Abednego: therefore he spake, and commanded that they should heat the furnace one seven times more than it was wont to be heated. (3:20) And he commanded the most mighty men that were in his army to bind Shadrach, Meshach, and Abednego, and to cast them into the burning fiery furnace. (3:21) Then these men were bound in their coats, their hosen, and their hats, and their other garments, and were cast into the midst of the burning fiery furnace. (3:22) Therefore because the king's commandment was urgent, and the furnace exceeding hot, the flames of the fire slew those men that took up Shadrach, Meshach, and Abednego.*

(3:23) And these three men, Shadrach, Meshach, and Abednego, fell down bound into the midst of the burning fiery furnace. (3:24) Then Nebuchadnezzar the king was astonied, and rose up in haste, and spake, and said unto his counsellors, Did not we cast three men bound into the midst of the fire? They answered and said unto the king, True, O king. (3:25) He answered and said, Lo, I see four men loose, walking in the midst of the fire, and they have no hurt; and the form of the fourth is like the Son of God. (3:26) Then Nebuchadnezzar came near to the mouth of the burning fiery furnace, and spake, and said, Shadrach, Meshach, and Abednego, ye servants of the most high God, come forth, and come hither. Then Shadrach, Meshach, and Abednego, came forth of the midst of the fire. (3:27) And the princes, governors, and captains, and the king's counsellors, being gathered together, saw these men, upon whose bodies the fire had no power, nor was an hair of their head singed, neither were their coats changed, nor the smell of fire had passed on them.

Cast into the Furnace. Nebuchadnezzar had been shown so much of the true God that we are amazed that he set up the golden image; that he set it up to be worshipped; that he would slay anyone who would not worship it; and now that he would slay these upon whom he had formerly bestowed the highest acclaim. But such is sin, once the ball begins rolling it is difficult to stop.

Instead of being convinced the king became more incensed. ***Then was Nebuchadnezzar full of fury, and the form of his visage was changed against Shadrach, Meshach, and Abednego*** (3:19). Their God honouring response made him *full of fury* and the *form of his visage was changed*. Nebuchadnezzar here exchanged the majesty of a prince upon his throne, or of a judge upon the bench, for the fury of a *wild bull in a net*.

Instead of mitigating their punishment the king increases it: ***therefore he spake, and commanded that they should heat the furnace one seven times more than it was wont to be heated*** (3:19). Seven times hotter, which would make them die the sooner; but by this the king would have all to know that he looked upon their crime as seven times more heinous than the crimes of others. God in this foolish instance of the tyrant's rage would bring glory to Himself, for their deliverance would be all the more illustrious. This term *seven times* has prophetic significance and points to Israel's dispersion during the *Times of the Gentiles* and ultimately of the seven year *Time of Jacob's Trouble* (Jer 30:7) when the earth shall experience the fierce heat of God's wrath.

> • *For, behold, the day cometh,* **that shall burn as an oven**; *and all the proud, yea, and all that do wickedly, shall be stubble: and the day that cometh shall burn them up, saith the LORD of hosts, that it shall leave them neither root nor branch. But unto you that fear my name shall the Sun of righteousness arise with healing in his wings; and ye shall go forth, and grow up as calves of the stall (Mal 4:1,2).*

> • *And if ye will not yet for all this hearken unto me, then I will punish you* **seven times** *more for your sins (Lev 26:18).*

> • *And if ye walk contrary unto me, and will not hearken unto me; I will bring* **seven times** *more plagues upon you according to your sins (Lev 26:21).*

> • *Then will I also walk contrary unto you, and will punish you yet* **seven times** *for your sins (Lev 26:24).*

> • *Then I will walk contrary unto you also in fury; and I, even I, will chastise you* **seven times** *for your sins (Lev 26:28).*

> • *Let his heart be changed from man's, and let a beast's heart be given unto him; and let* **seven times** *pass over him (Dan 4:16).*

> • *And whereas the king saw a watcher and an holy one coming down from heaven, and saying, Hew the tree down, and destroy it; yet leave the stump of the roots thereof in the earth, even with a band of iron and brass, in the tender grass of the field; and let*

DANIEL 3. THE GOLDEN IMAGE ON THE PLAINS OF DURA

it be wet with the dew of heaven, and let his portion be with the beasts of the field, till **seven times** *pass over him (Dan 4:23).*

• *That they shall drive thee from men, and thy dwelling shall be with the beasts of the field, and they shall make thee to eat grass as oxen, and they shall wet thee with the dew of heaven, and* **seven times** *shall pass over thee, till thou know that the most High ruleth in the kingdom of men, and giveth it to whomsoever he will (Dan 4:25).*

• *And they shall drive thee from men, and thy dwelling shall be with the beasts of the field: they shall make thee to eat grass as oxen, and* **seven times** *shall pass over thee, until thou know that the most High ruleth in the kingdom of men, and giveth it to whomsoever he will (Dan 4:32).*

Instead of regular soldiers, the mightiest in Babylon must perform this execution. ***And he commanded the most mighty men that were in his army to bind Shadrach, Meshach, and Abednego, and to cast them into the burning fiery furnace*** (3:20). The fire must be the hottest and the executioners the strongest. So it has been throughout the *Times of the Gentiles* and so it will be so especially during the Great Tribulation (Rev 13:7). See the famous older books that deal with the sufferings of God's people: *Foxe's Book of Martyrs*, *The Martyr's Mirror* (T.J. van Braght); *Miller's Church History* (Andrew Miller); *The Pilgrim Church* (E. H. Broadbent); *History of Ancient Christians* (Jean Paul Perrin); *The Ecclesiastical History of the Ancient Churches of Piedmont and of The Albigenses* (Peter Allix); *History of the Donatists* (David Benedict).

Instead of prison clothes they are bound in their own garments. ***Then these men were bound in their coats, their hosen, and their hats, and their other garments*** (3:21). They were bound that they might not give any resistance. They were bound in their clothes for haste and further detestation of their "crime." They were thus bound for the burning, but God's providence ordered it for the increase of the miracle. Their clothes were not so much as singed.

Instead of any last minute reprieve they ***were cast into the midst of the burning fiery furnace*** (3:21). It is a wonder that the tyrant was so hard-hearted to inflict such a punishment; and it is a great encouragement to faith that the confessors were so stout-hearted that they submitted to it rather than sin against God. But, what would this be in comparison to the *second death* (Rev 2:11; 20:6,14; 21:8): to that furnace into which *the tares shall be cast in bundles* (Matt 13:30,41,42), to that lake which burns eternally with fire and brimstone? Let Nebuchadnezzar heat his furnace as hot as he can, a few minutes will finish the suffering of the brave martyrs; but in hell-fire the *smoke of their torment ascendeth up for ever and ever: and they have no rest day or night who worship the beast and his image* (Rev. 14:10,11).

Instead of only delivering the condemned to the flames, the executioners were themselves consumed. ***Therefore because the king's commandment was urgent, and the furnace exceeding hot, the flames of the fire slew those men that took up Shadrach, Meshach, and Abednego*** (3:22). The *king's commandment was urgent*; they must be dispatched to the furnace with speed and efficiency. These strongest of soldiers hurried them to the very mouth of the furnace that they might throw them *into the midst* of it; but their haste was their eternal undoing and they were engulfed by the same flames. Perhaps these strong men were doing more than obeying the king's command. They were glad to be doing it and making a spectacle of it as they proudly marched the Hebrews to the furnace.

Instead of *only* entering the flames: ***these three men, Shadrach, Meshach, and Abednego, fell down bound into the midst of the burning fiery furnace*** (3:23). They *fell*. The fell ***down***. They fell down ***bound***. They fell down bound ***into the midst of the burning fiery furnace***. And, when they were falling they were still *believing*; *If it be so, our God whom we serve is able to deliver us from the burning fiery furnace* (3:17). Perhaps initially they thought it would be ***from*** the furnace. But now as they are falling their faith must have risen to a higher level. Our God will save us in *the midst of the burning fiery furnace*. Hebrews ll:33,34 confirms that *through faith...they quenched the violence of fire*.

This event is now memorialized. This is what befell **these three men**. Let us hear their names again: **Shadrach, Meshach, and Abednego**.

<u>Delivered from the Flames</u>. We find now that these three men: Did not *bow* before the image; Did not be *bend* before the king; Did not *burn* in the furnace. We find them, as always, calm and composed, and walking about in the furnace. **Then Nebuchadnezzar the king was astonied, and rose up in haste, and spake, and said unto his counsellors, Did not we cast three men bound into the midst of the fire? They answered and said unto the king, True, O king. He answered and said, Lo, I see four men loose, walking in the midst of the fire, and they have no hurt; and the form of the fourth is like the Son of God** (3:24,25).

<u>The Astonishment of Nebuchadnezzar</u>. The king has suddenly gone from rage to astonishment. **He was astonished, and rose up in haste**. Perhaps the slaying of the men that carried out his sentence had astonished and put him in a fright, and well it might, for he had reason to think his own turn would be next. It is of course beyond that. Now something beyond words has taken place and he must get as good a view as possible. God can strike with astonishment those whose hearts are most hardened against Him and against his people. *He that made him can make his sword to approach unto him* (cp. Job 40:19).

Nebuchadnezzar asks an astonished question. **Did not we cast three men bound into the midst of the fire?** To which he gets an obedient reply: **True, O king**. "We carried out your orders; the number we sent to their death was *three*." "But now," says the king, "I have been looking into the furnace and I *see four men, loose*."

<u>The State of the Hebrews</u>. When nothing left was expected to be seen of them, it was in fact quite the opposite. They were loosed from their bonds. The fire that did not so much as singe or leave the smell of smoke on their clothes, burnt the cords.

They were healthy and whole. **They have no hurt**. The flame did not scorch them; the smoke did not stifle them; they are alive and well in the midst of the flames. Here the God of nature can when he pleases control the powers of nature to make them serve his purposes. Here is a fulfilment of the gracious promise. Here was a fulfilment of the gracious promise.

> *When thou walkest through the fire, thou shalt not be burned; neither shall the flame kindle upon thee (Isa. 43:2).*

They **walked in the midst of the fire**. The furnace was large, so that they had room to walk; they were unhurt, so that they were able to walk; their minds were clear, so that they wanted to walk. It was all as if the furnace became a garden. They were not looking for an exit. They seem to have no inclination to escape. *Can a man walk upon hot coals and his feet not be burnt* (cp. Prov 6:28)? No, but they did.

<u>The Sight of The Son of God</u>. There was a Fourth Person seen with them in the fire, whose form in Nebuchadnezzar's judgment was *like the Son of God*. **Lo, I see four men loose...and the form of the fourth is like the Son of God** (3:25). He appeared as a Divine Person, a Messenger from heaven, not as a servant but as a Son. This was the eternal Son of God, the *Messenger of the covenant* (Mal 3:1), and not a created angel, but the Angel of the LORD to whom worship is given (Judg 13:15-20). Christ appeared often in the resemblance of our nature before He assumed our nature at His incarnation in *the fulness of time* (Gal 4:4). Here, in order to deliver them out of the fire, He came and walked with them in the fire. Here Christ showed that what is done against His people, He takes as done against Himself. Whoever throws them into the furnace does, in effect, bring Christ to the fire.

DANIEL 3. THE GOLDEN IMAGE ON THE PLAINS OF DURA

• I am Jesus, whom thou persecutes (Acts 9:5).

• In all their affliction he was afflicted, and the angel of his presence saved them: in his love and in his pity he redeemed them; and he bare them, and carried them all the days of old (Isa 63:9).

The Son of God or "a son of the gods"

Modern versions of the Bible diminish Messianic prophecy in the Old Testament (if not in the actual text, then in the footnotes). See for example Job 19:25,26; Psalms 22:16; Isaiah 7:14; Micah 5:2. Here they make Nebuchadnezzar to say that he saw *a son of the gods*. The *New King James Version* has *the Son of God* in the text, but with "*or a son of the gods*" in the footnote.

The Critic Says: "While the 'fourth person' may have been the Son of God, Nebuchadnezzar would not know this, and therefore speaks of him as 'a son of the gods'. This is confirmed in verse 28 where Nebuchadnezzar acknowledges that 'God sent his angel to deliver Shadrach, Meshach, and Abednego.' Further, the Aramaic form *elahin* is plural, and whenever used in the Aramaic section of Daniel seems to refer to the gods of the heathen; whereas the singular *elah* is used for the True God." (so The *New Scofield Bible*, *Ryrie Study Bible*, *NIV*, etc.)

Answer: In the passage before us, it is not only a question of how Nebuchadnezzar could speak about *the Son of God* but how could he also speak about *El Elyon* (In Chaldee it is Illai), the Most High God.) Verse 26 is the first instance of this title of Deity in Daniel. The answer can only be by Divine revelation! As in the case of Caiaphas and the Centurion, the Scriptures promise to *every man* a revelation of Christ:

• And one of them, named Caiaphas, being the high priest that same year, said unto them, Ye know nothing at all, Nor consider that it is expedient for us, that one man should die for the people, and that the whole nation perish not. And this spake he not for himself: but being high priest that year, he prophesied that Jesus should die for that nation (Jhn 11:49-51).

• Now when the centurion, and they that were with him, watching Jesus, saw the earthquake, and those things that were done, they feared greatly, saying, Truly this was the Son of God (Matt 27:54).

• That was the true Light which lighteth every man that cometh into the world (Jhn 1:9).

A.R. Fausset believes this to be the case concerning Nebuchadnezzar, "Unconsciously, like Saul, Caiaphas, and Pilate, he is made to utter divine truths, the full import of which he did not himself understand" (*JFB Commentary*).

As for the king's statement in Daniel 3:28, (*Blessed be the God of Shadrach, Meshach, and Abednego, who hath sent his angel, and delivered his servants that trusted in him*), Christ in Old Testament times was indeed the Angel of the Lord and the Messenger of the Covenant. The matter that is frequently overlooked is that Nebuchadnezzar in Chapter Two had already been given a revelation of Christ as **the Stone** (cp. Gen 49:24)!

• But there is a God in Heaven that revealeth secrets, and maketh known to the King Nebuchadnezzar what shall be in the latter days (Dan. 2:28).

• Thou sawest till that a stone was cut out without hands, which smote the image upon his feet ... and the stone that smote the image became a great mountain, and filled the whole earth (Dan. 2:34, 35).

There is certainly no problem with the plural *Son of elahin* in 3:25. *Elahin* is the Chaldee spelling of the plural *Elohim*. As *Elohim*, depending on the context, is used for the True God in the Trinity of His Being and also of false gods, so it would be with *Elahin* (see 6:20). In the idolatrous climate of Babylon in which captive Judah found itself, the singular *Elah* is used in Daniel (and Ezra) as a counter to that idolatry, while *Elahin* is used of the false deities. By believing that Nebuchadnezzar's words in 3:25 are a revelation rather than merely a startled exclamation, *Elahin/Elohim* is used here in its usual sense of the true God.

This was *The* Son of God in the fiery furnace with the three Hebrews. Whenever a singular angelic personage appears in the Old Testament, it is invariably the Preincarnate Christ. Christ had previously been in the flames of the bush speaking to Moses (Exod 3), and would shortly be in the lions' den with Daniel. Note also, *the Son of God* is the reading in the Septuagint.

<u>The Welcoming Return Nebuchadnezzar Gave to the Hebrews</u>. ***Then Nebuchadnezzar came near to the mouth of the burning fiery furnace, and spake, and said, Shadrach, Meshach, and Abednego, ye servants of the most high God, come forth, and come hither. Then Shadrach, Meshach, and Abednego, came forth of the midst of the fire*** (3:26). Nebuchadnezzar, now so completely chastened, calls them out of the furnace. He *comes near to the mouth of the burning fiery furnace,* and bids them *come forth and come hither.* He speaks with a great deal of tenderness and concern, and stands ready to lend them his hand and help them out. He does not as in the case of Paul at the jail in Philippi seek to *thrust them out privily; he will come himself and fetch them out* (Acts 16:37).

He addresses them with a respectful title: ye *servants of the most high God,* a God who now appears *able to deliver them out of his hand.* Sooner or later, God will convince the proudest of men that He is the *Most High God*, and above them, and too hard for them.

He receives these whom he had so shortly before abandoned. They *came forth out of the midst of the fire.* How the *fourth One* withdrew, and whether he vanished away or visibly ascended as in Judges 13:19-21, we are not told.

He bids all of the officials of Babylon to behold the wondrous sight. ***And the princes, governors, and captains, and the king's counsellors, being gathered together, saw these men, upon whose bodies the fire had no power, nor was an hair of their head singed, neither were their coats changed, nor the smell of fire had passed on them*** (3:27). These were the same ones he had commanded to worship his golden image. As they gathered all the amazed spectators were able to witness to the fact that they had not received the least damage during their time in the fire. All the great men came together to view them, and found that there was not so much as *a hair of their head singed.* During the Tribulation there will be a remnant of Jews (the 144,000; Rev 7 and 14) of whom this will be fulfilled to the letter: *There shall not a hair of your head perish* (Lu. 21:18).

Their clothes did not so much as change colour, nor smell of fire, much less were their bodies in the least bit affected by the fire. The Chaldeans worshipped the fire as a sort of the image of the sun, so it was here as in the days of Moses: *against all the gods of Egypt I will execute judgment: I am the LORD* (Exod 12:12). It is our God only that is *the consuming fire* (Heb 12:29).

The Proclamation of Nebuchadnezzar 3:28-30.

Then Nebuchadnezzar spake, and said, Blessed be the God of Shadrach, Meshach, and Abednego, who hath sent his angel, and delivered his servants that trusted in him, and have changed the king's word, and yielded their bodies, that they might not serve nor worship any god, except their own God. (3:29) Therefore I make a decree, That every people, nation, and language, which speak any thing amiss against the God of Shadrach, Meshach, and Abednego, shall be cut in pieces, and their houses shall be made a dunghill: because there is no other God that can deliver after this sort. (3:30)

DANIEL 3. THE GOLDEN IMAGE ON THE PLAINS OF DURA

Then the king promoted Shadrach, Meshach, and Abednego, in the province of Babylon.

The strict observations of *the princes, governors, and captains, and the king's counsellors* having seen *these men* contributed much to the verifying of the miracle and the magnifying of the power and grace of God. As with the Apostles and the lame man, those who would want to say otherwise were forced to acknowledge what had happened:

What shall we do to these men? for that indeed a notable miracle hath been done by them is manifest to all them that dwell in Jerusalem; and we cannot deny it (Acts 4:16).

The effect upon Nebuchadnezzar is great. He does not seek to rationalize or diminish what has happened. He gives a good testimony, though as we shall see it does not approach *New Testament* levels until the next chapter.

He Gives Glory to the God of Israel. **Then Nebuchadnezzar spake, and said, Blessed be the God of Shadrach, Meshach, and Abednego, who hath sent his angel, and delivered his servants that trusted in him, and have changed the king's word, and yielded their bodies, that they might not serve nor worship any god, except their own God** (3:28). This is a God proclaims Nebuchadnezzar who protects His own worshippers; who sends a Deliverer to rescue His worshippers; whose worshippers stand firm in the face of any other supposed god or dictate of man. They **changed the king's word**! Therefore, and before all assembled here I confess: **Blessed be the God of Shadrach, Meshach, and Abednego.**

He Pronounces a Decree in Behalf of the God of Israel. **Therefore I make a decree, That every people, nation, and language, which speak any thing amiss against the God of Shadrach, Meshach, and Abednego, shall be cut in pieces, and their houses shall be made a dunghill: because there is no other God that can deliver after this sort** (3:29). This is similar to the later Persian decree on behalf of the returning captives:

That they may offer sacrifices of sweet savours unto the God of heaven, and pray for the life of the king, and of his sons. Also I have made a decree, that whosoever shall alter this word, let timber be pulled down from his house, and being set up, let him be hanged thereon; and let his house be made a dunghill for this (Ezra 6:10,11).

We have reason to think that both the sins and the troubles of Israel have given Nebuchadnezzar and the Babylonians an excuse to speak lightly of and blaspheme the God of Israel. He now seeks to rectify this, and in so doing he gives religious liberty and protection to Hebrew captives living in Babylon. On matters of religious liberty the Times of the Gentiles have been *"Who's on the desk on the day."* They have persecuted; they have given religious liberty; they, like here, have become extreme. Compare Nebuchadnezzar is this decree with the higher *New Testament* level in the next chapter. There he almost sounds like the Apostle Paul in comparison:

Nebuchadnezzar the king, unto all people, nations, and languages, that dwell in all the earth; Peace be multiplied unto you. I thought it good to shew the signs and wonders that the high God hath wrought toward me. How great are his signs! and how mighty are his wonders! his kingdom is an everlasting kingdom, and his dominion is from generation to generation (Dan 4:1-3).

He Issues a promotion to Shadrach, Meshach, and Abednego. **Then the king promoted Shadrach, Meshach, and Abednego, in the province of Babylon** (3:30). Nebuchadnezzar not only reverses the sentence against the three men, and not only restores them to their former position in the land but promotes them to greater and more advantageous trusts than they had before. This was to their honour; it was to the comfort of their brethren in captivity, and it was to the honour of the LORD who by so delivering them in this land of idolatry provided a constant witness and reminder of their Deliverer.

This then is our first characteristic picture of the *Times of The Gentiles* in the Book of Daniel. The attempt of this great king of Babylon to unify the religions of his empire by self-deification will be repeated by the *Beast*, the last head of the Gentile world-dominion (Rev 13:11-15). Various levels of self-aggrandisement have repeatedly characterized Gentile authority in the earth (Dan 6:7; Acts 12:22); and compare the later Roman emperors).

All monarchs recognize that to consolidate their power they must have a state religion. This is man's wisdom. God is disowned by most in the governments of the Gentile world, but acknowledged by a little group of suffering believers. The three Jewish men, faithful to God while the great mass of their countrymen were still in unbelief, are a fit type of the Jewish remnant in the last days (Isa 1:9; Rom 11:5) and who will be faithful in the *furnace* of the Great Tribulation (Psa 2:5; Rev 7:14).

The *God of heaven* (Dan 2:18,19,28,37,44) is the Lord's distinguishing title during the *Times of the Gentiles*. God withdrew to Heaven; His visible presence (glory) is no longer seen in Jerusalem. Believers in the meantime await the fulfilment of the promised Messiah's physical Return to the Throne of David in Jerusalem.

> *And the angel said unto her, Fear not, Mary: for thou hast found favour with God. And, behold, thou shalt conceive in thy womb, and bring forth a son, and shalt call his name JESUS. He shall be great, and shall be called the Son of the Highest:* **and the Lord God shall give unto him the throne of his father David:** *And he shall reign over the house of Jacob for ever; and of his kingdom there shall be no end (Lk 1:30-33).*

THE TIMES OF THE GENTILES 1-7

C. THE CHARACTERISTICS OF THE TIMES OF THE GENTILES 3-6

2. A TIME OF EXPANSION AND INSTABILITY: NEBUCHADNEZZAR'S MADNESS 4

DANIEL 4. THE TREE AND THE BEAST VISION

To press home the point that Daniel Chapters 2-7 deals with the Tines of the Gentiles (Lk 21:24), the Holy Spirit records the events in a Gentile language rather than Hebrew. To press the point further the penman of this chapter is not a Hebrew but Nebuchadnezzar himself. The account here recorded is given in his own words and as he published it to the world. Daniel, a prophet by inspiration, places Nebuchadnezzar's account in his history, thus making it a part of the Sacred Scriptures, and a very remarkable part!

Nebuchadnezzar was as daring a rival with God Almighty as perhaps any mortal man ever had been; but here he confesses himself as completely conquered and that by the God of Israel. This king had given the example of the enforced state religion (Chapter 3) that would characterize the Times of the Gentiles; and now (before he comes to his senses) of the bazaar unstable behaviour of Gentile rulers during that time.

Nebuchadnezzar's Proclamation 4:1-3.

Nebuchadnezzar the king, unto all people, nations, and languages, that dwell in all the earth; Peace be multiplied unto you. (4:2) I thought it good to shew the signs and wonders that the high God hath wrought toward me. (4:3) How great are his signs! and how mighty are his wonders! his kingdom is an everlasting kingdom, and his dominion is from generation to generation.

<u>Note the Form In Which He Writes</u>. ***Nebuchadnezzar the king, unto all people, nations, and languages, that dwell in all the earth; Peace be multiplied unto you*** (4:1). Yes he had often addressed *all people, nations, and languages, that dwell in all the earth*. And he was still monarch over *all people, nations, and languages, that dwell in all the earth*. But here he lays aside the great swelling words of vanity that his subjects were so used to. Further, for even a good cause there is none of the fearsome tirade that we saw at the end of the last chapter.

Therefore I make a decree, That every people, nation, and language, which speak any thing amiss against the God of Shadrach, Meshach, and Abednego, shall be cut in pieces, and their houses shall be made a dunghill: because there is no other God that can deliver after this sort (3:29).

Here instead it is: ***Peace be multiplied unto you.*** This sounds almost like the Apostle Paul as he begins his Epistles.

To all that be in Rome, beloved of God, called to be saints: ***Grace to you and peace*** *from God our Father, and the Lord Jesus Christ (Rom 1:7).*

<u>Note the Subject of Which He Writes</u>.

<u>The Wonders of God</u>. ***I thought it good to shew the signs and wonders that the high God hath wrought toward me*** (4:2). This is *the high God* of which he writes, the True God. Not the gods he formerly worshipped or whose image he set up on the plains of Dura. Concerning this God he now feels it his duty and debt to tell all near and far about. If word had spread about his strange affliction and demise they must now hear of the wonders God had wrought toward him. If they heard he had been *lost in a wilderness* (4:33), they must now hear that he has been found.

The Extent of the Wonders of God.

He Admires God's Doings. ***How great are his signs! and how mighty are his wonders*** (4:3)*!* He speaks of them as one amazed. Nebuchadnezzar was now old; he had reigned above forty years. He had seen as much of the world as a man could see. But the vast empire, the high walls of Babylon on which three chariots could ride abreast, all the golden splendour and the hanging gardens etc. etc. can give just so much pleasure. He will say in this chapter, but it will soon be to his undoing:

> *Is not this great Babylon, that I have built for the house of the kingdom by the might of my power, and for the honour of my majesty (4:30)?*

All the bright things of the world soon become a burden and an empty shell. Nebuchadnezzar has now been touched by a far greater majesty than what his Babylon could offer. He has begun to see something of the King of Kings, Israel's King (whom he had long ignored) and His glory.

> *The stone which the builders refused is become the head stone of the corner. This is the LORD's doing; it is **marvellous in our eyes** (Psa 118:22,23).*

He Marvels at God's Kingdom. ***His kingdom is an everlasting kingdom, and his dominion is from generation to generation*** (4:3). Despite his best efforts; despite all the accolades: *O King live for ever* (2:4; 3:9), Nebuchadnezzar the foremost king during the *Times of the Gentiles* now knows that neither his life or kingdom is going to last very long. Other reigns are confined to one generation, and other dynasties to a few generations, but God will have a kingdom on earth whose *dominion is from generation to generation.* Nebuchadnezzar had heard it before, now he knows it.

> *And in the days of these kings shall the God of heaven set up a kingdom, which shall never be destroyed: and the kingdom shall not be left to other people, but it shall break in pieces and consume all these kingdoms, and it shall stand for ever (Dan 2:44).*

Nebuchadnezzar's Dream: The Circumstances 4:4-9.

> *I Nebuchadnezzar was at rest in mine house, and flourishing in my palace: (4:5) I saw a dream which made me afraid, and the thoughts upon my bed and the visions of my head troubled me. (4:6) Therefore made I a decree to bring in all the wise men of Babylon before me, that they might make known unto me the interpretation of the dream. (4:7) Then came in the magicians, the astrologers, the Chaldeans, and the soothsayers: and I told the dream before them; but they did not make known unto me the interpretation thereof. (4:8) But at the last Daniel came in before me, whose name was Belteshazzar, according to the name of my God, and in whom is the spirit of the holy gods: and before him I told the dream, saying, (4:9) O Belteshazzar, master of the magicians, because I know that the spirit of the holy gods is in thee, and no secret troubleth thee, tell me the visions of my dream that I have seen, and the interpretation thereof.*

Nebuchadnezzar, in his worldwide proclamation, tells of the warning he received that judgement was going to fall upon his proud head. He relates further that he ignored the warning, and then in a moment of self-glory the storm came and it was exactly as was foretold.

How the Alarm Came.

It Came at a Time of Peace. ***I Nebuchadnezzar was at rest in mine house, and flourishing in my palace*** (4:4). He had recently conquered Egypt, and with it completed his victories, ended his wars, and made himself monarch of all those parts of the world. This calculated from Ezekiel 29:17 would be about the 35th year of his reign. After these military accomplishments he had a warning dream which was fulfilled about a year after. The judgement described in the dream lasted (apparently) seven years and upon his recovery he

DANIEL 4. THE TREE AND THE BEAST VISION

penned this declaration. He lived about two further years and died in the 45th year of his reign. He had undertaken the fatigue and distress of many wars and dangerous campaigns on the field of battle; but now at length he is *at rest in his house,* and there is *no adversary, nor any evil occurrent* (1 Kng 5:4). God can reach the greatest of men with His terrors even when they are most secure, and think themselves *at rest and flourishing.*

It Came through a Fearful Dream. ***I saw a dream which made me afraid, and the thoughts upon my bed and the visions of my head troubled me*** (4:5). Nebuchadnezzar was used to looking the perils of war in the face. One would not think a little thing like a dream would frighten this *man of war from his youth* (1 Sam 17:33). Yet God can strike terror into heart of the greatest of men, and in the place he feels most at ease and secure. In this case it was his well-guarded bed chamber. Nebuchadnezzar had been the troubler of the world. Many thousands had been swept away by his conquests. Now something as normally insignificant as a dream troubles him. Having had a dream long before (Dan 2:1) he now reflects that it may have been sent by God on a special errand.

How a Solution was Found.

It Would Not Come from the *Old Crowd.* ***Therefore made I a decree to bring in all the wise men of Babylon before me, that they might make known unto me the interpretation of the dream.*** **(4:7)** ***Then came in the magicians, the astrologers, the Chaldeans, and the soothsayers: and I told the dream before them; but they did not make known unto me the interpretation thereof*** (4:6,7). Orders are immediately given to summon *all the wise men of Babylon* that were such fools as to pretend by magic, divination, inspecting the entrails of beasts, or observations of the stars, to predict things to come. They must *all* come together to see if any, or all of them in consultation could interpret the king's dream. They are no more successful than they were in the 2nd year of Nebuchadnezzar's reign (2:1,2). But the key of this dream was in a sacred prophecy (Ezek 31:3, etc.), where the Assyrian is compared, as Nebuchadnezzar here, to a *tree cut down* for his pride. *That was a book the magicians had not studied.* It was good for these magicians that the king was in a different frame of mind than with the first dream (2:4-13).

It Would Come from *Daniel.* ***But at the last Daniel came in before me*** (4:8). *At the last Daniel came in.* Many make God's Word and the prophecies of Daniel and Revelation their last refuge, and that only when all others fail. From his previous encounters he should have known to call Daniel first.

He Complements Daniel with Allusions to Idolatry. The compliments began with Daniel's name: ***whose name was Belteshazzar, according to the name of my God, and in whom is the spirit of the holy gods: and before him I told the dream, saying,*** **(4:9)** ***O Belteshazzar, master of the magicians, because I know that the spirit of the holy gods is in thee.*** He takes notice of the name given to Daniel, a name given under his authority (2:5-7). A name *according to the name of* Nebuchadnezzar's *god*: **Belteshazzar** (the *keeper of the hidden treasures of Bel*). He applauds Daniel's rare endowments: He has **the spirit of the holy gods**. With these "compliments" Daniel would have been extremely grieved. Nebuchadnezzar after the two previous encounters with the True God (Chapter 2 and 3) still retains the language and dialect of idolatry. He is not yet a convert to the faith and worship of the Living God of Israel. His previous professions (2:47; 3:29) had come short of Biblical faith.

He Compliments Daniel's Interpretive Ability: ***and no secret troubleth thee, tell me the visions of my dream that I have seen, and the interpretation thereof*** (4:9). He looked upon him as one that had such an insight, such a foresight, as none of his magicians had. There is no comparison between the *sure word of prophecy* in the Bible (2 Pet 1:19) and *the spirit of divination* (Rev 19:10; Acts 16:16). Again we ask: Why was Daniel not called first!

Nebuchadnezzar's Dream: The Description of Babylon 4:10-18.

Thus were the visions of mine head in my bed; I saw, and behold a tree in the midst of the earth, and the height thereof was great. (4:11) The tree grew, and was strong, and the height thereof reached unto heaven, and the sight thereof to the end of all the earth: (4:12) The leaves thereof were fair, and the fruit thereof much, and in it was meat for all: the beasts of the field had shadow under it, and the fowls of the heaven dwelt in the boughs thereof, and all flesh was fed of it. (4:13) I saw in the visions of my head upon my bed, and, behold, a watcher and an holy one came down from heaven; (4:14) He cried aloud, and said thus, Hew down the tree, and cut off his branches, shake off his leaves, and scatter his fruit: let the beasts get away from under it, and the fowls from his branches: (4:15) Nevertheless leave the stump of his roots in the earth, even with a band of iron and brass, in the tender grass of the field; and let it be wet with the dew of heaven, and let his portion be with the beasts in the grass of the earth: (4:16) Let his heart be changed from man's, and let a beast's heart be given unto him; and let seven times pass over him. (4:17) This matter is by the decree of the watchers, and the demand by the word of the holy ones: to the intent that the living may know that the most High ruleth in the kingdom of men, and giveth it to whomsoever he will, and setteth up over it the basest of men. (4:18) This dream I king Nebuchadnezzar have seen. Now thou, O Belteshazzar, declare the interpretation thereof, forasmuch as all the wise men of my kingdom are not able to make known unto me the interpretation: but thou art able; for the spirit of the holy gods is in thee.

<u>Nebuchadnezzar Saw a Stately Tree.</u>

Its Situation and Eminence. **Thus were the visions of mine head in my bed; I saw, and behold a tree in the midst of the earth, and the height thereof was great** (4:10). To the Gentile World Babylon was then geographically in *the midst of the earth*. As a term defining *the love of the world* (1 Jhn 2:15,16) Babylon is still *in the midst*. From the Biblical standpoint Jerusalem is *in the midst of the earth* (on the land bridge between three continents). But as Jerusalem is under Gentile dominion during the Times of the Gentiles, it is the Gentiles who to a greater or lesser extent control this **central point**.

Thus saith the Lord GOD; This is Jerusalem: I have set it in the midst of the nations and countries that are round about her (Ezek 5:5).

The eminency of Babylon above all other nations is signified by the height of this tree. **The height thereof was great**. As a symbol of its eminence Babylon began with the *Tower of Babel* (Gen 11:1-9). That principle continued with Nebuchadnezzar and will do so until the end of the age.

And the great city was divided into three parts, and the cities of the nations fell: and great Babylon came in remembrance before God, to give unto her the cup of the wine of the fierceness of his wrath (Rev 16:19).

Its Growth and Extent. **The tree grew, and was strong, and the height thereof reached unto heaven, and the sight thereof to the end of all the earth** (4:11). And so much were Nebuchadnezzar and his growing greatness the talk of the nations, so much had they their eye upon him (some a jealous eye, all a wondering eye), that the sight of this tree is said to be *to the end of all the earth*. But remember, we are looking beyond Nebuchadnezzar to the CHARACTERISICS of the Times of the Gentiles. These characteristics extend to the end of the Age and become more prominent as the Age draws to its close. Note again the emphasis given to the height of Babylon: **and the height thereof reached unto heaven, and the sight thereof to the end of all the earth.** As Babylon began with *a tower whose top may reach unto heaven,* and that in order to **make us a name** (Gen 11:4); so the same Babylonian spirit is behind the recent race to build ever taller skyscrapers around the world. A skyscraper is not

cost effective or efficient in comparison to buildings of more moderate height, but it is solely to *make us a name*. Skyscrapers used to be thought of in terms of New York or Chicago and in more recent times Hong Kong and Shanghai, but now hundreds of cities are trying to make their mark by building these huge but inefficient buildings.

Dubai: A Middle Eastern Illustration of Latter Day Babylon?

For sheer audacity in the construction of ultra-high buildings (above 1000 feet) nothing approaches the desert city of Dubai. It now in a very short time has built nearly as many buildings above 1000 feet as New York, Chicago, Hong Kong and Shanghai *combined*! Without necessarily being latter day Babylon, some wonder whether Dubai might symbolize *the latter day Babylonian spirt* of which the Bible speaks. From the site *High Time to Awake*, Craig C. White says the following.

Burj Khalifa

The world's tallest building at 2,717 feet is located in Dubai, U.A.E. Notice the spiral stair step form resembling the original "Tower of Babylon" concept. (Photo credit: Nicolas Lannuzel).

The people of Dubai said "let us build us a city and a tower, whose top may reach unto heaven; and let us make us a name". Read an article about the Burj Dubai on the web at blog.luxuryproperty.com. It is located in the United Arab Emirates. The UAE is on the south eastern tip of Saudi Arabia on the Persian Gulf. Dubai is a new city that was built to cater to the rich and powerful, and has miraculously risen out of the desert over the last thirty years. It is therefore a city that was not previously known. Dubai has the world's tallest building, the first 7 star hotel, the world's biggest shopping mall, the world's largest manmade port, the first indoor ski resort in the Middle East, a Tiger Woods golf course, diamonds, fashion, financial services, a vast slave labour force, and premier sex, drug and human trafficking rings.

Dubai is a major shipping port. It is ranked in the world's ten busiest ports. That is amazing for a city in only thirty years. It exports oil, natural gas, re-exports, fish and some produce. It imports immense amounts of building material along with all kinds of luxury goods.

Dubai is a hub for illicit drug shipping. I found the following on the CIA website (www.cia.gov).The UAE is a drug trans-shipment point for traffickers given its proximity to Southwest Asian drug-producing countries; the UAE's position as a major financial center makes it vulnerable to money laundering; anti-money-laundering controls are improving, but informal banking remains unregulated.

Dubai's slave labour problem is unbelievable. Workers borrow to pay for work permits only to discover that it takes two years wages to pay it back. Promises of pay are not kept. Passports are taken away by employers so workers cannot leave. That includes construction labourers, maids and service workers; not to mention the sex trade. Human trafficking is the way of life. If any person in Dubai does not pay their debts they are thrown into prison, and many are. Some 300,000 construction labourers are housed in large camps in Sonapur. They are packed into minimal housings without electricity, running water, or sanitation. Thousands die every year. No one knows exactly how many, because deaths are not reported.

Prostitution is imbibed into every pore of Dubai society. These women are also enslaved. Prostitutes can be found in bars, hotel lobbies, restaurants, mall gift shops, beaches, gas stations, grocery stores, labour camps, and everywhere else. Their presence entices the rich and powerful, local citizens, and visitors into Dubai's opulent net. You may read an article about Dubai prostitution by William Butler of *The Observer* in the British newspaper the *Guardian* on the web at www.guardian.co.uk.

Dubai is a city founded on a promise of opulence. Read a personal account of Dubai society by reporter Johann Hari in the London newspaper *The Independent* on the web at www.independent.co.uk. (http://hightimetoawake.com/dubai-a-case-for-mystery-babylon/)

Buildings Above 1000 Feet (the Height of London's *Shard*) in Five Skyscraper Cities

Chicago: 1007, 1128, 1136, 1389, 1451 **(5)**

Hong Kong: 1051, 1135, 1205, 1227, 1352, 1588 **(6)**

Shanghai: 1048, 1083, 1094, 1380, 1614, 2073 **(6)**

New York: 1005, 1046, 1050, 1171, 1200, 1250, 1268, 1396, 1775, 1776 **(10)**

Dubai: 1005, 1014, 1017, 1042, 1053, 1070, 1076, 1079, 1083, 1093, 1100, 1122, 1155, 1163, 1166, 1166, 1181, 1207, 1211, 1248, 1287, 1356, 1399, 1460, 2717 **(25)**

(The Skyscraper Center, May 2015. Including buildings under construction.)

"Is not this great Babylon that I have built" (Daniel 4:30)?

Returning now to the stately tree that Nebuchadnezzar saw:

Its Abundance and Refuge: ***The leaves thereof were fair, and the fruit thereof much, and in it was meat for all: the beasts of the field had shadow under it, and the fowls of the heaven dwelt in the boughs thereof, and all flesh was fed of it*** (4:12). This tree had everything that was *good for food and pleasant to the eyes* (cp. Gen). *The leaves thereof were fair,* denoting the pomp and splendour of Nebuchadnezzar's court, which was the wonder of the Ancient World. Babylon represents the world in all of its lavish opulence. In Babylon the welcome is extended to all that the fallen heart of man desires: material gain and sensual pleasure. It is the *world* the believer is not to *love* (1 Jhn 2:15). Yet Babylon was not for sight, desire and wonder only; it also gave provision and protection.

For protection: ***the beasts of the field had shadow under it, and the fowls of the heaven dwelt in the boughs thereof***. It is protection that draws allegiance and Babylon protected its subjects. The kings of the earth protect their subjects as the shadow of a *great tree*; but Christ is more substantial to his subjects as the *shadow of a great rock in a weary land* (Isa 32:2). And more so, because that which is strong may be cold, believers are said to be hidden under the *shadow of his wings* (Psa 17:8), where they are not only safe but warm.

For provision: The Assyrian was compared to a *cedar* (Ezek 31:6), which affords shadow only; but Babylon was a tree that had much fruit: ***meat for all*** and ***all flesh was fed of***

DANIEL 4. THE TREE AND THE BEAST VISION

it. Nebuchadnezzar was not only great but he did good. He did not impoverish, but enriched his kingdom and peoples. Those that *exercise authority* should also be *benefactors* (Lk 22:25).

New York: A Western Illustration of Latter Day Babylon?

Babylon was the market place of the nations and as with other great cities New York is also the market place of the world. It is the *Big Apple*! Its *Wall Street*, *Fifth Avenue* and *Times Square* (or *Broadway*) have long been the foremost bywords for finance, shopping and pleasure. Long before New York became the site of the United Nations it welcomed the *huddled masses* to its shores. It has the world's largest Jewish population outside of Israel; the largest Italian population outside of Rome and a larger Irish population than Dublin. Outside of South America and Spain, it has a larger Spanish speaking population than any city on earth. It is a city of immigrants. It is a microcosm of the world.

On a bronze plaque inside the Statue of Liberty are the famous words from the *New Colossus* written by the Jewish poetess Emma Lazarus:

> ...Give me your tired, your poor, Your huddled masses yearning to breathe free, The wretched refuse of your teeming shore. Send these, the homeless, tempest-tost to me, I lift my lamp beside the golden door!

Indeed the *boughs* and *shadow* of New York have provided sanctuary for many and most especially the Jewish People. This in no small measure has led to the greatness of New York. With its massive population, towering skyscrapers, banking, world trade, shopping, entertainment....New York more than any other city became known as the *world's greatest city*. But what the world calls *great* will rarely be *godly*. New York is a godless city! It is often compared with London which was formerly the world's largest city and also a *godless* city. London, however, had a Protestant spiritual heritage that New York did not have. As an immigrant city, New York soon had a larger Roman Catholic population than Rome and virtually became the *Rome of the New World* (it is this fact that may link it to the summary statement in Rev 18:24). Most of the Protestants that entered America through New York moved elsewhere. The city soon became infamous for its organised crime and the control exercised by its Mafia families. With these considerations and especially its very large Jewish population New York will always be under the spot light when reading the description of latter day Babylon in Revelation 18. If it be argued that New York may not exhaust all of the prophecy of that chapter (in fact it probably does!), there is more than enough said that makes one think of no other city.

What City is Like This Great City?

(18:1) And after these things I saw another angel come down from heaven, having great power; and the earth was lightened with his glory. (18:2) And he cried mightily with a strong voice, saying, **Babylon the great is fallen, is fallen**, *and is become the habitation of devils, and the hold of every foul spirit, and a cage of every unclean and hateful bird. (18:3) For* **all nations** *have drunk of the wine of the wrath of her fornication, and* **the kings of the earth** *have committed fornication with her, and* **the merchants of the earth** *are waxed rich through the abundance of her delicacies.*

(18:4) And I heard another voice from heaven, saying, **Come out of her, my people** [the frequent Biblical term used almost entirely of Jewish people; thus a special reference to New York's large Jewish population], *that ye be not partakers of her sins, and that ye receive not of her plagues. (18:5) For* **her sins have reached unto heaven**, *and God hath remembered her iniquities. (18:6) Reward her even as she rewarded you, and double unto her double according to her works: in the cup which she hath filled fill to her double. (18:7) How much she hath glorified herself, and lived deliciously, so much torment and sorrow give her: for she saith in her heart,* **I sit a queen**, *and am no widow, and shall see no sorrow. (18:8) Therefore shall her plagues come in one day, death,*

and mourning, and famine; and she shall be utterly burned with fire: for strong is the Lord God who judgeth her.

*(18:9) And **the kings of the earth** [home of the United Nations], who have committed fornication and lived deliciously with her, shall bewail her, and lament for her, when they shall see the smoke of her burning, (18:10) Standing afar off for the fear of her torment, saying, Alas, alas **that great city** Babylon, **that mighty city**! for in one hour is thy judgment come.*

*(18:11) And **the merchants of the earth** shall weep and mourn over her; for no man buyeth their merchandise any more: (18:12) The merchandise of gold, and silver, and precious stones, and of pearls, and fine linen, and purple, and silk, and scarlet, and all thyine wood, and all manner vessels of ivory, and all manner vessels of most precious wood, and of brass, and iron, and marble, (18:13) And cinnamon, and odours, and ointments, and frankincense, and wine, and oil, and fine flour, and wheat, and beasts, and sheep, and horses, and chariots, and slaves, and souls of men. (18:14) And the fruits that thy soul lusted after are departed from thee, and all things which were dainty and goodly are departed from thee, and thou shalt find them no more at all.*

*(18:15) **The merchants of these things**, which were made rich by her, shall stand afar off for the fear of her torment, weeping and wailing, (18:16) And saying, Alas, alas **that great city**, that was clothed in fine linen, and purple, and scarlet, and decked with gold, and precious stones, and pearls!*

*(18:17) For in one hour so great riches is come to nought. And **every shipmaster**, and **all the company in ships**, and sailors, and as many as **trade by sea**, stood afar off* [a great harbour city, thus ruling out London or Rome], *(18:18) And cried when they saw the smoke of her burning, saying, **What city is like unto this great city*** [what other city than New York]! *(18:19) And they cast dust on their heads, and cried, weeping and wailing, saying, Alas, alas **that great city**, wherein were made rich all that had ships in the sea by reason of her costliness! for in one hour is she made desolate.*

*(18:20) Rejoice over her, thou heaven, and ye holy apostles and prophets; for God hath avenged you on her. (18:21) And a mighty angel took up a stone like a great millstone, and cast it into the sea, saying, Thus with violence shall **that great city** Babylon be thrown down, and shall be **found no more at all**. (18:22) And the voice of harpers, and musicians, and of pipers, and trumpeters, shall be **heard no more at all in thee**; and no craftsman, of whatsoever craft he be, shall be found any more in thee; and the sound of a millstone shall be **heard no more at all in thee**; (18:23) And the light of a candle shall **shine no more at all in thee**; and the voice of the bridegroom and of the bride shall be **heard no more at all in thee**: for **thy merchants were the great men of the earth** [the great banking names of Wall street]; for by thy sorceries were all nations deceived.*

(18:24) And in her was found the blood of prophets, and of saints, and of all that were slain upon the earth. [This is a summary statement encompassing the Babylonian spirit in the world from beginning to end: religious, political, commercial. Babylon has always been and will always be opposed to Biblical faith].

The Woman in the Basket Prophecy

In addition to Revelation 18 (see also Isa 13,47; Jer 50,51), Zechariah 5 refers to Babylon in a latter day sense. Broadly Zechariah sees a symbol of commercialism (the ephah-basket) *going forth* to *Babylon*. Nebuchadnezzar's Babylon had already fallen; this "second" Babylon as in Revelation 18 is a great commercial centre of the last days. The general picture of the vision seems clear; but the addition of *the woman* in the basket and other details have perplexed students of the Bible.

*(5:5) Then the angel that talked with me went forth, and said unto me, Lift up now thine eyes, and see what is this **that goeth forth**. (5:6) And I said, What is it? And he said, This is an ephah that **goeth forth**. He said moreover, This is their resemblance through all the earth. (5:7) And, behold, there was lifted up a talent of lead: and this is **a woman***

DANIEL 4. THE TREE AND THE BEAST VISION

> *that sitteth in the midst of the ephah. (5:8) And he said,* **This is wickedness***. And he cast it into the midst of the ephah; and he cast the weight of lead upon the mouth thereof. (5:9) Then lifted I up mine eyes, and looked, and, behold, there came out* **two women***, and* **the wind was in their wings***; for they had wings like the wings of a stork: and they* **lifted up the ephah** *between the earth and the heaven. (5:10) Then said I to the angel that talked with me, Whither do these bear the ephah? (5:11) And he said unto me, To* **build it an house in the land of Shinar***: and* **it shall be established, and set there upon her own base***.*

The background to this Vision in the Book of Zechariah relates to the Babylon that had fallen to Persia and where despite their "right of return" many Jewish people preferred to remain rather than return to Israel. Judah was deported to Babylon because of her idolatry. There in the "capital of idolatry" they learned a hard lesson and have never returned to their former idolatries (Hosea 3:4,5). However in Babylon they learned something else (!). Formerly they were a pastoral and agricultural people; there they learned to become merchants, money lenders and ultimately bankers. Clay financial tablets from Babylon containing Jewish names (now at the British Museum) show that they soon excelled and eclipsed the Babylonians themselves as the world's primary money lenders. *Thou shalt lend unto many nations but thou shalt not borrow* (Deut 15:6). What they had learned in Babylon was an insatiate greed of gain (Neh 5:1-9; Mal 3:8); that intense commercial spirit which had been foreign to Israel, but which was thenceforward to characterize them through the ages. Thus one form of idolatry was exchanged for another. *The love of money is the root of all evil* (1 Tim 6:10).

This avarice is pictured as a woman placed in an ephah-basket (a symbol and unit of commercial enterprise) and taken to this latter day Babylon where she is *set on her base* (Zech 5:11). In considering where *this base* and *this other Babylon* might be, no other city appears to come as close as New York. As we will see the woman pictures other things!

The covering or lid of the ephah-basket is a lead disk. This speaks of the fixedness of what is happening. Despite the great distance being covered in the transport of this woman; despite the fact that the ephah is a symbol of commercial enterprise *through all the earth* (Zech 5:5), there is here *a special ephah* and it will be *set up on its base*. This is the commercial sense but there is also a religious aspect to this woman. Before the Jews were carried into Babylon many worshipped *the queen of heaven* (Jer 44:18). Could it be that the Jews in coming to their most populous end-time city they will be greeted by this *queen*!?

Babylon – Kabbalah – Freemasonary Link!

Scofield presents the general but not the specific religious aspect of the woman:

> Symbolically, a *measure* (or *cup*) stands for something which has come to the full, so that God must judge it (2 Sam 8:2; Jer 51:13; Hab 3:6,7; Matt 7:2; 23:32). A *woman*, in the bad ethical sense, is always a symbol of that which religiously is out of its place. The *woman* in Matthew 13:33 is dealing with doctrine, a sphere forbidden to her (1 Tim 2:12). In Thyatira a *woman* is suffered to teach (Rev 2:20). The Babylon phase of the apostate church is symbolized by an unchaste *woman*, sodden with the greed and luxury of commercialism (Rev 17:1-6; 18:3,11-20).

A woman with wicked teaching (in addition to commercialism) is placed in the ephah-basket. ***This is wickedness*** (Zech 5:8). In the above sense, wickedness is that which undermines faith in the Bible. The mystical Jewish Kabbalah had its origins in Nebuchadnezzar's Babylon. The Talmud which came later was associated with Babylon and its primary edition was known as the *Babylonian Talmud*. Both detract from a literal faith in Scripture. Both oppose faith in Jesus Christ as the Messiah. Masonic teaching and ritual are known to have substantial roots in Jewish Kabbalism and there has long been a strong if not always consistent link between Judaism and Freemasonry.

David J. Stewart writes:

Albert Pike and other Masonic leaders acknowledge their debt to Kabbalah and to the Babylonian Mystery Schools. In his book, *Morals and Dogma*, Pike states:

"Every lodge is a temple of religion, and its teaching instruction in religion... Masonry is the successor to the Mysteries."

The Jewish Kaballah, their more occult teachings, is said by many to have been influenced by the Babylonian Mystery religion, and it originated as oral teachings during the Babylonian Captivity of the Jews. Albert Pike (1809 to 1891), a highly influential 33rd Degree Freemason of the nineteenth century, acknowledged that the Masons derived many of their ideas from the Jewish Kabbalah. In his 1871 book, *Morals and Dogma of the Ancient and Accepted Scottish Rite of Freemasonry*, Pike, says of the Jewish Pharisee tradition... "The primary tradition... has been preserved under the name of the Kabbalah by the priesthood of Israel." (http://www.jesus-is-savior.com/False%20Religions/Freemasonry/infiltrate.htm)

Is the Roman Goddess Libertas the Woman in the Basket ?

No other major city is so prominently represented by a *woman* as New York, and few monuments anywhere are held is such esteem and affection as the Statue of Liberty. Even if it can be shown that there is *another side* to this revered icon; given the positive image it expresses as a symbol of America's greatness, and the hope it has conveyed to multitudes; should not this venerable lady be left in peace and allowed to remain undisturbed as that *beacon of hope*? Having lived for a while in New York (the northern end of Staten Island) and only a short distance from a clear vantage point of the Statue, I understand well the patriotic pride felt for this monument and its revered place in America's heritage. Nevertheless there is *another side*, and for believers we have a far different hope –

>My hope is built on nothing less
>
>Than Jesus blood and righteousness;
>
>I dare not trust the sweetest frame,
>
>But wholly lean on Jesus' name.

1. There is nothing *remotely Christian, Historical or even Secular* about the Statue of Liberty. It is the Statue of *Libertas*, the well-known Roman (and much earlier) goddess of liberty and freedom. Libertas under different names was venerated and worshipped throughout the Ancient World. This is the largest standing replica in the entire world of a pagan goddess. At the time of its placement, pastors voiced concern that a pagan deity was now looking down on the city of New York. Some other form of monument could have been built. Why a Roman goddess! *Libertas* is likely the *woman in the basket*, and as the following shows gives full cause for the epithet: ***This is wickedness*** (Zech 5:8)!

DANIEL 4. THE TREE AND THE BEAST VISION

The worship of Libertas goddess extends into ancient history. Her appearance in Rome and link to the Statue of Liberty is here described.

"In 238 BC, before the Second Punic War, having long been **a Roman deity** along with other personified virtues, **Libertas assumed goddess status**. Tiberius Gracchus ordered the construction of **her first temple** on Aventine Hill. A subsequent temple was built (58-57 BC) on Palatine Hill, though later removed. In 46 BC, the Roman Senate voted to build and dedicate a shrine to Libertas in recognition of Julius Caesar, but no temple was built; instead, a small statue of the goddess stood in the Roman Forum. **Libertas**, along with other Roman goddesses, **has served as the inspiration for many modern-day symbols**, including **the Statue of Liberty** on Liberty Island in the United States of America."
(http://en.wikipedia.org/wiki/Libertas)

Libertas

"The sculptor who made the Statue of Liberty was the Italian Freemason Frederic-Auguste Bartholdi. His work was greatly influenced by the ancient sculptor Phidias who made gigantic statues of ancient goddesses, particularly *Athena*, the goddess of wisdom and *Nemesis* (another name for Venus), **a goddess who held a cup in her right hand**. Before beginning the Statue of Liberty project, Bertholdi was seeking a commission to construct a giant statue of the goddess *Isis*, the Egyptian Queen of Heaven, to overlook the Suez canal. The statue of Isis was to be of "**a robed woman holding aloft a torch**". Bertholdi never made the statue of Isis for the Suez canal - but it seems obvious that he made it after all, fulfilling his life's ambition, when he constructed the Statue of Liberty for the United States!" (*Statue of Liberty: 1st Hundred Years*, Bernard Weisberger, p.30, quoted in *Beyond Babylon*, James Lloyd, p.103).

(http://yahushua.net/babylon/liberty/pagan_statue.htm)

The Rays of the Sun Signifying Illumination

"Bartholdi did not originate the concept of the statue. The idea for creating a statue of liberty and freedom was first proposed by another Frenchman and Freemason, Edward Laboulaye. Laboulaye proceeded to raise the financial support and commissioned Bartholdi to provide the sculpture of this goddess of illumination. What deity was this? It was the goddess known by various names. Laboulaye and Bartholdi referred to her as "Libertas" but she was also an early adoption by Romans of the **Babylonian goddess Ishtar**. *The American Babylonianism Introduction* (humansarefree.com).

Libertas was the goddess of personal freedom and liberty – in fact of a very wide range of freedoms! She was a multi-faceted deity. On the one hand she was worshipped as the goddess of slaves, immigrants and exiles; and also a goddess of war who fought for freedom. But she was also well-known as the matron of sexual freedom and prostitution. Many women who gained freedom later turned to prostitution to survive and thereby retained Libertas as their goddess. This was especially the case if they became priestesses in the Libertas cult. In the writings of the Roman historian and senator, Cicero, Libertas is referred to as the "Mother of Harlots"!

Cicero indicates that she was also the goddess of the Greeks before Roman civilization developed. The Greeks had Ishtar; acquired knowledge of this being from previous empires in the Middle East and Egypt. This goddess was called Ashtoreth in Hebrew. Ashtoreth becomes transliterated into the Greek as Astarte, which became the early Greek name for the goddess until it was later changed to Aphrodite. The Hebrew term Ashtoreth was itself a transliteration from the Babylonian dialect (Akkadian) term of Ishtar. Ishtar in ancient times was also referred to by the Sumerian dialect as Inanna or Ninanna meaning the Queen of Heaven. In Canaan this deity was called Ashtaroth. Isis was the name the Egyptians gave to her.

What was Ishtar's (Libertas') legacy in Babylon? She was the chief goddess of Babylon and all of Babylonia. There was no other goddess more honored than she. She was equated to have nearly the same power as the chief god of Babylon, the sun god Utu. (http://humansarefree.com/2014/04/the-secret-worship-of-illuminati-statue.html)

2. The Statue of Liberty was thoroughly Masonic. Freemasonry takes a few subjects from the Bible (the sons of Noah, the building of Solomon's Temple) and blends them with pagan mythology and Jewish mysticism. It is enormously influential, and so it was with the building of the Statue of Liberty.

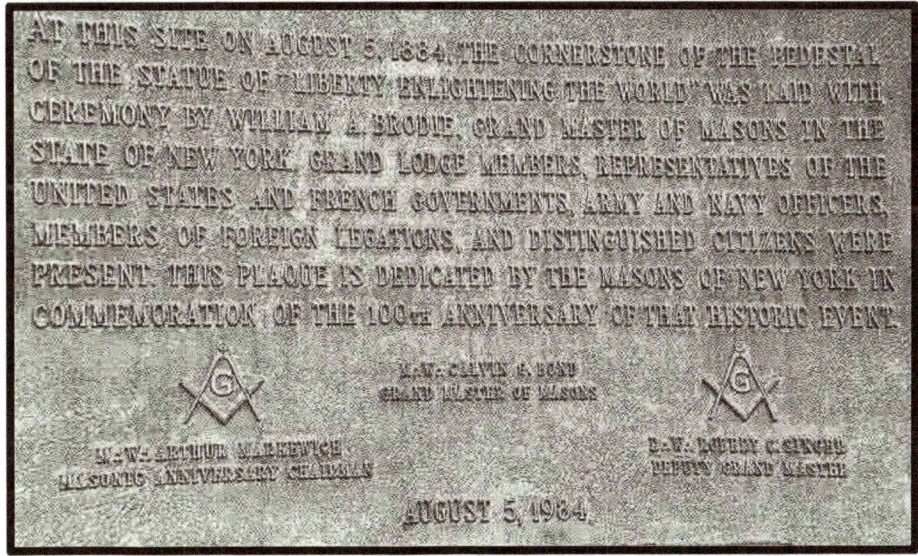

The Masonic Cornerstone of the Statue of Liberty

The *Friends of the American Revolution* write:

One of the many proofs of Freemasonry's influence… upon our culture and mentality, is the Statue of Liberty. This colossus in New York's harbor was conceived by Freemasons, financed by Freemasons, built by Freemasons, and installed by Freemasons in a Freemasonic ceremony. The maker of the statue was Freemason Frederic-Auguste Bartholdi. He had already made a statue of the Freemason Marquis de Lafayette for the city of New York, for the occasion of the centenary of the signing of the Declaration of Independence. Bartholdi sailed to America, at the suggestion of other Freemasons and kindred spirits in France, for the purpose of proposing the project. Although he had no drawings as he set sail, his Masonic biographer writes, as he entered New York harbor, "he caught a vision of a magnificent goddess, holding aloft a torch in one hand and welcoming all visitors to the land of freedom and opportunity". Returning to France, he managed to raise, through the help of a great deal of Masonic propaganda, the sum of 3,500,000 French francs, a very large sum for the 1870's. Although financial support for the statue was forthcoming in France, America was not willing to put up the money for the pedestal. It was Joseph Pulitzer [Jewish, Freemason], the owner and editor of the New York World, who managed to raise over $100,000 for the project. On Washington's Birthday in 1877, Congress accepted the statue as a gift from the French people. Bedloe's Island, now Liberty Island, was chosen as the site. In Paris the work gradually progressed. The statue was finished on May 21, 1884, and presented for shipment to Ambassador Levi Morton on July 4th of the same year by Ferdinand de Lesseps, builder of the Suez canal. The chairman of the American committee prepared the ceremony to receive the cornerstone and contacted the Grand Lodge of the "Free and Accepted Masons" of the State of New York. The ceremony was set for August 5, 1884. It poured rain. The decorated vessel 'Bay Ridge' carried about a hundred Freemasons, along with some civil officials, to Bedloe's Island. Freemason Richard M. Hunt, the principal architect of the pedestal, handed the working tools to the Masonic officers. Then Freemason Edward M.,L. Ehlers...read the list of items to be included in the copper box within the cornerstone: a copy of the United States Constitution; George Washington's Farewell Address; twenty bronze medals of Presidents up through Chester A. Arthur [including Washington, Monroe, Jackson, Polk, Buchanan, Johnson and Garfield, who were all Freemasons]...and a list on parchment of the Grand Lodge officers. The traditional Masonic ceremony was observed. The cornerstone being found square, level and plumb, the Grand Master applied the mortar and had the stone lowered into place. He then struck the stone three times, and declared it duly laid. Then the elements of "consecration" were presented, corn, wine, and oil. The "Most Worshipful" Grand Master then spoke a few words. He posed the question: "Why call upon the Masonic Fraternity to lay the cornerstone of such a structure as is here to be erected?" His answer was: **"No institution has done more to promote liberty and to free men from the trammels and chains of ignorance and tyranny than has Freemasonry."** https://21stcenturycicero.wordpress.com/american-icons/the-statue-of-liberty-a-masonic-goddess-from-top-to-bottom/

Libertas in Paris to be disassembled, packed into 214 cases and shipped to New York

3. The Statue of Liberty Packed in Cases and Brought in Two Ships (Isere and Flore) to New York.

"Liberty was dismantled in Paris, every copper plate and beam coded and packed into 214 cases, and the whole shipment transported on a 70-car train to the coast. After a month at sea on the *Isere* [accompanied by the *Flore*], she arrived at Bedloe's Island in June, 1885. It took 15 months to assemble the 225 tons of pure copper." MasonicWorld.com

Parallels with the Zechariah Prophecy

*(5:7) …this is **a woman that sitteth in the midst of the ephah**. (5:8) And he said, **This is wickedness**. And he cast it into the midst of the ephah; and he cast the weight of lead upon the mouth thereof.(5:9) Then lifted I up mine eyes, and looked, and, behold, there came out **two women**, and **the wind was in their wings**; for they had wings like the wings of a stork: and they **lifted up the ephah** between the earth and the heaven. (5:10) Then said I to the angel that talked with me, Whither do these bear the ephah? (5:11) And he said unto me, To **build it an house in the land of Shinar**: and **it shall be established, and set there upon her own base**.*

"The U.S. Navy art collection features a work by J.O. Davidson depicting the French warships <u>**Isere**</u> (in white) and <u>**Flore**</u> (firing salute) as they arrive in New York Harbour. The ships are delivering the disassembled Statue of Liberty."

<u>Time will tell but the parallels with the Prophecy of Zechariah are remarkable</u>:

(1) The Statue of Liberty *is* the goddess Libertas. There is reasonable probability that Libertas is **the woman in the basket**.
(2) This woman is called *wickedness*. Libertas was a multi-faceted object of worship for slaves, immigrants, exiles and prostitutes. Further, from beginning to end the Statue of Liberty was a Masonic project.
(3) This *woman in the basket* was packed in 214 cases for shipment to New York.
(4) Two ships (named after *two women*) and powered by steam and *wind* brought Libertas to this latter day Babylon.
(5) Libertas was **lifted up… and set there upon her own base… between the earth and the heaven,**

DANIEL 4. THE TREE AND THE BEAST VISION

Libertas Lifted to Her Pedestal and *Base*

"Is not this great Babylon that I have built" (Daniel 4:30)?

The Great Tree that Nebuchadnezzar saw refers not only to his day, but the spirit of the age generally and most especially the Babyon of the last days.

Babylon the great is fallen, is fallen (Rev 18:2).

We return now to the *Stately Tree* that Nebuchadnezzar saw in his dream. We have seen a number of features that made this tree so magnificent but now suddenly his dream takes a turn for the worst.

<u>Nebuchadnezzar Saw a Stately Tree.</u>

Its Situation and Eminence. ***Thus were the visions of mine head in my bed; I saw, and behold a tree in the midst of the earth, and the height thereof was great*** (4:10).

Its Growth, Extent and Benevolence. ***The tree grew, and was strong, and the height thereof reached unto heaven, and the sight thereof to the end of all the earth*** (4:11). ***The leaves thereof were fair, and the fruit thereof much, and in it was meat for all: the beasts of the field had shadow under it, and the fowls of the heaven dwelt in the boughs thereof, and all flesh was fed of it*** (4:12).

<u>Nebuchadnezzar Heard the Doom of the Tree.</u>

The Messenger of the Doom. ***I saw in the visions of my head upon my bed, and, behold, a watcher and an holy one came down from heaven*** (4:13). The sentence was passed upon it by an angel, whom he saw *come down from heaven,* and heard proclaim this sentence aloud. This angel is here called a *watcher*. Three times, and all in this chapter, the term is used of angels. Once it is used of men. In each case the watchers *utter a warning* of coming judgement.

- ***Make ye mention*** *to the nations; behold,* ***publish*** *against Jerusalem, that* ***watchers*** *come from a far country, and* ***give out their voice*** *against the cities of Judah (Jer 4:16).*

- *I saw in the visions of my head upon my bed, and, behold, a* ***watcher*** *and an holy one came down from heaven (Dan 4:13).*

- *This matter is by the* ***decree*** *of the* ***watchers****, and the* ***demand*** *by the word of the holy ones: to the intent that the living may know that the most High ruleth in the kingdom of men, and giveth it to whomsoever he will, and setteth up over it the basest of men (Dan 4:17).*

- *And whereas the king saw a* ***watcher*** *and an holy one coming down from heaven, and* ***saying****, Hew the tree down, and destroy it; yet leave the stump of the roots thereof in the earth, even with a band of iron and brass, in the tender grass of the field; and let it be wet with the dew of heaven, and let his portion be with the beasts of the field, till seven times pass over him (Dan 4:23).*

It is interesting to compare the *watchers* with the cherubim who are *full of eyes*.

- *As for their rings, they were so high that they were dreadful; and their rings were* ***full of eyes*** *round about them four (Ezek 1:18).*

- *And their whole body, and their backs, and their hands, and their wings, and the wheels, were* ***full of eyes*** *round about, even the wheels that they four had (Ezek 10:12).*

- *And before the throne there was a sea of glass like unto crystal: and in the midst of the throne, and round about the throne, were four beasts* ***full of eyes*** *before and behind (Rev 4:6).*

- *And the four beasts had each of them six wings about him; and they were* ***full of eyes*** *within: and they rest not day and night, saying, Holy, holy, holy, Lord God Almighty, which was, and is, and is to come (Rev 4:8).*

The Felling of the Tree. ***He cried aloud, and said thus, Hew down the tree, and cut off his branches, shake off his leaves, and scatter his fruit: let the beasts get away from under it, and the fowls from his branches*** (4:14). Orders are given that the great stately tree be cut down. Compare this with the thrice repeated judgement: *Babylon is fallen, is fallen* (Isa 21:9;

DANIEL 4. THE TREE AND THE BEAST VISION

Rev 14:18; 18:2). Now is *the axe is laid unto the root* of this tree (Matt 3:10). Though it is ever so high and ever so strong, Babylon's height and strength will mean nothing on the day that it falls. The beasts and fowls that sheltered in and under it are all driven away. The branches are cropped, the leaves shaken off and the fruit scattered. Worldly prosperity in its highest degree is a very uncertain thing. But the *trees of righteousness,* that are *planted in the house of the Lord* and bring forth fruit to him, shall not be cut down, nor shall their leaf wither.

> *To appoint unto them that mourn in Zion, to give unto them beauty for ashes, the oil of joy for mourning, the garment of praise for the spirit of heaviness; that they might be called* **trees of righteousness, the planting of the LORD***, that he might be glorified (Isa 61:3).*

The Preservation of the Stump. ***Nevertheless leave the stump of his roots in the earth, even with a band of iron and brass, in the tender grass of the field; and let it be wet with the dew of heaven, and let his portion be with the beasts in the grass of the earth*** (4:15). Care is taken that the root be preserved; *Leave the stump of it in the earth,* exposed to all weathers. There let it lie neglected and buried in the grass. Let the beasts that formerly sheltered themselves under the boughs now repose themselves upon the stump. But that it may not be raked to pieces, or trodden to dirt, and to show that it is yet reserved for better days, let it be *hooped* with *a band of iron and brass.* God in judgment remembers mercy; and may yet have good things in store for those whose condition seems most forlorn. There is *hope of a tree, if it be cut down, that it will sprout again, that through the scent of water it will bud* (Job 14:7-9).

But Note: In the middle of this verse the figure begins to change dramatically from the fate of the *tree* to that of a ***beast***!

The Change of the Figure.

From a Tree to a Beast. ***Let his heart be changed from man's, and let a <u>beast's heart</u> be given unto him; and let <u>seven times</u> pass over him*** (4:16). There is not only going to be a fall, but the one falling is going to be deposed from the dignity of a man. He is going to be deprived of the use of his reason and live like a beast out in the field where he saw the tree felled. To suddenly be deprived of reason is the sorest calamity imaginable! To fall and be cut down is bad but this is a lingering judgement that is far worse. This as we will see is a CHARACTERISTIC OF THE TIMES OF THE GENTILES. It happened to the first king and is repeated many times. Those on the throne and in high office can act in a very bizarre manner. There have been proud leaders who *set their heart as the heart of God* (Ezek 27:2), and find themselves deprived of normal human reason and take on the irrationality of a beast. So it will be for the "great" world leader during the coming Tribulation. He is called *the beast*!

The Times of the Gentiles Begin and End with a *Beast*

Chapters 3-6 of Daniel set out events which both characterize the Times of the Gentiles through the ages and which will also conclude this time. Thus it will begin and end with an ***image*** that must be worshipped (Dan 3; Rev 13). It will begin and end with a "magnificent" ***Babylon*** (Dan 4; Rev 18). And while Nebuchadnezzar out in the fields illustrates the bizarre behaviour of Gentile rule throughout the period; it also demonstrates that the Times of the Gentiles will begin and end with a ***beast*** (Dan 4, Rev 13,17). It is this singular fact that is so emphasized in the Book of Revelation. The following gives each time this term for the Antichrist is used in that Book.

> • *And when they shall have finished their testimony,* **the beast(1)** *that ascendeth out of the bottomless pit shall make war against them, and shall overcome them, and kill them (Rev 11:7).*

- And I stood upon the sand of the sea, and saw a **beast(2)** rise up out of the sea, having seven heads and ten horns, and upon his horns ten crowns, and upon his heads the name of blasphemy (Rev 13:1).

- And **the beast(3)** which I saw was like unto a leopard, and his feet were as the feet of a bear, and his mouth as the mouth of a lion: and the dragon gave him his power, and his seat, and great authority (Rev 13:2).

- And I saw one of his heads as it were wounded to death; and his deadly wound was healed: and all the world wondered after **the beast(4)** (Rev 13:3).

- And they worshipped the dragon which gave power unto **the beast(5)**: and they worshipped **the beast(6)**, saying, Who is like unto **the beast(7)**? who is able to make war with him (Rev 13:4)?

- And he exerciseth all the power of **the first beast(8)** before him, and causeth the earth and them which dwell therein to worship **the first beast(9)**, whose deadly wound was healed (Rev 13:12).

- And deceiveth them that dwell on the earth by the means of those miracles which he had power to do in the sight of **the beast(10)**; saying to them that dwell on the earth, that they should make an image to **the beast(11)**, which had the wound by a sword, and did live (Rev 13:14).

- And he had power to give life unto the image of **the beast(12)**, that the image of **the beast(13)** should both speak, and cause that as many as would not worship the image of **the beast(14)** should be killed (Rev 13:15).

- And that no man might buy or sell, save he that had the mark, or the name of **the beast(15)**, or the number of his name (Rev 13:17).

- Here is wisdom. Let him that hath understanding count the number of **the beast(16)**: for it is the number of a man; and his number is Six hundred threescore and six (Rev 13:18).

- And the third angel followed them, saying with a loud voice, If any man worship **the beast(17)** and his image, and receive his mark in his forehead, or in his hand (Rev 14:9).

- And the smoke of their torment ascendeth up for ever and ever: and they have no rest day nor night, who worship **the beast(18)** and his image, and whosoever receiveth the mark of his name (Rev 14:11).

- And I saw as it were a sea of glass mingled with fire: and them that had gotten the victory over **the beast(19)**, and over his image, and over his mark, and over the number of his name, stand on the sea of glass, having the harps of God (Rev 15:2).

- And the first went, and poured out his vial upon the earth; and there fell a noisome and grievous sore upon the men which had the mark of **the beast(20)**, and upon them which worshipped his image (Rev 16:2).

- And the fifth angel poured out his vial upon the seat of **the beast(21)**; and his kingdom was full of darkness; and they gnawed their tongues for pain (Rev 16:10).

- And I saw three unclean spirits like frogs come out of the mouth of the dragon, and out of the mouth of **the beast(22)**, and out of the mouth of the false prophet (Rev 16:13).

- So he carried me away in the spirit into the wilderness: and I saw a woman sit upon **a scarlet coloured beast(23)**, full of names of blasphemy, having seven heads and ten horns (Rev 17:3).

- And the angel said unto me, Wherefore didst thou marvel? I will tell thee the mystery of the woman, and of **the beast(24)** that carrieth her, which hath the seven heads and ten horns (Rev 17:7).

DANIEL 4. THE TREE AND THE BEAST VISION

> • **The beast(25)** *that thou sawest was, and is not; and shall ascend out of the bottomless pit, and go into perdition: and they that dwell on the earth shall wonder, whose names were not written in the book of life from the foundation of the world, when they behold* **the beast(26)** *that was, and is not, and yet is (Rev 17:8).*

> • *And* **the beast(27)** *that was, and is not, even he is the eighth, and is of the seven, and goeth into perdition (Rev 17:11).*

> • *And the ten horns which thou sawest are ten kings, which have received no kingdom as yet; but receive power as kings one hour with* **the beast(28)** *(Rev 17:12).*

> • *These have one mind, and shall give their power and strength unto* **the beast(29)** *(Rev 17:13).*

> • *And the ten horns which thou sawest upon* **the beast(30)**, *these shall hate the whore, and shall make her desolate and naked, and shall eat her flesh, and burn her with fire (Rev 17:16).*

> • *For God hath put in their hearts to fulfil his will, and to agree, and give their kingdom unto* **the beast(31)**, *until the words of God shall be fulfilled (Rev 17:17).*

> • *And I saw* **the beast(32)**, *and the kings of the earth, and their armies, gathered together to make war against him that sat on the horse, and against his army (Rev 19:19).*

> • *And* **the beast(33)** *was taken, and with him the false prophet that wrought miracles before him, with which he deceived them that had received the mark of* **the beast(34)**, *and them that worshipped his image. These both were cast alive into a lake of fire burning with brimstone (Rev 19:20).*

> • *And I saw thrones, and they sat upon them, and judgment was given unto them: and I saw the souls of them that were beheaded for the witness of Jesus, and for the word of God, and which had not worshipped* **the beast(35)**, *neither his image, neither had received his mark upon their foreheads, or in their hands; and they lived and reigned with Christ a thousand years (Rev 20:4).*

> • *And the devil that deceived them was cast into the lake of fire and brimstone, where* **the beast(36)** *and the false prophet are, and shall be tormented day and night for ever and ever (Rev 20:10).*

From a beast in a field to a beast over all the earth! Note the remarkable significance of the numbers. The beast when referring to Antichrist and his rule occurs 36 times in the Book of Revelation. That is **6 x 6 = 36**. But notice also:

1+2+3+4+5+6+7+8+9+10+11+12+13+14+15+16+17+18+19+20+21+22+23+24+25+26+27+28+29+30+31+32+33+34+35+36 = **666**

Again notice, ***Let his heart be changed from man's, and let a beast's heart be given unto him; and let seven times pass over him*** (4:16). Yes this most dreadful of calamities was to fall upon the mighty monarch Nebuchadnezzar. For him however there would be a humbling and a recovery. For many monarchs during the Times of the Gentiles there was no return to reasonable and benevolent governance. And as we know well, the final beast will seek to plunge the world into the depths of Satan.

For Nebuchadnezzar this judgement was to last for **seven times**. This is likely to be a period of seven years, But as we saw in Chapter 3 when the furnace was heated *seven times more* (3:19), this is a term with prophetic significance. It occurs four times in Chapter 4 (4:16,23,25,32), and also in Leviticus.

> • *And if ye will not yet for all this hearken unto me, then I will punish you* **seven times** *more for your sins (Lev 26:18).*

> • *And if ye walk contrary unto me, and will not hearken unto me; I will bring* **seven times** *more plagues upon you according to your sins (Lev 26:21).*

> • Then will I also walk contrary unto you, and will punish you yet **seven times** for your sins (Lev 26:24).
>
> • Then I will walk contrary unto you also in fury; and I, even I, will chastise you **seven times** for your sins (Lev 26:28).

The term *time* (referring to years) occurs in Revelation and is linked to 1260 days and 42 months (Rev 12:6; 11:2; 13:5; cp. Dan 12:11,12).

> And to the woman were given two wings of a great eagle, that she might fly into the wilderness, into her place, where she is nourished for **a time, and times, and half a time**, from the face of the serpent (Rev 12:14).

<u>Nebuchadnezzar Understood the General Warning of the Dream</u>. ***This matter is by the decree of the watchers, and the demand by the word of the holy ones: to the intent that the living may know that the most High ruleth in the kingdom of men, and giveth it to whomsoever he will, and setteth up over it the basest of men*** (4:17). Nebuchadnezzar is beginning to understand that *the heavens do rule* (4:26). God as the righteous Judge has determined it. He has signed this edict in conformity to His eternal counsels. The angels of heaven have subscribed to it and made it their own decree.

The *holy ones* likely refers to the *watchers*, the angels. But if it refers to God's suffering people, then we note that they had long groaned under the heavy yoke of Nebuchadnezzar's tyranny. They had cried to God for deliverance and when the *oppressed cry to God, he will hear*. This being the case, and if the dream refers to himself, Nebuchadnezzar accepts their cause as being just.

The *basest of men* Nebuchadnezzar (if that be the intent implied in the dream) takes this to himself. From his haughty pride, he now accepts this as a just description of his long years on the throne. He has now gone from the haughtiest to the basest.

<u>Nebuchadnezzar Requests the Specific Interpretation of the Dream</u>. ***This dream I king Nebuchadnezzar have seen. Now thou, O Belteshazzar, declare the interpretation thereof, forasmuch as all the wise men of my kingdom are not able to make known unto me the interpretation: but thou art able; for the spirit of the holy gods is in thee*** (4:18). Nebuchadnezzar fully and faithfully related his dream to Daniel, what he saw and what he heard. He likely has a sense, and is beginning to accept that sense as what and to whom the dream is referring. He accepts it as a general warning and wants now to know the specifics.

Nebuchadnezzar's Dream: The Interpretation 4:19-27.

> Then Daniel, whose name was Belteshazzar, was astonied for one hour, and his thoughts troubled him. The king spake, and said, Belteshazzar, let not the dream, or the interpretation thereof, trouble thee. Belteshazzar answered and said, My lord, the dream be to them that hate thee, and the interpretation thereof to thine enemies. (4:20) The tree that thou sawest, which grew, and was strong, whose height reached unto the heaven, and the sight thereof to all the earth; (4:21) Whose leaves were fair, and the fruit thereof much, and in it was meat for all; under which the beasts of the field dwelt, and upon whose branches the fowls of the heaven had their habitation: (4:22) It is thou, O king, that art grown and become strong: for thy greatness is grown, and reacheth unto heaven, and thy dominion to the end of the earth. (4:23) And whereas the king saw a watcher and an holy one coming down from heaven, and saying, Hew the tree down, and destroy it; yet leave the stump of the roots thereof in the earth, even with a band of iron and brass, in the tender grass of the field; and let it be wet with the dew of heaven, and let his portion be with the beasts of the field, till seven times pass over him; (4:24) This is the interpretation, O king, and this is the decree of the most High, which is come upon my lord the king: (4:25) That they shall drive thee from men, and thy dwelling shall be with the beasts of the field, and they shall make thee to eat grass as oxen, and they shall wet thee with the dew of heaven, and seven times shall pass

DANIEL 4. THE TREE AND THE BEAST VISION

over thee, till thou know that the most High ruleth in the kingdom of men, and giveth it to whomsoever he will. (4:26) And whereas they commanded to leave the stump of the tree roots; thy kingdom shall be sure unto thee, after that thou shalt have known that the heavens do rule. (4:27) Wherefore, O king, let my counsel be acceptable unto thee, and break off thy sins by righteousness, and thine iniquities by shewing mercy to the poor; if it may be a lengthening of thy tranquillity.

We have here the interpretation of Nebuchadnezzar's dream, and he soon discovers what he no doubt suspected — *Change but the name, the dream speaks of thee*. When, as soon as it is recounted, the reply can only be: *Thou art the man* (2 Sam 12:7). There needs little more to be said, Nebuchadnezzar has described it fully.

The Preface.

Daniels Reaction. **Then Daniel, whose name was Belteshazzar, was astonied for one hour, and his thoughts troubled him** (4:19). The recounting was so plain that Daniel, upon hearing it was *astonished for one hour*. He was struck with amazement and terror at so great a judgment coming upon so great a prince. But not only for Nebuchadnezzar but for its implications concerning Gentile rule during the age and for Gentile rule at the end of the age. He must bring *heavy tidings* not only to this king but to kings across the ages. Woeful days are coming. Those that come after the ruined sinner are said to be *astonished at his day*, as *those that went before were affrighted* (Job 18:20).

Nebuchadnezzar's Admonishment. **The king spake, and said, Belteshazzar, let not the dream, or the interpretation thereof, trouble thee** (4:19). This is quite a scene, whether Daniel in his stunned silence remained in Nebuchadnezzar's immediate presence for the entire hour, he was very much aware of Daniel's distress for that hour. The dream had made the king *afraid* and *troubled* him (4:4); Daniel is *afraid* and *troubled*, but whatever the outcome the king must have an answer. In the past he had received many times the adulation: *O king live forever* (2:4; 3:9); now he must know the truth.

Daniel's Reply. **Belteshazzar answered and said, My lord, the dream be to them that hate thee, and the interpretation thereof to thine enemies.** "Let the ill this dream foretells light on the head of your enemies, not on your head." But it is not to Nebuchadnezzar's enemies that this arrow of judgement is directed.

The Interpretation. The interpretation itself is a direct repetition of the dream, with application to the king. "As for **the tree** which you saw *flourishing* (4:20,21), *it is thou, O king* (4:22). But this is repeated for our admonition to emphasize again of what will not only happen to Nebuchadnezzar but will take place throughout the Times of the Gentiles. In view of what we have already seen above note the *line upon line* (Isa 28:13) presentation of these characteristics. As to the Greatness, it was a *rebellious* greatness, thirteen (a number of rebellion, (Gen 14:4) statements are made. Twelve statements are made concerning the judgement.

As to the Greatness.

> ***The tree that thou sawest,***
>   ***which grew,***
>   ***and was strong,***
>   ***whose height reached unto the heaven,***
>   ***and the sight thereof to all the earth*** (4:20);
>   ***Whose leaves were fair,***
>   ***and the fruit thereof much,***
>   ***and in it was meat for all;***
>   ***under which the beasts of the field dwelt, and***
>   ***upon whose branches the fowls of the heaven had their habitation*** (4:21):

It is thou, O king,
>   *that art grown and become strong:*
>   *for thy greatness is grown,*
>   *and reacheth unto heaven,*
>   *and thy dominion to the end of the earth* (4:22).

As to the Judgement.

And whereas the king saw a watcher and an holy one
coming down from heaven, and saying,
>   *Hew the tree down,*
>   *and destroy it;*
>   *yet leave the stump of the roots thereof in the earth,*
>   *even with a band of iron and brass,*
>   *in the tender grass of the field;*
>   *and let it be wet with the dew of heaven,*
>   *and let his portion be with the beasts of the field,*
>   *till seven times pass over him* (4:23);

This is the interpretation, O king, and this is the decree of the most High, which is come upon my lord the king (4:24):

>   *That they shall drive thee from men,*
>   *and thy dwelling shall be with the beasts of the field,*
>   *and they shall make thee to eat grass as oxen,*
>   *and they shall wet thee with the dew of heaven,*
>   *and seven times shall pass over thee,*
>   *till thou know that the most High ruleth in the kingdom of men,*
>   *and giveth it to whomsoever he will* (4:25).

As to Nebuchadnezzar's Restoration.

And whereas they commanded to leave the stump of the tree roots;
>   *thy kingdom shall be sure unto thee,*
>   *after that thou shalt have known that the heavens do rule* (4:26).

The Counsel. We are not told the manner in which Nebuchadnezzar received these words from Daniel. Was he concerned? Was he comforted? Was he indifferent? We do not know, but if this king had carefully heeded Daniel's counsel there may have been at least a temporary removal of the judgement as when Jonah warned Nineveh: *Yet forty days, and Nineveh shall be overthrown* (Jonah 3:4).

The Humbleness of the Counsel. **Wherefore, O king, let my counsel be acceptable unto thee** (4:27). Daniel speaks with earnestness and respect to the monarch. The apostle Paul beseeches hearers to *suffer the word of exhortation* (Heb. 13:22).

The Substance of the Counsel. **Break off thy sins by righteousness, and thine iniquities by shewing mercy to the poor** (4:27). Daniel had observed the wicked and ruthless side of Nebuchadnezzar for many years. Sin was on the throne in Babylon. In this he was a foreshadowing of the last king of Babylon:

> • Let no man deceive you by any means: for that day shall not come, except there come a falling away first, and **that man of sin** be revealed, **the son of perdition**; Who opposeth and exalteth himself above all that is called God, or that is worshipped; so that he as God sitteth in the temple of God, shewing himself that he is God (2 Thess 2:3,4).

DANIEL 4. THE TREE AND THE BEAST VISION

> *• And then shall **that Wicked** be revealed, whom the Lord shall consume with the spirit of his mouth, and shall destroy with the brightness of his coming: Even him, whose coming is **after the working of Satan** with all power and signs and lying wonders, And with all deceivableness of unrighteousness in them that perish; because they received not the love of the truth, that they might be saved (2 Thess 2:8-10).*

With Nebuchadnezzar there was a way back from the brink of doom; with the coming Antichrist there will be *no remedy* (2 Chron 36:16). True repentance and faith in Christ will result in one heeding the call to: *Wash you, make you clean; put away the evil of your doings from before mine eyes; cease to do evil* (Isa 1:16).

The Motive of the Counsel. ***If it may be a lengthening of thy tranquillity*** (4:27). Though it may not wholly prevent the judgment, yet by this means a reprieve may be obtained, as with one of Israel's most wicked kings.

> *Seest thou how Ahab humbleth himself before me? because he humbleth himself before me, I will not bring the evil in his days: but in his son's days will I bring the evil upon his house (1 Kng 21:29).*

Nebuchadnezzar's Dream: The Fulfilment 4:28-33.

> *(4:28) All this came upon the king Nebuchadnezzar. (4:29) At the end of twelve months he walked in the palace of the kingdom of Babylon. (4:30) The king spake, and said, Is not this great Babylon, that I have built for the house of the kingdom by the might of my power, and for the honour of my majesty? (4:31) While the word was in the king's mouth, there fell a voice from heaven, saying, O king Nebuchadnezzar, to thee it is spoken; The kingdom is departed from thee. (4:32) And they shall drive thee from men, and thy dwelling shall be with the beasts of the field: they shall make thee to eat grass as oxen, and seven times shall pass over thee, until thou know that the most High ruleth in the kingdom of men, and giveth it to whomsoever he will. (4:33) The same hour was the thing fulfilled upon Nebuchadnezzar: and he was driven from men, and did eat grass as oxen, and his body was wet with the dew of heaven, till his hairs were grown like eagles' feathers, and his nails like birds' claws.*

We have here Nebuchadnezzar's dream accomplished, and Daniel's application of it to the king justified and confirmed. *Know now that there shall fall unto the earth nothing of the word of the LORD* (2 Cor 10:10).

God's Patience with the King. ***All this came upon the king Nebuchadnezzar. At the end of twelve months*** (4:28,29). It came as prophesied, but it did not come until twelve months had passed. There had been a *lengthening of his tranquillity*, though it does not appear that he *broke off his sins,* or showed any *mercy to the poor* captives (4:27). He *opened not the house of his prisoners* (Isa 14:17). Daniel counselled Nebuchadnezzar to repent and God gave him time and space to repent. *Let it alone this year also* (Lk 13:8). There will be *one* year more! God is long-suffering with provoking sinners. He is not willing that *any should perish, but that all should come to repentance* (2 Pet 3:9).

The Pride and Haughtiness of the King.

How He Walked. ***He walked in the palace of the kingdom of Babylon*** (4:29). He walked in pomp and pride, pleasing himself with the view of that vast city, which with all the surrounding territories belonged to him and were under his command. What a splendid view he thought as he walked that day.

How He Talked. ***The king spake, and said, Is not this great Babylon, that I have built for the house of the kingdom by the might of my power, and for the honour of my majesty*** (4:30)? Was he speaking to himself, or his captains, or his servants, or foreign visitors? One thing is certain, he was not speaking to God. He was not giving any glory to Him. It was all *I* and *my*. Yes, in the world's view Babylon was great. It was of vast extent, some fifty miles of massive walls compassed the city about. It was full of inhabitants and many of them were full of wealth. It was a *golden city* (Isa. 14:4), and that by itself is enough to proclaim it to be great. See the grandeur of the houses, walls, towers, and public edifices.

Everything in Babylon he thinks looks *great*; *Is not this great Babylon that I have built.* Babylon was built many years before Nebuchadnezzar was born, but because he fortified, beautified and enlarged it, he could say this. He boasts as Augustus Caesar boasted concerning Rome —*I found it brick, but I left it marble.* This as we have seen is the boast of Babylon builders through the ages and especially in the last days.

> • *That thou shalt take up this proverb against the king of Babylon, and say, How hath the oppressor ceased! the golden city ceased (Isa 14:4)!*

> • *How much she hath glorified herself, and lived deliciously, so much torment and sorrow give her: for she saith in her heart, I sit a queen, and am no widow, and shall see no sorrow (Rev 18:7).*

Nebuchadnezzar's *Great Babylon*

The Judgement Upon the King. While Nebuchadnezzar was strutting and "adoring his own shadow", *while the* proud *word was in the king's mouth*, a powerful word came from heaven. By this word the king was immediately deprived of two things.

He is Sentenced to be Deprived of His Honour as a King. **While the word was in the king's mouth, there fell a voice from heaven, saying, O king Nebuchadnezzar, to thee it is spoken; The kingdom is departed from thee** (4:31). When he thought he had erected impregnable bulwarks for the preserving of his kingdom, now, in an instant, it *has departed from him.* When he thought it so well guarded that none could take it from him, behold, it departs of itself. The city that he claimed he had built with his own hands, he now finds taken from his hands.

DANIEL 4. THE TREE AND THE BEAST VISION

He is Sentenced to be Deprived of His Honour as a Man. *And they shall drive thee from men, and thy dwelling shall be with the beasts of the field: they shall make thee to eat grass as oxen, and seven times shall pass over thee, until thou know that the most High ruleth in the kingdom of men, and giveth it to whomsoever he will* (4:32). The tree part of his dream is not mentioned in Nebuchadnezzar's sentencing; it does not need to be! Only what happens at the foot of the tree is here stated. He loses his reason, and by that means loses his dominion; but the way he loses it is terrifying. He will be a beast in the field, out with the oxen, until he learns better than they. *The ox knoweth his owner, and the ass his master's crib: but Israel doth not know, my people doth not consider* (Isa 1:3).

He is Deprived of Both Honours Immediately. *The same hour was the thing fulfilled upon Nebuchadnezzar: and he was driven from men, and did eat grass as oxen, and his body was wet with the dew of heaven, till his hairs were grown like eagles' feathers, and his nails like birds' claws* (4:33). *They shall drive thee from men*, verse 32. And it was immediately fulfilled, verse 33: *he was driven from men,* and it was *the same hour*. Like a lightning bolt the mighty king fell stark mad, distracted in the highest degree. His understanding and memory were gone, and all the faculties of rational behaviour were broken. He became a beast in the shape of a man. He was on all fours and ran wild into the fields and forest. He was immediately *driven from men*, driven out by his own servants who soon saw that there was no hope for him in the palace are anywhere else.

He was like a beast, but thankfully not a beast of prey as the final beast and his kingdom are likened.

- *After this I saw in the night visions, and behold a fourth beast, dreadful and terrible, and strong exceedingly; and it had great iron teeth: it devoured and brake in pieces, and stamped the residue with the feet of it: and it was diverse from all the beasts that were before it; and it had ten horns (Dan 7:7).*

- *And the beast which I saw was like unto a leopard, and his feet were as the feet of a bear, and his mouth as the mouth of a lion: and the dragon gave him his power, and his seat, and great authority (Rev 13:2).*

Nebuchadnezzar was more of the farm-yard variety, he was made **to** *eat grass as oxen;* and, likely not being able to speak, lowed like oxen. Some think that his body was all covered with hair; however, *the hair* of his head and beard, being never cut nor combed, grew like *eagles feathers*, and **his nails like birds' claws**. *Is this the man that made the earth to tremble, that did shake kingdoms* (Isa 14:16). Never let the *wise man* then *glory in his wisdom*, nor *the mighty man in his might* (Jer 9:23), both can suddenly be taken away. God justly makes him less than a man, and puts him who set himself as a rival with his Maker on a level with the beasts in the field.

> *Cast abroad the rage of thy wrath: and behold every one that is proud, and abase him. Look on every one that is proud, and bring him low; and tread down the wicked in their place. Hide them in the dust together; and bind their faces in secret (Job 40:11-13).*

This then is an illustration of the bizarre behaviour of many Gentile leaders during the Times of the Gentiles, but especially of the *Beast* at the end of that time.

Nebuchadnezzar's Praise to God 4:34-37.

> *(4:34) And at the end of the days I Nebuchadnezzar lifted up mine eyes unto heaven, and mine understanding returned unto me, and I blessed the most High, and I praised and honoured him that liveth for ever, whose dominion is an everlasting dominion, and his kingdom is from generation to generation: (4:35) And all the inhabitants of the earth are reputed as nothing: and he doeth according to his will in the army of heaven, and among the inhabitants of the earth: and none can stay his hand, or say unto him, What doest thou? (4:36) At the same time my reason returned unto me; and for the glory of*

my kingdom, mine honour and brightness returned unto me; and my counsellors and my lords sought unto me; and I was established in my kingdom, and excellent majesty was added unto me. (4:37) Now I Nebuchadnezzar praise and extol and honour the King of heaven, all whose works are truth, and his ways judgment: and those that walk in pride he is able to abase.

Here the chapter ends as it began, with Nebuchadnezzar giving grateful thanks to God. Here is his recovery and his return.

The Time when He Recovered.

It was at the End of the Days. ***And at the end of the days*** (4:34). It was after ***seven times***. This was likely seven years for Nebuchadnezzar. As *seven times* is mentioned four times in Daniel Four (4:16,23,25,32) and four times in Leviticus Twenty-six (26:18,21,24,28) some have conjectured that with the Return of Christ, the Times of the Gentiles will end and "sanity" and repentance will return to the Jewish and Gentile world *after* 7x7x7x7 = 2401 years. This is tolerably close to the *Biblical* date that Daniel received the Seventy Weeks prophecy (see page 9). Others think that 360 is a *Jewish time*, with 7x360 = 2520 years. This is tolerably close to the *Biblical* date for the beginning of the Times of the Gentiles. We know not the day, hour or year, but these two computations may indicate that we are living in the general time of Christ's Return.

It was when He Looked Up. ***And at the end of the days I Nebuchadnezzar lifted up mine eyes unto heaven and mine understanding returned unto me*** (4:34). It was when he looked no longer downward towards the earth as a beast, but begun to look up as a man, as a man to heaven. As a humble penitent and petitioner for mercy, he began to look upward. When Nebuchadnezzar could look to no one else for advice or counsel (not even Daniel) he began to look upward to the God of Israel. With his restored reason Nebuchadnezzar glorified God. He had been told that he should continue in that forlorn state *until thou knowest that the Most High ruleth in the kingdom of men* (4:32). He now knows it! This praise and worship was the first act of Nebuchadnezzar's returning reason.

The Praise to God for His Recovery: ***and I blessed the most High, and I praised and honoured him that liveth for ever, whose dominion is an everlasting dominion, and his kingdom is from generation to generation*** (4:34): ***And all the inhabitants of the earth are reputed as nothing: and he doeth according to his will in the army of heaven, and among the inhabitants of the earth: and none can stay his hand, or say unto him, What doest thou*** (4:35)?

That God is Everlasting. ***The most High…liveth for ever*** (4:34). His flatterers often complimented him with, *O king live for ever.* But he is now knows the brevity and period of life, his life (!), and it is only the God of Israel who is everlasting.

That God's Kingdom Like Himself is Everlasting: ***Whose dominion is an everlasting dominion, and his kingdom is from generation to generation*** (4:34), There is no succession, no revolution, no termination in His Kingdom. As He lives, so He reigns. *Of the increase of his government there is no end* (Isa 9:6). This will be fully manifest at Christ's Return; at His Millennial Reign and throughout the Eternal Ages.

That Man in Comparison is as Nothing. ***And all the inhabitants of the earth are reputed as nothing*** (4:35). Apart from His grace He has no need of them. Despite their "claims to fame" their reputation is nothing. The greatest of men in comparison with Him are less than nothing.

DANIEL 4. THE TREE AND THE BEAST VISION

That His kingdom Encompasses Heaven and Earth. *He doeth according to his will in the army of heaven, and among the inhabitants of the earth* (4:35). Though now not yet seen on earth, the first request of the Lord's Prayer will shortly be answered.

After this manner therefore pray ye: Our Father which art in heaven, Hallowed be thy name. Thy kingdom come, Thy will be done in earth, as it is in heaven (Matt 6:9,10).

That His Power is Irresistible. *None can stay his hand, or say unto him, What doest thou?* Before the Day of the LORD, there may seem to be *the hiding of his power* (Hab 3:4), yet it will always come to this. God does according to His design and purpose, and for this He is not required to give an answer.

Woe unto him that striveth with his Maker! Let the potsherd [strive] with the potsherds of the earth. Shall the clay say to him that fashioneth it, What makest thou (Isa 45:9)?

Reflection Upon His Recovery. *At the same time my reason returned unto me; and for the glory of my kingdom, mine honour and brightness returned unto me; and my counsellors and my lords sought unto me; and I was established in my kingdom, and excellent majesty was added unto me* (4:36). This is a *returning* verse. He tells of seven things that returned (the number of completion):

(1) His *Reason* (in verse 34 he mentioned his *understanding*).

(2) *The glory of his kingdom* (over which there had been so long a dark shadow while the king was out in the fields).

(3) His *Honour* (which was far more honourable now). He had heeded Daniel's counsel to *break off thy sins by righteousness, and thine iniquities by shewing mercy to the poor* (4:27).

(4) His *Brightness* (the king's appearance, the wisdom of his pronouncements, now all much brighter than before). *The path of the just is as a shining light, that shineth more and more unto the perfect day* (Prov 4:18).

(5) His Servants. *My counsellors and my lords sought unto me*. The last time we saw them, they *drove him from men* (4:33). Now they return (he does not have to call them), The counsellors now come, not to counsel but to be counselled.

(6) His Establishment. *I was established in my kingdom* (and that upon far better principles of government than it ever was before).

(7) *Excellent Majesty*. This was not said to have returned but to have been **added**. *Excellent majesty was added unto me*. This was something entirely different than what he had when he went from kingdom to kingdom *conquering and to conquer* (Rev 6:2). When men are brought to honour, particularly by a penitent confession of sin and believing upon Christ's Finished Sacrifice, they receive *excellent majesty*. What the first Adam lost we regain through the Last Adam (1 Cor 15:45). This may be especially noteworthy in times of tribulation.

If ye be reproached for the name of Christ, happy are ye; for the spirit of glory and of God resteth upon you: on their part he is evil spoken of, but on your part he is glorified (1 Pet 4:14).

The King's Final Word of Praise.

Now I Nebuchadnezzar praise and extol and honour the King of heaven, all whose works are truth, and his ways judgment: and those that walk in pride he is able to abase (4:37).

Everything God Does is Well Done. His *works are truth,* for they all agree with his Word. *His ways are judgment,* both wise and righteous, exactly consonant with His prudence and equity. No fault is to be found with them.

All Arrogance (Including his own!) is Brought Down. He has power to humble the haughtiest. Pride will especially be a mark of the last days (2 Tim 3:1,2). *Those that walk in pride he is able to abase*; He is able to deal with those that are most confident of their own sufficiency. They will soon find their walk interrupted.

We may talk about "famous last words", and few Gentile kings have uttered better than these last ones we hear of Nebuchadnezzar. It was not long after this that he died. Abydenus, quoted by the historian, Eusebius (*Prap. Evang.* 1.9), reports, from the tradition of the Chaldeans, that upon his death-bed he foretold the taking of Babylon by Cyrus.

> "Whether he continued in the same good mind that here he seems to have been in we are not told, nor does anything appear to the contrary but that he did: and, if so great a *blasphemer and persecutor* did find mercy, he was not the last. We must admire free grace, by which he lost his wits for a while that he might save his soul for ever *Matthew Henry*.

In fact Daniel when addressing Belshazzar indicates that Nebuchadnezzar concluded his life on this earth over which he ruled as a righteous king.

> *O thou king, the most high God gave Nebuchadnezzar thy father a kingdom, and majesty, and glory, and honour: And for the majesty that he gave him, all people, nations, and languages, trembled and feared before him: whom he would he slew; and whom he would he kept alive; and whom he would he set up; and whom he would he put down. But when his heart was lifted up, and his mind hardened in pride, he was deposed from his kingly throne, and they took his glory from him: And he was driven from the sons of men; and his heart was made like the beasts, and his dwelling was with the wild asses: they fed him with grass like oxen, and his body was wet with the dew of heaven; till he knew that the most high God ruled in the kingdom of men, and that he appointeth over it whomsoever he will. And thou his son, O Belshazzar, hast not humbled thine heart, though thou knewest all this (Dan 5:18-22).*

THE TIMES OF THE GENTILES 1-7

C. THE CHARACTERISTICS OF THE TIMES OF THE GENTILES 3-6

3. A TIME OF SACRILEGE: BELSHAZZAR'S FEAST 5

DANIEL 5. BABYLON'S LAST NIGHT, THE HANDWRITING ON THE WALL

The Times of the Gentiles will be a time when the holy things of God are treated with the greatest contempt. Everything possible will be done to undermine the Bible, the great doctrines, righteous living, the Godly hymns…… *Evil men and seducers will wax worse and worse* against the precious landmarks of the faith (2 Tim 3:13). Unbelief, rationalism, false religion, the undermining of the very foundations of life on the earth (cp. abortion, gay marriage) will become rampant.

- *And because **iniquity shall abound**, the love of many shall wax cold (Matt 24:12).*

- *And as it was in **the days of Noe**, so shall it be also in the days of the Son of man. They did eat, they drank, they married wives, they were given in marriage, until the day that Noe entered into the ark, and the flood came, and destroyed them all. Likewise also as it was in **the days of Lot**; they did eat, they drank, they bought, they sold, they planted, they builded; But the same day that Lot went out of Sodom it rained fire and brimstone from heaven, and destroyed them all. Even thus shall it be in the day when the Son of man is revealed (Lk 17:26-30).*

- *Nevertheless when the Son of man cometh, **shall he find faith on the earth** (Lk 18:8).*

- *Now the Spirit speaketh expressly, that in the latter times some shall **depart from the faith**, giving heed to **seducing spirits**, and doctrines of devils (1 Tim 4:1).*

- *This know also, that in the last days **perilous times** shall come (2 Tim 3:1).*

- *For the time will come when they **will not endure sound doctrine**; but after their own lusts shall they heap to themselves teachers, having itching ears. And they shall **turn away their ears from the truth**, and shall be turned unto fables (2 Tim 4:3,4).*

- *But there were false prophets also among the people, even as there shall be **false teachers** among you, who privily shall bring in **damnable heresies**, even denying the Lord that bought them, and bring upon themselves swift destruction. And **many shall follow** their pernicious ways; by reason of whom the way of truth shall be evil spoken of (2 Pet 2:1,2).*

- *Knowing this first, that there shall come **in the last days scoffers**, walking after their own lusts, And saying, Where is the promise of his coming? for since the fathers fell asleep, all things continue as they were from the beginning of the creation (2 Pet 3:3,4).*

- *Little children, it is the last time: and as ye have heard that antichrist shall come, even now are **there many antichrists**; whereby we know that it is the last time (1 Jhn 2:18).*

The destruction of the kingdom of Babylon had been long and often foretold when its destruction was at a distance (Isa 13,47; Jer 50,51); in this chapter we have it accomplished, and a prediction of it on the very same night that it was accomplished. Belshazzar now reigned in Babylon. His name is well known from the cuneiform sources which show that he reigned for a while as a coregent with his father Nabonidus. These same sources "expressly state that Nabonidus entrusted the kingship to his son" (Unger, p. 1630). Chapter 7 begins with the *first year* of his reign and Chapter 8 with his *third year*. Here in Chapter 5 we may also have his third year, but if longer it is his last year; in fact his *last night*.

Historical sources tell us that about two years before this Cyrus king of Persia (coregent with Darius the Median, 5:31), a growing monarch, came against Babylon with a great army;

Belshazzar met him, fought him, and was routed by him in a pitched battle. He and his scattered forces retired into the city, where Cyrus besieged them. They were very secure, because the river Euphrates was their bulwark, and they had twenty years; provision in the city; but in the second year of the siege all of this was to prove to be of no avail to the inhabitants of Babylon and Cyrus took the city as here related.

Note: Babylon, the capital of idolatry, was a Seventy Year *schoolhouse* for the idolatrous Jewish People. There they saw idolatry in all of its pagan wickedness. After the lesson was learned (we assume), the schoolhouse was itself dismantled (*at least this stage of Babylon*).

Kings of Babylon During the Seventy Years

Years 1-43	Nebuchadnezzar (died; the kingdom went to his son)
Years 43-45	Evil-merodach (Jer 52:31; murdered by his brother-in-law who reigned)
Years 45-48	Nergal-sharezer (Jer 39:3,13; succeeded by his son)
Year 48	Labashi-marduk (murdered by a group that included Nabonidus who reigned)
Year 48-67?	Nabonidus (coregent with his son Belshazzar who was granted sole reign)
Year 67?-70	Belshazzar

We will see now that if the Jewish People learned a lesson concerning idolatry in Babylon; if Nebuchadnezzar learned that same lesson; it now becomes certain that the last king of Babylon has not learned this lesson. He instead has taken idolatry to a height not seen before in Babylon.

The Feast of the King 5:1-4.

Belshazzar the king made a great feast to a thousand of his lords, and drank wine before the thousand. 5:2 Belshazzar, whiles he tasted the wine, commanded to bring the golden and silver vessels which his father Nebuchadnezzar had taken out of the temple which was in Jerusalem; that the king, and his princes, his wives, and his concubines, might drink therein. 5:3 Then they brought the golden vessels that were taken out of the temple of the house of God which was at Jerusalem; and the king, and his princes, his wives, and his concubines, drank in them. 5:4 They drank wine, and praised the gods of gold, and of silver, of brass, of iron, of wood, and of stone.

Here is the riotous, idolatrous, sacrilegious feast that Belshazzar made, and in which he filled up the measure of his iniquity. Here is a picture of how the knowledge of the Lord will be treated during the Times of the Gentiles and in like manner for the individual or the world will fill up the measure of iniquity. Here we have Belshazzar the king very happy, but then all of a sudden very afraid. Here we see how he affronts God, and then how God affrights him. Here is a massive party, a thousand lords, and then with all the wives and concubines all toasting the king that night, but it was not enough to save him.

He Affronted The Judgments of God. **Belshazzar the king made a great feast to a thousand of his lords, and drank wine before the thousand** (5:1). It may have been an anniversary of some past victory, but no more victory marches now. It may have been his birthday or coronation-day; but it will be the king's last celebration. It may be in open defiance of the Persians who were then besieging Babylon; an act of bravado. But it turned out to be an empty act.

With the enemy at the gate; his life and kingdom lay in the balance; the hand of the Lord having gone out against him **Belshazzar the king made a great feast to a thousand of his** *lords, and drank wine before the thousand*. Belshazzar was not a stranger to the divine dealings of the Almighty. He knew very well of the judgements of God that had fallen on Nebuchadnezzar. He would have known that Assyria, the kingdom Babylon had conquered had been given a reprieve when they repented at the preaching of Jonah (Jonah 3). Had he called for *weeping, and mourning* Babylon might have been spared. But this king is resolved to walk in another direction: *joy and gladness, slaying oxen, killing sheep, eating flesh, and drinking wine,* as if he dared the Almighty to do his worst, (Isa 22:12,13).

<u>He Affronted the Temple of God</u>. ***Belshazzar, whiles he tasted the wine, commanded to bring the golden and silver vessels which his father Nebuchadnezzar had taken out of the temple which was in Jerusalem; that the king, and his princes, his wives, and his concubines, might drink therein. Then they brought the golden vessels that were taken out of the temple of the house of God which was at Jerusalem; and the king, and his princes, his wives, and his concubines, drank in them*** (5:2,3). His grandfather Nebuchadnezzar had destroyed that Temple as judgement of God for the idolatry that had taken root there. Many of the sacred vessels were now in Babylon. Now as **he tasted the wine** a blasphemous idea comes into his head (wine will do that!).

This seems to have been done as a show of malicious contempt to the God of Israel. The heart of Judah was very much upon these sacred vessels (Jer 27:16,18; Ezra 1:7). Some realized that the prophecy of Jeremiah concerning the Seventy Years in Babylon was now reaching its end (Jer 25:11,12). "Now we will dash any such hopes, send for those vessels."

These vessels which were used in the sacrifices of the Temple and which pointed to the Coming of the Messiah, Belshazzar now claims as his own for his own ends to use in the worship of his idols. This ripened Babylon for immediate ruin. This is a picture of the sacrilege that we may expect during the Times of the Gentiles. Here we are about to see that whether then or now *God will not be mocked* (Gal 6:7).

<u>He Affronted God Himself</u>. ***They drank wine, and praised the gods of gold, and of silver, of brass, of iron, of wood, and of stone*** (5:4). With these vessels now filled with wine they glorified their idols, the work of their own hands, images of their own imagination. They praised them either with sacrifices offered or with songs sung or loud cries. When their heads were giddy and their hearts merry with wine they were in the fittest frame to *praise the gods of gold and silver, wood and stone*; for one would think that men with clear heads would not be so stupid. *They have erred through wine* (Isa. 27:7), and never more so than on that night.

The Word of the LORD 5:5-9.

> In the same hour came forth fingers of a man's hand, and wrote over against the candlestick upon the plaister of the wall of the king's palace: and the king saw the part of the hand that wrote. (5:6) Then the king's countenance was changed, and his thoughts troubled him, so that the joints of his loins were loosed, and his knees smote one against another. (5:7) The king cried aloud to bring in the astrologers, the Chaldeans, and the soothsayers. And the king spake, and said to the wise men of Babylon, Whosoever shall read this writing, and shew me the interpretation thereof, shall be clothed with scarlet, and have a chain of gold about his neck, and shall be the third ruler in the kingdom. (5:8) Then came in all the king's wise men: but they could not read the writing, nor make known to the king the interpretation thereof. (5:9) Then was king Belshazzar greatly troubled, and his countenance was changed in him, and his lords were astonied.

We have seen how the king affronted the Lord, now the Lord alarms the king. Belshazzar and his huge entourage are in the midst of their revelry and it has now become a blasphemous revelry, the wine is flowing, the cups are going all around. Even with Cyrus at the gates there is nothing to fear, the Euphrates is wide, the walls are high, the provision within the city is abundant. But the mirth of this party is about to be spoiled, and a thick cloud of gloom will descend upon the proceedings. The Word of the Lord comes; the banquet is thrown into confusion! The hour had come when that must be fulfilled which had been long before spoken concerning the king of Babylon (nearly 200 years), when his city would be besieged by the Persians and Medes, and when allusion was made to this very feast. The manner in which Isaiah prophesied of Babylon's doom was as if he himself was Babylon.

> *A grievous vision is declared unto me; the treacherous dealer dealeth treacherously, and the spoiler spoileth.* **Go up, O Elam: besiege, O Media**; *all the sighing thereof have I made to cease. Therefore are my loins filled with pain: pangs have taken hold upon me, as the pangs of a woman that travaileth: I was bowed down at the hearing of it; I was dismayed at the seeing of it. My heart panted, fearfulness affrighted me:* **the night of my pleasure hath he turned into fear unto me** *(Isa 21:2-4).*

<u>The Word of the Lord *Appears*</u>. ***In the same hour came forth fingers of a man's hand, and wrote over against the candlestick upon the plaister of the wall of the king's palace: and the king saw the part of the hand that wrote*** (5:5). That divine hand that had written the two tables for a Law of Moses for His people now writes the doom of Babylon and Belshazzar upon the wall. There was no frightening noise, no threatening voice, no clap of thunder nor flashes of lightning, no destroying angel drawn sword drawn in his hand, only a hand, writing on the wall, *over against the candlestick,* where they might all see it. The king saw *the part of the hand that wrote,* but saw not the Person whose hand it was, which made the thing more frightful. If this be *the finger of God* (Exod 8:19), what is it when His *arm is made bare* (Isa 52:10)? And what is He?

- *Verily thou art a God that hidest thyself, O God of Israel, the Saviour (Isa 45:15).*

- *Lo, these are parts of his ways; but how little a portion is heard of him (Job 26:14)?*

(www. goodsalt.com)

DANIEL 5. BABYLON'S LAST NIGHT, THE HANDWRITING ON THE WALL

The Handwriting on the Wall
by Knowles Shaw

AT THE FEAST of Belshazzar and a thousand of his lords,
While they drank from golden vessels, as the Book of Truth records,
In the night as they reveled in the royal palace hall,
They were seized with consternation — 'twas the Hand upon the wall!

See the brave captive, Daniel, as he stood before the throng,
and rebuked the haughty monarch for his mighty deeds of wrong;
As he read out the writing — 'twas the doom of one and all,
For the kingdom now was finished — said the Hand upon the wall!

See the faith, zeal and courage, that would dare to do the right,
Which the Spirit gave to Daniel — this the secret of his might;
In his home in Judea, or a captive in the hall,
He understood the writing of his God upon the wall!

So our deeds are recorded — there's a Hand that's writing now:
Sinner, give your heart to Jesus, to His royal mandates bow;
For the day is approaching — it must come to one and all,
When the sinner's condemnation will be written on the wall!

<u>The King is Seized with Panic</u>. ***Then the king's countenance was changed, and his thoughts troubled him, so that the joints of his loins were loosed, and his knees smote one against another*** (5:6). The king immediately falls into a terror. *His countenance was changed* (his colour went and *went further*, from pale to *very* pale) *The joints of his loins were loosed*, no strength, staggering around. *His knees smote one against another.* This is the great king of Babylon! But what was the matter? Why is he in such a fright? He perceives not what is written, but he knows that it is bad and not good news. Why? Because he is a guilty sinner, and when he sees something that appears to be a message from Heaven his own guilty conscience flew in his face and told him that he had no reason to expect good news! This is also a picture of rulers who throughout the Times of the Gentiles and especially in the last days dare to fly in the face of Almighty.

> • But the wicked are like the troubled sea, when it cannot rest, whose waters cast up mire and dirt. There is no peace, saith my God, to the wicked (Isa 57:20,21).

> • Why do the heathen rage, and the people imagine a vain thing? The kings of the earth set themselves, and the rulers take counsel together, against the LORD, and against his anointed, saying, Let us break their bands asunder, and cast away their cords from us. He that sitteth in the heavens shall laugh: the LORD shall have them in derision. Then shall he speak unto them in his wrath, and vex them in his sore displeasure (Psa 2:1-5).

<u>The "Wise Men" are Called</u>. ***The king cried aloud to bring in the astrologers, the Chaldeans, and the soothsayers. And the king spake, and said to the wise men of Babylon, Whosoever shall <u>read this writing</u>, and <u>shew me the interpretation</u> thereof, shall be clothed with scarlet, and have a chain of gold about his neck, and shall be the third ruler in the kingdom. Then came in all the king's wise men: but they <u>could not read</u> the writing, nor make known to the king <u>the interpretation</u> thereof*** (5:7,8). The king *cried aloud* as one in haste and as one in earnest to gather the entire college of magicians, to try if they can to *read* and *interpret* this writing. We have often "been here before"! Unlike with Nebuchadnezzar there is no threat of death, but only a promise to *be clothed with scarlet, and have a chain of gold about his neck,* and even further to *be the third ruler in the kingdom*, little realizing that there will be little time to enjoy it.

The king is soon disappointed. They do not venture to read it or interpret it. The writing, as with the rest of Daniel 2-7 was in Aramaic. The characters appear to have been arranged in a way, perhaps in an acrostic style, or read from left to right rather than from right to left as normal. Apart from the divine revelation shortly to be given to Daniel, it was impossible for it to be read. Thus the mouths of the so-called wise men of Babylon were kept shut and their occultic arts shown to be powerless. Nevertheless before Jerusalem's fall the false prophets in Judah were where having a "field day." But it was soon shown to be a mirage. False prophecy is a dangerous practice to the listener and the "prophet." Note one example from the latter days of Jeremiah.

> • Thus saith the LORD of hosts, Hearken not unto the words of the prophets that prophesy unto you: they make you vain: **they speak a vision of their own heart**, and not out of the mouth of the LORD (Jer 23:16).
>
> • (28:1) And it came to pass the same year, in the beginning of the reign of Zedekiah king of Judah, in the fourth year, and in the fifth month, that Hananiah the son of Azur the prophet, which was of Gibeon, spake unto me in the house of the LORD, in the presence of the priests and of all the people, saying, (28:2) Thus speaketh the LORD of hosts, the God of Israel, saying, **I have broken the yoke of the king of Babylon**. (28:3) **Within two full years** will I bring again into this place all the vessels of the LORD's house, that Nebuchadnezzar king of Babylon took away from this place, and carried them to Babylon: (28:4) And **I will bring again to this place Jeconiah the son of Jehoiakim king of Judah, with all the captives of Judah**, that went into Babylon, saith the LORD: for I will break the yoke of the king of Babylon. (28:5) Then the prophet Jeremiah said unto the prophet Hananiah in the presence of the priests, and in the presence of all the people that stood in the house of the LORD, (28:6) Even the prophet **Jeremiah said, Amen: the LORD do so**: the LORD perform thy words which thou hast prophesied, to bring again the vessels of the LORD's house, and all that is carried away captive, from Babylon into this place.
>
> • (28:10) **Then Hananiah the prophet took the yoke from off the prophet Jeremiah's neck, and brake it**. (28:11) And Hananiah spake in the presence of all the people, saying, Thus saith the LORD; Even so will I break the yoke of Nebuchadnezzar king of Babylon from the neck of all nations within the space of two full years. And the prophet Jeremiah went his way. (28:12) Then the word of the LORD came unto Jeremiah the prophet, after that Hananiah the prophet had broken the yoke from off the neck of the prophet Jeremiah, saying, (28:13) Go and tell Hananiah, saying, Thus saith the LORD; **Thou hast broken the yokes of wood; but thou shalt make for them yokes of iron**. (28:14) For thus saith the LORD of hosts, the God of Israel; I have put a yoke of iron upon the neck of all these nations, that they may serve Nebuchadnezzar king of Babylon; and they shall serve him: and I have given him the beasts of the field also. (28:15) Then said the prophet Jeremiah unto Hananiah the prophet, Hear now, Hananiah; **The LORD hath not sent thee; but thou makest this people to trust in a lie**. (28:16) Therefore thus saith the LORD; Behold, I will cast thee from off the face of the earth: **this year thou shalt die**, because thou hast taught rebellion against the LORD. (28:17) **So Hananiah the prophet died** the same year in the seventh month.

The Banquet is Benumbed. ***Then was king Belshazzar greatly troubled, and his countenance was changed in him, and his lords were astonied*** (5:9). With the blank stares and silent tongues of the occult prophets, the king's confusion escalates, and that of everyone with him: *His lords* also. They that had been partners with him in his revelling are now sharing in his terror. All are astonished and at their wits end. Neither their numbers nor their wine, nor the lavish spread could keep the spirits up. The burden of an awakened conscience will be increased by the utter insufficiency of any real help at hand.

The Counsel of the Queen 5:10-12.

> Now the queen by reason of the words of the king and his lords came into the banquet house: and the queen spake and said, O king, live for ever: let not thy thoughts trouble thee, nor let thy countenance be changed: (5:11) There is a man in thy kingdom, in whom is the spirit of the holy gods; and in the days of thy father light and understanding and wisdom, like the wisdom of the gods, was found in him; whom the king

DANIEL 5. BABYLON'S LAST NIGHT, THE HANDWRITING ON THE WALL

Nebuchadnezzar thy father, the king, I say, thy father, made master of the magicians, astrologers, Chaldeans, and soothsayers; (5:12) Forasmuch as an excellent spirit, and knowledge, and understanding, interpreting of dreams, and shewing of hard sentences, and dissolving of doubts, were found in the same Daniel, whom the king named Belteshazzar: now let Daniel be called, and he will shew the interpretation.

The Report to the Queen. ***Now the queen by reason of the words of the king and his lords came into the banquet house: and the queen spake and said, O king, live for ever: let not thy thoughts trouble thee, nor let thy countenance be changed*** (5:10). Here is the wise counsel given to the king by the queen-mother concerning Daniel. It is supposed that this queen was the widow of Evil-Merodach, and was the famous Nitocris whom Herodotus mentions as a woman of extraordinary prudence. She was not present at the feast, as the king's *wives and concubines were* (5:2); it was not agreeable to her character, her age or her gravity to have a merry party considering that the enemy was at the gates. Tidings of the state in which the king and his lords found themselves were brought to her chamber.

She came herself to the banqueting-house, to recommend to the king a physician for his terrified state. She could not help him but she knew someone who could. She uses the old address (for the last time in Babylon!) *O king, live for ever*. She comes with a good solution but it will only be momentary. The king has entered his last few hours before stepping into eternity.

The Recommendation of Daniel.

His High Character. ***There is a man in thy kingdom, in whom is the spirit of the holy gods; and in the days of thy father light and understanding and wisdom, like the wisdom of the gods, was found in him*** (5:11). She expresses Daniel's character in the old pagan way (4:8), and has not learned what Nebuchadnezzar had of the true God of Israel working in Daniel. She knew that there was in Daniel something that was more than human. In her pagan way she acknowledges that in this aged prophet there was not only the spirit of a man, but also *the candle of the LORD* (Prov 20:27). Her recommendation expresses the fact that Daniel had both a good *head* and a good *heart*. His wisdom was not for self-adulation but for the good of others. He was of a humble, holy, heavenly spirit; a devout and gracious spirit, a spirit of zeal for the glory of God and the good of men.

His Honour from the Previous King: ***whom the king Nebuchadnezzar thy father, the king, I say, thy father, made master of the magicians, astrologers, Chaldeans, and soothsayers;***(5:12). Perhaps Belshazzar had sometimes, in his pride, spoken lightly of Nebuchadnezzar and his policies, and thought himself to be wiser. Therefore his mother stresses the point: ***the king, I say, thy father*** under whose good management you have what you have today. This king, says she, was prepared to put Daniel over all the wise men. The inference from the queen mother is clear: Nebuchadnezzar was prepared to consult one whom Belshazzar ignored.

The Motion that Daniel be Called.

His Qualities are Again Stated. ***Forasmuch as an excellent spirit, and knowledge, and understanding, interpreting of dreams, and shewing of hard sentences, and dissolving of doubts, were found in the same Daniel, whom the king named Belteshazzar*** (5:12). She lists six qualifications and attributes that Daniel had, and even though Belshazzar had ignored them, they had been manifested to many in Babylon.

His Name is Declared. ***Now let Daniel be called*** (5:12). Yes, many wanted to call Daniel by his Babylonian name, but Daniel as a testimony of his faith and Judean heritage made certain that his Hebrew name was used. The queen-mother now honours the aged prophet by making this formal proposal with his Hebrew name, Daniel (Elohim is my judge).

His Ministry will be Heard. *He will shew the interpretation* (5:12). By all this it is obvious that Daniel was now forgotten at court. Belshazzar was a stranger to him, knew not (probably cared not) that he had such a jewel in his kingdom. With the new king there came in a new outlook, and the old one was laid aside. But as Daniel spoke at the beginning of the Babylonian Empire, he now comes to the rostrum again, and that in Babylon's closing hours.

Thus do the righteous shine forth out of *obscurity* (cp. Isa 59:9).

The Appearance of the Prophet 5:13-16.

Then was Daniel brought in before the king. And the king spake and said unto Daniel, Art thou that Daniel, which art of the children of the captivity of Judah, whom the king my father brought out of Jewry? (5:14) I have even heard of thee, that the spirit of the gods is in thee, and that light and understanding and excellent wisdom is found in thee. (5:15) And now the wise men, the astrologers, have been brought in before me, that they should read this writing, and make known unto me the interpretation thereof: but they could not shew the interpretation of the thing: (5:16) And I have heard of thee, that thou canst make interpretations, and dissolve doubts: now if thou canst read the writing, and make known to me the interpretation thereof, thou shalt be clothed with scarlet, and have a chain of gold about thy neck, and shalt be the third ruler in the kingdom.

Daniel was now nearly ninety years of age, thus his years, and honours, and former preferments should have entitled him to a free admission into the king's presence; yet he was willing to be conducted in as a stranger.

How the King Addressed Daniel. **Then was Daniel brought in before the king. And the king spake and said unto Daniel, Art thou that Daniel, which art of the children of the captivity of Judah, whom the king my father brought out of Jewry** (5:13)? The king speaks with an air of haughtiness: *Art thou that Daniel who art of the children of the captivity?* Being a Jew, and a captive, the king appears to imply that it is beneath his dignity to be beholden to such a one any more than is necessary.

What the King Heard of Daniel. **I have even heard of thee, that the spirit of the gods is in thee, and that light and understanding and excellent wisdom is found in thee** (5:14). He has just now *heard* it from his mother. He has no excuse for not *knowing* it long ago. He now sent for him to determine whether this was true and whether Daniel deserved so high of a recommendation.

What the King Acknowledged Concerning His Own Wise Men. **And now the wise men, the astrologers, have been brought in before me, that they should read this writing, and make known unto me the interpretation thereof: but they could not shew the interpretation of the thing** (5:15). To this "Jewish Captive" he acknowledges that all the wise men of Babylon were baffled by what they saw. They could not *read* it, let alone interpret it. Note that all revelation in the writing of the Bible came through the Jews. No Gentile is mentioned as being an author of any of the sixty-six Books of Scripture. Not only is *salvation of the Jews* (Jhn 4:22), but so also is Biblical Revelation and Inspiration.

What the King Promised Daniel. **And I have heard of thee, that thou canst make interpretations, and dissolve doubts: now if thou canst read the writing, and make known to me the interpretation thereof, thou shalt be clothed with scarlet, and have a chain of gold about thy neck, and shalt be the third ruler in the kingdom** (5:16). He promises him the same rewards that he had promised to his own wise men. The only difference is, that to Daniel and a true man of God they meant absolutely nothing. To a man *of the world whose portion is in*

DANIEL 5. BABYLON'S LAST NIGHT, THE HANDWRITING ON THE WALL

this life (Psa 17:14), they meant absolutely everything. As the evening's proceedings would show, Daniel's evaluation was the correct one (5:17,31).

The Reprimand of the King 5:17-24.

> *Then Daniel answered and said before the king, Let thy gifts be to thyself, and give thy rewards to another; yet I will read the writing unto the king, and make known to him the interpretation. (5:18) O thou king, the most high God gave Nebuchadnezzar thy father a kingdom, and majesty, and glory, and honour: (5:19) And for the majesty that he gave him, all people, nations, and languages, trembled and feared before him: whom he would he slew; and whom he would he kept alive; and whom he would he set up; and whom he would he put down. (5:20) But when his heart was lifted up, and his mind hardened in pride, he was deposed from his kingly throne, and they took his glory from him: (5:21) And he was driven from the sons of men; and his heart was made like the beasts, and his dwelling was with the wild asses: they fed him with grass like oxen, and his body was wet with the dew of heaven; till he knew that the most high God ruled in the kingdom of men, and that he appointeth over it whomsoever he will. (5:22) And thou his son, O Belshazzar, hast not humbled thine heart, though thou knewest all this; (5:23) But hast lifted up thyself against the Lord of heaven; and they have brought the vessels of his house before thee, and thou, and thy lords, thy wives, and thy concubines, have drunk wine in them; and thou hast praised the gods of silver, and gold, of brass, iron, wood, and stone, which see not, nor hear, nor know: and the God in whose hand thy breath is, and whose are all thy ways, hast thou not glorified: (5:24) Then was the part of the hand sent from him; and this writing was written.*

<u>Now is Not the Time to Give Gifts</u>. **Then Daniel answered and said before the king, Let thy gifts be to thyself, and give thy rewards to another; yet I will read the writing unto the king, and make known to him the interpretation** (5:17). Daniel is not pleased with the offer. He is not in the ministry for the money. The gratuities Nebuchadnezzar formerly gave Daniel did not result in his own enrichment but enabled him to do more for the Jewish captives in Babylon. And of course it is far too late for any gift-giving now. Daniel sees the king's kingdom in its last gasp, thus anyone who wants to enjoy these things (either the king or his wise men) they had better hurry. So for us as we see the shadows gathering and the final period of this world hastening on, it is not a time for accumulating.

> *But this I say, brethren, **the time is short**: it remaineth, that....**they that buy, as though they possessed not**; And they that use this world, as not abusing it: for the fashion of this world passeth away (I Cor 7:29-31).*

<u>Now is the Time to Consider God's Previous Judgement</u>.

<u>How God Advanced Nebuchadnezzar</u>.

His Personal Excellence. (5:18) **O thou king, the most high God gave Nebuchadnezzar thy father a kingdom, and majesty, and glory, and honour** (5:18). It may seem strange to say that God gave *majesty, and glory, and honour* to a pagan monarch; but wherever there was *majesty, and glory, and honour* (albeit in a relative sense) during the Times of the Gentiles it came, as stated here, *from God*! At the beginning Nebuchadnezzar did not realize this, but eventually he did. It is clear that the first kings of the next kingdom (Cyrus and Darius) would understand this. Even, as Josephus shows, Alexander the Great would be made to see something of this principle.

His Governmental Authority. **And for the majesty that he gave him, all people, nations, and languages, trembled and feared before him: whom he would he slew; and whom he would he kept alive; and whom he would he set up; and whom he would he put down** (5:19). Nebuchadnezzar's Babylon for a time seemed irresistible and immovable. His forces were so strong, so numerous, so disciplined, that by a mere word without striking a blow he could subdue an enemy. When he entered the field of battle in whichever direction his sword turned it prospered. He captivated and subdued the world for *all people trembled and feared before him,*

The power which was allowed him, which descended upon him, was without contradiction, was absolute and despotic, none shared with him either in the legislative or in the executive part of it. *Whom he would he slew, and whom he would he saved alive.* However this verse coupled with the next shows that he became tyrannical in his powers, and his *rod of iron* government became a crushing and abusive rod. Christ's rule when He returns will also be will be as a *rod of iron*, but unlike Nebuchadnezzar, it will total *righteousness*.

- Behold, **a king shall reign in righteousness**, and princes shall rule in judgment (Isa 32:1).

- And out of his mouth goeth a sharp sword, that with it he should smite the nations: and **he shall rule them with a rod of iron**: and he treadeth the winepress of the fierceness and wrath of Almighty God (Rev 19:15).

How God Humbled Nebuchadnezzar.

The Reason for His Humbling. **But when his heart was lifted up, and his mind hardened in pride** (5:20). He behaved insultingly towards those that were under him, and grew tyrannical and oppressive. The description given of his power in the previous verse intimates his abuse of that power. He often condemned the innocent and acquitted the guilty. He deposed men of merit and preferred unworthy men. Thus at the beginning of the Times of the Gentiles Nebuchadnezzar demonstrated that it is a very hard and rare thing for men to have absolute arbitrary power, and not to make an ill use of it.

However these words in verse 20 show that he behaved insolently towards *the God above him* and not only the people beneath him. This was especially so after the threefold revelation of God to Nebuchadnezzar in Chapters Two, Three and Four.

The Means of His Humbling. **He was deposed from his kingly throne, and they took his glory from him:** (5:21) **And he was driven from the sons of men; and his heart was made like the beasts, and his dwelling was with the wild asses: they fed him with grass like oxen, and his body was wet with the dew of heaven; till he knew that the most high God ruled in the kingdom of men, and that he appointeth over it whomsoever he will** (5:20,21).

Daniel reminds Belshazzar of how far and fast his grandfather fell. As Nebuchadnezzar became unreasonable in his rule, his reason was taken from him. He acted like a brute over his subjects, he became a brute out in the fields. And, he stayed in those fields until he learned that primary and first principle: *that the most high God ruled in the kingdom of men.*

Now is the Time to Face God's Present Judgement. In God's name, Daniel sets out articles of impeachment against Belshazzar. Before he reads him his doom from the handwriting on the wall, he shows him his crime that God may be *justified when he speaks, and clear when he judges* (Psa 51:4).

Belshazzar Had Not Heeded the Former Judgement. **And thou his son, O Belshazzar, hast not humbled thine heart, though thou knewest all this** (5:22). It is very bad when a man knows enough to humble himself and will not; sees that others have fallen before what could only be construed as God judgement and yet continues on obstinately in the same sins. Others have fallen, but you will not stoop! Others have been broken but you will not bend!

Belshazzar Had Exceeded the Former Sins. **But hast lifted up thyself against the Lord of heaven; and they have brought the vessels of his house before thee, and thou, and thy lords, thy wives, and thy concubines, have drunk wine in them; and thou hast praised the gods of silver, and gold, of brass, iron, wood, and stone, which see not, nor hear, nor know:**

DANIEL 5. BABYLON'S LAST NIGHT, THE HANDWRITING ON THE WALL

(5:23). *Thou hast lifted up thyself against the Lord of heaven.* You have swelled with rage against Him, and taken up arms against His crown. You have defiled and profaned the vessels of His House. You have *praised the gods of silver and gold, which see not, nor hear, nor know* anything, as if they were to be preferred before the God that sees, and hears, and knows everything. Sinners that are resolved to go on in sin are quite satisfied with gods that *neither see, nor hear, nor know*, for this they think will allow them to sin unhindered. But they will find that these gods they chose, will not be the God they are judged by. Before the God of Israel they are judged by One to whom *all things are naked and open* (Heb 4:13).

Belshazzar Has Ignored God's Maintenance of His Life. **And the God in whose hand thy breath is, and whose are all thy ways, hast thou not glorified** (5:23). The young king was too utterly besotted in his pride to consider the simple fact that that a god of stone or metal, even the most precious metal, could never give him even one breath. This is the great, general charge against all lost sinners. On reflection it is only too obvious God has given us the air to breath and the ability to breath it.

- *In whose hand is the soul of every living thing, and the breath of all mankind (Job 12:10).*

- *For in him we live, and move, and have our being (Acts 17:28).*

Belshazzar Must Now Face the Writing on the Wall. **Then was the part of the hand sent from him; and this writing was written** (5:24). Having now come to such a height of wickedness and to descend so low as to trample upon the most sacred things of the Almighty, "you O king saw **the part of the hand sent from him,** sent from the Almighty whom you have affronted." It is He that now *writes bitter things against thee,* and *makes thee to possess thy iniquities* (Job 13:26).

The Meaning of the Words 5:25-31.

And this is the writing that was written, MENE, MENE, TEKEL, UPHARSIN. (5:26) This is the interpretation of the thing: MENE; God hath numbered thy kingdom, and finished it. (5:27) TEKEL; Thou art weighed in the balances, and art found wanting. (5:28) PERES; Thy kingdom is divided, and given to the Medes and Persians. (5:29) Then commanded Belshazzar, and they clothed Daniel with scarlet, and put a chain of gold about his neck, and made a proclamation concerning him, that he should be the third ruler in the kingdom. (5:30) In that night was Belshazzar the king of the Chaldeans slain. (5:31) And Darius the Median took the kingdom, being about threescore and two years old.

The Reading and Interpretation.

The Reading. **And this is the writing that was written, MENE, MENE, TEKEL, UPHARSIN** (5:25). The writing was not in a mystical script. Like the rest of Daniel 2-7 it was in Aramaic. Unless the meaning was only too obvious (!) and no one *dared* to read the words, the reason it could not be read is not known. It was perhaps the way the characters were arranged, or the very conciseness of the writing: *He has numbered, He has weighed, and they divide.* The Chaldean wise men, because they knew not who *He* was, could not read it. If a person does not know *HIM*, does not know the Author of the Bible, then except for the basic salvation passages they cannot really understand the Bible. God in honour of His Words may simply have blinded everyone to the meaning until His own prophet Daniel revealed the meaning.

The Interpretation. *This is the interpretation of the thing:*

MENE; God hath numbered thy kingdom, and finished it (5:26). MENE is repeated in verse 25, for the thing is both numbered and has come to a final end. *He has numbered and finished it.* The days of Babylon are now over. God in His counsels had numbered them to last

Seventy Years (Jer 24:12). The term has expired. It was not numbered to allow for any further reprieve. It is *MENE, MENE*. This is it!

TEKEL; Thou art weighed in the balances, and art found wanting (5:27). *TEKEL* in Aramaic signifies, *Thou art weighed,* and, in Hebrew, *Thou art too light.* This king and his actions and his kingdom have been weighed in the just and unerring scales of Divine equity. God does more perfectly know Belshazzar's true character than the goldsmith knows the dust of gold in his balances. God weighs the sinner before the sentence goes forth. There was nothing of the weight of truth and righteousness in the heart of this king. He had spurned all offers of *the grace of God that bringeth salvation and has appeared to every man* (Titus 2:11). The king was a vain, light, empty man; a man of no weight or consequence.

PERES; Thy kingdom is divided, and given to the Medes and Persians (5:28). *PERES is the singular of PHARSIN* in verse 25. The "U" means "and *PHARSIN*". It means to "break in two and divide." The use of PERES is close in sound and meaning to *Paras* (Persia or Persians) and is a wordplay upon Persia. Daniel puts both together: *Thy kingdom is divided, and given to the Medes and Persians.*

> "Mene, Tekel, Peres, may signify *death, judgment,* and *hell.* At death, the sinner's days are *numbered* and *finished;* after death the judgment, when he will be *weighed in the balance and found wanting;* and after judgment the sinner is cast into place of *the devil and his angels* (Matt 25:41)". Matthew Henry.

Daniel does not give Belshazzar the advice and encouragement to repent as he had to Nebuchadnezzar, because he saw the decree had gone forth (*MENE, MENE*) and he would not be allowed any further time to repent.

The Response. **Then commanded Belshazzar, and they clothed Daniel with scarlet, and put a chain of gold about his neck, and made a proclamation concerning him, that he should be the third ruler in the kingdom** (5:29). One would have thought that Belshazzar would be absolutely stunned at what Daniel has just declared, and, seeing his case so desperate would have continued to be in a panic or rage or both. But the king was so far being convicted or alarmed by the sentence read that he seems completely unconcerned. He rewards Daniel, and apparently endeavours to get on with the evenings revelry. There are no calls for mercy. No, *Sirs, what must I do to be saved* (Acts 16:31). No, *God be merciful to me a sinner* (Luke 18:13).

Though the king shows no concern at Daniels words, he will show respect to Daniel's person. Belshazzar is "a man of his word," and he performs what he had publically promised. He put on Daniel the *scarlet gown* and the *gold chain,* and proclaimed him the *third ruler in the kingdom.* Certainly the strangest coronation in history! Daniel must have received them with a sad smile, foreseeing what a useless exercise this was and how soon they would all wither and with him that bestowed them. They were like Jonah's *gourd,* which came up in a night and perished in a night (Jonah 4).

The Fulfilment.

The Death of Babylon. **In that night was Belshazzar the king of the Chaldeans slain** (5:30). The composure Belshazzar showed did not last long. He soon returned to his former terrors, and well he did for he was falling into the hands of the *king of terrors* (Job 18:14). After returning to the festivities with his heart merry with wine, the Persian besiegers broke into the city, aimed at the palace; there they found the king, and gave him his death blow. The king could find no place so secret to hide himself, or so strong to protect himself. The Historians, Herodotus and Xenophon testify that the city was entered by diverting the Euphrates River, and the enemy entered to find people in a drunken festival (cp. Jer 51:11,39).

The Accession of Media-Persia. **And Darius the Median took the kingdom, being about threescore and two years old** (5:31). From the head of gold we now descend to the breast and arms of silver (Chapter 2). *Darius the Mede took the kingdom* in partnership with, Cyrus the Persian. They were partners in war and conquest (Dan 6:28). Notice is taken of his age, that he was now sixty-two years old, for which reason Cyrus, who was his nephew, gave him the precedency. Some observe that being now sixty-two in the last year of the captivity, he was born in the eighth year of it, and that was the year when Jeconiah was carried captive (2 Kng 24:13–15). Just at that time when a fatal stroke was given by Babylon a prince born who in process of time would avenge Jerusalem upon Babylon, and heal the wound that was given. Thus deep are the counsels of God concerning his people, thus kind are his designs towards them (*Matthew Henry*).

THE TIMES OF THE GENTILES 1-7

C. THE CHARACTERISTICS OF THE TIMES OF THE GENTILES 3-6

4. A TIME OF ENSHRINING BAD LAWS: DARIUS' LIONS DEN 6

DANIEL 6. DANIEL IN THE LION'S DEN

Daniel 3-6 demonstrates the characteristics of the *Times of the Gentiles*, what one can expect during that long period from when Nebuchadnezzar conquered Jerusalem until Christ returns to Jerusalem (Lk 21:24; Zech 14:1-4). Four illustrations are given.

The Characteristics of the Times of the Gentiles Daniel 3-6

      1. A Time of Enforced False Religion: Nebuchadnezzar's Image 3

      2. A Time of Expansion and Instability: Nebuchadnezzar's Madness 4

      3. A Time of Sacrilege: Belshazzar's Feast 5

      4. A Time of Enshrining Bad Laws: Darius' Lion's Den 6

The general development of governmental rebellion against the God of the Bibles is prophetically pictured by the three monarchs of Daniel 3-6. Nebuchadnezzar associated idols *with God*; Belshazzar substituted idols *for God*; and Darius set himself up *instead of God*. All of this will culminate in the coming Antichrist. In describing these characteristics we have now passed from Babylon to Persia; from Belshazzar to Darius. In describing the next two chapters, we will return to Babylon and the reign of Belshazzar (the final chapters 9-12 are from Darius and the Persian reign).

The End of the Times of the Gentiles: Gentile Perspective (Babylon) 7

The End of the Times of the Gentiles: Jewish Perspective (Babylon) 8

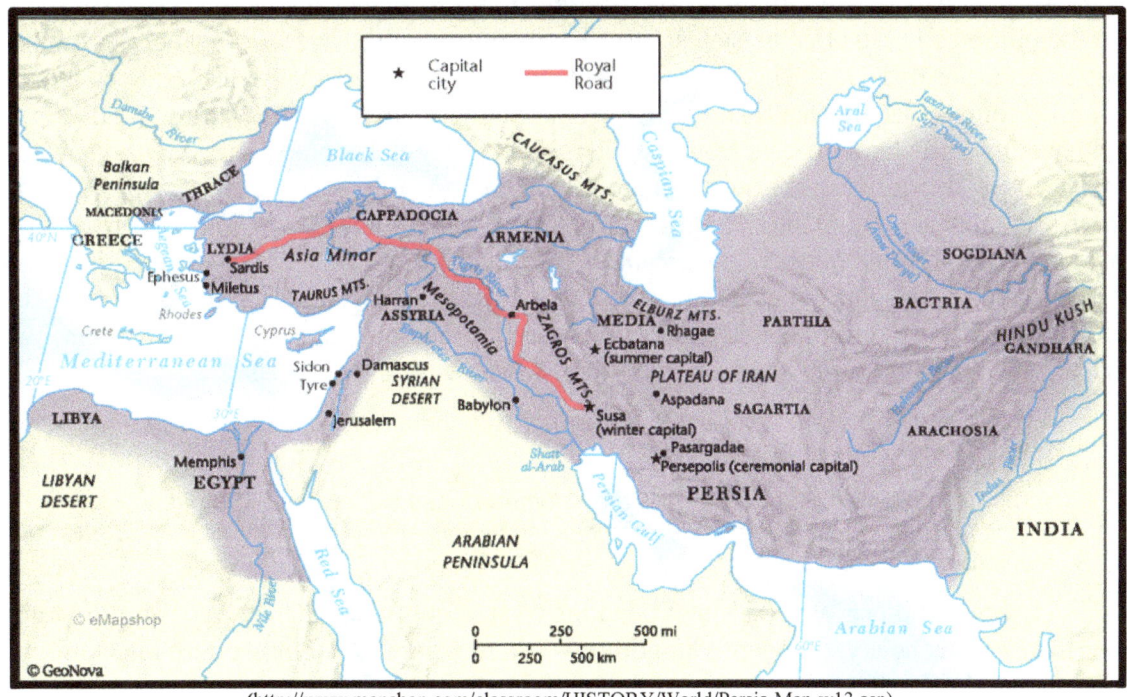

(http://www.mapshop.com/classroom/HISTORY/World/Persia-Map-w13.asp)

The Persian Empire

DANIEL 6. DANIEL IN THE LIONS DEN

From the famous chapter before us we see how Daniel by faith *stopped the mouths of lions*, and in so doing *obtained a good report* (Heb. 11:33). Daniel's three friends had been cast into the fiery furnace ***for refusing to pray*** to an idol; now he is cast into the lion's den ***for refusing to stop praying*** to God. Both attacks are used against believers during the Times of the Gentiles. Now in his nineties, Daniel remains as resolute as he was in the kings dining hall in Chapter One.

Daniel's Elevation by Darius 6:1-3.

It pleased Darius to set over the kingdom an hundred and twenty princes, which should be over the whole kingdom; (6:2) And over these three presidents; of whom Daniel was first: that the princes might give accounts unto them, and the king should have no damage. (6:3) Then this Daniel was preferred above the presidents and princes, because an excellent spirit was in him; and the king thought to set him over the whole realm.

<u>The Governance of Darius</u>. ***It pleased Darius to set over the kingdom an hundred and twenty princes, which should be over the whole kingdom*** (6:1). The first two verses describe the nature of the government of the Medo-Persian Empire. It was not the absolute monarchy that Babylon had been. It was as silver compared to gold, and thus we see the golden head of Babylon replaced by the two-part silver empire that comprised the two arms of the image that Nebuchadnezzar saw in his dream (Dan 2). The government was administered through one hundred twenty members of the royal households of Media and Persia. Each prince ruled over a province, and then a president was appointed over forty of the provinces. The responsibility of the president was to pass on to the princes the governmental policy and orders of the king. He was also to see that the princes were diligent and orderly in their duties. The government of the Medo-Persian Empire was actually a monarchal-republican form of government. The agreement between Darius and Cyrus and the institution of this particular type of government administration was reported by Xenophon the historian (*Hutchings*).

<u>The Advancement of Daniel</u>. (6:2,3) ***And over these three presidents; of whom Daniel was first: that the princes might give accounts unto them, and the king should have no damage Then this Daniel was preferred above the presidents and princes, because an excellent spirit was in him; and the king thought to set him over the whole realm*** (6:2,3). It is to the praise of Darius that he saw so much and so soon in the aged Daniel as to put him in a position such as this. Daniel had been a great man in the kingdom that was conquered (though out of the court under Belshazzar). The first thing many rulers do when coming to power is to purge out any influential officers from the old regime lest they become a threat to the new rule. But, Darius, it seems, was very quick-sighted in the judging of a leader's character and ability, and was soon aware that Daniel had something extraordinary about him. The king recognized what God put in Daniel: ***because an excellent spirit was in him*** (6:3). Many of the lost are *put off* when they see this in a believer. But, the king saw it, and for that reason he put (and so soon put) Daniel at his own right hand. Therefore while it turned out so completely different; what Belshazzar promised Daniel a short time before was now brought to pass.

* *Wherein they think it strange that ye run not with them to the same excess of riot, speaking evil of you (1 Pet 4:4).*

* *Then commanded Belshazzar, and they clothed Daniel with scarlet, and put a chain of gold about his neck, and made a proclamation concerning him, that he should be the third ruler in the kingdom (5:29).*

Darius had those who had long been his trusted confidants. They expected the king's preferment in this newly-conquered kingdom; yet in making the public welfare his chief goal, he knew that the aged prophet exceeded them all. Daniel excelled in prudence and virtue, and Darius likely heard of his pronouncements concerning the Word of God. When Darius looked at Daniel he knew he was looking at an "oak," not *a reed shaken with the wind* (Lk 7:24). He knew that what he saw in Daniel now was what was seen in Daniel for the past Seventy Years. He knew that he was not dealing with a man *given to change* (Prov 24:21).

Daniel's Entrapment by a Bad Law 6:4-10.

Then the presidents and princes sought to find occasion against Daniel concerning the kingdom; but they could find none occasion nor fault; forasmuch as he was faithful, neither was there any error or fault found in him. (6:5) Then said these men, We shall not find any occasion against this Daniel, except we find it against him concerning the law of his God. (6:6) Then these presidents and princes assembled together to the king, and said thus unto him, King Darius, live for ever. (6:7) All the presidents of the kingdom, the governors, and the princes, the counsellors, and the captains, have consulted together to establish a royal statute, and to make a firm decree, that whosoever shall ask a petition of any God or man for thirty days, save of thee, O king, he shall be cast into the den of lions. (6:8) Now, O king, establish the decree, and sign the writing, that it be not changed, according to the law of the Medes and Persians, which altereth not. (6:9) Wherefore king Darius signed the writing and the decree. (6:10) Now when Daniel knew that the writing was signed, he went into his house; and his windows being open in his chamber toward Jerusalem, he kneeled upon his knees three times a day, and prayed, and gave thanks before his God, as he did aforetime.

<u>The Malice of the Presidents.</u>

A Fruitless Search. ***Then the presidents and princes sought to find occasion against Daniel concerning the kingdom; but they could find none occasion nor fault; forasmuch as he was faithful, neither was there any error or fault found in him*** (6:4). Darius had placed three presidents over the 120 provinces of the Persian Empire. Each we assume were over forty of the provinces. Daniel was not only one of the three, he was the preferred president for *the king thought to set him over the whole realm* (6:3). With this, envy is now beginning to do its work and steps are being taken to prevent Daniel being given any further honour in the empire. The two co-presidents and their princes now "open a file on the Daniel case." Yet there is not a whiff of impropriety, scandal, treason, carelessness in the affairs of state etc. Daniel has been shown to be utterly faithful and honest in all respects. They come up with *a blank*! They ignore *the excellent spirit that was in him* (6:3), yet they concluded that *no error,* or *fault, could be found in him* (6:4). We can only wonder what the result would have been if they launched *the same investigative search of themselves.*

It is difficult to find a man in the Bible who is so utterly above reproach as Daniel. Unlike Abraham, Isaac, Jacob, Moses, David, Elijah, Peter, John the Baptist, John the Apostle…. there is never anything in Daniel that hints of a backward step. In the oppressive environment of Babylon he was faithful to every trust. He dealt fairly between the sovereign and the subject. We read of no mistake or blunder or indiscretion. These most spiteful and watchful enemies found Daniel's state so clean that they did not even bother to seek out false witnesses against him. Of course Daniel was a poor lost sinner like everyone else, but these facts demonstrate what God in grace can do through a man living in this world's *Babylon*.

A Valid Consideration. ***Then said these men, We shall not find any occasion against this Daniel, except we find it against him concerning the law of his God*** (6:5). From this we see that Daniel kept up the profession of his faith across the long years and now through the change of years from Babylon to Persia. He will live for the Messiah (9:26) in Persia just as he had in Babylon. Daniel did the king's business faithfully, but at the same time Daniel did not hide his faith *under a bushel* (Matt 5:18).

<u>The Enshrining of a Bad Law.</u>

The Gathering. ***Then these presidents and princes assembled together to the king, and said thus unto him, King Darius, live for ever*** (6:6). Daniel's adversaries could gain nothing

DANIEL 6. DANIEL IN THE LIONS DEN

against him from any law then in existence; therefore they contrive a *new* law. They do it with a *rush*! The idea came suddenly and now they come *suddenly*. The word for **assembled together** is *hargishu*, to "come together with excitement and tumult." Normally they would not approach the king in a reckless way like this, but with a proposal that appeals to the king's vanity they think it safe to rush in. They felt they had to act swiftly lest the king bestow any further authority to Daniel.

The Proposal. ***All the presidents of the kingdom, the governors, and the princes, the counsellors, and the captains, have consulted together to establish a royal statute, and to make a firm decree, that whosoever shall ask a petition of any God or man for thirty days, save of thee, O king, he shall be cast into the den of lions*** (6:7). It is pretended that this bill was the result of mature deliberation. And, because it was "good for both the king and his kingdom it was passed *unanimously*." Actually they do not have the majority of the *college of presidents* that they claim. It is not **all the presidents** but only two thirds! It is a CHARACTERISTIC of the Times of that Gentles that when with great assurance leaders claim to present "the will and sense of the nation" it is often not the case at all. During this time whether by decree, or parliament or popular vote, there will be the enshrinement of bad laws. Many examples could be given of laws which impinge upon the faith of Bible-believing Christians. The extremity to which this has reached is seen in the rush in many countries to legalize gay marriage. Few things could be so opposed to the Bible, to nature and to common sense. This is a strike against the Creator and the fundamental basis of human life upon the earth (Mk 10:6).

Whatever the empire thought of this new law, its proposal was bound to get a favourable response from the king: No prayer to any god for thirty days except to the king! Perhaps the pretext was that with many gods and the transition from the gods of Babylon to the gods of Persia, there needed to be this thirty day "review." The reason of course was to put Daniel quickly on an *unimpeded path* to **the den of lions**.

The Compulsion. ***Now, O king, establish the decree, and sign the writing, that it be not changed, according to the law of the Medes and Persians, which altereth not*** (6:8). Kingly interventio under Babylonian law could change and reverse previous legal statutes. But with the passage from *the head of gold* to the *silver* of Persia, a royal decree was immutable (Dan 6:12,15; Est 1:19; 8:8).

The Signing. ***Wherefore king Darius signed the writing and the decree*** (6:9). The king was foolish and vain; he will be "god for a month." Little did those who hatched the plot realise that as they joyfully witnessed the signing ceremony, they were watching the writing of their own death sentence.

<u>The Constancy of Daniel</u>. ***Now when Daniel knew that the writing was signed, he went into his house; and his windows being open in his chamber toward Jerusalem, he kneeled upon his knees three times a day, and prayed, and gave thanks before his God, as he did aforetime*** (6:10). Daniel did not retire into the country, nor abscond beyond the outer reaches of the empire. He will stay at his post; he will continue to serve the king; and while there he will continue to pray. *He will continue to keep his windows open toward heaven*! Every believer needs to keep *their* window open toward heaven.

He prayed though he **knew that the writing was signed**. There was no equivocation, no debate; he knew what he must do and what he would not do. He could have gone to the king about the matter, but he takes the business to God alone.

He prayed though **opened windows** and **three times a day**. He *opened the windows of his chamber* that the sight of the visible heavens might affect his heart with an awe of that God who dwells above the heavens. He prayed privately as the Lord taught us to *enter the closet* (Matt 6:6). He prayed *without ceasing* as the Apostle Paul taught (1 Thess 5:19), but at certain times he prayed in a noticeable way. Many, and now his enemies, knew when these times were. And so they gather to watch the windows on the westerly side of his chamber open in three daily intervals.

> *As for me, I will call upon God; and the LORD shall save me. Evening, and morning, and at noon, will I pray, and cry aloud: and he shall hear my voice (Psa 55:16,17).*

He prayed **toward Jerusalem**. Though the glory of the Lord's presence had now returned to Heaven (cp. Ezek 11:22,23); though the city was now in ruins; yet Jerusalem was where Jehovah placed His Name (2 Chron 6:6); where the Sacrifice would be offered (Gen 22:14), and to where Christ will return (Zech 14:1-4). The promises of the Messiah's Work are bound up in Jerusalem. By looking to Jerusalem, Daniel was exercising faith in these promises. He *opened his windows towards Jerusalem* to signify the affection he had for its very *stones* and *dust*, yet knowing that one day it will be a *praise in the earth*.

> • *Thou shalt arise, and have mercy upon Zion: for the time to favour her, yea, the set time, is come. For thy servants take pleasure in her stones, and favour the dust thereof (Psa 102:13,14).*

> • *Till he establish, and till he make Jerusalem a praise in the earth (Isa 62:7).*

> • *If I forget thee, O Jerusalem, let my right hand forget her cunning. If I do not remember thee, let my tongue cleave to the roof of my mouth; if I prefer not Jerusalem above my chief joy (Psa 137:5,6).*

He prayed **and gave thanks before his God**. Though long a captive in Babylon, though now once again facing a great crisis; Daniel prayed with a thankful heart. In *all* circumstances the believer is to maintain a thankful heart.

> • *In every thing give thanks: for this is the will of God in Christ Jesus concerning you (1 Thess 5:18).*

> • *Enter into his gates with thanksgiving, and into his courts with praise: be thankful unto him, and bless his name (Psa 100:4).*

He prayed *as he did aforetime*. Daniel was a man well-known for prayer (Ezek 14:14). This *aforetime* stretched back a long way. When he knew that *the thirty day writing was signed* he continued to do *as he did aforetime* and altered not one circumstance. He did not take *a thirty day* break.

Daniel's Descent into the Lion's Den 6:11-17.

> *Then these men assembled, and found Daniel praying and making supplication before his God. (6:12) Then they came near, and spake before the king concerning the king's decree; Hast thou not signed a decree, that every man that shall ask a petition of any God or man within thirty days, save of thee, O king, shall be cast into the den of lions? The king answered and said, The thing is true, according to the law of the Medes and Persians, which altereth not. (6:13) Then answered they and said before the king, That Daniel, which is of the children of the captivity of Judah, regardeth not thee, O king, nor the decree that thou hast signed, but maketh his petition three times a day. (6:14) Then the king, when he heard these words, was sore displeased with himself, and set his heart on Daniel to deliver him: and he laboured till the going down of the sun to deliver him. (6:15)* **Then these men assembled unto the king, and said unto the king, Know, O king, that the law of the Medes and Persians is, That no decree nor statute which the king establisheth may be changed. (6:16) Then the king commanded, and they brought Daniel, and cast him into the den of lions. Now the king spake and said unto Daniel, Thy God whom thou servest continually, he will deliver thee. (6:17) And a stone was brought, and laid upon the mouth of the**

DANIEL 6. DANIEL IN THE LIONS DEN

den; and the king sealed it with his own signet, and with the signet of his lords; that the purpose might not be changed concerning Daniel.

<u>Evidence for the King</u>. ***Then these men assembled, and found Daniel praying and making supplication before his God*** (6:11). It is the same word as in verse 6 (*hargishu*), they ***assembled*** with excitement and tumult. Compare its use in the Second Psalm, *Why do the heathen rage* (Psa 2:1)? They came together to visit Daniel, perhaps under pretence of business, but knowing very well that his at this time would be the *business* of prayer. Like David before him, Daniel could say - .

For my love they are my adversaries: but I give myself unto prayer (Psa 109:4).

<u>Complaint to the King</u>.

Inquiry Concerning the Law. ***Then they came near, and spake before the king concerning the king's decree; Hast thou not signed a decree, that every man that shall ask a petition of any God or man within thirty days, save of thee, O king, shall be cast into the den of lions? The king answered and said, The thing is true, according to the law of the Medes and Persians, which altereth not*** (6:12). When they had found evidence against Daniel concerning this *new bad law*, they lost no time seeking a guilty verdict. They quickly go through the formality of stating the law and the penalty of breaking the law, and then they get the king to admit that it was he who had ratified the law. This kind of action would never have never have taken place in the reign of Nebuchadnezzar. These presidents have virtually "put words into the king's mouth." This is an evidence of the descent from the *head of gold* to the *chest and arms* of silver (Dan 2).

Accusation Against Daniel. ***Then answered they and said before the king, That Daniel, which is of the children of the captivity of Judah, regardeth not thee, O king, nor the decree that thou hast signed, but maketh his petition three times a day*** (6:13). They proceed to accuse Daniel. They describe him in a way that is designed to diminish the aged prophet as much as possible in the eyes of the king. He is *of the children of the captivity of Judah*. He is a Jew; he is of Judah, that despicable people, and now justly a captive people. As a captive he can call nothing his own but what he has by the king's favour, and yet now he has shown great disfavour to the king. *He regardeth not thee, O king! nor the decree that thou hast signed.*

Distress of the King. ***Then the king, when he heard these words, was sore displeased with himself, and set his heart on Daniel to deliver him: and he laboured till the going down of the sun to deliver him*** (6:14). Darius now knew that whatever they pretended, it was not to honour him but to spite Daniel. Again, if he were Nebuchadnezzar he would not be *sorely displeased with himself*, but would immediately have these presidents "drawn and quartered." Darius turns the blame on himself for falling into such a vain-glorious trap and seeks to have the matter reversed. He learns as many have, that flatterers may turn out to be tormentors. He labours with the presidents both by argument and his authority to back off from prosecuting Daniel. But *by the going down of the sun* they were not to be moved.

Pressure upon the King. ***Then these men assembled unto the king, and said unto the king, Know, O king, that the law of the Medes and Persians is, That no decree nor statute which the king establisheth may be changed*** (6:15). We are not told what Daniel said; the King of kings Himself is his advocate, he commits himself to that One that though those opened windows he has been praying. But, the prosecutors insist that the law (even though it is a bad and contrived law) must take its course (cp. Est 1:19; 8:8). The Babylonians magnified the will of their king, by giving him a power to make and unmake laws at his pleasure. The Persians magnified their king in consultation with his presidents and princes by saying that whatever law was made it was so well made that it could not be unmade.

Sentence from the King. ***Then the king commanded, and they brought Daniel, and cast him into the den of lions. Now the king spake and said unto Daniel, Thy God whom thou servest continually, he will deliver thee. And a stone was brought, and laid upon the mouth of the den; and the king sealed it with his own signet, and with the signet of his lords; that the purpose might not be changed concerning Daniel*** (6:16,17).

The King Signs the Warrant for Daniel's Execution. He does this with the utmost reluctance and against his conscience. He acts far better than Pilate did, but in these proceedings he reminds us somewhat of Pilate. And now Daniel the venerable prophet who has such a combination of majesty and grace in his countenance; who had so often sat upon the bench to advise kings and more so had so continually knelt upon his knees to serve to serve the King of heaven, must now be *cast into the den of lions*.

The King Declares Daniel's Deliverance. ***Now the king spake and said unto Daniel, Thy God whom thou servest continually, he will deliver thee.*** He leaves it to God to free him from punishment, since he could not prevail to do it himself. Here at least he states the matter in the utmost; not merely that Daniel's God is *able* to deliver him, but He *will* deliver him.

Darius has reason to think He will do what He did for Daniel's companions in the fiery furnace. Darius justifies Daniel from guilt, declaring that his *crime* was only that he served his God continually, and continued to do so even when it was made a *crime*.

The King Oversees the Double Sealing of the Stone. ***And a stone was brought, and laid upon the mouth of the den; and the king sealed it with his own signet, and with the signet of his lords.*** The lords persuade the king to seal the stone *with his own signet*, and as they cannot trust him because of his sympathy to Daniel, they add their signets to the stone also. Thus, when Christ was buried, his adversaries *sealed the stone* that was rolled to the door of the sepulchre. In neither case did that stone and seal prevent it occupant from leaving.

Daniel's Deliverance from the Lion's Den 6:18-24.

Then the king went to his palace, and passed the night fasting: neither were instruments of musick brought before him: and his sleep went from him. (6:19) Then the king arose very early in the morning, and went in haste unto the den of lions. (6:20) And when he came to the den, he cried with a lamentable voice unto Daniel: and the king spake and said to Daniel, O Daniel, servant of the living God, is thy God, whom thou servest continually, able to deliver thee from the lions? (6:21) Then said Daniel unto the king, O king, live for ever. (6:22) My God hath sent his angel, and hath shut the lions' mouths, that they have not hurt me: forasmuch as before him innocency was found in me; and also before thee, O king, have I done no hurt. (6:23) Then was the king exceedingly glad for him, and commanded that they should take Daniel up out of the den. So Daniel was taken up out of the den, and no manner of hurt was found upon him, because he believed in his God. (6:24) And the king commanded, and they brought those men which had accused Daniel, and they cast them into the den of lions, them, their children, and their wives; and the lions had the mastery of them, and brake all their bones in pieces or ever they came at the bottom of the den.

<u>The Miserable Night</u>. ***Then the king went to his palace, and passed the night fasting: neither were instruments of musick brought before him: and his sleep went from him*** (6:18). It was a bad night for the king. He ate no supper; listened to no music and slept no sleep. The king had indeed said, that God would deliver Daniel out of the danger, but like the father in the Gospels, it was a struggle.

> *And straightway the father of the child cried out, and said with tears, Lord, I believe; help thou mine unbelief (Mk 9:24).*

<u>The Anxious Enquiry</u>. ***Then the king arose very early in the morning, and went in haste unto the den of lions. And when he came to the den, he cried with a lamentable voice***

DANIEL 6. DANIEL IN THE LIONS DEN

unto Daniel: and the king spake and said to Daniel, O Daniel, servant of the living God, is thy God, whom thou servest continually, able to deliver thee from the lions (6:19,20)? He was up early, *very early*; for how could he lie in bed with the tossings to and fro between Daniel being *delivered* and Daniel being *devoured*? He could not sleep for dreaming of Daniel, nor quietly lie awake for thinking of him.

He does not send a servant. No servant ever cared for his master as this king cared for his servant. Nor could he bear to wait for the servant's return. Darius must know *now*!

He comes to the den with some hope. He thinks that God may have graciously undone what he had wickedly done.

He cries **with a lamentable voice**. He is full of concern and trouble, *O Daniel!* art thou alive? He longs to know, yet trembles to ask the question, fearing the answer may be the lion's roar.

He addresses Daniel as the **servant of the living God**. If he rightly understood himself when he called him *the living God,* he could not doubt of His ability to keep Daniel alive, for He that has life in Himself is able to give and preserve life in His creatures.

The Joyful News. *Then said Daniel unto the king, O king, live for ever. My God hath sent his angel, and hath shut the lions' mouths, that they have not hurt me: forasmuch as before him innocency was found in me; and also before thee, O king, have I done no hurt* (6:21,22). Daniel knew the king's voice, though it was now a *lamentable* voice, and spoke to him with all the respect that were due to him: *O king, live for ever.* This was a title of respect, but unlike its use by the pagan princes, when both Daniel and the king exercise faith in the Living God, there is indeed a life that goes on *for ever*. Two things are especially noted in this joyful news.

God Has Preserved His Life. *My God hath sent his angel, and hath shut the lions' mouths, that they have not hurt me* (6:22). The same bright and glorious Being that was seen in the fiery furnace as *the Son of God* (3:25), has now appeared to Daniel. This was the Angel of the LORD, the pre-incarnate Son of God. He had enlightened the dark den and kept Daniel company and safe all night. The Angel's presence made even the lions' den Daniel's stronghold, Daniel's palace, Daniel's paradise; he had never had a better night in all his life. As at our Lord's temptation, the wild beasts knew Christ.

> • And he was there in the wilderness forty days, tempted of Satan; and was with the wild beasts; and the angels ministered unto him (Mk 1:13).

> • Who through faith subdued kingdoms, wrought righteousness, obtained promises, stopped the mouths of lions (Heb 11:33).

God Has Pleaded His Cause. **Forasmuch as before him innocency was found in me; and also before thee, O king, have I done no hurt** (6:22). The presidents had charged Daniel as a lawbreaker. We do not read that Daniel said anything in his own defence, but left it to God to deal with, and this God did in the lion's den. This practice of unjust accusation before civil authorities has been and will increasingly be a CHARACTERISTIC of the *Times of the Gentiles*.

> That make a man an offender for a word, and lay a snare for him that reproveth in the gate, and turn aside the just for a thing of nought (Isa 29:21).

The Immediate Discharge. *Then was the king exceedingly glad for him, and commanded that they should take Daniel up out of the den. So Daniel was taken up out of the den, and no manner of hurt was found upon him, because he believed in his God* (6:23). The prosecutors cannot but admit that the law is satisfied by the intervention of a higher court and law. It is here discovered that there is a higher court than that of the Medes and Persians. The condemned were duly brought to the executioners, but they were stopped by this higher court from doing their work. There was no further appeal against the accused and no just cause could be brought forward why Daniel should not be released.

When accusations come, we may seek counsel and defence, for since the days after the Flood (Gen 9) this is one of the privileges enshrined in human government. Yet in all this the key principle is, Daniel *believed in his God*.

The Swift Recompense. ***And the king commanded, and they brought those men which had accused Daniel, and they cast them into the den of lions, them, their children, and their wives; and the lions had the mastery of them, and brake all their bones in pieces or ever they came at the bottom of the den*** (6:24). We can never know how soon judgement may fall upon a false accuser. This we commit to the Lord; in this case the recompense came very swiftly. The prosecutors are now immediately led to the same prison and to the same executioners.

> • And the judges shall make diligent inquisition: and, behold, if the witness be a false witness, and hath testified falsely against his brother; Then shall ye do unto him, as he had thought to have done unto his brother: so shalt thou put the evil away from among you (Deut 19:18,19).
>
> • He made a pit, and digged it, and is fallen into the ditch which he made. His mischief shall return upon his own head, and his violent dealing shall come down upon his own pate (Psa 7:15,16).
>
> • The LORD is known by the judgment which he executeth: the wicked is snared in the work of his own hands. Higgaion. Selah (Psa 9:16).

The King's Severity. It was not only ***those men which had accused Daniel*** but also ***their children, and their wives***. We are not told to what extent they were complicit. We know that the laws of God established in the courts of Israel were far above the courts of the nations. Yet here as in other extraordinary cases (Achan, Saul, and Haman) they were put to death.

> The fathers shall not be put to death for the children, neither shall the children be put to death for the fathers: every man shall be put to death for his own sin (Deut 24:16).

The Lion's Ferocity. The death blow was immediate: ***the lions had the mastery of them, and brake all their bones in pieces or ever they came at the bottom of the den***. This magnified the miracle of the lions sparing Daniel. Mastiffs that are kept muzzled are the more fierce when the muzzle is taken off (*Matthew Henry*).

The King's Decree and Daniel's Prosperity 6:25-28.

> Then king Darius wrote unto all people, nations, and languages, that dwell in all the earth; Peace be multiplied unto you. (6:26) I make a decree, That in every dominion of my kingdom men tremble and fear before the God of Daniel: for he is the living God, and stedfast for ever, and his kingdom that which shall not be destroyed, and his dominion shall be even unto the end. (6:27) He delivereth and rescueth, and he worketh signs and wonders in heaven and in earth, who hath delivered Daniel from the power of the lions. (6:28) **So this Daniel prospered in the reign of Darius, and in the reign of Cyrus the Persian.**

The Decree of Darius. The Persian king Darius now *brings forth fruit meet for repentance* (Matt 3:8). He makes amends for the dishonour he had shown to God and to Daniel by yielding to pressure to issue the death warrant. He gives honour to God by issuing a counter-decree throughout the realm and to all his subjects. This unlike his previous pronouncement will not be a *thirty-day decree*; it will be much more in conformity to *the law of the Medes and Persians which altereth not* (6:8).

DANIEL 6. DANIEL IN THE LIONS DEN

<u>The Recipients of the Decree</u>. ***Then king Darius wrote unto all people, nations, and languages, that dwell in all the earth*** (6:25). This was sent to the *same* far flung geographic regions mentioned at the beginning, but with the exception that the offices of the presidents and many of the princes where *now filled by others*!

> It pleased Darius to set over the kingdom an hundred and twenty princes, which should be over the whole kingdom; And over these three presidents; of whom Daniel was first: that the princes might give accounts unto them, and the king should have no damage (6:2,3).

<u>The Preface of the Decree</u>. ***Peace be multiplied unto you*** (6:25). Like Nebuchadnezzar before, Darius has learned to address his kingdom with words of grace and peace. These were not the usual words of a powerful monarch; but like Nebuchadnezzar it is from one to whom grace has been shown, and the words are approaching those which we read of the Apostle Paul.

> • Nebuchadnezzar the king, unto all people, nations, and languages, that dwell in all the earth; **Peace be multiplied unto you.** (4:2) I thought it good to shew the signs and wonders that the high God hath wrought toward me. (4:3) How great are his signs! and how mighty are his wonders! his kingdom is an everlasting kingdom, and his dominion is from generation to generation (4:1-3).

> • To all that be in Rome, beloved of God, called to be saints: **Grace to you and peace** from God our Father, and the Lord Jesus Christ (Rom 1:7).

The Subject of the Decree. That *men tremble and fear before the God of Daniel.* ***I make a decree, That in every dominion of my kingdom men tremble and fear before the God of Daniel*** (6:26). This goes further than the earlier decree Nebuchadnezzar (3:29), for that only restrained people from *speaking amiss* of this God, but here he requires them to *fear before him*, and maintain their reverence of Him. It is good that it is that it is linked to *peace be multiplied unto you*, for the only foundation of true and abundant peace is laid in the *fear of God*.

The decree goes quite far and if adhered to would lead to the suppression of false religion and idolatry. However it fell short in specifically requiring the removal of the idols that were so ingrained in the Persian world. Further, it is not by decree but by the spread of the Gospel that idolatry can ever truly be rooted out. It is not by princes, but by the *power* of God in the Gospel (Rom 1:16).

> • The fear of the LORD is the beginning of wisdom: and the knowledge of the holy is understanding (Prov 9:10).

> • They feared the LORD, and served their own gods, after the manner of the nations whom they carried away from thence (2 Kng 17:33).

> • For from you sounded out the word of the Lord not only in Macedonia and Achaia, but also in every place your faith to God-ward is spread abroad; so that we need not to speak any thing. For they themselves shew of us what manner of entering in we had unto you, and how ye turned to God from idols to serve the living and true God (1 Thess 1:8,9).

<u>The Causes for the Decree</u>. ***For he is the living God, and stedfast for ever, and his kingdom that which shall not be destroyed, and his dominion shall be even unto the end. He delivereth and rescueth, and he worketh signs and wonders in heaven and in earth, who hath delivered Daniel from the power of the lions*** (6:27,28). With his limited knowledge of the God of Israel, the king Darius *professed a good profession before many witnesses* (1Tim 6:12).

> (1) God's Being is Transcendent. He is ***the living God***. He *lives* as a God; whereas the gods the Persians worship are dead things; they have no life or breath. They must be moved or carried, whereas He is the *Mover* of all things.

(2) God's Purposes are Immutable. He is *stedfast for ever*. He does not change; His purposes do not alter. The laws of the Medes and Persians may profess to be so but they are not. He is *the same yesterday, today and for ever* (Heb 13:8).

(3) God's Government is Everlasting. ***His kingdom that which shall not be destroyed, and his dominion shall be even unto the end***. The kings of Persia, as Babylon before, made this same two-fold claim but as Babylon was shown to be wrong on both counts so would Persia. With these statements *the spirit of prophecy* is no doubt entering the king (cp. 1 Pet 1:11; Rev 19:10; Jhn 11:51). Darius has never seen such an everlasting kingdom; such a kingdom has never been seen on earth; yet such a kingdom is coming.

> *Of the increase of his government and peace there shall be no end, upon the throne of David, and upon his kingdom, to order it, and to establish it with judgment and with justice from henceforth even for ever. The zeal of the LORD of hosts will perform this.(Isa 9:7).*

(4) God's Authority is Incontrovertible. ***He delivereth and rescueth, and he worketh signs and wonders in heaven and in earth.*** The power and ability of the God of Israel fully meets the dictates of His authority; and this, not only on earth but also in heaven. Nations and empires during the Times of the Gentiles would claim great authority but they lacked the power to effect it. From East to West Rome claimed total obedience over much of the ancient world, but in time it fell in on itself. The power to effect was lacking.

(5) God's Care is Personal: ***who hath delivered Daniel from the power of the lions.*** It may be easier to talk of God's *far off* power, but what of His *nearby* power. This miracle, and that of the deliverance from the fiery furnace were seen and published by two of the greatest monarchs in the history of the world. If this is what the God of Israel can do before my eyes, I have no doubt what He can do on the other side of the world or in heaven.

The Affluence of Daniel. ***So this Daniel prospered in the reign of Darius, and in the reign of Cyrus the Persian*** (6:28). God brought good out of the bad for the last years of his *good and faithful servant* (Matt 25:21,23). The death blow that his enemies aimed at his life resulted in it sweeping them aside instead. Those who had injurious thoughts against Daniel where were removed so that he could spend his last days in peace. What took place for Daniel in his old age would take place for our Saviour in His infancy.

> *But when Herod was dead, behold, an angel of the Lord appeareth in a dream to Joseph in Egypt, Saying, Arise, and take the young child and his mother, and go into the land of Israel: for they are dead which sought the young child's life (Matt 2:19,20).*

But note the special reason for Daniels prosperity during the reign of Cyrus. He ***prospered*** in the Word of God! Though now a very old man, and like his aged counterpart, the Apostle John on the isle of Patmos, the Lord continued to maintain His prophetic work through Daniel. The aged prophet saw Cyrus (in accordance with the Word of God) permit the Jews to return and rebuild Jerusalem and the Temple (Isa 45:13). Likewise Daniel's prophetic ministry continued. Likewise we too, prosper spiritually when we take careful heed to the Scriptures. True spiritual prosperity is bound up in making much of the Bible.

> • *In the third year of Cyrus king of Persia a thing was revealed unto Daniel, whose name was called Belteshazzar; and the thing was true, but the time appointed was long: and he understood the thing, and had understanding of the vision (Dan 10:1).*

DANIEL 6. DANIEL IN THE LIONS DEN

> *• Thus saith Cyrus king of Persia, The LORD God of heaven hath given me all the kingdoms of the earth; and he hath charged me to build him an house at Jerusalem, which is in Judah (Ezra 1:2).*
>
> *• We have also a more sure word of prophecy; whereunto ye do well that ye take heed, as unto a light that shineth in a dark place, until the day dawn, and the day star arise in your hearts (2 Pet 1:19).*
>
> *• I know thy works, and tribulation, and poverty, (but thou art rich)....(Rev 2:9).*

In these chapters (3-6) which give examples showing the characteristics of the Times of the Gentiles, we have seen examples of faith at its highest level when man was at his worst. It is especially illustrative of the coming Tribulation when the fires on earth both from the wrath of God and the wickedness of men will be heated *one seven times more than it was want to be heated* (Dan 3:19; Mal 4:1). In coming now to the final *Gentile-language* chapter of Daniel, we note again the Times of the Gentiles as given thus far.

I THE TIMES OF THE GENTILES 1- 7

    A. The Beginnings of the Times of the Gentiles 1

    B. The Overview of the Times of the Gentiles (*Aramaic* Begins) 2

    C. The Characteristics of the Times of the Gentiles 3-6

        1. A Time of Enforced False Religion: Nebuchadnezzar's Image 3

        2. A Time of Expansion and Instability: Nebuchadnezzar's Madness 4

        3. A Time of Sacrilege: Belshazzar's Feast 5

        4. A Time of Enshrining Bad Laws: Darius' Lion's Den 6

    D. The End of the Times of the Gentiles: Gentile Perspective 7

THE TIMES OF THE GENTILES 1-7

D. The End of the Times of the Gentiles: Gentile Perspective 7

DANIEL 7. FOUR ENDTIME *BEASTS* AND THE ADVENT OF THE MESSIAH

In this Seventh Chapter we have a vision that *Daniel himself received* and not as before one that he interpreted on behalf of others. Previously he had shown the meaning of Nebuchadnezzar's dream of the *metallic statue* in Chapter 2, and his dream of the *great tree* in Chapter 4. He had also shown Belshazzar the meaning of the *handwriting on the wall* in Chapter 5. Beginning in Chapter 7 however, the dreams and the visions continue, but they are Daniel's own.

In this Chapter we see the emphasis becoming much more prophetic and apocalyptic rather than historical. It is for these two basic reasons that many see this chapter as the beginning of the second half of Daniel rather than the conclusion of the first half

    1-6   Historical

    7-12   Prophetical

It seems best, however, to view Chapter 7 as the *conclusion* of the first section. This is for the basic reason that Chapter 7 continues to be written in the Gentile language (Aramaic) rather than Hebrew. The Hebrew section resumes (chapter 1 was in Hebrew) in Chapter 8. Further, as we have seen, there is along with the history a great deal of prophetic implication in chapters 1 – 6. Thus we have:

I THE TIMES OF THE GENTILES 1-7

II THE TIMES OF THE GENTILES REGARDING JERUSALEM 8-12

In this Seventh Chapter Daniel sees *four beasts* rise out of *the great sea*. Daniel also sees the Return of Christ to become ruler over the entire earth. Further, he sees the four beasts in **close proximity** to that Event. At the outset it is necessary to show the Interpretive Key of Chapter which demonstrates that the four beasts are *endtime* beasts and therefore not a mere repetition of the four ancient empires of Chapter 2.

The Interpretive Key to Chapter 7

(7:13) I saw in the night visions, and, behold, <u>one like the Son of man</u> came with the clouds of heaven, and came to the Ancient of days, and they brought him near before him. (7:14) And <u>there was given him dominion, and glory, and a kingdom, that all people, nations, and languages, should serve him</u>: his dominion is an everlasting dominion, which shall not pass away, and his kingdom that which shall not be destroyed. (7:15) I Daniel was grieved in my spirit in the midst of my body, and the visions of my head troubled me. (7:16) I came near unto one of them that stood by, and asked him the truth of all this. So he told me, and made me know the interpretation of the things. (7:17) <u>These great beasts, which are four, are four kings, which shall arise out of the earth.</u> (7:18) But <u>the saints of the most High shall take the kingdom</u>, and possess the kingdom for ever, even for ever and ever.

We show this passage for the beginning of our study of Chapter 7 as it demonstrates what is so frequently overlooked. The *four beasts* that **shall arise** out of *the great sea*, not only arise after Daniel's day, but they arise *so far after* that they are in existence in the time immediately before the Return of Christ.

It is commonly taught that Chapter 7 is really not much more than a repetition of Chapter 2, and that it presents the same ancient world empires (Babylon, Persia, Greece and Rome). It is believed that the *beasts* of Chapter 7 present *God's view* of these empires, while

DANIEL 7. FOUR ENDTIME *BEASTS* AND THE ADVENT OF THE MESSIAH

the *metals* of the great statue in Chapter 2 are how they appear to man. There is a parallel between the fourth *metal* and the fourth *beast* (the latter day aspect of the Roman Empire), but the emphasis of Chapter 7 is the appearance of four dominant powers **near the end** of the Times of the Gentiles.

When Daniel wrote these words, Greece had *already risen* as a strong and influential nation; Persia had *already risen* and was preparing to conquer Babylon; and, Babylon was not only, "*already risen,*" but in its final death throes as an empire.

Further, Daniel names *Babylon* in Chapter 2; he names *Media-Persia* in Chapters 5 and 6; he names *Persia and Greece* in Chapter 8 and he names *Persia and Greece* in Chapter 10; why does he not name any of the beasts in Chapter 7? The answer seems clear; these were nations which were (or for the most part) unknown in Daniel's day. This was the view of Josephus, he named the empires of Chapter 2 but made no attempt to name the beasts of Chapter 7. Thus ultimately the nations these beasts represent cannot be known until they are actually seen to arise. Whether or not they are identifiable in our own day, or are still yet future, is the question that we will now examine.

Noah Hutchings demonstrates further how untenable the common view is.

> The generally accepted interpretation of Daniel's vision concerning the four beasts corresponds to the four divisions of the image which Nebuchadnezzar saw in a dream (Dan 2). The beast like a lion with eagle's wings is Babylon; the bear with three ribs in his mouth is Medo-Persia; the beast like a leopard with four wings of a fowl is Greece; and the last beast, which was too dreadful and terrible for Daniel to describe, is Rome.
>
> The reason Bible scholars have given this interpretation to this vision in Daniel chapter seven is that the lion is the king of the beasts, and therefore the lion represented Babylon. The plucking off of the eagle's wings related to Nebuchadnezzar's downfall and his period of insanity. Thereafter, he was lifted from his beastlike existence and restored to his kingdom. The reason the bear is identified with the Medo-Persian Empire is because it is a huge lumbering beast, and the Medo-Persian military victories were due to its commitment to huge forces to battle whereby enemies were overcome by the superiority of numbers. The three ribs in the bear's mouth represent the triple alliance of Babylon, Egypt, and Lydia against Medo-Persia. After the bear comes the leopard. According to the traditional explanation, this beast is descriptive of the Grecian Empire. Just as the leopard is smaller and more swift in motion than the other beasts mentioned, Alexander overcame opposing armies with tactical superiority and maneuverability, even though he had a smaller military force. The terrible beast with iron teeth represents the Roman Empire, with the ten horns referring to the Revived Roman Empire and the little horn representative of Antichrist.....
>
> As declared by Josephus, Daniel was the greatest of the Old Testament prophets because he was explicit in his prophetic applications. He mentioned kingdoms by name and even gave the time in which his prophecies would be fulfilled. When Daniel interpreted Nebuchadnezzar's dream about the image, he pointed to the king and declared: "Thou art the head of gold!" The rest of the image fell into their proper places with the fall and rise of subsequent empires. When the prophet interpreted Nebuchadnezzar's dream about the tree, he again pointed to the monarch and said: "It is thou, O king!" Again, when he was called to interpret the handwriting on the wall, he boldly told Belshazzar: "Thou art weighed in the balance, and art found wanting. . . . Thy kingdom is given to the Medes and Persians. "The prophet was again explicit in the interpretation of the vision about the ram and the goat. He boldly stated that Greece would be victorious over Medo-Persia, and this was two hundred years before the rise of the Grecian Empire.
>
> Josephus gives all these prophecies as a witness to Daniel's greatness in the service of God; however, the historian does not even make mention of the vision of the four beasts. The reason for the omission is apparent. No one to that time, about 80 a.d., had connected the lion with eagle's wings as Babylon, the bear with three ribs in its

mouth as Medo-Persia, or the leopard as Greece. If the lion did indeed represent Babylon, why did not Daniel declare it? It is apparent from the ending of chapter seven that Daniel didn't know who these beasts represented, and it is apparent from Josephus that no one had connected them to nations or empires existing in his time.

Daniel knew only one thing about the rise of the four beasts, and that was, when the last beast was standing upon the great sea, the Lord would come to bring in His kingdom. Therefore, it is difficult to understand how anyone could be so dogmatic as to say that the lion has to be ancient Babylon, the bear has to be Medo-Persia, and the leopard has to be Greece.

The forces of Satan deceiving the nations, and preparing them to be drawn into the Middle East at the battle of Armageddon; the waves and the seas roaring; wars and rumors of wars; the major world powers' interest in the Mediterranean — all these things would place the setting entirely in the last generation. In fact, never in the history of the world until now, have these four beasts been identifiable according to national emblems. However, all four beasts are very much in evidence today and all four are very much concerned about the Mediterranean Sea. (*Exploring The Book of Daniel*, pp. 147-150).

It is therefore likely that Daniel Two presents about 2500 years of Gentile history whereas Daniel Seven presents the last century or so of that history. In both cases it is a history that relates especially to Israel and the Jewish People.

The Great Sea and the Four Beasts 7:1-8.

In the first year of Belshazzar king of Babylon Daniel had a dream and visions of his head upon his bed: then he wrote the dream, and told the sum of the matters. (7:2) Daniel spake and said, I saw in my vision by night, and, behold, the four winds of the heaven strove upon the great sea. (7:3) And four great beasts came up from the sea, diverse one from another. (7:4) The first was like a lion, and had eagle's wings: I beheld till the wings thereof were plucked, and it was lifted up from the earth, and made stand upon the feet as a man, and a man's heart was given to it. (7:5) And behold another beast, a second, like to a bear, and it raised up itself on one side, and it had three ribs in the mouth of it between the teeth of it: and they said thus unto it, Arise, devour much flesh. (7:6) After this I beheld, and lo another, like a leopard, which had upon the back of it four wings of a fowl; the beast had also four heads; and dominion was given to it. (7:7) After this I saw in the night visions, and behold a fourth beast, dreadful and terrible, and strong exceedingly; and it had great iron teeth: it devoured and brake in pieces, and stamped the residue with the feet of it: and it was diverse from all the beasts that were before it; and it had ten horns. (7:8) I considered the horns, and, behold, there came up among them another little horn, before whom there were three of the first horns plucked up by the roots: and, behold, in this horn were eyes like the eyes of man, and a mouth speaking great things.

<u>The Background and Circumstances of the Vision.</u>

<u>The Date of Vision.</u> ***In the first year of Belshazzar king of Babylon*** (7:1). We saw Belshazzar slain by the Persians at the conclusion of Chapter 5, but we now have the timing of Daniel's first vision in the ***first year of Belshazzar king of Babylon***; and as the subject matter of Daniel's second vision bears certain similarities to the first we will find Chapter 8 timed to ***the third year of the reign of king Belshazzar*** (8:1). This fact points to the *Babylonian spirit* that will dominate the world at the end of the age. Here as the Outline shows we have:

THE END OF THE TIMES OF THE GENTILES: GENTILE PERSPCTIVE 7

THE END OF THE TIMES OF THE GENTILES: JEWISH PERSPECTIVE 8

Matthew Henry notes the change in the king's name in Chapter 7.

"Belshazzar's name here is, in the original, spelt differently from what it used to be; before it was *Bel-she-azar—Bel is he that treasures up riches.* But this is *Bel-eshe-*

DANIEL 7. FOUR ENDTIME *BEASTS* AND THE ADVENT OF THE MESSIAH

> *zar—Bel is on fire by the enemy.* Bel was the god of the Chaldeans; he had prospered, but is now to be consumed."

(Note: a fair amount of what is given in the following is based on *Exploring the Book of Daniel* by Noah W. Hutchings).

<u>The Transmission of the Vision</u>. ***Daniel had a dream and visions of his head upon his bed: then he wrote the dream, and told the sum of the matters*** (7:1). The prophet was very explicit in what he saw, and the fact that he emphasized that he witnessed these things with his own eyes points out that this vision was real. Some seem to believe that just because the Scriptures say this happened in a vision, we can take it with a grain of salt. But a vision is a revelation from Heaven. A person's eyes may play tricks on him, but something that is seen in a Heaven-sent vision is beyond human error. Nine times in this chapter Daniel says: *I saw*, *I beheld*, or *I was beholding*. When such a vision was given to the writer of Scripture, the language is always symbolic in varying degrees, however the interpretation is literal. Symbols never symbolize symbols.

<u>The Symbols of the Vision</u>. ***Daniel spake and said, I saw in my vision by night, and, behold, the four winds of the heaven strove upon the great sea. And four great beasts came up from the sea, diverse one from another*** (7:2,3). Four symbolic expressions are given in these two verses: ***by night***, ***the four winds of Heaven***, ***the great sea***, and ***four great beasts***.

It was a Vision of the *Night*. ***I saw in my vision by night*** (7:2). The *great day of God's wrath* (Rev 6:17), the seven-year Tribulation in which the world's rebellion against the God of the Bible reaches its limit is consistently referred to in Scripture as *the night*, or a *time of darkness*. This fact certainly shows that the **night** vision of the beasts is not one of ancient empires as in Chapter 2, but one that will have its ultimate fulfilment during the Tribulation, yet perhaps with indications "pointing to that direction" before the Tribulation (Lk 21:28).

> • *A day of darkness and of gloominess, a day of clouds and of thick darkness, as the morning spread upon the mountains (Joel 2:2).*

> • *Woe unto you that desire the day of the LORD! to what end is it for you? the day of the LORD is darkness, and not light. As if a man did flee from a lion, and a bear met him; or went into the house, and leaned his hand on the wall, and a serpent bit him. Shall not the day of the LORD be darkness, and not light? even very dark, and no brightness in it (Amos 5:18-20)?*

> • *For yourselves know perfectly that the day of the Lord so cometh as a thief in the night (1 Thess 5:2).*

It was a Vision of *Four Winds*. ***Behold, the four winds of the heaven strove upon the great sea*** (7:2). Some believe *the four winds of Heaven* refer to **four angelic spirits** and are those mentioned in Zechariah 6:5, and, as indicated from the other particulars of the passage give rise to the four horsemen of Revelation 6.

> • *(6:1) And I turned, and lifted up mine eyes, and looked, and, behold, there came* **four chariots** *out from between two mountains; and the mountains were mountains of brass. (6:2) In the* **first** *chariot were red horses; and in the* **second** *chariot black horses; (6:3) And in the* **third** *chariot white horses; and in the* **fourth** *chariot grisled and bay horses. (6:4) Then I answered and said unto the angel that talked with me, What are these, my lord? (6:5) And the angel answered and said unto me, These are* **the four spirits of the heavens, which go forth from standing before the LORD of all the earth** *(Zech 6:1-5).*

Others see them as **four satanic spirits** (yet under the ultimate control of God, thus making the two views virtually the same) who strive against each other as they *strove upon the great sea*. Note how Matthew Henry describes it:

> They strove which should blow strongest, and, at length, blow alone. This represents the contests among princes for empire, and the shakings of the nations by these contests... One wind from any point of the compass, if it blow hard, will cause a great commotion in the sea; but what a tumult must needs be raised when the four winds strive for mastery! This is it which the kings of the nations are contending for in their wars, which are as noisy and violent as the battle of the winds; but how is the poor sea tossed and torn, how terrible are its concussions, and how violent its convulsions, while the winds are at strife which shall have the sole power of troubling it! Note, This world is like a stormy tempestuous sea; thanks to the proud ambitious winds that vex it.

This is like the storm which suddenly arose on the Sea of Galilee after our Saviour with the disciples set out by boat to Gadara to free the possessed men (Matt 8:23-28). There, the winds where whipped up by Satan, and so it will be with these four winds. Here Daniel sees satanic forces stir up nations to defy the God of Heaven. They blow from the four points of the compass. In Revelation 7:1 we read that before the judgments of the Tribulation begin, God will send four angels to hold back *the four winds of the earth* to allow for the sealing of the 144,000 Jewish evangelists (Rev 7:1-9). Further, Satan is called *the prince of the power* of the air and these powers are further described in Ephesians 6.

> • *And after these things I saw four angels standing on the four corners of the earth, holding* **the four winds of the earth**, *that the wind should not blow on the earth, nor on the sea, nor on any tree. And I saw another angel ascending from the east, having the seal of the living God: and he cried with a loud voice to the four angels, to whom it was* **given to hurt the earth and the sea**, *Saying, Hurt not the earth, neither the sea, nor the trees, till we have sealed the servants of our God in their foreheads (Rev 7:1-3).*
>
> • *Wherein in time past ye walked according to the course of this world, according to the prince of the power of the air, the spirit that now worketh in the children of disobedience (Eph 2:2).*
>
> • *For we wrestle not against flesh and blood, but against principalities, against powers, against the rulers of the darkness of this world, against spiritual wickedness in high places (Eph 6:12).*

It was a Vision of *the Great Sea*. The *four winds strove upon* **the great sea** (7:2). The vast population and nations of the earth are symbolically pictured in Scripture as waters and the restless sea. However, the term *the great sea* (found thirteen times in the Bible) refers specifically to the Mediterranean Sea and not the mass of mankind generally. The following comparison demonstrates this distinction.

> • *The* **waters** *which thou sawest, where the whore sitteth, are peoples, and multitudes, and nations, and tongues (Rev 17:15).*
>
> • *Woe to the multitude of many people, which make a noise like the* **noise of the seas**; *and to the rushing of nations, that make a rushing like the* **rushing of mighty waters** *(Isa 17:12).*
>
> • *And as for the western border, ye shall even have* **the great sea** *for a border: this shall be your west border (Num 34:6).*
>
> • *And the west border was to* **the great sea**, *and the coast thereof. This is the coast of the children of Judah round about according to their families (Josh 15:1).*
>
> • *And it shall come to pass, that the fishers shall stand upon it from Engedi even unto Eneglaim; they shall be a place to spread forth nets; their fish shall be according to their kinds, as the fish of* **the great sea**, *exceeding many (Exek 47:10).*
>
> • *And by the border of Gad, at the south side southward, the border shall be even from Tamar unto the waters of strife in Kadesh, and to the river toward* **the great sea** *(Ezek 48:28).*

*were as the **feet of a bear**, and his mouth as the **mouth of a lion**: and the dragon gave him his power, and his seat, and great authority. And I saw one of his heads as it were wounded to death; and his deadly wound was healed: and all the world wondered after the beast (Rev 13:1-3).*

THE LION AND EAGLES WINGS.

(7:4) The first was like a lion, and had eagle's wings: I beheld till the wings thereof were plucked, and it was lifted up from the earth, and made stand upon the feet as a man, and a man's heart was given to it.

The Britain View

"Numerous sources will confirm that the Lion is an international symbol for Great Britain. It was in 1914 that the First World War began, and the United Kingdom and the British Empire played an important role. At the turn of the 20th century, Great Britain was the dominant power in the world. The British navy had dazzled the world and ruled the waves for three centuries, and the British Commonwealth's domain was so vast that it was commonly stated that the sun never set on the British Empire. It was the British that defeated Napoleon at Waterloo, and Rommel at El Alamein. The Lion was a world power, but it had not yet become a beast. A beast is a symbol for an enemy of Israel, God's chosen people. Great Britain was blessed by God with great authority around the globe. God used Britain to assist the Jews in their return to the Holy Land, and in the establishment of the State of Israel. The League of Nations gave a mandate to the British to rule over Palestine (as it was called). This was an opportunity for a tremendous blessing for Britain, but it was only realized in a very limited extent. General Allenby's entrance into Jerusalem and the Balfour Declaration played a significant role in Israel's realization of statehood, but Britain gradually shifted its support away from the Jewish people. The period from 1917 to 1948 was a time of great conflict in the Land of Israel between the Jews and the Arabs. Satan and the rulers of darkness in the spiritual realm exerted much pressure and influence on Great Britain to alter its role in the restoration of the Jewish people. Britain became antagonistic towards the Jews and did much to hinder the establishment of the state of Israel. The Jewish people came close to total annihilation. Fortunately, God's prophetic Word prevailed, and God led a few Jewish men to meet in Tel Aviv on May 14, 1948. They established the new and independent state of Israel. God has intervened on numerous occasions since that time in order to preserve the state of Israel. The present-day existence of Israel can only be described as miraculous. Israel has been, and continues to be, the prophetic fulfillment of the burning bush: always in the fire, but never consumed.

God's judgment has fallen on Great Britain since that fateful time when it turned against God's chosen people. In Scripture, a beast symbolizes an enemy of God's people. Thus, the lion as a beast represents Great Britain in its opposition to the Jews. The eagle's wings represent the widespread power of Great Britain over the earth, but its wings are plucked. The eagle's wings also typify the daughter of Great Britain, which was the United States of America. Not only was the power of Great Britain decreased, but the USA was also plucked out of the control of Great Britain during the Revolutionary War when America won its independence from Great Britain. In the years since World War II, Great Britain's political, economic and military power has been greatly weakened, just as God stated in this prophecy about the Lion. The widespread power of Great Britain was plucked by God, no doubt because of its treatment of the Jews after World War II. It is also significant that the Lion was lifted up from the earth, made to stand on two feet like a man and was given a man's heart. It is not coincidence that Great Britain ceased its opposition to Israel after it became an independent state, and Britain has been generally favourable towards Israel right with America since that time. Thus, Great Britain is currently no longer a beast, since it is no longer hostile towards Israel [Note however the British and USA pressure on Israel since 2000 to give up Judea and Samaria to the Palestinians]. Unfortunately, this will very likely change in the near future when Great Britain becomes one of the horns on the Ten-Horned beast." (Lyn Mize, http://www.ffruits.org/v03/fourbeastsoutofthesea.html).

The Britain and America View

"With the signing of the Balfour Declaration recognizing Palestine as the rightful home of the Jewish People, the hands of God's prophetic clock began to move. Prophetic history of the Middle East from that time to the Second Coming of Christ is revealed in the seventh chapter of Daniel. In Daniel 7:4 we note that the first predatory beast is a lion with eagle's wings, and Daniel saw this lion coming up out of the Mediterranean Sea. After World War I, England dictated policy in the Middle East. The national symbol of England is the lion. We read in Webster's Dictionary: 'Lion: a large, powerful mammal of the animal family, found in Africa and southwest Asia. . . . It is also the symbol of Great Britain.' From 1918 to 1948, the Mediterranean Sea was an English sea. English ships sailed past Gibraltar, then on to the Suez Canal, and then on down to the Indian Ocean, and fluttering from the highest mast on each ship was the bold and fearless lion of Great Britain.

Next we notice that the Lion Daniel saw had on its back eagle's wings, and as it walked upon the Mediterranean Sea, the wings were plucked off. We read again from Webster's Dictionary: 'Eagle: any of a number of large, strong, flesh-eating birds of prey belonging to the falcon family. . . . The national emblem of the United States.' Wings, when spoken of symbolically in the Scriptures, indicate protection. Over and over in the Old Testament we read of God's protective wings over Israel. Christ declared in Matthew 23:37 that He would have gathered Jerusalem like a mother hen protects her chicks under her wings, but they would not. The United States, since World War I, has been England's protective wings. This nation had to come to England's aid in World War I and again in World War II, but England and the United States have drifted apart and England has declined as a world colonial power. We notice in Daniel's account in the vision, that as the eagle-wings are plucked off, the lion no longer is a predatory beast, but stands up and becomes a man. No longer is the lion the hunter, but rather as a man he becomes the hunted and must fear other predators.

Since World War II, England has lost its dominion. Today England is a relatively weak nation militarily. However, with the withdrawal of England from the Mediterranean after World War II, the eagle's wings that were plucked off, the United States, has controlled the great sea. Thus, for twenty years the Mediterranean was an American sea and the United States dictated policy in the Middle East. We remember President Eisenhower intervening to make Israel and England return the Suez Canal to Nasser, and then again when he landed Marines in Lebanon. But the area of American control over the Mediterranean and the surrounding territory began slipping in 1968 with the appearance of a Russian armada appeared on the scene.

The four beasts seen by Daniel are flesh-eating animals — predators. Empires act like beasts because there is only one way a nation becomes an empire: by devouring much flesh; by conquering other nations and then digesting them into a colonial system. As the eagle's wings are plucked off of the lion, it stands on its feet like a man and a man's heart was given to it (Dan. 7:4). The old saying that the sun never sets on the British Empire is no longer true. England has been divesting itself of its colonial system since World War II, and not only is England not beastlike any longer, but lost all heart for either restoring or even maintaining what is left of the British Empire." (Hutchings, pp. 150-153).

The Eagle has *Fallen* !

The White House is illuminated in celebration after the Supreme Court ruled that the Constitution guarantees a right to same-sex marriage, on Friday, June 26, 2015, in Washington. (AP Photo/Evan Vucci)

THE BEAR

(7:5) And behold another beast, a second, like to a bear, and it raised up itself on one side, and it had three ribs in the mouth of it between the teeth of it: and they said thus unto it, Arise, devour much flesh.

The Bear Empire is diverse from that of the Lion. The Bear is Russia. Russia is diverse: ethnically it is Slavic rather than Anglo-Saxon; its alphabet is Cyrillic rather than Roman; its religion is Orthodox or atheist rather than predominantly Protestant. The Bear **raised up itself on one side**, that is it has roused and prepared itself to strike. The obvious link of the Bear with Russia is demonstrated by Noah Hutchings. As again one of the perceptive prophecy teachers in recent times he brings out insights that are not so commonly seen. Here he notes that it is *the ribs in the mouth in the of the bear* that are speaking to the bear!

> Let us reconsider the second beast that is seen by Daniel coming upon the Mediterranean Sea. The United States is identified by the eagle, and it was no coincidence that the eagle was chosen to be our national emblem. Although the eagle is not a beast, it is a predatory bird. As a nation, the United States has never tried to conquer and devour other people in order to build an empire, but neither have we failed in courage to fight where our own needs and self-interest have been involved. After the departure of the lion from the Mediterranean, the eagle's wings lingered for twenty years. But the failure of the United States to fulfil contractual commitments to Israel in the Six-Day War of June 1967 marked the decline of U.S. naval power in the Mediterranean and the total collapse of our political influence in the Middle East outside the borders of Israel. On God's prophetic clock, it was time for the bear to take its bath in the great sea.
>
> What emblem, besides the hammer and sickle, is Russia known by? By the sign of the bear, of course. One can go anywhere in the world and find that

Russia is always identified in the press by the cartoon drawing of a giant lumbering bear. Nations have flags to identify them according to their political or racial structure, but they also adopt another symbol which identifies them according to national disposition. If you were to go to the zoo in your area and ask the keepers what animal they consider to be the most dangerous, they would likely say the bear. Most zookeepers say the bears are even more dangerous than the lions and tigers because not only can they claw and bite, but they can reach out and kill a person with a powerful stroke of one of the front legs. They are so huge and strong that a man has little chance of escape once he comes in contact with a wild or angry bear. Certainly, the bear is a fitting emblem of the national nature of Russia, because Russia is the most dangerous of all the predatory nations in modern times. It is big and cumbersome, yet tenacious and fierce.

With this in mind, let us read again Daniel 7:5: *And behold another beast, a second, like to a bear, and it raised up itself on one side, and it had three ribs in the mouth of it between the teeth of it: and they said thus unto it, Arise, devour much flesh.* Here we see a hungry bear with three bony ribs in its mouth. As it rises up on one side, the ribs, in a most precarious predicament themselves, speak to the bear and say: "Arise, devour much flesh." The traditional interpretation that the three ribs represent the ancient nations of Babylonia, Egypt, and Lydia does not satisfy the meaning. Why would Babylonia, Egypt, and Lydia entreat Medo-Persia to embark on aggression? They wouldn't because Medo-Persia was the enemy. What we actually have represented is a dangerous accommodation arrangement like the one existing between Russia and the Arab world. The Arabs are indeed in a most precarious position — trying to use the power of the bear by whetting its appetite, yet without being chewed up and swallowed by the beast. Russia has invested billions in the Middle East, but has yet to reap much harvest. The Arabs cannot keep Russia pacified forever, because the bear is out for bigger game — the Middle East oil fields, the Suez Canal, the riches of the Dead Sea, and the new cities, farms, and factories in Israel. Today the Russian bear is rising up one side toward the Mediterranean, as indicated in Daniel 7:5.

We definitely believe the three ribs in the bear's mouth represent three nations. It seems apparent that three nations in the Middle East from the Arab bloc will call upon Russia to fulfil its military commitments and attack Israel. This is evident in their calling on the bear *to rise and devour much flesh.* The result of Russia's invasion of Israel [in which she herself in devoured] is clearly prophesied in Ezekiel and Joel.

• *And I will call for a sword against him throughout all my mountains, saith the Lord God: every man s sword shall be against his brother. And I will plead against him with pestilence and with blood: and I will rain upon him, and upon his bands, and upon the many people that are with him, an overflowing rain, and great hailstones, fire, and brimstone. . . . Thou shalt fall upon the mountains of Israel, thou, and all thy bands (Ezek 38:21-22; 39:4).*

• *I will remove far off from you the northern army, and will drive him into a land barren and desolate, with his face toward the east sea, and his hinder part toward the utmost sea, and his stink shall come up, and his ill savour shall come up, because he hath done great things (Joel 2:20).*

The Russian army will be driven back all the way to Siberia, because Siberia lies between the Pacific Ocean, *the east sea,* and the Arctic Ocean. *the utmost sea.* (pp. 153-157).

Despite the Russian Bear's massive defeat, like the Lion, what is left of it will be assimilated into the Antichrist's composite Empire described in Revelation 13:2. That beast has *the mouth of a lion* (the English language), and *the feet of a bear* (Russia's brute nuclear force).

THE LEOPARD

(7:6) After this I beheld, and lo another, like a leopard, which had upon the back of it four wings of a fowl; the beast had also four heads; and dominion was given to it.

DANIEL 7. FOUR ENDTIME *BEASTS* AND THE ADVENT OF THE MESSIAH

The endtime identity of the Leopard is more problematic. The two common views are that the Leopard is either Germany or an Islamic Arab / African coalition.

Is it a German Leopard?

Twice during the Twentieth Century Germany has demonstrated its brutal military might. Along with its role in the Holocaust, its rise from the ashes of World War II to become a leading economic power and its strong currency – *the Mark*, Germany will always be considered as likely being at the centre of endtime events. The recently deceased and well-known prophecy teacher, J.R, Church, believed that Germany was the Leopard of Daniel 7.

> Germany is still my choice for the leopard. Though traditional theology has considered Greece, I find no evidence that the Greek empire ever used the leopard for a symbol. But Germany has! The most glaring use of the symbolic leopard today is the German tank. During World War II they were called panzers (leopards), but today they are referred to as leopards..
>
> The four heads with their respective wings may refer to the history of the German empire – commonly called the "Reich." The first Reich is reported to have been the kingdom of the Holy Roman Empire. The second Reich was developed under Otto Von Bismarck. Adolf Hitler instituted Germany's third Reich. The fourth Reich lies yet in the future. It is my opinion that Germany's involvement with a united Europe and its Euro currency may be represented by the fourth head on Daniel's leopard.
>
> Both of these modern nations – Russia and Germany – are notorious for persecuting the Jews. Both nations have launched genocide against the Chosen People. That seems to be the main theme in Daniel's vision. Why else would Daniel be so troubled by the dream? Why else would he tell us that the color drained from his countenance? (*Prophecy in the News*, November 11,1998).

There are several arguments against Germany being the Leopard. In a latter day context, except for a brief period in World War II, Germany has not been an empire, nor has she been a Mediterranean power. Germany has attempted both but unlike Britain or Russia has not succeeded.

The emphasis is made in Daniel 7 that these beasts are **diverse** from each other. If Britain is the Lion, it is doubtful that Germany is diverse enough to be the Leopard. There is a language link between them (with heavy influence from Latin, French and Greek). Both English and German are based on the same alphabet and derived from the same *Germanic* family of languages.

A recent study reported in the *Guardian* states that "Genetic study reveals that 30% of white British DNA has German ancestry." This is especially noteworthy in the British royal family. The Windsor name now used by Queen Elizabeth II and other British royals only dates back to 1917. Before that the British royal family bore the German name Saxe-Coburg-Gotha. The following from *Quora.com* gives the brief history of this drastic change.

> In the 17th Century the Kingdoms of England, Scotland and Ireland were ruled by the Scottish House of Stuart. This was a period of friction between the monarchy and Parliament, including the English Civil War and the Glorious Revolution, the outcome of which was that we retained a monarchy, but Parliament was firmly in charge of who the monarch was. As Parliament did not want a Catholic King, indeed most of the point of the Glorious Revolution was to depose the Catholic King James II&VII and install his daughter Mary, who was a Protestant, as Queen, by inviting her husband William of Orange (also a Protestant) to invade England from the Netherlands.
>
> This was okay as it went, but then William and Mary died childless, and the throne went to Mary's sister Anne, who also did not have children. The next few Stuarts in line were Catholics, and Parliament did not want that, so they issued the Act of Settlement 1701, which decreed that the throne would bypass the Catholics and go to the next person in line who was a Protestant, which happened to be **Sophia of Hanover**, daughter of

Frederick V, Elector Palatine and Elizabeth Stuart, who was the daughter of James VI&I of Scotland and England.

Sophia died two months before Anne did, so the claim passed to her eldest son, George, Elector of Hanover, who became **George I of Great Britain** in 1714. (England and Scotland had been unified as Great Britain by the Acts of Union 1707). Thus George became the first Hanoverian King of Britain, because his great-grandfather was a Stuart King of England and Scotland, and the British Parliament considered it more important to have a Protestant monarch than to have one from Britain...

George III (great-grandson of George I) was the third of the Hanoverian Kings and the first to be born in Britain and to speak English as his first language, indeed he never went to Hanover. The monarchs after him were called Hanover but were definitely more British than German, culminating in the last Hanoverian monarch,

Queen Victoria. Victoria, as a woman, could not inherit the throne of Hanover, so the connection between Hanover and the UK was severed here. Victoria may not have been German but her husband **Albert of Saxe-Coburg and Gotha** was so the British royal family got another injection of Germanises, and a change of name.

The House of Saxe-Coburg and Gotha had two British Kings, **Edward VII** and **George V**, before it was considered prudent to change the name because of anti-German sentiment among the public in WW1. So in the UK they became the House of Windsor.

George V, who was King during WW1, had no particular sympathies with the Germans, even though Kaiser Wilhelm II was his cousin. The fact he had some German ancestry would have made little difference to his dealings with Germany during the war.

Edward VIII actually served in the British army during WW1, and saw the front-line first hand, although obviously as heir to the throne he was kept out of immediate harm. He was only King for a matter of months before his abdication in 1936, but in 1937 he visited Germany, meeting with Hitler, giving Nazi salutes and generally being quite friendly to the Nazis. When WW2 started this was somewhat unhelpful, and was made Governor of the Bahamas, in order to make certain that he was a long way from Europe.

George VI, who became King when his brother Edward abdicated, did not share Edward's Nazi sympathies, and neither was he particularly German. His mother was a princess of Teck, which is in Germany, but she was born and raised in England. In any case, his partial German ancestry was not considered an issue in official dealings with Germany, before, during or after World War 2. And neither is that of his daughter Elizabeth II, the current monarch. (http://www.quora.com/How-did-Germans-the-ancestors-of-the-royal-family-take-over-and-become-the-British-Monarch)

Thus overall, if Britain is the Lion, it is doubtful that Germany is ***diverse*** enough to be the Leopard (unless of course it be argued that this diversity refers to the fact that Britain and Germany fought two devastating world wars against each other).

Further, there are three symptoms of weakness in this Leopard which do not fit so well with Germany. It has ***four wings*** which speak of its manoeuvrability and swiftness, but unlike the *eagle wings* on the Lion's back, they are only ***the wings of a fowl***. Germany had powerful wings! It had a powerful air force and powerful weaponry. It was the nation that was the forerunner of modern rocket technology.

The Leopard is next stated to have ***four heads***. The fact that this is mentioned after the wings indicates that these heads do not represent historical and sequential reigns and *Reichs*. The Leopard is four-headed when Daniel sees it rise from the sea. This points to a lack of centralized leadership.

Thirdly, rather than take power of and by itself as Germany did, ***dominion was given to*** this Leopard. Therefore from these considerations we conclude that it is unlikely this particular Leopard is Germany.

Nevertheless. when we compare the Fourth Beast of Daniel 7 with the statement that *the people of the prince that shall come shall destroy the city* (Dan 9:26), we will have to return to the German question. There is a link between Titus who destroyed Jerusalem in AD 70 (***the people of***), and the coming Antichrist (***the prince that shall come***). Before Titus destroyed Jerusalem, he was over a military garrison in Bavaria!

Is it an Islamic (Arab/African) Leopard?

The explosive rise of militant Islam in recent times has prompted many students of prophecy to view Daniel's third beast as an Islamic Leopard. Both in language and ethnicity such a Leopard would be ***diverse*** from the Lion and the Bear. Its brutal ferocity, sheer weight of numbers and yet having the three weaknesses mentioned above make it a likely candidate for the Leopard. Militant Islam has lesser military power (***wings of a fowl***). It fights against itself as much as it fights against non-Muslims and is completely fragmented in its leadership (***four heads***). As a bloc against Israel and the West it is shown favouritism in the United Nations (***dominion was given to it***). A number of authors have taken the matter further and believe the coming Antichrist will be Islamic. This seems unlikely. For a review of four books presenting an Islamic Antichrist, (see David Reagan at *Lamb and Lion Ministries.*
http://www.lamblion.com/articles/articles_islam4.php.)

Noah Hutchings back in 1990 presented a chiefly African and North African identity of Daniel's third beast the Leopard.

> Leopards are not native to Israel; however, from the Song of Solomon 4:8, it is evident that there were some of these animals in the mountains to the south of Israel. The Leopard is a ferocious beast and relatively small in comparison to a bear or lion. According to Jeremiah 5:6 and Hosea 13:7, we know they stalk their prey. While the nature of a lion is of a kingly bearing, protective toward its family, methodical in its hunting habits, and reticent to attack either man or other wild beast except when its domain is threatened, the characteristics of the third Mediterranean power is strikingly different from either the lion or the bear. The Leopard is a cunning animal with seemingly no self-protective instincts. It is one of the few animals in the world that will attack a man without provocation. The native habitat of the Leopard is the southern region of Asia and all of Africa with the exception of the desert areas. It is especially native to central Africa.

> While the Lion is the national emblem of England, the Bear of Russia, the eagle of the United States, no nation of international prominence claims the Leopard as its representative symbol. However, the Leopard has been the symbol of rising Black Nationalism in Africa. Black nationalistic terrorist groups in Africa of the past three decades have adopted the Leopard as their standard. The Mau Mau terrorists and other similar African organizations have worn leopard skins and fashioned weapons out of leopard claws tied or nailed to clubs and boards.

> The nature and characteristics of this third beast are indicative of the African bloc of nations, or an Afro-Asian alliance. The Asian nations would certainly be those of Southwest Asia. The African bloc in the United Nations has been demanding a greater voice in Middle Eastern affairs. [with few exceptions, notably Ghana, African with Asian countries vote against Israel]....These African nations are former French, Belgium, Netherland, and German colonies. They include Tunisia, Morocco, Central African Republic, Gabon, Congo, Republic of the Congo, Uganda, Tanzania, Kenya, Somalia, and five other smaller nations. These nations are associate members of the Common Market. These are also nations that are native to the Leopard.

> We read in Daniel 7:6 of the leopard kingdom that *dominion was given to it*. This is said of none of the other three beasts. Now, why would Daniel say this of only the leopard empire? If the leopard applied to Greece, then we would indeed have a difficult time explaining the meaning because Alexander was a classic of all the conquerors who either preceded or succeeded him. He overcame and took the Middle East just like Nebuchadnezzar, Cyrus, or the Caesars — by raw military power. When England took

possession of the Mediterranean, they simply moved their fleet in and said: "We're it. Who is strong enough to put us out?" Likewise, the United States and now Russia. The fact that dominion will be given to the leopard kingdom would indicate that this Mediterranean power will receive its authority from an outside source. The leopard kingdom will not have sufficient military power of itself to control the great sea, but it will receive an appointment and sufficient strength to enforce its will. This appointment may come from the United Nations or by direct agreement from several stronger nations. Of course, the African nations, membership-wise, constitute the strongest bloc in the United Nations (pp. 157-161).

More recently Eric Summers has proposed a somewhat different version of the Arab view of the Leopard and makes a number of noteworthy points. Time will tell whether he has placed too much emphasis upon Egypt. He begins by quoting from *The American Heritage Dictionary*:

"**leop·ard** n. **1.a.** A large, ferocious cat (Panthera pardus) of Africa and southern Asia, having either tawny fur with dark rosette-like markings or black fur. **b.** Any of several felines, such as the cheetah or the snow leopard. **c.** The pelt or fur of this animal. **2. Heraldry. A lion in side view, having one forepaw raised and the head facing the observer.** [Middle English, from Old French leupart, from Late Latin leopardus, from Greek leopardos : Greek le½n, lion; see LION + Greek pardos, pard; see PARD.]"

Definition number 2 above is the key to the identification of the third beast in Daniel 7. The sphinx matches this definition perfectly, and the sphinx is the international symbol for Egypt. Egypt's significant role in the prophetic events of the last days confirms that Egypt will be the beast "like a leopard."

The Four Wings on the Back of the Leopard Egypt: Syria, Jordan, Iraq and Saudi Arabia

The identification of the "four wings of a fowl" on the back of the leopard only requires a map of the Middle East. The four Arab countries of Syria, Iraq, Jordan and Saudi Arabia appear as the wings of a bird, and they are attached to the back of Egypt at the Sinai Peninsula. The Leopard with the four wings of a fowl can be discerned on the above map. [The Mediterranean and other bodies of water are coloured brown.]

It should be clear that the third great beast out of the sea will be an Arab coalition of Egypt, Syria, Iraq, Jordan and Saudi Arabia. The statement "the beast had also four heads" appears to mean that when the coalition forms one of these nations will have no leader. It is not yet known which nation will have no leader, but Basshar Assad of Damascus, Syria is a prime candidate as the missing leader, since Damascus will become a ruinous heap immediately before the leopard rises up. The total destruction of Damascus, Syria by a nuclear weapon would very likely cause Syria to be leaderless.

Please read my exegesis of Isaiah 17 for an understanding of the destruction of Damascus in the following link: The Burden of Damascus. [see also the authors, The Burden of Egypt]....Current events in Iraq could also leave that country leaderless, since the execution of Saddam Hussein and the occupation by American troops have left that country with only a tentative leader.... The last statement in the prophecy about the leopard with the four wings on its back states "and dominion was given to it." This simply means that this beast will have dominion or power over the other nations of the world. The oil that these five countries possess has already given them power or dominion over the other nations in the world, including the United States of America. These five Arab countries have about 60% of the world's known oil reserves, and America, Europe and Japan are all dependent upon their oil. Saudi Arabia alone could destroy the economies of America, Europe and Japan by simply turning off its oil pumps....Regardless of the details surrounding the rise to power of the beast "like a leopard," some major event in the very near future will cause Egypt, Syria, Iraq, Jordan and Saudi Arabia to form a confederation and utilize their oil resources to exert influence in world politics. This power or influence will result from the Arabs hatred of the Jews, and their desire to destroy Israel. The negative impact on the West will be critical, and this will cause the formation of the Ten-Horned beast with the Antichrist as its leader. (http://www.ffruits.org/v03/fourbeastsoutofthesea.html)

The Leopard Nations and Psalm 83

Before leaving Daniel's third *Leopard* Beast, we need to look at the view that Israel launches a pre-emptive attack on hostile nations surrounding her borders. This is believed to take place just after the Tribulation begins or, as the view is usually expounded, before it begins. The devastating victory will allow Israel to have a measure of peace in the early part of the Tribulation. It would allow for the "peace and safety" described when Gog and Magog invades Israel.

> • *After many days thou shalt be visited: in the latter years thou shalt come into the land that is brought back from the sword, and is gathered out of many people, against the mountains of Israel, which have been always waste: but it is brought forth out of the nations, and **they shall dwell safely all of them** (Ezek 38:8).*

> • *And thou shalt say, I will go up to the land of unwalled villages; I will go to **them that are at rest, that dwell safely, all of them dwelling without walls, and having neither bars nor gates** (Ezek 38:11).*

> • *Therefore, son of man, prophesy and say unto Gog, Thus saith the Lord GOD; In that day when my people of Israel **dwelleth safely**, shalt thou not know it (Ezek 38:14)?*

It is proposed that Psalm 83 describes this victory over the immediate threat of hostile nations surrounding the borders of Israel. Eleven nations are mentioned.

> *(83:1) Keep not thou silence, O God: hold not thy peace, and be not still, O God. (83:2) For, lo, thine enemies make a tumult: and they that hate thee have lifted up the head. (83:3) They have taken crafty counsel against thy people, and consulted against thy hidden ones. (83:4) They have said, **Come, and let us cut them off from being a nation; that the name of Israel may be no more in remembrance.** (83:5) For they have consulted together with one consent: they are confederate against thee: (83:6) The tabernacles of **Edom**, and the **Ishmaelites**; of **Moab**, and the **Hagarenes**; (83:7) **Gebal**, and **Ammon**, and **Amalek**; the **Philistines** with the inhabitants of **Tyre**; (83:8) **Assur** also is joined with them: they have holpen the **children of Lot**. Selah. (83:9) Do unto them as unto the Midianites; as to Sisera, as to Jabin, at the brook of Kison: (83:10) Which perished at Endor: they became as dung for the earth. (83:11) Make their nobles like Oreb, and like Zeeb: yea, all their princes as Zebah, and as Zalmunna: (83:12) Who said, Let us take to ourselves the houses of God in possession. (83:13) O my God, make them like a wheel; as the stubble before the wind. (83:14) As the fire burneth a wood, and as the flame setteth the mountains on fire; (83:15) So persecute them with thy tempest, and make them afraid with thy storm. (83:16) Fill their faces with shame; that they may seek thy name, O LORD. (83:17) Let them be confounded and*

troubled for ever; yea, let them be put to shame, and perish: (83:18) That men may know that thou, whose name alone is JEHOVAH, art the most high over all the earth.

Bill Salus is the primary proponent of the Psalm 83 view. His book *Psalm 83 – The Missing Prophecy Revealed*, has been widely read. The author believes the events of Psalm 83 take place before the Tribulation. It is our view that the Rapture is imminent! There are no endtime Biblical prophecies that must be fulfilled before the Rapture before the Rapture can take place. It is also a near certainty that the Rapture does not take place on the day when the Seven Year Tribulation begins. The Tribulation begins specifically when the Antichrist *confirms the covenant with many for one week* (*one week* of years; Dan 9:27). As such a "confirming" could be foreseen (removing the principle of immanence for the Rapture), we conclude that the Rapture takes place before that event (likely a short time before). Therefore, if the proposal of Bill Salus is correct, I view it as taking place in this gap between the Rapture and the confirming of the covenant.

Mr. Salus also follows the generally accepted view that the Battle of Gog and Magog takes place in the early part of the Tribulation. This may be correct and is based in part on *seven years* being spent in clearing away the weaponry of the defeated Russian army (Ezek 39:9). However, there are quite a number of passages in Ezekiel 38 and 39 that do not seem to fit in with that timing and almost appear to merge with Armageddon at the end of the Tribulation Note, for example, that four of the seven sons of Noah's son Japheth are involved in the Gog and Magog invasion of Israel.

- *The sons of Japheth;* **Gomer**, *and* **Magog**, *and Madai, and Javan, and* **Tubal**, *and* **Meshech**, *and Tiras (Gen 10:2).*

- *Son of man, set thy face against Gog, the land of* **Magog**, *the chief prince of* **Meshech** *and* **Tubal**, *and prophesy against him, (Ezek 38:2).*

- *Gomer, and all his bands (Ezek 38:6).*

In fact it is difficult to see how the following passages could be fulfilled *before* the worldwide adulation of the Antichrist at the middle of the Tribulation (**Compare** Ezekiel 38:16,17,20,23; 39:6-8,13,16-18,21,22,28,29 **with** Revelation 13:7,8). Nevertheless, Bill Salus' view appears to be sound that neither Psalm 83 nor a significant number of other OT passage can refer to either Armageddon or Gog and Magog and therefore must refer to a previous battle. A survey of these passages points further to the belief that Daniel's third beast is an *Islamic* Leopard.

The following (shortened, and with Scriptures from the KJV) is from Bill Salus' online presentation, *Are We Living In The Last Days?*
(http://www.arewelivinginthelastdays.com/road/mewar.html)

> We are a front row witness to the prophetic setting of the stage for the War of Gog and Magog. We have seen alliances form between lifelong enemies Russia and Iran while at the same time countries like Turkey move from leaning to the west to a path of strategic alliance with Russia and Iran. We are very close to the War of Gog and Magog, but before this happens there will be a Middle East war that will quickly start, rapidly conclude, and then soon followed by the War of Gog and Magog... The Arab Nations around Israel that are defeated in the war described in Psalm 83 are conspicuously absent from the Russian/Iranian led coalition which includes Ethiopia, Libya, and Turkey along with several modern nations.

Salus applies the *"pricking briar around Israel"* passage (Ezek 28:24-26) to the temporary "peace and safety" passages of Ezekiel 38 (38:8,11,14). The passage likely refers ultimately to the Millennial peace, but as the language is similar and in fact uses identical statements to those found in Ezekiel 38 and 39 there may a reference to the earlier defeat of the Psalm 83 nations.

- *(28:24) And there shall be no more a pricking brier unto the house of Israel, nor any grieving thorn of all that are round about them, that despised them; and they shall know that I am the Lord GOD. (28:25) Thus saith the Lord GOD; When I shall have gathered the house of Israel from the people among whom they are scattered, and shall be sanctified in them in the sight of the heathen, then shall they dwell in their land that I have given to my servant Jacob. (28:26) And they shall dwell safely therein, and shall build houses, and plant vineyards; yea, they shall dwell with confidence, when I have executed judgments upon all those that despise them round about them; and they shall know that I am the LORD their God.*

Using this passage as a precedent, Salus goes on to list other warfare passages that he feels predate both Gog and Magog, and Armageddon and thereby coincide with Psalm 83.

We know that the Russian-Iranian led coalition will attempt to invade a militarily secure Israel. This condition of security becomes a reality only after the judgments are executed upon the surrounding Psalm 83 nations. The adversaries of Israel who **seek to cut Israel off from being a nation** (Psa 83:4) will form their own coalition. Unfortunately for them, they are described in Ezekiel 28:24-26 as **all that are round about them**, **that despised them**; and that they **shall be no more....**Many have confused the events of the War of Gog and Magog [and Armageddon] with a preceding war describe in Psalm 83, Ezekiel, Obadiah, Jeremiah, Isaiah, and Zephaniah. Keep in mind that it is God and God alone who destroys the Russian/Iranian coalition. However, in this war (the Psalm 83 War), it is the Israeli army who, blessed by God, destroys a different Arab coalition.

*Therefore thus saith the Lord GOD; I will also stretch out mine hand upon Edom, and will cut off man and beast from it; and I will make it desolate from Teman; and they of Dedan shall fall by the sword. And **I will lay my vengeance upon Edom <u>by the hand of my people Israel</u>**: and they shall do in Edom according to mine anger and according to my fury; and they shall know my vengeance, saith the Lord GOD (Ezek 25:13,14).*

The Psalm 83 Coalition

*The **tabernacles of Edom**, and the **Ishmaelites**; of **Moab**, and the **Hagarenes**; **Gebal**, and **Ammon,** and **Amalek**; the **Philistines** with the inhabitants of **Tyre**; **Assur** also is joined with them: they have holpen the **children of Lot**. Selah (Psalm 83:6-8).*

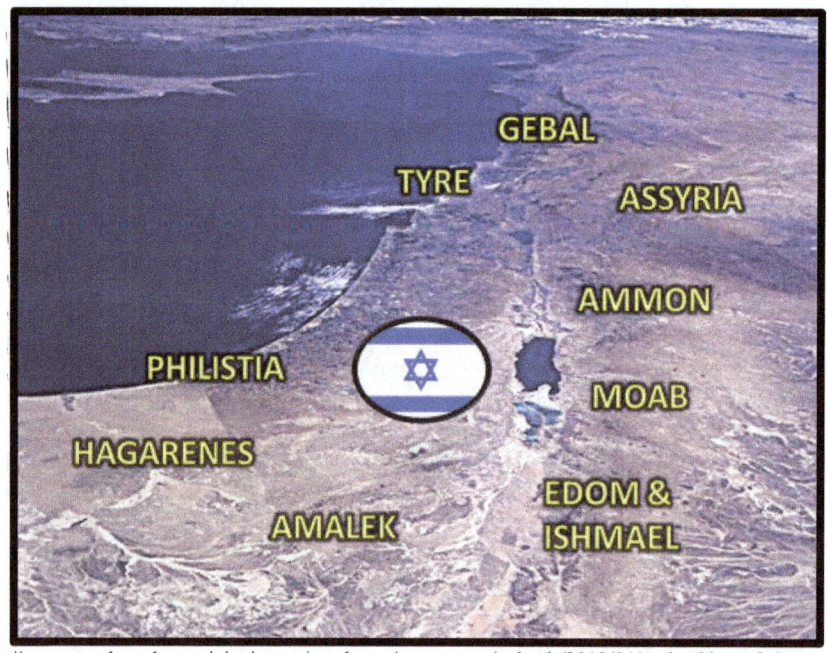

(http://www.prophecydepotministries.net/wordpress/wp-content/uploads/2012/04/psalm-83-confederates.jpg)

The "Pricing Briers" Around Israel

(1) Tabernacles (tents) of Edom = decedents of Esau, Palestinian Refugees and Southern Jordanians

(2) Ishmaelites = Saudi Arabians

(3) Moab = Palestinian Refugees and Central Jordanians

(4) Hagarenes = Egyptians

(5) Gebal = Northern Lebanese

(6) Ammon = Palestinian Refugees and Northern Jordanians

(7) Amalek = Arabs South of Israel

(8) Philistines = Palestinian Refugees and Hamas of Gaza Strip

(9) Inhabitants of Tyre = Hezbollah and Southern Lebanese

(10) Assur = Syrians and perhaps Northern Iraqis

(11) Children of Lot = Moab and Ammon

The term *Palestinian* is the ethnic label used loosely in modern times to identify three predominantly Arab groups of people: the Palestinians of the Gaza Strip, the Palestinians of the West Bank, and the Palestinian refugees. These groups inhabit the territories that most closely approach the borders of modern-day Israel. We generally understand that these groups are comprised of a mixture of peoples who descend from various origins, the main one of these being traceable back to Esau, father of the Edomites.

It is to be noted that it is Assur (Assyria) rather than Syria that is listed in the Psalm 83 coalition. This likely refers to the Arab peoples (Issis?) living in that geographic area. That Syria is not mentioned here or in Ezekiel 38,39 points to the conclusion that by this time Isaiah 17:1 has been fulfilled. *The burden of Damascus. Behold, Damascus is taken away from being a city, and it shall be a ruinous heap.* In the following Salus gives his view on the nations that join Russia's invasion of Israel.

The Gog and Magog Coalition

• *Son of man, set thy face against* **Gog**, *the* **land of Magog**, *the* **chief prince of Meshech** *and* **Tubal**, *and prophesy against him, And say, Thus saith the Lord GOD; Behold, I am against thee, O Gog, the chief prince of Meshech and Tubal (Ezek 38:2,3).*

• **Persia**, **Ethiopia**, *and* **Libya** *with them; all of them with shield and helmet:* **Gomer, and all his bands;** **the house of Togarmah** *of the north quarters, and all his bands: and many people with thee (Ezek 38:5,6).*

• Sheba, and <u>Dedan</u>, and the <u>merchants of Tarshish</u>, with all <u>the young lions</u> thereof, *shall say unto thee, Art thou come to take a spoil? hast thou gathered thy company to take a prey? to carry away silver and gold, to take away cattle and goods, to take a great spoil (Ezek 38:13)?*

(1) Magog ("chief prince" is the Aramaic *rosh*) = Russia and the former Soviet republics

(2) Persia = Iran

(3) Cush = Sudan, Ethiopia, and Possibly Eritrea

(4) Put = Libya, Algeria, and Tunisia

(5) Gomer, Meshech, and Tubal = Turkey (and possibly Germany and Austria)

(6) Togarmah = Turkey, Armenia, and the Turkish-speaking people of Asia Minor & Central Asia

None of Israel's immediate Arab neighbours take part with Russia in her invasion of Israel. The reason being they are destroyed in the prior battle described in Psalm 83 and a substantial number of other passages. These other Scriptures are listed below, and as Salus contends are generally wrongly timed with Armageddon or Gog and Magog. Given that Israel

DANIEL 7. FOUR ENDTIME *BEASTS* AND THE ADVENT OF THE MESSIAH

faces an *immediate* threat today from her *immediate* neighbours, and as these countries likely relate to Daniel's third *Leopard* beast, it is essential that we consider Salus' view of the looming conflict.

The Rapidly Approaching War

This impending war in the Middle East will be a major and devastating war. The Arab confederacy of Psalm 83 will be defeated and destroyed by the army of Israel:

• *Therefore, behold, the days come, saith the LORD, that I will cause an alarm of war to be heard in **Rabbah of the Ammonites**; and it shall be a desolate heap, and her daughters shall be burned with fire: then shall Israel be heir unto them that were his heirs, saith the LORD (Jer 49:2).*

• *Flee ye, turn back, dwell deep, O **inhabitants of Dedan**; for I will bring the calamity of Esau upon him, the time that I will visit him (Jer 49:8).*

• *Behold, he shall come up like a lion [confederacy of Esau] from the swelling of Jordan against the habitation of the strong: but I will suddenly make him run away from her: and who is a chosen man, that I may appoint over her? for who is like me? and who will appoint me the time? and who is that shepherd that will stand before me (Jer 49:19)?*

These are just three of the many Scriptures that point to a Middle East war that is fast approaching. Interestingly enough, many Bible scholars apparently do not recognize how soon. Some scholars place this war within the seven-year Tribulation period. This is however not the case.

• *For **the day of the LORD is near** upon all the heathen: as thou hast done, it shall be done unto thee: thy reward shall return upon thine own head. For as ye have drunk upon my holy mountain, so shall all the heathen drink continually, yea, they shall drink, and they shall swallow down, and they shall be as though they had not been (Obad 1:15,16).*

Obadiah 1:15-16 is a key Scripture which reveals that Esau's judgment will happen before Tribulation or *The Day of the LORD*.

And the house of Jacob shall be a fire, and the house of Joseph a flame, and the house of Esau for stubble, and they shall kindle in them, and devour them; and there shall not be any remaining of the house of Esau; for the LORD hath spoken it

Israel, represented by the house of Jacob and Joseph reduces Southern Jordan, which is represented by Esau, to rubble. This defeat is thorough leaving no survivors.

• *And thy mighty men, **O Teman**, shall be dismayed, to the end that every one of the mount of Esau may be cut off by slaughter (Obad 1:9).*

Obadiah 1:9 describes the soldiers of Teman, as having been slaughtered. This emphasizes the severity of Israel's victory over the Palestinian descendants of Edom. Teman's modern day equivalent may be Taiwan, about 3 miles east of Petra. However Teman and the mountains of Esau appear to be representative of the entire region of Edom in this passage.

• *Therefore thus saith the Lord GOD; I will also stretch out mine hand upon **Edom**, and will cut off man and beast from it; and I will make it desolate from **Teman**; and they of **Dedan** [from Teman to Dedan: Saudi Arabia] shall fall by the sword. And I will lay my vengeance upon Edom **by the hand of my people Israel** [Israeli Defense Force]: and they shall do in Edom according to mine anger and according to my fury; and they shall know my vengeance, saith the Lord GOD (Ezek 25:13,14).*

This war extends into Saudi Arabia.

• *Flee ye, turn back, dwell deep, O **inhabitants of Dedan**; for I will bring the calamity of Esau upon him, the time that I will visit him (Jer 49:8).*

This is a warning to the Saudis to disengage from their confederate allegiance with the Palestinians. They are instructed to flee from the slaughter and go back into the depths of Saudi Arabia. The historical location of *Dedan* was in Northwest Saudi Arabia. Ezekiel tells us that the Saudis do not heed Jeremiah's warning.

• *Therefore thus saith the Lord GOD; I will also stretch out mine hand upon **Edom**, and will cut off man and beast from it; and I will **make it desolate from Teman; and they of Dedan shall fall by the sword** (Ezek 25:13).*

This reference to Dedan, Arabia offers a connection to the confederacy of Esau/Edom found in Psalm 83:4-8 and Obadiah 1:7. In Psalm 83:6, the Saudis are represented by their ancestor Ishmael and are labelled as the Ishmaelites....The army of Israel advances beyond the southern border of Jordan into northwest Saudi Arabia, represented by Dedan, as far south as the Red Sea.

• *Therefore hear the counsel of the LORD, that he hath taken against **Edom**; and his purposes, that he hath purposed against **the inhabitants of Teman**: Surely the least of the flock shall draw them out: surely he shall make their habitations desolate with them. The earth is moved at the noise of their fall, at the cry the noise thereof was heard in **the Red sea** (Jer 49:20,21).*

This places the confederate members of Saudi Arabia, Southern Jordan, and Egypt within this war's scope. The army of Israel will cut off its confederate adversaries and then come down upon the Gaza territory. In continuing their conquest, they plunder the people of the East, which according to its scriptural usage in Genesis 29:1, would be Syria. They then lay their hands on all of Jordan causing its capitol to fall under Jewish sovereignty. Ammon represents northern Jordan, the location of the capitol city of Amman. Isaiah says the people of Ammon shall obey them, depicting the surrender of Jordanian sovereignty.

As this war rages, Isaiah 17 describes what will happen in the north with Syria. Isaiah 17:1-9, is describing one of two events:

(1) Syria (who we know has chemical and bio-weapons:
(http://www.meforum.org/493/guile-gas-and-germs-syrias-ultimate-weapons)
launches some kind of chemical or biological attack that kills many in northern Israel which is then follow by a nuclear attack from Israel that wipes out Damascus.
OR EITHER
(2) Israel fighting on all fronts and facing a Syrian army sweeping through the north utilize a limited version of its Samson Option to avoid being overrun.
(http://en.wikipedia.org/wiki/Samson_Option)

This nuclear strike is clearly going hit Damascus which is just over the Israeli northern border. It could be that Isaiah 17:4-6 is describing the radiation poisoning experienced in the north due to the fallout. The results (from either event) are clearly spelled out. Damascus, the oldest continually inhabited city on earth, will be instantly and completely destroyed and Syria will be crushed by the Israeli Defence Force.

• *The burden of Damascus. Behold, **Damascus is taken away from being a city**, and it shall be a ruinous heap (Isa 17:1).*

• *In that day shall his strong cities be as a forsaken bough, and an uppermost branch, which they left because of the children of Israel: and **there shall be desolation** (Isa 17:9).*

• *And behold at eveningtide trouble; and **before the morning he is not**. This is the portion of them that spoil us, and the lot of them that rob us (Isa 17:14).*

• *But they shall fly upon the shoulders of the Philistines **toward the west**; they shall spoil them **of the east** together: they shall lay their hand upon Edom and Moab; and the children of Ammon shall obey them (Isa 11:14).*

From Isaiah 11:14 and Isaiah 17:1 we know that Israel will destroy Damascus and completely take over Syria. Presently, almost every known Middle Easter terrorist organization has representation in Damascus. How fitting that the city that is the most adversarial to the nation of Israel will cease to exist.

Both Jeremiah and Isaiah tell us how Egypt, another member of this Arab coalition, will react to the news of what the Israeli Defence Force has done to Syria:

• *In that day shall Egypt be like unto women: and it shall be afraid and fear because of the shaking of the hand of the LORD of hosts, which he shaketh over it. And **the land of Judah shall be a terror unto Egypt**, every one that maketh mention thereof shall be afraid in himself, because of the counsel of the LORD of hosts, which he hath determined against it (Isa 19:16,17).*

The picture that Isaiah aptly portrays is that of a fragile, unarmed female fighting a skilled male warrior wielding a mighty sword. The woman is freighted as the warrior waves his sword in the air.

• ***Concerning Damascus.** **Hamath** is confounded, and **Arpad**: for they have heard evil tidings: they are fainthearted; there is sorrow on the sea; it cannot be quiet. **Damascus is waxed feeble**, and turneth herself to flee, and fear hath seized on her: anguish and sorrows have taken her, as a woman in travail. **How is the city of praise not left**, the city of my joy! Therefore her young men shall fall in her streets, and all the men of war shall be cut off in that day, saith the LORD of hosts (Jer 49: 23-26).*

Israel's Borders Expand

The Bible tells us that as a result of this massive military victory given to Israel from God via the Israel Defence Force, the face of the Middle East will drastically change. Israel will significantly increase in size. The tiny nation of Israel as we currently know it will soon encompass a major portion of the Middle East. The nations that form this Arab coalition fall for the most part within the scope of land from the covenant that God made with Abraham. At the end of this war, Israel's borders will be reset to that of, or very close to, the borders that God established for Israel in His covenant with Abraham.

• *In the same day the LORD made a covenant with Abram, saying, Unto thy seed have I given this land, **from the river of Egypt unto the great river, the river Euphrates** (Gen 15:18).*

• *And they of the south shall possess **the mount of Esau** [Southern Jordan]; and they of **the plain the Philistines** [Gaza Strip]: and they shall possess **the fields of Ephraim**, and **the fields of Samaria** [West Bank]: and Benjamin shall possess **Gilead** [West Bank and Golan Heights]. And the captivity of this host of the children of Israel shall possess that of the Canaanites, even **unto Zarephath** [between Tyre and Sidon]; and the captivity of Jerusalem, which is in **Sepharad**, shall possess **the cities of the south** [coastal and southern coastal plan] (Obad 19,20).*

• *Therefore, behold, the days come, saith the LORD, that I will cause an alarm of war to be heard in Rabbah of the Ammonites; and it shall be a desolate heap, and her daughters shall be burned with fire: then shall Israel be heir unto them that were his heirs, saith the LORD [Jer 49:2].*

• *In that day shall **five cities in the land of Egypt speak the language of Canaan**, and swear to the LORD of hosts; one shall be called, The city of destruction. In that day shall there be **an altar to the LORD in the midst of the land of Egypt**, and **a pillar at the border thereof to the LORD** (Isa 19:18,19).*

Isaiah tells us that the expansion of Israeli sovereignty in the region will even reach into Egypt to some degree. Five Hebrew speaking cities will be established in the land of Egypt. There will be an altar erected to God as well as a pillar erected to God on the border. Israel will be elevated to a condition of regional superiority due to their decisive victory over the Arab confederacy. As such, they dwell securely in the Middle East (for a time).

Prisoners of War are Taken

Israel will take prisoners of war. They will establish future detention camps in the regions of Southern Lebanon and the Negev.

• *Howl, O Heshbon, for Ai is spoiled: cry, ye daughters of Rabbah, gird you with sackcloth; lament, and run to and fro by the hedges; for their king **shall go into captivity**, and his priests and his princes together…And afterward I will bring again the captivity of the children of Ammon, saith the LORD (Jer 49:3,6).*

• *Leave thy **fatherless children**, I will preserve them alive; and let thy **widows** trust in me (Jer 49:11).*

The refugees left behind are the *fatherless* and the *widows*. The *mighty men* (soldiers) as they are called in Obadiah 1:9 are slaughtered in defeat, and the refugees left behind are instructed to trust in the Lord.

• *And thy mighty men, O Teman, shall be dismayed, to the end that every one of the mount of Esau may be cut off by slaughter (Obad 9).*

According to Obadiah, these fatherless children and widows are transported to internment camps.

• *And the house of Jacob shall be a fire, and the house of Joseph a flame, and the house of Esau for stubble, and they shall kindle in them, and devour them; and there shall not be any remaining of the house of Esau; for the LORD hath spoken it. And they of the south **shall possess** the mount of Esau; and they of the plain the Philistines: and they **shall possess** the fields of Ephraim, and the fields of Samaria: and Benjamin **shall possess** Gilead. And **the captivity of this** <u>host</u> of the children of Israel **shall possess** that of the Canaanites, even unto Zarephath; and the captivity of Jerusalem, which is in <u>Sepharad</u>, **shall possess** the cities of the south (Obad 18-20).*

Some teach that the "the captives of Jerusalem who are in Sepharad" refers to the return of Jewish people back into Israel from Spain and other associated areas. However, the Hebrew word Obadiah uses for "this host", is *cheyl*, which is defined as "a collateral form of; an army; also (by analogy) an entrenchment, or bulwark." "This Host," the ones referred to in verse 18 as the "houses of Jacob and Joseph" and known in verse 19 as "the possessors" of the expanded territories; "This Host" in verse 20 relocates Palestinian exiles. The Hebrew word used here by Obadiah for "possess," is *yaresh*…The inference here is that the Israeli army will take prisoners of war and detain them in designated areas. Israel will establish two camps for these POWs: one in the north *as far Zarephath*, which is modern day Lebanon, and one *to the south*, referring to the Negev.

The Nations are Astonished

• *The **earth is moved** at the **noise** of their fall, at the cry the **noise** thereof was heard in the Red sea (Jer 49:21).*

This shows the magnitude of the affect that this war will have on the international community. The Hebrew word used here is *rash*, which expresses the trembling experienced during a devastating earthquake and its aftershock. Isaiah describes this further:

• *Woe to the multitude of many people, which make a noise like the noise of the seas; and to the **rushing** of nations, that make a **rushing** like the **rushing** of mighty waters! The nations shall **rush** like the **rushing** of many waters: but God shall rebuke them, and they shall flee far off, and shall be chased as the chaff of the mountains before the wind, and like a rolling thing before the whirlwind (Isa 17:12-13).*

Although the peoples roar like the roar of surging waters (in response to Israel's victory), when he rebukes them they flee far away like tumbleweed before a gale.

The Setting of the Stage for the Antichrist

It is also important to understand what the prophet Daniel declared regarding Edom and the end-time faithful Jewish remnant. He states that the Antichrist enters into the Glorious Land which is Israel with her new pre-ordained borders which at that time should encompass parts of what are modern day Lebanon, Syria, Jordan, and Egypt.

• *He shall enter also into the glorious land, and many countries shall be overthrown: but these shall escape out of his hand, even **Edom**, and **Moab**, and the chief of the children of **Ammon** (Dan 11:41).*

The Antichrist comes in heavy-handedly conquering many countries, but he does not overthrow Edom, Moab, and Ammon. These three territories comprise what is today referred to as the nation of Jordan. Jordan became a nation in 1946 but prior to this was referred to down through the generations as Edom, Moab, and Ammon which as we already know will be under Jewish control. Daniel declares that Jordan escapes the hands of the Antichrist, yet Isaiah informs us that Jordanians do not escape the grasp of Israel's army.

The sequence of events prophesied over Edom, Moab, and Ammon are first that the people of Jordan align themselves with the Psalm 83:6-8 confederacy. Second, this confederacy goes to war against Israel. Third, Israel defeats them. Fourth, Israel establishes sovereignty over Jordan. Fifth, the Antichrist initiates a campaign to destroy Israel. Sixth, the Antichrist avoids Jordan, and marches through Israel proper instead. We can tell by the path the Antichrist will take that his aim is to kill the Jews.

By connecting the dots, we can determine that the people whom Isaiah says, *Ammon shall obey* (11:14), are those reigning over them. Since the events Daniel describes occur after the events Isaiah describes, we can surmise *the chief of the children of Ammon* referred to by Daniel are those governing Jordan at the time that the Antichrist marches into Israel. According to Isaiah, those sovereign over Jordan at the time are the Jews. Therefore *the chief of the children of Ammon* whom Daniel declares will escape the march of the Antichrist will either be Jewish governors or some form of vassal Jordanian government subservient to Israeli sovereignty. Because the Antichrist is on a campaign to overthrow the Jews and kill them, his focus is on the supreme leadership of the Jews headquartered in Israel, rather than their ambassadors stationed in Amman (Amman, with an "a", is the present day capital of Jordan). This could be the reason they escape.

Daniel 11:42,43 tells us that he will then go down into Egypt and he will take their treasure. He will probably use the excuse of taking out the Jewish cities (by then established there) as a reason for moving into the area but Daniel makes it clear that he will be taking the treasure from this area.

• *He shall stretch forth his hand also upon the countries: and the land of Egypt shall not escape. But he shall have power over the treasures of gold and of silver, and over all the precious things of Egypt: and the Libyans and the Ethiopians shall be at his steps (Dan 11:42,43).*

As stated at the beginning of this study by Bill Salus, much that takes place in the Tribulation and after the Rapture will likely cast its shadow before the Rapture. Nevertheless the Rapture itself is imminent. It is this that we look for! We do not wait for the full development of any prophecy to take place before the Rapture. We currently see the *pricking briar* closing in around Israel, but we do not necessarily await the destruction of the *pricking briar* nations before the Rapture. It is in this sense that we consider Bill Salus' *A Signal to Christians*.

• *And when these things **begin to come to pass**, then look up, and lift up your heads; for your redemption draweth nigh (Lk 21:28).*

A Signal to Christians

The judgment to befall Edom will serve as a precursor to the judgment that will come in the Day of the Lord upon all the nations. Zephaniah 2 makes clear that this judgment against Edom, which also extends to the other confederate member nations, is to serve as an example to the other nations but more importantly it is a call to the meek of the Earth to get right *before the day of the Lord* and the Rapture of the Church occurs.

• ***Seek ye the LORD, all ye meek of the earth**, which have wrought his judgment; seek righteousness, seek meekness: it may be ye shall be **hid in the day of the LORD's anger**. For **Gaza** shall be forsaken, and **Ashkelon** a desolation: they shall drive out **Ashdod** at the noon day, and **Ekron** shall be rooted up. Woe unto the inhabitants of the sea coast, the nation of the Cherethites! the word of the LORD is against you; O Canaan, the land of the Philistines, I will even destroy thee, that there shall be no inhabitant (Zeph 2:3-5).*

> Zephaniah sets the stage as follows: The Jews return into the land of Israel then conquer the Arab alliance which is really an Iranian plot. As a result, Israeli fortunes are greatly enhanced. Then Zephaniah appears to allude to the advance against the regionally superior Israel by the Russian/Iranian coalition spoken of in chapters 38 and 39 of Ezekiel, which is commonly referred to as the war of Gog & Magog.
>
> Lastly, he declares that these events occur before the day of the Lord arrives, which is the period of time known as Tribulation. He prophesizes all of the above for the primary purpose of invoking *the meek of the Earth* (Christians) into the worship of God.
>
> Included with the return of the Jewish people to their homeland is the restoration of their fortunes. This is an important area of Biblical prophecy not to be overlooked! Zephaniah, in his call to caution, causes the meek of the earth to consider very carefully this important episode. When they you witness Israel empowered, they are to recognize that the time to take action and be hidden from the day of the Lord is running out.

Bill Salus is to be credited with drawing attention to a significant number of passages regarding Israel's conflict with the surrounding Islamic nations. These passages have been generally linked with Armageddon, but in our survey this looks not to be the case. They depict an earlier conflict that removes the immediate threat and gives Israel a temporary semblance of peace at the beginning of the Tribulation. They lend evidence also to Daniel's third beast being an *Islamic* Leopard.

Islamic State

We cannot leave the question of Daniels Third Beast without dealing with an Islamic phenomenon that until recent times had barely been considered: the explosive rise of Islamic State. Its sheer brutality and seemingly unstoppable trans-border growth has shocked the world. How could what appears to be a ragtag army accomplish so much in such a short time?

ISIL, not just ISIS, *The Plot Thickens*!

In a presentation on *Meghan Monday* (Sep 15, 2014) Glenn Beck states the implications when the President of the United States chooses to call this terrorist movement ISIL rather than ISIS. The subject of the particular program was entitled: "Why Obama's use of the term ISIL instead of ISIS is actually really important".

> ISIL. ISIS. IS. DAISH. You have probably heard each one of those acronyms at least once over the last several months as the media and politicians attempt to determine the best way to refer to the terror group that declared a caliphate spanning Syria and Iraq. IS simply stands for the Islamic State, while ISIS stands for the Islamic State of Iraq and Syria. ISIL is the acronym for the Islamic State of Iraq and the Levant....
>
> They changed their name because they started saying, 'We are bigger than this. We are bigger than Iraq and Syria. We are Iraq, Syria, and Levant...ISIL includes Levant, which includes the area we like to call Israel. Obama has come under fire for underestimating this threat wreaking havoc across the Middle East and threatening the western way of life, and yet he continuously refers to them as ISIL...
>
> I don't know what that means, but, believe me, the President does... What that means is: They have designs that go from Iran through Egypt. There is no Israel. So by the President saying 'this is ISIL,' he is sending the message: 'I know who you are. I know what lands you are planning to take'... The President knows who they are. But he is not telling you who they are. He is trying to downplay that they are putting together a caliphate from Egypt to Iran
> (edited and abridged http://www.glennbeck.com/2014/09/15/why-obamas-use-of-the-term-isil-instead-of-isis-is-actually-reallyimportant/?utm)

How is Islamic State Supplied ?

The obvious question as to how such an army is supplied. It is certainly more than just captured weaponry! Here we see an example from Daniel 7:6. ***And dominion was given unto it.*** "Germany's international broadcaster Deutsche Welle (DW) published a video report of immense implications – possibly the first national broadcaster in the West to admit that the so-called Islamic State (ISIS) is supplied not by 'black market oil' or 'hostage ransoms' but billions of dollars worth of supplies carried into Syria across NATO member Turkey's borders via hundreds of trucks a day."

> The current conflict consuming the Middle East, particularly in Iraq and Syria where the so-called "Islamic State" (ISIS) is operating and simultaneously fighting and defeating the forces of Syria, Lebanon, Iraq, and Iran, we are told, is built upon a logistical network based on black market oil and ransom payments.
>
> The fighting capacity of ISIS is that of a nation-state. It controls vast swaths of territory straddling both Syria and Iraq and not only is able to militarily defend and expand from this territory, but possesses the resources to occupy it, including the resources to administer the populations subjugated within it.
>
> For military analysts, especially former members of Western armed forces, as well as members of the Western media who remember the convoys of trucks required for the invasions of Iraq in the 1990s and again in 2003, they surely must wonder where ISIS' trucks are today. After all, if the resources to maintain the fighting capacity exhibited by ISIS were available within Syrian and Iraqi territory alone, then certainly Syrian and Iraqi forces would also posses an equal or greater fighting capacity but they simply do not.
>
> And were ISIS' supply lines solely confined within Syrian and Iraqi territory, then surely both Syrian and Iraqi forces would utilize their one advantage – air power – to cut front line ISIS fighters from the source of their supplies. But this is not happening and there is a good reason why.
>
> Recent maps showing ISIS' territory show obvious supply lines leading from Jordan and Turkey. Should Syria and its allies manage to cut these supply lines, one wonders just how long ISIS' so-far inexplicable winning streak would last. ISIS' supply lines run precisely where Syrian and Iraqi air power cannot go. To the north and into NATO-member Turkey, and to the southwest into US allies Jordan and Saudi Arabia. Beyond these borders exists a logistical network that spans a region including both Eastern Europe and North Africa.
>
> Terrorists and weapons left over from NATO's intervention in Libya in 2011 were promptly sent to Turkey and then onto Syria – coordinated by US State Department officials and intelligence agencies in Benghazi – a terrorist hotbed for decades. The London Telegraph would report in their 2013 article, "**CIA 'running arms smuggling team in Benghazi when consulate was attacked'**," that:[CNN] said that a CIA team was working in an annex near the consulate on a project to supply missiles from Libyan armouries to Syrian rebels.
>
> Weapons have also come from Eastern Europe, with the New York Times reporting in 2013 in their article, "**Arms Airlift to Syria Rebels Expands, With Aid From C.I.A.**," that: From offices at secret locations, American intelligence officers have helped the Arab governments shop for weapons, including a large procurement from Croatia, and have vetted rebel commanders and groups to determine who should receive the weapons as they arrive, according to American officials speaking on the condition of anonymity.
>
> And while Western media sources continuously refer to ISIS and other factions operating under the banner of Al Qaeda as "rebels" or "moderates," it is clear that if billions of dollars in weapons were truly going to "moderates," they, not ISIS would be dominating the battlefield.

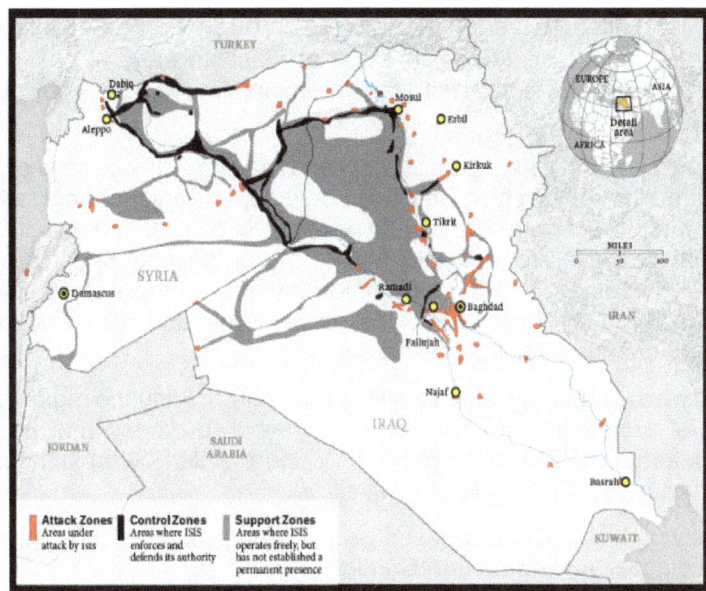

Recent revelations have revealed that as early as 2012 the United States Department of Defense not only anticipated the creation of a "Salafist Principality" straddling Syria and Iraq precisely where ISIS now exists, it welcomed it eagerly and contributed to the circumstances required to bring it about.

Just How Extensive Are ISIS' Supply Lines?

While many across the West play willfully ignorant as to where ISIS truly gets their supplies from in order to maintain its impressive fighting capacity, some journalists have traveled to the region and have video taped and reported on the endless convoys of trucks supplying the terrorist army.

Were these trucks traveling to and from factories in seized ISIS territory deep within Syrian and Iraqi territory? No. They were traveling from deep within Turkey, crossing the Syrian border with absolute impunity, and headed on their way with the implicit protection of nearby Turkish military forces. Attempts by Syria to attack these convoys and the terrorists flowing in with them have been met by Turkish air defenses.Germany's international broadcaster Deutsche Welle (DW) published the first video report from a major Western media outlet illustrating that ISIS is supplied not by "black market oil" or "hostage ransoms" but billions of dollars worth of supplies carried into Syria across NATO member Turkey's borders via hundreds of trucks a day.

German national broadcaster DW reported on convoys of hundreds of trucks per day crossing into Syria from NATO-member Turkey with impunity, enroute to ISIS terrorists, finally explaining the source of the terrorist army's fighting capacity. The trucks were reported by DW to have originated from deep within Turkish territory – most likely NATO air bases and ports.

> The report titled, "IS' supply channels through Turkey," confirms what has been reported by geopolitical analysts since at least as early as 2011 – that ISIS subsides on immense, multi-national state sponsorship, including, obviously, Turkey itself.
>
> Looking at maps of ISIS-held territory and reading action reports of its offensive maneuvers throughout the region and even beyond, one might imagine hundreds of trucks a day would be required to maintain this level of fighting capacity. One could imagine similar convoys crossing into Iraq from Jordan and Saudi Arabia. Similar convoys are likely passing into Syria from Jordan. In all… there is no other plausible explanation to ISIS's ability to wage war within Syria and Iraq besides immense resources being channeled to it from abroad…
>
> What we are currently left with is NATO literally holding the region hostage with the prospect of a catastrophic regional war in a bid to defend and perpetuate the carnage perpetrated by ISIS within Syria, fully underwritten by an immense logistical network streaming out of NATO territory itself.
>
> Tony Cartalucci, Bangkok-based geopolitical researcher and writer, especially for the online magazine *New Eastern Outlook*.
> *(www.informationclearinghouse.info/article40347.htm)*

Though we constantly read about western forces attacking Islamic State, the above reports makes it appear that all is not what it seems. And, more of the same can be seen in a July 2, 2015 *Daily Telegraph* report.

> The United States has blocked attempts by its Middle East allies to fly heavy weapons directly to the Kurds fighting Islamic State jihadists in Iraq, The Telegraph has learnt.
>
> Some of America's closest allies say President Barack Obama and other Western leaders, including David Cameron, are failing to show strategic leadership over the world's gravest security crisis for decades.
>
> They now say they are willing to "go it alone" in supplying heavy weapons to the Kurds, even if means defying the Iraqi authorities and their American backers, who demand all weapons be channeled through Baghdad.
>
> High level officials from Gulf and other states have told this newspaper that all attempts to persuade Mr Obama of the need to arm the Kurds directly as part of more vigorous plans to take on Islamic State of Iraq and the Levant (Isil) have failed.
>
> The Senate voted down one attempt by supporters of the Kurdish cause last month. The officials say they are looking at new ways to take the fight to Isil without seeking US approval.
> Con Coughlin, *Daily Telegraph* Defence Editor

The rise of the fourth Beast that Daniel saw will not result in the destruction of the Lion, Bear and Leopard. Their dominion will be taken away but their characteristics will be assimilated into the Fourth Beast.

> • As concerning the rest of the beasts, they had their **dominion taken away**: yet their **lives were prolonged** for a season and time (Dan 7:12).
>
> • And the beast which I saw was like unto a **leopard**, and his feet were as the feet of a **bear**, and his mouth as the mouth of a **lion**: and the dragon gave him his power, and his seat, and great authority (Rev 13:2).

THE FOURTH BEAST, THE TEN HORNS AND THE LITTLE HORN

> *(7:7) After this I saw in the night visions, and behold a fourth beast, dreadful and terrible, and strong exceedingly; and it had great iron teeth: it devoured and brake in pieces, and stamped the residue with the feet of it: and it was diverse from all the beasts that were before it; and it had ten horns. (7:8) I considered the horns, and, behold, there came up among them another little horn, before whom there were three of the first*

horns plucked up by the roots: and, behold, in this horn were eyes like the eyes of man, and a mouth speaking great things.

The indescribably terrible Fourth Beast represents the kingdom of Antichrist. Daniel saw this beast devouring all peoples, kingdoms and nations; he saw it breaking the nations and what it could not devour and break, it utterly trampled beneath into the earth. There appears to be no escape anywhere upon earth from the enslavement of this voracious fourth beast and the *Little Horn* who rules and directs its conquests.

The Beast Itself

The *Night* Times of the Fourth Beast. ***After this I saw in the night visions*** (7:7). Daniel's ***night*** vision continues and the fourth beast is seen in the ***night***. The three previous beasts, the lion, bear and leopard were also seen in the same *night* vision. This indicates that however active these kingdoms may have been before the Tribulation begins, the climax of their destiny and activity lies in the dark days of the coming Tribulation. The English speaking world, Russia, and the Muslim powers are energetically pursuing their goals today, but it will be in the world's *night* that this fourfold prophecy finds its complete fulfilment.

> • *Behold, the day of the LORD cometh, cruel both with wrath and fierce anger, to lay the land desolate: and he shall destroy the sinners thereof out of it. For the stars of heaven and the constellations thereof* **shall not give their light***: the sun shall be* **darkened** *in his going forth, and the moon shall* **not cause her light to shine***. And I will punish the world for their evil, and the wicked for their iniquity; and I will cause the arrogancy of the proud to cease, and will lay low the haughtiness of the terrible (Isa 13:9-11).*

> • *For the day is near, even the day of the LORD is near,* **a cloudy day***; it shall be the time of the heathen (Ezek 30:3).*

> • *A day of* **darkness** *and of* **gloominess***, a day of* **clouds** *and of* **thick darkness***, as the* **morning spread upon the mountains***: a great people and a strong; there hath not been ever the like, neither shall be any more after it, even to the years of many generations (Joel. 2:2).*

> • *Woe unto you that desire the day of the LORD! to what end is it for you? the day of the LORD is* **darkness***, and* **not light***. As if a man did flee from a lion, and a bear met him; or went into the house, and leaned his hand on the wall, and a serpent bit him. Shall not the day of the LORD be* **darkness***, and* **not light***? even very dark, and* **no brightness** *in it (Amos 5:18-20)?*

> • *(5:2) For yourselves know perfectly that the day of the Lord so cometh as a thief in the* **night***. (5:3) For when they shall say, Peace and safety; then sudden destruction cometh upon them, as travail upon a woman with child; and they shall not escape. (5:4) But ye, brethren, are* **not in darkness***, that that day should overtake you as a thief. (5:5) Ye are all the children of light, and the children of the day: we are not of the* **night***, nor of* **darkness***. (5:6) Therefore let us not sleep, as do others; but let us watch and be sober. (5:7) For they that sleep sleep in the* **night***; and they that be drunken are drunken in the* **night***. (5:8) But let us, who are of the day, be sober, putting on the breastplate of faith and love; and for an helmet, the hope of salvation.*

Its Enumeration as the Fourth Beast. ***And behold a fourth beast*** (7:7). It is as is stated, the *Fourth Beast*; but also the *fourth* in a twofold sense. It is mentioned after the Lion, Bear and Leopard, and as they were latter day beasts, so this also is a *fourth latter day beast*. It also clearly parallels the *fourth*, iron and *Roman* section of the Colossus Vision in Chapter Two. Unlike the Babylonian, Persian and Greek sections of the statue, the Roman section is shown to *directly* extend to the last days. It is primarily the Roman section that is destroyed by Christ, ***the stone cut out without hands*** (2:34). In like manner this fourth beast of Chapter Seven is also destroyed by Christ (7:11). Therefore the Fourth Beast is *Roman*, but as Ancient Rome assimilated the different empires preceding it, so the final stage of Rome will assimilate the Lion, Bear and Leopard.

The Likeness and Power of the Fourth Beast. It was ***dreadful and terrible, and strong exceedingly; and it had great iron teeth: it devoured and brake in pieces, and stamped the residue with the feet of it: and it was diverse from all the beasts that were before it*** (7:7). It is described but unlike the first three beasts it is not *initially* given a likeness. There is a nameless terror in this ***dreadful and terrible*** beast. The description is similar to that given the Roman part of the image in Daniel. The Fourth Beast is ***diverse*** from all before it and *conquers* all before it; yet as shown in Revelation 13 it also *assimilates* what came before it.

> • And the fourth kingdom shall be strong as **iron**: forasmuch as **iron** breaketh in pieces and subdueth all things: and as **iron** that breaketh all these, shall it break in pieces and bruise (Dan 2:40).
>
> • And the beast which I saw was like unto a **leopard**, and his feet were as the feet of a **bear**, and his mouth as the mouth of a **lion**: and the dragon gave him his power, and his seat, and great authority (Rev 13:2).
>
> • And he opened his mouth in blasphemy against God, to blaspheme his name, and his tabernacle, and them that dwell in heaven. And it was given unto him to make war with the saints, and to overcome them: and **power was given him over all kindreds, and tongues, and nations**. And **all that dwell upon the earth shall worship him**, whose names are not written in the book of life of the Lamb slain from the foundation of the world (Rev 13:6-8).

The *Roman* Identity of the Fourth Beast. It is a *Roman* Beast, but it does not have its own unique identity. It does not necessarily have ethnic characteristics that make it diverse from the beasts which came before. What makes it different is that it is a composite and assimilation of major parts of the world's peoples. In the ancient empires, Babylon (Chaldea) had a relatively unique ethnicity, language and geographic location. The same was the case for Persia and Greece. But Rome had it all! It included all and in this sense was different.

Daniel's Fourth Beast is the world empire of the Antichrist. From Daniel 7 and Revelation 13 we see that this last days *Roman* Empire will have the characteristics of each of Noah's three sons: it will be *like a Leopard* (Shem and Ham); it will have the *mouth of a Lion* (Japheth); it will have the *feet of a Bear* (Japheth). It will utilize English as the global language. It will have the raw nuclear might of Russia. It will have the power either by coercion or consent to unite the Japhetic powers with the Shemitic and Hamitic nations (Muslim, Hindu, Buddhist). Thus, according to Revelation 13:2 the Leopard characteristic is prominent in the Fourth Beast.

Religious Unity and the Fourth Beast

Through Satanic power the Fourth Beast will unite the world's religions to divert their worship to the Antichrist. Again, this will either be by coercion or consent.

> • And he saith unto me, The waters which thou sawest, where the whore sitteth, are peoples, and multitudes, and nations, and tongues. And the ten horns which thou sawest upon the beast, these shall hate the whore, and shall make her desolate and naked, and shall eat her flesh, and burn her with fire (Rev 17:15,16).
>
> • And **all that dwell upon the earth shall worship him**, whose names are not written in the book of life of the Lamb slain from the foundation of the world (Rev 13:8).

We see many moves today that are leading toward the kind of religious unity that will make *much more easy* the ultimate worship of the Antichrist. Most notably there are the large interfaith gatherings of the Catholic Church. These are intended for the strengthening of the Vatican, but as shown in Revelation 17, it will turn out otherwise and the Fourth Beast which she formerly supported will destroy her. Contemporary Christian Music is often the *glue* in the march for a world church. Popular, doctrineless, feel-good preaching like that of Joel Osteen is an ingredient. Rick Warren has been called "America's Pastor" and many follow him. Consider his push toward the *Chrislam* view in uniting Christians and Muslims.

> Saddleback Church in Orange County, California, home to **super-pastor Rick Warren** (Obama inauguration, Purpose Driven Life, etc.) has joined forces with Southern California mosques to adopt a three-step plan for ending enmity between evangelical Christians and Muslims.
>
> The plan's first step calls for **Muslims and Christians to recognize they worship the same God**. Interfaith reconciliation has been proceeding for years between Muslims and mre liberal-leaning mainline Protestant denominations.
>
> This is the first such effort I've heard of by an evangelical mega-church. Many evangelicals regard Islam as Christianity's number one enemy, and they do not at all agree that the two faiths worship the same God….
>
> The effort, informally dubbed King's Way, caps years of outreach between Warren and Muslims. Warren has broken Ramadan fasts at a Mission Viejo mosque, met Muslim leaders abroad and addressed 8,000 Muslims at a national convention in Washington D.C.   http://www.exposingchrislam.com/

Note further:

> On Monday, November 17, 2014, **Pope Francis** will host a global ecumenical conference featuring Muslim leaders, pagans, and Chrislam founder **Rick Warren** from Saddleback Church in California. The official website says that the Colloquium is sponsored by the Congregation for the Doctrine of the Faith and co-sponsored by the **Pontifical Council for Inter-religious Dialogue**, and   the **Pontifical Council for the Promotion of Christian Unity**.
>
> The conference will be held Nov. 17-19 at the Vatican, and is expected to feature more than 30 speakers from over 20 countries. According to the Catholic News Service,

those of the Jewish, Islamic, Buddhist, Hindu, Jaina Shasana, Taoist and Sikh religions will be present, as well as Roman Catholics and professing Christians.
http://www.nowtheendbegins.com/blog/?p=28081

The Ten Horns

The Ten Horns of the Fourth Beast. ***And it had ten horns*** (7:7). The Ten Horns clearly parallel the Ten Toes of the image of Daniel 2 and the Ten Horns on the Beast in Revelation 17. As the Ten Toes are Roman, the Ten Horns must also be Roman. This fact by itself demonstrates that the recent teaching of a Muslim fourth kingdom and antichrist is in error.

> • *And the fourth kingdom shall be strong as iron: forasmuch as iron breaketh in pieces and subdueth all things: and as iron that breaketh all these, shall it break in pieces and bruise. And whereas thou sawest the feet and* **toes**, *part of potters' clay, and part of iron, the kingdom shall be divided; but there shall be in it of the strength of the iron, forasmuch as thou sawest the iron mixed with miry clay. And as the* **toes** *of the feet were part of iron, and part of clay, so the kingdom shall be partly strong, and partly broken (Dan 2:40-42).*

> • *So he carried me away in the spirit into the wilderness: and I saw a woman sit upon a scarlet coloured beast, full of names of blasphemy, having seven heads and* **ten horns** *(Rev 17:3).*

> • *And the angel said unto me, Wherefore didst thou marvel? I will tell thee the mystery of the woman, and of the beast that carrieth her, which hath the seven heads and* **ten horns** *(Rev 17:7).*

> • *And the* **ten horns** *which thou sawest are ten kings, which have received no kingdom as yet; but receive power as kings one hour with the beast (Rev 17:12).*

> • *And the* **ten horns** *which thou sawest upon the beast,* ***these shall hate the whore, and shall make her desolate and naked, and shall eat her flesh, and burn her with fire*** *(Rev 17:16).*

The Ten Horns are ten powerful nations that "whip" the rest of the world into submission and worship of the Antichrist. One example of this is that during the Tribulation they destroy the Roman Catholic Church and direct its adherents to the worship of the Antichrist. As much of Europe is Catholic, and as many are thoroughly appalled by the abuse and corruption of the Roman Catholic Church we have here further support for the long held view that these horns are ten powerful *Roman* nations who are either European or have their origins from(or were colonized by) Roman/European powers. Seven (*) of the ten most powerful could be said to fall into this category. Spain with other Spanish speaking countries, Canada and possibly Australia would follow.

	GDP in billion U.S. dollars
*United States	17,416.25
China	10,355.35
Japan	4,769.8
*Germany	3,820.46

	GDP in billion U.S. dollars
*France	2,902.33
*United Kingdom	2,847.6
*Brazil	2,244.13
*Italy	2,129.28
*Russia (? Crimea)	2,057.3
India	2,047.81

Whatever their power was before, it is through their submission to the Antichrist that these *horns* derive their ultimate power. The effect that the Antichrist will have on the leaders of these nations and the "example" that is made of *three of these horns* before there is total submission is seen in the following.

> • And the **ten horns** which thou sawest are **ten kings**, which have received no kingdom as yet; but receive power as kings one hour with the beast. These have one mind, and shall give their power and strength unto the beast (Rev 17:12,13).
>
> • And of the ten horns that were in his head, and of the other which came up, and **before whom three fell**; even of that horn that had eyes, and a mouth that spake very great things, whose look was more stout than his fellows (Dan 7:20).

The Little Horn

The Little Horn of the Fourth Beast. *I considered the horns, and, behold, there came up among them another little horn, before whom there were three of the first horns plucked up by the roots: and, behold, in this horn were eyes like the eyes of man, and a mouth speaking great things* (7:8).

The Diminutiveness of the Little Horn. He will apparently come from a less significant country (not from one of the ten *horns*). He will not be someone that people "have had their eye on for some time." His lineage and physical appearance will not be what we read of King Saul. It will be something other than these things that will make the coming Antichrist a *towering personality*.

> • *Now there was a man of Benjamin, whose name was Kish, the son of Abiel, the son of Zeror, the son of Bechorath, the son of Aphiah, a Benjamite, **a mighty man of power**. And he had a son, whose name was Saul, **a choice young man**, and a goodly: and there **was not among the children of Israel a goodlier person** than he: **from his shoulders and upward he was higher than any of the people*** (1 Sam 9:1, 2).

The Relation of the Little Horn to the Ten Horns. *I considered the horns, and, behold, there came up among them another little horn.* That there is a relationship is shown by the fact that though he does not come from one the *ten horns*, he does come **up among them**. The first thought is that he comes from one of the smaller nations of Europe.

The People of the Prince that Shall Come and The Recent Muslim Antichrist View

A number of books and speakers are presenting the view that the little horn, the Antichrist will be Muslim. One particular argument set forth seems at first hearing to be convincing and has led a not inconsiderable number to re-evaluate the long held Roman/European view of the Antichrist. Three prominent expositions of this idea include:

Phillip Goodman, *The Assyrian Connection* (Tulsa, Oklahoma: Prophecy Watch Books, 1993 — revised edition in 2003), 136 pages.

Joe VanKoevering, *Unveiling The Man of Sin* (St. Petersburg, FL: God's News Publishing, 2007), 175 pages.

Joel Richardson, *Antichrist: Islam's Awaited Messiah*, (Enumclaw, WA: Pleasant Word, 2006), 276 pages.

One of the key arguments that the Antichrist will be Roman/European is given in Daniel 9:26. The Antichrist will be *as Roman* as was Titus who was born in Rome; who was a lieutenant over Roman forces in Germania and Britannia, and who led four Roman legions in the destruction of Jerusalem in AD 70. In Daniel 9:26, Titus and his legions are called ***the people of the prince that shall come*** (the *prince* being the last days Antichrist). It is the *people* of this coming prince that ***shall destroy the city*** in AD 70). The *prince that shall come* will *confirm* a seven year covenant with Israel during the Tribulation. Here then is a clear link between Titus and the Antichrist of the Tribulation.

> • (9:26) And after threescore and two weeks shall Messiah be cut off, but not for himself: and **the people of the prince that shall come shall destroy the city** and the sanctuary; and the end thereof shall be with a flood, and unto the end of the war desolations are determined. (9:27) And **he shall confirm the covenant with many for one week**: and in the midst of the week he shall cause the sacrifice and the oblation to cease, and for the overspreading of abominations he shall make it desolate, even until the consummation, and that determined shall be poured upon the desolate.

Proponents of a Muslim Antichrist take a counter view of this key passage and present what they view as their strong argument. They say that many of the soldiers in the legions Titus led against Jerusalem *were Arabic*, and therefore it will be from Arabic ranks (not European) that Antichrist will come. They have gathered statements primarily from two early sources to support this contention.

Do Early Sources Show *Arabic* Romans Destroying Jerusalem in AD 70?

Hope of Israel Ministries (HOIM) in presenting the Muslim Antichrist view quote two early sources (Tacitus and Josephus).

> **Publius Cornelius Tacitus** was both a senator and a historian of the Roman Empire that wrote extensively concerning the specific period that we are now examining. The surviving portions of his two major works -- the *Annals* and the *Histories* -- have become a vital source of information from this period of the Roman Empire. Speaking of the Roman attack of Jerusalem, Tacitus details the specific legions and the peoples that primarily composed the attacking army:

> "Titus Caesar...found in Judaea three legions, the 5th, the 10th, and the 15th...To these he added the 12th from Syria, and some men belonging to the 18th and 3rd, whom he had withdrawn from Alexandria. This force was accompanied...by *a strong contingent of Arabs*, who hated the Jews with the usual hatred of neighbors..." (Tacitus, *The History*, New Ed edition Book 5.1).

There are several important bits of information that we can gain from this reference. First, we learn that the Roman legions had been stationed in Judea, Syria and Egypt. Secondly, we learn that beyond the Roman legions, there was also "a strong contingent of Arabs, who hated the Jews" who accompanied the soldiers.

Titus Flavius Josephus, another irreplaceable historian from this period also confirms the report of Tacitus:

"So Vespasian sent his son Titus [who], came by land into Syria, where he gathered together the Roman forces, with a considerable number of auxiliaries from the kings in that neighbourhood" (Flavius Josephus, *The Complete Works of Josephus*, *The Wars of the Jews* or *The History of the Destruction of Jerusalem*, Book III, Chapter 1, Paragraph 3).

Once again, Josephus reveals that the Roman legions used to attack Jerusalem were stationed in Syria. This is where Titus gathered them together as he proceeded toward the Jewish capital. He also details that "a considerable number" of auxiliaries, or volunteers, from Syria and the surrounding regions were also gathered for the attack. Later, Josephus also details the specific number of Arab soldiers who joined forces with the invading armies:

"Malchus also, the king of Arabia, sent a thousand horsemen, besides five thousand footmen, the greatest part of which were archers; so that the whole army, including the auxiliaries sent by the kings, as well horsemen and footmen, when all were united together, amounted to sixty thousand" (Flavius Josephus, *The Complete Works of Josephus*, *The Wars of the Jews* or *The History of the Destruction of Jerusalem*, Book III, Chapter 4, Paragraph 20...)

Note that the quotes are brief; that the place of gathering the armies (Judea, Syria) appears to differ in Tacitus and Josephus; that the Arab contingent who "hated the Jews" is distinguished from the rest of the army: and that out of an army totalling sixty thousand, the Arab contingent was six thousand. **Therefore these two early sources do not support the idea of an *Arabic* Roman army destroying Jerusalem!**

Nevertheless, despite the smallness of the Arab contingent, the authors continue to press their case by arguing that the four legions destroying Jerusalem were composed of a composite mixture "eastern provincials" rather than Italian or European.

Modern Roman scholars across the boards all thoroughly validate the claim that by 70 A.D. the Roman soldiers were almost exclusively non-Italian peoples. Antonio Santosuosso in *Storming the Heavens: Soldiers, Emperors, and Civilians in the Roman Empire* confirms that during the first half of the 1st century, approximately 49% of the soldiers were Italians, but by 70 A.D. that number had fallen to only 22%. (Westview Press, 2001, page 97-98).

Despite this line of argument, the prophecy of Daniel 9:26 declares plainly that the people who destroyed Jerusalem **would be identifiable** and would thereby provide the link to the coming Antichrist. If they are not primarily Italian, or Arabic but only a composite mixture of "eastern provincials" then how could they be identified? The prophecy loses its force and becomes too generalized.

Whatever the degree of ethnic diversity in the army that destroyed Jerusalem, the city fell to the *iron* **legions** of Rome. It was a *Roman* Army, and with its soldiers under the iron-clad grip of *Roman* discipline. Its orders were from *Rome*. Its generals and leaders were *Roman*. Its strategy was *Roman*. Its weaponry was *Roman*. It is therefore linked to the latter day *Roman* empire, and to this that Daniel 9:26 directs our attention. Note briefly the key historical factors that demonstrate this link.

DANIEL 7. FOUR ENDTIME *BEASTS* AND THE ADVENT OF THE MESSIAH

Distinguishing Between the *Legions* and *Auxiliaries* in the Roman Army

The *HOIM* editors do not explain clearly the difference between the **legions** and the **auxiliaries** that existed in the Imperial Army Rome. Notice again that Tacitus says *legions* and *contingents* attacked Jerusalem, while Josephus refers to them as *Roman forces* and *auxiliaries* (clearly by *Roman forces*, "legions" are meant and *contingents* must mean "auxiliaries").

> Titus Caesar...found in Judaea **legions**, the 5th, the 10th, and the 15th...To these he added the 12th from Syria, and some men belonging to the 18th and 3rd, whom he had withdrawn from Alexandria. This force was accompanied...by a **strong contingent of Arabs**, who hated the Jews with the usual hatred of neighbors...

> So Vespasian sent his son Titus [who], came by land into Syria, where he gathered together the **Roman forces**, with a considerable number of **auxiliaries** from the kings in that neighbourhood...

The two terms cannot be combined and lumped together. The composition of a *legion* is much more identifiable than that of an *auxiliary*. The Wikipedia sources explain the difference.

> The imperial Roman army was the standing force deployed by the Roman Empire during the Principate era (30 BC – AD 284). Under the founder–emperor Augustus, **the legions**, which were formations numbering about 5,000 heavy infantry **recruited from the ranks of Roman citizens only**, were transformed from mixed conscript and volunteer corps soldiers serving an average of 10 years, to all-volunteer units of long-term professionals serving a standard 25-year term. (Conscription was only decreed in emergencies.) In the later 1st century, the size of a legion's First Cohort was doubled, increasing the strength of a legion to about 5,500.

> To complement the legions, Augustus established **the auxilia**, a regular corps with numbers similar to those of the legions, but **recruited from the peregrini or non-citizen** inhabitants of the empire. Peregrini constituted approximately 90 percent of the Empire's population in the 1st century. In addition to large numbers of heavy infantry equipped in a similar manner to legionaries, the auxilia provided virtually all the army's cavalry, light infantry, archers and other specialists. The auxilia were organised in units about 500 strong. These units were termed cohortes if they consisted of infantry, alae if they consisted of cavalry and cohortes equitatae if they were composed of infantry with a cavalry contingent attached.

> Until about AD 68, the auxilia were recruited by a mix of conscription and voluntary enlistment. After that time, the auxilia also became largely a volunteer corps, with conscription resorted to only in emergencies. Auxiliaries were required to serve a minimum of 25 years, although many served for longer periods. On completion of their minimum term, auxiliaries were awarded Roman citizenship. [emphasis mine] https://en.wikipedia.org/wiki/Imperial_Roman_army

Therefore as we are primarily dealing with *legions* that attacked Jerusalem and as they are composed of Roman citizens, that army is not the "indeterminable mix" the Muslim Antichrist view seeks to convey.

The Roman General Titus

Christ said that *not one stone would be left upon another* in the judgement that would befall Jerusalem in AD 70 (Lk 21:6). We have here notice of the man who was the instrument of that monumental judgement. There is no doubt that when Daniel 9:26 speaks of the *people* who would destroy Jerusalem, it directs our attention to the *leader* of that people. The information especially to be noted are his birth in **Rome** and his positions in **Britain** and **Germania**. Later it will be noted that the attack on Jerusalem was planned from **Greece**.

Before AD 70, Titus Served in Germania (southern) and Britannia

Titus was born in Rome, probably on 30 December 39 AD, as the eldest son of Titus Flavius Vespasianus—commonly known as Vespasian. As a military commander, Vespasian gained early renown by participating in the Roman invasion of Britain in 43. What little is known of Titus's early life has been handed down to us by Suetonius, who records that he was brought up at the imperial court in the company of Britannicus, the son of emperor Claudius, who would be murdered by Nero in 55.

From c. 57 to 59 he was a military tribune in Germania. He also served in Britannia, perhaps arriving c. 60 with reinforcements needed after the revolt of Boudica. In c. 63 he returned to Rome and married Arrecina Tertulla, who died c. 65. Titus then took a new wife of a much more distinguished family, Marcia Furnilla.
https://en.wikipedia.org/wiki/Titus

The Roman Advance on Jerusalem

Simon Baker writes:

Needing people he could rely on, Vespasian called upon his eldest son, Titus, to join him in **Greece** where together they drew up plans for the Roman campaign.....now that the father and son were together, it was agreed that, although only a quaestor, Titus be given the command of the 15th Legion based in Alexandria, while Vespasian took charge of the 10th Legion and the 5th Legion based in Syria. The General decided against making use of the disgraced 12th Legion defeated by the Jews at Beth-horan. The three legions would rendezvous at the coastal city of Ptolemais in Galilee before launching their attack on the rebels....They were reinforced by a mixture of auxiliary and regular cohorts from Caesarea and Syria, and also with allied forces contributed by the pro-Roman kings in the region – Agrippa, Antiochus and Soaemus. With an army at least 60,000 strong thus deployed, Vespasian and Titus decided on the strategy for war...

To win a psychological advantage over the Jewish rebels, Vespasian and Titus decided on a war of terror, a standard Roman tactic. The key principle was to show no mercy: to kill everyone fit to bear arms, and enslave those who could not resist; to plunder and ravage all that came into the Roman army's path. In short, the plan was to terrorize Jerusalem into submission. The sight of the column alone was daunting. Light-armed auxiliaries and bowmen were followed by heavy-armed infantry, some with the responsibility of marking out camps. Then came the road-makers, laden with their tools for levelling surfaces and straightening bends obstructing the path. A cavalry force and body of spearmen protected the personal baggage of the high command. After them could be seen the train of mules carrying the mass of artillery, the battering rams and missile engines. Then came the group comprising Vespasian, Titus and the senior officers with their bodyguard. Appropriately, the military standards, surrounding the symbol of the eagle - 'the king of birds and most fearless of all' -divided the generals from the main body of soldiers, while servants and camp followers brought up the rear.
(*Ancient Rome, The Rise and Fall of an Empire*. BBC Books, 2006, pp.258-263).

DANIEL 7. FOUR ENDTIME *BEASTS* AND THE ADVENT OF THE MESSIAH

The Roman Legions that Attacked Jerusalem

According to the Roman Senator Tacitus, "Titus Caesar…found in Judaea three legions, the 5th, the 10th, and the 15th…To these he added the 12th from Syria." Others elaborate: "Titus surrounded the city, with three legions (V *Macedonica*, XII *Fulminata*, XV *Apollinaris*) on the western side and a fourth (X *Fretensis*) on the Mount of Olives to the east" (Barbara Levick, *Vespasian,* Routledge, 1999, pp. 116–119). Simon Baker above says, "The General decided against making use of the disgraced 12th Legion defeated by the Jews at Beth-horan."

The Siege and Destruction of Jerusalem, by David Roberts (1850)

V Macedonian Legion (European)

The Legion usually mentioned first in the Roman attack on Jerusalem was the Fifth Macedonian. It was levied in 43 BC and was based in the Balkan provinces of Macedonia, Moesia (Serbia) and Dacia (Romania).

The Fifth was sent to fight the Parthians in the east (62 AD), and was in the east until the Jewish Revolt. In 67, Sepphoris in Galilee and Mount Gerizim in Samaria fell to this legion. Before its attack on Jerusalem the Fifth was stationed in Emmaus where several tombstones of its soldiers remain. After the fall of Jerusalem it left Judaea and returned to Oescus (Bulgaria). In the 2nd century the Fifth was in Dacia protecting the Danube frontier. Its symbol was the bull, but the eagle was used as well. (https://en.wikipedia.org/wiki/Legio_V_Macedonica)

XII Fulminata Legion (Eastern)

Inscription in Boyukdash, (near Baku) Azerbaijan left by XII Fulminata

The Twelfth or Thunderbolt legion was levied by Julius Caesar in 58 BC. Its emblem was a thunderbolt (*fulmen*). The Twelfth was commonly stationed on the eastern frontiers of the Empire and was still guarding the Euphrates River crossing near Melitene at the beginning of the 5th century. During the latter part of Caesar Augustus' reign (died AD 14) the Twelfth served in Syria. In the Parthian War of 58–63 it with other legions was defeated by the Parthians and Armenians at the battle of Rhandeia. The legions were shamed and removed from the war theater.

In 66, after the Jewish revolt had destroyed the Roman garrison in Jerusalem, the XII Fulminata, with detachments of IV Scythica and VI Ferrata, were sent to retaliate, but was sent back by the legate of Syria when he saw that the legion was weak. On its return, XII Fulminata was ambushed and defeated by Eleazar ben Simon at Beit-Horon, and lost its eagle-standard (*aquila*). However, the Twelfth fought well in the last part of the Jewish war and supported its commander Titus in his bid for the imperial throne. At the end of the overthrow, XII Fulminata was sent to guard the Euphrates border at Melitene.
(https://en.wikipedia.org/wiki/Legio_XII_Fulminata)

XV Apollinaris Legion (European)

"Apollo's" Fifteenth Legion" was recruited by Augustus Caesar in 41/40 BC. Its emblem was probably a picture of the Greek god Apollo, or of one of his animals. It was sent to garrison Illyricum (Yugoslavia), where it probably remained until 6 BC. Thereafter it was sent to Carnuntum (Austria, between Vienna and Bratislava). The Fifteenth remained in Carnuntum until being sent to Syria and possibly Armenia by Nero in 61 or 62. After the conclusion of the war with Parthia, the legion was sent to Alexandria but soon found itself engaged in the fierce fighting of the Jewish Revolt. It was the Fifteenth that captured the Jewish general later to become famous historian Josephus.

After the suppression of the revolt, the legion returned to Carnuntum and rebuilt its fortress. Elements of the XVth fought in the Dacian Wars (Romania) although the main body of the legion remained in Pannonia (Hungary).
(https://en.wikipedia.org/wiki/Legio_XV_Apollinaris)

X Fretensis Legion (Judaea, Syria)

This Legion was also founded by Augustus Caesar (41/40 BC). In 36 BC it fought in the Battle of Naulochus and earned the name *Fretensis* (strait). The battle took place near the Strait of Messina. Various Greek gods provided the symbols under which it fought. Tiles found in Caesarea Maritima, built in the second decade BC, suggest that the legion was at that time based in Judaea. By 6 AD it was stationed in Syria. However, for almost half a century we have no evidence for the whereabouts and actions of Fretensis. Under Nero (58-63), the legion participated in the campaigns against the Parthians.

In 66, the X Fretensis and V Macedonia were sent to Alexandria for an invasion of Ethiopia planned by Nero. However, they were diverted to Judaea to suppress the Jewish revolt. In the summer of 68, X Fretensis destroyed the monastery of Qumran, where the Dead Sea Scrolls are believed to have originated. Its winter camp was at Jericho.

By 70, the rebellion in all of Judaea had been crushed, except for Jerusalem and a few fortresses, including Masada. In that year X Fretensis, in conjunction with V Macedonia, XII Fulminata, and XV Apollinaris, began the siege of Jerusalem. The Tenth camped on the Mount of Olives. During the siege they gained fame in their use of war machines. It was noted that they were able to hurl stones that weighted a talent (about 25 kg) a distance of two furlongs (400 m) or further. The projectiles of their *ballistae* caused heavy damage to the ramparts. The siege lasted five months and the besieged population experienced all the terrible rigors of starvation. Finally, the combined assaults of the legions succeeded in taking Jerusalem, which was then subjected to complete destruction.

After the fall of Jerusalem it was the Tenth with auxiliary troops that that was used in overcoming the few remaining Jewish strongholds. Most notable of these was Masada. In the autumn of 72, after demands for surrender were rejected a siege was imposed against the elevated fortress. When the Romans finally broke through the walls of the citadel, they discovered that the Jewish defenders had chosen death with a mass suicide.

After the conclusion of the Jewish revolt, the Tenth was garrisoned at Jerusalem. Their main camp was positioned on the Western Hill, located in the southern half of the old city, now leveled of all former buildings. Their camp buildings were built using the surviving portions of the walls of Herod's Palace, demolished by order of Titus. X Fretensis became the sole legion assigned to maintain the peace in Judaea. It took the lead in putting down the Bar Kokhba revolt (132-135) and remained in Jerusalem until the end of the 3rd century.
https://en.wikipedia.org/wiki/Legio_X_Fretensis

The Theory that the AD 70 Conquerors of Jeruasalem were Arabic, and that the Future Antichrist will be Muslim is Not Sustained by the Evidence

(1) Titus was born in Rome and served in Germany and Britain before leading the attack on Jerusalem. Daniel 9:26 clearly links Titus and his army to the coming Antichrist.

(2) Though Titus wanted to spare the Temple, it was by his direct command and in accord with the prophecy of Daniel 9:26 that he gave the command for *the city to be destroyed.*

(3) Titus had wanted to dedicate the Temple to the Emperor and see it transformed as a pantheon to the Greek and Roman gods.

(4) The Roman Legions that attacked Jerusalem were first and foremost *Roman* and are to be distinguished from the Auxiliaries.

(5) The banners under which the Legions fought were *Greek*, not Arabic gods.

(6) The large arch commemorating the destruction of Jerusalem is in Rome.

Consider also;

(1) Could a Muslim Antichrist obtain the technology and military might to rule the world (Rev 13:4)?

(2) Would Israel agree to a seven year covenant initiated by a Muslim Antichrist (Dan 9:27)?

(3) What 10 nations would unite and *whip the rest of the world* into submission to a Muslim Antichrist (Rev 17:12,13)?

(4) Would a Muslim Antichrist proclaim himself to be god instead of Allah (2 Thess 2:4)?

(5) Would a Muslim Antichrist **not** *worship the god of his fathers* (Dan 11:37)?

(6) Could it be said of a Muslim Antichrist that *by peace he shall destroy many* (Dan 8:25)?

We cannot leave this inquiry into the ethnicity of the conquerors of Jerusalem without giving a brief consideration of the siege itself. The Fall of Jerusalem was one of the great catastrophes of history and was an event foretold in Scripture.

The Destruction of Jerusalem in 70 AD

* *Therefore shall Zion for your sake be **plowed as a field**, and Jerusalem shall become heaps, and the mountain of the house as the high places of the forest (Micah 3:12).*

* *And when he was come near, he beheld the city, and wept over it, Saying, If thou hadst known, even thou, at least in this thy day, the things which belong unto thy peace! but now they are hid from thine eyes. For the days shall come upon thee, that thine enemies shall cast a trench about thee, and compass thee round, and keep thee in on every side, And shall **lay thee even with the ground**, and thy children within thee; and they shall not leave in thee one stone upon another; because thou knewest not the time of thy visitation (Lk 19:41-44).*

* *And as some spake of the temple, how it was adorned with goodly stones and gifts, he said, As for these things which ye behold, the days will come, in the which **there shall not be left one stone upon another**, that shall not be thrown down (Lk 21:5,6).*

The following from Wikipedia describes the horror of the event:

The Siege of Jerusalem in AD 70 was the decisive event of the First Jewish–Roman War. The Roman army, led by the future Emperor Titus, with Tiberius Julius Alexander as his second-in-command, besieged and conquered the city of Jerusalem, which had been occupied by its Jewish defenders in AD 66.

The siege ended with the sacking of the city and the destruction of its famous Second Temple. The destruction of both the first and second temples is still mourned annually as the Jewish fast Tisha B'Av. The Arch of Titus, celebrating the Roman sack of Jerusalem and the Temple, still stands in Rome.

Despite early successes in repelling the Roman sieges, the Zealots fought among themselves, and they lacked proper leadership, resulting in poor discipline, training, and preparation for the battles that were to follow.

Titus surrounded the city, with three legions(V *Macedonica*, XII *Fulminata*, XV *Apollinaris*) on the western side and a fourth (X *Fretensis*) on the Mount of Olives to the east. He put pressure on the food and water supplies of the inhabitants by allowing pilgrims to enter the city to celebrate Passover, and then refusing to allow them back out. After Jewish allies killed a number of Roman soldiers, Titus sent Josephus, the Jewish historian, to negotiate with the defenders; this ended with Jews wounding the negotiator with an arrow, and another sally was launched shortly after. Titus was almost captured during this sudden attack, but escaped.

***Catapulta*, by Edward Poynter (1868)**

In mid-May Titus set to destroying the newly built Third Wall with a ram, breaching it as well as the Second Wall, and turning his attention to the Fortress of Antonia just north of the Temple Mount. The Romans were then drawn into street fighting with the Zealots, who were then ordered to retreat to the temple to avoid heavy losses. Josephus failed in another attempt at negotiations, and Jewish attacks prevented the construction of siege towers at the Fortress of Antonia. Food, water, and other provisions were dwindling inside the city, but small foraging parties managed to sneak supplies into the city, harrying Roman forces in the process. To put an end to the foragers, orders were issued to build a new wall, and siege tower construction was restarted as well.

After several failed attempts to breach or scale the walls of the Antonia Fortress, the Romans finally launched a secret attack, overwhelming the sleeping Zealots and taking the fortress. Overlooking the Temple compound, the fortress provided a perfect point from which to attack the Temple itself. Battering rams made little progress, but the fighting itself eventually set the walls on fire; a Roman soldier threw a burning stick onto one of the Temple's walls. Destroying the Temple was not among Titus' goals, possibly due in large part to the massive expansions done by Herod the Great mere decades earlier. Titus had wanted to seize it and transform it into a temple dedicated to the Roman Emperor and the Roman pantheon. The fire spread quickly and was soon out of control. The Temple was destroyed on Tisha B'Av, in the beginning of August, and the flames spread into the residential sections of the city.

The Roman legions quickly crushed the remaining Jewish resistance. Part of the remaining Jews escaped through hidden underground tunnels, while others made a final stand in the Upper City. This defence halted the Roman advance as they had to construct siege towers to assail the remaining Jews. The city was completely under Roman control by September 7 and the Romans continued to pursue those who had fled the city.

A COMMENTARY AND SURVEY SERIES: DANIEL

(http://www.bible-history.com/archaeology/rome/arch_of_titus_menorah-copy.jpg)

Relief of the Sack of the Temple on the *Arch of Titus* in Rome

Josephus claims that 1.1 million people were killed during the siege, of which a majority were Jewish, and that 97,000 were captured and enslaved. "The slaughter within was even more dreadful than the spectacle from without. Men and women, old and young, insurgents and priests, those who fought and those who entreated mercy, were hewn down in indiscriminate carnage. The number of the slain exceeded that of the slayers. The legionaries had to clamber over heaps of dead to carry on the work of extermination."

Many fled to areas around the Mediterranean. Titus reportedly refused to accept a wreath of victory, saying that the victory did not come through his own efforts but that he had merely served as an instrument of God's wrath.
(https://en.wikipedia.org/wiki/Siege_of_Jerusalem_(AD_70)

The Daniel Chapters 7/8/9/11 Link to the *Origin* of the Coming Antichrist

(1) **The Antichrist will come from among the Ten** (Daniel 7). As the Ten Horns are clearly the same as the Ten *Roman* Toes of the great image (Daniel 2), the Antichrist will come from *among* ten powerful nations that had their origin in the Roman Empire. He does not directly come from one of the Ten, but from *among* one of these Ten.

> • *After this I saw in the night visions, and behold **a fourth beast, dreadful and terrible**, and strong exceedingly; and it had great iron teeth: it devoured and brake in pieces, and stamped the residue with the feet of it: and it was diverse from all the beasts that were before it; and **it had ten horns**. I considered the horns, and, behold, **there came up among them another little horn**, before whom there were three of the first horns plucked up by the roots: and, behold, in this horn were eyes like the eyes of man, and a mouth speaking great things (Dan 7:7,8).*

(2) **The Antichrist will come from among Four of the Ten** (Daniel 8). The Antichrist is seen coming from among the Four divisions of Alexander's Grecian Empire. These four divisions became part of the eastern half of the Roman Empire.

> • *Therefore the he goat waxed very great: and when he was strong, the great horn was broken; and for it came up **four notable ones toward the four winds of heaven**. And*

DANIEL 7. FOUR ENDTIME *BEASTS* AND THE ADVENT OF THE MESSIAH

out of one of them came forth a little horn, which waxed exceeding great, toward the *south*, and toward the *east*, and toward *the pleasant land* (Dan 8:8,9).

He is not said to come directly from one of these four divisions, but rather *out of them* (he could hardly come from *each* of the four); thus the Antichrist has a special association with the Four without necessarily coming from one of them. This could possibly mean that he is Greek Catholic (Orthodox) rather than Roman Catholic. The four regions taken by Alexander's generals were vast, but the language here indicates that their extent may ultimately be greater. They are *four notable ones toward the four winds of heaven*. Regarding the division of Alexander's domain between his generals, Unger writes.

> **Seleucus in the east** gained control of Syria, Babylonia, Media, and so on. **Cassander in the west** obtained Macedon, Thessaly, and Greece. **Ptolemy in the south** got Egypt and Cyprus, **Lysimachus in the north** came into possession of Thrace, Cappadocia, and the northern parts of Asia Minor (*Unger's Old Testament Commentary*).

In order for the Little Horn to *wax exceeding great, toward the south, and toward the east, and toward the pleasant land*, he would have to come either from the northwest of Alexander's Empire or from its north-western edge.

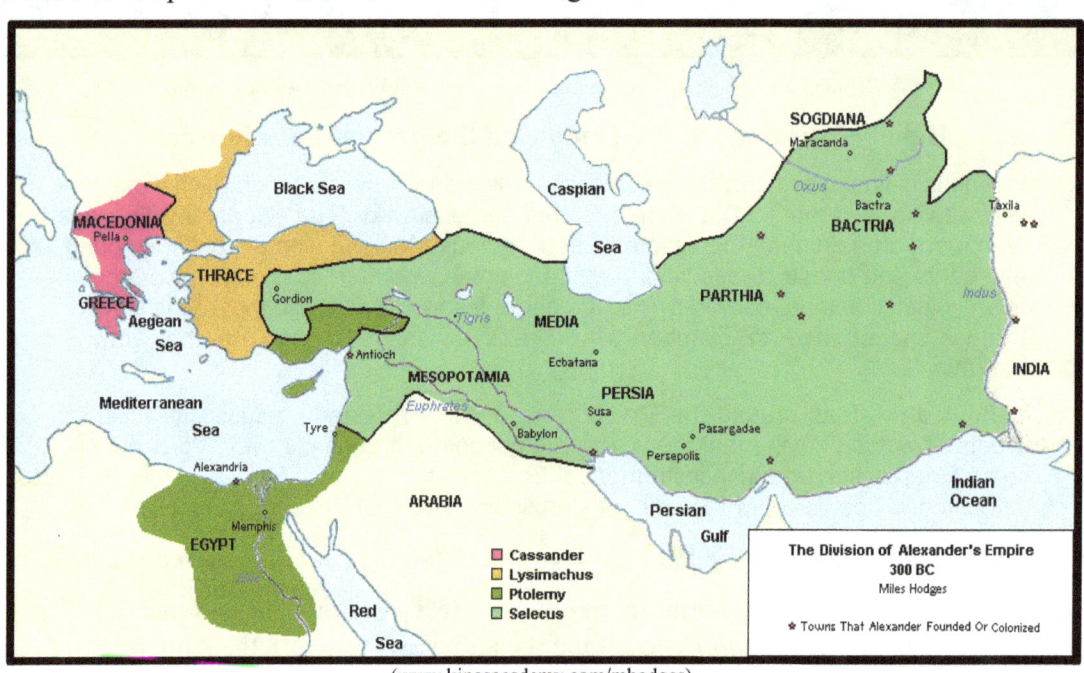

(www.kingsacademy.com/mhodges)

The Four Divisions of Alexander's Empire

(3) **The Antichrist is linked to Titus and the Legions which destroyed Jerusalem** (Daniel 9). As for Titus himself, he was born in Rome. Before leading the onslaught on Jerusalem he served in Britannicus and was a military tribune in Germania. He then joined his father Vespasian in Greece where they drew up plans for the attack on the city. The Legion usually mentioned first in the attack on the city was the Fifth Macedonian. It was based in the Balkan provinces of Macedonia, Moesia (Serbia) and Dacia (Romania). After the fall of Jerusalem it left Judaea and returned to Oescus (Bulgaria). In the 2nd century the Fifth was in Dacia protecting the Danube frontier.

The north western setting of these historical facts lend an interesting parallel to the prophecy that the Little Horn will *wax exceeding great, toward the south, and toward the east, and toward the pleasant land* (thus from the northwest). We could speculate and say that the coming Antichrist may be Orthodox rather than Catholic, and if not associated with Greece itself could be living in western Europe and perhaps Germany.

Two prominent European leaders are atheist: Hollande of France and Tsipras of Greece; also Milanovic of Croatia. Note also

> • When I have bent Judah for me, filled the bow with Ephraim, and **raised up thy sons, O Zion, against thy sons, O Greece**, and made thee as the sword of a mighty man. And the LORD shall be seen over them, and his arrow shall go forth as the lightning: and the LORD God shall blow the trumpet, and shall go with whirlwinds of the south (Zech 9:13,14).

(4) The Antichrist is distinguished from the King of the North and the King of the South (Daniel 11). Some have thought that the Little Horn will rise out of Syria and be the final King of the North. Daniel 11 foretells the breakup of Alexander's empire and the ongoing struggles over the next several centuries between Syria (the King of the North, the Seleucids) and Egypt (the King of the South, the Ptolemy's). At the end of the age the *Willful King*, the Antichrist is clearly distinguished from the Kings of the North and South. They both attempt to fight against him (Dan 11:40).

> (11:36) And **the king shall do according to his will**; and he shall exalt himself, and **magnify himself above every god**, and shall speak marvellous things against the God of gods, and shall prosper till the indignation be accomplished: for that that is determined shall be done. (11:37) **Neither shall he regard the God of his fathers, nor the desire of women**, nor regard any god: for he shall magnify himself above all. (11:38) But in his estate shall he honour the God of forces: and a god whom his fathers knew not shall he honour with gold, and silver, and with precious stones, and pleasant things. (11:39) Thus shall he do in the most strong holds with a strange god, whom he shall acknowledge and increase with glory: and he shall cause them to rule over many, and shall divide the land for gain. (11:40) And **at the time of the end shall the king of the south push at him**: and **the king of the north shall come against him** like a whirlwind, with chariots, and with horsemen, and with many ships; and he shall enter into the countries, and shall overflow and pass over. (11:41) **He shall enter also into the glorious land**, and many countries shall be overthrown: but these shall escape out of his hand, even Edom, and Moab, and the chief of the children of Ammon. (11:42) He shall stretch forth his hand also upon the countries: and the land of Egypt shall not escape. (11:43) But he shall have power over the treasures of gold and of silver, and over all the precious things of Egypt: and the Libyans and the Ethiopians shall be at his steps. (11:44) But tidings out of the east and out of the north shall trouble him: therefore he shall go forth with great fury to destroy, and utterly to make away many. (11:45) And **he shall plant the tabernacles of his palace between the seas in the glorious holy mountain**; yet he shall come to his end, and none shall help him.

We have now considered the likely relation of the Antichrist the (Little Horn), to the Ten Horns of this Fourth Beast. Before our vista changes to Someone and Something infinitely *higher* (Daniel 7:9), two further features are given concerning the Little Horn. Previously we commented on his *diminutiveness*. He is in fact called *the Little* Horn. He will apparently come from a less significant country (not one of the ten *horns*). He will not be someone that people "have been looking for some time." As we have seen, his lineage and physical appearance will not be what was said of King Saul. He will not be *head and shoulders* over everyone. It will be something else that will make him a *towering personality*. His **eyes and mouth** are here mentioned.

> And, behold, in this horn were eyes like the eyes of man, and a mouth speaking great things (7:8).

The devil has sent three beasts into the Mediterranean region to prevent the re-establishment of Israel as a nation whereby Christ will return and rule on David's throne, but while they are still trying, they have not been successful. The Devil now sends his master stroke. A fourth beast appears, and one that is totally energized by Satan. The Little Horn that rules over this empire is practically an incarnation of Satan. It is this that removes the *little* and makes him a towering personality.

> • *Woe to the inhabiters of the earth and of the sea! for the devil is come down unto you, having great wrath, because he knoweth that he hath but a short time (Rev 12:12).*

> • *And **his mouth** as the mouth of a lion: and **the dragon gave him his power**, and his seat, and great authority . . . and all the world wondered after the beast. And they worshipped **the dragon which gave power unto the beast**: and they worshipped the beast, saying, Who is like unto the beast? who is able to make war with him? And there was given unto him **a mouth speaking great things and blasphemies**; and power was given unto him to continue forty and two months (Rev 13:2-5).*

> • *I beheld then because of the voice of **the great words which the horn spake** (Dan. 7:11).*

> • *And **he shall speak great words** against the most High, and shall wear out the saints of the most High, and think to change times and laws (Dan 7:25).*

As for his *eyes*: Eyes express intelligence (Ezek 1:18); so the serpent's promise was that man's *eyes would be opened*, if he would but rebel against God (Gen 3:5). The Antichrist will be the consummation godless wisdom begun at the fall (*JFB*). He will be the supreme example of wicked and godless intelligence. It is this that will give him *his look*.

> • *And of the ten horns that were in his head, and of the other which came up, and before whom three fell; even of that horn that **had eyes**, and a mouth that spake very great things, **whose look was more stout than his fellows** (Dan 7:20).*

When we come to Chapter 8 we will see some of the further characteristics of this *man of sin* that will be revealed after the Rapture (2 Thess 2:3,7). For example:

> • *And in the latter time of their kingdom, when the transgressors are come to the full, a king of **fierce countenance**, and **understanding dark sentences**, shall stand up. And **his power shall be mighty**, but not by his own power: and he **shall destroy wonderfully**, and **shall prosper**, and practise, and shall destroy the mighty and the holy people. And through his policy also he shall **cause craft to prosper** in his hand; and he shall **magnify himself in his heart**, and **by peace shall destroy many**: he **shall also stand up against the Prince of princes**; but he shall be broken without hand (Dan 8:23-25).*

Daniel in Chapter 7 saw things on earth, but he also saw things in Heaven. And, here in the next verse we go from unimaginable depths to unutterable heights.

The Ancient of Days and the Son of Man 7:9-14.

I beheld till the thrones were cast down, and the Ancient of days did sit, whose garment was white as snow, and the hair of his head like the pure wool: his throne was like the fiery flame, and his wheels as burning fire. (7:10) A fiery stream issued and came forth from before him: thousand thousands ministered unto him, and ten thousand times ten thousand stood before him: the judgment was set, and the books were opened. (7:11) I beheld then because of the voice of the great words which the horn spake: I beheld even till the beast was slain, and his body destroyed, and given to the burning flame. (7:12) As concerning the rest of the beasts, they had their dominion taken away: yet their lives were prolonged for a season and time. (7:13) I saw in the night visions, and, behold, one like the Son of man came with the clouds of heaven, and came to the Ancient of days, and they brought him near before him. (7:14) And there was given him dominion, and glory, and a kingdom, that all people, nations, and languages, should serve him: his dominion is an everlasting dominion, which shall not pass away, and his kingdom that which shall not be destroyed.

Now men have their day, and every pretender thinks he should have his day and struggles for it. But, *He that sits in heaven laughs at them,* for he sees that *his day is coming,*

(Psa 37:13). No matter how formidable the forces of evil may be, everything launched against Christ, the Bible, believers in Christ and Israel – will come to an end. Here in Daniel 7 is a description of that end which is set out in many passages of Scripture.

> • *For they are the spirits of devils, working miracles, which go forth unto the kings of the earth and of the whole world,* **to gather them to the battle of that great day of God Almighty** *(Rev 16:14).*

> • *And the seventh angel sounded; and there were great voices in heaven, saying,* **The kingdoms of this world are become the kingdoms of our Lord, and of his Christ**; *and he shall reign for ever and ever (Rev 11:15).*

The Destruction of the Horns and Their Thrones. *I beheld till the thrones were cast down* (7:9). As Daniel watched this fourth terrible beast stand upon the earth with its ten horns pointing in all directions, He saw that the horns met an end and were broken off, signifying that the ten-nation federation which gave the Antichrist and his empire its authority was destroyed. By whom were they destroyed? Certainly, not by earthly power because we read in Revelation 13 that no one on earth during the last half of the Tribulation could *make war with the beast* (Rev 13:4). The ten-nation alliance is destroyed by the Lord Jesus Christ; and He now appears. These kings were greatly elated to be beckoned by the Beast to their lofty thrones. Little did they realise how *short-lived* it would be!

> • *And the ten horns which thou sawest are ten kings, which have received no kingdom as yet; but* **receive power as kings one hour** *with the beast (Rev 17:12).*

> • *That the triumphing of the wicked* **is** *short, and the joy of the hypocrite but for* **a moment** *(Job 20:5)?*

The Appearance of the Father. ***And the Ancient of days did sit, whose garment was white as snow, and the hair of his head like the pure wool: his throne was like the fiery flame, and his wheels as burning fire*** (7:9).

The Throne Upon Which He is Sitting. Here the Eternal God is sitting. We have had enough of the Ten Horns reigning one hour with the Beast. Here we have an entirely different kind of throne. In the midst of the convulsions and revolutions of states and kingdoms, it is comforting to know that there is another kind of Throne, where another King sits.

> • *The Lord has prepared his throne in the heavens and his kingdom ruleth over all (Ps. 103:19).*

> • *So that a man shall say, Verily there is a reward for the righteous: verily he is a God that judgeth in the earth (Psa 58:11).*

The Name by Which He is Presented. He is *the Ancient of days.* He is God *from everlasting to everlasting* (Psa 90:2). Among men we reckon that *with the ancient is wisdom,* and *length of days is understanding* (Job 12:12). That being the case, shall not all flesh then be *silent* before Him who is *the Ancient of days?* He now sits as Judge. There is no recourse to a court of higher appeal.

> • *The eternal God is thy refuge, and underneath are the everlasting arms: and he shall thrust out the enemy from before thee; and shall say, Destroy them (Deut 33:27).*

> • *But the LORD is in his holy temple: let all the earth keep silence before him (Hab 2:20).*

The Righteousness of His Judgements.

As Demonstrated by His Judicial Robe. It is a ***garment*** that is ***white as snow***, hereby denoting righteousness in all the administrations that He undertakes and is about to undertake. This is *now* about to be demonstrated. It is *now* to *go forward.* Judicial robes here below are dark; there they are white. His judgements are not as man's.

DANIEL 7. FOUR ENDTIME *BEASTS* AND THE ADVENT OF THE MESSIAH

> • Therefore **the law is slacked, and judgment doth never go forth**: for the wicked doth compass about the righteous; therefore wrong judgment proceedeth (Hab 1:4).

As Demonstrated by His Countenance. The sagacity of the execution of His wrath is evidenced by **the hair of his head like the pure wool**. His knowledge of man's sin goes back to the beginning. He needs none to gather evidence on His behalf. He has perfect recall of everything that has happened. He has seen all that was done in the *open* and all in *secret*, even to the thoughts of the heart.

> • In the day when **God shall judge the secrets of men by Jesus Christ** according to my gospel (Rom 2:16).

> • **Can any hide himself in secret places that I shall not see him?** saith the LORD. Do not I fill heaven and earth? saith the LORD (Jer 23:24).

As Demonstrated By the Source of the Burnings. *His throne was like the fiery flame, and his wheels as burning fire. A fiery stream issued and came forth from before him* (7:9,10). The throne is very formidable. It is *like the fiery flame,* dreadful to the wicked that shall be summoned before it and to those who will be punished from it. The wrath that will engulf the earth when it *burns like an oven* (Mal 4:1), will come from *His Throne*. For all the faithful, there *proceeds out of the throne of God and the Lamb a pure river of water of life* (Rev. 22:1), so to all his implacable enemies there *issues and comes forth from* His throne a *fiery stream, a stream of brimstone* (Isa 30:33), a *fire* that shall *devour before him.*

The *wheels* of God's chariots are mentioned in connection with His Throne. They are *as burning fire* to devour all in their path with *everlasting burnings* (Isa 33:14). Here is a judgement that will fly to the most distant parts of the earth. Compare the Lord's angelic chariots is Psalms and Isaiah with His Throne-chariot and its wheels in Ezekiel.

> • The **chariots of God are twenty thousand**, even thousands of angels: the Lord is among them, as in Sinai, in the holy place (Psa 68:17).

> • For, behold, **the Lord will come with fire, and with his chariots like a whirlwind**, to render his anger with fury, and his rebuke with flames of fire. For by fire and by his sword will the Lord plead with all flesh: and the slain of the Lord shall be many (Isa 66:15,16).

> • And Elisha prayed, and said, LORD, I pray thee, open his eyes, that he may see. And the LORD opened the eyes of the young man; and he saw: and, behold, the mountain was full of horses and **chariots of fire** round about Elisha (2 Kng 6:17).

> • As for **their rings**, they were so high that they were dreadful; and **their rings were full of eyes** round about them four. And when the living creatures went, **the wheels** went by them: and when the living creatures were lifted up from the earth, the wheels were lifted up. Whithersoever the spirit was to go, they went, thither was their spirit to go; and **the wheels** were lifted up over against them: for **the spirit of the living creature was in the wheels** (Ezek 1:18-20).

> • And it came to pass, that when he had commanded the man clothed with linen, saying, **Take fire from between the wheels**, from between the cherubims; then he went in, and stood beside **the wheels**. And one cherub stretched forth his hand from between the cherubims unto the fire that was between the cherubims, and took thereof, and put it into the hands of him that was clothed with linen: who took it, and went out. And there appeared in the cherubims the form of a man's hand under their wings. And when I looked, behold **the four wheels** by the cherubims, **one wheel** by one cherub, and **another wheel** by another cherub: and the appearance of the wheels was as the colour of a beryl stone. And as for their appearances, they four had one likeness, as if **a wheel had been in the midst of a wheel**. When they went, they went upon their four sides; they turned not as they went, but to the place whither the head looked they followed it; they turned not as they went. And their whole body, and their backs, and their hands, and their wings, and **the wheels, were full of eyes** round about, even the

wheels that they four had. **As for the wheels, it was cried unto them in my hearing, O wheel** *(Ezek 10:6-13).*

Here we understand the Scripture that says *Our God is a consuming fire* (Heb 12:29). Here is the source of the flames which shall shortly engulf the earth during the Tribulation, and which is so often stated in Scripture.

- *Thou shalt make them as **a fiery oven** in the time of thine anger: the LORD shall swallow them up in his wrath, and **the fire shall devour them** (Psa 21:9).*

- *The earth also is defiled under the inhabitants thereof; because they have transgressed the laws, changed the ordinance, broken the everlasting covenant. Therefore hath the curse devoured the earth, and they that dwell therein are desolate: therefore **the inhabitants of the earth are burned, and few men left** (Isa 24:4,5).*

- *Thou shalt be visited of the LORD of hosts with thunder, and with earthquake, and great noise, with storm and tempest, and **the flame of devouring fire** (Isa 29:6).*

- *For, behold, **the LORD will come with fire**, and with his chariots like a whirlwind, to render his anger with fury, and his rebuke with **flames of fire**. For **by fire** and by his sword will the LORD plead with all flesh: and the slain of the LORD shall be many (Isa 66:15,16).*

- *But the day of the Lord will come as a thief in the night; in the which the heavens shall pass away with a great noise, and **the elements shall melt with fervent heat, the earth also and the works that are therein shall be burned up** (2 Pet 3:10).*

- *The first angel sounded, and there followed hail and fire mingled with blood, and they were cast upon the earth: and **the third part of trees was burnt up, and all green grass was burnt up** (Rev 8:7).*

- *And the fourth angel poured out his vial upon the sun; and power was given unto him to **scorch men with fire. And men were scorched with great** heat, and blasphemed the name of God, which hath power over these plagues: and they repented not to give him glory (Rev 16:8,9).*

<u>The Multitude of His Attendants</u>. ***Thousand thousands ministered unto him, and ten thousand times ten thousand stood before him: the judgment was set, and the books were opened*** (7:10). The attendants are numerous and very splendid. Both groups, those *ministering* and *standing* are thought to be the same, i.e. the redeemed who are the attendants and witnesses to the coming judgements (1 Cor 6:2). The scene is connected with that of Revelation 5 and should also be compared with the great gathering before the Throne in Revelation 7.

- *And I saw in the right hand of him that sat on the throne a book written within and on the backside, sealed with seven seals. And I saw a strong angel proclaiming with a loud voice, Who is worthy to open the book, and to loose the seals thereof? And no man in heaven, nor in earth, neither under the earth, was able to open the book, neither to look thereon. And I wept much, because no man was found worthy to open and to read the book, neither to look thereon. And one of the elders saith unto me, Weep not: behold, the Lion of the tribe of Juda, the Root of David, hath prevailed to open the book, and to loose the seven seals thereof. And I beheld, and, lo, in the midst of the throne and of the four beasts, and in the midst of the elders, stood a Lamb as it had been slain, having seven horns and seven eyes, which are the seven Spirits of God sent forth into all the earth. And he came and took the book out of the right hand of him that sat upon the throne (Rev 5:1-7).*

- *After this I beheld, and, lo, **a great multitude, which no man could number, of all nations, and kindreds, and people, and tongues, stood before the throne**, and before the Lamb, clothed with white robes, and palms in their hands; And cried with a loud voice, saying, Salvation to our God which sitteth upon the throne, and unto the Lamb. And all the angels stood round about the throne, and about the elders and the four beasts, and **fell before the throne on their faces, and worshipped God**, Saying, Amen: Blessing, and glory, and wisdom, and thanksgiving, and honour, and power,*

DANIEL 7. FOUR ENDTIME *BEASTS* AND THE ADVENT OF THE MESSIAH

and might, be unto our God for ever and ever. Amen. And one of the elders answered, saying unto me, **What are these** *which are arrayed in white robes? and whence came they? And I said unto him, Sir, thou knowest. And he said to me,* **These are they which came out of great tribulation, and have washed their robes, and made them white in the blood of the Lamb** *(Rev 7:9-14).*

Note: Those *standing* in this vast assembly before the throne will not be standing for long, for along with the believers caught up in the Pretribulational Rapture, vast multitudes will return with Christ to earth for His Millennial Reign.

- *The LORD my God shall come, and all the saints with thee (Zech 14:5).*
- *Behold, the Lord cometh with ten thousands of his saints (Jude 14).*

The Judgement here described is in the broadest perspective that of the destruction of Gentile world power (Dan 2:34,35). This is a judgement which in four stages will take place before the Millennial Reign can be established.

(1) The Judgement upon the Antichrist as head of the ten-horned empire (Dan 7:11,12: Rev 16:10; 19:19-21).

(2) The Judgement and Salvation of Israel (Ezek 20:33-44; Matt 25:1-11; Rom 11:26).

(3) The Judgement of the Nations (Matt 25:31-41). This includes both the military at Armageddon (Rev 16:16-13) and the non-military (Rev 19:11-20).

(4) The Judgement of Satan, demons and the satanic world system (Rev 20:1-3; 1 Cor 6:2,3)

The Doom of the Little Horn.

He is Slain. *I beheld then because of the voice of the great words which the horn spake: I beheld even till the beast was slain, and his body destroyed, and given to the burning flame* (7:11). The Antichrist will have his day during the Tribulation but it will be a short one. His words, deeds and followers will come to an ignominious end. *Great words* are but *idle words* for which men must give account in the *great day*. And see now where it all ends for this beast that has talked so big. Does the mouth of the enemy *speak great things?* Here are far greater things which the mouth of the Lord has spoken.

- *And there was given unto him* **a mouth speaking great things and blasphemies;** *and power was given unto him to continue forty and two months. And* **he opened his mouth in blasphemy** *against God, to blaspheme his name, and his tabernacle, and them that dwell in heaven (Rev 13:5,6).*

- *And I saw* **the beast, and the kings of the earth,** *and their armies, gathered together* **to make war against him that sat on the horse,** *and against his army. And the beast was taken, and with him the false prophet that wrought miracles before him, with which he deceived them that had received the mark of the beast, and them that worshipped his image. These both were* **cast alive into a lake of fire burning with brimstone.** *And the remnant were slain with the sword of him that sat upon the horse, which sword proceeded out of his mouth: and all the fowls were filled with their flesh (Rev 19:19-21).*

His Kingdom is Vanquished. *As concerning the rest of the beasts, they had their dominion taken away: yet their lives were prolonged for a season and time* (7:12). While judgement will fall during the Tribulation upon great swaths of the world's population, and that to the extent that a *few men are left* (Isa 24:6); yet here as in Psalm 2 and Zephaniah 3 there is a window of opportunity for mercy. Some additional time is given to **the rest of the beasts** (the lion, bear and leopard). Note this in two extended passages:

- **I have cut off the nations**: *their towers are desolate; I made their streets waste, that none passeth by: their cities are destroyed, so that there is no man, that there is none*

> inhabitant. I said, **Surely thou wilt fear me**, thou wilt receive instruction; so their dwelling should not be cut off, howsoever I punished them: but they rose early, and corrupted all their doings. **Therefore wait ye upon me**, saith the LORD, until the day that I rise up to the prey: **for my determination is to gather the nations**, that I may assemble the kingdoms, to pour upon them mine indignation, even all my fierce anger: **for all the earth shall be devoured with the fire of my jealousy. For then will I turn to the people a pure language**, that they may all call upon the name of the LORD, to serve him with one consent (Zeph 3:6-9).
>
> • **Why do the heathen rage**, and the people imagine a vain thing? (2:2) The kings of the earth set themselves, and the rulers take counsel together, against the LORD, and against his anointed, saying, Let us break their bands asunder, and cast away their cords from us. **He that sitteth in the heavens shall laugh**: the LORD shall have them in derision. Then shall he speak unto them in his wrath, and vex them in his sore displeasure. **Yet have I set my king upon my holy hill of Zion**. I will declare the decree: the LORD hath said unto me, Thou art my Son; this day have I begotten thee. Ask of me, and I shall give thee the heathen for thine inheritance, and the uttermost parts of the earth for thy possession. **Thou shalt break them with a rod of iron**; thou shalt dash them in pieces like a potter's vessel. **Be wise now therefore, O ye kings**: be instructed, ye judges of the earth. Serve the LORD with fear, and rejoice with trembling. **Kiss the Son, lest he be angry**, and ye perish from the way, when his wrath is kindled but a little. Blessed are all they that put their trust in him (Psa 2:1-12).

<u>The Coming of the Son of Man.</u>

<u>His Investiture</u>. *I saw in the night visions, and, behold, one like the Son of man came with the clouds of heaven, and came to the Ancient of days, and they brought him near before him* (7:13).

The Dark Times. It is seen in **the night visions**. The entirety of Daniel 7 has been a night vision (7:1). It has been of earth's darkest midnight. But above there is light and shortly that light will be seen on earth. Then the world will know the fullness of what Christ said when He came the first time:

> • I am the light of the world (Jhn 8:12).

The Name Given. ***And, behold, one like the Son of man.*** The Messiah is here called the *Son of man*, for he was *made in the likeness of sinful flesh* (Rom 8:3), and was *found in fashion as a man* (Phil 2: 5-8). He thusly became *the Mediator between God and man* (1 Tim 2:5,6). He is *like unto the son of man*, but is indeed the *Son of God*. Our Saviour plainly refers to this vision when He said to the religious leaders that the *Father* has therefore *given him authority to execute judgment* because He is *the Son of man* (Jhn 5:27). He is the One whom Daniel saw in vision and to whom a *kingdom* and *dominion* were to be given. This name, the *Son of man*, is the Name under which the Eternal Son of God, now incarnate (Jhn 1:14) restores to man all that the first man, Adam, lost.

Yet, though He bears this title, and though He is distinguished from the Father, *the Ancient of Days*, His descriptions given elsewhere show how much like the Father He is, even to the extent of being called *the Mighty God, the Everlasting Father* in Isaiah 9:7. Therefore we see the *oneness* of Persons in the Godhead, and yet at the same time their *distinction*. It is He alone who could open the seals to the Title Deed of the earth (Rev 5), and come to righteously take to Himself the earth's dominion (Dan 7:14).

> • And in the midst of the seven candlesticks one like unto **the Son of man**, clothed with a garment down to the foot, and girt about the paps with a golden girdle. **His head and his hairs were white like wool**, as white as snow; and **his eyes** were as a flame of fire; And **his feet** like unto fine brass, as if they burned in a furnace; and **his voice** as the sound of many waters (Rev 1:13-15).

DANIEL 7. FOUR ENDTIME *BEASTS* AND THE ADVENT OF THE MESSIAH

• *I and my Father are one. Then the Jews took up stones again to stone him (Jhn 10:30,31).*

• *Philip saith unto him, Lord, **shew us the Father**, and it sufficeth us. Jesus saith unto him, Have I been so long time with you, and yet hast thou not known me, Philip? **he that hath seen me hath seen the Father**; and how sayest thou then, Shew us the Father? Believest thou not that **I am in the Father, and the Father in me**? the words that I speak unto you I speak not of myself: but the Father that dwelleth in me, he doeth the works. Believe me that **I am in the Father, and the Father in me**: or else believe me for the very works' sake (Jhn 14:8-11).*

The Attending Clouds. He **came with the clouds of heaven**. The *four beasts came up from the sea* (Dan 7:2). The empires of the world come from the murky depths, but Christ's kingdom is from above: *The heavens do rule* (Dan 4:26). He is the *Lord from heaven* (I Cor 15:47). These are the Shekanah, or the *presence* clouds which attend the presence of Deity. They are the clouds that filled the Tabernacle (Exod 40:3,4), and the Temple (1 Kng 8:10). In His First Coming He descended, as it where, *in the clouds of heaven,* or the One who came is *God manifest in the flesh* (1Tim 3:16). Compare:

• *And the angel answered and said unto her, The Holy Ghost shall come upon thee, and **the power of the Highest shall overshadow thee**: therefore also that holy thing which shall be born of thee shall be called the Son of God (Lk 1:35).*

• *And suddenly there was with the angel **a multitude of the heavenly host** praising God, and saying, Glory to God in the highest, and on earth peace, good will toward men (Lk 2:13,14).*

When he returned to the Father the eye of his disciples followed Him until *a cloud received him out of their sight* (Acts 1:9). As Matthew Henty said "He made that cloud his chariot, wherein he rode triumphantly to the upper world." At the Rapture and the Return to earth seven years later, there will be *clouds*, for the Christ who is coming is *God* (Zech 14:5; Titus 2:13).

• *For **the Lord himself shall descend from heaven** with a shout, with the voice of the archangel, and with the trump of God: and the dead in Christ shall rise first: Then we which are alive and remain **shall be caught up together with them in the clouds**, to meet the Lord in the air: and so shall we ever be with the Lord (1 Thess 4:16,17).*

• ***Behold, he cometh with clouds**; and every eye shall see him, and they also which pierced him: and all kindreds of the earth shall wail because of him. Even so, Amen (Rev 1:7).*

The Presentation to the Father. **And they brought him near before him** (7:13). At His Investiture, He comes before the Father with clouds of glory; for He is the eternal God, the eternal Son of God. Though taking humanity into union with Deity the Father has long bid Him to *come near*. The Son was *in the bosom of the Father* from past eternity (Jhn 1:18). His work on the behalf of sinners was so completely accepted that Heaven sent an angel to remove the stone on the morning of His Resurrection (Matt 28:3). Angels were also sent to bring Him to Heaven at His Ascension (Acts 1:9-11). And, once ascended He was made to sit down on *the right hand of the Father*. As He draws near, we in Him draw near.

• *So then after the Lord had spoken unto them, he was received up into heaven, and **sat on the right hand of God** (Mk 16:19).*

• *Having therefore, brethren, boldness to enter into the holiest by the blood of Jesus, By a new and living way, which **he hath consecrated for us, through the veil**, that is to say, his flesh (Heb 10:19,20).*

• *But this man, after he had offered one sacrifice for sins for ever, **sat down on the right hand of God; From henceforth expecting till his enemies be made his footstool** (Heb 10:12,13).*

The long appointed time has now come when *his enemies will be made His footstool*, and when *the kingdoms of this world will become the kingdoms of our Lord and of His Christ* (Rev. 12:9). To mark the enormity of what is about to happen the Bible says: **They brought him near before him** (7:13).

His Kingdom. ***And there was given him dominion, and glory, and a kingdom, that all people, nations, and languages, should serve him: his dominion is an everlasting dominion, which shall not pass away, and his kingdom that which shall not be destroyed*** (7:14). Let the nations rage if they want, God will *set his King upon his holy hill of Zion* (Psa 2:6). Nebuchadnezzar saw it as *stone cut out of the mountain without hands* (2:34,45); that it would *smite the image on the feet* (2:34) and that it would *fill the whole earth* (2:35). What has long been called the *Lord's Prayer* is now answered.

- Its First Petition: *Thy kingdom come. Thy will be done on earth, as it is in heaven* (Matt 6:10).

- Its Closing Affirmation: *For thine is the kingdom, and the power, and the glory, for ever. Amen* (Matt 6:13).

The Righteous Glory of Christ's Kingdom. ***And there was given him dominion, and glory, and a kingdom.*** The glory of all previous sovereigns has been a tarnished glory. No head of state has ruled with absolute righteousness over their dominion. There is here the Investiture for One who will so reign.

- *Behold, a king shall reign in righteousness, and princes shall rule in judgment (Isa 32:1).*

- *Behold, the days come, saith the LORD, that I will raise unto David a righteous Branch, and a King shall reign and prosper, and shall execute judgment and justice in the earth (Jer 23:5).*

The Endless Extent of Christ's Kingdom. ***That all people, nations, and languages, should serve him.*** The reign of Christ will be absolute. All resistance will be put down before the Millennial Reign begins (Psa 10:16); all rebellion will be vanquished at the end of the Millennial Reign (Rev 20:7-10). Christ's Kingdom will extend and continue to extend throughout the New Heavens and the New Earth. The rule of all previous sovereigns has been riddled with rebellion and dissent. They have never been served by *all people, nations, and languages*. There is here the Investiture for One who will so reign.

- ***All the ends of the world*** *shall remember and turn unto the LORD: and* ***all the kindreds of the nations*** *shall worship before thee (Psa 22:27).*

- *Say unto God, How terrible art thou in thy works! through the greatness of thy power shall thine enemies submit themselves unto thee.* ***All the earth*** *shall worship thee, and shall sing unto thee; they shall sing to thy name. Selah (Psa 66:3,4).*

- *O let* ***the nations*** *be glad and sing for joy: for thou shalt judge the people righteously, and govern* ***the nations*** *upon earth. Selah (Psa 67:4).*

- *Wherefore God also hath highly exalted him, and given him a name which is above every name: That at the name of Jesus* ***every knee should bow****, of things in heaven, and things in earth, and things under the earth; And that* ***every tongue should confess*** *that Jesus Christ is Lord, to the glory of God the Father (Phil 2:9-11).*

- ***Of the increase of his government and peace there shall be no end****, upon the throne of David, and upon his kingdom, to order it, and to establish it with judgment and with justice from henceforth even for ever. The zeal of the LORD of hosts will perform this (Isa 9:7).*

- *For, behold,* ***I create new heavens and a new earth****: and the former shall not be remembered, nor come into mind (Isa 65:17).*

DANIEL 7. FOUR ENDTIME *BEASTS* AND THE ADVENT OF THE MESSIAH

• *And the city had no need of the sun, neither of the moon, to shine in it: for the glory of God did lighten it, and the Lamb is the light thereof. And **the nations** of them which are saved shall walk in the light of it: and **the kings** of the earth do bring their glory and honour into it (Rev 21:23,24).*

The Everlasting Tenure of Christ's Kingdom. ***His dominion is an everlasting dominion, which shall not pass away, and his kingdom that which shall not be destroyed*** (7:14). His *dominion* shall not *pass away* to any successor, much less to any invader. All other kingdoms *have come to a period.* The most powerful kingdom the world has known (and is about to know!), the kingdom of the Antichrist, will last in its zenith for 42 months (Rev 13:5). The horns who made the Beast their lord are said to reign only *one hour* (Rev 17:12). Our Lord's Kingdom will extend and remain *forever* throughout the New Jerusalem, the New Earth and the New Heaven (Rev 21:1). The contrast could not be greater:

• *Thus saith the Lord GOD; **Remove the diadem, and take off the crown**: this shall not be the same: exalt him that is low, and abase him that is high. **I will overturn, overturn**, overturn, it: and it shall be no more, **until he come whose right it is**; and I will give it him (Ezek 21:26,27).*

• *The LORD is King **for ever and ever**: the heathen are perished out of his land*

(Psa 10:16).

• *Thy throne, O God, is **for ever and ever**: the sceptre of thy kingdom is a right sceptre (Psa 45:6).*

• *Then will I cause you to dwell in this place, in the land that I gave to your fathers, **for ever and ever** (Jer 7:7).*

• *But the saints of the most High shall take the kingdom, and possess the kingdom for ever, even **for ever and ever** (Dan 7:18).*

• *And he shall reign over the house of Jacob **for ever**; and of his kingdom **there shall be no end** (Lk 1:33).*

• *Unto him be glory in the church by Christ Jesus **throughout all ages, world without end**. Amen (Eph 3:21).*

• *But unto the Son he saith, Thy throne, O God, is **for ever and ever**: a sceptre of righteousness is the sceptre of thy kingdom (Heb 1:8).*

• *And hath made us kings and priests unto God and his Father; to him be glory and dominion **for ever and ever**. Amen (Rev 1:6).*

• *The kingdoms of this world are become the kingdoms of our Lord, and of his Christ; and he shall reign **for ever and ever** (Rev 11:15).*

• *And there shall be no night there; and they need no candle, neither light of the sun; for the Lord God giveth them light: and they shall reign **for ever and ever** (Rev 22:5).*

• *Of the increase of his government and peace there shall be no end (Isa 9:7).*

The Four Recountings of Daniels Vision in Chapter 7

It will now be noted that Daniel's vision is stated four times. The first account in which he receives the vision is the fullest; but the three restatements add additional information.

(1) Daniel receives the vision, 7:1-14.

(2) Daniel inquires and is answered concerning the vision generally, 7:15-18.

(3) Daniel inquires concerning the fourth beast and little horn specifically 7:19-22.

(4) Daniel is answered concerning the fourth beast and little horn 7:23-28

The First Inquiry and Answer: The Four Beasts Generally 7:15-18.

I Daniel was grieved in my spirit in the midst of my body, and the visions of my head troubled me. (7:16) I came near unto one of them that stood by, and asked him the truth of all this. So he told me, and made me know the interpretation of the things. (7:17) These great beasts, which are four, are four kings, which shall arise out of the earth. (7:18) But the saints of the most High shall take the kingdom, and possess the kingdom for ever, even for ever and ever.

The Prophet's Perplexity.

His Grief. ***I Daniel was grieved in my spirit in the midst of my body, and the visions of my head troubled me*** (7:15). Although Daniel has set down in detail the main features of the vision, he confessed his lack of understanding of what he saw and his great foreboding at what was implied in the rise of these four beasts and especially the fourth. If this vision, as most interpret it, was only a restatement of the four great empires of Chapter 2, Daniel would not have been in this state of mind; for as we have seen the identity of three of these beasts have been previously given. Here we see also that the Old Testament prophets did not necessarily understand what they prophesied. Compare the following.

> • *Of which salvation the prophets have **enquired and searched diligently**, who prophesied of the grace that should come unto you: **Searching what, or what manner of time** the Spirit of Christ which was in them did signify, when it testified beforehand the sufferings of Christ, and the glory that should follow. Unto whom it was revealed, that not unto themselves, but unto us they did minister the things, which are now reported unto you by them that have preached the gospel unto you with the Holy Ghost sent down from heaven; which things the angels desire to look into (1 Peter 1:10-12).*

His Inquiry. ***I came near unto one of them that stood by, and asked him the truth of all this. So he told me, and made me know the interpretation of the things*** (7:16). The identity of the one who helped Daniel is not made known, but we assume it was an angel. We know that an angelic guide aided the Apostle John in the book of Revelation; as also did an angel for the Prophet Zechariah (cp. Rev 1:1; Zech 2:3,4).

The Angel's Assistance.

Concerning the Beasts. ***These great beasts, which are four, are four kings, which shall arise out of the earth*** (7:17). Note again, *they shall arise*. Thus it could not be Babylon, Persia or Greece as in Chapter 2, for they had already arisen. These are four empires (British speaking, Russian speaking, Arabic speaking and a fourth under Antichrist) that will prowl the Mediterranean Sea during the last days and especially during the Tribulation. They are clearly *empires*, yet here it emphasises the *kings* who ruled over them. It is when these kings throw their lot in with the Beast (the Antichrist) and are *subsumed* by him, that they become *beasts* in the full sense. Note again how the *lion*, *bear* and *leopard* become a composite part of the Antichrist's Empire.

> • *And I stood upon the sand of the sea, and saw a beast rise up out of the sea, having seven heads and ten horns, and upon his horns ten crowns, and upon his heads the name of blasphemy. And the beast which I saw was like unto a **leopard**, and his feet were as the feet of a **bear**, and his mouth as the mouth of a **lion**: and the dragon gave him his power, and his seat, and great authority. And I saw one of his heads as it were wounded to death; and his deadly wound was healed: and all the world wondered after the beast (Rev 13:1-3).*

Concerning the Saints. ***But the saints of the most High shall take the kingdom, and possess the kingdom for ever, even for ever and ever*** (7:18). The interpreter informed Daniel that in spite of the four beasts that will prowl the Mediterranean, the saints of the most High would possess the kingdom, the centre of which will be Israel. The word ***saints*** appears in both the Old and New Testaments, and it always refers to God's people. In the Old Testament it means Israel (Exod 19:6; Matt. 27:52,53). In the Church Age, a *saint* is a believer in Christ (1 Cor 1:2; Eph 1:1; Phil 1:1). A *saint* is also a person who will be saved in the Tribulation by refusing to take the mark of Antichrist because he believes in the true Christ (Rev. 13:7). As Israel will be the chief nation during the Millennium, this term here, in the first instance, refers to them, but it also to the Apostles (Matt 19:28), and believers of the church age (Rev 2:26).

- *And ye shall be unto me **a kingdom of priests**, and an holy nation (Exod 19:6).*

- *And the LORD shall make thee **the head, and not the tail** (Deut 28:13).*

- *And it shall come to pass in the last days, that **the mountain of the LORD's house** shall be established in the top of the mountains, and shall be exalted above the hills; and **all nations shall flow unto** it. And many people shall go and say, Come ye, and let us go up to the mountain of the LORD, to the house of the God of Jacob; and he will teach us of his ways, and we will walk in his paths: for **out of Zion shall go forth the law, and the word of the LORD from Jerusalem** (Isa 2:2,3).*

- *Thus saith the LORD of hosts; It shall yet come to pass, that **there shall come people**, and the inhabitants of many cities: And the inhabitants of one city shall go to another, saying, **Let us go speedily to pray before the LORD**, and to seek the LORD of hosts: I will go also. Yea, many people and strong nations shall come to seek the LORD of hosts in Jerusalem, and to pray before the LORD. Thus saith the LORD of hosts; In those days it shall come to pass, that **ten men shall take hold out of all languages of the nations, even shall take hold of the skirt of him that is a Jew**, saying, We will go with you: for we have heard that God is with you (Zech 8:20-23).*

- *And Jesus said unto them [the Apostles], Verily I say unto you, That ye which have followed me, in the regeneration **when the Son of man shall sit in the throne** of his glory, **ye also shall sit upon twelve thrones**, judging the twelve tribes of Israel (Matt 19:28).*

- *And he that overcometh, and keepeth my works unto the end, to him will I give **power over the nations** (Rev 2:26).*

The Second Inquiry: The Fourth Beast and Little Horn 7:19-22.

Then I would know the truth of the fourth beast, which was diverse from all the others, exceeding dreadful, whose teeth were of iron, and his nails of brass; which devoured, brake in pieces, and stamped the residue with his feet; (7:20) And of the ten horns that were in his head, and of the other which came up, and before whom three fell; even of that horn that had eyes, and a mouth that spake very great things, whose look was more stout than his fellows. (7:21) I beheld, and the same horn made war with the saints, and prevailed against them; (7:22) Until the Ancient of days came, and judgment was given to the saints of the most High; and the time came that the saints possessed the kingdom.

We have dealt with much of the interpretation of Daniel's vision concerning the four beasts; however there are some additional factors in these subsequent accounts that are now given. Daniel was particularly concerned about the fourth beast because it was the ruler of this kingdom that would make war against Israel and prevail against them for a time. It is this beast that was the strangest, the strongest and the most terrifying of all the beasts. It is this beast that will be destroyed by Christ at His Second Coming and the Battle of Armageddon.

The Bible has to say something only once for us to pay careful attention; but when it repeats a matter it is to be especially noted. In this inquiry there additional factors are given.

<u>(1) The Nails of Brass of the Fourth Beast</u>. ***Then I would know the truth of the fourth beast, which was diverse from all the others, exceeding dreadful, whose teeth were of iron, and his nails of brass; which devoured, brake in pieces, and stamped the residue with his feet*** (7:19). It is as we saw in verse 7, but now with the addition of *the nails of brass*.

> • *After this I saw in the night visions, and behold a fourth beast,*
> *dreadful and terrible, and strong exceedingly;*
> *and it had great iron teeth:*
> *it devoured and brake in pieces,*
> *and stamped the residue with the feet of it:*
> *and it was diverse from all the beasts that were before it;*
> *and it had ten horns (7:7).*

Not only was this Fourth Beast capable of stamping with its great *feet* and devouring with its *iron teeth*; it would also ravage with its **brass nails**. The kingdom of Antichrist is totally vicious. It will deface, destroy, mutilate all and everything that gets in its way. It will fulfil the utter wrath of Satan who knows that he has only a *short time (42 months*, Rev 13:5) to ravage against God's creation.

> • **Woe to the inhabiters of the earth** *and of the sea! for* **the devil is come down** *unto you, having great wrath, because he knoweth that he hath but* **a short time** *(Rev 12:12).*
>
> • *And* **the dragon was wroth** *with the woman, and went to make war with the remnant of her seed, which keep the commandments of God, and have the testimony of Jesus Christ (Rev 12:17).*
>
> • *And they worshipped* **the dragon which gave power unto the beast**: *and they worshipped the beast, saying, Who is like unto the beast?* **who is able to make war with him** *(Rev 13:4)?*
>
> • *And it was* **given unto him** *to make war with the saints, and to overcome them: and* **power was given him** *over all kindreds, and tongues, and nations (Rev 13:7).*

(2) The Stout Look of the Little Horn. ***And of the ten horns that were in his head, and of the other which came up, and before whom three fell; even of that horn that had eyes, and a mouth that spake very great things, whose look was more stout than his fellows*** (7:20). For reasons that will only be known when the Beast begins to be manifest, he is called the *Little Horn*; yet in every other respect he is an overwhelming personality. He will have a presence that other leaders will not be able to counter. Initially this will be demonstrated in what is evidently a power struggle within the beast kingdom, and three of the ten kings are overthrown. It is thought that this may be the same time that the Antichrist himself will receive a *deadly wound*. This *stout look* may be associated with an assassination attempt.

> • *And I saw one of his heads as it were* **wounded to death**; *and his deadly wound was healed: and all the world wondered after the beast (Rev 13:3).*
>
> • *And he exerciseth all the power of the first beast before him, and causeth the earth and them which dwell therein to worship the first beast,* **whose deadly wound was healed** *(Rev 13:12).*
>
> • *And deceiveth them that dwell on the earth by [the means of] those miracles which he had power to do in the sight of the beast; saying to them that dwell on the earth, that they should make an image to the beast,* **which had the wound by a sword, and did live** *(Rev 13:14).*
>
> • *The beast that thou sawest was, and is not; and shall* **ascend out of the bottomless pit***, and go into perdition: and they that dwell on the earth shall wonder, whose names were not written in the book of life from the foundation of the world, when they behold the beast that was, and is not, and yet is (Rev 17:8).*

(3) The War Against the Saints by the Little Horn. ***I beheld, and the same horn made war with the saints, and prevailed against them*** (7:21). The Antichrist will wage war against the Jewish people. Christ in His Olivet Discourse warned of this:

DANIEL 7. FOUR ENDTIME *BEASTS* AND THE ADVENT OF THE MESSIAH

> *• When ye therefore shall see **the abomination of desolation**, spoken of by Daniel the prophet, stand in the holy place, (whoso readeth, let him understand:) Then **let them which be in Judaea** flee into the mountains: Let him which is on the housetop not come down to take any thing out of his house: Neither let him which is in the field return back to take his clothes. And woe unto them that are with child, and to them that give suck in those days! But pray ye that your flight be not in the winter, neither on the sabbath day: For **then shall be great tribulation**, such as was not since the beginning of the world to this time, no, nor ever shall be (Matt 24:15-21).*

It is also indicated in Revelation 12:13-16 that God will have to intervene directly and protect the remnant of Israel in a place called *the wilderness* for three and a half years. Many believe this place to be in Petra, but it is also indicated that they may be scattered throughout the area that comprised ancient Edom and Moab. We read in Daniel 11:41 that Edom, Moab, and Ammon will escape out of the hands of Antichrist (*Hutchings*).

The Antichrist will wage *economic warfare* against every Jew and Gentile who come to faith in Christ during the Tribulation and refuse to take the mark.

> *• And **he causeth all**, both small and great, rich and poor, free and bond, **to receive a mark** in their right hand, or in their foreheads: And that **no man might buy or sell, save he that had the mark**, or the name of the beast, or the number of his name. Here is wisdom. Let him that hath understanding count the number of the beast: for it is the number of a man; and his number is Six hundred threescore and six (Rev 13:16-18).*

The Answer: The Extent of the Fourth Beast, the Little Horn and the Kingdom of the Messiah 7:23-28.

> *Thus he said, The fourth beast shall be the fourth kingdom upon earth, which shall be diverse from all kingdoms, and shall devour the whole earth, and shall tread it down, and break it in pieces. (7:24) And the ten horns out of this kingdom are ten kings that shall arise: and another shall rise after them; and he shall be diverse from the first, and he shall subdue three kings. (7:25) And he shall speak great words against the most High, and shall wear out the saints of the most High, and think to change times and laws: and they shall be given into his hand until a time and times and the dividing of time. (7:26) But the judgment shall sit, and they shall take away his dominion, to consume and to destroy it unto the end. (7:27) And the kingdom and dominion, and the greatness of the kingdom under the whole heaven, shall be given to the people of the saints of the most High, whose kingdom is an everlasting kingdom, and all dominions shall serve and obey him. (7:28) Hitherto is the end of the matter. As for me Daniel, my cogitations much troubled me, and my countenance changed in me: but I kept the matter in my heart.*

Daniel in his second inquiry made three further statements concerning the Fourth Beast, the Ten Horns and the Little Horn (7:19-22). Now in this second answer (see page 179), further information is given regarding the ends achieved by the Fourth Beast, the Little Horn and the Kingdom of the Messiah.

(1) The Extent of the Fourth Kingdom's Dominion. ***Thus he said, The fourth beast shall be the fourth kingdom upon earth, which shall be diverse from all kingdoms, and shall devour the whole earth, and shall tread it down, and break it in pieces*** (7:24). Ponder this statement. No kingdom has ever ***devoured the whole earth***. The Bible does not exaggerate, whether they be English speaking, Chinese, African, European, Asian, Muslim, Russian; the Antichrist will *devour, tread down, break in pieces* the entire earth. The Bible gives the description of a soon to come time on earth which before was unimaginable!! We stress again what Scripture stresses:

> *• Alas! for that day is great, so that **none is like it**: it is even the time of Jacob's trouble, but he shall be saved out of it (Jer 30:7).*

> • And at that time shall Michael stand up, the great prince which standeth for the children of thy people: and there shall be **a time of trouble, such as never was** since there was a nation even to that same time: and at that time thy people shall be delivered, every one that shall be found written in the book (Dan 12:1).
>
> • A day of darkness and of gloominess, a day of clouds and of thick darkness, as the morning spread upon the mountains: a great people and a strong; **there hath not been ever the like**, neither shall be any more after it, even to the years of many generations (Joel 2:2).
>
> • For then shall be great tribulation, such as was not since the beginning of the world to this time, no, nor ever shall be (Matt 24:21).

(2) The Extent of the Little Horn's Dominion. *And the ten horns out of this kingdom are ten kings that shall arise: and another shall rise after them; and he shall be diverse from the first, and he shall subdue three kings. And he shall speak great words against the most High, and shall wear out the saints of the most High, and think to change times and laws: and they shall be given into his hand until a time and times and the dividing of time. But the judgment shall sit, and they shall take away his dominion, to consume and to destroy it unto the end* (7:24-26). In addition to what we have already been told about the Little Horn, we are now told that he will *think to change times and laws: and they shall be given into his hand until a time and times and the dividing of time* (7:25).

He Will Think To Change Times. As *he speaks great words against the Most High*, any observance of Christmas, Easter, Pentecost and other Christian or Jewish days will be abolished. But as *he exalteth himself above all that is called God* (2 Thess 2:4), any Muslim, Hindu, Buddhist or other religious days will also be ruled out. All public religious observance is directed to him alone.

> • And the king shall do according to his will; and **he shall exalt himself, and magnify himself above every god**, and shall speak marvellous things against the God of gods, and shall prosper till the indignation be accomplished: for that that is determined shall be done. Neither shall he regard the God of his fathers, nor the desire of women, nor regard any god: for he shall magnify himself above all (Dan 11:36,37).
>
> • Let no man deceive you by any means: for that day shall not come (Christ's Return after the Tribulation, as stated previously in 2 Thess. 1:7,8), except there come a falling away first, and that man of sin be revealed, the son of perdition; Who **opposeth and exalteth himself above all that is called God**, or that is worshipped; so that he as God sitteth in the temple of God, shewing himself that he is God (2 Thess 2:3,4).

The Antichrist will trample upon all laws and customs, human and divine. He will "change square into round" (*Matthew Henry*). He may try as they did during the French Revolution to change the seven day week (the mark of the Creator; Gen. 1) to a ten day "week." He would be happy with the steps England's second largest city took a number of years ago.

> Winterval was a season of public events in Birmingham, England organised by Birmingham City Council in each of two consecutive winters: first from 20 November to 31 December 1997, and then again from mid-October 1998 to mid-January 1999. The intention was to encourage people into the newly rejuvenated city centre, with secular and religious events marking religious and other occasions during the relevant period. The name "Winterval" has since become used in the UK as shorthand for what are presented as attempts to "rebrand" Christmas so as not to exclude non-Christians. https://en.wikipedia.org/wiki/Winterval

He Will Not Extend Beyond God's Times. *And they shall be given into his hand until a time and times and the dividing of time* (7:25; also 7:22). If he meant to alter *the ordinances of heaven* themselves (Job 38:33), he will soon be disappointed. These daring attempts would for a time prosper, but it would be a short time. It would last for only *Until the Ancient of days came, and judgment was given to the saints of the most High; and the time came that the*

DANIEL 7. FOUR ENDTIME *BEASTS* AND THE ADVENT OF THE MESSIAH

saints possessed the kingdom (7:22)*.* Only **until time, times, and half a time** (that is, for three years and a half years).This is the prophetic measure of time for the second half of the Tribulation given in Revelation. It is the same as the two other designations: *forty-two months* and *1260 days*.

> • *And to the woman were given two wings of a great eagle, that she might fly into the wilderness, into her place, where she is nourished for **a time, and times, and half a time**, from the face of the serpent (Rev 12:14).*

> • *But the court which is without the temple leave out, and measure it not; for it is given unto the Gentiles: and the holy city shall they tread under foot **forty and two months**. And I will give power unto my two witnesses, and they shall prophesy **a thousand two hundred and threescore days**, clothed in sackcloth (Rev 11:2,3).*

> • *And the woman fled into the wilderness, where she hath a place prepared of God, that they should feed her there **a thousand two hundred and threescore days** (Rev 12:6).*

> • *And there was given unto him a mouth speaking great things and blasphemies; and power was given unto him to continue **forty and two months** (Rev 13:5).*

(3) The Extent of the Messiah's Dominion. ***And the kingdom and dominion, and the greatness of the kingdom under the whole heaven, shall be given to the people of the saints of the most High, whose kingdom is an everlasting kingdom, and all dominions shall serve and obey him*** (7:27).

As to the Geography of this Kingdom: It will be unending. However far ***the whole heaven*** will extend, there it will extend also. As far as the New Heavens and the New Earth reach (Rev 21:1), there the Kingdom of Messiah will be.

As to the Tenure of the Kingdom: It will be *everlasting*. It will be as its King who is *everlasting*. The Kingdom will never die, or decline, or wane, or weaken. On the contrary, *Of the **increase** of his government and peace there shall be no end* (Isa 9:7).

As to the Governance of the Kingdom: ***All dominions shall serve and obey him.*** There will be no pockets of resistance or non-recognition. All will accede. Heaven and earth will be one and under One. Though this governance will be shared with the ***people of the saints***, yet there will be perfect accord among those reigning; no debate, dispute, discord. Each will serve to their highest ability and in perfect harmony with everyone else. In that day heaven and earth will be one, and *the heavens will rule* (Dan 4:26). Even the different administrations of the Father, the Son and the Holy Spirit – made necessary by the fall of man – will be removed in that day. There will be no veils, no approaches, no separations; but God will be *all in all* (1 Cor 15:28). Consider for example the following:

> • *For as in Adam all die, even so in Christ shall all be made alive. But every man in his own order: Christ the firstfruits; afterward they that are Christ's at his coming. Then cometh the end, when he shall have delivered up the kingdom to God, even the Father; when he shall have put down all rule and all authority and power. For he must reign, till he hath put all enemies under his feet. The last enemy that shall be destroyed is death. For he hath put all things under his feet. But when he saith all things are put under him, it is manifest that he is excepted, which did put all things under him. And when all things shall be subdued unto him, then shall the Son also himself be subject unto him that put all things under him, **that God may be all in all** (1 Cor 15:22-28).*

Daniel Acknowledges His Fearful Awe At What He had Seen. ***Hitherto is the end of the matter. As for me Daniel, my cogitations much troubled me, and my countenance changed in me: but I kept the matter in my heart*** (7:28). As Mary did with the message of Gabriel, Daniel kept the matter in his heart (cp. Lk 2:51). It was not to be kept from, but kept for God's people. It was to be kept in the security of his heart until it was *Inscripturated*, and kept in that volume where *not on jot or tittle passes away* (Matt 5:18). Not only was this vision for a long-off day; but before Christ came there was greater fearfulness in the hearts of those through whom the inspired words were given.

> • *But thou, O Daniel, shut up the words, and seal the book, even to the time of the end: many shall run to and fro, and knowledge shall be increased (Dan 12:4).*

> • *But is now made manifest by the appearing of our Saviour Jesus Christ, who hath abolished death, and hath brought life and immortality to light through the gospel (2 Tim 1:10).*

Nevertheless, no one could be informed about what was coming upon this world at the end of this present age without being troubled. As we look at our world today, it is no wonder that Daniel was troubled. But, *the blessed hope* as presented in this marvellous chapter is the coming of the Son of man to save the world for both Jew and Gentile (*Hutchings*).

With Daniel's fearful awe of all that he has seen and heard in Chapter 7, we conclude the first half of this Book that bears his name. These seven chapters began with Daniel as a *young man* interpreting Nebuchadnezzar's dream. The dream gave an overview of the Times of the Gentiles, some 2500 years when Gentile powers will to a greater or lesser extent rule over Israel and Jerusalem. As an *old man* he has now in this chapter been given a vision of the end time Gentile powers that will oppress the Land of Israel. In the intervening chapters (3-6) historical evets are recorded which give the characteristics of this time. To further illustrate these times a phenomenon occurs that is uniquely rare in the Old Testament: rather than Hebrew, these seven chapters are written in a Gentile language, Aramaic. In addition, the location and descriptions are primarily the capitals of the Gentile world.

With Chapter 8, the Hebrew language now resumes. The emphasis is now primarily Jerusalem. The contrast is remarkable between Chapter 7 which concludes the Aramaic section and Chapter 8 that introduces the returns to the Hebrew. Both deal with Gentile powers that are in the immediate proximity of the Return of Christ, but the perspective is different. Note this and how they connect the two main sections of the Book.

THE END OF THE TIMES OF THE GENTILES: GENTILE PERSPCTIVE 7

THE END OF THE TIMES OF THE GENTILES: JEWISH PERSPECTIVE 8

I THE TIMES OF THE GENTILES 1- 7

    A. The Beginnings of the Times of the Gentiles 1

    B. The Overview of the Times of the Gentiles (*Aramaic* Begins) 2

    C. The Characteristics of the Times of the Gentiles 3-6

        1. A Time of Enforced False Religion: Nebuchadnezzar's Image 3

        2. A Time of Expansion and Instability: Nebuchadnezzar's Madness 4

        3. A Time of Sacrilege: Belshazzar's Feast 5

        4. A Time of Enshrining Bad Laws: Darius' Lion's Den 6

    D. The End of the Times of the Gentiles: Gentile Perspective 7

II THE TIMES OF THE GENTILES REGARDING JERUSALEM 8-12

    A. The End of the Times of the Gentiles: Jewish Perspective (*Hebrew Resumes*) 8

    B. The Seventy Weeks of Years upon Jerusalem and the Jewish People 9

C. The Desolations and Final Blessing of Jerusalem 10-12

    1. Desolations and The Glory of Christ 10

    2. Desolations: Future to Daniel 11:1-35

    3. Desolations and Glory: Future to Us 11:36-12:13

Here again in Chapter 8, we will see the Little Horn, the Antichrist. But we will see him more in respect of his actions against Jerusalem rather than the Gentile world.

II THE TIMES OF THE GENTILES REGARDING JERUSALEM 8-12

A. THE END OF THE TIMES OF THE GENTILES: JEWISH PERSPECTIVE (Hebrew Resumes) 8

DANIEL 8. THE VISION OF THE RAM, GOAT AND LITTLE HORN

Chapter 8 marks the beginning of a new section as indicated by the change of language from Aramaic back to Hebrew. The overall subject is still the *Times of the Gentiles*, but now it is Gentile history as it more directly affects Jerusalem and the Jewish People. There are more than twice as many references to Jerusalem in Daniel 8-12 as there where in Chapters 1-7. Especially central to these chapters and that which demonstrates the emphasis is the *Seventy Weeks Prophecy*. It is a prophecy which finds a parallel in many other passages.

> • **Seventy weeks are determined upon thy people and upon thy holy city**, to finish the transgression, and to make an end of sins, and to make reconciliation for iniquity, and to bring in everlasting righteousness, and to seal up the vision and prophecy, and to anoint the most Holy. **Know therefore and understand, that from the going forth of the commandment to restore and to build Jerusalem unto the Messiah the Prince** shall be seven weeks, and threescore and two weeks: the street shall be built again, and the wall, even in troublous times. And after threescore and two weeks shall Messiah be cut off, but not for himself: and **the people of the prince that shall come shall destroy the city and the sanctuary**; and the end thereof shall be with a flood, and unto the end of the war desolations are determined. And **he shall confirm the covenant with many for one week: and in the midst of the week he shall cause the sacrifice and the oblation to cease**, and for the overspreading of abominations he shall make it desolate, even until the consummation, and that determined shall be poured upon the desolate (Dan 9:24-27).

> • Behold, **I will make Jerusalem a cup of trembling unto all the people round about**, when they shall be in the siege both against Judah and against Jerusalem. And in that day will **I make Jerusalem a burdensome stone for all people**: all that burden themselves with it shall be cut in pieces, though all the people of the earth be gathered together against it. In that day, saith the LORD, I will smite every horse with astonishment, and his rider with madness: and I will open mine eyes upon the house of Judah, and will smite every horse of the people with blindness. And the governors of Judah shall say in their heart, **The inhabitants of Jerusalem shall be my strength in the LORD of hosts their God.** In that day will I make the governors of Judah like an hearth of fire among the wood, and like a torch of fire in a sheaf; and they shall devour all the people round about, on the right hand and on the left: and **Jerusalem shall be inhabited again in her own place, even in Jerusalem** (Zech 12:2-6).

Here in Chapter 8, further information is given concerning the *Little Horn*, the Antichrist. Here though it is not only his worldwide control as in Chapter 7, but the special focus is his control over Jerusalem. For example:

> • Yea, he magnified himself even to the prince of the host, and **by him the daily sacrifice was taken away, and the place of the sanctuary was cast down**. And an host was given him against **the daily sacrifice** by reason of transgression, and it cast down the truth to the ground; and it practised, and prospered. Then I heard one saint speaking, and another saint said unto that certain saint which spake, How long shall be the vision concerning **the daily sacrifice**, and the transgression of desolation, to give both **the sanctuary** and the host to be trodden under foot? And he said unto me, Unto **two thousand and three hundred days**; then shall **the sanctuary be cleansed** (8:11-14).

DANIEL 8. THE VISION OF THE RAM, GOAT AND LITTLE HORN

* *And he shall confirm the covenant with many for one week: and in the midst of the week **he shall cause the sacrifice and the oblation to cease** (Dan 9:27).*

* *And **he shall plant the tabernacles of his palace between the seas in the glorious holy mountain**; yet he shall come to his end, and none shall help him (Dan 11:45).*

IF I FORGET THEE O JERUSALEM !

As the focus of Chapters 8-12 begins to shift more and more to Jerusalem, it is vital that we have a basic overview of this city and its Temple Mount that is so much at the heart of Biblical history and prophecy, and very much also at the centre of world events today.

* *Since the day that I brought forth my people out of the land of Egypt **I chose no city** among all the tribes of Israel to build an house in, that my name might be there; neither chose I any man to be a ruler over my people Israel: But **I have chosen Jerusalem, that my name might be there**; and have chosen David to be over my people Israel (2 Chron 6:5,6).*

* *Thus saith the Lord GOD; **This is Jerusalem: I have set it in the midst of the nations** and countries that are round about her (Ezek 5:5).*

* *I was glad when they said unto me, Let us go into the house of the LORD. **Our feet shall stand within thy gates, O Jerusalem**. Jerusalem is builded as a city that is compact together: Whither the tribes go up, the tribes of the LORD, unto the testimony of Israel, to give thanks unto the name of the LORD. For there are set thrones of judgment, the thrones of the house of David. **Pray for the peace of Jerusalem: they shall prosper that love thee**. Peace be within thy walls, and prosperity within thy palaces. For my brethren and companions' sakes, I will now say, Peace be within thee. **Because of the house of the LORD our God I will seek thy good** (Psa 122:1-9).*

* *If I forget thee, O Jerusalem, let my right hand forget her cunning. If I do not remember thee, let my tongue cleave to the roof of my mouth; **if I prefer not Jerusalem above my chief joy** (Psa 137:5,6).*

An Overview of Biblical Jerusalem

The following is from is from *Bible History Online*.

The Jebusites

During the time of Joshua the city of Jerusalem was named Jebus or Jebusi, and a Canaanite people called the Jebusites dwelt there. Though Joshua had conquered the land there, he never fully drove out the Jebusites, and David had to actually take possession of the stronghold of Zion. Apparently there were some Jebusites who were still living in this area during the time of David, because we find David actually purchasing the ground on which the Temple would be built from Araunah the Jebusite.

Mount Moriah

The Lord had appeared to David at the threshing floor of the Jebusite and this is the exact spot where David instructed his son Solomon to build the house of the Lord, at Mount Moriah. This was also the place in Hebrew history were Abraham bound his son Isaac upon an altar in order to sacrifice him according to the word of the Lord, but an angel of the Lord held back his hand when he drew the knife, for this was only a test of Abraham's obedience and a wonderful picture of God's plan of redemption with the sacrificing of His own Son, the Jewish Messiah Jesus Christ.

Today Mount Moriah, the top of the Temple hill, is where the Mosque of Omar, more correctly, the Dome of the Rock, now stands. The Arabs call it the Sakhrah Rock. It is a strangely shaped mass of rock, protruding 10 feet above the ground, and is about 50 feet in diameter. It is believed to be the actual site of the altar of burnt offering in Solomon's Temple. Jews, Christians, and Muslims, according to tradition have regarded it as "the stone of foundation," the Foundation Rock of which the Jews claim that it was the precise site of the Holy of Holies of Solomon's Temple and the place where God's Schekinah glory appeared between the Cherubim, above the Ark of the

Covenant and the Mercy Seat. [This is the view believed generally today, but as shown below the Temple was likely built to the north of the Dome of the Rock and in line with the Eastern Gate].

Geography

The city of Jerusalem rests on a limestone plateau 2500 feet above sea level. It is located in the central hill country, and is near the border of the Judean desert. It is far removed from any major trade routes. On the west side of Jerusalem are the Judean mountains, on the east side is the Judean desert which descends 4000 feet in 10 miles at the Dead Sea. The rugged terrain of Jerusalem was a definite military advantage, it was easy to defend because the city can only be reached on its northern side. The east, west, and southern sides had steep valleys.

Jerusalem's Four Mountains

His foundation is in the holy mountains (Psa 87:1)

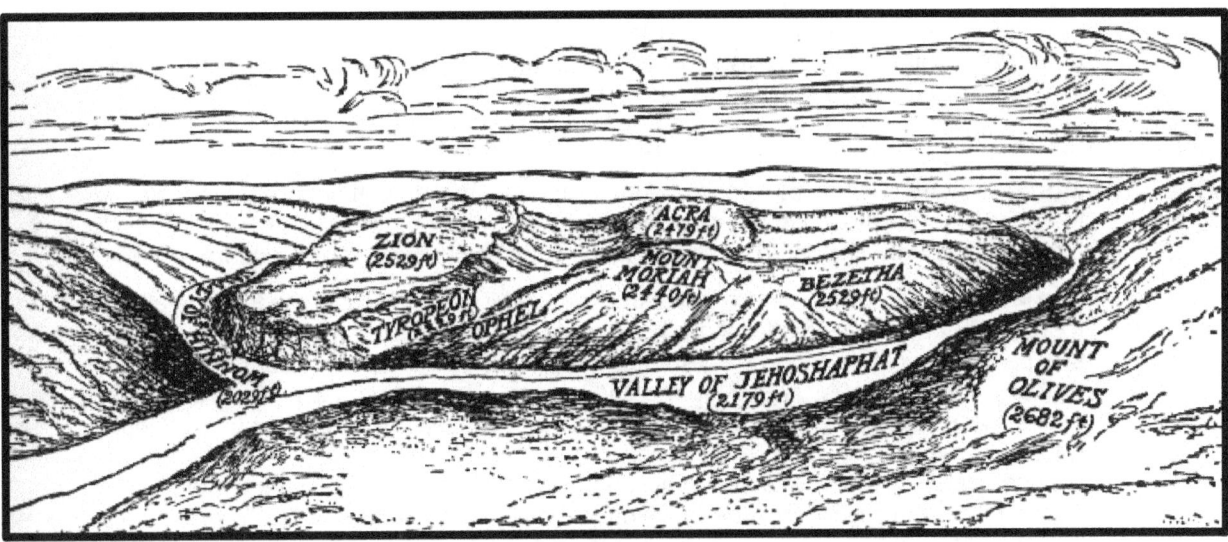

Jerusalem rests upon four hills or mountains, but only two of them have biblical names, Mount Zion and Mount Moriah. Between these mountains there is a large valley that the Romans called the Tyropoean. Mount Zion was referred to geographically as the southwestern hill of Jerusalem. But Zion has much greater significance in the Bible and it is frequently mentioned as the place of the Temple and of the King. When David said that he would not rest until he had *found out a place for the LORD, a habitation for the mighty God of Jacob... the Lord replied: For the LORD hath chosen Zion; He hath desired it for his habitation place: This is my rest forever; Here will I dwell, for I have desired it* (Psa 132:5,13,14).

The hill on the north was called Bezetha, or the New City. The hill on the northwest was called the Akra, or Fortress, and according to tradition was called the "stronghold of Zion."

Mount Zion is the largest of the hills in Jerusalem, it stands 2,550 feet high. Mount Zion is mentioned throughout the Old Testament and seven times in the New Testament (spelled Sion and used in its larger designation). Mount Zion in its limited sense is located on the southwest side of Jerusalem between the Tyropoeon Valley and the Hinnom Valley and this is the location of the Upper City where the wealthy lived during the time of Christ.. This is also the hill where the Jebusites built a stronghold but were eventually conquered by David. David built a palace there and it became the palace and home for the kings of Israel. David and most of his successors were buried on Mount Zion (1 Kng 2:10; 9:43; 14:31).

Mount Moriah is located to the northeast of Mount Zion, in the southeast side of Jerusalem between the Kidron Valley and Tyropoeon Valley. It is 2440 feet high. The Bible sometimes calls Mount Moriah by the name of Zion as well. King Solomon

DANIEL 8. THE VISION OF THE RAM, GOAT AND LITTLE HORN

increased the size of Mount Moriah who built a high platform and wall on three sides (east, south, and west) and this formed an extremely high summit on the southeast corner. This summit is where the Temple was built, the highest point was the location of the Holy of Holies, the same spot where Abraham was tested to offer his son Isaac (Gen. 22:2). The southern slope of Mount Moriah, extending from the southern wall down to the point where the three valleys meet, was called Ophel (Neh 3:26, 27).

Mount Acra is located in Jerusalem on the north side of Mount Zion along the Tyropoeon Valley. It is interesting that Simon Maccabeus nearly filled up the Tyropoeon Valley which is located between Mount Bezetha and Mount Acra. He also reduced the height of Mount Acra in order to make it lower than Mount Moriah where the Temple stood. Antiochus Epiphanes, ruler of the Seleucid Empire built a fortress in Jerusalem on Mount Acra after he conquered the city in 168 BC. It was here that the Syrians governed the Jews. Later this fortified compound was destroyed by Simon Maccabeus. Mount Acra was important in the Maccabean Revolt and the formation of the Hasmonean Kingdom.

Mount Bezetha is located to the north of the Temple Mount, and in the first century was just to the north of the Roman Antonia fortress. Mount Bezetha was not included in the city until the first century after the third wall was built, and received the name *New City*.

Two Other *Mountains*

Mount Calvary (Golgotha) was located near the Damascus Gate on the north side of the city. According to Catholic tradition Christ was crucified at the site now called the Church of the Holy Sepulchre but recent investigations have confirmed the former view.

The Mount of Olives is located east of the Temple Mount just across the Kidron Valley. It stood about 300 feet higher than the Temple Mount and over 100 feet higher than any part of the city. On the eastern slope of the Mount of Olives was the village of Bethany, the home of Mary and Martha and Lazarus. From here at the Mount of Olives Jesus looked over the beautiful city and wept because of Jerusalem's rebellious leaders. Overlooking the Temple on the Mount of Olives was the garden of Gethsemane, where Christ suffered his agony, betrayal and arrest. In the center of the mount the so-called Church of Ascension stands at an elevation of 2,682 where it is traditionally taught that Christ ascended into Heaven.

Jerusalem's Deep Valleys

Jerusalem was surrounded on the west, south, and east by deep ravines the which are 200-400 feet deep and therefore made it impossible for an enemy to attack from either these directions. Therefore Herod's Jerusalem was considered unapproachable, except from the north side which was actually protected by the outermost wall which was over 100 feet high and had 90 towers according to Josephus.

The deep valley on the west and the southwest side of the city was called the valley of Hinnom (the abhorred place). The deep valley on the east side of the city was called the valley of the Kidron, or Jehoshaphat, where the prophet Joel saw a futuristic vision where the nations of the world would be summoned for judgment. The place where these ravines met was called "Enrogel" or The Well of Joab (2 Sam 17:17).

These deep valley's made the inhabitants of Jerusalem to feel safe and secure, as though God Himself were protecting it. It was so secure from an enemy attack that Titus, the Roman General who conquered Jerusalem in 70 A.D. said that "if it had not been for the internal dissensions, the city could never have been taken."

The **Kidron Valley** also called the Valley of Jehoshaphat formed the eastern boundary of the city of Jerusalem and a separation of Mount Zion from the Mount of Olives. The Bible also refers to the Kidron Valley as the King's Dale (2 Sam 18:18).

The **Tyropoean Valley** also called the Valley of the Cheese Makers, joins the Kidron Valley on the south side of Mount Moriah and runs to the north between Mount Zion and Mount Moriah. The Tyropoean Valley separates at the north part causing a fork and Mount Acra is located between the forks.

The **Hinnom Valley** created a western and southern boundary for the city. The southern part of the Valley of Hinnom was called Gehenna or Tophet, "the place of fire" (Jer 7:31). It was here is in the Valley of Hinnom that Moloch was worshipped and therefore later became a garbage heap during the first century AD.

The Walls and Gates of Jerusalem

Do good in thy good pleasure unto Zion: build thou the walls of Jerusalem (Psa 51:18).

Jerusalem was surrounded by massive walls. David's prayer was answered when his son Solomon built the wall of Jerusalem around the city, and repaired the breaches of the city of David. He also built the Millo (rampart), a fortification which apparently existed when it was inhabited by the Jebusites. Two accounts of wall building and repair are described in the reigns of Hezekiah and Manesseh.

• *Also he strengthened himself, and built up all the wall that was broken, and raised it up to the towers, and another wall without, and repaired Millo in the city of David, and made darts and shields in abundance (2 Chron 32:5).*

• *Now after this he built a wall without the city of David, on the west side of Gihon, in the valley, even to the entering in at the fish gate, and compassed about Ophel, and raised it up a very great height, and put captains of war in all the fenced cities of Judah (2 Chron 33:14).*

By the time of Christ, according to Josephus, there were three walls that surrounded Jerusalem, "90 towers stood in the first wall, 14 in the second, and 60 in the third." The third wall was built by Herod Agrippa I.
http://www.biblehistory.com/jerusalem/firstcenturyjerusalem_the_land_of_jerusalem.html

The fullest Biblical account of the Walls and Gates of Jerusalem is given in Nehemiah Chapter 3. Here there is a detailed account of the rebuilding work that took place after the Babylonian captivity.

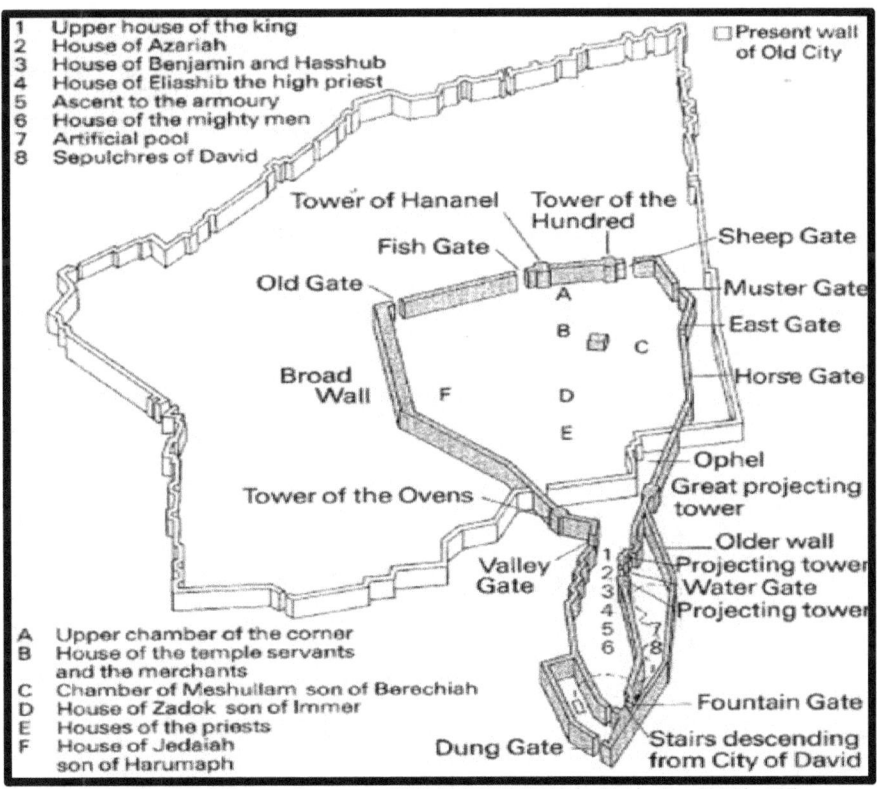

(https://kzlam36.files.wordpress.com/2009/07/1247279328-hr-994.jpg?w=500&h=577)

The Walls and Gates During Nehemiah's Time Superimposed upon the Current Walls

DANIEL 8. THE VISION OF THE RAM, GOAT AND LITTLE HORN

H. A. Ironside in his commentary on Nehemiah made a helpful spiritual application concern the twelve gates of Nehemiah's time.

> The first gate mentioned in the chapter is the **sheep gate**. This naturally suggests the Cross to one familiar with the Bible, and the sacrifice upon it of the Lamb of God. This gate was built by a priest; Christ offered Himself for us as our great High Priest (Heb 7:26,27). Then came the **fish gate**, which brings to mind the Lord's promise *I will make you fishers of men* (Matt. 4:19). The one saved through Christ's blood is himself to become an evangelist, winning others to the Lord. The **old gate** suggests subjection to the revealed will of God (Je. 6:16). The **valley gate** makes us think of humility (Psa 84:6); the **dung gate** of cleansing from defilement (1 Jhn 1:7-9). The **fountain gate** brings to our thoughts sanctification by the Spirit and by the Word of God (Eph 5:25,26). The **water gate**, which seems to have been still intact, reminds one of the Word of God which needs no repair. The **horse gate** speaks of war (the horse being used then as an animal of warfare), which brings to mind the judgments of the tribulation period (Rev 6:1-8), and also of One who will return from heaven *on a white horse* (Rev. 19:11). The **east gate** points to the coming day when *the Sun of righteousness will rise* (Mal 4:2). The **Miphkad gate**, the "gate of judgment," should make us meditate on the judgment seat of Christ (2 Cor 5:10). (*Notes on Ezra, Nehemiah and Esther*, pp. 24-52).

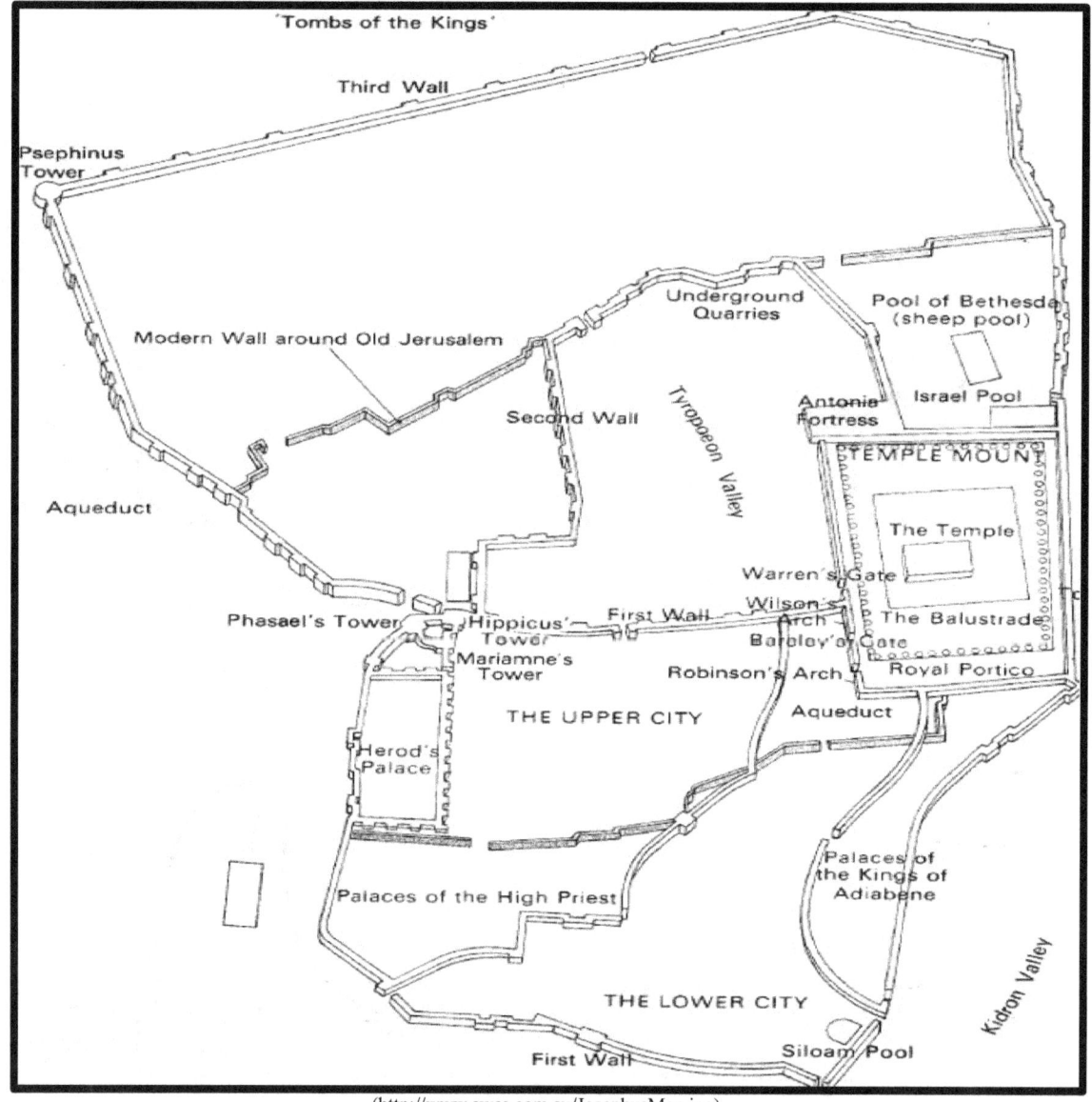

(http://www.swcs.com.au/JosephusMap.jpg)

Jerusalem at the Time of Christ

The Gates and Walls of Old Jerusalem Today

Beginning at the Lions Gate and ending at the Eastern Gate, the following gives an anti-clockwise survey of the Eight Gates of Jerusalem as they are today. This is from Jerry Golden | PO Box 10268 | Jerusalem 91102 Israel. Source: *The Golden Report*

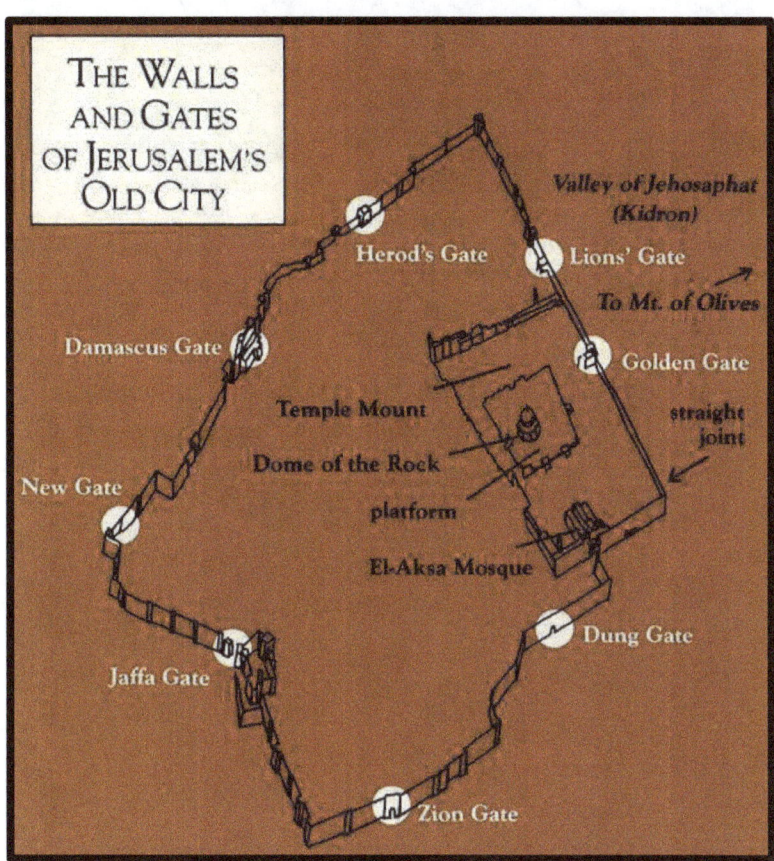

LION'S GATE

Also known as St. Stephen's Gate, it is the location that Paul (Saul) witnessed the stoning of Steven. The Lion's Gate is located in the east wall, and leads to the Via Dolorosa. Near the top of the Lion's Gate are four figures of lions, two on the left and two on the right. Israeli paratroops came through this gate during the Six Day War in 1967.

DANIEL 8. THE VISION OF THE RAM, GOAT AND LITTLE HORN

HEROD'S GATE

Located on the North Wall of the Old City and leads into the Moslem quarter of the Old City.

DAMASCUS GATE

The road to Damascus once came out of this Gate, you will also notice a smaller Roman Gate to the left, it would have been the Gate the Messiah came through with the Cross. It is the busiest of Jerusalem's gates. It consists of one large center gate originally intended for use by persons of high station, and two smaller side entrances.

NEW GATE

The New Gate is located on the Northwest corner of the old city walls. Yes, the New Gate is about 600 years old and is the newest gate.

JAFFA GATE

Located on the Western wall, this gate has a lot of history over the past 100 years. It marks the end of the highway leading from the Jaffa coast and now leads into the Muslim and Armenian quarters. A road allows cars to enter the Old City through a wide gap in the wall between Jaffa Gate and the Citadel. This passage was originally opened in 1898 when Kaiser Wilhelm II of Germany visited Jerusalem. The ruling Ottoman Turks opened it so the German Emperor would not have to dismount his carriage to enter the city.

ZION GATE

The Zion Gate is located in the south part of the Old City. It was used by the Israel Defense Forces in 1967 to enter and capture the Old City. The stones surrounding the gate are still pockmarked by weapons fire. This entrance leads to the Jewish and Armenian quarters.

DUNG GATE

Located in the south wall this Gate leads into the Temple Mount area and the Western Wall of the Temple Mount. Solomon's stables were nearby. Since the 2nd century, refuse has been hauled out of the city through this gate.

GOLDEN / EASTERN GATE

This is the oldest and most important of Jerusalem's gates. You will notice that unlike the others it is closed, The Moslems know the Jewish Messiah will come through this Gate and they filled it with 16 feet of cement. They also know a Gadol Cohen (High Priest) cannot walk in a graveyard so they bury their dead there. The Golden Gate faces the Mount of Olives on the East wall of the Old City. We will show now that this gate is in direct alignment with the Holy of Holies of Israel's past two Temples.

THE TEMPLE MOUNT, THE WORLD'S FLASHPOINT !

The Temple Mount and Eastern/Golden Gate
Viewed from the East Above the Mount of Olives

Daniel is the Book of the Times of the Gentiles, but in its latter part it is more pre-eminently the Times of Jerusalem and her Temple Mount. There is no place on earth more emotive than the Temple Mount. When one denies that the Temple of Solomon and the rebuilt Temple of Herod once stood there they have brought new meaning to the adage, *In Denial*. The Muslim world denies it; and the rush to political correctness now calls it the *El Aqsa Compound*!

The *New York Times* (not a good friend of the Nation Israel) had even questioned whether the Temple ever stood there, but then amended the statement a day later.

> The New York Times walked back an article that questioned whether two Jewish temples ever existed on the site of the Temple Mount in Jerusalem. The article, written by Rick Gladstone, a Times foreign editor, originally published on October 8 (2015), read: "The question, which many books and scholarly treatises have never definitively answered, is whether the 37-acre site, home to Islam's sacred Dome of the Rock shrine and Al-Aqsa Mosque, was also the precise location of two ancient Jewish temples, one built on the remains of the other, and both long since gone."

> The article was amended the following day and a correction published in the newspaper. The correction stated: "An earlier version of this article misstated the question that many books and scholarly treatises have never definitively answered concerning the two ancient Jewish temples. The question is where precisely on the 37-acre Temple Mount site the temples had once stood, not whether the temples had ever existed there." www.timesofisrael.com/ny-times-amends-article-questioning-jewish-temples-existence-on-temple-mount/

The Eastern Gate and the Ancient Holy of Holies

There is a growing view today that the Muslim's did not as claimed build their Dome of the Rock edifice over the site of the ancient Jewish Holy of Holies. According to Josephus and the Talmud this holy place, where the Ark of the Covenant rested, was *directly in line* with a prominent eastern gate known as the Shushan Gate. It now seems increasingly likely that as there is little on the Eastern Wall to indicate the remains of another prominent gate; the Eastern or Golden Gate (now known to be built upon the foundations of an earlier gate) **is the location of the gate** to which the Talmud and Josephus referred.

The following is from *Bible History Online*.

> During the time of the First Temple the Eastern Gate (also called Shushan or HaKohan gate) was the main entrance into the Temple area. It was also the gate that Jesus entered on a humble donkey in His triumphal entry. If one were to stand on the Mount of Olives he could look over this Eastern Gate into the huge area presently north of the Dome of the Rock and see all the gates (at different levels) in a perfect line: the

DANIEL 8. THE VISION OF THE RAM, GOAT AND LITTLE HORN

East (Shushan) Gate --Outer Court Gate --Inner Court Gate --Temple Entrance. The Talmud makes an interesting observation:

"All the walls which were there were high, except the wall in the east, so that the priest who burned the heifer, standing on the top of the Mount of Olives, and directing himself to look, saw through the gateway of the sanctuary, at the time when he sprinkled the blood." [Mishnah, Middot 2:4].

The Golden Gate (Eastern Gate) in the eastern wall of Jerusalem gave access to the courtyards of the Temple from the Kidron valley.

Tradition

According to Jewish tradition [but based on Scriputre!] [sic.] the Messiah (Mashiach) will enter Jerusalem from the east. The gate has a special holiness; legend has it that the Shechinah (Divine Presence) used to appear through this gate and will appear again, and that in the meantime it must be left untouched. The Arabs (Moslems) call this gate The Mercy Gate (Bab el Rahmeh) and according to the Koran, the just will pass through this gate on the Day of Judgment.

The Sealed Gate

It is interesting that this gate is the only one of the eight gates in Jerusalem that is sealed. The Arabs believe that since the Jews expect that Messiah would come through this gate (Sha'ar harachamim) they would try to prevent any possibility of His return.

The East gate was walled up by its Muslim conquerors (the Ottoman Turks) with great stones in 1530 A.D. and a cemetery was planted in front of it thinking that the Jewish Messiah could not set foot in a cemetery and therefore would not be able to come. Many believe this was done to prevent the entrance of the Jewish Messiah through that gate as was foretold by known Old Testament prophecies.

The East Gate and the Return of the Messiah

Christ entered Jerusalem through the East gate around 32 A.D. (long before it was blocked by the Ottomans) as he came down from the Mount of Olives and entered the temple according to our understanding of Luke 19:28-48. He would have entered through the original gate in the wall which was destroyed with the city by the Romans in 70 A.D. Jesus, having entered the city, said that he would not be seen again until Jerusalem acknowledges Him (Matthew 23:37-39). (http://www.bible-history.com/jewishtemple/JEWISH_TEMPLEThe_Golden_Gate.htm

Note: Compare the sealing of the current Eastern Gate with the Eastern Gate of the Millennial Temple. The latter will also be shut!

• *Then he brought me back the way of the gate of the outward sanctuary which looketh toward the east; and it was shut. Then said the LORD unto me; This gate shall be shut, it shall not be opened, and no man shall enter in by it; because the LORD, the God of Israel, hath entered in by it, therefore it shall be shut (Ezek 44:1,2).*

The Research of Asher Kaufman

A prized volume in my library is the large paged volume by Asher Kaufman, *The Temple Mount: Where Is The Holy of Holies.* For many years Dr. Kaufman served as professor at The Hebrew University of Jerusalem. His work is a primary reference source indicating that the Temple of Solomon was located to the north of Dome of the Rock Mosque. It is one of the most extensive works of research available on this subject.

The Following by Rickard Levitt Sawyer of Family Bible Messianic Ministries gives a brief overview of Kaufman's conclusions.

I believe that the archaeological evidence shows that the Muslim Dome of the Rock is in fact **not** standing on the site of the Second Temple as most suppose, but nearly 50 yards to the south of that spot. Two of the major evidences to that opinion are the location of the Golden (Eastern) Gate and the Dome of the Tablets, which is also known as the Dome of the Spirits.

**The Temple Mount looking west from above
the Golden Gate, showing the alignment of
the Dome of the Tablets**

The Dome of the Rock is situated approximately 50 yards south of a direct east-west line from the middle of the Golden Gate. If you were designing a Temple to the God of the Universe with a surrounding security wall, and you wanted visitors to the Temple to be totally awe-struck as they see it for the first time, does it not make sense that you would locate that Temple in a direct line with the main entrance to the enclosure? You would want people entering through the main gate of the city to be immediately struck with a view of the magnificent Temple itself the instant they enter the gate. If the Temple were located at the position of the Dome of the Rock, then worshippers would have to enter the city through the Golden Gate, turn left and travel 50 yards south along the inside of the city wall, make a hard right turn and climb the stairs to the main platform, then enter through the main gate of the Temple grounds into the court of the Gentiles, where they would finally actually see the Temple for the first time. Much less dramatic!

It makes more sense that there would be a direct east-west line from the center of the Golden Gate, through the main gate of the Temple proper, through the door to the Holy Place, directly into the Most Holy Place. That being the case, the Most Holy Place, and the Ark of the Covenant within it, would logically be located due west of the Golden Gate. Interestingly enough, that is the **exact** location of the Dome of the Tablets (marked by the red arrow), as shown in the photograph above.

The Dome of the Tablets is a small Islamic cupola on the bedrock of the Temple Mount, approximately 50 yards north of the Dome of the Rock (to your left as you look at this picture). Nobody knows for sure why it is called "the Dome of the Tablets" but conjecture is that "Dome of the Tablets" traces back to the "Dome of the Tablets of the Covenant inside the ark in the Holy of Holies," and that "Dome of the Spirits" [as it also called] traces back to "Dome of the Spirit of God that dwelt in the Holy of Holies." Archeologist Asher S. Kaufman claims that it marks the exact spot where the Tablets of the Torah sat within the Ark of the Covenant in the Most Holy Place. ("Where the Ancient Temple of Jerusalem Stood. Extant 'foundation stone' for the Ark of the Covenant is identified." *Biblical Archaeology Review*, 9:02, Mar/Apr 1983.)

**Detail of the Dome of the Tablets
with the Dome of the Rock in the background and the Al Aqsa Mosque in the far left background behind the Dome of the Rock**

(A) The Dome of the Tablets, (B) The Dome of the Rock, (C) The El Asqa Mosque

A Possible "Compromise Temple" Location
with the Holy of Holies situated where the Dome of the Tablets now stands. The Eastern Gate creates a direct line through this Temple into the Holy of Holies

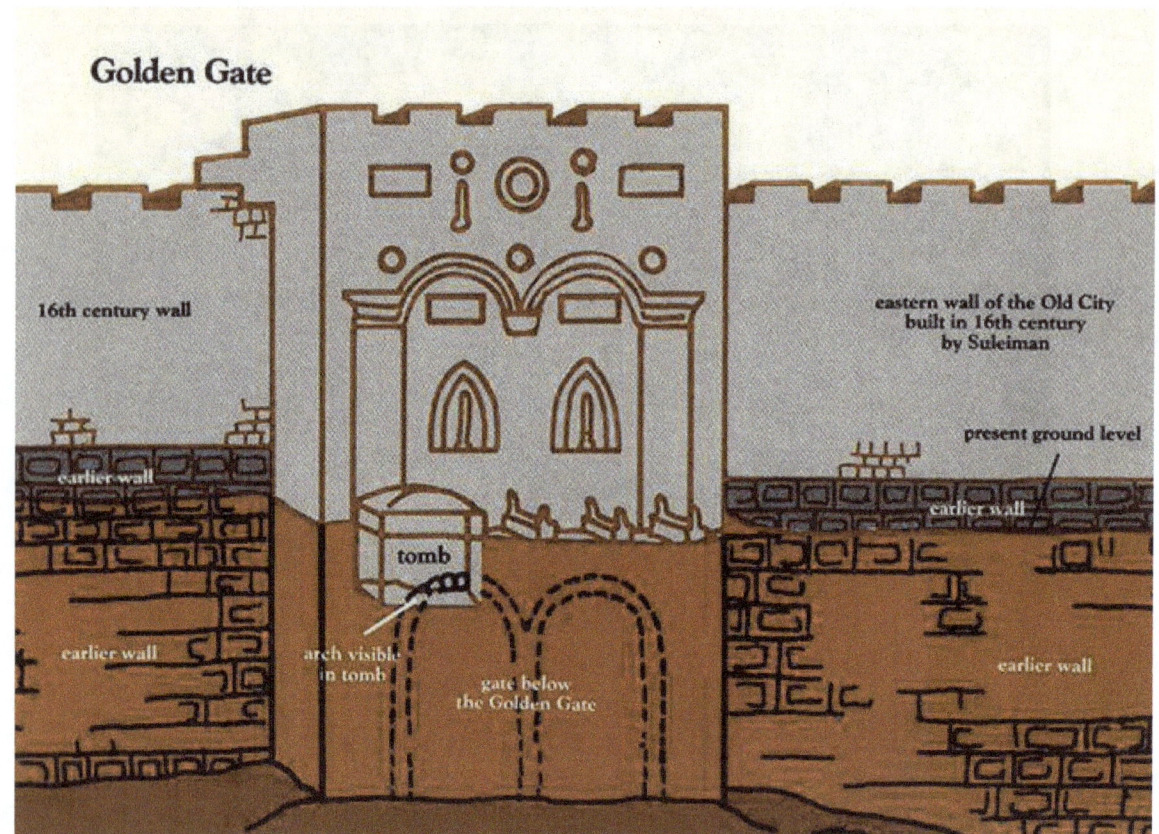

(http://www.templemount.org/jerusalemgates/gates.html)

The Foundations of the Earlier Eastern Gate

The Eastern Gate is the oldest of the current gates in Jerusalem's Old City Walls. According to Jewish tradition, the Shekhinah (Divine Presence) used to appear through this gate, and will appear again when the Messiah comes (Ezekiel 44:1-3) and a new gate replaces the present one. Jewish people have prayed for mercy at this gate. Hence the name Sha'ar Harachamim the Gate of Mercy. This is the gate that Jesus passed through on Palm Sunday.

The date when the present Eastern Gate was built is disputed. It was probably built in the 520s AD, as part of Justinian I's building program in Jerusalem, and on top of the ruins of the earlier gate in the wall. An alternate theory holds that it was built in the later part of the 7th century by Byzantine artisans employed by the Umayyad khalifs.

The Ottoman Sultan Suleiman sealed off the Golden Gate in 1541. While some say this was purely for defensive reasons, it is likely that he took to heart the Biblical promises that the Messiah at His Second Coming will enter Jerusalem from the east and through this gate (Zech 14:1-4; Ezek 43:1-7). The Muslims have sought further to prevent the Messiah's entrance by building a cemetery in front of the gate. These two measures have long been a prominent monument to the foolish and contradictory nature of unbelief in Christ's Second Coming. See: http://www.crystalinks.com/jerusalemgates.html

In 1969 James Fleming discovered beneath the current gate remains of the much earlier gate dating to the time of the Second Temple (Herod's). *Biblical Archaeological Review* gives the following account of this discovery:

> The Golden Gate is located in a turret protruding from the eastern wall of the Old City of Jerusalem. The two arched portals of the Golden Gate are now mortared closed, but if you could walk through them, you would find yourself on the Temple Mount, which is located in the southeastern corner of the Old City. In short, the southern part of the

eastern wall of the Old City is also the eastern wall of the Temple Mount, and if it were open, the Golden Gate would lead into the Old City directly onto the Temple Mount.

On the interior (western side) of the Gate is an elaborate structure that includes domed chambers that may be entered from steps leading down from the Temple Mount. Outside the Golden Gate is a Moslem cemetery. It covers the slope down to the Kidron Valley.

In the drawing [above], we see, above ground, the Golden Gate and the eastern wall. We also see also the sealed Lower Gate below the Golden Gate and an underground eastern wall. The author [James Fleming] of this article stumbled into the large tomb in front of the left portal of the Golden Gate. At the bottom of the tomb, on the face of the wall, he observed wedge-shaped stones, indicating the top of an arch. In the drawing above, the stones that he actually saw are drawn in solid lines inside the tomb. If the partial arch he saw is, in fact, complete, it forms an arched gateway exactly under the left portal of the Golden Gate. Presumably, a similar arched portal is under the right portal of the Golden Gate, thus forming a double-portaled Lower Gate. Except for the stones in the left arch of the Lower Gate that were actually observed, the Lower Gate is drawn with dotted lines to show that it is a reconstruction. "The Undiscovered Gate Beneath Jerusalem's Golden Gate" by James Fleming—*BAR*, Jan/Feb 1983).

Picture taken within the tomb showing the upper part of the arch of the earlier Eastern Gate

With the ever increasing desire of the Jewish People to worship on the Temple Mount, Israel will make a covenant with a political leader who will not only allow them to worship on the Temple Mount but also enable them to build a Temple there. As the influence of this leader spreads around the world, it is obvious that he did not reckon upon the entry of the Two Witnesses into Jerusalem. Few can imagine the all surpassing power the Two Witnesses will have in Jerusalem and on its Temple Mount. For three and one half years, despite all of his efforts to the contrary, the **Antichrist will be powerless to do anything about it!**

After our survey of Jerusalem and its Temple Mount we now return to Chapter 8, which we find is divided into two parts of equal length: the *Vision* and the *Interpretation*. Unlike the interpretation of Chapter 7, the Interpretation here is given as a single unit.

The Vision Given To Daniel 8:1-14.

In the third year of the reign of king Belshazzar a vision appeared unto me, even unto me Daniel, after that which appeared unto me at the first. (8:2) And I saw in a vision; and it came to pass, when I saw, that I was at Shushan in the palace, which is in the

DANIEL 8. THE VISION OF THE RAM, GOAT AND LITTLE HORN

province of Elam; and I saw in a vision, and I was by the river of Ulai. (8:3) Then I lifted up mine eyes, and saw, and, behold, there stood before the river a ram which had two horns: and the two horns were high; but one was higher than the other, and the higher came up last. (8:4) I saw the ram pushing westward, and northward, and southward; so that no beasts might stand before him, neither was there any that could deliver out of his hand; but he did according to his will, and became great. (8:5) And as I was considering, behold, an he goat came from the west on the face of the whole earth, and touched not the ground: and the goat had a notable horn between his eyes. (8:6) And he came to the ram that had two horns, which I had seen standing before the river, and ran unto him in the fury of his power. (8:7) And I saw him come close unto the ram, and he was moved with choler against him, and smote the ram, and brake his two horns: and there was no power in the ram to stand before him, but he cast him down to the ground, and stamped upon him: and there was none that could deliver the ram out of his hand. (8:8) Therefore the he goat waxed very great: and when he was strong, the great horn was broken; and for it came up four notable ones toward the four winds of heaven. (8:9) And out of one of them came forth a little horn, which waxed exceeding great, toward the south, and toward the east, and toward the pleasant land. (8:10) And it waxed great, even to the host of heaven; and it cast down some of the host and of the stars to the ground, and stamped upon them. (8:11) Yea, he magnified himself even to the prince of the host, and by him the daily sacrifice was taken away, and the place of the sanctuary was cast down. (8:12) And an host was given him against the daily sacrifice by reason of transgression, and it cast down the truth to the ground; and it practised, and prospered. (8:13) Then I heard one saint speaking, and another saint said unto that certain saint which spake, How long shall be the vision concerning the daily sacrifice, and the transgression of desolation, to give both the sanctuary and the host to be trodden under foot? (8:14) And he said unto me, Unto two thousand and three hundred days; then shall the sanctuary be cleansed.

The Introduction to the Vision.

The Time. ***In the third year of the reign of king Belshazzar a vision appeared unto me, even unto me Daniel, after that which appeared unto me at the first.*** (8:1). Though Chapter 6 brought us to beginning of the Persian era, with Darius as king; the revelations of Chapters 7 and 8 were given in the last years of Babylon, in Belshazzar's first and third years. The revelations are likely presented in this way to demonstrate that it is primarily Babylon rather than the following kingdoms that characterise to the greater extent the *Time of the Gentiles*. It will be more *Babylonian* than it is Persian, Grecian or even Roman. Thus at the close of the Age and the Bible, two chapters are devoted to Babylon (Rev 17,18).

The Means. *A vision appeared unto me*. This second revelation given directly to Daniel appeared not as before, when he was asleep, but when he was awake. Formerly he had ***a dream and visions of his head upon his bed*** (Dan 7:1). We can be glad that the revelation has been made known to us and placed in Scripture, though the reasons for the different means are not made known.

> • *God, who at sundry times and **in divers manners** spake in time past unto the fathers by the prophets (Heb 1:1).*

The Place. ***And I saw in a vision; and it came to pass, when I saw, that I was at Shushan in the palace, which is in the province of Elam; and I saw in a vision, and I was by the river of Ulai*** (8:2). In the vision, Daniel saw himself supernaturally transported to Shushan (Susa), much like Ezekiel was transported to Jerusalem in the famous Temple vision (Ezek. 40-48), although he also remained physically in Babylon.

It is significant that the prophet was projected geographically into the future of the Persian and Greek empires, concerning which his great vision was to furnish prophetic revelation. The fact that he saw himself in Susa, in the province of Elam, a city that later became one of the principal residences of Persian monarchs, shows that the prophet was to be granted important information concerning the political and governmental powers that were to come into ascendancy there, and which would have such an important effect on Daniel's people, the Jews.

The Assyrians under Ashurbanipal sacked Shushan and sent its inhabitants to exile in Samaria (Ezra 4:9,10), but it flourished again under the Persians and became one of the three royal cities (Neh 1:1) and figures prominently in the book of Esther (1:2,5; 2:3; 3:15, etc.). The site of Susa was first excavated in 1851.

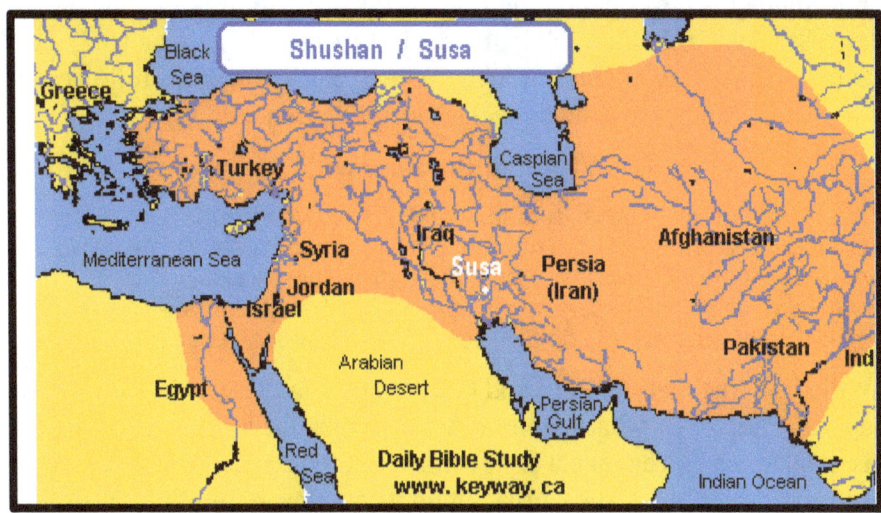

The Persian Empire

Susa was located in **Elam** ("highland", part of present day Iran), the region beyond the Tigris river east of Babylonia (Gen 10:22; 14:1; Isa 11:11; Jer 25:25; Ezek 32:24). In the vision Daniel found himself supernaturally projected alongside *the river of Ulai*, the Ulaeus of classical writers, an artificial canal that flowed close by Susa (*Unger*).

(www.aitotours.com/uploads/files/Iran%20by%20City%20Photos/Susa-Chogha-Zanbil.jpg)

Shushan Today

Thus while Daniel was still a captive in Babylon he is transported some 250 miles to the east by the Spirit of God to the kingly city in the empire that is shortly to conquer Babylon. The body may be bound but the Holy Spirit is not. The spiritual projection Daniel would

DANIEL 8. THE VISION OF THE RAM, GOAT AND LITTLE HORN

experience was similar to that of the Apostle John on the Isle of Patmos. Both were transported into the future Day of the Lord.

> • *I John, who also am your brother, and companion in tribulation, and in the kingdom and patience of Jesus Christ, was in the isle that is called Patmos, for the word of God, and for the testimony of Jesus Christ. I was in the Spirit on the Lord's day, and heard behind me a great voice, as of a trumpet (Rev 1:9,10).*

Many interpret this to mean that John was in spiritual communion with the Lord on *Sunday*, but Sunday is never called *the Lord's day* in Scripture, it is always *the first day of the week* (Matt 28:1; Mk 16:2,9; Lk 24:1; Jhn 20:1,19; Acts 20:7; 1 Cor 16:2). John was projected into the events of the Day of the Lord (the seven year Tribulation followed by the Millennial Reign of Christ); Daniel will now have the same experience.

The Vision of the Ram with Two Horns.

> *Then I lifted up mine eyes, and saw, and, behold, there stood before the river a ram which had two horns: and the two horns were high; but one was higher than the other, and the higher came up last. I saw the ram pushing westward, and northward, and southward; so that no beasts might stand before him, neither was there any that could deliver out of his hand; but he did according to his will, and became great (8:3,4).*

While it is true that the Ram and Goat (Persia and Greece) composed the *midriff* of the great image in Chapter 2; what Daniel now sees goes far beyond those two ancient empires. Unless, as in Chapter 7, we make a firm connection to the end of the age, the rise of Antichrist and the Return of the Lord Jesus Christ, attempts at interpreting these visions will be met with confusion. Here we see how end time events can have their roots in early history, but they are nevertheless *end time*. They occur at the time of Christ's Return.

(americaslastdays.blogspot.com)

The Ram and Goat Vision

The representations given here of the ram and the goat accord with the historical emblems of Persia and Greece. The national emblem of Persia was a ram, and Persian coins had a ram's head engraved on one side. Noah Hutchings gives the following summary:

> What we are dealing with here is horns. The beasts on which these horns appear are of secondary importance. Horns are symbolic of kings and rulers, and the eighth chapter deals not so much with empires and governmental administration as it does with the identification and nature of notable potentates who would rule over the earth until Christ comes again.

We have no trouble at all with the vision as far as it pertains to the ram and the he goat. Even a child should be able to interpret it from the explanation given to Daniel by the archangel Gabriel. According to verse twenty, the ram represented the united kingdom of Media and Persia. The two horns on the ram represent the first two kings of this empire. We read: The ram which thou sawest having two horns are the kings of Media and Persia. As depicted by the ram, Medo-Persia moved westward and conquered Babylon; it moved southward to Egypt; and it moved northward to Greece. This was the extent of the Medo-Persian conquests. The two horns on the ram spoke of the two most notable kings of the dual empire. One horn came up on the ram, and then another horn came up which overshadowed the first.

The first horn represented Darius the Mede, and although Darius was a relatively good man, as far as ancient monarchs could be called good, he was not a strong king. He relied heavily on his three presidents and his prime minister, Daniel, for advice and counsel. His reign was also brief, lasting only two years. The second king of Medo-Persia, Cyrus, completely overshadowed Darius. Cyrus was the conqueror, the strong man, and we know that he ruled the kingdom for at least twenty years, and possibly longer. Therefore, we have no difficulty in determining that the ram is Medo-Persia. The short horn on the ram is Darius and the long horn on the ram is Cyrus. The agnostic or atheist might say that this was not a revelation — that Daniel would have known at that time that Babylon would be defeated by the Medes and Persians, and as Darius and Cyrus were both leaders of their own countries, they would be the new rulers over the kingdom. However, in this same vision God showed Daniel that in the more distant future (and thus far beyond Daniel's time) the Medo-Persian Empire would be overrun by Greece (pp. 183,184).

The Vision of the Goat.

<u>The Great Horn</u>. ***And as I was considering, behold, an he goat came from the west on the face of the whole earth, and touched not the ground: and the goat had a notable horn between his eyes*** (8:5). The national emblem of Greece was a goat and the coins of this nation carried the outline of a goat. The ancient capital of Greece was Aegae, which meant "the goat city." Alexander himself was nicknamed "The Goat," and his son by Roxana was called Aegus, "the son of a goat." Inasmuch as Persia and Greece are so clearly identified by their national emblems, we should also expect the beasts of Daniel chapter seven to relate to nations with similar emblems — namely, England, the United States, Russia, the Afro-Asian Muslim bloc, and the Revived Roman Empire (*Hutchings*).

Though Greece had long been an influential nation, with the introduction of ***the notable horn*** (Alexander), it swiftly arose to become an empire.

<u>The Attack Against the Ram</u>. ***And he came to the ram that had two horns, which I had seen standing before the river, and ran unto him in the fury of his power. And I saw him come close unto the ram, and he was moved with choler against him, and smote the ram, and brake his two horns: and there was no power in the ram to stand before him, but he cast him down to the ground, and stamped upon him: and there was none that could deliver the ram out of his hand*** (8:6,7). The fierce anger of the goat points to Alexander. Josephus records the Grecian emperor often went into a rage when he was defied or if battle plans did not develop as he expected. The immense armies of Persia were powerless to save it from the smaller forces of Alexander, which were fired with rage for earlier Persian attacks against the Greek mainland. In lightning advances, Alexander won three decisive battles against the Persians: at Granicus (334 BC); Issus (333 BC) and Gaugamela (near Nineveh, 331 BC). After Gaugamela the Persian Empire crumbled and swiftly fell under Alexander's dominion. In 330 BC the great Persian capital of Persepolis was burned. The few terse words of the inerrant words of prophecy given to Daniel describe perfectly the overwhelming force, swiftness and manoeuvrability of Alexander's legions. His Persian conquest determined the history of the Middle East for the next two hundred years.

DANIEL 8. THE VISION OF THE RAM, GOAT AND LITTLE HORN

<u>The Great Horn Broken</u>. ***Therefore the he goat waxed very great: and when he was strong, the great horn was broken*** (8:8). History records that Alexander died just after he had conquered – very unexpectedly and very suddenly. Like Saddam Hussein, Alexander died attempting to rebuild Nebuchadnezzar's Babylon.

Alexander's Death After Attempting to Rebuild Babylon

Daniel wrote about the fall of Alexander from Babylon. It is very remarkable that the notable horn of Greece, Alexander (Dan 8:21), would die after making plans to rebuild Babylon. While it is true that the Babylonian spirit will characterize the Times of the Gentiles, and that the end of the time will see the rise of religious and commercial Babylon (Rev 17,18); yet in accordance with prophecy the ancient city itself would not be rebuilt. The tooth of time would leave Babylon as desolate as Sodom and Gomorrah. Alexander and Saddam attempted to defy this prophecy and both died in the process!

> • *And Babylon, the glory of kingdoms, the beauty of the Chaldees' excellency, shall be as when God overthrew Sodom and Gomorrah.* **It shall never be inhabited, neither shall it be dwelt in from generation to generation**: *neither shall the Arabian pitch tent there; neither shall the shepherds make their fold there (Isa 13:19,20).*

> • *And I will render unto Babylon and to all the inhabitants of Chaldea all their evil that they have done in Zion in your sight, saith the LORD. Behold, I am against thee, O destroying mountain, saith the LORD, which destroyest all the earth: and I will stretch out mine hand upon thee, and roll thee down from the rocks, and will make thee a burnt mountain. And* **they shall not take of thee a stone for a corner, nor a stone for foundations; but thou shalt be desolate for ever**, *saith the LORD (Jer 51:24-26).*

History records that the destruction and desolation of ancient Babylon took place in stages. Though conquered by the Persians, it still initially retained importance, and though a regional administrative centre, was increasingly beset with destructive turmoil. Alexander the Great died in Babylon (323 BC) shortly after he announced plans to rebuild the city. This should be viewed as Gods judgement upon an attempt to restore that which the Bible declared would be *desolate forever* (Jer. 51:26).

> According to a Babylonian astronomical diary, Alexander died between the evening of June 10 and the evening of June 11, 323 BC. This happened in the palace of Nebuchadnezzar II in Babylon.
> wikipedia.org/wiki/Death_of_Alexander_the_Great

Thereafter the city went into steep decline. A tablet dated 275 BC, states that the inhabitants of Babylon were transported to Seleucia. With this the history of Babylon (the city) seems practically to come to an end. By 141 BC, when the Parthian Empire took over the region, Babylon was in complete desolation and obscurity. In 20 BC the Greek historian Strabo described it as a "vast desolation." In the AD era, the historian Dio Cassius (c.150-235 AD) quoted a visitor to Babylon as "finding nothing but mounds and stones and ruins."

1 Peter 5:13 refers to *the church that is at Babylon*, and both Philo and Josephus say that many Jews inhabited Babylon during the Apostolic era. Later, from Babylon the *Babylonian Talmud* was prepared. This, however, refers to Babylon the *region* with its centres' of population, not the *ruins* of the 300 kilometer sq. ancient city.

In recent times Saddam Hussein put forward grandiose plans and spent large sums to rebuild Nebuchadnezzar's Babylon and for his efforts met the same fate as Alexander: Saddam is dead and the site remains desolate. *It shall never be inhabited, neither shall it be dwelt in from generation to generation* (Isa 13:20). There will be (and likely already is!) a latter day Babylon (Rev. 17, 18), but it will not be built upon the ruins of the ancient city. Those ruins will *never be inhabited*.

<u>The Four Divisions of Alexander's Empire</u>. *And for it came up four notable ones toward the four winds of heaven* (8:8).

Alexander's Empire Divided Among His Four Generals

After Alexander's death, his four generals divided the empire into four divisions, with each taking a province for his own dominion. Cassander took over Macedonia and Greece; Lysimachus claimed Asia Minor (Thrace and Bithynia); Seleucus took Syria and Babylonia; and Ptolemy took Egypt and North Africa. Out of one of these four divisions (which were to become the eastern half of the Roman Empire) come the Little Horn. Many believe there is a historical fulfilment to this Little Horn.

Is the Little Horn Antiochus Epiphanes?

There has been a great deal of disagreement among Bible students concerning the identity of this *Little Horn*. Is it the same Little Horn as in Chapter 7 that arose from among Ten Horns? YES! Was it fulfilled as many think in past history with the rise Antiochus Epiphanes? NO! Noah Hutchings writes the following:

> Many believe that this prophecy was fulfilled when Antiochus Epiphanes (175-164 BC), the governor of Syria, took Jerusalem and defiled the temple by offering a sow upon the altar. There is a great similarity between the little horn of chapter eight and Antiochus Epiphanes. The antiochus, or ruler of Syria, who preceded Epiphanes was the grandfather of Seleucus, the Grecian general. This antiochus died, and his brother Epiphanes became the new king to carry on the Syrian dynasty established by General Seleucus. We read in verse nine: "And out of one of them [doubtless meaning Seleucus], came forth a little horn"

> Antiochus Epiphanes did offer an initial fulfilment of Daniel's prophecy. In our studies about this man from The History of the Jews by Josephus, we find that he was without a doubt the most despicable man in the world. He was a confirmed liar. He used the women in his own household as pawns to gain political favour. He tried to unify the four divisions of the old Grecian Empire, but he was turned back at Egypt when the Romans began to advance into that part of the world. Antiochus dealt unmercifully with the Jews. He killed anyone who possessed a copy of the Law of Moses, and he crucified one hundred thousand in Jerusalem who refused to worship his false gods. He hung all the young Jewish boys who had been circumcised; he horribly mutilated the Jewish women; and he offered a sow upon the altar in the temple. Josephus considered this deed the abomination of desolation prophesied by Daniel.

> The Jews, under the leadership of Judah the Maccabee, threw off the Syrian yoke and cleansed the temple. This was in the Jewish month of Kislev, the twenty-fifth day; this date corresponds to December 25, or Christmas. The day that the temple was cleansed and the perpetual lamp was lit has since been observed by the Jews as Hanukkah, the Feast of Lights.

DANIEL 8. THE VISION OF THE RAM, GOAT AND LITTLE HORN

> In spite of the fact that those things which Antiochus Epiphanes did seemed to have satisfied the prophecy about the little horn of Daniel chapter eight, he was not the man depicted in the vision. Even those who make the application do so with great uncertainty. In almost every commentary on chapter eight that makes the connection to Antiochus Epiphanes, it is explained that he could possibly have been the little horn, or that the author is uncertain. Martin Luther said: "This chapter in Daniel refers to both Antiochus and Antichrist." The majority seem to concur with Luther's opinion — the prophecy was fulfilled in type in Antiochus, but the real little horn will be the Antichrist. In other words, the little horn of chapter eight that grew up out of one of the four notable horns is the same little horn of chapter seven who comes up in the middle of the ten horns on the head of the terrible beast. How can we be certain of this?
>
> The four horns first point toward the four winds of heaven (Dan 8:8), indicating an end-time application. It will be in the latter time when the transgressors are come to the full (8:23). (pp. 187-189).

As bad as Antiochus Epiphanes was, what is revealed in Daniel Chapter 8 points far beyond that terrible man.

The Vision of the Little Horn.

Antichrist's Warfare in the Eastern Mediterranean. ***And out of one of them came forth a little horn, which waxed exceeding great, toward the south, and toward the east, and toward the pleasant land*** (8:9). On his road to world domination (Rev 13:4,7), we see here the direction of the Antichrist's conquests in the crucial eastern Mediterranean. From the central starting point in his kingdom, he will move toward the south, then he will turn eastward toward the *pleasant land*, or Israel. This could not apply to Antiochus Epiphanes, because he moved southward out of Syria and then turned westward toward Jerusalem. This route of conquest would indicate that the Antichrist will move southward into Egypt and Libya from Europe, and then turn eastward and move against Jerusalem (see *Hutchings*). This means that the Antichrist will probably come from the north-western part of the Grecian empire.

We have previously noted that the Fifth Macedonian Legion was at the forefront of the legions under Titus in the AD 70 destruction of Jerusalem. We now see further that Macedonia (the area given to Alexander's general, Cassander) was at the north-western corner of the divided Grecian Empire (see pp. 161, 167,193). If this scenario is correct it demonstrates the threefold origin of the Antichrist as given in Daniel. He comes from the among the Ten Horns; from Four of the Ten, and he is linked to on the most prominent legion of Titus.

The Threefold Origin of Antichrist as Given in Daniel

> • And of the **ten horns** that were in his head, and of **the other which came up**, and before whom three fell; even of that horn that had eyes, and a mouth that spake very great things, whose look was more stout than his fellows (Dan 7:20).

> • Therefore the he goat waxed very great: and when he was strong, the great horn was broken; and for it came up **four notable ones** toward the four winds of heaven. And out of one of them came forth **a little horn**, which waxed exceeding great, toward the south, and toward the east, and toward the pleasant land (Dan 8:8,9).

> • And after threescore and two weeks shall Messiah be cut off, but not for himself: and **the people of the prince that shall come** shall destroy the city and the sanctuary; and the end thereof shall be with a flood, and unto the end of the war desolations are determined (Dan 9:26).

This same stage of the Little Horn's eastern Mediterranean campaign is described further in in Daniel 11. There the King of the North and the King of the South unsuccessfully attempt to resist his advance.

> • **He shall enter also into the glorious land**, and **many countries shall be overthrown**: but these shall escape out of his hand, even Edom, and Moab, and the

*chief of the children of Ammon. He shall stretch forth his hand also upon the countries: and **the land of Egypt shall not escape**. But he shall have power over the treasures of gold and of silver, and over all the precious things of Egypt: and the Libyans and the Ethiopians shall be at his steps. But **tidings out of the east and out of the north** shall trouble him: therefore **he shall go forth with great fury to destroy**, and utterly to make away many. And **he shall plant the tabernacles of his palace between the seas in the glorious holy mountain**; yet he shall come to his end, and none shall help him (Dan 11:41-45).*

Antichrist's Warfare Against Heaven. ***And it waxed great, even to the host of heaven; and it cast down some of the host and of the stars to the ground, and stamped upon them*** (8:10). Daniel 10:12,13 reveals an instance of angelic warfare during Daniel's time, but here is a description of angelic warfare at the end of the Age during the Tribulation. The Antichrist being empowered by Satan will extend his warfare into the heavens themselves and will even cast down some of the angels to the earth. While the nature and implications of this conflict are not revealed, it is described further in Revelation 12 and demonstrates again the terrible times that await those who enter the Tribulation. This raises a difficult question!

Are Both Good and Evil Angels Cast Down During the Tribulation?

(1) Good Angels: Daniel 8:10 and perhaps Revelation 12:3,4?

• *And it waxed great, even to the host of heaven; and it **cast down some of the host and of the stars to the ground**, and stamped upon them (Dan 8:10).*

• *And there appeared another wonder in heaven; and behold **a great red dragon**, having seven heads and ten horns, and seven crowns upon his heads. And **his tail drew the third part of the stars of heaven, and did cast them to the earth**: and the dragon stood before the woman which was ready to be delivered, for to devour her child as soon as it was born (Rev 12:3,4).*

(2) Evil Angels: Revelation 12:7-10.

• *And **there was war in heaven**: Michael and his angels fought against the dragon; and the dragon fought and his angels, And prevailed not; neither was their place found any more in heaven. And **the great dragon was cast out**, that old serpent, called the Devil, and Satan, which deceiveth the whole world: he was cast out into the earth, **and his angels were cast out with him**. And I heard a loud voice saying in heaven, Now is come salvation, and strength, and the kingdom of our God, and the power of his Christ: for the accuser of our brethren is cast down, which accused them before our God day and night (Rev 12:7-10).*

While it is clear that Satan's angels are cast to earth during the Tribulation, Scripture also seems clearly to state that God's angels are also cast down during that time. Most say that Revelation 12:4 is referring to the original fall of Satan and his angels (cp. Isa 14:12-15; Ezek 28:16; Matt 25:41; Lk 10:18); nevertheless the context of both Daniel 8:10 and Revelation 12:4 is the future Tribulation, not past history.

Antichrist's Warfare Against Michael the Archangel. ***Yea, he magnified himself even to the prince of the host*** (8:11). Here we are informed that the power of the Antichrist's wrath will extend even to Michael, the prince of the heavenly host. Note the five times this mighty angel is mentioned is the Bible. These passages give further insights to the future angelic warfare.

• *But the prince of the kingdom of Persia withstood me one and twenty days: but, lo, **Michael, one of the chief princes**, came to help me; and I remained there with the kings of Persia (Dan 10:13).*

• *But I will shew thee that which is noted in the scripture of truth: and there is none that holdeth with me in these things, but **Michael your prince** (Dan 10:21).*

DANIEL 8. THE VISION OF THE RAM, GOAT AND LITTLE HORN

> *• And at that time shall **Michael** stand up, **the great prince** which standeth for the children of thy people: and there shall be a time of trouble, such as never was since there was a nation even to that same time: and at that time thy people shall be delivered, every one that shall be found written in the book (Dan 12:1).*
>
> *• Yet **Michael the archangel**, when contending with the devil he disputed about the body of Moses, durst not bring against him a railing accusation, but said, The Lord rebuke thee (Jude 9).*
>
> *• And there was war in heaven: **Michael and his angels** fought against the dragon; and the dragon fought and his angels (Rev 12:7).*

Antichrist's Warfare Against Jewish Temple Worship. ***And by him the daily sacrifice was taken away, and the place of the sanctuary was cast down. And an host was given him against the daily sacrifice by reason of transgression, and it cast down the truth to the ground; and it practised, and prospered*** (8:11,12). The Antichrist will make a seven year treaty with Israel. This will allow the Jewish People to have a place of worship on the Temple Mount and resume animal sacrifices. In the midst of these seven years the antichrist will break the covenant causing the sacrifices to cease. In trampling down Israel's sacrificial worship (as *misguided* as that worship is; see Rev 11:1,2), the Antichrist will be declaring to the world that he is God. Over the past decades substantial preparation have been made in preparation for the restoration of Temple worship. Note the key Biblical passages describing this:

> *• And he shall confirm the covenant with many for one week: and in the midst of the week he shall cause the sacrifice and the oblation to cease, and for the overspreading of abominations he shall make it desolate, even until the consummation, and that determined shall be poured upon the desolate (Dan 9:27).*
>
> *• And he shall plant the tabernacles of his palace between the seas in the glorious holy mountain; yet he shall come to his end, and none shall help him (Dan 11:45).*
>
> *• And from the time that the daily sacrifice shall be taken away, and the abomination that maketh desolate set up, there shall be a thousand two hundred and ninety days Blessed is he that waiteth, and cometh to the thousand three hundred and five and thirty days (Dan 12:11,12).*
>
> *• When ye therefore shall see the abomination of desolation, spoken of by Daniel the prophet, stand in the holy place, (whoso readeth, let him understand:) Then let them which be in Judaea flee into the mountains (Matt 24:15,16).*
>
> *• Who opposeth and exalteth himself above all that is called God, or that is worshipped; so that he as God sitteth in the temple of God, shewing himself that he is God (2 Thess 2:4).*
>
> *• And there was given me a reed like unto a rod: and the angel stood, saying, Rise, and measure the temple of God, and the altar, and them that worship therein. But the court which is without the temple leave out, and measure it not; for it is given unto the Gentiles: and the holy city shall they tread under foot forty and two months (Rev 11:1,2).*

The Length of Antichrist's Warfare Against the Temple. ***Then I heard one saint speaking, and another saint said unto that certain saint which spake, How long shall be the vision concerning the daily sacrifice, and the transgression of desolation, to give both the sanctuary and the host to be trodden under foot? And he said unto me, Unto two thousand and three hundred days; then shall the sanctuary be cleansed*** (8:13,14). In these verses Daniel is prophetically brought into a conversation of ***two saints*** seeking information concerning the terrible blasphemy of the Antichrist in breaking his covenant with Israel. It is a discussion regarding his taking absolute control of Jerusalem; literally treading down the city with the feet of his army; stopping the daily sacrifices; and then sitting in the temple to declare himself to be the Messiah.

The Questioners. These *two saints* are likely the Two Witnesses described in the Books of Zechariah and Revelation.

> *• And I answered again, and said unto him, What be these two olive branches which through the two golden pipes empty the golden oil out of themselves? And he answered me and said, Knowest thou not what these be? And I said, No, my lord. Then said he, **These are the two anointed ones**, that stand by the LORD of the whole earth (Zech 4:12-14).*

> *• And I will give power unto **my two witnesses**, and **they shall prophesy a thousand two hundred and threescore days**, clothed in sackcloth. **These are the two olive trees**, and the two candlesticks standing before the God of the earth (Rev 11:3,4).*

The Question. The question is addressed by the *one saint* who is listening to the *second saint* who is speaking. The inquiry concerns the length of time for the Tribulation sacrifices of the Jews and their desecration. *How long shall be the vision* **(1)** *concerning the daily sacrifice,* **(2)** *and the transgression of desolation, to give both the sanctuary and the host to be trodden under foot* **(8:14)?** The question is two-fold; it concerns the length of time that the daily sacrifice would be offered and the time of the Antichrist's desecration of that sacrifice by setting up his own image, and after which the Temple site would be restored.

The Answer. The *second saint* now addresses the answer to Daniel. ***And he said unto me, Unto two thousand and three hundred days; then shall the sanctuary be cleansed*** **(8:14)**. Note: at the end of the chapter these ***two thousand and three hundred days*** are described as ***evenings and mornings***.

> *• And the vision of the **evening and the morning** which was told is true: wherefore shut thou up the vision; for it shall be for many days (8:26).*

Three Common But UnteniableViews of the 2300 Days

Many suggestions are offered for these 2300 days (about six and one half years). At the outset we are impressed that it is specific time. It is 2300 days, not 2000 days. The most prominent views are:

(1). The most popular view is that it refers to a time within the reign of Antiochus IV (Epiphanes) who reigned from 175 to 164/3 BC. But as Walter K. Price writes: "No two significant events, 2300 days apart, can be found in the history of this era between 175 and 163 B.C., to form the boundary of this period. Even if the 2300 mornings and evenings are reduced to 1150 full days, this period of just over three years has no two outstanding events in Antiochus' history to mark off the beginning and end of its boundary." (*The Coming Antichrist*, Moody Press, p. 47). "Further, his actual desecration lasted only about three years." (John F Walvoord; Daniel, *The Key to Prophetic Revelation*, Moody Press, p. 190). While admitting no beginning or end in Antiochus' history, it is remarkable that both of these authors try to place the 2300 days is his times. Further, the statements made in Chapter 8 concerning the Little Horn go far beyond Antiochus. The setting is the Tribulation, not the Second Century BC.

(2). Others suggest the *evenings and mornings* statement of verse 26 indicates that the 2300 days are half days with the total being 1150 whole days. This would make the time a little over three years. But this would still fall short of the three and a half year periods of the Tribulation, or somewhat more than the approximately three years that Antiochus desecrated the Temple. The chief argument against this idea is as C. K. Keil states: "A Hebrew reader could not possibly understand the period of 2300 evening-mornings of 2300 half days or 1150 whole days, because evening and morning at the Creation constituted not the half but the whole day… We must therefore take the words as they are…2300 whole days". (C. F. Keil, *Biblical Commentary on the Book of Daniel*, Eerdmans, p. 304).

DANIEL 8. THE VISION OF THE RAM, GOAT AND LITTLE HORN

(3). Some appeal to the day-year theory. The one clear precedent in Scripture where days represent an exact number of years are in the symbolic acts which God told Ezekiel to perform. There he was specifically told: *And when thou hast accomplished them, lie again on thy right side, and thou shalt bear the iniquity of the house of Judah forty days:* ***I have appointed thee each day for a year*** (Ezek 4:6). No similar instruction was given to Daniel concerning the 2300 days. Further, whether these "2300 years" be viewed as solar (365 days) or lunar (360 days), the years since Alexander the Great died (323 BC) have now exceeded 2300 years (cp. Dan 8:8,9).

Note that Daniel is told to ***shut thou up the vision; for it shall be for many days*** (8:26). This is similar to what Daniel was told later: *But thou, O Daniel,* ***shut up the words and seal the book, even to the time of the end*** (12:4). This militates against the idea that the 2300 days occurred in past history (Antiochus) or that they occur as years across history.

A Look At The Numbers

There are substantial weaknesses in the three common views that render them untenable. The key and emphatic point stated in Daniel 8:14 is that ***after 2300 days the sanctuary will be cleansed***. This must be seen in relation to the other numbers given. The seven years (Dan 9:27) of the Tribulation are divided into two lunar-year periods of 1260 days (though it appears that the two times this figure is given refers to the second half the Tribulation).

> • And I will give power unto my two witnesses, and they shall prophesy **a thousand two hundred and threescore days**, clothed in sackcloth (Rev 11:3).

> • And the woman fled into the wilderness, where she hath a place prepared of God, that they should feed her there **a thousand two hundred and threescore days** (Rev 12:6).

The Tribulation is a period of 2520 days, and thus 220 days in excess of the 2300 days. As we find at the end of Chapter 12, two further periods totalling 75 days are added.

> • And from the time that the daily sacrifice shall be taken away, and the abomination that maketh desolate set up, there shall be **a thousand two hundred and ninety days**. Blessed is he that waiteth, and cometh to **the thousand three hundred and five and thirty days** (Dan 12:11,12).

Here are the numbers: To the 2520 days (1260 + 1260) there is first an added 30 days, and then a further 45 days: 1260 + 1260 + 30 + 45 = 2595 days, This would give a total excess of 295 days beyond the 2300 days. We are not able to ascertain exactly where within these seven-year-plus time frames the 2300 years occur. Yet the limits are clear: whether it is within the 2595 days, or the 2550 days, or the 2520 days – there will be these ominous 2300 days.

Will the Antichrist and False Prophet Make an Evening and Morning Telecast from the Temple Mount for 2300 Days?

In considering a possible and we think *likely* scenario for the 2300 days, we will look again at this passage and its related *evening and morning* passage. Note again and especially that the 2300 days have two component parts.

> • Then I heard one saint speaking, and another saint said unto that certain saint which spake, How long shall be the vision concerning **(1) the daily sacrifice**, and **(2) the transgression of desolation**, to give both the sanctuary and the host to be trodden under foot? And he said unto me, Unto two thousand and three hundred days; then shall the sanctuary be cleansed (8:13,14).

> • And the vision of the **evening and the morning** which was told is true: wherefore shut thou up the vision; for it shall be for many days (8:26).

It seems clear that the 2300 day vision comprises two proceedings: **(1)** *the daily sacrifice,* and **(2)** *the transgression of desolation,* Daniel sees the sacrifices taking place, and he sees also their abolition by the Antichrist and resulting desolation. Therefore the 2300 days do not begin with the abolition of the sacrifices at the midpoint of the Tribulation but rather when they begin. Further, the *evening and morning* in verse 26 must certainly refer to the *daily sacrifices* which were at the heart of the Old Testament Temple worship.

> • Command the children of Israel, and say unto them, My offering, and my bread for my sacrifices made by fire, for a sweet savor unto me, shall ye observe to offer unto me **in their due season**. And thou shalt say unto them, This is the offering made by fire which ye shall offer unto the LORD; **two lambs of the first year without spot day by day, for a continual burnt offering. The one lamb shalt thou offer in the morning**, and **the other lamb shalt thou offer at even**; And a tenth part of an ephah of flour for a meat offering, mingled with the fourth part of an hin of beaten oil. **It is a continual burnt offering, which was ordained in mount Sinai** for a sweet savor, a sacrifice made by fire unto the LORD (Num 28:2-6).

The Antichrist having made the Covenant with Israel and allowing them to resume sacrifices on the Temple Mount, would assure that he himself receives maximum publicity for his action. A daily world-wide telecast, every morning and every evening, will present this *great man of peace* (Dan 8:25) on the Temple Mount. For the first two or three years he will appear as Israel's benefactor and will give warm "lip service" to the God of Israel. But all will change. He will unexpectedly be seen in an altogether different light; and for the remaining years he appears as the *object* of the world's worship. If interest wanes during the latter part of this 2300 day telecast, *there will be means to assure that everyone is tuned in*.

Note especially that during this time, and in reference to the Temple Mount and the Jewish sacrifices – the Antichrist will be *showing himself*.

> • **When ye therefore shall see** the abomination of desolation, spoken of by Daniel the prophet, stand in the holy place, (whoso readeth, let him understand:). (Matt 24:15).

> • Who opposeth and exalteth himself above all that is called God, or that is worshipped; so that he as God sitteth in the temple of God, **shewing himself** that he is God (2 Thess 2:4).

As Titus Did in 70AD, Antichrist Will Terminate Israel's Christ-less Sacrifices: The Three Accounts of the Olivet Discourse Compared

The terrible act of the Beast will in fact be a judgement upon the *Christ-less* sacrifices that Israel will introduce during the Tribulation. Their temple services will not *measure up* (!), and in judgement will be brought to an end by Antichrist much like Titus did in 70 AD.

> • And there was given me a reed like unto a rod: and the angel stood, saying, Rise, and **measure the temple** of God, and **the altar**, and **them that worship** therein. But the court which is without the temple leave out, and measure it not; for it is given unto the Gentiles: and the holy city shall they tread under foot forty and two months (Rev 11:1,2).

Both 70 AD and the Tribulation are linked in the three accounts of the Olivet Discourse (Lk 21:12-24; Matt 24:15-22; Mk 13:14-20). Luke deals with both events and presents *the long period* between them. Luke in describing the Tribulation does not deal with the Antichrist's desecration of the Temple. Matthew and Mark deal only with the Tribulation and give an account of the Antichrist's desecration. AD 70 was a foreshadowing of what the Antichrist would do in the Temple. There is similar language in the three accounts but also notable differences.

DANIEL 8. THE VISION OF THE RAM, GOAT AND LITTLE HORN

Both 70 AD and the End Time Tribulation are Described in Luke; But no Description is Given of the Temple Desecrations

*• Then said he unto them, **Nation shall rise against nation**, and kingdom against kingdom: And **great earthquakes** shall be in divers places, and famines, and pestilences; and fearful sights and great signs shall there be from heaven (Lk 21:10,11). **But before all these,** they shall lay their hands on you, and persecute you, delivering you up to the synagogues, and into prisons, being brought before kings and rulers for my name's sake....And **when ye shall see Jerusalem compassed with armies**, then know that the desolation thereof is nigh. **Then let them which are in Judaea flee to the mountains**; and let them which are in the midst of it depart out; and let not them that are in the countries enter thereinto. For these be the days of vengeance, that all things which are written may be fulfilled [see Micah 3:12]. But **woe unto them that are with child**, and to them that give suck, in those days! **for there shall be great distress in the land**, and wrath upon this people. And they shall fall by the edge of the sword, **and shall be led away captive into all nations: and Jerusalem shall be trodden down of the Gentiles, until the times of the Gentiles be fulfilled** (Luke 21:12, 20-24).*

Luke goes on to describe the Tribulation (continued from 21:8-11), but without dealing with the Antichrist's desecration of the Temple.

Only the Tribulation (and with the Tribulation Temple Descration) is Described in Matthew and Mark

• For nation shall rise against nation, and kingdom against kingdom: and there shall be famines, and pestilences, and earthquakes, in divers places. All these are the beginning of sorrows (Matt 24:7,8)... When ye therefore shall see the abomination of desolation, spoken of by Daniel the prophet, stand in the holy place, (whoso readeth, let him understand:) Then let them which be in Judaea flee into the mountains: Let him which is on the housetop not come down to take any thing out of his house: Neither let him which is in the field return back to take his clothes. And woe unto them that are with child, and to them that give suck in those days! But pray ye that your flight be not in the winter, neither on the sabbath day: For then shall be great tribulation, such as was not since the beginning of the world to this time, no, nor ever shall be. And except those days should be shortened, there should no flesh be saved: but for the elect's sake those days shall be shortened (Matt 24:15-22).

*• **For nation shall rise against nation**, and kingdom against kingdom: and there shall be **earthquakes in divers places**, and there shall be famines and troubles: these are the **beginnings of sorrows** (Mk 13:8)... **But when ye shall see the abomination of desolation, spoken of by Daniel the prophet**, standing where it ought not, (let him that readeth understand,) then let them that be in Judaea flee to the mountains: And let him that is on the housetop not go down into the house, neither enter therein, to take any thing out of his house: And let him that is in the field not turn back again for to take up his garment. But woe to them that are with child, and to them that give suck in those days! And pray ye that your flight be not in the winter. **For in those days shall be affliction, such as was not from the beginning of the creation which God created unto this time**, neither shall be. And except that the Lord had shortened those days, no flesh should be saved: but for the elect's sake, whom he hath chosen, he hath shortened the days (Mk 13: 14-20).*

The Interpretation Given To Daniel 8:15-27.

And it came to pass, when I, even I Daniel, had seen the vision, and sought for the meaning, then, behold, there stood before me as the appearance of a man. (8:16) And I heard a man's voice between the banks of Ulai, which called, and said, Gabriel, make this man to understand the vision. (8:17) So he came near where I stood: and when he came, I was afraid, and fell upon my face: but he said unto me, Understand, O son of man: for at the time of the end shall be the vision. (8:18) Now as he was speaking with me, I was in a deep sleep on my face toward the ground: but he touched me, and set me upright. (8:19) And he said, Behold, I will make thee know what shall be in the last end of the indignation: for at the time appointed the end shall be. (8:20) The ram which thou sawest having two horns are the kings of Media and Persia. (8:21) And the rough goat is the king of Grecia: and the great horn that is between his eyes is the first king. (8:22) Now that being broken, whereas four stood up for it, four kingdoms shall stand up out of the nation, but not in his power. (8:23) And in the latter time of their kingdom, when the transgressors are come to the full, a king of fierce countenance, and understanding dark sentences, shall stand up. (8:24) And his power shall be mighty, but not by his own power: and he shall destroy wonderfully, and shall prosper, and practise, and shall destroy the mighty and the holy people. (8:25) And through his policy also he shall cause craft to prosper in his hand; and he shall magnify himself in his heart, and by peace shall destroy many: he shall also stand up against the Prince of princes; but he shall be broken without hand. (8:26) And the vision of the evening and the morning which was told is true: wherefore shut thou up the vision; for it shall be for many days. (8:27) **And I Daniel fainted, and was sick certain days; afterward I rose up, and did the king's business; and I was astonished at the vision, but none understood it.**

The Interpreter is Sent to Daniel.

Daniel Seeks the Meaning *And it came to pass, when I, even I Daniel, had seen the vision, and sought for the meaning, then, behold, there stood before me as the appearance of a man* (8:15). Those that are given the truths of God cannot but want to know all they can about them. *To you that hear shall more be given* (Mk 2:24). Daniel considered the vision, compared it with the former revelations, tried to understand it, but now seeks by prayer (as he had done in 2:18) for an understanding. He did not seek in vain.

Gabriel Appears to Daniel. He was sent suddenly. As the angel Michael fights on behalf of God's people (Dan 12:1), so the angel Gabriel (*valiant one of God*) instructs God's people. The fact that Gabriel (the first instance in Scripture of a holy angel being mentioned by name) was called to interpret the vision to Daniel emphasises the importance of the disclosure it contains.

> • *Yea, whiles I was speaking in prayer, even the man* **Gabriel**, *whom I had seen in the vision at the beginning, being caused to fly swiftly, touched me about the time of the evening oblation. And he informed me, and talked with me, and said, O Daniel, I am now come forth to give thee skill and understanding (Dan 9:21,22).*

> • *And the angel answering said unto him, I am* **Gabriel**, *that stand in the presence of God; and am sent to speak unto thee, and to shew thee these glad tidings (Lk 1:19).*

> • *And in the sixth month the angel* **Gabriel** *was sent from God unto a city of Galilee, named Nazareth (Lk 1:26).*

Christ Commissions Gabriel. *And I heard a man's voice between the banks of Ulai, which called, and said, Gabriel, make this man to understand the vision* (8:16). Only Deity can command an angel. The One who here speaks from the midst of the river is Christ Himself. He was with the three Hebrews in the fiery furnace (a picture of the Tribulation), He will now commission Daniel's further instruction concerning the Tribulation. The scene here is similar to that which appears later.

> • *And in the four and twentieth day of the first month, as I was by the side of* **the great river**, *which is Hiddekel; Then I lifted up mine eyes, and looked, and* **behold a certain man clothed in linen**, *whose loins were girded with fine gold of Uphaz: His body also was like the beryl, and* **his face as the appearance of lightning**, *and his eyes as lamps of fire, and his arms and his feet like in colour to polished brass, and the voice of his words like the voice of a multitude. And I Daniel alone saw the vision: for the men that were with me saw not the vision; but a great quaking fell upon them, so that they fled to hide themselves. Therefore I was left alone, and saw this great vision, and there remained no strength in me: for my comeliness was turned in me into corruption, and I retained no strength. Yet heard I the voice of his words: and when I heard the voice of*

DANIEL 8. THE VISION OF THE RAM, GOAT AND LITTLE HORN

his words, then was I in a deep sleep on my face, and my face toward the ground. **And, behold, an hand touched me,** *which set me upon my knees and upon the palms of my hands. And he said unto me, O Daniel, a man greatly beloved,* **understand the words** *that I speak unto thee, and stand upright: for* **unto thee am I now sent**. *And when he had spoken this word unto me, I stood trembling (Dan 10:4-11).*

• *Then I Daniel looked, and, behold,* **there stood other two,** *the one on this side of the bank of the river, and the other on that side of the bank of the river. And one said to* **the man clothed in linen, which was upon the waters** *of the river, How long shall it be to the end of these wonders (Dan 12:5,6)?*

As with the interpreting angel to the Apostle John in the Book of Revelation (and also frequently in the Book of Zechariah to Zechariah) orders are now given to the angel Gabriel to inform Daniel concerning this vision.

<u>The Times of the Vision and its Effect upon Daniel</u>. (8:17) *So he came near where I stood: and when he came, I was afraid, and fell upon my face: but he said unto me, Understand, O son of man: for at the time of the end shall be the vision.* (8:18) *Now as he was speaking with me, I was in a deep sleep on my face toward the ground: but he touched me, and set me upright.* (8:19) *And he said, Behold, I will make thee know what shall be in the last end of the indignation: for at the time appointed the end shall be.*

<u>Daniel is Overwhelmed</u>. He *was afraid*. Daniel was a man of great prudence and courage, and had been previously conversant with the visions of the Almighty and certainly not without fearful awe…

• *Then Daniel, whose name was Belteshazzar, was* **astonied for one hour**, *and his thoughts troubled him. The king spake, and said, Belteshazzar, let not the dream, or the interpretation thereof, trouble thee. Belteshazzar answered and said, My lord, the dream be to them that hate thee, and the interpretation thereof to thine enemies (Dan 4:19).*

• *Hitherto is the end of the matter. As for me Daniel,* **my cogitations much troubled me, and my countenance changed in me**: *but I kept the matter in my heart (Dan 7:28).*

Yet now the approach of an extraordinary messenger from heaven puts Daniel into a great fear.. He *fell upon his face*, he could not look upon the lustre of the glory of this messenger. With his physical properties so overwhelmed, he *fell into a deep sleep*. The disciples in the Garden were *sleeping for sorrow* (Lk 22:45); and on the Mount of Transfiguration were *heavy with sleep* (Lk 9:32), so here, *the spirit was willing, but the flesh was weak* (Matt 26:41). Daniel would have kept awake but could not.

<u>Gabriel Gives Assistance</u>. He *touched him,* and *set him upon his feet*. Thus also with John in Revelation, Christ *laid his right hand upon him, and said, fear not am the first and the last* (Rev 1:17, He promised to inform him: *Understand, O son of man*. The Messiah was in the previous chapter was called the *Son of man* (7:13). Christ is not ashamed to call us *brethren* (Heb 2:11). As much as possible it was God's will that Daniel understand the prophecy he was give, but as we shall see he did not.

• *Surely the Lord GOD will do nothing, but he revealeth his secret unto his servants the prophets (Amos 3:7).*

• *And I Daniel fainted, and was sick certain days; afterward I rose up, and did the king's business; and I was astonished at the vision, but none understood it (Dan 8:27).*

<u>The Vision Concerns the End Time</u>. Gabriel tells Daniel that he will be made to know *what shall be in the last end of the indignation*. In the ultimate sense the coming Tribulation will be *indignation*! But it will not continue, it will have its *last end*. Daniel is informed that *at the time appointed the end shall be*. It is fixed in the Divine counsels which will allow for

no further extension. From Daniel's standpoint the first part of the vision concerned events of the nearer future, but most of the vision concerns the terrible events of the of the end time. This is *the time of Jacob's trouble* (Jer 30:5-7), the *Great Tribulation* (Dan 12:1; Psa 2:5; Matt 24:21; Rev. 7:14), preceding the setting up of the Kingdom over Israel (Acts 1:6,7; cp. Deut 28:13; Rev 20:4-6), a theme emblazoned everywhere upon the pages of Old Testament prophecy (Isa 2:6-22; 26:16-21;34:8; Micah 4:1-13; Zeph 3:11-13; Hag 2:20-23; Zech 3:7-9; Mal 4:1) and elucidated in the New Testament (Matt 24:1-51; 2 Thess 2:4; Rev 6:1—20:3).

It will come suddenly (1 Thess 5:2-4) and suddenly come also to an abrupt end!

- *For yet a very little while, and **the indignation shall cease**, and mine anger in their destruction (Isa 10:25).*

- *Come, my people, enter thou into thy chambers, and shut thy doors about thee: hide thyself as it were for a little moment, **until the indignation be overpast** (Isa 26:20).*

- *Now therefore be ye not mockers, lest your bands be made strong: for I have heard from the Lord GOD of hosts **a consumption, even determined upon the whole earth** (Isa 28:22).*

- *For he will finish the work, and cut it short in righteousness: because a short work will the Lord make upon the earth (Rom 9:28).*

- *And except those days should be shortened, there should no flesh be saved: but for the elect's sake those days shall be shortened (Matt 24:22).*

- *For it is the day of the LORD's vengeance, and the year of recompences for the controversy of Zion (Isa 34:8).*

<u>The Historical Fulfilment of the Vision.</u> (8:20) ***The ram which thou sawest having two horns are the kings of Media and Persia. (8:21) And the rough goat is the king of Grecia: and the great horn that is between his eyes is the first king. (8:22) Now that being broken, whereas four stood up for it, four kingdoms shall stand up out of the nation, but not in his power.***

Here again (Dan 2:32;38,39; 8:2-8) we see the two monarchies of Persia and Greece. At the time of the writing (Dan 2:1; 8:1), Babylon had not yet fallen to Persia, yet Daniel not only saw the rise of Persia but the rise of her conqueror Greece. He saw the great king of Greece, Alexander, and his sudden fall (Alexander died of a fever in Babylon, 323 BC). He saw that the fourfold division of Alexander's kingdom and the subsequent diminishing of its strength. This is an example of the historical fulfilment of Biblical prophecy and is seen frequently in the Scriptures and *nowhere else*. Note the challenge to compare prediction with fulfilment in the pages of the Bible; ***none shall want her mate***.

- *Seek ye out of the book of the LORD, and read: no one of these shall fail, **none shall want her mate**: for my mouth it hath commanded, and his spirit it hath gathered them (Isa 34:16).*

<u>The End Time Fulfilment of the Vision.</u>

(8:23) And in the latter time of their kingdom, when the transgressors are come to the full, a king of fierce countenance, and understanding dark sentences, shall stand up. (8:24) And his power shall be mighty, but not by his own power: and he shall destroy wonderfully, and shall prosper, and practise, and shall destroy the mighty and the holy people. (8:25) And through his policy also he shall cause craft to prosper in his hand; and he shall magnify himself in his heart, and by peace shall destroy many: he shall also stand up against the Prince of princes; but he shall be broken without hand. (8:26) And the vision of the evening and the morning which was told is true: wherefore shut thou up the vision; for it shall be for many days.

DANIEL 8. THE VISION OF THE RAM, GOAT AND LITTLE HORN

<u>The Antichrist: His Time and Origin</u>. ***And in the latter time of their kingdom,*** (8:23). The *latter times*, the *transgressors coming to the full* coupled with the *four winds of heaven* point to the appearing of the end time Antichrist and his ultimate wickedness. In all of this we have further confirmation that this is the end time Antichrist and not Antiochus Epiphanes.

> • Therefore the he goat waxed very great: and when he was strong, **the great horn was broken**; and **for it came up four notable ones toward the four winds of heaven**. And out of one of them came forth **a little horn**, which waxed exceeding great, toward the south, and toward the east, and toward the pleasant land (8:8.9).

The Antichrist will come from the four divisions of Alexanders empire, but in a ***latter time***, *four winds of heaven* context. His movements *toward the south, and toward the east, and toward the pleasant land* (8:9), indicate that he comes from the north-western part of Alexander's domain – Greece itself, Macedonia or perhaps further into central Europe. Daniel saw that his rise to power from small beginnings would be *exceeding great* (8:9).

<u>The Antichrist: His Supreme Wickedness</u>. ***When the transgressors are come to the full*** (8:23). As the *Man of Sin* (2 Thess 2:3) he will appear on earth when wilful and arrogant wickedness have reached their ***full***. Compare, *the iniquity of the Amorites is not yet full* (Gen 15:16). In that however it will be full! The full measure that was reached in Noah and Lot's day will be reached then (Lk 17:26-30). The Antichrist and his followers (Psa 2:1-3; Rev 16:13-16; 19:19), who will think to expel God and His Christ from the earth and take over in Satan's name (Rev. 19:11-20:3) will now come to the fore. Such supreme rebellion did not occur in Antiochus' day and will not occur until this still future revelation of *the mystery of iniquity* in the career of the Antichrist (2 Thess 2:4-12; cp. Luke 18:8). Nor until then will Israel's guilt come to the full, when they who rejected Christ will receive Antichrist (Jhn 5:43; cp. Matt. 23:39).

<u>The Antichrist: His Appearance</u>. ***A king of fierce countenance*** (8:23). Though called *a little horn* (8:9), perhaps because of his stature or insignificant origin, he will be anything but that in appearance. He will be commandingly *fierce*. His insolence and stern-face will far exceed anyone the world has known.

> • *Whose **look was more stout** than his fellows* (Dan 7:20).

<u>The Antichrist: His Satanic Dealings</u>. ***And understanding dark sentences*** (8:23).

He will be a master of diabolical intrigue (Rev. 13:1-16; 2 Thess 2:4; Dan. 11:36-40). He will be will become the epitome of extraordinary intelligence, but it will be satanic. He will know as no man has ever known, *the depths of Satan* (Rev 2:24). In any forum, before any assembly, in front of the world's media, he will show complete mastery. The Bible reveals both his wisdom and ultimate confusion.

> • In this horn were eyes like the **eyes of man** (Dan 7:8).

> • And the fifth angel poured out his vial upon the seat of the beast; and his kingdom was **full of darkness** (Rev 16:10).

<u>The Antichrist: His Compelling Entrance</u>. He ***shall stand up*** (8:23).

(http://www.traditioninaction.org/History/HistImages/G_006_Crowd.jpg)

Hitler *Standing* Before the Multitudes

The sudden and compelling entrance of Adolf Hitler in 1930s Germany was a precursor of the Antichrist. Hitler was a relatively small man from an insignificant background (a paper hanger) who suddenly ***stood up*** with a "solution" to Germany's economic ills. When Hitler *stood up* crowds in hitherto unimaginable numbers gathered to be mesmerized. The Antichrist will likewise suddenly ***stand up***. The fact that he stands up indicates that before this he was *sitting down*. That is, as with Hitler, no one was paying much attention to him. With his sudden and compelling entrance, the Antichrist will present a convincing solution to the world's problems. Multitudes from around the world in far greater numbers will gather to listen to this scintillating orator. And, unlike Hitler he will appear as a man of peace (initially at least!).

When the hindering influence of the *Salt* and the *Light* – the Holy Spirit indwelt Body of Christ – is removed, this man will arise as the world's deliverer.

> • Ye are the **salt of the earth**: but if the salt have lost his savour, wherewith shall it be salted? it is thenceforth good for nothing, but to be cast out, and to be trodden under foot of men. Ye are the **light of the world**. A city that is set on an hill cannot be hid. Neither do men light a candle, and put it under a bushel, but on a candlestick; and it giveth light unto all that are in the house. Let your light so shine before men, that they may see your good works, and glorify your Father which is in heaven (Matt 5:13-16).

> • For the mystery of iniquity doth already work: only he who now letteth will let, until he be taken out of the way. And then shall that Wicked be revealed, whom the Lord shall consume with the spirit of his mouth, and shall destroy with the brightness of his

DANIEL 8. THE VISION OF THE RAM, GOAT AND LITTLE HORN

coming: Even him, whose coming is after the working of Satan with all power and signs and lying wonders (2 Thess 2:7-9).

The Antichrist: His Power. ***And his power shall be mighty, but not by his own power*** (8:24). When Hitler spoke, and even with those who did not speak German, it soon became apparent that there was something that went beyond powerful oratory. So when the Antichrist speaks, it will be far more than compelling oratory. Although his power will be ***mighty***, his strength will be superhuman and demonic. That strength will not be by his own power and personality, but by Satan's, who will be permitted to work through him in a practically unrestricted way (2 Thess 2:9-12; Rev.13:2; 17:13), causing him to succeed in everything diabolical that he attempts (Dan 8:12), The Scriptures paint a grim picture of how power (from Satan and in concert with the False Prophet) will be manifest on earth through this man during the Tribulation.

> • *Even him, **whose coming is after the working of Satan with all power and signs and lying wonders**, And with all deceivableness of unrighteousness in them that perish; because they received not the love of the truth, that they might be saved (2 Thess 2:9,10).*
>
> • ***The dragon gave him his power** (Rev 13:2).*
>
> • *And they worshipped **the dragon which gave power unto the beast**: and they worshipped the beast, saying, Who is like unto the beast? who is able to make war with him (Rev 13:4)?*
>
> • *And I beheld another beast coming up out of the earth; and he had two horns like a lamb, and he spake as a dragon. And **he exerciseth all the power of the first beast** before him, and causeth the earth and them which dwell therein to worship the first beast, whose deadly wound was healed. And **he doeth great wonders**, so that **he maketh fire come down from heaven on the earth** in the sight of men, And deceiveth them that dwell on the earth by the means of **those miracles which he had power to do** in the sight of the beast; saying to them that dwell on the earth, that they should make an image to the beast, which had the wound by a sword, and did live (Rev 13:11-14).*

The Antichrist: His Rampage. ***He shall destroy wonderfully, and shall prosper, and practise, and shall destroy the mighty and the holy people*** (8:24). In Daniel's account of his vision we saw the Antichrist as he goes forth to war. No nation (where will America be at this time!), no matter how powerful will be able to stand before him. Many will submit without a fight, but many will not; thus we are told: ***He shall destroy wonderfully***. Whether the North or South America, Africa, Asia, Europe or Israel; wherever military force is necessary, with diabolical power he will ***destroy wonderfully***. And, *the world will wonder*!

> • *Who is like unto the beast? **who is able to make war with him** (Rev 13:4)?*
>
> • *And it was given unto him to **make war with the saints**, and to overcome them: and **power was given him over all kindreds, and tongues, and nations**. And all that dwell upon the earth shall worship him, whose names are not written in the book of life of the Lamb slain from the foundation of the world (Rev 13:7,8).*
>
> • *But tidings out of the east and out of the north shall trouble him: therefore **he shall go forth with great fury to destroy, and utterly to make away many** (Dan 11:44).*

The Antichrist: His "Peacemaking." ***And through his policy also he shall cause craft to prosper in his hand; and he shall magnify himself in his heart, and by peace shall destroy many*** (8:25). Here we have the greatest contrast to what is described above. He will have power not only to destroy and make war make war but also to make and enforce peace. But notice, that while he will be a "peacemaker", in the "same breath" this passage says he will ***destroy***. In the beginning his is *little* (8:9; 7:8), but by ***craft*** and deceit the *little horn* will become mighty, making a covenant of "peace" with Israel (9:27) and then treacherously breaking it. By this pretended peace he shall *destroy many* in Israel (Rev. 12:7-13:16). Our Lord gave a warning of this in His Olivet Discourse.

> • *Because ye have said, We have made **a covenant with death**, and with hell are we at agreement; when the overflowing scourge shall pass through, it shall not come unto us: for we have made lies our refuge, and under falsehood have we hid ourselves (Isa 28:15).*

> • *And **your covenant with death** shall be disannulled, and your agreement with hell shall not stand; when the overflowing scourge shall pass through, then ye shall be trodden down by it (Isa 28:18).*

> • ***When ye therefore shall see the abomination of desolation**, spoken of by Daniel the prophet, stand in the holy place, (whoso readeth, let him understand:) **Then let them** which be in Judaea flee into the mountains: **Let him** which is on the housetop not come down to take any thing out of his house: **Neither let him** which is in the field return back to take his clothes. **And woe** unto them that are with child, and to them that give suck in those days! **But pray** ye that your flight be not in the winter, neither on the sabbath day (Matt 24:15-20).*

> • *And it shall come to pass, **that in all the land**, saith the LORD, **two parts therein shall be cut off and die**; but the third shall be left therein. And **I will bring the third part through the fire**, and will refine them as silver is refined, and will try them as gold is tried: they shall call on my name, and I will hear them: I will say, It is my people: and they shall say, The LORD is my God (Zech 13:8,9).*

By his pretended peace he will also destroy many others in the world (directly or indirectly). This will result in *the reduction of the world's population by at least one half* (Rev 6:8; 9:18). The Antichrist for all intents and purposes is the rider on the **white**, **red**, **black** and **pale** horse.

> • *For when they shall say, Peace and safety; then sudden destruction cometh upon them, as travail upon a woman with child; and they shall not escape (1 Thess 5:3).*

> • *And I saw, and behold **a white horse**: and he that sat on him had a bow; and a crown was given unto him: and he went forth conquering, and to conquer. And when he had opened the second seal, I heard the second beast say, Come and see. And there went out **another horse that was red**: and power was given to him that sat thereon to take peace from the earth, and that they should kill one another: and there was given unto him a great sword. And when he had opened the third seal, I heard the third beast say, Come and see. And I beheld, and lo **a black horse**; and he that sat on him had a pair of balances in his hand. And I heard a voice in the midst of the four beasts say, A measure of wheat for a penny, and three measures of barley for a penny; and see thou hurt not the oil and the wine. And when he had opened the fourth seal, I heard the voice of the fourth beast say, Come and see. And I looked, and behold **a pale horse**: and his name that sat on him was Death, and Hell followed with him. And **power was given unto them over <u>the fourth part</u> of the earth, to kill with sword, and with hunger, and with death, and with the beasts of the earth.** And when he had opened the fifth seal, I saw under the altar **the souls of them that were slain for the word of God**, and for the testimony which they held (Rev 6:2-9).*

> • *And the number of the army of the horsemen were two hundred thousand thousand: and I heard the number of them. And thus I saw the horses in the vision, and them that sat on them, having breastplates of fire, and of jacinth, and brimstone: and the heads of the horses were as the heads of lions; and out of their mouths issued fire and smoke and brimstone. **By these three was <u>the third part</u> of men killed**, by the fire, and by the smoke, and by the brimstone, which issued out of their mouths (Rev 9:16-18).*

> • *Therefore hath the curse **devoured the earth**, and they that dwell therein are desolate: therefore the inhabitants of the earth are burned, and **few men left** (Isa 24:6).*

<u>The Antichrist: His Blasphemy</u>. ***He shall also stand up against the Prince of princes*** (8:26). In his vision, Daniel saw that the Antichrist's warfare was not restricted to the earth,

but he was so energized by Satan that he declared war against Heaven itself (8:10-12), against angels, against Michael the leader of angels; he now takes the ultimate step and fights against Christ Himself. He shall magnify himself in his heart to such an extent that he is prepared to take this daring step of total and complete blasphemy (Isa. 14:12-14; 2 Thess. 2:4; Rev. 13:6).

He will stand up against the **Prince of princes**, the *King of kings*, the *Lord of lords* (Rev 19:16). Satan as before the Creation (Isa 14:12-14) seeks by this man to usurp the Throne of the Lord of the earth, the One who is the Creator and the Redeemer. He has already destroyed many of the peoples of the earth; but he will fail, both in Heaven and on earth.

> • *And the great dragon was cast out, that old serpent, called the Devil, and Satan, which **deceiveth the whole world**: he was cast out into the earth, and his angels were cast out with him (Rev 12:9).*

> • *And I saw three unclean spirits like frogs come out of the mouth of the dragon, and out of the mouth of the beast, and out of the mouth of the false prophet. For they are the spirits of devils, working miracles, which **go forth unto the kings of the earth** and of the whole world, to gather them to the battle of that great day of God Almighty (Rev 16:13,14).*

Empowered by Satan, he will stir the earth to blaspheme God:

> • *And there was given unto him **a mouth speaking great things and blasphemies**; and power was given unto him to continue forty and two months. And he opened his mouth in blasphemy against God, to **blaspheme his name**, and his tabernacle, and them that dwell in heaven (Rev 13:5,6).*

> • *And men were scorched with great heat, and **blasphemed the name of God**, which hath power over these plagues: and they repented not to give him glory (Rev 16:9).*

> • *And **blasphemed the God of heaven** because of their pains and their sores, and repented not of their deeds (Rev 16:11).*

> • *And there fell upon men a great hail out of heaven, every stone about the weight of a talent: and men **blasphemed God** because of the plague of the hail; for the plague thereof was exceeding great (Rev 16:21).*

The Antichrist: His End. **But he shall be broken without hand** (8:26). The Antichrist will fight against Heaven and he will fight on earth; he and all with him will come to an ignoble end, and that *without hand*. Compare **broken without hand** with the following:

> • *Thou sawest till that **a stone was cut out without hands**, which smote the image upon his feet that were of iron and clay, and **brake them to pieces**. Then was the iron, the clay, the brass, the silver, and the gold, broken to pieces together, and became like the chaff of the summer threshingfloors; and the wind carried them away, that no place was found for them: and the stone that smote the image became a great mountain, and filled the whole earth (Dan 2:34,35).*

> • *In a moment shall they die, and the people shall be troubled at midnight, and pass away: and the mighty shall be taken away **without hand** (Job 34:20).*

"Although Antiochus's horrible death — caused by worms and ulcers while he was on his way to Judea to take vengeance on the Maccabees for the humiliating defeat of his armies — was a foreshadowing of God's judgment upon the last great enemy of the Jews, it fell far short of the scope and purely supernatural destruction of the Antichrist of the end time. Antichrist will be apprehended red-handed and "cast alive" into gehenna (Rev. 19:20; 20:10)." (*Unger's Commentary on the Old Testament*).

The Antichrist will gather the nations of earth to fight against Christ. He is a *fool* for doing so, and likewise those who follow him are *fools*. It will be over before it begins; *no hand* will be needed to slay them. Note the three things that the Apostle John *saw*:

> • *And I saw heaven opened, and behold a white horse; and he that sat upon him was called Faithful and True*, *and in righteousness he doth judge and make war. His eyes were as a flame of fire, and on his head were many crowns; and he had a name written, that no man knew, but he himself. And he was clothed with a vesture dipped in blood: and his name is called The Word of God. And the armies which were in heaven followed him upon white horses, clothed in fine linen, white and clean. And **out of his mouth goeth a sharp sword**, that with it he should smite the nations: and he shall rule them with a rod of iron: and he treadeth the winepress of the fierceness and wrath of Almighty God. And he hath on his vesture and on his thigh a name written, KING OF KINGS, AND LORD OF LORDS (Rev 19:11-16). • **And I saw an angel standing in the sun**; and he cried with a loud voice, saying to all the fowls that fly in the midst of heaven, Come and gather yourselves together unto the supper of the great God; That ye may eat the flesh of kings, and the flesh of captains, and the flesh of mighty men, and the flesh of horses, and of them that sit on them, and the flesh of all men, both free and bond, both small and great (19:17,18).*
>
> • **And I saw the beast, and the kings of the earth, and their armies**, *gathered together to make war against him that sat on the horse, and against his army. And the beast was taken, and with him the false prophet that wrought miracles before him, with which he deceived them that had received the mark of the beast, and them that worshipped his image.* **These both were cast alive into a lake of fire burning with brimstone**. *And the remnant were slain with the sword of him that sat upon the horse, which sword proceeded out of his mouth: and all the fowls were filled with their flesh (19:19-21).*

The Conclusion. *And the vision of the evening and the morning which was told is true: wherefore shut thou up the vision; for it shall be for many days* (8:26). The great subject of this chapter is the 2300 day period mentioned in Daniel 8:14. The Seven Year Tribulation is a period of 2520 days and during that time (as explained) it is very likely that the Antichrist will be the "Master of Ceremonies" in a daily 2300 day telecast from Jerusalem's Temple Mount. Every morning at 9 AM and afternoon at 3 PM, with the world's media watching, the Jewish people will be allowed to renew and offer as described in the Old Testament their morning and evening sacrifices. But, in the midst of the seven years (Dan 9:27) this compelling Master of Ceremonies will change the order of service. Note again this crucial passage:

> • *Then I heard one saint speaking, and another saint said unto that certain saint which spake, How long shall be* **the vision concerning the daily sacrifice**, *and* **the transgression of desolation**, *to give both the sanctuary and the host to be trodden under foot? And he said unto me, Unto two thousand and three hundred days; then shall the sanctuary be cleansed (8:13,14).*

As we saw, it seems clear that the 2300 day vision comprises two proceedings: **(1)** *the daily sacrifice, and* **(2)** *the transgression of desolation*, Daniel sees the sacrifices taking place, and he sees also their abolition by the Antichrist and resulting desolation. Therefore the 2300 days do not begin with the abolition of the sacrifices at the midpoint of the Tribulation but rather when they begin. Further, the *evening and morning* in verse 26 must certainly refer to the *daily sacrifices* which were at the heart of the Old Testament Temple worship.

> • *And thou shalt say unto them, This is the offering made by fire which ye shall offer unto the LORD;* **two lambs of the first year without spot day by day, for a continual burnt offering**. *The one lamb shalt thou offer* **in the morning**, *and the other lamb shalt thou offer* **at even** *(Num 28:3,4).*

With the catastrophic demise of its Master of Ceremonies who will be *broken without hand* (8:25), this "telecast" will also come to an abrupt end! Note again that these *evening and morning* presentations are from the standpoint of Daniel's day - *in the distant future*. They are not as some teach an overview of history; they are a primary feature of the Seven Year Tribulation. Thus Daniel is told to *shut thou up the vision; for it shall be for many days*.

DANIEL 8. THE VISION OF THE RAM, GOAT AND LITTLE HORN

Note also that despite the implications of the astounding revelations given in Daniel 8, they are, as with all the other revelations of Bible prophecy, *true*! Note how the veracity of Bible prophecy was in a like manner confirmed by the interpreting angel to the Apostle John:

- *And he saith unto me, Write, Blessed are they which are called unto the marriage supper of the Lamb. And he saith unto me,* **These are the true sayings of God** *(Rev 19:9).*

- *And he that sat upon the throne said, Behold, I make all things new. And he said unto me, Write: for* **these words are true and faithful** *(Rev 21:5).*

- *And he said unto me,* **These sayings are faithful and true**: *and the Lord God of the holy prophets sent his angel to shew unto his servants the things which must shortly be done (Rev 22:6).*

The Effect Upon Daniel. *And I Daniel fainted, and was sick certain days; afterward I rose up, and did the king's business; and I was astonished at the vision, but none understood it* (8:27). Daniel has seen into the heart of a man who will one day rule over the world and over his people Israel. The sight left him exhausted and ill, and in spite of the aid of the interpreting angel, it was beyond his power to comprehend. It was beyond understanding because it was projected so far into the future. But the prophet understood enough of it to know that the Tribulation though which Israel would have to endure at the hands of the *Little Horn* would be temporary and that Israel as a nation, along with the rest of the rest of the redeemed would enter the Kingdom of Messiah.

The prophecies of Daniel will nevertheless be *sealed* and *shut up* until last days leading up to the Lord's Return.

- *Wherefore* **shut thou up the vision**; *for it shall be for many days (Dan 8:26).*

- *But thou, O Daniel, shut up the words, and* **seal the book**, *even to the time of the end: many shall run to and fro, and knowledge shall be increased (Dan 12:4).*

- **Blessed is he that readeth**, *and they that hear the words of this prophecy, and keep those things which are written therein: for the time is at hand (Rev 1:3).*

- *And he saith unto me,* **Seal not the sayings of the prophecy of this book**: *for the time is at hand (Rev 22:10).*

We now come to the second prophecy in the Hebrew half of the Book of Daniel. It is a prophecy that is foundational to both *Bible Prophecy* and *Bible Chronology*. It is the prophecy of "God's Clock for Israel" – *The Seventy Weeks of Daniel*.

II THE TIMES OF THE GENTILES REGARDING JERUSALEM 8-12

A. THE END OF THE TIMES OF THE GENTILES: JEWISH PERSPECTIVE (Hebrew Resumes) 8

B. THE SEVENTY WEEKS OF YEARS UPON JERUSALEM AND THE JEWISH PEOPLE 9

DANIEL 9. THE PROPHECY OF THE SEVENTY WEEKS

"Chapter Nine of the Book of Daniel stands out as the paragon of Bible prophecy. This chapter proves beyond a shadow of a doubt that God revealed the future course of world events to faithful men of God, and they wrote about things to come as they were led by the Holy Spirit. Dr. H.A. Ironside called the ninth chapter of Daniel, *the greatest-of-all-time-prophecies*. Sir Edward Denny called it, *the backbone of prophecy*. The prophecy recorded in this chapter proves that Jesus Christ is the Messiah of Israel. Chapter eight tells about a little horn, the Antichrist, who will rise up in the last days to challenge the Christ of God. This little horn will magnify himself and command millions to be killed for failing to worship him as God. He will rule over a ten-nation kingdom, and gain control of the whole earth. The prophecy about the little horn began in chapter seven where his kingdom is described and its chronological appearance is given. Chapter eight describes his evil nature and his great power. Chapter nine tells about his deceitful dealings with the nation of Israel. Chapter nine also tells us about *a greater horn* than the little horn. This great horn will…be of David, the royal house of Israel.

- *There I will make **the horn of David** to bud: I have ordained a lamp for mine household. His enemies will I clothe with shame: but upon himself shall his crown flourish (Psa 132:17).*

- *Blessed be the Lord God of Israel; for he hath visited and redeemed his people, And hath raised up **an horn of salvation** for us in the house of his servant David; As he spake by the mouth of his holy prophets, which have been since the world began (Lk 1:68-70).*

The prophecy of the seventy weeks of Daniel tells how *the horn of David, the Messiah* of Israel, would be cut off from His people until the abomination of the little horn had run its course." (Noah Hutchings).

(https://principlesforlifeministries.files.wordpress.com/2011/06/israelcl4.jpg)

Israel and Her Seventy Weeks is the Clock by Which God Marks Prophetic Time

DANIEL 9. THE PROPHECY OF THE SEVENTY WEEKS

The Time and the Occasion of the Seventy Weeks Prophecy 9:1,2.

In the first year of Darius the son of Ahasuerus, of the seed of the Medes, which was made king over the realm of the Chaldeans; (9:2) In the first year of his reign I Daniel understood by books the number of the years, whereof the word of the LORD came to Jeremiah the prophet, that he would accomplish seventy years in the desolations of Jerusalem.

As Daniel is the Prophet of the Times of the Gentiles, it is remarkable to note again that the prophecies of this Book are directly linked to the reigns of Gentile kings. The only time where the reign of a Jewish king is given is in the first verse of the Book.

- *(1:1) In **the third year of the reign of Jehoiakim** king of Judah came Nebuchadnezzar king of Babylon unto Jerusalem, and besieged it.*

- *(1:21) And Daniel continued even unto **the first year of king Cyrus**.*

- *(2:1) And in **the second year of the reign of Nebuchadnezzar** Nebuchadnezzar dreamed dreams, wherewith his spirit was troubled, and his sleep brake from him.*

- *(5:30) In that night was Belshazzar the king of the Chaldeans slain. (5:31) And **Darius the Median took the kingdom**, being about threescore and two years old.*

- *(6:28) So this Daniel prospered in **the reign of Darius**, and in **the reign of Cyrus** the Persian.*

- *(7:1) In **the first year of Belshazzar** king of Babylon Daniel had a dream and visions of his head upon his bed: then he wrote the dream, and told the sum of the matters.*

- *(8:1) In **the third year of the reign of king Belshazzar** a vision appeared unto me, even unto me Daniel, after that which appeared unto me at the first.*

- *(9:1) In **the first year of Darius** the son of Ahasuerus, of the seed of the Medes, which was made king over the realm of the Chaldeans; (9:2) In **the first year** of his reign I Daniel understood by books the number of the years, whereof the word of the LORD came to Jeremiah the prophet, that he would accomplish **seventy years in the desolations of Jerusalem**.*

- *(10:1) In **the third year of Cyrus** king of Persia a thing was revealed unto Daniel, whose name was called Belteshazzar; and the thing was true, but the time appointed was long: and he understood the thing, and had understanding of the vision.*

- *(11:1) Also I in **the first year of Darius** the Mede, even I, stood to confirm and to strengthen him.*

<u>The Time of the Seventy Week Prophecy</u>. ***In the first year of Darius the son of Ahasuerus, of the seed of the Medes, which was made king over the realm of the Chaldeans*** (9:1). We left Daniel at the close of Chapter 8 employed in the ***king's business***, but here we have him employed in a better business than any earthly king could have for him; once again he is hearing from the King of kings.

The prophecies of the previous chapter where given in *the third year of the reign of king Belshazzar*, the king of Babylon (8:1); but in this chapter it is ***the first year of Darius the son of Ahasuerus, of the seed of the Medes***. Babylon has fallen to Media Persia. A king who wanted little to do with Daniel has fallen with his empire to a king who wanted a great deal to do with Daniel. The setting now is only a year or so (if that long) after the *brazen* Belshazzar had fallen to the *benevolent* Darius and Cyrus.

- *In that night was Belshazzar the king of the Chaldeans slain. And Darius the Median took the kingdom, being about threescore and two years old (5:30, 31).*

- *(6:28) So this Daniel prospered in the reign of Darius, and in the reign of Cyrus the Persian.*

Darius the Mede took the kingdom in partnership with, Cyrus the Persian. They were partners in war and conquest. We have previously noted that Darius was now *sixty-two years old,* "for which reason Cyrus, who was his nephew, gave him the precedency. It is observed that being now sixty-two in the last year of the captivity, he was born in the eighth year of it, and that was the year when Jeconiah was carried captive (2 Kng 24:13–15). Just at that time when a fatal stroke was given by Babylon a prince born who in process of time would avenge Jerusalem upon Babylon, and heal the wound that was given. Thus deep are the counsels of God concerning his people, thus kind are his designs towards them" (see *Matthew Henry*).

Darius was the son of **Ahasuerus**. This is also the *titular* (title) name of a later king who would oppose the Jews in their rebuilding of Jerusalem (Ezra 4:5), and the king who would marry Esther (Est 1:1). Like "Pharaoh," *Darius, Ahasuerus,* and *Artaxerxes* were titular names given to the Medo-Persian kings. These titles may be interchanged to designate the kings status during a particular time of his reign. We will show that the **first seven weeks** (49 years) of the 70 week prophecy are linked to a later *Darius,* but who is also called by these other titles. Failure to recognize this fact and linkage (as most do) makes these 49 years an *empty gap* as far as Biblical history is concerned! When recognized they provide a harmonious chronology for the last 49 years of Israel's Old Testament history (*Haggai, Zechariah, Ezra, Nehemiah, Esther, Malachi*).

The Bible Reading That Led to the Prophecy. *In the first year of his reign I Daniel understood by books the number of the years, whereof the word of the LORD came to Jeremiah the prophet, that he would accomplish seventy years in the desolations of Jerusalem* (9:2). After the defeat of Babylon and the institution of the Persian government in Babylon, Daniel begins to contemplate what effect this turn of events would have on the status of the Jews in this foreign country. The prophet began studying the Books of Scripture and most notably the Book of Jeremiah. Daniel would have used his high office under both the Babylonian and Persian Governments (which ruled over Israel) to make certain that he had copies of the Word of God. He likely requested that copies of Scripture in Jerusalem be brought to him in Babylon. Daniel probably read first from Jeremiah 25:11 and then found great hope for Israel in Jeremiah 29:10.

> • And this whole land shall be **a desolation**, and an astonishment; and these nations shall serve the king of Babylon **seventy years** *(Jer 25:11).*

> • For thus saith the Lord, That after **seventy years** be accomplished at Babylon I will visit you, and perform my good word toward you, in causing you to return to this place *(Jer 29:10).*

The *first year* of Darius is repeated twice for emphasis (9:1,2). About 68 years have now elapsed since Daniel was brought to Babylon by Nebuchadnezzar in the first deportation. Nebuchadnezzar's pressure upon Jerusalem before the deportation brings the number to about 70 years.

As Daniel read the books by Jeremiah he understood that his fellow prophet wrote as he himself did — by *the Word of the Lord.* He realized that from these prophecies of Jeremiah and other Scriptures the time had arrived for God to look again upon His people, to hear their cries, and deliver them from their bondage.

> • *For the prophecy came not in old time by the will of man: but holy men of God spake as they were moved by the Holy Ghost (2 Pet 1:21).*

> • *If my people, which are called by my name, shall humble themselves, and pray, and seek my face, and turn from their wicked ways; then will I hear from heaven, and will forgive their sin, and will heal their land (2 Chron 7:14).*

DANIEL 9. THE PROPHECY OF THE SEVENTY WEEKS

As shown in the Introduction (pages 3-10), this commentary follows what is believed to be the *Biblical* rather than the *Current* (or *Ptolemaic*) Chronology. The chief difference between the two is that in the Biblical Chronology *permission is given to rebuild Jerusalem (including the Temple) shortly after Daniel receives the Seventy Week Prophecy*; whereas in the Current Chronology it is only the Temple that is permitted to be built. Jerusalem itself is rebuilt only 93 years after Daniel receives the prophecy. Therefore *Jerusalem will be in desolation for a further 93 years after Daniel receives the prophecy*. One of *many* reasons why this cannot be correct is shown by contradiction this makes with the length of time Jeremiah said Jerusalem would be in *desolation*.

> • In the first year of his reign I Daniel understood by books the number of the years, whereof the word of the LORD came to Jeremiah the prophet, that he would **accomplish seventy years in the desolations of Jerusalem** (Dan 9:2).

> • And this whole land shall be a desolation, and an astonishment; and these nations shall serve the king of Babylon seventy years (Jer 25:11).

To say that Jerusalem must lie waste for another 93 years imposes a huge denial upon what the Bible clearly states. Where do these 93 years come from? Why are they allowed by nearly everyone to intrude into the Biblical Chronology! From what was stated in the Introduction, note the following basic fact.

The Intrusion of Ptolmy's 93 Years into Daniel's Prophecy

(http://www.thefamouspeople.com/profiles/images/claudius-ptolemy-1.jpg)

Claudius Ptolemy (AD c100-168) The Most Renowned Astronomer, Mathematician, Geographer and Historian of the Ancient World

Few are aware that the well-known dates given for the times in which Daniel lived have 93 years added from a secular source. For a start this is at variance with the fact that *the Bible itself* (without any addition or subtraction from secular sources) *gives a complete chronology from Adam to the crucifixion of Christ*. For example, from among the Bible's many chronological statements, Luke 3 gives an unbroken genealogy from Adam to Christ; and the Seventy Week prophecy of Daniel 9 gives the years from the Cyrus Decree to rebuild Jerusalem (at the end of the captivities in Babylon) to the Crucifixion of Christ.

When one reads Daniel 9 in conjunction with the passages dealing with the Cyrus Decree, it is clear that the *counting* of the Seventy Week prophecy was to begin *shortly after*

Daniel received the prophecy (Dan 9:1,2; 18-27). It is also clear that the Cyrus Decree not only allowed the Jews to return and rebuild the Temple, ***but also rebuild Jerusalem***

(Isa 44:28; 45:13). This latter point is denied because it completely refutes any idea of adding 93 further years from secular history before Jerusalem is rebuilt!

According to the prophecy, there will be 69 weeks of years (483 year) *from the going forth of the command to restore and to build Jerusalem* (9:25) until the Messiah is *cut off* (9:27). This *command* can only be the Cyrus Decree to which Scripture gives substantial emphasis (later Persian kings also gave permission, but this was not a new decree but based on the Cyrus Decree). With our Lord crucified in 33 AD it should be a simple matter to subtract 483 years and arrive at a date of about 450 BC for the Cyrus Decree and the beginning of the count of the *weeks*. Daniel then would have received the prophecy a short time before 450 BC.

With such a direct and Biblical computation, why then do we have the intrusion of this 93 year addition? The answer is *depressingly simple*! Some 600 or more years after Daniel, the esteemed astronomer, *astrologer*, mathematician and geographer Claudius Ptolemy (died c168 AD) compiled his *Canon of Kings*. This is considered the primary source for dating the reigns of rulers in the ancient world. On the basis of what Ptolemy considered were the length of Persian, Greek and Roman king-reigns, he pushed back Persia's capture of Babylon by nearly a century earlier than what the Book of Daniel shows. The scholarly world (with a few exceptions) has chosen to follow Ptolemy rather than the Bible with the result that the "standard dates" commonly accepted and often printed in our Bibles have been inflated by these 93 years.

The decision to follow Ptolemy turns a blind eye to the well-known fact that while the length of Roman reigns is accurate; that of Greek reigns (mainly before Alexander) is much less so, and that of Persian reigns is so unreliable that what Ptolemy listed for Persian kings is not much more than an educated guess. History has been shown to give a reasonably accurate length of time from Alexander's defeat of Persia (331 BC) unto Christ; but with the Persian period before Alexander, there is not only great uncertainty as to the length of the reigns but also to the number of Persian kings.

We have no such uncertainty when we recognize that Seventy Week Prophecy is not only the cornerstone of prophecy but also for chronology. It provides the certain link from Daniel to the Death of Christ.

Daniels Prayer: His Confession 9:3-15.

And I set my face unto the Lord God, to seek by prayer and supplications, with fasting, and sackcloth, and ashes: (9:4)And I prayed unto the LORD my God, and made my confession, and said, O Lord, the great and dreadful God, keeping the covenant and mercy to them that love him, and to them that keep his commandments; (9:5) We have sinned, and have committed iniquity, and have done wickedly, and have rebelled, even by departing from thy precepts and from thy judgments: (9:6) Neither have we hearkened unto thy servants the prophets, which spake in thy name to our kings, our princes, and our fathers, and to all the people of the land. (9:7) O Lord, righteousness belongeth unto thee, but unto us confusion of faces, as at this day; to the men of Judah, and to the inhabitants of Jerusalem, and unto all Israel, that are near, and that are far off, through all the countries whither thou hast driven them, because of their trespass that they have trespassed against thee. (9:8) O Lord, to us belongeth confusion of face, to our kings, to our princes, and to our fathers, because we have sinned against thee. (9:9) To the Lord our God belong mercies and forgivenesses, though we have rebelled against him; (9:10) Neither have we obeyed the voice of the LORD our God, to walk in his laws, which he set before us by his servants the prophets. (9:11) Yea, all Israel have transgressed thy law, even by departing, that they might not obey thy voice; therefore the curse is poured upon us, and the oath that is written in the law of Moses the servant of God, because we have sinned against him. (9:12) And he hath

DANIEL 9. THE PROPHECY OF THE SEVENTY WEEKS

confirmed his words, which he spake against us, and against our judges that judged us, by bringing upon us a great evil: for under the whole heaven hath not been done as hath been done upon Jerusalem. (9:13) As it is written in the law of Moses, all this evil is come upon us: yet made we not our prayer before the LORD our God, that we might turn from our iniquities, and understand thy truth. (9:14) Therefore hath the LORD watched upon the evil, and brought it upon us: for the LORD our God is righteous in all his works which he doeth: for we obeyed not his voice. (9:15) And now, O Lord our God, that hast brought thy people forth out of the land of Egypt with a mighty hand, and hast gotten thee renown, as at this day; we have sinned, we have done wickedly.

(1) Here We See the Preparations of Daniel's Prayer.

His Prayer as Concerning Himself. ***And I set my face unto the Lord God, to seek by prayer and supplications, with fasting, and sackcloth, and ashes*** (9:3): When he understood that the seventy years were just about to expire (note that his fellow prophet Ezekiel frequently recorded the years of the captivity), he *set his face to seek God by prayer*. God's promises are intended, not to supersede but to excite and encourage our prayers. When we see the day of the Lord's Return approaching, we should become more earnest in prayer. God had said to Ezekiel that though Daniel, among others, prayed before Him, the judgement of the captivity would not be prevented (Ezek 14:14), but now that *the warfare is accomplished* (Isa 40:2), he prays that it may soon be lifted. When the day of deliverance is dawning, it is time for God's praying people to pray even more.

Note the Intensity of His Mind. *I set my face unto the Lord God to seek Him*. Here we see the fixedness of his thoughts, the firmness of his faith, and the fervour of his affections. Probably as before (6:10), and in token of God's promises concerning Jerusalem, he *set his face* towards Jerusalem, the place of God's Name and earthly dwelling.

> • *Now when Daniel knew that the writing was signed, he went into his house; and his windows being open in his chamber **toward Jerusalem**, he kneeled upon his knees three times a day, and prayed, and gave thanks before his God, as he did aforetime (Dan 6:10).*
>
> • *But I have **chosen Jerusalem**, that my name might be there; and have chosen David to be over my people Israel (2 Chron 6:6).*
>
> • *Yet if they bethink themselves in the land whither they are carried captive, and turn and pray unto thee in the land of their captivity, saying, We have sinned, we have done amiss, and have dealt wickedly; If they return to thee with all their heart and with all their soul in the land of their captivity, whither they have carried them captives, and **pray toward their land**, which thou gavest unto their fathers, and **toward the city** which thou hast chosen, and **toward the house** which I have built for thy name (2 Chron 6:37,38).*

Note the *Dying* of Self. In token of his deep humiliation, his own unworthiness and the sins of his people; he *fasted*, put on *sackcloth*, and lay in *ashes*. This also put Daniel in mind of the desolations of Jerusalem which he was now praying for the repair of. Nothing of the world, *nothing at all* was to be a distraction in this prayer. Not its needs (food and clothing); not its abundance (seen now as *ashes*).

His Prayer as Concerning the LORD. ***And I prayed unto the LORD my God, and made my confession, and said, O Lord, the great and dreadful God, keeping the covenant and mercy to them that love him, and to them that keep his commandments*** (9:4).

He is a God to be Reverenced. He is to be reverenced as to His Name. The three primary Old Testament Names of God are given in verse 4. He is *Jehovah* (LORD). He is *Elohim* (God). He is *Adonai* (Lord). He is to be reverenced as to His Person. He is ***the great and dreadful God***. As a God to be feared, and before whom it is our duty to always stand in awe, He is able to deal with the greatest and most terrible of Israel's and the believer's enemies.

- *Thou shalt not be affrighted at them: for the LORD thy God is among you, **a mighty God and terrible** (Deut 7:21).*

- *Now therefore, our God, the great, **the mighty, and the terrible God**, who keepest covenant and mercy, let not all the trouble seem little before thee, that hath come upon us (Neh 9:32).*

He is a God to be Trusted. ***Keeping the covenant and mercy to them that love him, and to them that keep his commandments***. The Abrahamic and Davidic covenants will be fulfilled with the Nation Israel but it is nevertheless with those in Israel who come to *love* Him.

- *Not as though the word of God hath taken none effect. For **they are not all Israel, which are of Israel** (Rom 9:6).*

- *For I would not, brethren, that ye should be ignorant of this mystery, lest ye should be wise in your own conceits; that blindness in part is happened to Israel, until the fulness of the Gentiles be come in. And so **all Israel shall be saved**: as it is written, There shall come out of Sion the Deliverer, and shall turn away ungodliness from Jacob: **For this is my covenant unto them, when I shall take away their sins**. As concerning the gospel, they are enemies for your sakes: but **as touching the election, they are beloved for the father's sakes** (Rom 11:25-28).*

He will be to his people as good as his word, for He keeps *covenant* with them and not one iota of His promise shall fall to the ground. And, more than that, He sends *mercy* to them. It was proper for Daniel to have his eye upon God's mercy now that he was to lay before Him the *miseries* of Israel.

(2) Here We See the Confessions of Daniel's Prayer.

What Israel Did. ***We have sinned, and have committed iniquity, and have done wickedly, and have rebelled, even by departing from thy precepts and from thy judgments*** (9:5). When we seek God for national mercies we ought to humble ourselves before him for national sins (National calls to prayer have not always done this). Note the variety of words that Daniel uses to set forth the greatness and the provocation of Israel's sins (a true penitent *loads sin* upon himself): *We have sinned* in many particular instances. *We have committed iniquity*; it is deeply dyed, we have made sin *our trade*. *We have done wickedly* with a hard heart and a stiff neck. *We have rebelled*; we have taken up arms against the King of kings, against His crown and against His dignity. Here then is the procuring cause of all the calamities which Daniel's people had for so many years been groaning under.

What Israel Did Not Do. ***Neither have we hearkened unto thy servants the prophets, which spake in thy name to our kings, our princes, and our fathers, and to all the people of the land*** (9:6). They did not listen to the Bible! They had heard it again and again and rejected it. Israel like many professing Christians today had ignored and violated the Word of God. It had been given to them repeatedly. They had slighted the fair warnings. God had given them prophets, which in every age He had sent to them, *rising up betimes and sending them* (2 Chron 36:15). They delivered the message faithfully, with a universal respect to all orders and degrees of men, to *our kings and princes*, with whom they had the courage and confidence to speak, and *to our fathers*, and to all the *people of the land*, whom they had the compassion to speak. Yet in all this, they did not *hearken*. They did not hear, heed, comply with. Note that mocking God's messengers, and despising His Words, were Jerusalem's *measure-filling* sins.

- *And the LORD God of their fathers sent to them by his messengers, rising up betimes, and sending; because he had compassion on his people, and on his dwelling place: But **they mocked the messengers of God**, and despised his words, and misused his prophets, until the wrath of the LORD arose against his people, **till there was no remedy** (2 Chron 36:15,16).*

DANIEL 9. THE PROPHECY OF THE SEVENTY WEEKS

Daniel was among the few who did not commit these sins, yet in total humility and abasement he says *we* and not *they*. With Daniel as their representative and intercessor, the second person pronoun expresses the fact that Israel did it as a corporate body. But it goes further; Daniel is foreshadowing One who would be *made sin* and who (at the end of this chapter) would be *cut off, but not for himself.*

- *For he hath made him to be sin for us, who knew no sin; that we might be made the righteousness of God in him (2 Cor 5:21).*

- *After threescore and two weeks shall Messiah be cut off, but not for himself (9:26).*

(3) Here We See Where the Cause **Belongs** for Israel's Troubles.

Note the parallel statements in verses 9:7-9.

O Lord,
>   righteousness <u>belongeth</u> unto thee,
>   *but unto us confusion of faces, as at this day;*
>   *to the men of Judah, and to the inhabitants of Jerusalem, and unto*
>   *all Israel, that are near, and that are far off, through all the*
>   *countries whither thou hast driven them, because of their trespass*
>   *that they have trespassed against thee* (9:7).

O Lord,
>   *to us <u>belongeth</u> confusion of face, to our kings, to our princes, and to*
>   *our fathers, because we have sinned against thee* (9:8).
>   **To the Lord our God <u>belong</u> mercies and forgivenesses, though we have**
>   **rebelled against him** (9:9);

In true repentance there is full acknowledgement where the fault *belongs*. God is righteous when he judges, and the sinner must bear *all* the blame. It was sin that plunged Israel into all these troubles. Israel is *dispersed* through *all the* countries; some *near,* where they are known and therefore the more ashamed, others *afar off,* where they are not known and therefore abandoned. They mingled themselves with the nations and willing allowed themselves to be corrupted by them, and now God mingles them with the nations that they might be plundered by them.

- *The LORD is righteous; for I have rebelled against his commandment: hear, I pray you, all people, and behold my sorrow: my virgins and my young men are gone into captivity (Lam 1:18).*

(4) Here We See Israel's Rejection of the Bible.

<u>Their Sin Against the Bible</u>. **Neither have we obeyed the voice of the LORD our God, to walk in his laws, which he set before us by his servants the prophets. Yea, all Israel have transgressed thy law, even by departing, that they might not obey thy voice** (9:10,11) Notice the first and last statements here. **Neither have we obeyed….. that they might not obey**. They did not obey *personally* in order that they would not obey *nationally*. In between are two further statements. They not only refused to **walk** in His Laws, but they brazenly **transgressed** the Law. Though the Bible was faithfully and continually set before them by **his servants the prophets** they wanted nothing to do with it.

- *Yet the LORD testified against Israel, and against Judah, by all the prophets, and by all the seers, saying, Turn ye from your evil ways, and keep my commandments and my statutes, according to all the law which I commanded your fathers, and which I sent to you by my servants the prophets. Notwithstanding **they would not hear**, but **hardened their necks**, like to the neck of their fathers, that did not believe in the LORD their God. And they **rejected his statutes**, and his covenant that he made with their fathers, and his testimonies which he testified against them; and they **followed vanity**,* *and became vain, and went after the heathen that were round about them, concerning whom the LORD had charged them, that they should not do like them (2 Kng 17:13-15).*

• *Because they **obeyed not** the voice of the LORD their God, but transgressed his covenant, and all that Moses the servant of the LORD commanded, and **would not hear** them, nor do them (2 Kng 18:12).*

Their Judgement From the Bible. (9:11) ***Therefore the curse is poured upon us, and the oath that is written in the law of Moses the servant of God, because we have sinned against him.** (9:12) **And he hath confirmed his words, which he spake against us, and against our judges that judged us, by bringing upon us a great evil: for under the whole heaven hath not been done as hath been done upon Jerusalem.** (9:13) **As it is written in the law of Moses, all this evil is come upon us: yet made we not our prayer before the LORD our God, that we might turn from our iniquities, and understand thy truth*** (9:11-13). Like many people, they might have thought that they were through with the Bible, *but the Bible was not through with them!* The catastrophic judgement came exactly as it had been *written* in the Bible and *spoken* by the prophets.

And lest they at the first should think that these were "the common lot of mankind" type of troubles, they soon realized that *under the whole heaven hath not been done as hath been done upon Jerusalem* (9:11). So also many today are taking lightly the Bible warnings of the Seven Year Tribulation (***The Seventieth Week of Daniel***). As we have shown, it will be like nothing the world has ever seen before.

• *Alas! for that day is great, so that **none is like it**: it is even the time of Jacob's trouble, but he shall be saved out of it (Jer 30:7).*

• *And at that time shall Michael stand up, the great prince which standeth for the children of thy people: and there shall be a time of trouble, **such as never was since there was a nation even to that same time**: and at that time thy people shall be delivered, every one that shall be found written in the book (Dan 12:1).*

• *A day of darkness and of gloominess, a day of clouds and of thick darkness, as the morning spread upon the mountains: a great people and a strong; **there hath not been ever the like**, neither shall be any more after it, even to the years of many generations (Joel 2:2).*

• **For then shall be great tribulation, such as was not since the beginning of the world to this time, no, nor ever shall be** *(Matt 24:21).*

• *Thine hand shall find out all thine enemies: thy right hand shall find out those that hate thee. Thou shalt make them as **a fiery oven in the time of thine anger**: the LORD shall swallow them up in **his wrath, and the fire shall devour them**. Their fruit shalt thou destroy from the earth, and their seed from among the children of men (Psa 21:8-10).*

• *Therefore I will shake the heavens, and the earth shall remove out of her place, in **the wrath of the LORD of hosts, and in the day of his fierce anger** (Isa 13:13).*

• *Come near, ye nations, to hear; and hearken, ye people: let the earth hear, and all that is therein; the world, and all things that come forth of it. For **the indignation of the LORD is upon all nations, and his fury upon all their armies**: he hath utterly destroyed them, he hath delivered them to the slaughter. Their slain also shall be cast out, and their stink shall come up out of their carcases, and the mountains shall be melted with their blood. And all the host of heaven shall be dissolved, and the heavens shall be rolled together as a scroll: and all their host shall fall down, as the leaf falleth off from the vine, and as a falling fig from the fig tree (Isa 34:1-4).*

• *But the LORD is the true God, he is the living God, and an everlasting king: **at his wrath the earth shall tremble, and the nations shall not be able to abide his indignation** (Jer 10:10).*

DANIEL 9. THE PROPHECY OF THE SEVENTY WEEKS

Just as the promises of judgement were fulfilled to the letter in Daniel's day, so they will be likewise fulfilled in the near to come future day. The judgements of the *mouth* and *pen* (the prophets and their Scriptures), were fulfilled exactly as stated by the *hand, God's Hand*!

<u>(5) Here We See the Summary of Daniel's Confession.</u>

<u>It Was a *Watched Over* Judgement</u> . ***Therefore hath the LORD watched upon the evil, and brought it upon us: for the LORD our God is righteous in all his works which he doeth: for we obeyed not his voice*** (9:14). It was controlled entirely by Him. God measured and ordered the intensity of the judgement. And, it was entirely deserved.

<u>It Was a Judgement From One Who Had Formerly Delivered Them</u>. ***And now, O Lord our God, that hast brought thy people forth out of the land of Egypt with a mighty hand, and hast gotten thee renown, as at this day; we have sinned, we have done wickedly*** (9:15). God had formerly glorified himself by delivering them out of Egypt; "wilt thou not now with the same mighty hand bring them out of Babylon?" Were they then formed into a people, and shall they not now be reformed and new-formed? Are their oppressors now mighty and haughty, and were they not then mighty and haughty? Will He bury in Babylon those that He brought out of Egypt! Note: the following passage looks not only to Israel's deliverance from Babylon but to their latter day regathering.

> • *Therefore, behold, the days come, saith the LORD, that it shall no more be said, The LORD liveth, that brought up the children of Israel* **out of the land of Egypt**; *But, The LORD liveth, that brought up the children of Israel* **from the land of the north**, *and* **from all the lands whither he had driven them**: *and I will bring them again into their land that I gave unto their fathers (Jer 16:14,15).*

Daniels Prayer: His Petition 9:16-19.

> O LORD, according to all thy righteousness, I beseech thee, let thine anger and thy fury be turned away from thy city Jerusalem, thy holy mountain: because for our sins, and for the iniquities of our fathers, Jerusalem and thy people are become a reproach to all that are about us. (9:17) Now therefore, O our God, hear the prayer of thy servant, and his supplications, and cause thy face to shine upon thy sanctuary that is desolate, for the Lord's sake. (9:18) O my God, incline thine ear, and hear; open thine eyes, and behold our desolations, and the city which is called by thy name: for we do not present our supplications before thee for our righteousnesses, but for thy great mercies. (9:19) O Lord, hear; O Lord, forgive; O Lord, hearken and do; defer not, for thine own sake, O my God: for thy city and thy people are called by thy name.

Here is Daniel's importunate and urgent request to God for the restoring of the poor captive Jews. Here is the plea for ***thy city*** for Jerusalem to be restored. Here, and with this we give the greatest emphasis, **is the plea for God to do it now!** The urgency of this appeal is in the sharpest contrast to the standard Ptolemaic chronology which says this prayer will not be answered for another 93 years. To say such a thing misses the total thrust of this chapter.

After reading from Jeremiah that God ***would accomplish seventy years in the desolations of Jerusalem*** (9:2), and realizing that *time was just about up*, Daniel has immediately gone to prayer with the urgent plea that it *now* be done. Note how Daniel presses this. Note how he presses it for Jerusalem and not only the Temple. It is commonly taught that permission was granted by Cyrus only for the rebuilding of the Temple and not for the city at large. This ignores that Cyrus distinctly decreed that the city itself was to be rebuilt (Isa 44:28; 45:13). This ignores *common sense*; how could a Temple be built in a ruined and uninhabited city. This ignores the urgency of Daniels prayer for immediate action.

Daniel Prayed for Jerusalem Itself to be Rebuilt *Immediately* (Not Only the Temple)

- *I beseech thee, let thine anger and thy fury be turned away from **THY CITY JERUSALEM** (9:16). Not 93 years later!*

- ***NOW** therefore, O our God, hear the prayer of thy servant (9:17). Not 93 years later!*

- *Cause thy face to shine upon **THY SANCTUARY** that is desolate, for the Lord's sake (9:17). Not 93 years later!*

- *O my God, incline thine ear, and hear; open thine eyes, and behold our desolations, and **THE CITY** which is called by thy name (9:18). Not 93 years later!*

- *O Lord, hear; O Lord, forgive; O Lord, **HEARKEN AND DO** (9:19). Not 93 years later!*

- ***DEFER NOT**, for thine own sake, O my God: for **THY CITY** and thy people are called by thy name (9:19). Not 93 years later!*

In this section, verses 15 to 19, Daniel addressed God as Adonai (***Lord***) and Elohim (***God***) rather than Jehovah (***LORD***) as in verses 4 to 14. In the first section Daniel used *Jehovah* for that was God's redemptive and covenant Name. By using this Name he is appealing to God's covenant promises to Israel. He now uses *Adonai*, a Name which expresses the Master to servant relationship and by which the servant is instructed. Daniel further looks to the divine power expressed in the Name *Elohim* to accomplish the tremendous petitions presented.

Note: That in praying for the restoration of Jerusalem Daniel was anticipating his own release from Babylon as well of that of his countrymen. While the aged Daniel would not be leaving, he is now to discover that the answer to his prayer will extend far beyond the Jews release after *seventy years*. There will be *seventy weeks of years*!

The Answer to Daniels Prayer: The Seventy Week Prophecy 9:20-27.

And whiles I was speaking, and praying, and confessing my sin and the sin of my people Israel, and presenting my supplication before the LORD my God for the holy mountain of my God; (9:21) Yea, whiles I was speaking in prayer, even the man Gabriel, whom I had seen in the vision at the beginning, being caused to fly swiftly, touched me about the time of the evening oblation. (9:22) And he informed me, and talked with me, and said, O Daniel, I am now come forth to give thee skill and understanding. (9:23) At the beginning of thy supplications the commandment came forth, and I am come to shew thee; for thou art greatly beloved: therefore understand the matter, and consider the vision. (9:24) Seventy weeks are determined upon thy people and upon thy holy city, to finish the transgression, and to make an end of sins, and to make reconciliation for iniquity, and to bring in everlasting righteousness, and to seal up the vision and prophecy, and to anoint the most Holy. (9:25) Know therefore and understand, that from the going forth of the commandment to restore and to build Jerusalem unto the Messiah the Prince shall be seven weeks, and threescore and two weeks: the street shall be built again, and the wall, even in troublous times. (9:26) And after threescore and two weeks shall Messiah be cut off, but not for himself: and the people of the prince that shall come shall destroy the city and the sanctuary; and the end thereof shall be with a flood, and unto the end of the war desolations are determined. (9:27) And he shall confirm the covenant with many for one week: and in the midst of the week he shall cause the sacrifice and the oblation to cease, and for the overspreading of abominations he shall make it desolate, even until the consummation, and that determined shall be poured upon the desolate.

We have here the answer that was immediately sent to Daniel's prayer, and it is a very memorable one, for it tells of the Messiah being *cut off* in Jerusalem and of His bringing about *everlasting righteousness* to Jerusalem. From this we may know that what happens in Jerusalem will have its bearing upon the entire earth.

- *Let them know that God ruleth in Jacob unto the ends of the earth. Selah (Psa 59:13).*

DANIEL 9. THE PROPHECY OF THE SEVENTY WEEKS

The Time of the Answer:

It Was a Time of Prayer. *And whiles I was speaking, and praying, and confessing my sin and the sin of my people Israel, and presenting my supplication before the LORD my God for the holy mountain of my God* (9:20). Daniel was still praying. This fact he stated with great emphasis and is repeated in the next verse. *Yea, whiles I was speaking in prayer.* The answer came before he rose from his knees, and while there was yet more which he intended to say. *While they are yet speaking, I will hear* (Isa. 65:24).

He Was Praying About Sin. *My sin and the sin of my people.* Daniel was a very great and good man, and yet he finds sins of his own to confess before God. *There is not a just man upon earth that doeth good and sinneth not* (Eccl 7:20), *If we say that we have no sin we deceive ourselves* (1 Jhn 1:8). He also as an intercessor confessed the *sin of his people.*

He Was Praying About Jerusalem. *The holy mountain of my God.* Jerusalem is God's earthly *mountain.* Though at this time of this prayer it seems *low* and *not holy* and was in *ruins,* yet a **holy mountain** is what it should be and what it will be. This is Jerusalem's name throughout the Scriptures.

* Great is the LORD, and greatly to be praised in the city of our God, in **the mountain of his holiness**. Beautiful for situation, the joy of the whole earth, is **mount Zion**, on the sides of the north, the city of the great King (Psa 48:1,2).

* Thus saith the LORD; I am returned unto Zion, and will dwell in the midst of Jerusalem: and Jerusalem shall be called a city of truth; and **the mountain** of the LORD of hosts **the holy mountain** (Zech 8:3).

It Was the Time of the Evening Sacrifice. *Yea, whiles I was speaking in prayer, even the man Gabriel, whom I had seen in the vision at the beginning, being caused to fly swiftly, touched me about the time of the evening oblation* (9:21). The altar in Jerusalem was in in ruins; for a very long time there had been no 9 AM and no 3 PM oblations offered upon its altar. Nevertheless for the believing Jews it was well remembered.

* Lord, I cry unto thee: make haste unto me; give ear unto my voice, when I cry unto thee. Let my prayer be set forth before thee as incense; and the lifting up of my hands as **the evening sacrifice** (Psa 141:1,2).

* And thou shalt say unto them, This is the offering made by fire which ye shall offer unto the LORD; two lambs of the first year without spot day by day, for a continual burnt offering. The one lamb shalt thou offer **in the morning**, and the other lamb shalt thou offer **at even** (Num 28:3,4).

About the Time of the Evening Oblation

The six hours between the two sacrifices pointed to the six hours Christ would be on the Cross. The evening oblation was a type of the great sacrifice which Christ was to offer in the evening of the world (Heb 9:26), and it was in the virtue of that future sacrifice that Daniel's prayer and those of the Old Testament believers could be offered and accepted. Note: The Lamb *opened the seals* (Rev 6) in the virtue of His own shed Blood (Rev 5:9).

Contrast the true morning and *evening* sacrifice pointed to in this chapter and to a *Messiah* who will *be cut off, but not for himself* (9:26), with that of the false evening and morning observance orchestrated by the Antichrist in the previous chapter (8:13,14,26; cp. 9:27).

It Was at This Time Gabriel Appeared.

His Swift Approach. ***The man Gabriel, whom I had seen in the vision at the beginning, being caused to fly swiftly, touched me*** (9:21). The answer was not given in a vision as in Chapter 8 to which Gabriel came afterwards to interpret (8:1,15). Here Daniel has received nothing yet, and Gabriel comes directly with the full message. He came a long way for he *stands in the presence of God* (Lk 1:19) and must therefore be *caused to fly swiftly*. If the Messiah's Coming is from, and at a great *distance*, its message must be brought to the *door* and that *swiftly*.

Angels are messengers, quick in their journeys, and without delay they execute their orders. They run and *return like a flash of lightning* (Ezek 1:14). But it seems here that in some cases they are called upon to make an even quicker despatch. This was one of those times. Gabriel was *caused to fly swiftly*.

Again, if we ask, *How Swiftly*? Gabriel's flight to Daniel could not have taken over an hour because the Jewish oblation lasted from Three to Four in the afternoon. It is called the *ninth hour* in the Scriptures. The reason the sacrifice had to be offered during the ninth hour was because the animal sacrifice looked forward to the eternal sacrifice, Jesus Christ the Lamb of God. It was in the *ninth hour* that Jesus Christ finished His atoning work on the Cross and died for the sins of the world (see *Hutchings*).

> • Now from the sixth hour there was darkness over all the land unto the ninth hour. And about the ninth hour Jesus cried with a loud voice, saying, Eli, Eli, lama sabachthani? that is to say, My God, my God, why hast thou forsaken me? . . . Jesus, when he had cried again with a loud voice, yielded up the ghost (Matt 27:45-46, 50).

As the sacrifice was being offered the priest would pray for the acceptance of the sacrifice for the sins of Israel, and they prayed for Israel to become holy and righteous in God's sight so that Messiah would come and bring in the Kingdom promised in the covenants. Therefore, it was according to Biblical instruction and Jewish tradition for Daniel to be praying at the Oblation Time and for the answer to come at that time. Daniel wanted to know that Israel's sins would be forgiven, The Angel now flies swiftly to tell Daniel **when** this will happen and by **what means** it will happen.

Note further, if as the standard Ptolemaic chronology states, another 93 years must elapse before Jerusalem is to be rebuilt, there would be no need for this haste!

His Stated Purpose.

As to Daniel's Enablement. ***And he informed me, and talked with me, and said, O Daniel, I am now come forth to give thee skill and understanding*** (9:22). Gabriel *talked with* Daniel, talked familiarly with him, as one friend talks with another, that might not as previously be overwhelmed at his presence and message (8:27). Daniel will not only be *shown* (9:23), but in a now greater measure he will have *skill* to *understand*.

As to the Immediacy of the ***Commandment***. ***At the beginning of thy supplications the commandment came forth, and I am come to shew thee*** (9:23). By this it appears that it was

DANIEL 9. THE PROPHECY OF THE SEVENTY WEEKS

not so much of what Daniel said that moved God, for the answer was given as he *began* to pray, not when he finished. *At the beginning of thy supplications the commandment came forth.* While most take this as the command to Gabriel to minister to Daniel, when compared with the same word in verse 25 it appears to be otherwise.

> • Know therefore and understand, that from **the going forth of the commandment** to restore and to build Jerusalem (9:25).

The commandment in both verses likely refer to the same thing – the edict of King Cyrus to allow the Jews to return and to restore and rebuild Jerusalem. "The thing was done *this very day;* the proclamation of liberty to the Jews was signed this morning, just when you began to pray for it, Daniel." As it were, the jubilee-trumpet has already sounded to proclaim liberty and the restoration of Jerusalem.

<u>As to Daniel's Commendation</u>. *For thou art greatly beloved: therefore understand the matter, and consider the vision* (9:23). He assured him that he was a favourite of Heaven; else he would not have had this intelligence sent to him. Paul in the Epistles to the churches referred to believers as *beloved*. He did not mean that they were beloved by him, although they were as much as man can love his brothers and sisters in Christ. He meant that they were beloved of God. While it means a great deal to know you are beloved among fellow believers, it means infinitely more to know that you are beloved of God. But even in this, though God loves all of His children, yet there are some that are ***greatly beloved***. Christ had one such among the disciples, the Apostle John, *the beloved disciple* who was entrusted with the key prophetic vision of the New Testament, as here Daniel was in the Old Testament. With such a high and holy calling, Daniel is to give it his greatest attention. *Therefore understand the matter, and consider the vision.* So today, believers who place great emphasis on the Second Coming of Christ are a special object of Heaven's affection.

> • **Blessed** are those servants, whom the lord when he cometh shall find **watching**: verily I say unto you, that he shall gird himself, and make them to sit down to meat, and will come forth and serve them (Lk 12:37).

> • Henceforth there is laid up for me **a crown of righteousness**, which the Lord, the righteous judge, shall give me at that day: and not to me only, but unto all them also that **love his appearing** (2 Tim 4:8).

> • **Blessed** is he that **readeth**, and they that **hear** the words of this prophecy, and **keep** those things which are written therein: for the time is at hand (Rev 1:3).

Consider The Vision !

It will seem strange that the Seventy Week Prophecy given *verbally* by Gabriel to Daniel should here be called a *vision* (9:23). Certainly what follows and onward to Chapters 10-12 gives a *panoramic overview* of what will take place from Daniel's time down to the Second Coming of Christ, yet in the strict sense of the word as previously used this is a Divine revelation and instruction rather than a *vision*. It may therefore be that this vision now stated refers to what Daniel has already seen in the previous two chapters – but now it is supplemented with specific chronological detail. At the end of both of these chapters we left Daniel in a very unsettled state concerning the *visions* he had seen.

> • In the first year of Belshazzar king of Babylon Daniel had a dream and **visions** of his head upon his bed: then he wrote the dream, and told the sum of the matters (Dan 7:1).

> • Daniel spake and said, I saw in **my vision** by night, and, behold, the four winds of the heaven strove upon the great sea (Dan 7:2).

> • After this **I saw in the night visions, and behold a fourth beast, dreadful and terrible**, and strong exceedingly; and it had great iron teeth: it devoured and brake in

> *pieces, and stamped the residue with the feet of it: and it was diverse from all the beasts that were before it; and it had ten horns (Dan 7:7).*
>
> • *I **Daniel was grieved** in my spirit in the midst of my body, and **the visions** of my head troubled me (Dan 7:15).*
>
> • *Hitherto is the end of the matter. As for me Daniel, **my cogitations much troubled me, and my countenance changed in me**: but I kept the matter in my heart. of the evening and the morning which was told is true: wherefore shut thou up **the vision**; for it shall be for many days. vision of the evening (Dan 7:28).*
>
> • *In the third year of the reign of king Belshazzar **a vision** appeared unto me, even unto me Daniel, after that which appeared unto me at the first (Dan 8:1).*
>
> • *And out of one of them came forth **a little horn**, which waxed exceeding great, toward the south, and toward the east, and toward the pleasant land (Dan 8:9).*
>
> • *And **the vision** of the evening and the morning which was told is true: wherefore shut thou up the vision; for it shall be for many days. and the morning which was told is true: wherefore shut thou up the vision; for it shall be for many days (Dan 8:26).*
>
> • *And I Daniel **fainted, and was sick certain days**; afterward I rose up, and did the king's business; and I was **astonished at the vision**, but none understood it (Dan 8:27).*

What Daniel saw in in the two previous chapters (during the first and third years of the last Babylonian king, *Belshazzar*), was in effect *one connected vision* of the coming Antichrist, his kingdom and its destruction by the Lord Jesus Christ. Thus the Seventy Weeks Prophecy directly complements what had been revealed before by vision and what Daniel had just inquired concerning – Israel's sin! Daniel is now told the relationship of this vision and Israel's sins to *time* and *chronology*. With the Seventy Year Captivity now ending, Daniel is introduced to something much greater - Seventy Weeks of Years.

The Seventy Week Prophecy

The Seventy Weeks: Its Overview.

<u>Its Time and Recipients</u>. ***Seventy weeks are determined upon thy people and upon thy holy city y*** (9:24). As to its time it will be a period of seventy weeks *of years*. That this is the case and that these are not seventy weeks of *days* (490 day) can immediately be seen by the fact that they extend to be the Death of Christ and the everlasting righteousness that will prevail at His Second Coming

The particular employment here of a multiple of sevens (the number that signifies perfection and completion) points to the fact that this is an *epoch of judgement*. The period of seven times seventy, which equals 490 years, is related in part to the warning given Israel for violating her Sabbatical years. The Seventy Year Captivity had been a punishment for violating seventy Sabbatical years over a period of 490 years.

> • *And them that had escaped from the sword carried he away to Babylon; where they were servants to him and his sons until the reign of the kingdom of Persia: To fulfil the word of the LORD by the mouth of Jeremiah, **until the land had enjoyed her sabbaths: for as long as she lay desolate she kept sabbath, to fulfil threescore and ten years** (2 Chrono 36:20,21).*
>
> • *For thus saith the LORD, That **after seventy years be accomplished** at Babylon I will visit you, and perform my good word toward you, in causing you to return to this place (Jer 29:10).*

However the Seventy Weeks of Years which are now revealed extend far beyond this and conform to the ***seven times more warnings*** given in Leviticus 26.

DANIEL 9. THE PROPHECY OF THE SEVENTY WEEKS

> • *And if ye will not yet for all this hearken unto me, then I will punish you* **seven times more** *for your sins (Lev 26:18).*
>
> • *And if ye walk contrary unto me, and will not hearken unto me; I will bring* **seven times more** *plagues upon you according to your sins (Lev 26:21).*
>
> • *Then will I also walk contrary unto you, and will punish you* **yet seven times** *for your sins (Lev 26:24).*
>
> • *Then I will walk contrary unto you also in fury; and I, even I, will chastise you* **seven times** *for your sins (Lev 26:28).*

The Divine Objectives to Be Accomplished. *To finish the transgression, and to make an end of sins, and to make reconciliation for iniquity, and to bring in everlasting righteousness, and to seal up the vision and prophecy, and to anoint the most Holy* (9:24). The Seventy Weeks that *are determined upon* Jerusalem and the Jewish people are in the sense of something that is burdensome, disciplinary and hostile to their comforts. It is that which will be necessary to bring them to the place of repentance and will enable them to see the establishment and fulfilment of the Davidic-Messianic Kingdom on earth (2 Sam. 7:1-17; 1 Chron. 17:3-15; Acts 1:6-7; Rom. 11:26-32; Rev. 20:4-6).

There are *six objectives* to be accomplished. The first three are negative and are marked out by three important Hebrew words for *sin*. The second three are positive and speak of righteousness and blessing. They will all be fulfilled at the end of the Seventieth Week, but they are in turn based on the Messiah being *cut off* at the end of the Sixty-ninth Week (9:26).

Three Negative Objectives of the Seventy Weeks.

(1) ***To finish the transgression (pasha)***. Joseph's brethren were guilty of many sins but their great overriding sin was their rejection of Joseph. The *transgression of Israel* is her rejection of the Messiah. The word ***transgression*** has special reference to the breaking of God's revealed laws. The Hebrew word speaks of revolt and rebellion against authority, and in this instance the authority of Scripture. Israel has flagrantly broken the very laws and Scriptures that she was ordained channel of bringing into the world. This has resulted in her domination by the nations and her being scattered throughout the world. Israel's full restoration, for which Daniel prayed, will be answered by the end of the Seventieth week. It is then that Isaiah 53 will become their *Confession of Faith*.

> • *And I will pour upon the house of David, and upon the inhabitants of Jerusalem, the spirit of grace and of supplications: and* **they shall look upon me whom they have pierced**, *and they shall mourn for him, as one mourneth for his only son, and shall be in bitterness for him, as one that is in bitterness for his firstborn. In that day shall there be a great mourning in Jerusalem, as the mourning of Hadadrimmon in the valley of Megiddon (Zech 12:10,11).*
>
> • *In that day* **there shall be a fountain opened to the house of David** *and to the inhabitants of Jerusalem for sin and for uncleanness (Zech 13:1).*
>
> • *According to their uncleanness and according to their transgressions have I done unto them, and hid my face from them. Therefore thus saith the Lord GOD; Now will* **I bring again the captivity of Jacob, and have mercy upon the whole house of Israel**, *and will be jealous for my holy name; After that they have borne their shame, and all their trespasses whereby they have trespassed against me, when they dwelt safely in their land, and none made them afraid. When I have brought them again from the people, and gathered them out of their enemies' lands, and am sanctified in them in the sight of many nations (Ezek 39: 24-27).*
>
> • *And so* **all Israel shall be saved**: *as it is written, There shall come out of Sion the Deliverer, and shall turn away ungodliness from Jacob: For this is my covenant unto them, when I shall take away their sins (Rom 11: 26,27).*

(2) *To make an end of sins* (*chata*). The Hebrew word means to habitually miss the mark, to stumble, to fall short. It is a word that describes the natural course of the fallen nature. It is a path where actions will always be opposed to and turn away from God. *The end of sins* and its condemnation for the sinner comes when the sinner repents and believe on the One who died for their sins. There is no ***end*** of sins until there is faith in the One who said on the Cross ***It is finished*** (Jhn 19:30). But that which Gabriel especially speaks here is when Israel comes to her Messiah. The *fountain has long been opened for sin and for uncleanness* (Zech 13:1) but the great bulk of Israel nationally will not avail herself of that fountain until Christ returns. It is then that she will confess –

> • Surely he hath borne our griefs, and carried our sorrows: yet we did esteem him stricken, smitten of God, and afflicted. But **he was wounded for our transgressions, he was bruised for our iniquities: the chastisement of our peace was upon him**; and with his stripes we are healed. All we like sheep have gone astray; we have turned every one to his own way; and the LORD hath laid on him the iniquity of us all (Isa 53:4-6).

(3) *To make reconciliation for iniquity (avon)*. This is a word that describes the deep bent, perversity and stain of sin. It is not "surface"; it is *from the sole of the foot even to the head* (Isa 1:6). This looks at Calvary's atonement as it becomes effective for Daniel's people at the Messiah's Second Advent and the establishment of His Millennial Reign. Then they will *come with weeping* to their Messiah. Then their iniquity will be purged away.

> • In those days, and in that time, saith the LORD, the children of Israel shall come, they and the children of Judah together, going and **weeping**: they shall go, and seek the LORD their God. They shall ask the way to Zion with their faces thitherward, saying, Come, and let us join ourselves to the LORD in a perpetual covenant that shall not be forgotten (Jer 50:4,5).

> • And I will bring Israel again to his habitation, and he shall feed on Carmel and Bashan, and his soul shall be satisfied upon mount Ephraim and Gilead. In those days, and in that time, saith the LORD, **the iniquity of Israel shall be sought for**, and there shall be none; and **the sins of Judah, and they shall not be found**: for I will pardon them whom I reserve (Jer 50:19,20).

> • Behold, he cometh with clouds; and every eye shall see him, and they also which pierced him: and all kindreds of the earth **shall wail because of him**. Even so, Amen (Rev 1:7).

Three Positive Objectives of the Seventy Weeks.

(4) *To bring in everlasting righteousness*. This is the imputed righteousness of Jesus Christ effected by His death on Calvary. But like His *making reconciliation for iniquity*, it will not become effective for Israel (nor to the earth as a whole, Rev 1:7) till Israel as *the crown of the nations*; turns in faith to her Messiah-Saviour at His Second Coming and experiences regeneration and inward moral transformation (Jer 31:33,34).

> • But this shall be the covenant that I will make with the house of Israel; After those days, saith the LORD, I will put my law in their inward parts, and write it in their hearts; and will be their God, and they shall be my people. And they shall teach no more every man his neighbour, and every man his brother, saying, Know the LORD: for they shall all know me, from the least of them unto the greatest of them, saith the LORD: for I will forgive their iniquity, and I will remember their sin no more (Jer 31:33,34).

Christ's death for all sinners (Dan 9:26; Heb 9:26; 1 Jhn 2:2) provides the basis for His reign, and not only as Israel's King in that day, but also as *King of kings* of the nations. By virtue of His *obedience unto death* (Phil 2:6-9), He is given authority over all nations to restore all things in the mediatorial reign that will bridge the thousand years and then continue into the

DANIEL 9. THE PROPHECY OF THE SEVENTY WEEKS

perfect, sinless phase of the eternal state. This will be the grand culmination of *the everlasting righteousness* spoken of here.

> • *Let them know that God ruleth in Jacob unto the ends of the earth. Selah (Psa 59:13).*
>
> • *The kingdoms of this world are become the kingdoms of our Lord, and of his Christ; and he shall reign for ever and ever (Rev 11:15).*
>
> • *But with **righteousness** shall he judge the poor, and reprove with equity for the meek of the earth: and he shall smite the earth: with the rod of his mouth, and with the breath of his lips shall he slay the wicked. And **righteousness** shall be the girdle of his loins, and faithfulness the girdle of his reins (Isa 11:4,5).*
>
> • *Behold, the days come, saith the LORD, that I will raise unto David **a righteous Branch**, and a King shall reign and prosper, and shall execute judgment and justice in the earth. In his days Judah shall be saved, and Israel shall dwell safely: and this is his name whereby he shall be called, **THE LORD OUR RIGHTEOUSNESS** (Jer 23:5,6).*
>
> • *In those days, and at that time, will I cause **the Branch of righteousness** to grow up unto David; and he shall execute judgment and **righteousness** in the land. In those days shall Judah be saved, and Jerusalem shall dwell safely: and this is the name wherewith she shall be called, **The LORD our righteousness** (Jer 33:15,16).*

(5) *To seal up the vision and prophecy.* The Lord will confirm, ratify, authenticate and fulfil the entirety of the vast contents of Biblical prophecy and vision. Everything that the Old and New Testament state regarding Israel and the nations will be fulfilled, and that to the letter.

> • *Seek ye out of the book of the LORD, and read: no one of these shall fail, **none shall want her mate**: for my mouth it hath commanded, and his spirit it hath gathered them (Isa 34:16).*
>
> • *Verily I say unto you, This generation shall not pass away, **till all be fulfilled**. Heaven and earth shall pass away: but my words shall not pass away (Lk 21:33,34).*
>
> • *And the LORD answered me, and said, Write the vision, and make it plain upon tables, that he may run that readeth it. For the vision is yet for an appointed time, but at the end it shall speak, and not lie: **though it tarry, wait for it**; because it will surely come, it will not tarry (Hab 2:2,3).*

Noah Hutchings states further concerning this *sealing* and its relationship to Joel 2:27.28. Note: he is *not* saying that it is the same as the extra Biblical revelation claimed today by the Charismatic movement. It is Israel who that in the days of Christ's Return will expound fully what had been previously revealed in the Scriptures.

> This does not mean the particular vision and prophecy which Gabriel delivered to Daniel. It means all visions and all prophecies recorded in the Bible. All the prophecies given in the Bible were revealed to Israelites, and all prophecy is sealed up in Israel. Daniel was commanded to seal up the book of his prophecy until the end, meaning when the Jew began to return to the land. And only when the Jews began to return to their land did men begin to understand the prophecies that applied to the last days. Gentile ministers today expound the prophecies which were given to the Jews, but the time is coming when Christ returns that the gift of prophecy and vision will again be sealed up in God's covenant people.
>
> *And ye [Israel] shall know that I am in the midst of Israel, and that I am the Lord your God. . . And it shall come to pass afterward, that I will pour out my spirit upon all flesh; and your sons and your daughters shall prophesy, your old men shall dream dreams, your young men shall see visions (Joel 2:27,28).*
>
> Some churches today try to claim this promise for themselves, but it applies only to the sons and daughters of Israel during the millennium (Hutchings pp. 213,214).

(6) *And to anoint the most Holy.* This does not refer to Heaven itself or the New Jerusalem, for there is no Temple there.

*• And **I saw no temple** therein: for the Lord God Almighty and the Lamb are the temple of it (Rev 21:22).*

The reference is instead to the consecration of the great Temple which will stand in Jerusalem during the millennial reign of Christ.

*• Afterward he brought me to the gate, even the gate that looketh toward the east: And, behold, **the glory of the God of Israel** came from the way of the east: and his voice was like a noise of many waters: and the earth shined with his glory (Ezek 43:1,2).*

*• And **the glory of the LORD** came into the house by the way of the gate whose prospect is toward the east (Ezek 43:4).*

*• And he said unto me, Son of man, **the place of my throne, and the place of the soles of my feet**, where I will dwell in the midst of the children of Israel for ever, and my holy name, shall the house of Israel no more defile, neither they, nor their kings, by their whoredom, nor by the carcases of their kings in their high places (Ezek 43:7).*

*• In that day shall the branch of the LORD be beautiful and glorious, and the fruit of the earth shall be excellent and comely for them that are escaped of Israel. And it shall come to pass, that he that is left in Zion, and **he that remaineth in Jerusalem, shall be called holy**, even every one that is written among the living in Jerusalem: When the Lord shall have **washed away the filth** of the daughters of Zion, and shall have **purged the blood** of Jerusalem from the midst thereof by the spirit of judgment, and by the spirit of burning. And the LORD will create upon every dwelling place of mount Zion, and upon her assemblies, a cloud and smoke by day, and the shining of a flaming fire by night: for upon all the glory shall be a defence. And there shall be a tabernacle for a shadow in the day time from the heat, and for a place of refuge, and for a covert from storm and from rain (Isa 4:2-6).*

*• And it shall come to pass, that from one new moon to another, and from one sabbath to another, shall **all flesh come to worship** before me, saith the LORD (Isa 66:23).*

*• And the inhabitants of one city shall go to another, saying, **Let us go speedily to pray before the LORD**, and to seek the LORD of hosts: I will go also. Yea, many people and strong nations shall come to seek the LORD of hosts in Jerusalem, and to pray before the LORD. Thus saith the LORD of hosts; In those days it shall come to pass, that ten men shall take hold out of all languages of the nations, even shall take hold of the skirt of him that is a Jew, saying, We will go with you: for we have heard that God is with you (Zech 8:21-23).*

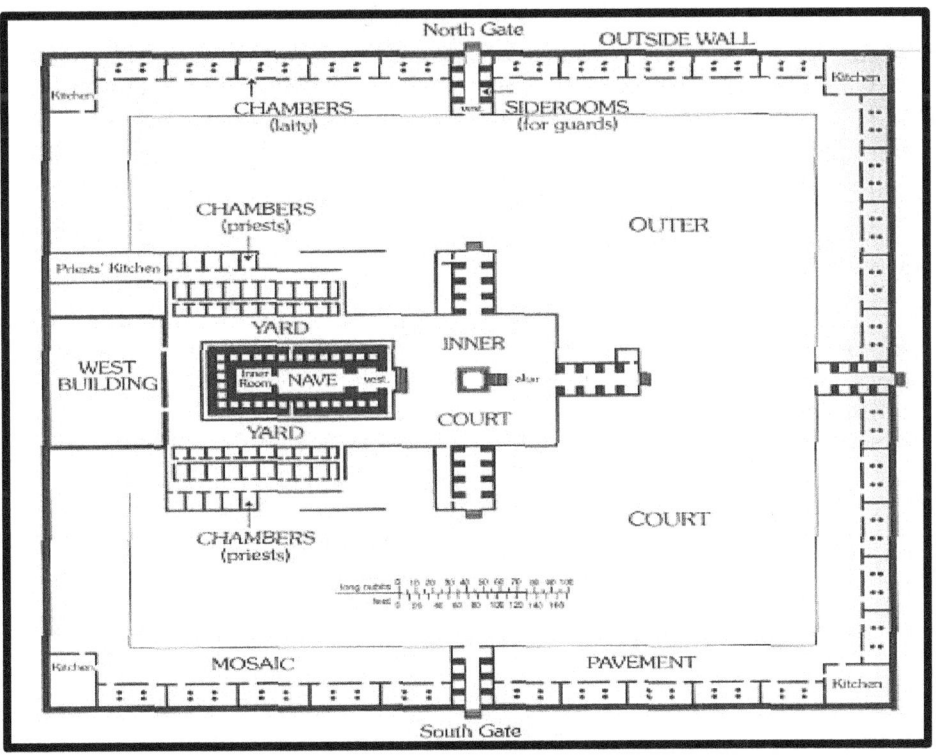

DANIEL 9. THE PROPHECY OF THE SEVENTY WEEKS

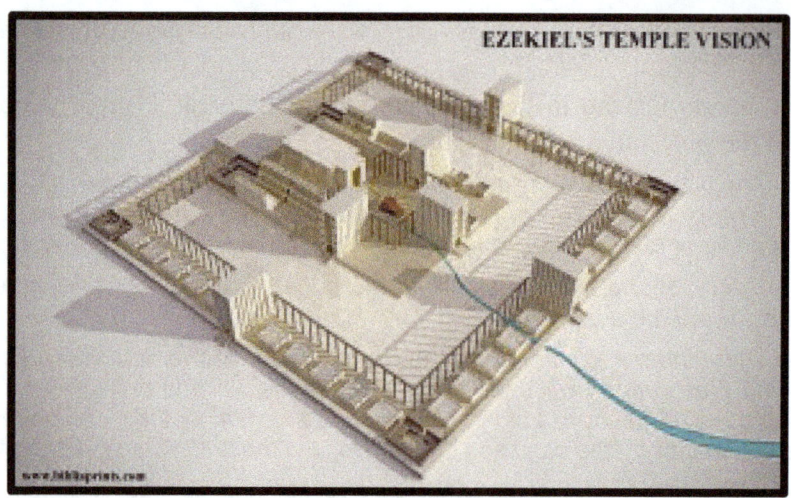

The Millennial Temple of Ezekiel 40-48
(templemount.org/ezektmp.htmlhttp://www.templemount.org/ezektmp.html)
(treybailey.net/2014/06/the-mystery-of-the-temples-in-ezekiel-40-41/)

The Seventy Weeks: Its Parts. Daniel 9:25-27 states that the Seventy Weeks are composed of three segments. It shows further that a time-gap exists between the second and third segment, and that the third (the Seventieth Week) is divided into two parts.

> *(9:25). Know therefore and understand, that from the going forth of the commandment to restore and to build Jerusalem unto the Messiah the Prince shall be **seven weeks**, and **threescore and two weeks**: the street shall be built again, and the wall, even in troublous times. (9:26) And after threescore and two weeks shall Messiah be cut off, but not for himself: and the people of the prince that shall come shall destroy the city and the sanctuary; and the end thereof shall be with a flood, and unto the end of the war desolations are determined. (9:27) And he shall confirm the covenant with many for **one week**: and in the **midst of the week** he shall cause the sacrifice and the oblation to cease, and for the overspreading of abominations he shall make it desolate, even until the consummation, and that determined shall be poured upon the desolate.*

Three Events Between the End of the Sixty-Ninth Week and the Beginning of the Seventieth Week.

> *(9:26) And after threescore and two weeks **shall Messiah be cut off**, but not for himself: and the people of the prince that shall come **shall destroy the city** and the sanctuary; and **the end thereof shall be with a flood, and unto the end of the war desolations are determined**.*

(1) The Crucifixion of Christ will take place *five days* after the 69th Week. Luke 19:42 indicates that the 69th Week ended on the *Palm Sunday* that Christ presented Himself to the Nation.

> • *And when he was come near, he beheld the city, and wept over it, Saying, **If thou hadst known, even thou, at least in this thy day**, the things which belong unto thy peace! but now they are hid from thine eyes. For the days shall come upon thee, that thine enemies shall cast a trench about thee, and compass thee round, and keep thee in on every side (Lk 19:41-43).*

(2) Jerusalem will be Destroyed by Titus. This took place in AD 70 about *33 years* after the death of Christ.

(3) The Entire Age. This will extend *to the end* (mentioned twice) and clearly refers to the end time events of Christ's Second Coming and the beginning of the Seventieth Week.

The Seventy Weeks: Its Beginning. *Know therefore and understand, that from the going forth of **the commandment to restore and to build Jerusalem unto the Messiah the Prince** shall be seven weeks, and threescore and two weeks* (9:25). This commandment can only refer to the Decree of Cyrus and is likely the same *commandment* mentioned previously.

- *At the beginning of thy supplications **the commandment** came forth (9:23).*

The Decree of Cyrus is the Commandment that Launches the Seventy Weeks

Given its emphasis in Scripture and the fact that it is the subject of a two hundred year old prophecy (Isa. 44,45), and occurring so soon after Daniel received the prophecy, it seems highly unlikely that any decree other than that of Cyrus could be considered as the starting point for the Seventy Weeks. It is ***The Decree***, and the basis and precedent for any further decrees. None of these other decrees were a subject of prophecy. Nevertheless for most today the Cyrus Decree cannot be considered because as their chronology is based on Ptolemy's *King List*, the Weeks would fall some over fifty years short of the birth of Christ. We are told by virtually all commentators, including those of our premillennial school -

> Daniel was told that this 490-year period would begin "from the going forth of the commandment to restore and to build Jerusalem" (Dan 9:24). In the Scriptures are contained several decrees that have to do with the restoration of the Jews from the Babylonian captivity. There was the decree of Cyrus in 2 Chron. 36:22,23; the decree of Darius in Ezra 6:3-8; and the decree of Artaxerxes in Ezra 7:7. However, in all these permission was granted for the rebuilding of the temple and nothing was said about the rebuilding of the city ... When we turn to the decree of Artaxerxes, made in his twentieth year, recorded in Neh. 2:1-8, for the first time is permission granted to rebuild the city of Jerusalem (Dwight Pentecost, *Things to Come*, p.244).

This statement, however much we respect its source, is blatantly incorrect! It is the standard answer based on Ptolemy. There is compelling Scripture evidence that points conclusively to Cyrus.

(1) The Scriptures Specifically State that Cyrus Would *Build* Jerusalem.

- *That saith of Cyrus, He is my shepherd and shall perform all my pleasure: even **saying to Jerusalem, Thou shalt be built**; and to the temple, Thy foundation shall be laid (Isa. 44:28).*

- *I have raised him up in righteousness, and I will direct all his ways: **he shall build my city**, and he shall let go my captives, not for price nor for reward, saith the Lord of Hosts (Isa. 45:13).*

What could be plainer! Was Cyrus going to send them back to a city which could not be built for another 93 years? It is likely that God *stirred* the heart of Cyrus toward this action by acquainting him with the prophecy of Isaiah 44:28-45:13. Note the statement by *Josephus*:

> This was known to Cyrus by his reading the book which Isaiah left behind him of the Prophecies. (XI.5-7).

(2) The Jews' Enemies Complained that the Early Returnees had Begun to Rebuild Jerusalem.

- *Be it known unto the king, that the Jews which came up from thee to us are come unto Jerusalem, **building the rebellious and the bad city**, and **have set up the walls** thereof, and **joined the foundations** (Ezra 4:12).*

(3) The Cyrus Decree for Jerusalem was the Basis and Precedent for Subsequent Decrees by Persian kings. The Cyrus' Decree was primary, while those of Darius in his 2nd year (Ezra 5:9-6:8) and Artaxerxes in his 7th and 20th years (cp. Ezra 6:14) were secondary, and an adjunct to the original. Notice how *Josephus* confirms this principle.

DANIEL 9. THE PROPHECY OF THE SEVENTY WEEKS

> And all that Cyrus intended to do before him, relating to the restoration of Jerusalem, Darius also ordained should be done accordingly (XI.63).

(4) <u>The Seventy *Weeks* were the Lord's Answer to Daniel's Prayer Regarding the Seventy *Years* (Dan 9:2)</u>. They are linked! The Decree of Cyrus provided the *conclusion* to the Seventy years and it provided the *commencement* to the Seventy Weeks. This was ***not*** a prayer that was to be answered 93 years later. It was answered immediately.

Daniel asked God to *defer not* (9:19); the Lord then told Daniel: *At the beginning of thy supplication the commandment came forth* (9:23; cp. 9:25).

(5) <u>The Start of the Seventy Weeks was Something Daniel Could *Know*</u>. As Daniel actually saw the decree go forth from Cyrus and was perhaps party to it, he would assume that with it the Weeks were now commencing. It was something he would know *experientially*. This explains the emphasis on the word "know".

> • Know therefore and understand that from the going forth of the commandment to restore and to build Jerusalem ... (9:25).

(6) <u>Only the Cyrus Decree Would Alert the Jews to Start Counting to The Messiah</u>. While most premillennialists believe the 20th year of Artaxerxes Longimanus is the starting point for the *Seventy Week Count*, few have considered how minor this so-called decree was in comparison with that issued by Cyrus. In fact it was not a decree but rather the granting of a request by Nehemiah (Neh 2:4,8). The king provided a guard and wrote letters of authorization to the Persian authorities enabling Nehemiah to reach Judah and to obtain timber for the work (2:7-9), but in all other respects his coming to Jerusalem was unannounced, and with only a few accompanying him (2:11,12,16). The extent of the rebuilding was limited to a three-fold objective:

> • That he may give me timber to make beams for the gates of the **palace** which appertained to the house, and for the **wall** of the city and for the **house** that I shall enter into (Neh 2:8).

The reader must ask whether the Jewish People would be sufficiently alerted by such a restrained and unannounced event to ***know*** (Dan.9:25) that the counting of Weeks to Messiah was then to begin. Contrast this with the worldwide proclamation given in the Cyrus Decree:

> • **The LORD stirred up the spirit of Cyrus king of Persia, that he made a proclamation throughout all his kingdom,** and put it in writing, saying, Thus saith Cyrus king of Persia, The LORD God of heaven hath given me all the kingdoms of the earth; and he hath charged me to build him an house at Jerusalem ... (Ezra 1:1,2).

(7) <u>Only the Cyrus Decree Could be a Basis for the Calculations of the Wise Men</u>. Scripture specifically points to a linkage between Daniel and the wise men of Babylon, and it may be reasonably assumed that the wise men in paying homage to the infant Christ based and timed their journey according to the Seventy Weeks prophecy.

> • Then the king made Daniel a great man , and gave him many great gifts, and made him ruler over the whole province of Babylon, and chief of the governors over <u>all the wise men</u> of Babylon (Dan. 2:48).

With the other "decrees" so little known, it is difficult to conceive that the wise men would commence the count from anything other than the Decree of Cyrus. The very fact that they were looking for Christ's birth (Mt. 2:2), rather than his ministry and death 33 years later shows that the decree of Cyrus must have been about 451/0 BC; i.e. 451 + 33 (-1 for BC/AD) = 483 years.

(8) Jerusalem's Desolation was to be *Limited* to 70 Years and its Rebuilding would Span 49 Years, The Other Decrees would Make the Desolation Last Much Longer.

• *In the first year of his reign I Daniel understood by books the number of the years, whereof the word of the LORD came to Jeremiah the prophet, that he would accomplish* **seventy years in the desolations of Jerusalem** *(Dan. 9:2).*

• *That from the going forth of the commandment to restore and to build Jerusalem ... shall be* **seven weeks** *... the street shall be built again, and the wall even in troublous times (Dan.9:25).*

Realizing that this revelation was in answer to Daniel's prayer, it would be natural for him to assume that though he could not personally return to Jerusalem he *could* have the joy of knowing that work was shortly to begin and would be largely completed in 49 years. But there would be no personal satisfaction if major restoration was only to start in 93 years (538-445 BC), and completion not until 142 years (93 + 49). Certainly this would not be an answer to the *immediacy* of Daniel's prayer and that it be not deferred (9:19). Therefore, the decree to rebuild must occur at the close of the Seventy Years, and this must be the starting point of the Seventy Weeks.

Later, Ezra in his prayer acknowledges that repairs to the ***desolations*** were well in place by the time of his own arrival in Jerusalem.

• *For we were bondmen; yet our God hath not forsaken us in our bondage, but hath extended mercy to us in the sight of the kings of Persia, to give us a reviving, to set up the house of our God, and to* **repair the desolations** *thereof, and to give us* **a wall** *in Judah and in Jerusalem (Ezra 9:9).*

(9) Josephus Said The Cyrus Decree Applied to the City and not Only the Temple.
Whatever modern interpreters may think, Josephus, who lived before Ptolemy, leaves us in no doubt that Cyrus' decree mandated the city at large:

In the **first year of Cyrus**, which was the **seventieth** from the day that our people were removed out of their own land ... God stirred up the mind of Cyrus, and made him write this throughout all Asia:- "Thus saith Cyrus the king; Since God Almighty hath appointed me to be king of the inhabited earth, I believe he is that God which the nation of the Israelites worship; for indeed he foretold my name by the prophets, and that I should build him a house at Jerusalem, in the country of Judaea." (XI.1-4).

This was known to Cyrus by his reading the book which Isaiah left behind him of his prophecies ... Accordingly when Cyrus read this, and admired the divine power, an earnest desire and ambition seized upon him to fulfil what was so written; so he called for the most eminent Jews that were in Babylon, and said to them that he gave them leave to go back to their own country, and **to rebuild their city Jerusalem**, and the temple of God. (XI.5-6).

When Cyrus had said this to the Israelites, the rulers of the two tribes of Judah and Benjamin, with the Levites and priests, went in haste to Jerusalem, yet did many of them stay in Babylon ... so they performed their vows to God, and offered the sacrifices that had been accustomed of old time; I mean this upon **the rebuilding of their city**, and the revival of the ancient practices relating to their worship ... Cyrus also sent an epistle to the governors that were in Syria, the contents whereof here follow:- ... I have given leave to as many of the Jews that dwell in my country as please to return to their own country, **and to rebuild their city**, and to build the temple of God at Jerusalem. (XI.8-9,12).

(10) Many Contradictions Arise if the Seventy Weeks do not begin with the Cyrus Decree.
This has been noted in the introduction and is discussed fully in the authors *Bible Chronology: The Two Great Divides*, but notice again from the ***emboldened statements*** some of the many anomalies that appear when comparing the Ptolemaic with the unbroken Biblical Chronology.

DANIEL 9. THE PROPHECY OF THE SEVENTY WEEKS

CURRENT PTOLEMAIC CHRONOLOGY: LIVING ON BOTH SIDES OF A LONG GAP.

"There are "many sprightly 130-year-olds"

We have seen that the famous scientist Issac Newton studied the prophecies and chronology of the Book of Daniel. As far back as 1728 he wrestled with the fact that the Ptolemaic reckoning faced a very big problem when its dates are compared with the lists of names in Nehemiah 10 and 12 (And that is only the beginning!). Others have seen the same thing. A brief outline of these **traditional dates** will show what the problem is.

605 1st Deportation to Babylon.

   Daniel taken. *Time of Gentiles begins.*

597 2nd Deportation: Ezekiel taken with King Jehoiachin.

586 3rd Deportation: Jerusalem destroyed. ***Ezra's father Seraiah, slain*** (2 Kg 25:18; Ezra 7:1-5).

539 Persia (Darius the Mede, Dan 5:31) conquers Babylon.

538 Daniel is given 70 Week prophecy: 1st year of Darius (Dan 9:1).

536 Cyrus Decree (1st year of reign, Ezra 1:1):70 years after 1st Deportation.

- Jews allowed to build Temple.
- **Zerubbabel brings back first exiles.** *Many leaders among exiles "still active" 91 years later in time of Nehemiah.*

535 Temple begun, but work stopped.

520-15 Ministries of Haggai and Zechariah.

515 Temple completed. (Note: The times between the events down to this point are accurate, but because they are pushed back, the dates are wrong).

515-458 GAP: NOTHING BUT PTOLEMY'S KING LIST

458
- **Ezra brings back second group of exiles**.
- Institutes reforms.
- *Even if Ezra was not born until his father died (586), he is now at least 128!!*

445
- *Nehemiah weeps over report of fallen walls of Jerusalem 141 years after they were destroyed* (Neh 1)! He returns to rebuild wall of Jerusalem.
- **COUNT OF THE WEEKS BEGIN:** *93 years after given to Daniel But 483 years (69 weeks) added to 445 BC overruns the AD 32/33 Crucifixion by about 5 years!*
- 17 Priests/ Levites return with Zerubbabel (Neh 12) and aid Nehemiah's reforms (Neh 10). To be leaders in 536, they were *likely 130 years old in 445*!
- For further examples of **leaders that are too old** see *Bible Chronology: The Two Great Divides.*

Sir Robert Anderson's "Solution" for the Overlap

We now see that there is a further problem for the standard chronology. Adding 483 years (69 weeks) to the Ptolemaic 445 BC date for the beginning of these weeks will result in the Crucifixion taking place in 37/38. This gives an overrun of about five years and as many eight years for those who propose a 30 AD Crucifixion.

Sir Robert Anderson followed the Ptolemaic dates. In his *Daniel in the Critics Den* he proposed that this overrun could be eliminated by using Jewish lunar years of 360 days (instead of solar years of 365 days). Reckoning the 483 lunar years in days (360 days x 69 = 24,840 days) from Nisan (March 14, 445 BC), Anderson, finds the period culminates on April 6, AD. 32, the day Christ offered Himself to the Nation as the promised Messiah (Lk 19:42), and some five days before the Crucifixion.

This view has been widely accepted, but there is a major problem. Short periods of time can be timed by a lunar year, but not a long period. The Jewish people follow a luni-solar year in which the lunar sequence is compensated to the solar sequence. In late winter they watch for the blossoms on the almond tree, then they look for the first shoots of the barley crop, and finally the year will begin when the next new moon appears. (Note this assumes the Biblical beginning of the year in the Spring not the Autumn as they currently reckon; Exodus 12:2).

This ancient practice synchronizes the lunar year to the solar year, and makes the overall count of years, solar. Therefore their Festal calendar was lunar from Passover to Tabernacles; the length of the Flood was given by lunar counting; the Tribulation will be lunar for the days and months (Rev 11:2); but time over an extended period *must be counted* in normal solar years. To say there are 483 *uncompensated lunar years* to the Death of Christ contradicts the way the Jews measured extended time.

BIBLICAL CHRONOLOGY: BASED ON THE <u>CORNERSTONE</u>.

Sixty-Nine Weeks (483 years) from the Cyrus Decree to the Crucifixion. <u>*The First Week*</u> *(49 years) dates the closing period of Old Testament History.*

520   1st Deportation to Babylon.

- 3rd year of Johoiakim's 11 year reign (Dan 1:1).
- Daniel taken.
- Beginning of *Times of the Gentiles* (cp. Lk 21:24).

511   2nd Deportation to Babylon.

- 11th year of Johoiakim's reign and 3rd months of Jehoiachin's reign (2 Kng 24:6-8).
- Ezekiel and Jehoiachin taken.

500   3rd Deportation to Babylon and Jerusalem destroyed.

- 11th year of Zedekiah's reign (2 Kng 25:1-10).
- Ezra's father Seraiah, is slain (2 Kg 25:18; Ezra 7:1-5).

484   Last dated prophecy in Ezekiel: 27th year of Jehoichin's captivity (Ezek 29:17).

474   Last dated event in the captivity: Jehoiachin released from prison.

- 37th year of Jehoiachin's captivity (Jer 52:31), and 1st year of Evil-merodach, King of Babylon's reign (Jer 52:31).
- After Evil-merodach, Daniel gives the 1st year (7:1), 3rd year (8:1) and death (ch. 5) of Belshazzar the last king of Babylon. It does not give the years connecting them.

DANIEL 9. THE PROPHECY OF THE SEVENTY WEEKS

453   Persia (Darius the Mede, Dan 5:31) conquers Babylon.

452   **Daniel is given the 70 Week prophecy**: 1st year of Darius the Mede (Dan 9:1).

- Daniel has been in Babylon for nearly 70 years.

- Daniel (9:2) had been reading Jeremiah 25:11,12. *And this whole land shall be desolation, and an astonishment; and these nations shall serve the king of Babylon* **seventy years**. *And it shall come to pass,* **when seventy years are accomplished**, *that I will punish the king of Babylon...*

- Daniel had also been reading 2 Chronicles 36:19-23. *And they* **burnt the house of God, and brake down the wall of Jerusalem**, *and burnt all the palaces thereof with fire, and destroyed all the goodly vessels thereof.* (36:20) *And them that had escaped from the sword* **carried he away to Babylon**; *where they were servants to him and his sons* **until the reign of the kingdom of Persia**: (36:21) **To fulfil the word of the LORD by the mouth of Jeremiah, until the land had enjoyed her sabbaths**: *for as long as she lay desolate she kept sabbath, to fulfil* **threescore and ten years**. (36:22) *Now* **in the first year of Cyrus king of Persia**, *that the word of the LORD spoken* **by the mouth of Jeremiah** *might be accomplished, the LORD stirred up the spirit of Cyrus king of Persia, that he made a proclamation throughout all his kingdom, and put it also in writing, saying,* (36:23) *Thus saith Cyrus king of Persia, All the kingdoms of the earth hath the LORD God of heaven given me; and* **he hath charged me to build him an house in Jerusalem**, *which is in Judah. Who is there among you of all his people? The LORD his God be with him, and* **let him go up**.

450   **BEGINNING OF SEVENTY WEEKS:Cyrus Decree (1st year of reign, Ezra 1:1):70 years after 1st Deportation.**

- **Count of the Weeks begin: 483 years to the Crucifixion of Christ.**

- **SEVEN WEEKS BEGIN: 49 Years to 402/1 and conclusion of Nehemiah's reforms.**

- **Jews allowed to rebuild Jerusalem and Temple.**

- **Zerubbabel brings back the first exiles.**

434   1st year of Darius Hystapes King of Persia. The remainder of the First Week of Years (33 years) is dated to Darius' reign.

- He is the *third king* of Daniel 11:1-3; following Cyrus and Cambyses.

- He is also known in Scripture as *Ahasuerus* and *Artaxerxes* (an additional honour).

432   2nd year of reign: After stoppage, work on Temple/ City resumes (Ezra 4:24).

- Ministry of Haggai during 2nd year of reign (Hag 1:1).

- Ministry of Zechariah during 2nd and 4th year of reign (Zech 1:1; 7:1).

431   3rd year of reign: Vashti in Book of Esther deposed (Est 1:1).

428   6th year of reign: Temple finished (Ezra 6:15). A little over 70 years since destruction.

427   7th year of reign: **Ezra brings back second group of exiles** (Ezra 7:7).

422   12ᵗʰ year of reign: Haman's plot foiled (Est 3:7).

414   20ᵗʰ year of reign: **Nehemiah's trip to rebuild walls of Jerusalem** (Neh 2:1).

402/1 32ⁿᵈ year of reign: Nehemiah's 2ⁿᵈ trip to Jerusalem (Neh 13:6).

- Further reforms concluded.

- Malachi's ministry occurs here or shortly after.

- **CONCLUSION OF FIRST SEVEN WEEKS (49 years), 62 Weeks (434 years) remaining to Crucifixion of Christ.**

331   Persia falls to Alexander the Great. The Ptolemaic *King List* is accurate from this point onward, but becomes increasingly inaccurate before Alexander.

The Seventy Weeks: Seven Weeks followed by Sixty-Two Weeks.

Know therefore and understand, that from the going forth of the commandment to restore and to build Jerusalem unto the Messiah the Prince shall be seven weeks, and threescore and two weeks: the street shall be built again, and the wall, even in troublous times (9:25).

The Biblical outline of the first Seven Weeks (49 years) are shown above. They begin in the first year of Cyrus' reign and the sending forth of his Decree to rebuild Jerusalem. They end in the 32ⁿᵈ year of the reign Darius Hystaspes (under the Artaxerxes title, Neh. 13:6), With Nehemiah's second trip to Jerusalem and the ministry of the Prophet Malachi, this concludes the history of Israel as recorded in the Old Testament. Note: the above demonstrates that these 49 years are a period that is *full of Biblical History*!

These 49 years are here described as both *building times*, but also ***troublous times***. Ezra, Nehemiah, Esther, Haggai, Zechariah, Malachi describe the extent to which they were ***troublous times***.

Note what happens when, as in the Ptolemaic chronology, Nehemiah is placed at the ***beginning*** of these 49 years rather than in his proper place towards their end; ***nearly all of these 49 years will become a Biblical Blank***! No further Biblical events take place and much of what is listed above must take place before the Seven Weeks begin. Under this scheme there is nothing to show how or with what the Seven Weeks end. Commentators on Daniel Nine struggle with this fact. The following is typical:

> An interesting but difficult question arises in connection with the division of the sixty-nine weeks from Artaxerxes' decree to the Messiah the Prince into a period of seven plus sixty-two weeks. **There is no clear reason given** for distinguishing the two periods... *Unger's Commentary on the Old Testament*, p. 1666; emphasis mine.

There is *every clear reason given* as to the events of these 49 years when the Biblical rather than the Ptolemaic chronology is followed. This is also demonstrated when the last 32 years of these 49 years are dated to the reign of Darius Hystaspes and that he at different times in his reign is given the titles Ahasuerus and Artaxerxes. For a full discussion see Chapter Three of the author's *Bible Chronology: The Two Great Divides* (available from Amazon, or online at bethelbaptistlondon.com).

Next we are told that ***Three Climatic Events*** will occur after the Sixty-Ninth Week but before the Seventieth Week. The most fundamental of these is the ***First Event***.

The Seventy Weeks: After Sixty-Nine Weeks, (1) The Messiah is Cut Off, (2) Jerusalem is Destroyed, (3) Desolations Unto the Time of the End.

And after threescore and two weeks shall Messiah be cut off, but not for himself: and the people of the prince that shall come shall destroy the city and the sanctuary; and

DANIEL 9. THE PROPHECY OF THE SEVENTY WEEKS

the end thereof shall be with a flood, and unto the end of the war desolations are determined (9:26).

(1) The Messiah is Cut Off In A *Substitionary* Death. *And after threescore and two weeks shall Messiah be cut off, but not for himself.* The explanation drawn from Noah Hutchings regarding the *breach of promise* is especially noteworthy with regard to this crucial passage and the gap of time between the Sixty-Ninth and Seventieth Week.

> Daniel is told that after the Messiah would be cut off from His people Israel, and Jerusalem with Temple would be destroyed. This would be the judgement upon the people who had refused to accept Jesus Christ as the One who would end their transgressions and take away their sin as Daniel had prayed.
>
> In the Temple Discourse of Matthew 23, Christ laid the sins of Israel bare, He thundered out: Ye serpents, ye generation of vipers, how can ye escape the damnation of hell? (Matt 23:33). When He left the Temple after delivering this fearful denunciation, His disciples followed, and in perhaps a misguided attempt to placate Him, pointed out to the beauty of the Temple. Likely they were trying to show that there was something good and beautiful left in Israel and something worth saving. But Christ would not be placated. He said of the temple in Matthew 24:2: I say unto you, There shall not be left here one stone upon another, that shall not be thrown down.
>
> After the Messiah was crucified, the city and the Temple were destroyed exactly as prophesied, and that because Israel had cut off their own Messiah. Now who would be the agent of destruction? . . . The people of the prince that shall come shall destroy the city and the sanctuary (Dan. 9:26).
>
> Notice in Daniel 9:26 that there is no mention at any time of the four hundred ninety years being consumed from the cutting off of Messiah to the destruction of the Temple. The reason for this is when the Messiah was cut off, God stopped the clock. This was the iniquity that caused God to breach His promise of four hundred ninety years to the bringing in of the kingdom. The time stopped at the end of the sixty-ninth week, and it has not started again to this day. There is still one week of the seventy prophetic weeks to be fulfilled. This period of time that has been going on from the end of the sixty-ninth week to the time it begins in the seventieth week is called a gap, and this particular gap is the dispensation of grace. God calls it a breach in His promise to Israel. We read in Numbers 14:34: After the number of the days in which ye searched the land, even forty days, each day for a year, shall ye bear your iniquities, even forty years, and ye shall know my breach of promise.
>
> It was quite common a few decades ago, and still happens occasionally, for a woman to sue a man for breach of promise. The man would promise to marry a woman, and for one reason or another, he would not show up for the wedding. The jilted bride would sue the man for breach in his promise, and she would bring suit for real and personal damages. This is where it comes from — from God breaching His promise to His faithless wife, Israel. We should remember that God does not breach His promise without good cause. We read in Isaiah 30:13: Therefore this iniquity shall be to you as a breach ready to fall, swelling out in a high wall, whose breaking cometh suddenly at an instant. The instant Israel crucified the Son of God, the iniquity was so great God not only turned away from His only begotten Son as the sins of the world were laid upon Him, but He also turned His face away from His covenant people who were responsible. The clock ticking off the time on the seventy prophetic weeks was stopped just as if you would pull the plug on your electric clock.
>
> But let us keep in mind that the promise which God made to Israel has only been breached, it has not been cancelled. Everything that God has said he would do from the creation of the world will be done. But because of Israel's iniquity, salvation has come to the Gentiles during the breach. We read in Romans 11:30: For ye [Gentiles] in times past have not believed God, yet have now obtained mercy through their [Israel's] unbelief. We read also in Roman 11:26: And so all Israel shall be saved: as it is written, There shall come out of Sion the Deliverer, and shall turn away ungodliness from Jacob. When will the breach be healed and time begins again on Daniel's seventieth and last prophetic week? The Word of God tells us in Isaiah 30:25-26: And

there shall be upon every high mountain, and upon every high hill, rivers and streams of waters in the day of the great slaughter, when the towers fall. Moreover the light of the moon shall be as the light of the sun, and the light of the sun shall be sevenfold, as the light of seven days, in the day that the Lord bindeth up the breach of his people. The breach will be closed and the Seventy Weeks Time will resume when the Tribulation period begins (Hutchings, pp. 222-226).

Here then, in this prophecy to the Jewish People, is the inescapable declaration that their Messiah would be cut off 483 years after Cyrus decreed that their city be rebuilt. It was in fact so *inescapable* that during the Talmudic period they undertook *two fundamental means* which they hoped would enable them to *escape* it!

To Avoid This Truth Israel Shortened Her National Chronology. Documentation was presented in the Introduction to demonstrate that in the decades after the Crucifixion, Jewish leaders were faced with the unbearable dilemma that their own Prophet Daniel so emphatically gave the exact time of the Crucifixion of Christ. Something therefore had to be done to show that the *Weeks* could point to someone else. The solution was to shorten their national history so that Daniel's Weeks would shoot well beyond the Crucifixion of AD 33. The history of Persia from the fall of Babylon to its defeat by Alexander was the logical place to apply the editorial knife.

The compiler of the new chronology was the influential Akiva ben Joseph (known as Rabbi Akiva), a greatly loved, and leading contributor to the Talmud. His *The Sedar Olam Rabbah* ("The Great Order of the World") adapted Israel's national chronology in such a way that the *Weeks* of Daniel could point tolerably close to one of Israel's national heroes. That man was Bar Kokhba, who died fighting the Romans in 135 AD.

To Avoid This Truth Daniel was Placed in a "Back Room" of the Hebrew Scriptures. In our Bible Daniel is found in its rightful place among the four Major Prophets. This however is not the case with the Hebrew Scriptures. The Hebrew *Tanakh* has a threefold division: the Law (*Torah*), the Prophets (*Nebhiim*) and the Writings (*Kethubhim*). Daniel is not found in the second division (the Prophets) but in the third division (the Writings). Therefore in the Hebrew Bible Daniel is not included among the Major Prophets – Isaiah, Jeremiah, Ezekiel, or among the twelve so-called Minor Prophets – Hosea to Malachi.

Josephus in his day points to Daniel being in the *Prophets* rather than the *Writings*; but shortly afterwards, in AD 90, there is an account of Daniel being officially placed in the *Writings* of the Jewish Canon. And there it remains unto this day.

> But what happened to the writing called the scroll of Daniel? From what we can ascertain, sometime between AD. 70-110. probably 90 AD., (perhaps the Sanhedrin itself) the Rabbis determined at the Council of Jamnia that the book of Daniel would be placed in and fixed in the third section of the TANAKH / or Kethuvim (Writings)...
> The formation of the Writings/Kethuvim was developed between 105 BC and 16 BC...It was the Patriarch Gamaliel II who presided over the Sanhedrin during the council of Jamnia in which a scroll of Daniel was officially placed in the Kethuvim Writings (Charles Eisenberg, *The Book of Daniel-A Well Kept Secret*, p.21).

Here then is a prophecy of the precise time of the Death of Christ. And, it is a *Substitutional Death*, for it will **not be for himself**. How grand and far-reaching is this prophetic revelation of the Saviour of the world, who would not only be *cut off* in physical death, but be made the sin offering and be cut off from His Father (Psa 22:1; Matt 27:46) to accomplish man's redemption.

> • The next day John seeth Jesus coming unto him, and saith, **Behold the Lamb of God, which taketh away the sin of the world** (Jhn 1:29).

DANIEL 9. THE PROPHECY OF THE SEVENTY WEEKS

• For **he hath made him to be sin for us**, who knew no sin; that we might be made the righteousness of God in him (2 Cor 5:21).

• Christ hath redeemed us from the curse of the law, **being made a curse for us**: for it is written, Cursed is every one that hangeth on a tree (Gal 3:13).

• **Who his own self bare our sins in his own body** on the tree, that we, being dead to sins, should live unto righteousness: by whose stripes ye were healed (1 Pet 2:24).

• For **Christ also hath once suffered for sins, the just for the unjust**, that he might bring us to God, being put to death in the flesh, but quickened by the Spirit (1 Pet 3:18).

(2) Jerusalem's AD 70 Destruction is Linked to the Last Days Antichrist. *And the people of the prince that shall come shall destroy the city and the sanctuary* (9:26). The second far-reaching event predicted to occur after the Sixty-Ninth Week and before the Seventieth Week is the destruction of Jerusalem in 70 AD. That event occurred about 37/38 years after the death of the Messiah the Prince, necessitating a gap of at least that length between the Sixty-Ninth week and the start of the Seventieth Week. But the hiatus is much longer, for the events of AD 70 did not consummate the Seventieth Week of the 490 years.

There is a remarkable combination of events in the words - *the people of the prince that shall come shall destroy the city and the sanctuary*. That **prince** (Antichrist) stands in contrast to **Messiah, the Prince** (9:25). Thus the prophecy speaks of *two princes*. The *people of the prince that shall come* were the Romans under Titus (AD 70), but Titus, though a prince, is not *the prince shall come* (for he did not in any sense fulfil the actions of verse 27), this *prince that shall come* can only refer to the last days Antichrist. Thus this prophecy spans the period from the AD 70 destruction of Jerusalem to the final days of the Antichrist. This prophecy also links the Romans under Titus and the Romans under Antichrist. Consider the current antisemitism in Europe, and the continual political pressure by the EU against Israel. This span from AD 70 to the end, demonstrates conclusively that an extensive time period exists between the end of the Sixty-Ninth week and the beginning of the Seventieth Week.

For a full discussion of this passage and its connection with the ***origin*** of *the Little Horn* (Antichrist) refer back to the notes beginning at Daniel 7:8

(3) Desolation of War From AD 70 Unto the Final End Times. *And the end thereof shall be with a flood, and unto the end of the war desolations are determined* (9:26). The Jewish nation and its Temple worship were destroyed by the Roman legions. It came as a *flood* and with unspeakable horrors. The *flood* is a figure to describe a warring army that overruns and annihilates all in its wake. This was a description of AD 70, and overwhelming warfare as *a flood with its desolations* will characterize the age generally, but especially the end of the age.

• Now therefore, behold, the Lord bringeth up upon them **the waters of the river, strong and many**, even the king of Assyria, and all his glory: and he **shall come up over all his channels, and go over all his banks**: And he shall pass through Judah; he shall overflow and go over, he **shall reach even to the neck**; and the stretching out of his wings shall fill the breadth of thy land, O Immanuel (Isa 8:7,8).

• So shall they fear the name of the LORD from the west, and his glory from the rising of the sun. **When the enemy shall come in like a flood**, the Spirit of the LORD shall lift up a standard against him (Isa 59:19).

• The LORD is good, a strong hold in the day of trouble; and he knoweth them that trust in him. But **with an overrunning flood** he will make an utter end of the place thereof, and darkness shall pursue his enemies (Nah 1:7,8).

AND UNTO THE END OF THE WAR DESOLATIONS ARE DETERMINED

(Meczenstwo Walka, Zaglada Aydów w Polsce 1939-1945. Poland. No. 282.)

Auschwitz-Birkenau

The Jewish Holocaust Country by Country: *The National WWII Museum, New Orleans*

Country	Minimum Loss	Maximum Loss	% of Jewish Population
Austria	50,000	50,000	27%
Belgium	28,900	28,900	44%
Bohemia and Moravia	78,150	78,150	66%
Bulgaria	0	0	0%
Denmark	60	60	0.7%
Estonia	1,500	2,000	44%
Finland	7	7	0.3%
France	77,320	77,320	22%
Germany	134,500	141,500	25%
Greece	60,000	67,000	86%
Hungary	550,000	569,000	69%
Italy	7,680	7,680	17%

Latvia	70,000	71,500	78%
Lithuania	140,000	143,000	85%
Luxembourg	1,950	1,950	56%
Netherlands	100,000	100,000	71%
Norway	762	762	45%
Poland	2,900,000	3,000,000	90%
Romania	271,000	287,000	47%
Slovakia	68,000	71,000	80%
Soviet Union	1,000,000	1,100,000	36%
Yugoslavia	56,200	63,300	81%
Totals	**5,596,029**	**5,860,129**	

(http://www.museumsyndicate.com/images/6/*56541*.jpg)

Dresden

The desolations wrought by man will be brought to an end by the desolations wrought by Christ during the Tribulation and at His Second Coming. Come, behold the works of the LORD, what **desolations** he hath made in the earth.**He maketh wars to**

The Seventy Weeks: The Last and Seventieth Week 9:27.

And he shall confirm the covenant with many for one week: and in the midst of the week he shall cause the sacrifice and the oblation to cease, and for the overspreading of abominations he shall make it desolate, even until the consummation, and that determined shall be poured upon the desolate.

Who is the *he* that is going to confirm the covenant with *many* in Israel for *one week*? What is this *covenant* that he is going to *confirm*? What is he going to do in the Temple in the *midst* of the Seventieth Week? And what is it *that* is *determined* to *be poured upon the desolate*? These are questions concerning events that are shortly to have a catastrophic impact upon Middle East and the World.

(1) The Antichrist is a *Prince*. There is only one possible antecedent of the pronoun *he*, and that person is the *prince* described in the previous verse, **the prince that shall come**. This is the prince of the final stage of the Roman Empire. It is true that Titus was a prince as well as a military commander. How do we know that Titus was a prince? He was the son of a sovereign. His father Vespasian was made emperor very shortly before the siege of Jerusalem. The *Collins English Dictionary* says that a "prince is a son of the sovereign or of one of the sovereign's sons."

> Certainly, Titus made no treaty nor confirmed any covenant with the Jews. They used Josephus to intervene, and time and time again, Josephus tried to get the Jews to make a treaty with Titus, and they would not. It was their stubbornness to concede defeat that brought about their destruction. The reason they refused to agree to a peace treaty was that until the very last moment, they were expecting the Messiah to come and save them...They rejected to the very end the truth that Jesus Christ was the promised Saviour (Hutchings p.228).

Thus to the list of attributes already compiled in Chapters seven and eight, we must now add another descriptive feature; *the Antichrist is a prince*. That is, (if we understand this rightly) before he reigns as the world's king, he will be recognized as *having royal blood*! But what kind of *royal blood*?! *Of which Sovereign is he the son*?

• Now is the judgment of this world: now shall **the prince of this world** be cast out (Jhn 12:31).

• Hereafter I will not talk much with you: for **the prince of this world cometh**, and hath nothing in me (Jhn 14:30).

• Of judgment, because **the prince of this world** is judged (Jhn 16:11).

• Wherein in time past ye walked according to the course of this world, according to **the prince of the power of the air**, the spirit that now worketh in the children of disobedience (Eph 2:2).

• And when they shall have finished their testimony, **the beast that ascendeth out of the bottomless pit** shall make war against them, and shall overcome them, and kill them (Rev 11:7).

(2) The Antichrist will *Confirm The Covenant*. This as Hutchings points out will not be just any ordinary run-of-the-mill treaty. It will be *the* covenant. God has confirmed several covenants with Israel, but when the Scripture refers to *the covenant*, there is only one in consideration. It is the first covenant that God made with Abraham; an agreement entered into between Abraham and God that the Land of Israel would be given to the Patriarch's physical descendants and that as an everlasting inheritance (Gen 12:1,2). This is stated frequently in the Scriptures.

DANIEL 9. THE PROPHECY OF THE SEVENTY WEEKS

> *• And I will make thee exceeding fruitful…And I will establish my covenant between me and thee and thy seed after thee in their generations for an everlasting covenant… And I will give unto thee, and to thy seed after thee, the land wherein thou art a stranger, all the land of Canaan, for an everlasting possession (Gen 17:6-8.*

World powers today do not (to their own hurt) recognize *the* Abrahamic Covenant. To them there is only one "covenant" and that is *The United Nations Resolution on Palestine, Number 242*. This resolution in concert with other resolutions requires Israel to relinquish control of the "West Bank" that is to give up Judea and Samaria (Ephraim and Manasseh) which was given in the Abrahamic Covenant. The Antichrist will *confirm* (make strong, bring to fruition) this already existing covenant (likely UN 242), but in the end it will be the Abrahamic Covenant this is confirmed.

> *• God hath spoken in his holiness; I will rejoice, I will divide **Shechem**, and mete out the **valley of Succoth**. **Gilead** is mine, and **Manasseh** is mine; **Ephraim** also is the strength of mine head; **Judah** is my lawgiver (Psa 60:6,7).*

> *• God hath spoken in his holiness; I will rejoice, I will divide **Shechem**, and mete out the **valley of Succoth**. **Gilead** is mine; **Manasseh** is mine; **Ephraim** also is the strength of mine head; **Judah** is my lawgiver (Psa 108:6-8).*

> *• Because ye have said, **We have made a covenant with death**, and with hell are we at agreement; when the overflowing scourge shall pass through, it shall not come unto us: for we have made lies our refuge, and under falsehood have we hid ourselves: Therefore thus saith the Lord GOD, **Behold, I lay in Zion for a foundation a stone, a tried stone, a precious corner stone**, a sure foundation: he that believeth shall not make haste. Judgment also will I lay to the line, and righteousness to the plummet: and the hail shall sweep away the refuge of lies, and the waters shall overflow the hiding place. And **your covenant with death shall be disannulled**, and your agreement with hell shall not stand; when the overflowing scourge shall pass through, then ye shall be trodden down by it (Isa 28:15-18).*

> *• For it is the day of the LORD's vengeance, and the year of recompences for **the controversy** of Zion (Isa 34:8).*

Today we see the government of Israel trying desperately to get the Arab nations, the European Union, the United States, the United Nations or any representative coalition of nations, to recognize their right to the Land of Israel promised in the Abrahamic Covenant. There is no relenting on the part of the nations; she must give up Judea (with part of Jerusalem) and Samaria. Many of the Arab nations refuse to acknowledge that the Jews have any right at all in the Land.

But as we have seen a covenant is going to be enforced by ***the prince that shall come***, and this will not only give the Jewish People a foothold in the Land, but also *a very surprising foothold*! They will be allowed to build a house of worship on the Temple Mount and resume their Old Testament sacrifice. We can only speculate what they have had to give in return for this agreement.

The *vision* of the altar fires burning morning and evening (Dan 8:14,26) will be sent around the world. The *man of peace* is overseeing the spectacle and seems to be taking more of a role than one would expect. The fears however of many Jewish people seem to have been allayed and the agreement appears to be holding. The daily telecast from the Temple Mount has brought a certain sense of *peace and safety* (1 Thess 5:3). They should have been looking at the Book of Daniel:

(antichristconspiracy.com/PopeInnocentXEUsigning.jpg)

Not a Picture of the Antichrist, Nor of His Image! But an Illustration of Where the World is Heading!

(3) **The Antichrist will *Break The Covenant*.** Without warning to those who had ignored the prophecies of Scripture and especially the Jewish People who had relegated the Daniel to the end of their Scriptures, the Antichrist will command a halt to the proceedings. Immediately, from being a kind of *master of ceremonies*, he becomes the centre of attention. An image of himself will be erected on the Temple Mount and he will himself become the object of the world's worship. This will send shockwaves to every Jewish person. Now they know that they have made *a covenant with death* (Isa 28: 15-18). Again we note our Lord's warning:

• **When ye therefore shall see the abomination of desolation, spoken of by Daniel the prophet, stand in the holy place**, *(whoso readeth, let him understand:) Then let them which be in Judaea flee into the mountains: Let him which is on the housetop not come down to take any thing out of his house: Neither let him which is in the field return back to take his clothes. And woe unto them that are with child, and to them that give suck in those days! But pray ye that your flight be not in the winter, neither on the sabbath day:* **For then shall be great tribulation, such as was not since the beginning of the world to this time, no, nor ever shall be**. *And except those days should be shortened, there should no flesh be saved… (Matt 25:15-22).*

• *Who opposeth and exalteth himself above all that is called God, or that is worshipped; so that he* **as God sitteth in the temple of God, shewing himself that he is God** *(2 Thess 2:3,4).*

(4) **The Antichrist will Incite The Overspreading of Abominations.** An abomination to Israel was the worship of false gods, the eating of things sacrificed to idols, or the polluting of the sanctuary with worship of other gods. The Antichrist himself will be the *abomination of desolation* — he will stand in the holy temple. His claiming to be the Messiah, the anointed One of God, will be the greatest abomination ever committed on the earth. Satan will be seen to have succeeded in setting up own false Christ upon the *holy hill of Zion* (contrast Psa. 2:6). *Exploding* (!) from the Temple Mount the world will be whipped into an orgy of the vilest idolatrous "worship." The *man of sin* in defiance of the Creator will lead the will into depths of sin crazed madness which even by today's standards are not thought possible. The most blasphemous rock concert now performed will seem mild in comparison. When *the Man of*

Sin "takes the stage" he will leave no doubt as to why he has been given that epithet in the Scriptures.

There are others sins (but not many) that are called an *abomination* in the Scripture. One of these is homosexuality. It is a strike against the foundation of life upon earth. Global legislation has now enshrined same-sex marriage. It is widely promoted in the world's media and educational systems. Christ Himself said it would be a primary mark of the last days (Lk 17:28,29). It is a certain precursor of *the overspreading of abominations* in the days of Antichrist. *Thou shalt not lie with mankind, as with womankind: it is abomination* (Lev 18:22).

The Overspreading of Abominations in Our Day and *Everywhere*!

(Photo credit:courtesyJerusalem Municipality)

Zion Square Jerusalem circa 1939, To be Renamed *Tolerance* Square

"Zion Square, in the historic heart of downtown Jerusalem – which for many years attracted protests, demonstrations and clashes – will soon become a square to represent tolerance and mutual respect in the spirit of the late Shira Banki, murdered during the Gay Pride Parade," the municipality said in a statement. *Jerusalem Post* 16 Feb. 2016.

(http://i.telegraph.co.uk/multimedia/archive/00682/parade_682944n.jpg)

The Annual Jerusalem Gay Pride Parade

• *And their dead bodies shall lie in the street of the great city, which spiritually is called* **Sodom** *and Egypt, where also our Lord was crucified (Rev 11:8).*

(5) The Antichrist will be a Desolator and be Desolated. *And for the overspreading of abominations he shall make it desolate, even until the consummation, and that determined shall be poured upon the desolate* (9:27). Sin desolates! The Man of Sin will turn the world into a desolate wilderness. Compare the vast areas of urban desolation in American cites. In turn, the empire of the Antichrist having brought about spiritual, economic and agricultural desolation will itself fall under the desolating judgements of the *Seals*, *Trumpets* and *Vials* (Rev 6-16).

> • For the LORD shall rise up as in mount Perazim, he shall be wroth as in the valley of Gibeon, that he may do his work, his strange work; and bring to pass his act, his strange act. Now therefore be ye not mockers, lest your bands be made strong: for I have heard from the Lord GOD of hosts **a consumption, even determined upon the whole earth** (Isa 28:21,22).

With These Overspreading and Desolating Abominations The Antichrist Will Be All That His Names Say He Is!

THE ANTICHRIST

> • Who is a liar but he that denieth that Jesus is the Christ? He is **antichrist,** that denieth the Father and the Son (1 Jhn 2:22).

This is the title by which he is best known. It has a double significance. Its primary meaning is one who is opposed to Christ; but its secondary meaning is one who is instead of Christ. In both of these he will muster all Satanic power to oppose the True Christ and to divert worship from Christ to himself (Jhn 5:43).

THE BEAST

> • And when they shall have finished their testimony the Beast that ascendeth out of the bottomless pit shall make war against them, and shall overcome them, and kill them (Rev 11:7).

This is the title by which he is most frequently designated in the Book of Revelation: there are thirty-six references to him under this name in the last book of the Bible. The Greek word signifies a *wild beast*. This name *the Beast* contrasts the Antichrist from the true Christ who is *the Lamb of God*. The Lamb is the Saviour of sinners; the Beast is the persecutor and slayer of the saints. The Lamb calls attention to the gentleness of Christ; the Beast tells of the ferocity of the Antichrist. The Lamb reveals Christ as the Harmless One (Heb 7:26); the Beast manifests the Antichrist as the cruel and heartless one. Under the Law lambs were ceremonially clean and used in sacrifice, but beasts were unclean and unfit for sacrifices.

THAT MAN OF SIN, THE SON OF PERDITION

> • Let no man deceive you by any means: for that day shall not come, except there come a falling away first, and **that man of sin be revealed, the son of perdition** (2 Thess 2:3).

This double appellation is probably the most awful, the most important, and the most revealing title given to the Antichrist in the Bible. It diagnoses his personality and exposes his awful character. It tells us he will be possessed of a twofold nature: he will be a man, and yet more than a man. He will be Satan's parody of the God-Man. He will be an incarnation of the Devil. The world today is talking of and looking for the Super-man. This is exactly what the Antichrist will be. He will be the Serpent's masterpiece. As *Man of Sin*. The sin of man will culminate in the Man of Sin. The Christ of God was sinless; the Christ of Satan will not only be sinful, but the Man of Sin. "Man of Sin" intimates that he will be the living and active embodiment of every form and character of evil. "Man of Sin" signifies that he will be sin itself personified. "Man of Sin" denotes there will be no lengths of wickedness to which he will not go, no forms of evil to which he will be a stranger, no depths of corruption that he will not bottom. As *Son of Perdition*. Not only is he a human degenerate, but the offspring of the Dragon. Not only the worst of human kind, but the incarnation of the Devil. Not only the most depraved of all sinners, but an emanation from the Pit itself. "Son of Perdition" denotes that he will be the culmination and consummation of satanic craft and power. All the evil, malignity, cunning, and power of the Serpent will be embodied in this terrible man.

THAT WICKED

* *And then shall that **Wicked** be revealed, whom the Lord shall consume with the spirit of his mouth, and shall destroy with the brightness of his coming (2 Thess 2:8). He is so much the personification of wickedness that Scripture must label him in in the most stark and singular of terms – That Wicked !*
(drawn from biblebelievers.com/Pink/antichrist06.htm).

The End and Objective of the Seventy Week Prophecy is Very Good

Despite the turmoil across the Seventy Weeks generally, and the desolations and abominations of the Seventieth Week specifically, the conclusion will be very good. At the beginning of the prophecy (9:24), six immeasurable blessings for Israel and the earth are foretold. The first three speak about what will be taken away, the last three, what will be bestowed.

To finish the transgression
To make an end of sins
To make reconciliation for iniquity
To bring in everlasting righteousness
To seal up the vision and prophecy
To anoint the most Holy

He which testifieth these things saith, Surely I come quickly.
Amen. Even so, come, Lord Jesus (Rev 22:20).

II THE TIMES OF THE GENTILES REGARDING JERUSALEM 8-12

C. The Desolations and Final Blessing of Jerusalem 10-12
   1. Desolations and The Glory of Christ 10
   2. Desolations: Future to Daniel 11:1-35
   3. Desolations and Final Blessing 11:36-12:13
   4. Desolations and The Glory of Christ 10

DANIEL 10. INTRODUCTION TO THE LAST PROPHECY OF DANIEL

This chapter with the following two make up one entire vision and prophecy. In fact the vision (and a glorious vision it is, there could not be a better!) introduces the prophecy given at large in Chapter 11. Chapter 12 continues the prophecy but in the form of a momentous conclusion to the entire Book.

The Time of the Prophecy and the State of the Prophet 10:1-3.

In the third year of Cyrus king of Persia a thing was revealed unto Daniel, whose name was called Belteshazzar; and the thing was true, but the time appointed was long: and he understood the thing, and had understanding of the vision. (10:2) In those days I Daniel was mourning three full weeks. (10:3) I ate no pleasant bread, neither came flesh nor wine in my mouth, neither did I anoint myself at all, till three whole weeks were fulfilled.

Josephus wrote that because the Medes and the Persians held Daniel in such high regard, they built him a tower at Ecbatana in Media. It was in his own private castle on the bank of the Hiddekel River, also called the Tigris, that Daniel spent the remaining years of his life (*Hutchings*).

<u>The Date the Prophecy</u>. ***In the third year of Cyrus king of Persia*** (10:1). The time of the previous prophecy in Chapter 9 was *the first year of Darius* (9:1). As Darius and the younger man Cyrus were practically co-regents this would not be much more than three years after the fall of Babylon to Persia. It is now three years since Cyrus has given his Decree allowing the Jews to return and rebuild Jerusalem. As the Decree specified the rebuilding of Jerusalem (Isa 45:13: cp. Dan 9:25; how could they return and *not rebuild* their city!), the counting of the Seventy Weeks was now in its third year.

> • Now in **the first year of Cyrus** king of Persia, that the word of the LORD by the mouth of Jeremiah might be fulfilled, **the LORD stirred up the spirit of Cyrus** king of Persia, that **he made a proclamation throughout all his kingdom**, and put it also in writing, saying, **Thus saith Cyrus king of Persia, The LORD God of heaven hath given me all the kingdoms of the earth; and he hath charged me to build him an house at Jerusalem**, which is in Judah. Who is there among you of all his people? his God be with him, and **let him go up to Jerusalem, which is in Judah, and build the house of the LORD God of Israel, (he is the God,) which is in Jerusalem** (Ezra 1:1-3).

<u>The Nature and Times of the Prophecy</u>. ***A thing*** (*debar*, a communication, a matter of great substance and weight, not a wisp or trifle) ***was revealed unto Daniel, whose name was called Belteshazzar*** (his court name throughout the seventy years in Babylon and now remaining so in the Persian realm)***; and the thing was true, but the time appointed was long*** (10:1). As with all Biblical prophecy, the great length of time to the fulfilment does not diminish the truthfulness.

DANIEL 10. INTRODUCTION TO THE LAST PROPHECY OF DANIEL

> • *For the vision is yet for an appointed time, but at the end it shall speak, and not lie:* **though it tarry, wait for it**; *because it will surely come, it will not tarry (Hab 2:3).*

It is commonly thought that Chapter 11:1-35 deals with the *nearer future* to Daniel, with the remainder of Chapter 11 and on to Chapter 12 dealing with the end time Tribulation. We will show that it is likely that that the nearer future extends only as far as 11:20. Thus as stated here, for the most of what was now revealed to Daniel *the time appointed was long*.

Here it is also stated that unlike at Chapters 7 and 8 where Daniel confesses an inability to understand the prophecies he was give there, here he *understood*: ***and he understood the thing, and had understanding of the vision.***

<u>The State of the Prophet</u>. ***In those days I Daniel was mourning three full weeks. I ate no pleasant bread, neither came flesh nor wine in my mouth, neither did I anoint myself at all, till three whole weeks were fulfilled.*** (10:2,3). Daniel understood the prophecy and he understood it only too clearly! While there are rays of sunshine at the end of the revelation, before the *long-time appointed* to that end, his people Israel would undergo a great deal of suffering. But there was also another reason.

When Daniel was sad and troubled, it was always over his Nation. According to Ezra 1:1-4, it had now been three years since Cyrus signed the Decree permitting the Jewish People to return to their homeland, but only 49,697 had returned. Life for them had been fairly good under the Babylonians and now under the benevolent reigns of Darius and Cyrus, it became better still. They had established homes, planted fields, built businesses, made friends, had long family roots; therefore, they were reticent to pull up stakes and go back to a Land they had never seen. The vast majority had been born in Babylon and felt no urgent need to rebuild in Israel. Also, the land had been under the heel of oppressors for over seventy years. Jerusalem lay in ruins and the rest of the Land was desolate. Bands of robbers and Canaanite tribes roamed the mountains and valleys of Judah. They did not look kindly upon the return of the Jews.

However, when the Jewish People get too comfortable and too well situated in a foreign land, God has a way of stirring them up.

> • *For the LORD's portion is his people; Jacob is the lot of his inheritance. He found him in a desert land, and in the waste howling wilderness; he led him about, he instructed him, he kept him as the apple of his eye. As an eagle stirreth up her nest, fluttereth over her young, spreadeth abroad her wings, taketh them, beareth them on her wings: So the LORD alone did lead him, and there was no strange god with him (Deut 32:9-12).*

Israel is God's chosen earthly people, and He has given them a particular Land for their everlasting inheritance (Gen 17:8). When they become satisfied in a foreign nation, and begin to develop a national affinity for the nation in which they live, like an eagle, God stirs up their nest. When it becomes time for young eagles to get out of the nest and provide for themselves, the mother eagle will throw out the down, leaving only the rough sticks and sharp thorns. Then she will beat her wings over the young eagles to make them think she is going to attack them. She literally forces them out of their once comfortable nest. And as they flutter and fall down the rock cliffs, she catches them on her wings and bears them safely to a resting place (*Hutchings*). Note also a more extreme example:

> • *But, The LORD liveth, that brought up the children of Israel from the land of the north, and from all the lands whither he had driven them: and I will bring them again into their land that I gave unto their fathers. Behold,* **I will send for many fishers**, *saith the LORD, and they shall fish them; and* **after will I send for many hunters**, *and they shall hunt them from every mountain, and from every hill, and out of the holes of the rocks (Jer 16:15,16).*

The Vision of Christ 10:4-9.

And in the four and twentieth day of the first month, as I was by the side of the great river, which is Hiddekel; (10:5) Then I lifted up mine eyes, and looked, and behold a certain man clothed in linen, whose loins were girded with fine gold of Uphaz: (10:6) His body also was like the beryl, and his face as the appearance of lightning, and his eyes as lamps of fire, and his arms and his feet like in colour to polished brass, and the voice of his words like the voice of a multitude. (10:7) And I Daniel alone saw the vision: for the men that were with me saw not the vision; but a great quaking fell upon them, so that they fled to hide themselves. (10:8) Therefore I was left alone, and saw this great vision, and there remained no strength in me: for my comeliness was turned in me into corruption, and I retained no strength. (10:9) Yet heard I the voice of his words: and when I heard the voice of his words, then was I in a deep sleep on my face, and my face toward the ground.

The Date and Place of The Visitation. ***And in the four and twentieth day of the first month, as I was by the side of the great river, which is Hiddekel;*** The date of this encounter was 9 days after Passover. There are other references in Scripture to the ***four and twentieth day***. Here important events are noted, but this is the only occurrence in the first month. Each of the others occur some fifteen years later in the reign of Darius Hystapes with the Jews being urged to recommence the delayed building of the Temple. Therefore this became an important day in the post captivity era and a day (beginning here in Daniel) of special revelation from God.

• *In **the four and twentieth day of the sixth month**, in the second year of Darius the king (Hag 1:15).*

• *In **the four and twentieth day of the ninth month**, in the second year of Darius, came the word of the LORD by Haggai the prophet, saying (Hag 2:10).*

• *Consider now from this day and upward, from the **four and twentieth day of the ninth month**, even from the day that the foundation of the LORD'S temple was laid, consider it (Hag 2:18).*

• *And again the word of the LORD came unto Haggai in **the four and twentieth day of the month**, saying (Hag 2:20),*

• *Upon **the four and twentieth day of the eleventh month**, which is the month Sebat, in the second year of Darius, came the word of the LORD unto Zechariah, the son of Berechiah, the son of Iddo the prophet, saying (Zech 1:7).*

Daniel was by the side of the ***river Hiddekel*** (Tigris), probably walking there as Matthew Henry says not for diversion, but devotion and contemplation, as Isaac walked in the field, to meditate (Gen 24:63). Being aged and a person of distinction, he had his servants attending him but at some distance.

The Appearance of Christ. ***Then I lifted up mine eyes, and looked, and behold a certain man clothed in linen, whose loins were girded with fine gold of Uphaz: His body also was like the beryl, and his face as the appearance of lightning, and his eyes as lamps of fire, and his arms and his feet like in colour to polished brass, and the voice of his words like the voice of a multitude*** (10:5,6). That this is Christ and not an angel can be seen by the similarity to the description of Christ in Revelation 1:13-16 and 19:11-16. Further, as He is standing on the river, He is distinguished by two angels standing on either side of the river (12:5,6) and who come to minister to Daniel (10:10). In Chapter 9 it was revealed that the *Messiah shall be cut off* (9:26). Here we see Him in His pre-incarnate glory.

• *Then I Daniel looked, and, behold, **there stood other two**, the one on this side of the bank of the river, and the other on that side of the bank of the river. And one said to **the man clothed in linen, which was upon the waters of the river**, How long shall it be to the end of these wonders (Dan 12:5,6)?*

DANIEL 10. INTRODUCTION TO THE LAST PROPHECY OF DANIEL

The Appearance of Christ in Revelation 1:13-16

- *And in the midst of the seven candlesticks one like unto the Son of man.*
- *Clothed with a garment down to the foot.*
- *Girt about the paps with a golden girdle.*
- *His head and his hairs were white like wool, as white as snow.*
- *His eyes were as a flame of fire.*
- *His feet like unto fine brass, as if they burned in a furnace.*
- *His voice as the sound of many waters.*
- *He had in his right hand seven stars.*
- *Out of his mouth went a sharp twoedged sword.*
- *His countenance was as the sun shineth in his strength.*

The Appearance of Christ in Revelation 19:11-16

- *And I saw heaven opened, and behold a white horse.*
- *He that sat upon him was called Faithful and True.*
- *In righteousness he doth judge and make war.*
- *His eyes were as a flame of fire,*
- *On his head were many crowns.*
- *He had a name written, that no man knew, but he himself.*
- *He was clothed with a vesture dipped in blood.*
- *His name is called The Word of God.*
- *Out of his mouth goeth a sharp sword, that with it he should smite the nations.*
- *He treadeth the winepress of the fierceness and wrath of Almighty God.*
- *He hath on his vesture and on his thigh a name written, KING OF KINGS, AND LORD OF LORDS.*

The Appearance of Christ in Daniel 10:5,6

- *Then I lifted up mine eyes, and looked, and behold a certain man*
- *Clothed in linen.*
- *Whose loins were girded with fine gold of Uphaz.*
- *His body also was like the beryl.*
- *His face as the appearance of lightning.*
- *His eyes as lamps of fire.*
- *His arms and his feet like in colour to polished brass.*
- *The voice of his words like the voice of a multitude.*

In Daniel it is the Same Person as in Revelation, but in Daniel Christ appears more as Priest to minister and discern than as a King to conquer.

His clothing was priestly, for he is *the High Priest of our profession* (Heb 3:1). He was **clothed in linen**, as the High Priest himself was on the Day of Atonement.

His loins were girded with a golden girdle of the finest gold, that of ***Uphaz***, for everything about Christ is the best in its kind. The *girding of the loins* denotes His ready and diligent application in the work of our redemption.

His form was Heavenly. **His body like the beryl**, a precious stone of a sky-colour. For *He that cometh from above is above all* (John 3:31).

His countenance was awe inspiring, for His *face was as the appearance of lightning*, which dazzles the eyes, both to brighten and to threaten, depending on the state of the one beholding.

His eyes were as lamps of fire. They pierce all depths and look behind all masks. There is no hiding *in the dens and in the rocks of the mountains from the face of him that sitteth on the throne, and from the wrath of the Lamb* (Rev 6:15,16).

His arms and his feet like in colour to polished brass. There is perfect justice in His works and ways. His judgements are just. He is the *just justifier* (Rom 3:26).

His voice and words were *like the voice of a multitude*. The *Vox Dei*—*voice of God* overpowers the *vox populi*—*voice of the people*.

Thus before Christ walked on the waters of Galilee to the storm-tossed disciples (Matt 14:25) He here appears to aged Daniel on the waters of *the great river, which is Hiddekel* (10:4).

The Effect of the Visitation.

The Fear of the Attendants. **And I Daniel alone saw the vision: for the men that were with me saw not the vision; but a great quaking fell upon them, so that they fled to hide themselves** (10:7). They did not see the vision but they were moved by it! They could not bear to be in the presence of that which they had *not* seen; ***a great quaking fell upon them, so that they fled to hide themselves***. The Scriptures are for all, but these special manifestations were reserved for the select few through whom the Scriptures were written. Paul's companions were aware of the *light,* but *saw no man* (Acts 9:7; 22:9). Only Moses saw the burning bush. Only Ezekiel saw the departure and return of the Lord's Glory (Ezek 1-10; 43). By this God set apart and set a fence around the writers of Scripture. This is a sign and counter to all who claim verbal revelation apart from the Scriptures.

> •Thus saith the LORD of hosts, Hearken not unto the words of the prophets that prophesy unto you: they make you vain: **they speak a vision of their own heart**, and not out of the mouth of the LORD (Jer 23:16).

Note that the fright of Daniel's attendants, without seeing what frightened them, was a further confirmation of the vision. It could not have been a product of Daniel's imagination for it to have such a powerful effect upon those around him.

The Faintness of Daniel . **Therefore I was left alone, and saw this great vision, and there remained no strength in me: for my comeliness was turned in me into corruption, and I retained no strength. Yet heard I the voice of his words: and when I heard the voice of his words, then was I in a deep sleep on my face, and my face toward the ground** (10:8,9). Daniel saw it, and saw it alone, but he was not able to bear the sight of it. It not only dazzled his eyes, but overwhelmed his spirit to the extent that ***there remained no strength in him***, He said as Moses, *I exceedingly fear and quake* (Heb 12:21). It left him lifeless; all strength was gone. It left him pale; his colour was gone, his *comeliness* in him (whatever as an old man he still had!) was *turned into corruption.* Certainly (at least before Christ died on the Cross) the greatest and best of men could not bear the immediate fullness of the Divine Glory.

Though Daniel was left so utterly awe-struck by the vision of Christ, he still **heard the voice of his words** (10:9). Thus it was also with the *holy men of God* (2 Pet 1:21) through whom Scriptures came, if overwhelmed by God's Presence, they were by the Holy Spirit's inspiration very precise in recording God's Words. Thus believers today also, whatever their spiritual, physical or emotional state, must be diligent to hear God's Words, the Bible. That must come first.

DANIEL 10. INTRODUCTION TO THE LAST PROPHECY OF DANIEL

> ...I was not disobedient to the heavenly vision.
> Acts 26:19

(chrisaomministries.com/2016/02/08/visions-of-glory-walking-out-your-heavenly-vision/)

The Threefold Ministry to Daniel 10:10-21.

And, behold, an hand touched me, which set me upon my knees and upon the palms of my hands. (10:11) And he said unto me, O Daniel, a man greatly beloved, understand the words that I speak unto thee, and stand upright: for unto thee am I now sent. And when he had spoken this word unto me, I stood trembling. (10:12) Then said he unto me, Fear not, Daniel: for from the first day that thou didst set thine heart to understand, and to chasten thyself before thy God, thy words were heard, and I am come for thy words. (10:13) But the prince of the kingdom of Persia withstood me one and twenty days: but, lo, Michael, one of the chief princes, came to help me; and I remained there with the kings of Persia. (10:14) Now I am come to make thee understand what shall befall thy people in the latter days: for yet the vision is for many days. (10:15) And when he had spoken such words unto me, I set my face toward the ground, and I became dumb. (10:16) And, behold, one like the similitude of the sons of men touched my lips: then I opened my mouth, and spake, and said unto him that stood before me, O my lord, by the vision my sorrows are turned upon me, and I have retained no strength. (10:17) For how can the servant of this my lord talk with this my lord? for as for me, straightway there remained no strength in me, neither is there breath left in me. (10:18) Then there came again and touched me one like the appearance of a man, and he strengthened me, (10:19) And said, O man greatly beloved, fear not: peace be unto thee, be strong, yea, be strong. And when he had spoken unto me, I was strengthened, and said, Let my lord speak; for thou hast strengthened me. (10:20) Then said he, Knowest thou wherefore I come unto thee? and now will I return to fight with the prince of Persia: and when I am gone forth, lo, the prince of Grecia shall come. (10:21) But I will shew thee that which is noted in the scripture of truth: and there is none that holdeth with me in these things, but Michael your prince.

The First Ministration.

The Strengthening, Gradual. **And, behold, an hand touched me, which set me upon my knees and upon the palms of my hands.** (10:11) **And he said unto me, O Daniel, a man greatly beloved, understand the words that I speak unto thee, and stand upright: for unto thee am I now sent. And when he had spoken this word unto me, I stood trembling** (10:10,11). Daniel in the presence of Christ by the riverside is in the same state of weakness as the three disciples on the Mount of Transfiguration.

> • *And as he prayed,* **the fashion of his countenance was altered, and his raiment was white and glistering**. *And, behold, there talked with him two men, which were Moses and Elias: Who appeared in glory, and spake of his decease which he should accomplish at Jerusalem. But Peter and they that were with him* **were heavy with sleep: and when they were awake, they saw his glory**, *and the two men that stood with him* (Lk 9:29-32).

A great deal is now being done to bring Daniel to the state where he is able to bear the revelation of the turbulent days which lie ahead. The hand that **touched him** is that of the attending angel rather than Christ Himself. This is shown by the angels words that he was restrained by another opposing angel, the prince of Persia (10:13). Compare the angel who instructed the Apostle John (Rev 1:1).

Note that strength and comfort come to Daniel by degrees: first *upon **his knees and upon the palms of his hands**,* Afterwards he is helped up and he **stands upright** but he *stood trembling* . So, a recovering of composure by a child of God may also come by degrees. Yet Daniel is so overcome by the Divine Glory that he *set his face towards the ground and became dumb* (10:15). At length he recovered not only the use of his feet but the use of his tongue; but when he *opened his mouth* it was with great timidity (10:16). Yet more strengthening was necessary (10:18,19). Remember also that Daniel has been fasting for three weeks (10:2).

Daniels *Strengthening* in Chapter 10

- *he set me upon my knees and upon the palms of my hands.* (10:10).
- *stand upright* (10:11).
- *I stood trembling* (10:11)
- *I set my face toward the ground, and I became dumb* (10:15).
- *I opened my mouth, and spake* (10:16).
- *my sorrows are turned upon me, and I have retained no strength* (10:16).
- *the vision my sorrows are turned upon me, and I have retained no strength* (10:16).
- *straightway there remained no strength in me* (10:17).
- *neither is there breath left in me* (10:17).
- *he strengthened me* (10:18).
- *I was strengthened, and said, Let my lord speak* (10:19).
- *thou hast strengthened me* (10:19).

Of Israel in the last days it is said:

*• Come, and let us return unto the LORD: for he hath torn, and he will **heal us**; he hath smitten, and he will **bind us up**. **After two days will he revive us: in the third day he will raise us up**, and we shall **live in his sight**. Then shall we know, if we follow on to know the LORD: his going forth is prepared as the morning; and he shall come unto us as the rain, as the latter and former rain unto the earth (Hosea 6:1-3).*

<u>The Instruction, Delayed</u>.

<u>The Reason for the Delay</u>.

Then said he unto me, Fear not, Daniel: for from the first day that thou didst set thine heart to understand, and to chasten thyself before thy God, thy words were heard, and I am come for thy words. But the prince of the kingdom of Persia withstood me one and twenty days: but, lo, Michael, one of the chief princes, came to help me; and I remained there with the kings of Persia (10:12,13).

Daniel has been fasting and praying for three weeks (10:2), but here we discover that there has been angelic warfare during these same three weeks.

Who is the prince of Persia? He was clearly an evil angelic adversary to the good kings of Persia. Darius and Cyrus who had recently been set on throne of not only Persia, but Babylon and all other countries under Persia's domain. Belshazzar, Babylon's last king, had been

DANIEL 10. INTRODUCTION TO THE LAST PROPHECY OF DANIEL

Satan's man in Babylon. If Babylon must fall to Persia, Satan would again want one of his own over the realm. Thus we read here of angelic warfare between the angels of God and the fallen angels of Satan; and this warfare concerns what kind of king will be on the throne – one for Satan or one for God.

The Archangel Michael overcame the Satanic prince of Persia and his human protégé. The angel now talking to Daniel had then been enabled to **remain there with the kings of Persia** and confirm their position on the throne. Here the curtain is pulled back to give an insight of what may not be an altogether infrequent occurrence in the rise and fall of nations.

> • *Put on the whole armour of God, that ye may be able to stand against the wiles of the devil. For we wrestle not against flesh and blood, but against principalities, against powers, against* **the rulers of the darkness of this world, against spiritual wickedness in high places** *(Eph 6:11,12).*

> • *And there was* **war in heaven**: *Michael and his angels fought against the dragon; and the dragon fought and his angels, And prevailed not; neither was their place found any more in heaven. And the great dragon was cast out, that old serpent, called the Devil, and Satan, which deceiveth the whole world: he was cast out into the earth, and his angels were cast out with him.(Rev 12:7-9).*

> • *Behold, the Lord, the LORD of hosts, shall lop the bough with terror: and* **the high ones** *of stature shall be hewn down, and the haughty shall be humbled (Isa 10:33).*

> • *And it shall come to pass in that day, that the LORD shall punish* **the host of the high ones that are on high**, *and the kings of the earth upon the earth (Isa 24:21).*

Daniel himself would have been at the heart of this angelic warfare. The demonic prince of Persia incited the jealousy of the Persian princes and provoked a foolish decree by the good king Darius which led to Daniel going to the lion's den. There must also have been huge angelic turmoil over Cyrus issuing his Decree allowing the Jews to return, Jerusalem to be rebuilt and the count of the Seventy Weeks to commence.

Josephus in his *The Wars of the Jews* records that the phenomena of spiritual warfare was said to take place at the fall of Jerusalem in 70 AD.

> A few days after the feast, on the one and twentieth day of the month of Jyar, a certain prodigious and incredible phenomenon appeared: I suppose the account of it would seem to be a fable, were it not related by those that saw it, and were not the events that followed it of so considerable a nature as to deserve such signals; for before sun setting, chariots and troops of soldiers in their armour were seen running about among the clouds, and surrounding the cities.

> Moreover, at that feast which we call Pentecost, as the priests were going by night into the inner temple, as their custom was, to perform their sacred ministrations, they said that, in the first place, they felt a quaking, and heard a great noise, and after that they heard a sound as of a great multitude, saying, 'Let us remove hence.' But, what is still more terrible, there was one Jesus, the son of Ananus, a plebian and a husbandman, who, four years before the war began, to cry aloud, 'A voice from the east, a voice from the west, a voice from the four winds, a voice against Jerusalem and the holy house, a voice against the bridegrooms and the brides, and a voice against this whole people! (quoted from Hutchings).

<u>The Message that was Given</u>. *Now **I am come to make thee understand what shall befall thy people in the latter days: for yet the vision is for many days. And when he had spoken such words unto me, I set my face toward the ground, and I became dumb** (10:14,15).* It is a message concerning **the latter days**. It will not be fulfilled for **many days**. This is generally language that points to the Seventieth Week, the Seven Year Tribulation. The visions of the previous chapters culminated in that time, in fact *they rushed toward* that time! Whatever in Chapters 2,7,8 and 9 refers to a near fulfilment of the prophecies given, is passed over briefly

in order to place the great emphasis upon the Seven Year Tribulation. Daniel is now told that this final vision, that is when the Glorified Christ will appear on earth and for Israel as He now appears on the river (10:1,4,5) would be only after a *long time*.

> *• In the third year of Cyrus king of Persia a thing was revealed unto Daniel, whose name was called Belteshazzar; and the thing was true, but **the time appointed was long**: and he understood the thing, and had understanding of the vision (10:1).*

This raises the question; why is it now in the giving of this final prophecy to Daniel that we read about angelic warfare? There seems to have been no delay in Daniel receiving his previous revelations; but now there was an interference that resulted in a three week delay.

When we come to Chapter 11 we will find that the common view is that thirty-five of the forty-five verses deal with *near-times* rather than the *end-times*. Most believe that the great bulk of the prophecies in Chapter 11, while giving important information about the Syrian and Egyptian conflicts of the third and second centuries BC, have no direct bearing upon the days when Christ returns. Could it be that there is more for the last generation in this Chapter than has previously been realized? Would this not indicate that this warfare incited by evil angels was to prevent important information from reaching us? And further, now that it has reached us, to make only a part of past history? These are questions (and there are problems with this newer view!) which we will examine shortly, but for now note again **the end-time emphasis** given thus far (and at the beginning of Chapter 11) in this final revelation to Daniel. (For an example of making nearly all of Chapter 11 refer to the last days see:
http://rightwordtruth.com/have-any-of-the-prophecies-of-daniel-eleven-been-fulfilled/).

> *• the time appointed was long (10:1).*
>
> *• what shall befall thy people in the latter days (10:14).*
>
> *• yet the vision is for many days (10:14).*
>
> *• And in the end of years they shall join themselves together (11:6).*

When Daniel heard that the lifting of Jerusalem's troubles would not be for a far distant day, he collapsed in sorrow ***And when he had spoken such words unto me, I set my face toward the ground, and I became dumb*** (10:15). In our day there is every indication that those days which seemed so impossibly distant to Daniel are now drawing near.

<u>The Second Ministration</u>. ***And, behold, one like the similitude of the sons of men touched my lips: then I opened my mouth, and spake, and said unto him that stood before me, O my lord, by the vision my sorrows are turned upon me, and I have retained no strength. For how can the servant of this my lord talk with this my lord? for as for me, straightway there remained no strength in me, neither is there breath left in me*** (10:16,17).

The prophecy which was given to Daniel concerning Israel's future sufferings was in greater detail than any previous revelation he received. From the first day that Daniel entered Babylon he prayed daily before His window for God to forgive the sins of Israel, restore Jerusalem and the Temple, and bring in the everlasting kingdom of peace and righteousness. But now instead of peace, Daniel was made to understand that there would be wars and bloodshed over Jerusalem for many hundreds of years before Messiah would bring peace. As Daniel considered the extent of this warfare over the Holy Land given in covenant to his people by the Abrahamic Covenant, it was more than he could bear. He saw his people continuing in unbelief and idolatry, and he saw foreign armies marching back and forth across his country, murdering and pillaging. It was more than he could bear (from *Hutchings*).

DANIEL 10. INTRODUCTION TO THE LAST PROPHECY OF DANIEL

Again an angel ministers to Daniel lifting him out of his despair and enabling him to speak aright. One touch from heaven brings us to our knees, sets us on our feet and opens our lips.

The Third Ministration.

Daniel is Strengthened. *Then there came again and touched me one like the appearance of a man, and he strengthened me, And said, O man greatly beloved, fear not: peace be unto thee, be strong, yea, be strong. And when he had spoken unto me, I was strengthened, and said, Let my lord speak; for thou hast strengthened me* (10:18,19). Never did a loving mother comfort and quiet her child more than this attending angel does Daniel. He *came again and touched* him, and by that touch he *strengthened* him.

He assured him again of Heaven's favour; *O man greatly beloved.* Nothing is more likely to revive the drooping spirits of the believer more than to be assured of God's love to them. Those are greatly beloved indeed whom God loves.

He urges him to replace *fear* with *strength*. And, will enable him to do so. Is there a stronger encouragement to strength in the entire Bible?

- *Fear not: peace be unto thee, **be strong**, yea, **be strong**. And when he had spoken unto me, **I was strengthened**, and said, Let my lord speak; for **thou hast strengthened me** (10:19).*

- *Will he plead against me with his great power? No; but **he would put strength in me** (Job 23:6).*

Daniel is Informed. *Then said he, Knowest thou wherefore I come unto thee? and now will I return to fight with the prince of Persia: and when I am gone forth, lo, the prince of Grecia shall come. But I will shew thee that which is noted in the scripture of truth: and there is none that holdeth with me in these things, but Michael your prince* (10:20, 21). On what errand did this angel come to Daniel? He tells him (10:14): *I have come to make thee understand what shall befall thy people in the latter days.* Now he begins to enlarge upon this. Very likely the speaker here and before is Gabriel (8:16;9:21), and in this warfare he is here teamed with the archangel Michael (mentioned by name five times in the Scriputurs).

He is Informed Concerning Angelic Warfare. The Lord and His angels were victorious over the prince of Persia, Satan's evil angel. The kings of Persia did deal kindly with Israel, and they allowed the Jews to return to rebuild Jerusalem and the Temple. Nevertheless, Satan will continue to stir up rulers and nations against Israel, and that until the very end. This explains the roots of antisemitism. Apart from Satan himself there is no reason or rational for the Jewish People to be so singled out for hatred and abuse. Daniel, however, was assured that Michael their prince was ever ready to fight for Israel and to see that the plan and purpose of God for His earthly people would be fulfilled.

After the seven year reign of Cyrus, his eldest son Cambyses came to the throne of Persia and reigned eight years. Against the background of the angelic warfare here revealed, Cambyses put a stop to the rebuilding efforts in Jerusalem. Work was resumed through the prophetic ministries of Haggai and Zechariah and during second year of the benevolent reign of Darius Hystapes.

Gabriel tells Daniel that after Persian rule is brought into harmony with the wellbeing of Israel, another foe will arise. *I will return to fight with the prince of Persia: and when I am gone forth, lo, the prince of Grecia shall come* (10:20). This looks forward to the fall of Persia to Alexander the Great and the conflicts Israel will have with the remnants of his empire (Dan 8:8,9; 11:2-4…).

> • When I have bent Judah for me, filled the bow with Ephraim, and **raised up thy sons, O Zion, against thy sons, O Greece**, and made thee as the sword of a mighty man (Zech 9:13).

He is Informed Concerning the Revelation of Further Scripture. ***But I will shew thee that which is noted in the scripture of truth*** (10:21). This is a remarkable passage and gives added weight to the enormity of the prophecy now to be uttered. What we now know as the Scriptures were in the Mind of God *from past eternity*. In time their words were revealed and inscripturated through the ministries of the prophets and apostles. Again, while this was always the case concerning revelation and inspiration, it is highly significant that at this point the process in mentioned.

> • For ever, O LORD, thy word is settled in heaven (Psa 119:89).

He is informed Concerning the Uniqueness of the Angel Michael. Unger says, "Apparently to Michael alone, of all the angels, was delegated the special office of protecting Israel (Dan 12:1) in conjunction with the angel now speaking to Daniel. All the world powers, with potent demonic forces working through their human agents of government, were against Israel." Note also that apart from Gabriel, Michael is the only angel mentioned by name. Five passages give his name.

> • But the prince of the kingdom of Persia withstood me one and twenty days: but, lo, **Michael, one of the chief princes**, came to help me; and I remained there with the kings of Persia (Dan 10:13).

> • But I will shew thee that which is noted in the scripture of truth: and there is none that holdeth with me in these things, but **Michael your prince** (Dan 10:21).

> • And at that time shall **Michael** stand up, the great prince which standeth for the children of thy people: and there shall be a time of trouble, such as never was since there was a nation [even] to that same time: and at that time thy people shall be delivered, every one that shall be found written in the book (Dan 12:1).

> • Yet **Michael the archangel**, when contending with the devil he disputed about the body of Moses, durst not bring against him a railing accusation, but said, The Lord rebuke thee (Jude 9).

> • And there was war in heaven: **Michael and his angels** fought against the dragon; and the dragon fought and his angels (Rev 12:7).

II THE TIMES OF THE GENTILES REGARDING JERUSALEM 8-12

C. The Desolations and Final Blessing of Jerusalem 10-12

1. Desolations and The Glory of Christ 10

2. Desolations: Future to Daniel 11:1-35

3. Desolations and Glory: Future to Us 11:36-12:13

DANIEL 11. JERUSALEM'S CONFLICT: ANCIENT DAYS AND LAST DAYS

The importance of Chapter 11 is demonstrated by an entire Chapter given to its introduction, and an entire Chapter to its conclusion. It is a pivotal revelation of the role and warfare of angels in the rise and fall of nations – particularly with reference to Israel. The Chapter begins with *ancient days* and ends with *the last days*. Increasingly among students of Daniel 11 there has been debate as to where in the Chapter the last days begin. The Chapter is divided into four clearly marked out sections.

1. Five Kings of Persia followed by a Mighty King of Greece 11:1-4

2. The Kings of the South and Kings of the North 11:5-20

3. A Vile King 11:21-35

4. A Wilful King 11:36-44

Where in Daniel 11 is the Beginning Point of the Tribulation?

As the beginning of Chapter 12 is clearly describing the Tribulation and the beginning of Chapter 11 deals with the Persian Kings of Daniel's day and immediately after, the question is asked as to where the dividing lines are in Chapter 11. Most premillennial students believe the *final long time* mentioned in Chapter 10:1,14 (the Tribulation) begins at Chapter 11:36 with the mention of the *wilful king* and then continues into Chapter 12.

> • (11:35) *And some of them of understanding shall fall, to try them, and to purge, and to make them white, **even to the time of the end**: because it is yet for a time appointed. (11:36) And **the king shall do according to his will**; and he shall exalt himself, and magnify himself above every god, and shall speak marvellous things against the God of gods, and shall prosper till the indignation be accomplished: for that that is determined shall be done. (11:37) Neither shall he regard the God of his fathers, nor the desire of women, nor regard any god: for he shall magnify himself above all.*

> • (12:1) *And **at that time** shall Michael stand up, the great prince which standeth for the children of thy people: and there shall be **a time of trouble, such as never was** since there was a nation even to that same time: and at that time thy people shall be delivered, every one that shall be found written in the book.*

> • (12:4) *But thou, O Daniel, shut up the words, and **seal the book, even to the time of the end**: many shall run to and fro, and knowledge shall be increased.*

Most have believed that the *vile person* in 11:21 is the Syrian king Antiochus Epiphanes who in 167 BC desecrated the Jewish Temple by sacrificing a pig and setting up an altar to Zeus. But others believe that as Antiochus *did not set up an image of himself* and that as ***the abomination that maketh desolate*** (cp. Dan 9:27; Matt 24:15; Lk 21:20-24; 2 Thess 2:4; Rev 13:14) is so specifically mentioned in 11:31, the passage must look beyond Antiochus and point to the final Antichrist. Thus in this view the Tribulation begins in 11:21.

The argument against is that the events of 11:21-35 seem difficult to fit into the career of the Antichrist (certainly during the Tribulation and likely also before). Further 11:20 refers to a previous *king of the north* (a raiser of taxes) who immediately precedes the *vile person*. Just as the raiser of taxes is said to *stand up* in the *estate* of the previous king, so the vile person *stands* in the *estate* of the raiser of taxes. This would make *the vile person* a direct part of the long succession of the events involving the kings of the north and south before him (11:5-20).

It may also be argued that the *abomination of desolation* spoken of by Christ refers to Daniel 9:27 (which is clearly the Antichrist) and that 11:31 is only a precursor under Antiochus. Note also that the term *desolation* is used of the 70 AD destruction of Jerusalem (Lk 21:20-24). Therefore it seems likely that there are two precursor desolations (Dan 11:31; Lk 21:12,20, 24) with the final desolation being that of Antichrist (Dan 9:27; Matt 24:15,16; 2 Thess 2:3,4; Rev 13:14,15)

In both Chapter 8 and Chapter 11 we have two similar statements concerning Alexander's empire being scattered *to the four winds of heaven*. In Chapter 8 this is immediately followed by an account of the little horn, the Antichrist. In Chapter 11 this same kind of statement is followed immediately by the extended passage concerning the kings of the south and of the north. It is therefore argued that as the former passage projects into the end-time, so must the latter. Therefore in this view and further supported by the *end of years* statement in 11:6, it is proposed that the generation before the Rapture and Tribulation will see this succession of wars, covering quite a number of years, between the kings of south and the kings of the north. In fact they must wait to see this lengthy conflict before they can see the Rapture! Note the similarities of the two *projecting* passages.

> • And I saw him come close unto **the ram**, and he was moved with choler against him, and **smote the ram**, and brake his two horns: and there was no power in the ram to stand before him, but he cast him down to the ground, and stamped upon him: and there was none that could deliver the ram out of his hand. Therefore the **he goat waxed very great: and when he was strong, the great horn was broken**; and for it came up four notable ones **toward the four winds of heaven**. And **out of one of them came forth a little horn**, which waxed exceeding great, toward the south, and toward the east, and toward the pleasant land (Dan 8:7-9).

> • And now will I shew thee the truth. Behold, there shall stand up yet **three kings in Persia**; and the **fourth** shall be far richer than they all: and by his strength through his riches **he shall stir up all against the realm of Grecia**. And **a mighty king shall stand up**, that shall rule with great dominion, and do according to his will. And when he shall stand up, his kingdom **shall be broken**, and shall be **divided toward the four winds of heaven**; and not to his posterity, nor according to his dominion which he ruled: for his kingdom shall be plucked up, even for others beside those. And **the king of the south** shall be strong, and one of his princes; and he shall be strong above him, and have dominion; his dominion shall be a great dominion (Dan 11:2-5).

Thus both passages present: (1) Persia, (2) followed by Alexander, (3) Alexander's sudden death, (4) and his kingdom *divided to the four winds of heaven*. Chapter 8 then goes directly to the Little Horn, the Antichrist; while Chapter 11 goes to the King of the South followed by the **end of years** statement in 11:6. Therefore, some are viewing 11:5-20 as referring to the last days. However, as it is impossible to envisage these verses taking place within the Tribulation, to place them before the Rapture undermines completely the Biblical doctrine of imminence. We look for Christ not a long protracted war between Egypt and Syria!

Daniel 11:2-5 is a *projecting* passage, but unlike 8:7-9 it details the events leading up to a forerunner of Antichrist and then deals with the end-time Antichrist himself. Therefore the traditional view seems best, that is – Daniel 11:1-35 is a prophecy of events from Daniel's day up to and including Antiochus Epiphanes; and that from verse 36 it describes the man of

DANIEL 11. JERUSALEM'S CONFLICT: ANCIENT DAYS AND LAST DAYS

whom Antiochus was a type, *the wilful king* the Antichrist. Note the statement denoting a long gap of time in verse 35.

> *And some of them of understanding shall fall, to try them, and to purge, and to make them white, **even to the time of the end**: because it is **yet for a time appointed** (11:35).*

From these considerations we conclude that Scripture presents two precursor events foreshadowing the coming Antichrist and his abomination of desolation:

Two Precursor Desolations: Antiochus (175-164 BC) and Titus (70 AD)

> *And arms shall stand on his part, and they shall pollute the sanctuary of strength, and shall take away the daily sacrifice, and they shall place **the abomination that maketh desolate** (Dan 11:31).*

> *But before all these....And when ye shall see Jerusalem compassed with armies, then know that **the desolation thereof is nigh**....And they shall fall by the edge of the sword, and shall be led away captive into all nations: and Jerusalem shall be trodden down of the Gentiles, until the times of the Gentiles be fulfilled (Lk 21:12, 20, 24).*

The Primary Desolation: Antichrist During the Tribulation

> *And he shall confirm the covenant with many for one week: and in the midst of the week he shall cause the sacrifice and the oblation to cease, and for **the overspreading of abominations he shall make it desolate**, even until the consummation, and that determined shall be **poured upon the desolate** (Dan 9:27).*

> *When ye therefore shall see **the abomination of desolation, spoken of by Daniel the prophet, stand in the holy place**, (whoso readeth, let him understand:). Then let them which be in Judaea flee into the mountains (Matt 24:15,16).*

> *Let no man deceive you by any means: for that day shall not come [not the Rapture but the Return as described just before (1:7-10)], except there come a falling away first, and that man of sin be revealed, the son of perdition; Who opposeth and exalteth himself above all that is called God, or that is worshipped; **so that he as God sitteth in the temple of God**, shewing himself that he is God (2 Thess 2:3,4).*

> *And deceiveth them that dwell on the earth by the means of those miracles which he had power to do in the sight of the beast; saying to them that dwell on the earth, that they should make **an image to the beast**, which had the wound by a sword, and did live.*
> *And he had power to give life unto **the image of the beast**, that **the image of the beast** should both speak, and cause that as many as would not worship **the image of the beast** should be killed (Rev 13:14,15).*

Five Kings of Persia followed by a Mighty King of Greece 11:1-4.

Also I in the first year of Darius the Mede, even I, stood to confirm and to strengthen him. (11:2) And now will I shew thee the truth. Behold, there shall stand up yet three kings in Persia; and the fourth shall be far richer than they all: and by his strength through his riches he shall stir up all against the realm of Grecia. (11:3) And a mighty king shall stand up, that shall rule with great dominion, and do according to his will. (11:4) And when he shall stand up, his kingdom shall be broken, and shall be divided toward the four winds of heaven; and not to his posterity, nor according to his dominion which he ruled: for his kingdom shall be plucked up, even for others beside those.

The angel Gabriel (cp. 8:16; 9:21) in this chapter performs his promise to Daniel that he would show *what shall befall* his *people in the latter days* (10:14). Here we discover that before going to the very last days the revelation begins with Daniel's days. Here is a succession of kings that will march across the stage of Persia's history. The last Persian king will be strong and rich but it will lead to Persia's undoing; it will incite the rise of a much stronger Grecian king.

Darius the Mede (and Cyrus)

Also I in the first year of Darius the Mede, even I, stood to confirm and to strengthen him (11:2). This ***first year*** began with the fall of Belshazzar and Babylon.

> • In that night was Belshazzar the king of the Chaldeans slain. And **Darius the Median took the kingdom**, being about threescore and two years old (Dan 5:30,31).

Gabriel was instrumental in the pivotal victory on that night. As prophesied in Genesis 9:27 it saw the transfer of world dominion from the powerful Hamitic empires (Egypt, Babylon) to the empires of Japheth (Persia, Greece, Rome). The golden head was broken and the axe was laid to the root of the tree (Dan 2,4). Gabriel also enabled Darius to confirm the return of the Jews (which likely met with much opposition). He confirmed Darius in his kindness and sympathy toward Daniel and that despite the opposition of the princes (Dan 6). Here is a "behind the scenes report" of the kind which we do not see often in the Bible. Gabriel ***stood to confirm and to strengthen*** Darius the Mede.

A major factor in the strengthen of Darius and the confirming of Persian rule was through the support of his co-regent Cyrus and to whom so much reference is made in Scripture.

> • So this Daniel prospered in **the reign of Darius, and in the reign of Cyrus the Persian** (Dan 6:28).

> • And Daniel continued even unto **the first year of king Cyrus** (Dan 1:21).

> • **In the third year of Cyrus** king of Persia a thing was revealed unto Daniel, whose name was called Belteshazzar; and the thing was true, but the time appointed was long: and he understood the thing, and had understanding of the vision (Dan 10:1).

> • Now in **the first year of Cyrus** king of Persia, that the word of the LORD spoken by the mouth of Jeremiah might be accomplished, the LORD stirred up the spirit of Cyrus king of Persia, that he made a proclamation throughout all his kingdom, and put it also in writing, saying (2 Chron 36:22).

> • Thus saith **Cyrus king of Persia**, The LORD God of heaven hath given me all the kingdoms of the earth; and he hath charged me to build him an house at Jerusalem, which is in Judah (Ezra 1:2).

> • **That saith of Cyrus, He is my shepherd**, and shall perform all my pleasure: even saying to Jerusalem, Thou shalt be built; and to the temple, Thy foundation shall be laid (Isa 44:28).

> • **Thus saith the LORD to his anointed, to Cyrus**, whose right hand I have holden, to subdue nations before him; and I will loose the loins of kings, to open before him the two leaved gates; and the gates shall not be shut (Isa 45:1).

Though a practice long recognized in royal households, the interchange of titular names by the Persians (Darius, Ahasuerus, Artaxerxes) has especially complicated the identification of their kings. Concerning Darius the Mede, Unger writes:

> Scholars who recognize Darius the Mede as a historical person, and defend the book's historical reliability, commonly identify him with Gubaru, the governor appointed over Babylon by Cyrus. That view has been restudied by John C. Whitcomb, Jr. (*Darius the Mede*), with the intent of counteracting Rowley's attack on that identification and the overall authenticity of the book of Daniel. Whitcomb distinguishes Gubaru from Ugbaru, (governor of Gutium, the general under Cyrus who conquered Babylon and died three weeks later, according to the Nabonidus Chronicle).

> Gubaru is frequently mentioned in cuneiform documents during the following fourteen years as "Governor of Babylon and the Region Beyond the River"....That view accords with Daniel 5:31—6:3 that Darius the Mede received the kingdom as a sub-king, that is, from Cyrus the Great, and organized it under 120 satraps, with three administrators over them. The fact that Darius the Mede is styled "king" is not an inaccuracy, even

though he was a subordinate of Cyrus. Belshazzar was called "king" even though he was second ruler under Nabonidus (*Unger's Old Testament Commentary*, pp.1634,1635).

Note that the statements in Daniel give the reign of Darius only to his first year (5:31; 9:1; 11:1), whereas the latest for Cyrus is his third year (10:1). Early historians with cuneiform tablets state that Cyrus reigned seven years after the fall of Babylon. According to Herodotus Cyrus was killed near the Aral Sea during a campaign to protect the north-eastern borders of his empire. At his death, his son Cambyses II succeeded him.

The First King After Daniel: Cambyses

And now will I shew thee the truth. Behold, there shall stand up yet three kings in Persia (11:2). The count begins with the kings following Darius and Cyrus. *Behold, there shall stand up yet three kings.* Good men often appear to be cut of too soon. The Lord calls Cyrus, *His anointed* (Isa 45:1), yet after doing so much good for Israel, he died on the field of battle, only to be replaced by a far less worthy king, his son Cambyses. Grace does not run in the bloodline (cp. Isa 57:1).

Daniel had died some time before Cyrus' death (cp. Dan 1:21; 10:1), and this may help to explain that despite Cyrus' Decree, the rebuilding work was allowed to be disrupted before his reign ended. The disruption that Cyrus allowed (perhaps through carelessness), was formally enforced by Cambyses. Note that the *Ahasuerus* in Ezra 4:6 is Cambyses (the king before Darius Hystaspes). Note further that this same king who receives the letter of complaint and orders a halt to the construction is called *Artaxerxes* throughout the rest of the chapter. In both instances the titles *Ahasuerus* and *Artaxerxes* can only refer to the same king, Cambyses, for both titles appear immediately before Darius Hystaspes, (4:6, 23). This is an example of the Persian practice of making *Artaxerxes* the greater title, for in this chapter it only in his first year that Cambyses is called *Ahasuerus* (4:6).

The following from Ezra 4 gives the account of the complaint made to Cambyses and his commanding that the work of rebuilding Jerusalem and the Temple be halted.

> • *(4:1) Now **when the adversaries of Judah and Benjamin heard that the children of the captivity builded the temple** unto the LORD God of Israel; (4:2) Then they came to Zerubbabel, and to the chief of the fathers, and said unto them, **Let us build with you**: for we seek your God, as ye do; and we do sacrifice unto him since the days of Esarhaddon king of Assur, which brought us up hither. (4:3) But Zerubbabel, and Jeshua, and the rest of the chief of the fathers of Israel, said unto them, Ye have nothing to do with us to build an house unto our God; but **we ourselves together will build unto the LORD God of Israel, as king Cyrus the king of Persia hath commanded us**.(4:4) Then the people of the land weakened the hands of the people of Judah, and troubled them in building, (4:5) And hired counsellors against them, to frustrate their purpose, **all the days of Cyrus king of Persia, even until the reign of Darius king of Persia**. (4:6) And **in the reign of Ahasuerus, in the beginning of his reign** [Cambyses], wrote they unto him an accusation against the inhabitants of Judah and Jerusalem.*

> • *(4:7) And **in the days of Artaxerxes wrote** Bishlam, Mithredath, Tabeel, and the rest of their companions, unto **Artaxerxes** king of Persia; and the writing of the letter was written in the Syrian tongue, and interpreted in the Syrian tongue. (4:8) Rehum the chancellor and Shimshai the scribe wrote a letter against Jerusalem to Artaxerxes the king in this sort:*

> • *(4:12) Be it known unto the king, that the Jews which came up from thee to us are come unto Jerusalem, **building the rebellious and the bad city, and have set up the walls thereof, and joined the foundations**.*

> • **(4:17) Then sent the king an answer** unto Rehum the chancellor, and to Shimshai the scribe, and to the rest of their companions that dwell in Samaria, and unto the rest beyond the river, Peace, and at such a time.
>
> • **(4:23) Now when the copy of king Artaxerxes' letter was read** before Rehum, and Shimshai the scribe, and their companions, they went up in haste to Jerusalem unto the Jews, and **made them to cease by force and power.** (4:24) Then ceased the work of the house of God which is at Jerusalem. **So it ceased unto the second year of the reign of Darius king of Persia**.

Following Cyrus' conquest of the Near East and Central Asia, Cambyses further expanded the Persian empire into Egypt. However his invasion of the Kingdom of Kush (now the Republic of Sudan) met with little success. His throne was seized by a man posing as his brother Bardiya (his Greek name was Smerdis). Cambyses attempt to resist the overthrow resulted in his death, and this under disputed circumstances. Herodotus says he reigned seven years and five months, while the tablets give him a full eight years.

Little in the historical accounts is revealed about him personally; however from the Biblical record Cambyses will be remembered as the king who *stood up* (Dan 11:2) to block the reconstruction of Jerusalem (Ezra 4).

(factfiend.com/cambyses-ii-cat-throwing-king-persia/)

Persian Seal of Cambyses Capturing Pharaoh Psamtik III

The Second King After Daniel: Pseudo Smerdis

After the fall of Babylon to Persia, Cyrus and Cambyses each *stood up* for seven and eight years, the next king *stands up* for only seven months. Some would not number Pseudo Smerdis in this prophesy, but as the third king is clearly Darius Hystaspes and Xerxes is the fourth, who "stirred up the Greeks" (11:2), the second king can only be the one whom history records as Pseudo Smerdis (and a number of other names).

Cambyses' long campaigns in Egypt and elsewhere gave opportunity for intrigue to arise at the throne in Persia. Control was seized by a man posing as his brother Bardiya the son of Cyrus (Bardia's Greek name was Smerdis). The usurper was a magician named Gaumata. Concerning Bardia/Smerdis himself, Cambyses considered him to be a rival claimant to the throne and had him murdered. As his death was kept secret and with the passage of time Gamauta took his opportunity to seize the throne. Taking advantage of popular support and the continued absence of Cambyses', Gamauta under the name of Bardia/Smerdis proclaimed himself king of Persia.

The despotic rule of Cambyses, coupled with the promise of tax relief contributed to widespread acceptance of the usurper. Cambyses began to march against him, but died in disputed circumstances. Before his death he confessed to the murder of his brother, and publicly explained the whole fraud, but was not generally believed.

(iranchamber.com/history/darius/images/biston3.jpg)

Behistun Inscription of Darius Hystaspe Placing Foot on Pseudo Smerdis

When the new king transferred the seat of government to Media, a group of seven Persian nobles formed a plot to kill him. He was stabbed to death after reigning seven months. One of the seven, Darius Hystaspes, was proclaimed as king shortly after. The Behistun inscription of Darius Hystaspes, Herodotus' *Histories* and Ctesias are the source of account. (*Wikipedia*).

Ezra records that during his short reign the ban on the rebuilding of Jerusalem remained.

(4:24) Then ceased the work of the house of God which is at Jerusalem. **So it ceased unto the second year of the reign of Darius king of Persia**.

The Third King After Daniel: Darius Hystaspes

The ways in which the reign of this third king is intertwined with the closing events of the Old Testament makes him one of the most important Gentile kings of the Bible. Darius the Great was the son of Hystaspes, a leading figure in Persia. He belonged to the Achaemenid family, as did Cyrus and his son Cambyses, but to a different branch of this family.

(iranchamber.com/history/darius/darius.php#sthash.q49UYHcc.dpuf)

Relief of Darius Hystaspes in Persepolis

Darius ruled the Persian Empire at its peak: the entire Middle East, the Caucasus, Central Asia, parts of the Balkans (Bulgaria-Romania-Panonia), portions of north and northeast Africa including Egypt (Mudraya), eastern Libya, coastal Sudan, Eritrea), as well as northeast portions of and greater India (Pakistan and northwest India), the Aegean Islands and northern Greece/Thrace-Macedonia. Darius allowed peoples to keep their own customs and religion. He divided the empire into districts known as Satrapies and built a system of roads still used today. Under his reign two new capital cities were established, one at Susa and the other at Persepolis. He is well and truly the third king *to stand up* after Daniel.

The Regnal Years Given to Artaxerxes and Ahasuerus in Ezra, Nehemiah and Esther Likely Refer to Darius Hystaspes

A great deal of evidence is gathered in *Bible Chronology: The Two Great Divides* which demonstrates that the prominent Persian king in Ezra, Nehemiah and Esther, whether he be called by the title Ahasuerus or Artaxerxes is almost always referring to Darius Hystaspes during his **thirty-six year** reign.

(1) He is the *Darius* in Haggai, Zechariah and Ezra 4:5 who allows the work in Jerusalem to recommence in his **second year** (Hag 1:1).

(2) Darius (not Xerxes, as commonly believed) is the *Ahasuerus* who married Esther in his **seventh year**. Xerxes in his *seventh year* suffered a devastating defeat at hands of the Greeks. Persia then began its precipitous decline. The opposite was true for the flourishing times of Ahasuerus. In Esther extended to his **twelfth year** (Est 1:1; 3:7; 10:1,2).

(3) Darius is the *Artaxerxes* that supported Ezra and Nehemiah in their reforms and rebuilding work in Jerusalem and which extended to his **thirty-second year** (Neh 13:6). This recognition removes the *impossible* gap of time between points (1) and (2) as required by the Ptolemaic chronology.

The Regnal Years of the One King Darius Hystaspes (with Titles) Demonstrates the Chronological Close to Old Testament History

Although the royal titles are different, a listing of each date and year of reign demonstrates the kind of development and harmony we would expect if but one king is the subject.

2nd year, Darius

6th month 1st day	Appeal to Zerubbabel and Joshua to build (Hag 1:1).
6th month 24th day	Zerubbabel and Joshua stirred to work (Hag 1:15).
7th month 21st day	The glory of the latter house (Hag 2:1).
8th month - day	Zechariah to appeal for repentance (Zech 1:1).
9th month 24th day	"From this day will I bless you" (Hag 2:10).
11th month 24th day	Zechariah's 1st vision, 70 yrs. Indignation (Zech 1:7).

3rd year, Ahasuerus

- month - day	Ahasuerus' feast, Vashti deposed (Est 1:1,3).

4th year, Darius

9th month 4th day	Question of fasts during 70 yrs. (Zech 7:1).

DANIEL 11. JERUSALEM'S CONFLICT: ANCIENT DAYS AND LAST DAYS

6th year, Ahasuerus

   - month - day   Esther brought to Shushan (Est 2:8,12,16).

6th year, Darius

   12th month 3rd day   Temple finished (Ezra 6:15).

   1st month 14th day   Passover observed (6:19).

7th year, Ahasuerus

   10th month - day   Esther's marriage and feast (Est 2:16-18).

7th year, Artaxerxes

   1st month 1st day   Ezra leaves Babylon (Ezra 7:7,9).

   5th month 1st day   Ezra arrives in Jerusalem (7:9).

   9th month 20th day   Convocation begun, foreign wives (10:9).

   1st month 1st day   Convocation ended (10:17).

12th year, Ahasuerus

   1st month, to 16th day Haman's plot foiled (Est 3:7,12; 5:1,8).

   3rd month 23rd day   Mordecai's posts sent to 127 provinces (8:9).

   12th month, days 13-15 Jews defend themselves (9:1,15,18).

20th year, Artaxerxes

   9th month - day   Report of Jerusalem's broken state (Neh 1:1).

   1st month - day   Nehemiah sent to Jerusalem (2:1).

   6th month 25th day   Wall finished in 52 days (6:15).

   7th month, days 1-2   Ezra reads the Law (8:2,13).

   7th month, days 15-24 Feast of Tabernacles, separation (8:14-9:1).

32nd year, Artaxerxes

   - month - day   Nehemiah's temporary leave (Neh 5:14; 13:6).

The Regnal Years of Darius Hystaspes (with Titles) and the Three Previous Kings Occur in the First Seven Weeks (49 Years) of the Seventy Week Prophecy

450   • <u>**FIRST SEVEN WEEKS (49 years) OF SEVENTY WEEKS (483 years to Crucifixion of Christ)**</u>

     • The Darius/Cyrus co-regency (11:1,2).

     Cyrus soon begins 7 year sole reign (6:1; 9:1; 10:1; 11:1).

     Decree to Rebuild Jerusalem in 1st year of Cyrus' reign (Ezr 1:1; Isa 44:18; 45:13).

     Zerubbabel brings back the first exiles (Ezra 1,2).

     • <u>**Daniel's 1st King after Darius/Cyrus**</u>. **Cambyses** begins 8 year reign, Called *Ahasuerus* and *Artaxerxes* (Ezr. 4:6,7).

     Stops work on Temple.

     • <u>**Daniel's 2nd King**</u>. **Pseudo Smerdis** reigns 7 months.

434   • <u>**Daniel's 3rd King**</u>. **Darius Hystapes** begins long reign.

     The remainder of the First Week of Years (33 years) is dated to Darius' reign.

     Darius is also known in Scripture as *Ahasuerus* and *Artaxerxes*. (see *Bible Chronology: The Two Divides*, pp. 114-131).

432   2nd year of reign: work on Temple/ City resumes (Ezra 4:24).

        2nd year of reign: ministry of Haggai (Hag 1:1).

        2nd and 4th year of reign: ministry of Zechariah (Zech 1:1; 7:1).

431   3rd year of reign: Vashti in Book of Esther deposed (Est 1:1).

428   6th year of reign: Temple finished (Ezra 6:15). A little over 70 years since destruction of Jerusalem.

427   7th year of reign: **Ezra brings back second group of exiles** (Ezra 7:7).

422   12th year of reign: Haman's plot foiled (Est 3:7).

414   20th year of reign: **Nehemiah's trip to rebuild walls of Jerusalem** (Neh 2:1).

402/1 32nd year of reign: Nehemiah's 2nd trip to Jerusalem (Neh 13:6). Further reforms concluded.

Malachi's ministry occurs here or shortly after.

- **CONCLUSION OF FIRST SEVEN WEEKS (49 years), 62 Weeks (434 years) remaining to Crucifixion of Christ.**
  - **Daniel's 4th King. Xerxes** begins reign. In 7th year defeated by Greece. Thereafter, apart from Ptolemy's king list, history says very little about Persian rule and rulers.

It is proposed that the first list gives the chronicle of but one king, Darius Hystaspes. If however this is the record of two or three kings we are faced with the puzzling question as to why Darius disappears from the Biblical record after only six years of his thirty-six year reign. After his kindness to the Jews in actively supporting the building and completion of the Temple it would be strange not read any more about him. Yet if indeed there is one king here, then what follows, i.e. his kindness towards Esther and Nehemiah, is but a natural continuance of what he had already displayed toward Israel.

There is compelling harmony in this proposal; the regnal years when applied solely to Darius fit in perfectly with the latter two-thirds of the 49 years (7 Weeks) of the Seventy Week prophecy. It is shown to be a time of extensive Biblical activity (the Ptolemaic system leaves much of it as a *gap*).

There is nothing contradictory in applying these consecutive regnal years to one monarch. Yet anomalies would certainly appear if an attempt were made to take regnal data from three kings (Darius, Xerxes and Artaxerxes Longimanus) and apply them solely to Darius.

After Xerxes' defeat by the Greeks in seventh year Persian history seems to nearly *evaporate,* we are left with little except Ptolemy's king list.

A major event in Darius's reign was his expedition to punish Athens and Eretria for their aid in the Ionian Revolt, and subjugate Greece. Although ultimately ending in failure at the Battle of Marathon, Darius succeeded in the re-subjugation of Thrace, expansion of the empire through the conquest of Macedon, the Cyclades, and the island of Naxos, and the sacking and enslavement of the city of Eretria.

Though friendly to Jerusalem and the Jewish People, Darius was not a believer in the God of Israel. After his first failed attempt to occupy the Greek mainland, *Herodotus* records the following.

> Darius asked for his bow, he placed an arrow upon the string and he discharged it upwards towards heaven, and as he shot into the air he said: "Zeus, grant me to take vengeance upon the Athenians!". Also he charged one of his servants, to say to him, every day before dinner, three times: "Master, remember the Athenians."

The "prayer" was never answered, his long reign of 36 years ended while preparing for a second invasion of Greece. Darius' famous cliff-face inscription on Mount Behistun records his devotion to Persian idolatry. In this he wrote the sequence of events that occurred after the death of Cyrus down to his own reign and mentions several times that he is the rightful king by the grace of Ahura Mazda, the Zoroastrian god (*Wikipedia*).

(bible-history.com/archaeology/persia/behistun-relief-bw.jpg)

Darius' Behistun Stone, Inscribed in Three Languages Beneath Carved Figures

The Fourth King After Daniel: Xerxes

...and the fourth shall be far richer than they all: and by his strength through his riches he shall stir up all against the realm of Grecia (11:2).

(iranchamber.com/history/xerxes/xerxes.php)

Relief of Xerxes at Persepolis

The prophecy states two things: the fourth king would be *far richer* than his predecessors, and he would use his wealth to wage war against Greece. However given that his father Darius gathered gold in abundance and began a system of coinage, such increased wealth might like a "tall order" to be fulfilled by the prophecy. But of course it was not, the prophecies of God's Word are always precise.

The following demonstrates that the fulfilment was exactly as stated in the prophecy. Note also the key insight into the Grecian part of the prophecy

> The palace of Xerxes at Persepolis was twice as large as the Palace of Darius. A terrace connected the two royal mansions, which are not very far apart. Yet, compared to the palace of Darius, the house of Xerxes is badly damaged. A likely explanation is that it received a special treatment when Alexander the Great destroyed Persepolis in 330. His men were especially interested in the palace of the man who had once sacked Athens. livius.org/pen-pg/persepolis/persepolis_palace_xerxes.html

According to Plutarch, Alexander carried away its treasures on 20,000 mules and 5,000 camels. The magnificent palace complex at Persepolis was founded by Darius Hystaspes as the seat of government and a centre and showplace for receptions and ceremonial festivities. The wealth of the Persian empire was evident in all aspects of its construction.

Darius lived long enough to see only a small part of his plans executed. His brilliant and grandiose ideas by his son Xerxes, who, according to an excavated foundation inscription, said: "When my father Darius went (away from) the throne, I by the grace of Ahuramazda became king on my father's throne. After I became king . . . what had been done by my father, that I also (did), and other works I added." Actually, the Persepolis we know is mostly the work of Xerxes.

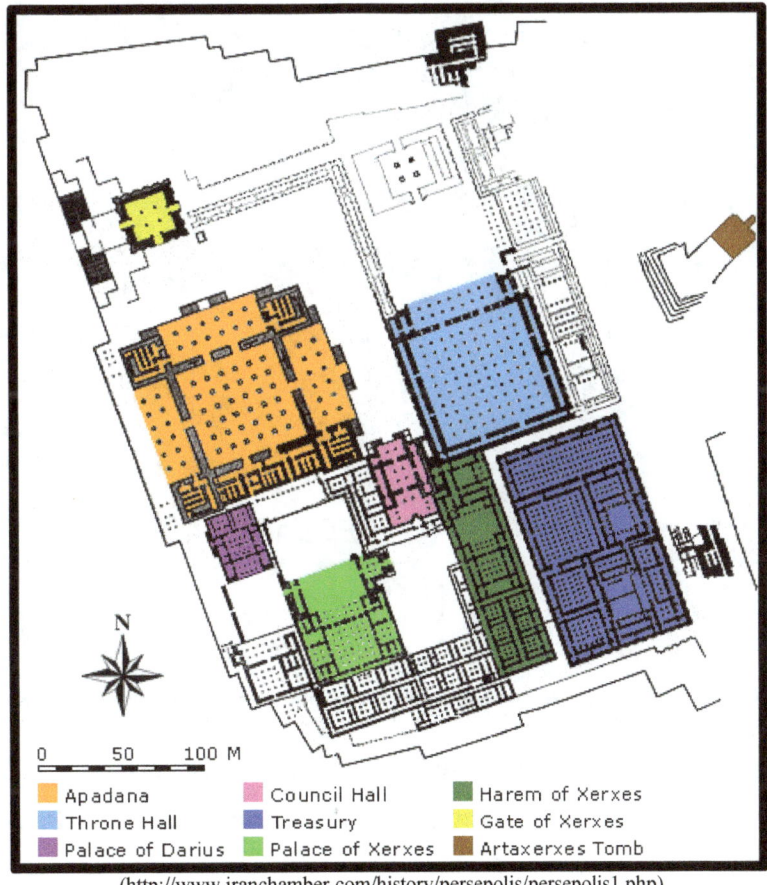

(http://www.iranchamber.com/history/persepolis/persepolis1.php)

The Persepolis Complex Built Mainly by Xerxes.
Compare the Palaces of Darius and Xerxes

We go now to the second, Grecian part of prophecy: *by his strength through his riches he shall stir up all against the realm of Grecia.* Xerxes at the beginning of his reign found himself dealing with several other matters before embarking on the long planned second invasion of Greece. He quickly suppressed a revolt in Egypt and then then broke with the policy followed by Cyrus and Darius of ruling foreign lands with a fairly light hand and compatible with local traditions. He ruthlessly ignored Egyptian forms of rule and imposed a solely Persian system. Plans for Greece were delayed further by supressing a major revolt in Babylonia.

But several years of continuing the preparations started by Darius, Xerxes in the fifth year of his reign began the long anticipated invasion of the Greek mainland. The vast army financed by his huge wealth, from all over the empire was estimated by Herodotus to be as many as a million. This again accords with the prophecy, **by his strength through his riches he shall stir up all against the realm of Grecia**. Having wintered at Sardis in Asia Minor, Xerxes, now at last led the combined land and sea invasion. This second invasion of Greece is one of the major battles of ancient history. It provides pivotal evidence for the comparison of solely Biblical chronology for the period as opposed to that of Ptolemy. It demonstrates why Daniel's prophecy concerning Persia concludes with **the fourth king**.

(http://edsitement.neh.gov/sites/edsitent.neh.gov/files/greece_outline.jpg)

Xerxes Land and Sea Invasion of Greece

The following is drawn and abridged from the stirring account by Paul Chrastina, *King Xerxes Invades Greece*:

> Xerxes ordered a fleet of a thousand warships to sail along the coast of the Aegean Sea, following his army and carrying provisions for the long march to Greece. Xerxes called a temporary halt when his army reached the stormy straits of the Dardanelles, at the mouth of the Black Sea. To transport his army across the mile-wide waterway, Xerxes sent hundreds of ships from his fleet into the channel, where they were tied

together with thick ropes to create a floating bridge. A violent storm destroyed this bridge before the Persian army was able to cross it.

Enraged, Xerxes ordered that the waters of the Dardanelles be whipped and branded with hot irons. The soldiers sent to perform this symbolic act of punishment recited the following royal proclamation: "O vile waterway! Xerxes lays on you this punishment because you have offended him, although he has done you no wrong! The great king Xerxes will cross you even without your permission, for you are a treacherous and foul river!"

(http://900igr.net/kartinki/istorija/Marafonskaja-bitva/029-BITVA-U-FERMOPIL-480-god-do-n.-e.html)

The Lashing of the Hellespont (Dardanelles)

When a second and dual bridge was completed (and after putting to death the engineers of the first bridge), Xerxes and his army crossed the straits into the kingdom of Thrace. The Thracians knew that Xerxes's primary goal was to destroy the powerful city of Athens and offered no resistance.

Passing through northern Greece, Xerxes met no opposition until he reached the rocky seashore of Thermopylae, about ninety miles from Athens. There, a small army of eight thousand Greek soldiers had reinforced an ancient stone wall across the road, where it followed a narrow beach between steep cliffs and the sea. Xerxes was astonished to see that this puny force of Greeks intended to challenge his giant army and refused his demand to surrender.

Xerxes fumed for three days, hoping for the arrival of his fleet, which he thought might be able to sail in behind the Greek position and launch an attack from the sea. The fleet, however, did not arrive. On the morning of the fourth day, Xerxes ordered his army to attack the Greek wall. The front ranks were composed entirely of slaves. By afternoon, the bodies of hundreds of Persians lay heaped in front of the Greek spearmen, who stood firm. Xerxes was furious. He ordered his elite troops, the Immortals, to attack the Greek line. They did no better and retreated at the end of the day after suffering heavy losses. The next morning, Xerxes ordered another attack on the Greek stronghold, but again the Persians failed to break through the Greek defenc. Messengers arrived from the Persian fleet and informed the king that 200 of his warships had been driven aground and wrecked in a fierce storm. It was only after a Greek traitor slipped into the Persian encampment and revealed a hidden mountain pass, that the Persians were able to encircle and defeat the brave Greek defenders.

After Thermopylae, no obstacle stood between Xerxes and the city of Athens, He learned that the Greek army was retreating to a position south of Athens, abandoning the city to its enemy. Instead of attacking Athens immediately, Xerxes sent his army into the surrounding countryside to pillage. Clouds of smoke hung heavy over the land as crops, farms, forests and entire villages were burned to the ground by the rampaging Persians. Temples and marketplaces were desecrated and looted. For three weeks the Persian army plundered the rich Greek countryside.

By the time Xerxes decided to move against Athens, the civilian population of the city had escaped to an offshore island called Salamis. The Persians ravaged the abandoned city; thus the stated goal of the Persian invasion was fully accomplished. Xerxes had avenged his father's defeat by the Athenians at Marathon.

All that remained was to round up and enslave the Athenian refugees on the island of Salamis. The mountainous terrain of the island provided protection for the refugees. Further, the narrow sea channel was guarded by about two hundred Greek warships. Xerxes soon realized that he faced an impasse similar to the one he had at Thermopylae, but Xerxes was anxious to enslave the Athenian refugees and to finish off the Greek fleet.

He ordered his ships into the channel. To witness the final destruction of the Athenian fleet, Xerxes ordered that a golden throne be set up on a mountain that overlooked Salamis. Watching from this high vantage point, Xerxes observed the Greek ships waiting in defensive formation as his Persian fleet approached the narrow channel. Suddenly, many Greek ships broke formation and fled back toward the beach at Salamis, where hundreds of Athenian refugees stood nervously. The Greek fleet was disintegrating before Xerxes's eyes.

Xerxes commanded more of his ships to attack. As the Persian ships jammed into the narrow channel between Salamis and the mainland, the retreating Greek ships suddenly paused in their flight. At the sound of a trumpet, the Greek ships encircled and attacked the Persians. Soon, hundreds of separate battles were raging on the decks of the outermost Persian warships. As damaged Persian ships began backing out of the channel, they stalled the progress of new ships that were trying to get to the fighting. In the confusion, shipwrecks tangled the Persian fleet.

From his golden throne, Xerxes watched helplessly as the Greek navy systematically destroyed his fleet. By the end of the day, according to the Greek playwright Aeschylus, who was present at the battle, "Crushed ships lay upturned on the sea so thick that none could see the water, choked with wrecks and slaughtered men; while the shores and reefs were strewn with Persian corpses."

Xerxes decided that it was time to go back to Persia. He called off the attack on the Greek navy. Leaving part of his army behind to occupy Greece, the great king marched north and east to the Dardanelles, where he found that storms and high tides had severely damaged the floating bridges. Ferried across the straits by the surviving ships of the Persian fleet, Xerxes returned to his old empire. A year later, Xerxes heard that the army he had left behind in Greece had been destroyed. Xerxes spent the rest of his life in his luxurious capital at Persepolis of which little of note is reported.

Fifteen years after the defeat at Salamis, Xerxes was murdered in his sleep by one of his ministers, setting off a chain of assassinations that left the Persian Empire to his son Artaxerxes. (http://www.adam2.org/eastons/ebd/xerxes.html)

Not the Time nor the King of Esther's Marriage!

Again we note how nearly impossible it is to place the defeat of Xerxes and the demise of Persia in what history records as his *seventh year* (and the years proceeding) with the marriage of Esther to Ahasuerus in what the Bible records as his *seventh year* (Est 2:16). It is far more likely that the marriage took place in the seventh year of the previous king, Darius Hystaspes. The events in Esther do not picture a defeated and declining Persian Empire.

> • So Esther was taken unto king Ahasuerus into his house royal in the tenth month, which is the month Tebeth, in **the seventh year of his reign**. And the king loved Esther above all the women, and she obtained grace and favour in his sight more than all the

*virgins; so that he set the royal crown upon her head, and made her queen instead of Vashti. Then the king made **a great feast unto all his princes** and his servants, even Esther's feast; and he made **a release to the provinces**, and gave gifts, according to the state of the king (Est 2:16-18).*

• *And he sent the letters unto all the Jews, to **the hundred twenty and seven provinces of the kingdom** of Ahasuerus, with words of peace and truth (Est 9:30).*

• *And the king Ahasuerus laid a **tribute upon the land, and upon the isles of the sea** (Est 10:1).*

In the crippled state of Persia after the disastrous expedition into Greece, Xerxes was in no position to lay *tribute upon the land, and upon the isles of the sea*.

Still further evidence that Ahasuerus is Darius Hystaspes rather than Xerxes is to be found in the apocryphal book of I Esdras. The first two verses of chapter three summarize Esther 1:1-3, except that **"Ahasuerus" is called "Darius."**

Unlike the other apocryphal books which tell their own unique and often fanciful story, 1 Esdras (Ezra) is different in that except for one section, it presents a divergent account of several parts of the Old Testament. It reproduces the substance of II Chronicles 35:1 - 36:23, the whole of Ezra, Nehemiah 7:73 - 8:12 and Esther 1:1-3. Thus for our enquiry it gives an insight into second century BC Jewish thought concerning the identity of Persian kings; and, concerning the king who married Esther, it is Darius rather than Xerxes. (See *Bible Chronology: The Two Divides* pp. 118-121.)

How Many Years from Xerxes to Alexander the Great?

The Brevity of the Persian Evidence

Both the Biblical and the Ptolemaic chronologies agree that Persia fell to Alexander the Great in 331 BC. However, the Ptolemaic gives 465 BC as the end for Xerxes reign (the 21st year); whereas the Biblical (assuming a 21 year reign) puts his death in 381. Thus the difference between the two is substantial.

        Biblical Chronology   50 years

        Ptolemaic Chronology 134 years

Before dealing with Alexander, Daniel 11:2 alerts us to *four* Persian kings that would follow Daniel. In the providence of God, near contemporary historians, mainly Herodotus, wrote concerning the same *four* kings (with Cyrus before) down to Xerxes' seventh year and defeat by Greece. But thereafter, and down to Alexander, there is only a smattering of information from early historians and that usually in the much later *Library of History* by Diodorus of Sicily (50 BC). The question may reasonably be asked whether all of the kings traditionally listed did in fact exist. And if they did, do they reign as long as Ptolemy says?

An example of the scarcity of historical evidence, can be seen in *Persia and the Bible* by Edwin Yamauchi. The author devotes his first seven chapters to the following subjects:

        1. The Medes
        2. Cyrus
        3. Cambyses
        4. Darius
        5. Xerxes
        6. Artaxerxes I
        7. Susa [a capital of Persia, no further formal discussion of kings !!!]

DANIEL 11. JERUSALEM'S CONFLICT: ANCIENT DAYS AND LAST DAYS

After describing so fully the reigns and times of the first five kings (Xerxes to his 7th year, and much less for years 8-21 and less still for Artaxerxes I), we would expect him to take us further than Artaxerxes I. Instead there is only a brief footnote:

For the confused situation that followed Artaxerxes I, in which there were several rivals for the throne, see D.M. Lewis, *Sparta and Persia*, (Leiden: Brill, 1977), pp.70-78.1.

Actually, there is not much to say! And the above is an example illustrating this well known fact. From the end of the first seven years of Xerxes' reign unto the Darius defeat by Alexander, one is hard-pressed to find material describing the **six Persian kings** which Ptolemy says reigned during this time.

The "fullest" account available for the years and Persian kings who supposedly reigned over a 148 year period (134 + 14) from Xerxes eighth year to the defeat of Persia by Alexander is found in *The Library of History* by Diodorus of Sicily (50 BC). Using the Ptolemaic chronology, the following shows the actual years cited for each king by Diodorus.

Xerxes, 21 years, 486-465 BC (after his eighth year 478 BC)
471
470
465 = events from 3 of his last 14 years are mentioned

Artaxerxes I Longimanus, 40 years, 465-425 BC
463
462
461
460
450
449
425 = events from 7 of his 40 years are mentioned

Darius II Ochus – Nothus, 19 years, 423-404 BC
424
412
405 = events from 3 of his 19 years are mentioned

Artaxerxes II Mnemon 43 years 405-362 BC
404
403
401
400
399
396
395
394
391
390
387
386
385
377
375
374
372

369
366
362 = events from 20 of his 43 years

Artaxerxes III Ochus 23 years 362-339 BC
351
350
349
341 = events from 4 of his 23 years are mentioned

Arses 2 years 339-337 BC
000 = no events from his 2 years are mentioned

Darius III Codomanus 7 years 337-330 BC
335
334
333
331
330 = events from 5 of his 7 years and murder after the fall of Persia are mentioned.

Thus between Xerxes and the Darius who fell to Alexander, there is only one Persian king given a "respectable amount of information" and that was a second Artaxerxes named Mnemon (perhaps there was only one Artaxerxes). This then demonstrates the brevity of historical substance that Diodorus was able to bring to bear upon this time. Nevertheless he is for the most part our sole and earliest available literary witness; and he is likely the primary source for Ptolemy. He wrote nearly three hundred years after the fall of Persia, and **he comments on only 41 of the supposed 147 years from Xerxes 8th year to the fall of Persia.**

The "Shortness" of the Jewish Evidence

This same historical brevity is seen in Egypt and also in Judea. The esteemed Jewish historian Josephus (93 AD) mentions only **three Persian kings**. In chapter XI of his *Antiquities,* Josephus briefly tells of these kings and their relation to the Jewish high priests who spanned the time from Xerxes to Alexander.

> Upon the death of **Darius**, **Xerxes** his son took the kingdom (XI.120) ... Now about this time a son of Jeshua, whose name was Joacim, was the high priest (XI.121) ... After the death of Xerxes, the kingdom came to be transferred to his son Cyrus, whom the Greeks called **Artaxerxes** (XI.184) ... And this was the state of the Jews under the reign of Artaxerxes (XI.296). When Eliasib the high priest was dead, his son Judas succeeded in the high priesthood: and when he was dead, his son John took that dignity; on whose account it was also that Bagoses, the general of **another Artaxerxes'** army, polluted the temple (XI.297) ... Now when John had departed this life, his son Jaddua succeeded in the high priesthood. He had a brother, whose name was Manasseh. Now there was one Sanballat who was sent by **Darius, the last king**, [of Persia] into Samaria (XI.302).

Josephus goes on to describe Darius' defeat at the hands of Alexander, and Jaddua going out to meet Alexander (XI.313-339). Therefore, between Xerxes and Alexander, the respected historian mentions only three kings in what was the fifty year death-throes of the once mighty Persian Empire.

It will startle the reader to find that with the writing of Israel's national chronology during Talmudic era the three Persian kings Josephus mentioned are reduced to only ***ONE***!

The Sedar Olam Rabbah (150 AD) makes the Darius who allowed the post-exilic Jews to finish their Temple to be the same Darius who was defeated by Alexander - Darius Hystaspes!

This is of course wrong, but it is the system Jewish people have traditionally followed. It is the basis for their current date (April 1, 2016 = 5776). In the introductory pages we demonstrated how the rabbis of the second century AD deliberately shortened the Persian period and altered their own national chronology in order to make the Seventy Weeks point to Bar Kokhba (died 135 AD) rather than to Christ. It would have been impossible for the Talmudic rabbis to have succeeded in this radical abridgement were it not for the general belief that Gentile chronology for the period was unstable.

The Inherent Weakness in the Greek Evidence

Only in Greece do we seem to have an impressive history for this period. In fact, the chronology of these other places is often written through "Grecian eyes". But the evidence for the Xerxes to Alexander period is not as sound as may first appear.

In the first case the only substantial near-contemporary account is Thucydides' twenty-two year history of the Peloponnesian War. This same historian gives a brief overview of the years before, as does Xenophon for the period after, but it is only Diodorus of Sicily who has left us with a connected year-by-year account of what was happening in Greece between time of Alexander and Xerxes. Again, he wrote nearly 300 years after the fall of Persia to Alexander. His travels from Sicily are known to have included trips to Rome and Egypt, but apart from his *Library of History* very little is known about the man himself.

But in addition to the lack of on-the-spot witnesses to these years there is a second major fault line in the Greek evidence. Unlike what we have seen of Persian history which is structured upon the reigns of kings, Greek history and especially in its most prominent place, Athens, there were no kings for the period under review. Instead, the historical assessments of how much time elapsed were structured upon *events*. But without the events being linked to the reign of a king, there will be the question as to what extent these events have floated with reference to each other. Note the following tor this period from *Encyclopaedia Britannia*:

> There was no all-important power center and no dominant rulership before Hellenistic [i.e. before Alexander] and Roman times: thus the geographical scattering of records was extreme, although naturally with some focuses of emphasis such as Athens ("History", 20th Edition, p. 600).

In *Bible Chronology: The Two Great Divides*, two further fault lines are demonstrated. For the supposed 148 years from Xerxes eighth year to Alexander's conquest of Persia, some **twenty prominent men** of Greece are shown to have to have been *Too Long in the Limelight*. Spanning much of the period in question, their active lives were almost impossibly too long.

A fourth fault line was discovered by actual search. There is an *Artefact Gap* at the British Museum. Few places on earth have as much of the ancient world on display as the British Museum on Great Russel Street in London. During the late 1990s I searched through sixteen galleries displaying their vast collection of Greek artefacts for the 125 year period in question (475-350 BC). Though this was a time that represents "its most illustrious era," there were substantially fewer artefacts than the 125 year periods before and after.

- 645-475 BC   1115 artefacts
- **475-350 BC**   **435 artefacts**
- 350-250 BC   602 artefacts

Again, as demonstrated in *Bible Chronology: The Two Great Divides* (pp. 198-214), the other commonly appealed to sources do not provide anything approaching a framework that spans the years in question.

- Ephorus
- Eratosthenes
- Apollodorus
- The Spartan King List
- The Olympiads
- The Archons (Athletes) of Athens
- The Marmor Parium

Daniel 11 begins with the words:

*• And now will I shew thee **the truth**. Behold, **there shall stand up yet three kings in Persia**; and **the fourth** shall be far richer than they all: and by his strength through his riches he shall stir up all against the realm of Grecia (11:2).*

*• And **a mighty king shall stand up**, that shall rule with great dominion, and do according to his will (11:3).*

We have seen that as with all else in Scripture, this was **the truth**! After Daniel's time, four kings did *stand up* in Persia. The fourth, Xerxes, did indeed stir up all the realm of Greece. For his efforts Persia went into a steep decline and moribund existence. During these last years no further kings were said in the prophecy to *stand up* in Persia – certainly not in the sense of the previous kings. No king would truly **stand up** in a real sense until a **mighty king** came, Alexander the Great.

That the years from Xerxes to Alexander as shown from Scripture are correct and the years as given by Diodorus and Ptolemy are nearly a century too long is tacitly admitted by the standard reference sources.

Encyclopaedia Judaica is typical:

With one or two notable exceptions, our information for the remaining 100 years of Persian rule dries up. ("History", Vol. VII, p.624).

Cambridge Ancient History admits:

We have as yet very meagre sources for fourth-century historical developments at Samaria and Jerusalem ... ("Judah", Second Edition, 1994, Vol. VI, p.289).

Therefore, to review, before he died, Daniel saw the rise of the first two Persian kings (who reigned for a while as co-regents): Darius the Mede and Cyrus. He then prophesied of four further kings who would rule Persia.

*Also I in the first year of Darius the Mede, even I, stood to confirm and to strengthen him. And now will I shew thee the truth. Behold, **there shall stand up yet three** kings in Persia; and **the fourth** shall be far richer than they all: and by his strength through his riches he shall stir up all against the realm of Grecia (11:1,2).*

1. Cambyses
2. Pseudo Smerdis
3. Darius Hystaspes
4. Xerxes

These kings were said to **stand up**! Persia after Xerxes went into terminal decline, thus the next king to *stand up* was not from Persia but from Greece.

The Mighty Grecian King: Alexander the Great

(11:3) And a mighty king shall stand up, that shall rule with great dominion, and do according to his will. (11:4) And when he shall stand up, his kingdom shall be broken, and shall be divided toward the four winds of heaven; and not to his posterity, nor according to his dominion which he ruled: for his kingdom shall be plucked up, even for others beside those.

Coin of Alexander the Great, *British Museum*

In his unique way, Matthew Henry says the following about one of history's most famous kings.

> Daniel foretells Alexander's conquests and the partition of his kingdom, v. 3. He is that mighty king that shall stand up against the kings of Persia, and he shall **rule with great dominion**, over many kingdoms, and with a despotic power, for he shall **do according to his will**, and undo likewise, which, by the law of the Medes and Persians, their kings could not. When Alexander, after he had conquered Asia, would be worshipped as a god, then this was fulfilled, that he shall *do according to his will*. That is God's prerogative, but was his pretension.

> But (v. 4) his *kingdom* shall soon be **broken**, and **divided** into four parts, **but not to his posterity**, nor shall any of his successors reign *according to his dominion*; none of them shall have such large territories nor such an absolute power. His *kingdom was* **plucked up for others besides those** of his own family. Arideus, his brother, was made king in Macedonia; Olympias, Alexander's mother, killed him, and poisoned Alexander's two sons, Hercules and Alexander. Thus was his family rooted out by its own hands. See what decaying perishing things worldly pomp and possessions are, and the powers by which they are got. Never was the vanity of the world and its greatest things shown more evidently than in the story of Alexander. *All is vanity and vexation of spirit* (Eccl 1:14;2:17).

This is the second time that Daniel prophesied of the sudden rise and even more *sudden* fall of Alexander. Under the figure of a swift and powerful goat, Chapter 8 records Alexander's dramatic conquest of Persia (the ram).

> • *(8:5) And as I was considering, behold, an* **he goat came from** *the west on the face of the whole earth, and touched not the ground: and the goat had* **a notable horn** *between his eyes. (8:6) And he came to the ram that had two horns, which I had seen standing before the river, and ran unto him in the fury of his power. (8:7) And I saw him come close unto the ram, and* **he was moved with choler against him, and smote the ram**, *and brake his two horns: and there was no power in the ram to stand before him, but he cast him down to the ground, and stamped upon him: and there was none that could deliver the ram out of his hand.(8:8) Therefore* **the he goat waxed very great: and when he was strong, the great horn was broken; and for it came up four notable ones toward the four winds of heaven.** *(8:9) And* **out of one of them came forth a little horn**, *which waxed exceeding great, toward the south, and toward the east, and toward the pleasant land. (8:10) And it waxed great, even to the host of heaven; and it cast down some of the host and of the stars to the ground, and stamped upon them (Dan 8:5-10).*

After conquering Persia, and expressing plans to rebuild Nebuchadnezzar's Babylon, Alexander contracted what some have called "swamp fever" and died in Babylon. His empire was then divided among four generals. The fact that in both Chapter 8 and 11 this is described as a judgement *toward the four winds of heaven* (8:8; 11:4) and that in Chapter 8 this is immediately followed by a description of the Little Horn, the end time Antichrist, leads a number of teachers to believe that the same principle will hold for Chapter 11. They propose that the conflict here described between successive kings of the north and kings of the south is an end time conflict between Syria and Egypt culminating in the rise of the Vile King (Antichrist. 11:5-21).

However, these wars have not taken place in modern times, nor, except for the period from the death of Alexander to the rise of Rome, is there any other period where we find them as here described. As shown above, they cannot be fit into the beginning of the Tribulation; and to place them before the Tribulation destroys the doctrine of the imminence. Scripture does not tell us to look for upwards of six wars between Syria and Egypt before the Rapture can take place.

Here in Chapter 11, *the four winds* statement introduces a series of conflicts that culminate in a precursor to the Antichrist (Antiochus Epiphanes).

Note Again: Josephus' Account of Alexander the Great Meeting the Jewish High Priest and Being Shown the Book of Daniel

We cannot leave Alexander without noting again (see on Daniel 2:39) the remarkable account Josephus gives of Alexander meeting the Jewish High Priest and being shown the Book of Daniel. There is historical evidence that as the God of Israel dealt with Nebuchadnezzar, Cyrus and Darius the Mede, He also dealt with Alexander. The Jewish historian *Josephus* gives the following remarkable account of Alexander's conquests when he was about to attack Jerusalem. It should also be noted that Josephus mentions both Sanballat and Jaddua the High Priest (from the book of Nehemiah) in connection with Alexander. This is further confirmation of the relative shortness of the Persian era. See *Bible Chronology: The Two Great Divides*, pp. 106,107.

DANIEL 11. JERUSALEM'S CONFLICT: ANCIENT DAYS AND LAST DAYS

Alexander Meeting the Jewish High Priest at the Gates of Jerusalem

"And when he understood that he was not far from the city, he went out in procession, with the priests and the multitude of the citizens. ... [And] Alexander, when he saw the multitude at a distance, in white garments, while the priests stood clothed with fine linen, and the high priest in purple and scarlet clothing with his mitre on his head having the golden plate on which the name of God was engraved, he approached by himself, and adored that name, and first saluted the high priest. The Jews also did all together, with one voice, salute Alexander, and encompass him about: whereupon the kings of Syria and the rest were surprised at what Alexander had done, and supposed him disordered in his mind. However, Parmenio alone went up to him, and asked him how it came to pass, that when all others adored him, he should adore the high priest of the Jews? To whom he replied, "I did not adore him, but that God who hath honored him with that high priesthood; for I saw this very person in a dream, in this very habit, when I was at Dios, in Macedonia, who, when I was considering with myself how I might obtain the dominion of Asia, exhorted me to make no delay, but boldly to pass over the sea thither, for that he would conduct my army, and would give me the dominion over the Persians ... And when he had said this to Parmenio, and had given the high priest his right hand, the priests ran along by him, and he came into the city; and when he went up into the temple, he offered sacrifice to God, according to the high priest's direction, and magnificently treated both the high priest and the priests. **And when the book of Daniel was showed him, wherein Daniel declared that one of the Greeks should destroy the empire of the Persians**, he supposed that himself was the person intended; and as he was then glad, he dismissed the multitude for the present, but the next day he called them to him, and bade them ask what favors they pleased of him: whereupon the high priest desired that they might enjoy the law of their forefathers and might pay no tribute on the seventh year. He granted all they desired." (XI.313-347).

After Alexander's death, his four generals divided the empire into four divisions, with each taking a province for his own dominion. Cassander took over Macedonia and Greece; Lysimachus claimed Asia Minor (Thrace and Bithynia); Seleucus took Syria and Babylonia; and Ptolemy took Egypt and North Africa. It was Syria and Egypt that become dominant the protagonists now described.

Alexander's Empire Divided Among His Four Generals

The Seleucid and Ptolemaic Wars From Alexander to Antiochus Epiphanes 11:5-20

The prophecy at this point narrows in scope to describe the wars between the kings of the south and the kings of the north. While these are commonly referred to as Egypt and Syria, it must be noted that the Seleucid region especially extended far beyond what today is Syria. It encompassed both Iran and Iraq. This must be kept in mind when seeking to interpret these terms in the end time (11:40). Daniel was made to understand that after the fall of the Persian and Greek Empire, his nation would become a buffer state between the Ptolemaic and Seleucid powers. Israel would be between *the upper and lower millstones* and a battle ground continually for next century and a half. This was one reason for Daniel's distress (10:15). Notice that in this section the Scriptures place greater emphasis on the Seleucid side. Ten of the sixteen verses centre on one Seleucid king – Antiochus the Great. The following is from *Noah Hutchings*.

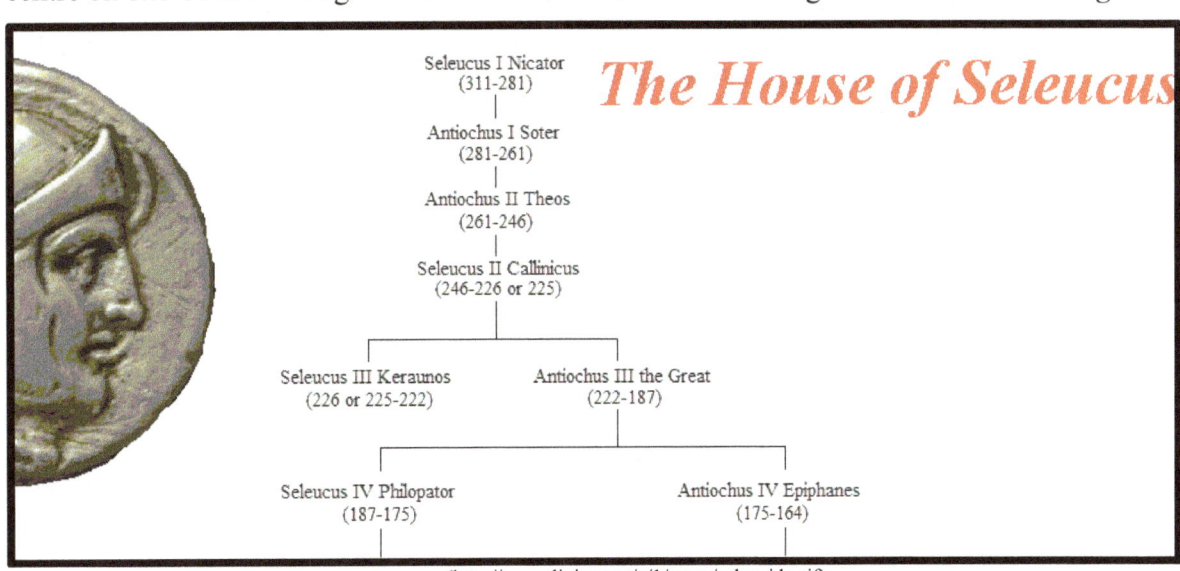

(http://www.livius.org/a/1/maps/seleucids.gif)

The Seleucid Dynasty; Seleucus I to Antiochus Epiphanes

Ptolemy I Soter and Seleucus I Nicator

(11:5) And the king of the south shall be strong, and one of his princes; and he shall be strong above him, and have dominion; his dominion shall be a great dominion.

Concerning verse five, the king of the south was **Ptolemy Soter** who ruled Egypt well and made of it a strong nation. At the time the kingdom was divided, **Seleucus Nicator** was made vice-regent of Babylonia, but a man by the name of **Antigonus** conspired to take over the province and Nicator had to flee to Egypt. In Egypt Nicator was received by his old friend Ptolemy and was made a prince of his empire. Ptolemy financed a military expedition for Seleucus Nicator, and he regained his position of authority in Babylon. From that starting point, he enlarged his province until it extended from India and included Syria and Assyria. Therefore, his dominion became a greater dominion than Egypt.

The Daughter of Ptolemy II is Given in Marriage to Antiochus II Theos

(11:6) And in the end of years they shall join themselves together; for the king's daughter of the south shall come to the king of the north to make an agreement: but she shall not retain the power of the arm; neither shall he stand, nor his arm: but she shall be given up, and they that brought her, and he that begat her, and he that strengthened her in these times.

Verse 6 describes the political intrigue that arose when it was decided that it would be to the advantage of both Syria and Egypt to join the two countries together in a mutual aid treaty. The daughter of the king of the south, **Bernice**, was given by **Ptolemy II** of Egypt, to **Antiochus Theos** of Syria, called the Divine. Ptolemy sent along a handsome dowry with his daughter. The demand made by Ptolemy upon Antiochus of Syria was that he must divorce his wife, **Laodice**, and declare his two children by her as illegitimate offspring of another man. Ptolemy planned to place his own heir upon the throne of Syria, and possibly bring about the unification of the two countries into one nation.

But soon after Bernice married Antiochus Theos, her father, Ptolemy II died. Antiochus then demoted her to the status of a concubine and brought back Laodice as his queen. But Laodice, playing the part of a jealous and spurned woman, murdered both Antiochus and Bernice. Therefore, as the prophecy indicated, Bernice was given up and the entire plot ended in disaster for all concerned. Upon hearing that Bernice had been murdered, her brother Euergetes set out to avenge his sister's death. He plundered Syria, burned their temples, and brought back to Egypt much gold, silver, and idols. Jerusalem served as a way station for the Egyptian army, and much suffering and hardships were brought upon the Jews.

Ptolemy Euergetes and Seleucus Callinicus

(11:7) But out of a branch of her roots shall one stand up in his estate, which shall come with an army, and shall enter into the fortress of the king of the north, and shall deal against them, and shall prevail: (11:8) And shall also carry captives into Egypt their gods, with their princes, and with their precious vessels of silver and of gold; and he shall continue more years than the king of the north. (11:9) So the king of the south shall come into his kingdom, and shall return into his own land.

The exploits of **Ptolemy Euergetes** in revenge for the murders of his sister in Syria are prophesied in verses 7-9: Jerome wrote that Euergetes brought back from Syria forty thousand talents of silver, four thousand talents of gold, and two thousand costly idol statues. But this Egyptian campaign only served to perpetuate the bitterness that existed between Syria and Egypt; and Israel continued to serve as a pawn and a battleground between the two powers. All this was revealed to Daniel and it proves the divine inspiration of our Holy Bible.

Antiochus III the Great Comes to Power

(11:10) But his sons shall be stirred up, and shall assemble a multitude of great forces: and one shall certainly come, and overflow, and pass through: then shall he return, and be stirred up, even to his fortress.

Coin of Antiochus III the Great, *British Museum*

After the sacking of Syria by Egypt, the sons of Antiochus Theos and the sons of former Syrian rulers put aside their differences to raise a large army to avenge their honor and recapture the national wealth. After an assassination and much power grabbing, the command ended up in the hands of another Syrian Antiochus (**Antiochus III the Great**), and by this time, another Ptolemy was on the throne in Egypt — **Ptolemy Philopater**. As indicated in the prophecy, Antiochus marched southward through Jerusalem with his huge army, and the Jews and their holy city were again trodden underfoot by the Gentiles. The city was robbed of all food and provisions, the men were killed in the streets, and the women were raped. After passing through Israel, the Syrian army attacked the Egyptian fortress in Gaza, the strongpoint that guarded the eastern approach. This was in the year 218 BC and this event brings us to the end of verse ten.

Antiochus III the Great is the prominent king in this section, and his history extends down to verse 19.

Antiochus III is Defeated by Ptolemy III

(11:11) And the king of the south shall be moved with choler, and shall come forth and fight with him, even with the king of the north: and he shall set forth a great multitude; but the multitude shall be given into his hand. (11:12) And when he hath taken away the multitude, his heart shall be lifted up; and he shall cast down many ten thousands: but he shall not be strengthened by it.

History records that the Egyptian fortress at Gaza delayed the Syrian army long enough for Philopater to marshal his entire army. The two forces met at Raphia near Gaza. The surprise effect which the Syrian hoped for was gone, and the Egyptian army, being fresher and better supplied, soundly defeated the invaders. Philopater, being somewhat of a playboy, was delighted with the victory because it seemed to prove to the masses that he could also be a general of the army. But also being enraged at the Syrians, he ordered many captives to be slaughtered. And tens of thousands were cast down as the prophecy states — they were killed without mercy. Had Philopater decided to march on Syria, all the land from Damascus to India would have been his; and so in order to bring peace, he made an agreement with Antiochus, and the Syrian king took what remained of his army and marched back to his own country.

Josephus records that Philopater's father, the brother of Bernice, was a godly man. He did not honour the gods of Egypt, but rather came to Jerusalem to offer up a sacrifice to the God of Israel. Philopater, although not an honorable man, inherited a friendship toward the

Jews from his father. The entire business affairs of Egypt were entrusted to the Jews and thousands moved from Israel to Alexandria to become merchants. After the death of Philopater, (also called Philometer), the new king decided to kill the Jews. Josephus writes that all the Jews in Alexandria were gathered together in the town square and stripped. Elephants belonging to the Egyptian army were first made drunk, and then turned loose on the helpless Jews. But instead of charging and trampling the Jews, the elephants turned on their handlers and the soldiers guarding them and many were killed. The Jews were subsequently spared.

After Fourteen Years Antiochus Attacks Egypt (Ptolemy V)

(11:13) For the king of the north shall return, and shall set forth a multitude greater than the former, and shall certainly come after certain years with a great army and with much riches.

The importance of this verse is to expose the folly of Philopater in making a peace treaty with Antiochus of Syria. The Syrian ruler began immediately to rebuild his army to start a new invasion of Egypt.

(11:14) And in those times there shall many stand up against the king of the south: also the robbers of thy people shall exalt themselves to establish the vision; but they shall fall.

This verse indicates a time of turmoil and rebellion in Egypt, and it contains a reference to the persecution of the Jews in Alexandria which we have already mentioned. The revolt in Egypt failed, the Jews were saved, and an infant king was instituted as the new royal monarch. It was also at this time that the Romans began to exert influence and a mutual aid treaty was signed between Rome and Egypt.

Antiochus III Moves Again Against Egypt; But Instead Gives His Daughter Cleopatra to the Egyptian King; This Attempt at Political Union Failed.

(11:15) So the king of the north shall come, and cast up a mount, and take the most fenced cities: and the arms of the south shall not withstand, neither his chosen people, neither shall there be any strength to withstand. (11:16) But he that cometh against him shall do according to his own will, and none shall stand before him: and he shall stand in the glorious land, which by his hand shall be consumed. (11:17 He shall also set his face to enter with the strength of his whole kingdom, and upright ones with him; thus shall he do: and he shall give him the daughter of women, corrupting her: but she shall not stand on his side, neither be for him.

In order to reach Egypt, Antiochus the Great had to first conquer Israel, which was at that time was under the protection of Egypt and guarded by an Egyptian army. Antiochus was successful in overrunning the Egyptian garrison stationed in Israel, and in Israel he was able to *do according to his will* (11:16) because the Jews, relying upon the protection of Egypt, had no army to resist him.

As Antiochus regrouped his forces for a march on Egypt, some rather disturbing news came to his attention. The Egyptians had signed a mutual aid pact with the Romans, a powerful new nation was rising up in the west. Therefore, he changed his plans. The monarch of Egypt at that time was a young boy, seven years old. His name was **Ptolemy Epiphanes**. Antiochus had a young daughter about the same age, so he left his army behind and travelled on to Egypt as an ambassador of good will, taking his daughter with him. The name of his daughter was **Cleopatra**. He proposed the royal household of Egypt and the royal household of Syria be united in peace by arranging a marriage between Cleopatra and Epiphanes. Now here is a remarkable fulfilment of prophecy. We are told that the king of the north, Antiochus, would corrupt the young girl that he would give to the king of the south for political reasons. As soon as the marriage was consummated, Cleopatra was supposed to gain control of Egypt and turn the nation over to her greedy father. Therefore, Cleopatra was exposed to deceit and intrigue at a very early age...The marriage between Cleopatra and Epiphanes was brought about when both were twelve years of age — five years after Antiochus brought her to Egypt.

Cleopatra learned her lesson well, and she began her career of deceit and trickery by betraying her own father. She exposed his plan to her young husband, and in turn he encouraged the Romans to attack Syrian shipping. Cleopatra herself sent congratulations to the Romans for their victories over her father.

Antiochus III is Defeated by the Roman Navy

(11:18) After this shall he turn his face unto the isles, and shall take many: but a prince for his own behalf shall cause the reproach offered by him to cease; without his own reproach he shall cause it to turn upon him.(11:19) Then he shall turn his face toward the fort of his own land: but he shall stumble and fall, and not be found.

All this political mystery, intrigue, and bitterness is embedded deep within the history of the Middle East, and time has not washed away these ugly memories. This is another reason why there can be no peace in the Middle East between Israel and the Arabs until Christ returns. As far as Cleopatra's father is concerned, he finally was goaded into defending his ships against the Roman navy. He fitted out three hundred warships to fight the ships of Rome and plunder their ports. This was the fulfilment of the prophecy that *he would turn his face toward the isles and take many*. However, his venture soon ended in disaster. A young naval commander of Rome, a member of Caesar's household by the name of **Scipio Asiasticus**, led a fleet of Roman warships against him, and the bulk of his Mediterranean naval force was sunk. This fulfilled the prophecy that a prince would end his reproach. After Antiochus returned to Antioch, he sent an ambassador to the Romans to affect a peace arrangement. The peace terms laid down by the Romans were harsh. He had to relinquish all his holdings in Europe and much of Western Turkey. He also had to pay twenty-three hundred thirty talents to Rome at the signing of the peace treaty, and one thousand talents a year for the next twelve years. A few months later, when robbing the temples in his own provinces for money to pay the war obligation, he was killed in the temple of Bel in Elymais. Therefore, the consummation of the prophecy concerning Antiochus that he would stumble and fall in his own land was fulfilled in every detail! The downfall of Antiochus was brought about by his own daughter. All was prophesied by Daniel some two hundred years before.

Seleucus Philopator, the Raiser of Taxes

(11:20) Then shall stand up in his estate a raiser of taxes in the glory of the kingdom: but within few days he shall be destroyed, neither in anger, nor in battle.

Antiochus the Great, the father of Cleopatra, was succeeded upon the throne of Syria by his oldest son, **Seleucus Philopater**. The new ruler of Syria inherited the heavy war debt imposed upon his father by the Romans. In order to meet the yearly assessment of one thousand talents, he placed a heavy tax upon all the Jews in Israel. Philopater had been on the throne for twelve years, and being extremely pressed to meet the last payment to Rome, sent his treasurer to Jerusalem to confiscate the gold and silver vessels in the Temple. However, within a few days, as the prophecy states, he was poisoned. It is not known who poisoned him. We can only guess that it may have been by a Jew in order to save the holy vessels. In any event, though the Jews were forced to help pay off the war debt of Syria, the Temple was spared for a time. We again see how Israel suffered under the reign of the Syrian ruler, Seleucus Philopater, and will now see how she suffers a great deal more.

Antiochus Epiphanes: A Forerunner to the Antichrist 11:21- 35

DANIEL 11. JERUSALEM'S CONFLICT: ANCIENT DAYS AND LAST DAYS

Antiochus IV Epiphanes, Altes Museum in Berlin

Yes, Daniel was made to understand that after the fall of Alexander's Greek Empire, his nation would become a buffer state between the Ptolemaic and Seleucid powers. Israel would be between *the upper and lower millstones* and a battle ground continually for the next century and a half. With the coming of as fourth Syrian *Antiochus* we now come to the worst of this time. In fact little in Israel's history up to this point can be compared with it.

The man who now came to the throne was the son of Antiochus III and the previous king's (Seleucus Philopator) young brother. He was also the young brother of Cleopatra, and it would appear that he was born after Cleopatra had been betrothed to Ptolemy Epiphanes of Egypt, for he seems to have been named after Cleopatra's first husband. He thus became known as, and what became a name of infamy, Antiochus Epiphanes!

History records that Antiochus Epiphanes was every bit as deceitful, treacherous, and cunning as his sister, Cleopatra. The Bible at the outset calls him a "vile person."

The following from *Bible History.com* gives an excellent summary of the wickedness of this man and also enforces the point that we are dealing here with a time when Greek culture nearly overwhelmed Israel. We are also

A Summary of the *Vile Person*

Antiochus IV (175-164 BC), was the 8th ruler of the Seleucid empire. He gave himself the surname "Epiphanes" which means "the visible god" (that he and Jupiter were identical). He acted as though he really were Jupiter and the people called him "Epimanes" meaning "the madman". He was violently bitter against the Jews, and was determined to exterminate them and their religion. He devastated Jerusalem in 168 BC, defiled the Temple, offered a pig on its altar, erected an altar to Jupiter, prohibited Temple worship, forbade circumcision on pain of death, sold thousands of Jewish families into slavery, destroyed all copies of Scripture that could be found, and slaughtered everyone discovered in possession of such copies, and resorted to every conceivable torture to force Jews to renounce their religion. This led to the Maccabaean revolt, one of the most heroic feats in history. The Antiochus bust discovery is important in the study of Biblical archaeology, it reveals an image of the man who was mentioned in the Book of Daniel.

Antiochus IV usurped the throne of his brother Seleucus IV after his death. He was determined to Hellenise Israel and make them a people who were worthy of bordering Egypt, he needed a loyal Hellenised population there. The Jews were quickly becoming more Greek than any other time in history. A group of Jews came to Antiochus with a plan. They proposed that the high priest Onias III should be removed and his hellenized brother Jason should take his place. They should set up a Greek Constitution and coin Greek money.

The plan was followed and all the Jews were outraged. It was the first time since the Babylonian Captivity that a non-Jewish government had interfered with the priesthood (treating the sacred office as though it were nothing other than a governmental office). But the worst was yet to come. Now the hellenizers had full control of the government in Jerusalem and they began to build gymnasiums within the city and encouraged the young to spent all their time there. The young priests engaged in sports, Jerusalem was filled with Greek styles, Greek clothes, Greek names, Greek language and worst of all, Greek religion and Greek morals.

The most radical Hellenizers felt that things were not moving fast enough so they convinced Antiochus to remove Jason and replace him with Menelaus who was not even a member of the priestly family. Menelaus had no sympathy for the Jewish traditions whatsoever and was only concerned about his own power. The Temple treasury did not contain enough money to pay Antiochus what he had promised to Rome so he sold some of the holy vessels of the Temple to raise the money he needed. It was now the goal that Judaism was to be destroyed. In the mind of Antiochus to be un-hellenized was stiff-necked nonsense. If Judaism stood in the way then Judaism was to be destroyed so he gave the orders.

The Syrian army marched into Jerusalem and many of the people were killed and others escaped to the hills. Only the known Hellenists were allowed to remain. Orders were given: NO Sabbath, NO Holy Days, and NO Circumcision. A Statue of Zeus/Antiochus was placed in the Temple above the altar. The most detestable animals (the pig) were brought and sacrificed on the altar. An abominable act was perpetrated on Kislev 25, 168 BC according to the Book of Maccabees that "left the Jewish people desolate." (They call this the Abomination of Desolation in Daniel) but Jesus taught that this was a preliminary occurrence of a greater fulfilment coming in the last days, during the seventieth week of Daniel.

http://www.bible-history.com/archaeology/greece/2-antiochus-iv-bust-bb.html

Antiochus Epiphanes: His Early Reign 11:21-23.

And in his estate shall stand up a vile person, to whom they shall not give the honour of the kingdom: but he shall come in peaceably, and obtain the kingdom by flatteries. (11:22) And with the arms of a flood shall they be overflown from before him, and shall be broken; yea, also the prince of the covenant. (11:23) And after the league made with him he shall work deceitfully: for he shall come up, and shall become strong with a small people.

1. He Obtains the Kingdom by Deceit.

And in his estate shall stand up a vile person, to whom they shall not give the honour of the kingdom: but he shall come in peaceably, and obtain the kingdom by flatteries (11:21).

Antiochus IV Epiphanes is foreseen seizing the throne by deceit and intrigue rather than obtaining it honourably. Like his sister Cleopatra, he was a great manipulator and good talker. He was not the rightful heir to the throne. Demetrius, son of Seleucus Philopator, was the legitimate heir to his murdered father's throne, but he was then a hostage in Rome. Meanwhile, Heliodorus, the wily finance minister of the murdered king (11: 20), was hatching another conspiracy to seize power under the pretext of acting as regent of the younger son of Seleucus. But as soon as Antiochus heard of Seleucus' death, he rushed to Antioch and succeeded not only in nullifying the conspiracy but in murdering the puppet king (Demetrius), and by sly machinations he rapidly climbed to power.

DANIEL 11. JERUSALEM'S CONFLICT: ANCIENT DAYS AND LAST DAYS

2. His Early Military Ventures.

And with the arms of a flood shall they be overflown from before him, and shall be broken.

He scattered Heliodorus' troops and the army of Egypt, which attempted to deprive him of Coela-Syria (the Beqaa Valley where modern Lebanon, Syria and Israel join) soon after he came into the kingship. In 170 BC Antiochus attacked Egypt and defeated the Egyptians on the coast, halfway between Gaza and the Delta.

3. He Overthrows the Jewish High Priest.

...and shall be broken; yea, also the prince of the covenant. (11:23) And after the league made with him he shall work deceitfully: for he shall come up, and shall become strong with a small people (11:22,23).

This *prince of the covenant* refers to the Jewish high priest, Onias III, whose death was ordered by Antiochus in 172 BC, and who was the de facto head of the theocratic Jewish state. The term *covenant* (11:28,32) was the spiritual and governmental constitution of Israel; and which was under attack by the Hellenizers.

A priest named Jason gave Antiochus a large sum of money (a bribe) and was installed in the priesthood. Jason's intention was to further the moves to set up a Greek constitution in Israel and Greek coinage. As shown above, "the most radical Hellenizers felt that things were not moving fast enough so they convinced Antiochus to remove Jason and replace him with Menelaus (after giving Antiochus a larger bribe) who was not even a member of the priestly family. Menelaus had no sympathy for the Jewish traditions whatsoever and was only concerned about his own power."

4. His Further Intrigues.

....for he shall come up, and shall become strong with a small people (11:23).

This may refer to his intrigues regarding the Jewish priesthood; or it may refer to his dealings with the Romans and the Egyptians. Antiochus was a polished liar. He made arrangements and kept them only as long as it was to his advantage. When he dealt with the Romans, in order not to arouse their opposition, he pretended to have only a small army, but then he suddenly attacked Egypt with a huge army. In the struggle for control of Egypt between Ptolemy Philometer and Ptolemy Euergetes, (Antiochus' nephews), Antiochus aided the former, but only with crafty cunning and an eye to his own advancement.

Antiochus Epiphanes: His Expanding Power 11:24-28.

He shall enter peaceably even upon the fattest places of the province; and he shall do that which his fathers have not done, nor his fathers' fathers; he shall scatter among them the prey, and spoil, and riches: yea, and he shall forecast his devices against the strong holds, even for a time. (11:25) And he shall stir up his power and his courage against the king of the south with a great army; and the king of the south shall be stirred up to battle with a very great and mighty army; but he shall not stand: for they shall forecast devices against him. (11:26) Yea, they that feed of the portion of his meat shall destroy him, and his army shall overflow: and many shall fall down slain. (11:27) And both of these kings' hearts shall be to do mischief, and they shall speak lies at one table; but it shall not prosper: for yet the end shall be at the time appointed. (11:28) Then shall he return into his land with great riches; and his heart shall be against the holy covenant; and he shall do exploits, and return to his own land.

1. His Power at Home.

He shall enter peaceably even upon the fattest places of the province; and he shall do that which his fathers have not done, nor his fathers' fathers; he shall scatter among them the prey, and spoil, and riches: yea, and he shall forecast his devices against the strong holds, even for a time (11:24).

He laid claim to Coela-Syria, Israel and Phoenicia. His father had been saddled with the huge Roman debt and used the plunder from these areas to satisfy the Romans. With the debt being paid off, Antiochus bought loyalty by dividing the spoils among his close friends and army officers. However, in contrast to the previous Seleucid kings he squandered much of the spoil on his own extravagant lifestyle (1 Maccabees 3:20; Josephus 12.7.2). All the while he was devising schemes to plunder every stronghold that was in his reach. But like all who make wealth their goal, it was only *for a time*. Regardless of his wealth and power, his military prowess and cunning, Antiochus would not exceed the limits allotted him by the Lord of history.

- *He that loveth silver shall not be satisfied with silver; nor he that loveth abundance with increase: this is also vanity (Eccl 5:10).*

<u>2. His Power Against Egypt</u>.

<u>The Egyptian King is Given Bad Advice</u>.

And he shall stir up his power and his courage against the king of the south with a great army; and the king of the south shall be stirred up to battle with a very great and mighty army; but he shall not stand: for they shall forecast devices against him Yea, they that feed of the portion of his meat shall destroy him, and his army shall overflow: and many shall fall down slain (11:25,26).

Antiochus brought his army against Ptolemy VI Philometor (his nephew). The Egyptian king was weak and actually a puppet of two ambitious advisers, who foolishly urged the young king to recapture Israel and the other areas Antiochus had taken. Despite Egypt's huge army, Ptolemy VI was disastrously defeated in 169 BC. His advisors promised him victory but their counsel resulted in the opposite a *device forecast against him*. It was the opposite of the following passage.

- *Every purpose is established by counsel: and with good advice make war (Prov 20:18).*

<u>Intrigue at the Egyptian *Peace Talks*</u>. ***And both of these kings' hearts shall be to do mischief, and they shall speak lies at one table; but it shall not prosper: for yet the end shall be at the time appointed*** (11:27). The victorious Antiochus and his defeated nephew, Ptolemy Philometor entered into negotiations; but this was only to exchange lies and seek to outwit the other. Antiochus was pretending to be a protector of Philometor's interests and crown. The two had apparently become allied against Philometor's brother and who had meanwhile been crowned as Ptolemy VII by a rival faction in Alexandria. Antiochus was "double-dealing" in hopes of exploiting the situation to weaken Egypt by strengthening this internal rivalry.

The attempt would not prosper. Antiochus' scheme to drive a wedge between his two nephews was thwarted when the two Ptolemy's were later reconciled and agreed to a joint rule. Further, in this intricate account of prophecy which is now history we are reminded that the course of events is not determined by the machinations of man but by the Lord: ***for yet the end shall be at the time appointed.***

<u>His Power Against Israel</u>. ***Then shall he return into his land with great riches; and his heart shall be against the holy covenant; and he shall do exploits, and return to his own land (11:28).*** Antiochus took vast spoil from the cities of Egypt (1 Maccabees 1:19,20) and left the country with only part of his plan accomplished. One reason for leaving Egypt early was reports of turmoil in Jerusalem, which was the aftermath of Antiochus's wicked interference in the office of the high priest. As noted, having deposed Onias III who opposed

DANIEL 11. JERUSALEM'S CONFLICT: ANCIENT DAYS AND LAST DAYS

his Hellenising policies, he had replaced him with his pro-hellenizing brother, Jason; and then later replaced with Menelaus, who had offered the king a higher bribe. An effort by Jason to reinstate himself in office, which Antiochus interpreted rebellion to his authority, caused the enraged king to invade Jerusalem, where he massacred 40,000 Jews and looted the Temple, carrying its treasures back to his capital, Antioch (1 Maccabees 1:20-24; 2 Mac. 5:5-21). By these blasphemous and barbaric actions, Antiochus *set his heart against the holy covenant* (a designation of the Jewish nation embracing the knowledge and worship of the true God, verses 22,30). We can now understand why Daniel wept when he was shown what was to come upon his people.

Antiochus Epiphanes: His Waning Power and Persecution of the Jews. 11:29-31.

At the time appointed he shall return, and come toward the south; but it shall not be as the former, or as the latter. (11:30) For the ships of Chittim shall come against him: therefore he shall be grieved, and return, and have indignation against the holy covenant: so shall he do; he shall even return, and have intelligence with them that forsake the holy covenant. (11:31) And arms shall stand on his part, and they shall pollute the sanctuary of strength, and shall take away the daily sacrifice, and they shall place the abomination that maketh desolate.

1. He Attempts to Invade Egypt. ***At the time appointed he shall return, and come toward the south; but it shall not be as the former, or as the latter*** (11:29). *At the time appointed* (i.e. by God) Antiochus was foreseen to return toward the south in his second war with Egypt in 168 BC, but it would not be as before.

2. He is Stopped by Rome. ***For the ships of Chittim shall come against him*** (11:30). *The ships of Chittim* (Cyprus), is a symbolic representation of the rising maritime power of Rome. Ships carrying a delegation headed by Gais Popillius Laenas, would demand that he leave Egypt. Antiochus' objective had been to take Alexandria. But when his army arrived at Alexandria, a Roman fleet lay anchored in the bay. The fleet commander met Antiochus and informed him that by a decree from the Roman senate, he must leave Egypt alone and return to his own country or he would be opposed by the Roman army and navy. To gain time, Antiochus told the Roman commander that he would have to consult with his advisers first. But knowing the deceitful ways of the Syrian, Popilius promptly drew a circle around him and said: "Before you step out of that circle give such an answer as I may report to the senate." Antiochus, seeing that his hand was called, agreed to leave.

3. He Returns to Israel.

The Apostate Jews Support Antiochus: ***therefore he shall be grieved, and return, and have indignation against the holy covenant: so shall he do; he shall even return, and have intelligence with them that forsake the holy covenant*** (11:30). Humiliated by the Roman block, and indignant at hearing that God's worship had been restored at Jerusalem, the brutal king would vent his wrath on the Jews. Antiochus would, however, show favourable consideration to the renegade Jews as Menelaus and other apostates who forsook the God of Israel. He paid money to some of the ungodly Jews to spy on their own people, and anyone who said anything against him was hung in public as a warning.

The Temple is Desecrated. ***And arms shall stand on his part, and they shall pollute the sanctuary of strength, and shall take away the daily sacrifice, and they shall place the abomination that maketh desolate*** (11:31). Besides massacring thousands and pillaging the city, Antiochus polluted the Temple's holy altar by offering a sow upon it and forbidding the daily sacrifices (cp. 1 Mac. 1:44-54). He also forbade the Jews to continue their worship, and he set up an idol (apparently the image of Zeus) in the holy place. That supreme act of blasphemy typically foreshadows the last-day abomination that *maketh desolate* of Antichrist, referred to by Christ in Matthew 24:15 (cp. Dan 8:23-25; 2 Thess 2:4; Rev 13:1-16).

Noah Hutchings in his quotation from Josephus elaborates further:

> *And when the king had built an idol altar upon God's altar, he slew swine upon it, and so offered a sacrifice neither according to the law, nor the Jewish religious worship.*

> We understand by Josephus that Antiochus first tore out the altar of God, and built an idol altar in its place. It was upon this idol altar that the swine was offered. This idol altar was actually an image of their false god, with a place to burn their sacrifice at the bottom. This was representative of what the Antichrist will do when he stops the daily sacrifice in the temple during the Tribulation and places his own image in the Temple.

> In verse 31 we notice that this deed is referred to as the abomination that maketh desolate. The abomination of desolation is mentioned specifically four times in the Bible. In Daniel 9:27 it is stated explicitly that it will occur in the middle of the Tribulation. Here in Daniel 11:31 it is indicated that it was committed by Antiochus Epiphanes, but this deed was only representative of the greater abomination and the great desolation in Israel that will come with Antichrist standing in the temple. In Daniel 12:11 the abomination of desolation is again placed in the middle of the Tribulation, and it is also placed in the Tribulation by Christ in Matthew 24:15,21:

> • *When ye therefore shall see the abomination of desolation, spoken of by Daniel the prophet, stand in the holy place, (whoso readeth, let him understand:) . . . For then shall be great tribulation, such as was not since the beginning of the world to this time, no, nor ever shall be.*

Antiochus Epiphanes: Israel in the Storm From That Day to the Last Days 11:32-35.

> *And such as do wickedly against the covenant shall he corrupt by flatteries: but the people that do know their God shall be strong, and do exploits. (11:33) And they that understand among the people shall instruct many: yet they shall fall by the sword, and by flame, by captivity, and by spoil, many days. (11:34) Now when they shall fall, they shall be holpen with a little help: but many shall cleave to them with flatteries. (11:35) And some of them of understanding shall fall, to try them, and to purge, and to make them white, even to the time of the end: because it is yet for a time appointed.*

1. <u>Those Who Yield to Compromise</u>. ***And such as do wickedly against the covenant shall he corrupt by flatteries*** (11:32). There are many who are only too willing to compromise concerning the truth of Scripture. Satan knows this and Antiochus knew it. This prophecy states that Antiochus would attempt by flatteries and smooth talk to corrupt those Jews who were living in disobedience to the Scriptures and the covenant based on the Scriptures. Those who do not stand for the Bible will fall for just about anything. In this case it was Antiochus' pagan Hellenistic religion.

2. <u>Those Who Stand with Conviction</u>.

<u>They Know Their God</u>: ***but the people that do know their God shall be strong, and do exploits*** (11:32). This is a prophetic reference to the Maccabees and their followers (1 Maccabees 1:62-63) and the glorious page in Jewish history they wrote, choosing death rather than to deny the Lord and His covenant with them. Their victory over Antiochus and cleansing of the Temple he desecrated is described below.

<u>They Understand</u>. ***And they that understand among the people shall instruct many*** (11:33). They who understand and keep the truth of God are foreseen to instruct many in their duty to God and the Scriptures. To know God leads to understanding. *The knowledge of the holy is understanding* (Prov 9:10).

3. <u>Those Who Fall in Persecution</u>:

DANIEL 11. JERUSALEM'S CONFLICT: ANCIENT DAYS AND LAST DAYS

The Severity: *yet they shall fall by the sword, and by flame, by captivity, and by spoil, many days* (11:33). Josephus specifies three years as the duration of the persecution under Antiochus (*Antiquities* 12.7; 6.7; cp. 1 Maccabees 1:59; 4:54; 2 Macc. 10:1-7).

The Help and Hindrance. *Now when they shall fall, they shall be holpen with a little help: but many shall cleave to them with flatteries* (11:34). The freedom won by the heroism of the Maccabees did not last permanently. The Roman, and then the Herodian, yoke was soon placed around the nation's neck, and at the fall of Jerusalem in 70 AD, the Jews were mercilessly scattered among the nations. Even their establishment as a nation in 1948, although a sign of eventual restoration, shows that the entire period of Gentile rule will be a period of strife for the Jewish People, extending from the Babylonian Exile to the Second Advent and Millennial Kingdom.

But many shall cleave to them with flatteries. Many joined with the Maccabees in hypocrisy. Large numbers of Jews joined Judas Maccabeus in his successful battles against Antiochus. However, they did so purely out of expediency (1 Maccabees 5:55-57; 2 Macc. 12:40), not by deep conviction in the Scriptures.

4. Those Who Suffer Across the Centuries. *And some of them of understanding shall fall, to try them, and to purge, and to make them white, even to the time of the end: because it is yet for a time appointed* (11:35). Others who are spiritually perceptive will fall, that is, give in under the terrible pressures of persecution to be tried, purged, and made white (Dan 12:10; Deut 8:16; Prov 17:3; Zech 13:9; Mal 3:2,3).

This chastening and refining process will go on throughout the course of the times of Gentile dominion until the end time (the end of Israel's woes at the Second Advent of the Messiah and the Kingdom).

This verse forms a bridge spanning the period from the times of the persecutions of Antiochus to the rise of him of whom Antiochus is a type, the Antichrist of the end time during Israel's Tribulation, preceding their final furnace of purging and refining, a necessary prelude to the Davidic-Messianic earthly Kingdom. The amazingly detailed prophecies (about 135 in number, all now fulfilled) "constitute an impressive introduction to the events that are yet future, beginning in verse 36 (J. F. Walvoord, quoted in *Unger's Commentary on the Old Testament*).

The Maccabean Revolt

The following account describes the spark that ignited the revolt against Antiochus Epiphanes and the Seleucid control of Israel.

> The Maccabean revolt in particular and the Pharisaic party in general are to be explained as measures of resistance against the Hellenization of the Jewish people. This was the Jew's memorable struggle for freedom under the leadership of the Hasmonaean Judas Maccabaeus and his brothers. He gave back to Israel for the last time its political independence for a century. Jewish history and poetry have amply glorified the heroism, the courage to confess, the readiness to die of the Maccabean soldiers of the faith.
>
> In a little town outside Jerusalem, a Greek official attempted to force an aged Jewish Levite priest to sacrifice to Greek gods. The name of the priest was Mattathias, of the Hasmonean house and after he had killed the official, other Jews joined in the fight. They became known as the Maccabees, the Hebrew word for hammer - for in battle after battle they dealt 'hammer blows' to the Seleucid armies. Mattathias died 166 BC and his mantle fell on his son Judas, a warrior of amazing military genius. Led by the five sons of Mattathias, the rebellion mushroomed from a spontaneous guerrilla operation into full-scale warfare. They won battle after battle against unbelievable and impossible odds. In 164 or 165 BC, the Jews shattered the armies and recaptured

A COMMENTARY AND SURVEY SERIES: DANIEL

> Jerusalem. They were able to cleanse and purify the Temple and throw out the heathen alter with which Antiochus had most horribly defiled the Temple for three years. The temple was purged of all idols and rededicated to Jehovah, giving birth to the feast of Hanukkah, which commemorates the victory. This was the origin of the Feast of Dedication (Jhn 10:22). Judea again became a theocracy, under the Hasmonean dynasty of priest kings.
>
> Simon, the son of Mattathias and older brother of Judas was never anointed king but he nevertheless is regarded as the first of the Hasmonean dynasty. Officially he was the High Priest of Jerusalem and governor of Judah. Judas united the priestly and civil authority in himself, and thus established the line of Asmonean priest-rulers and for 100 years governed an independent Judea.
>
> The fate of the Maccabean epoch was sealed when the Roman general Pompey appeared in Syria in 63 BC. http://latter-rain.com/ltrain/macc.htm

Antiochus Epiphanes died in Syria of malnutrition. His loss of Israel so disturbed him that he could not eat and he died. With the victory over his Jerusalem army by the Jews, he realized that he could never become a ruler of all the world. His vision of a world empire crumbled, and like his sister Cleopatra who shared the same ambitions, he died in his own disillusionment and misery.

The Feast of Hanukkah (*Dedication*), Also Called *The Feast of Lights*

(https://spoonuniversity.com/wp-content/uploads/sites/31/2014/12/dt.common.streams.StreamServer.cls_.jpeg)

The Eight Hanukkah Candles

We are often told that the traditional date of the birth of Christ (December 25th) was the time of a pagan Roman solar feast, *Dies Natalis Solis Invicti* (Birth of the Unconquered Sun). However it was not until 274 AD that the Roman Emperor Aurelian declared this to be a time of celebration. Regarding the other pagan feast of the time *Saturnalia* (the worship of Saturn) we find that originally it was observed considerably earlier than December 25th.

> Saturnalia originated as a farmer's festival to mark the end of the autumn planting season in honour of Saturn (*satus* means sowing). Numerous archaeological sites from the Roman coastal province of Constantine, now in Algeria, demonstrate that the cult of Saturn survived there until the early third century AD. Saturnalia grew in duration and moved to progressively later dates under the Roman period. During the reign of the Emperor Augustus (63 BC-AD 14), it was a two-day affair starting on December 17th. By the time Lucian described the festivities, it was a seven-day event. Changes to the Roman calendar moved the climax of Saturnalia to December 25th, around the time of the date of the winter solstice.
>
> (http://www.historytoday.com/matt-salusbury/did-romans-invent-christmas)

The traditional date for the birth of Christ has absolutely nothing to do with the dating of either *Dies Natalis Solis Invicti* or *Saturnalia*. Early believers would not "adapt" a memorial for the Birth of Christ with a pagan feast. Without going into a number of substantial reasons that point to the traditional date as being approximately the correct time of Christ's Birth, the following concerning Hanukah or the *Feast of Lights* has special significance.

Concerning this Feast and after describing what we have seen above concerning Antiochus Epiphanes, David Reagan writes:

> Though Mattathias did not live to see it, shortly after his death his son Judas entered the city as a victor.
>
> Judas spent several months cleansing the temple and its environs. He then proclaimed the 25th of Kislev as the beginning of a holy feast given to the rededication of the temple for the priestly service. This date marked the third anniversary from the time the temple was originally desecrated by Antiochus. Though the calendars do not match perfectly, **the eight day feast of Hanukkah generally corresponds to the Christmas season.**
>
> Hanukkah is celebrated each year by the eating of special foods like the potato pancakes called *latkes* and other fried foods. (They are fried in oil because of the miracle of the oil told below.) Children play a game with a holiday top called a *dreidel*. Also, the people give gifts to one another. This last part of the celebration used to be a minor part. However, many Jewish parents now feel that they must compete with Christmas so they often give their children gifts for each of the eight days of the feast.
>
> But probably the most characteristic tradition of the feast is the lighting of the Hanukkah candles. This is why Hanukkah is also called the Festival of Lights. Tradition teaches that when the priests went in to light the menorah (or candlestick), they only found one unopened and uncontaminated cruse of oil that could be used for the lighting of the lamps. And, it only had enough oil for one day. But, when they filled the lamps and lit them, the oil miraculously lasted for eight days. The lighting of the eight Hanukkah candles commemorates this miracle. Though Hanukkah is a Jewish feast, the New Testament teaches that Christ honored this feast with His attendance.
>
> • *And it was at Jerusalem the feast of the dedication, and it was winter. And Jesus walked in the temple in Solomon's porch (Jhn 10:22,23).*
>
> Since Christ attended this festival, we should not be surprised that many aspects of its celebration has lessons to His followers today. Let us look at some of these lessons.
>
> Hanukkah means "dedication". Its initial purpose was to rededicate the Temple that had sat filthy and had been used for the worship of false gods. This feast celebrated that fact that once again the House of God was cleansed and sanctified for His use alone. In like manner, we who have trusted in Jesus Christ as Saviour should cleanse our lives and set them apart for God's use. We should dedicate ourselves to God and live only for Him.
>
> The two great Jewish teachers, Shammai and Hillel, argued over how the candles should be lit. Shammai taught that all the candles should be lit the first night of the feast and that one should be snuffed out each succeeding evening. Hillel, whose view won out, said that one candle should be lit each night until all of the candles were lit at the end of the eight days. His argument was that we should be increasing in holiness and not decreasing. We should still be increasing and not decreasing; we should grow in the grace of the knowledge of Jesus Christ.
>
> According to Jewish tradition, the candles are placed in the Hanukkah candlestick (when facing it) from right to left. However, the candles are lit from left to right. This way, the candles that are set in place last are lit first and the candles that are set in place first are lit last. This reminds us of the saying of Jesus that "the last shall be first, and the first last." He is teaching that those who seem to be the most important may not have an equal place in heaven. And, those who seem to be lowly here may have a much higher position in the world to come.
>
> In a similar teaching, both men and women are to have part in the lighting of the candles. This is not true in many of the Jewish ceremonies. Usually, men do most of that which is visible. However, Hanukkah teaches that both men and women had an

equal part in the deliverance of the Jewish people in the time of the Maccabees. Many stories of the heroism of women are told. Also, under the teaching of the New Testament, women often take a back seat in the public ministry. However, the apostle Paul makes it clear that all, including male and female, are one in Christ Jesus. Different roles do not indicate different standings with God.

Each family is to place its Hanukkah candlestick so that it is visible to the outside—whether in a window or in a special place near a door. So, Christ tells us not to light our candle and put it under a bushel. We should put it on a candlestick and let it shine as a testimony to all men. Also, each candle is to be lit right after sundown. As this world gets darker and darker, so we should be lights in the world.

The Hanukkah menorah is purposely designed to be different from the Temple menorah. The Temple menorah has seven lamps. The Hanukkah candlestick has eight (plus the ninth, which will be explained in the next paragraph). Also, it is actually called the *hanukkia* in order to distinguish it from the holy menorah. It is like the Temple menorah but it is not to be confused with it. So, we are to be like Christ. He is our example in every aspect of the Christian life. We are to be recreated in His image. However, we should never get the idea that we are identical to Him. We will always come far short of the His glory. He will always be *the First and the Last*.

Finally, the Hanukkah menorah has a ninth candle called the *shamash* which means "servant." None of the eight candles are ever to be used to light any of the other eight candles. All of them are to be lit from the ninth, or servant, candle. God the Father calls Jesus Christ "my servant, whom I have chosen." Jesus came not to be ministered unto but to minister. We cannot find our light in the light of another believer. Each of us must have our candle lit by the light of all mankind, by Jesus Christ Himself. He is truly the Servant and the sole source of our light.

As we come to the season of the Festival of Lights, the Feast of Hanukkah, I wonder. Do you know the light of the world? Are you lit by His flame? Are you showing your candle to the outside world for all to see? There is so much for us to learn from this feast attended by Christ—the Feast of Dedication.
http://www.learnthebible.org/festival-of-lights.htmlFestival of Lights

Antiochus Epiphanes, A Biblical Foreview of the Coming Antichrist

In this final vision given to the prophet Daniel, upwards of fifteen verses concern Antiochus Epiphanes (Dan 11:21-35). From verse thirty-five, where it says **even unto the time of the end**, the prophecy passes all the way over to the Seventieth Week of Daniel and the Willful King, the Antichrist. This demonstrates that the *beastly* reign of Antiochus presented a picture of the end time Beast.

Larry Cockerham, in his *Antiochus IV Epiphanes: The Antichrist of the Old Testament*, shows the parallel between these two evil personages. The following is drawn from his material. While as shown in our notes on Daniel 8, I do not follow the author's view that Antiochus is actually the Little Horn of Daniel 8 (8:9-14; 23-25), nevertheless the parallels he makes are valid.

Antiochus IV Epiphanes (175—164 BC) was the eighth in a succession of twenty-six kings who ruled over the Syrian section of Alexander's empire. The name Epiphanes means the "Illustrious One," although his contemporaries nicknamed him Epimanes, meaning "madman. He is undoubtedly one of the greatest prototypes of the Antichrist in all of God's Word. Bible students call the account given to him as a ***double reference prophecy.***

(1) BOTH INVOLVE TWO END-TIME PERIODS. When it comes to the larger picture, these two periods of persecution leading up to the first and second coming of Christ are portrayed in both the exploits of Antiochus IV as well as those of the coming Antichrist. Lehman Strauss explains thusly: "Both of these periods witness the wrath of God being extended to His chosen people. The first of these periods of wrath commenced with the Babylonian captivity and concluded with the atrocities of

DANIEL 11. JERUSALEM'S CONFLICT: ANCIENT DAYS AND LAST DAYS

Antiochus, after which there was deliverance. The second of these periods is yet future. It will commence with the beginning of the Seventieth week (Dan 9:24-27) and conclude with the atrocities of Antichrist, after which there will be deliverance.

(2) BOTH COME TO GREAT POWER FROM A SMALL BEGINNING. Antiochus began as *a vile person, to whom they shall not give the honour of the kingdom* (Dan 11:21), and the Antichrist will begin as a *little horn* (Dan 7:8; 8:9) He will begin as an insignificant political figure and will soon gain control over *all kindreds, and tongues, and nations* (Rev 13:7).

(3) BOTH PERSECUTE THE SAINTS OF GOD. The cruel and violent persecutions of Antiochus Epiphanes are recorded in the annals of history for all to observe. In 168 BC he turned his vengeance upon Jerusalem. He killed over eighty thousand men, women, and children and sold forty thousand into slavery (2 Macc. 5:5-14). But the carnage of the impious Syrian king is only a foretaste of what lies ahead for those who will be swept away during the Great Tribulation. The persecution of God's saints under the *Beast* will be much more intense and far-reaching. The Apostle John *saw the souls of them that were beheaded for the witness of Jesus, and for the word of God, and which had not worshipped the beast, neither his image, neither had received his mark upon their foreheads, or in their hands* (Rev 20:4).

(4) BOTH BLASPHEME THE GOD OF HEAVEN. Antiochus compelled everyone under his domain to worship the gods of Greece and blaspheme the God of Heaven. His blasphemy will typify the future *Man of Sin*. The Apostle John witnessed the approaching Beast rising from the sea *and upon his heads the name of blasphemy* (Rev 13:1); *And he opened his mouth in blasphemy against God, to blaspheme his name, and his tabernacle, and them that dwell in heaven* (Rev 13:6).

(5) BOTH USE PEACE TO ACHIEVE THEIR AIMS. Of the Syrian king it is said *he shall come in peaceably, and obtain the kingdom by flatteries* (11:21). Of Antichrist it is said that *by peace he shall destroy many* (Dan. 8:25). He is presented as *a rider on a white horse* (Rev 6:1,2) who has a *bow* but no arrows. He will ascend to power through the voluntary alliance of ten Western European nations uniting under a one-world government (Rev 17:12, 13). As the *prince that shall come* (Dan. (9:26), he will lead Israel into signing a covenant (Dan. 9:27), which Isaiah describes as a *covenant with death, and with hell* (Isa 28:15,18). This *white horse* of conquest is quickly followed by the *red horse* of war (Rev 6:4), the *black horse* of famine (Rev 6:5), and the *pale horse* of death (Rev 6:8). The world will suddenly be plunged into utter devastation that ultimately leads to the battle of Armageddon and the Second Coming of Christ (Rev 19:11-21).

(6) BOTH DESECRATE THE JEWISH TEMPLE. Antiochus robbed the Temple of its treasures and dedicated it to Jupiter Olympus. It was defiled by offering a sow upon the altar and scattering its juice over all the sanctuary and vessels. He substituted the Jewish feasts with the drunken revelry of Bacchanalia, forcing the Jews to worship Bacchus, the god of pleasure and wine. The licentious festival of Saturnalia, the worship of Saturn, was also brought into the Temple. This is a matter of extensive historical record. Yet little did Antiochus realise that he was portraying a future defilement. His terrible act was called *the abomination that maketh desolate* (Dan 11:31), and the same term is used shortly after of the future desecration by Antichrist: *the abomination that maketh desolate* (12:11). Christ Himself used these same words when speaking of this terrible future event. *When ye therefore shall see the abomination of desolation spoken of by Daniel the prophet, stand in the holy place, whoso readeth, let him understand* (Matt 24:15).

(7) BOTH CLAIMED TO BE GOD. Concerning the Syrian king Antiochus, was demon possessed. Beyond the normal use of the terms, he was inordinately proud, lifted up, and ambitious. When Antiochus came to reign, he imprinted on his coins, **Theos Antiochus, Theos Epiphanes,** "Antiochus, God manifest." So it will be for the coming Antichrist.

• *Who opposeth and exalteth himself above all that is called God, or that is worshipped; so that he as God sitteth in the temple of God, **shewing himself that he is God** (2 Thess 2:4).*

Seeing that Christ was the "Seed of the woman", therefore Antichrist will be the "seed of the serpent" (Gen. 3:15). John Phillips notes that "in his human form he is the beast 'out of the sea,' a brilliant and dynamic world leader with charisma and vision, demon-possessed as Hitler was. He will be killed, will have a 'second coming,' and from then on will be the beast 'out of the bottomless pit.' As such he will be superhuman, awesome, and in a position to command and receive the worship of mankind" (*Exploring the Future*, p. 88).

(8) BOTH SHALL BE BROKEN WITHOUT HAND. This is specifically stated of the Antichrist (Dan 8:25). This means that his power will be broken apart from the intervention of man, but instead by God's special visitation. Antiochus was afflicted by a horrible death of worms and ulcers, when on his way to Judea, intending to take vengeance for the defeat by Maccabees (*JFB*). It is Christ, the Smiting Stone, who suddenly strikes the Antichrist at His Second Coming (Dan 2:34,35; Rev 19:11-21).

(9) BOTH PERIODS CONCLUDE WITH DELIVERANCE. Antiochus sent Appolonius who halted the sacrifices in June 167 B.C. and in December 25 of the same year set up the heathen altar and the heathen sacrifices began. On December 25, 164 BC, Judas Maccabeus restored the sanctuary and sacrificial system.
(http://www.prophecyforum.com/antiochus.html)

(www.123rf.com/photo_3952150_apamea)
Apamea, City of the Seleucid Kings on the Orontes River

The End Time Antichrist will come to the Same Desolation!

From verse thirty-five where it says, *even unto the time of the end*, the prophecy passes over the remainder of the Old Testament Age and the Present Church Dispensation unto the SEVENTIETH WEEK OF DANIEL. From our own pivotal point in time, the Eleventh Chapter of Daniel changes from history to prophecy. As the following shows, an age-spanning gap in the Scriptures is a common occurrence (Hutchings).

Several Examples of the Age Spanning Gaps in the Bible

E.W. Bullinger writes:

"There are many places in Scripture in which this passing over of the present Church Dispensation is very plainly evident; and where, in our reading, we have, like our Lord, to "close the book" (Lk 4:16-20).s If we fail to do this, and if we refuse to notice these so-called "gaps," we cannot possibly understand the Scriptures which we read.

We give a few by way of example, placing this mark **(—)** to indicate the parenthesis of this present Dispensation, which comes between the previous Dispensation of Law, and the next Dispensation of Judgment which is to follow this Present Dispensation of Grace. (*How to Enjoy the Bible*, pp.103,104).

• *The stone which the builders refused* ***(—)*** *is become the head-stone of the corner (Psa 118:22).*

• *For unto us a child is born, unto us a son is given:* ***(—)*** *and the government shall be upon his shoulder: and his name shall be called Wonderful, Counsellor, The mighty God, The everlasting Father, The Prince of Peace. (Isa 9:6; cp. Lk 1:31,32).*

• *It pleased the Lord to bruise him; he hath put him to grief; when thou shalt make his soul an offering for sin* ***(—)*** *he shall see his seed, he shall prolong his days, and the pleasure of the Lord shall prosper in his hands. He shall see of the travail of his soul and be satisfied (Isa 53:10,11).*

• *Rejoice greatly, O daughter of Zion; shout, O daughter of Jerusalem; behold, thy King cometh unto thee: he is just, and having salvation: lowly, and riding upon an ass, and upon a colt the foal of an ass.* ***(—)*** *And I will cut off the chariot from Ephraim, and the horse from Jerusalem, and the battle bow shall be cut off: and he shall speak peace unto the heathen: and his dominion shall be from sea even to sea, and from the river even to the ends of the earth (Zech 9:9,10).*

• *And, behold, thou shalt conceive in thy womb, and bring forth a son, and shalt call his name Jesus.* ***(—)*** *He shall be great, and shall be called the Son of the Highest: and the Lord God shall give unto him the throne of his father David (Lk 1:31,32).*

The Willful King, the Antichrist of the Last Days 11:36-45.

We are now introduced to the *Willful King* of the End Time. He is the Antichrist, and as the Antichrist he will ***do according to his will; and he shall exalt himself, and magnify himself above every god, and shall speak marvellous things against the God of gods*** *(11:36).* Daniel sees him exactly as the Apostles Paul and John saw him.

• *And out of one of them came forth* ***a little horn, which waxed exceeding great****, toward the south, and toward the east, and toward the pleasant land. And* ***it waxed great, even to the host of heaven****; and it cast down some of the host and of the stars to the ground, and stamped upon them. Yea,* ***he magnified himself even to the prince of the host****, and by him the daily sacrifice was taken away, and the place of the sanctuary was cast down (Dan 8:9-11).*

• *Who* ***opposeth and exalteth himself above all that is called God****, or that is worshipped; so that he as God sitteth in the temple of God, shewing himself that he is God (2 Thess 2:4).*

• *And they worshipped the dragon which gave power unto the beast: and* ***they worshipped the beast, saying, Who is like unto the beast?*** *who is able to make war with him (Rev 13:4)?*

The Willful King is Not the King of the North

Beginning at verse five of Chapter Eleven we have seen the warfare between successive kings of the north and south. Much more has been recorded concerning the kings of the north. This conflict has extended down to the description of Antiochus Epiphanes. A number of teachers believe that as Antiochus is clearly a type and foreshadowing of the Antichrist, and that as he is a king of the north, it is natural to expect that when we come to the End Time section of Daniel 11, the Willful King, who is clearly the Antichrist, is also the King of the

North. Many believe that he will be from the same geographic area as Antiochus (Syria or the general area) and will perhaps also be a lineal physical descendent of Antiochus Epiphanes.

Nevertheless as we begin reading this final section of Daniel 11, the term king of the north is not applied the Willful King. Nor is it found until verse 40, and here the King of the North is clearly distinguished from the previous description of the Willful King. In fact both the King of the North and the and King of the South are fighting against the Willful King!

> • And at the time of the end shall the king of the south push at **him**: and the king of the north shall come against **him** like a whirlwind, with chariots, and with horsemen, and with many ships; and **he** shall enter into the countries, and shall overflow and pass over (11:40).

Thus, there are *three* kings at war here. Yet this fact does not introduce a precedent in Daniel 11. In the previous section there was also a *third force*; and it was a *Roman Force*! The rising power of Rome, *the ships of Chittim*, began to intervene in the warfare of Antiochus the Great and Antiochus Epiphanes against Egypt. Likewise in the latter section, the Wilful King is the Roman Prince *that shall come* (Dan 9:26), and who will also be engaged with the latter day kings of the north and south.

> • After this shall he turn his face unto the isles, and shall take many: **but a prince for his own behalf shall cause the reproach offered by him to cease**; without his own reproach he shall cause it to turn upon him (11:18).

> • At the time appointed he shall return, and come toward the south; but it shall not be as the former, or as the latter. For **the ships of Chittim** shall come against him (11:29,30).

The pronouns further demonstrate the distinction between the Willful King and the King of the North. Throughout the ten verses (11:36-45) the pronouns (*he, him, himself*) naturally refer to the Willful King, the Antichrist, they do not, as some teach, transfer at verse 41 to the King of the North. To help the reader see this, the pronouns are highlighted. Reading the passage a number of times will I believe demonstrate that in every instance the thirty-one pronouns refer to the same individual, the Willful King, the Antichrist who is the subject of the entire passage. Note the pronouns in the three sections:

1. The Religion of the Willful King 11:36 -39

2. The Warfare of the Willful King 11:40-44

3. The Exaltation and End of the Willful King 11:45

The Religion of the Willful King 11:36 -39.

And the king shall do according to his will; and he shall exalt himself, and magnify himself above every god, and shall speak marvellous things against the God of gods, and shall prosper till the indignation be accomplished: for that that is determined shall be done. (11:37) Neither shall he regard the God of his fathers, nor the desire of women, nor regard any god: for he shall magnify himself above all. (11:38) But in his estate shall he honour the God of forces: and a god whom his fathers knew not shall he honour with gold, and silver, and with precious stones, and pleasant things. (11:39) Thus shall he do in the most strong holds with a strange god, whom he shall acknowledge and increase with glory: and he shall cause them to rule over many, and shall divide the land for gain.

The coming Antichrist will be willful. That is he will accept no will on earth but his own. The time for anything remotely approaching democracy is now over. Consensus in government; parliamentary democracy, counsel from advisors within a cabinet is no longer permitted. A king marches out on to the world stage that will do ***according to his will***. He ascends to a level never before seen; he is the Willful King. In order to stake his claim to such, he goes beyond man to God and claims that he is God. This passage describes three basic ways in which he does this:

(1) Self Exaltation 11:36.

(2) No Previous Precedents 11:37

(3) A New Kind of God 11:38,39

(1) Self Exaltation.

He Magnifies Himself Above All Religions. ***And the king shall do according to his will; and he shall exalt himself, and magnify himself above every god*** (11:36). Foreshadowed in this prophetic portrait of the Antichrist appears the final form of apostate religion succeeding the destruction of the *harlot system* of Revelation 17 by that sinister character himself. This religious monstrosity will be a combination of gross materialism, unbridled wickedness (the worship of sin by the Man of Sin), and brutal militarism. He is not only an absolute autocratic ruler; he is the ominous, self-deified king of kings. He will claim all divine honours to himself, magnifying himself above every god (2 Thess 2:4; Rev 13:6,7, 15), and compelling all, upon pain of death, to worship him (Rev 13:16-18).

He Blasphemes the True God: ***and shall speak marvellous things against the God of gods*** (11:36). The Antichrist will be worshipped, but this worship will include "in the same breath" blasphemy toward the God of Heaven.

> • And he opened his mouth in blasphemy against God, to blaspheme his name, and his tabernacle, and them that dwell in heaven (Rev 13:6).

He is Successful For a Time: ***and shall prosper till the indignation be accomplished: for that that is determined shall be done*** (11:37). This blasphemous self-deification will result in worldwide success. His dominion will prosper and enlarge. He will overcome all opposition. Tribulation believers if not martyred will go into hiding; Jews will flee the Land of Israel. The devil's man will have his day. He will have his day because the people of the world will become so sinful and wicked that they will want a wicked man to rule over them. When Israel cried for a king, God told Samuel to anoint them a dictator. The world is turning their backs on Christ today and crying for an Antichrist, and God will allow the nations to have their Antichrist *for a season*. God in judicial judgement will permit it to happen, but the *season* will be short. It will prosper, but only ***till the indignation be accomplished: for that that is determined shall be done*** (11:36).

> • Knowest thou not this of old, since man was placed upon earth, That the triumphing of the wicked is short, and the joy of the hypocrite but for a moment (Job 20:4,5).

(2) No Previous Precedents. ***Neither shall he regard the God of his fathers, nor the desire of women, nor regard any god: for he shall magnify himself above all*** (11:37). Three further statements are made. A great deal has been written about them, particularly the first and second. The fact that the statements are linked together indicates that they are speaking about the same general thing: *the religious policies of the Antichrist*. That means that the second statement, the *desire of women*, must have a connection with the first and third.

A COMMENTARY AND SURVEY SERIES: DANIEL

(http://greeceeu.weebly.com/uploads/2/8/5/6/28565437/2449611_orig.jpg)

Does "*Not Regard the God of His Fathers*" Refer to the Greek Orthodox Church ??

The Willful King Disregards His Ancestor's Faith. *Neither shall he regard the God of his fathers.* Many believe this means that the coming Antichrist will be Jewish. Certainly his covenant with the Jewish people in restoring their Temple and sacrifices on the Temple Mount points to this possibility; and even more so if they actually view him as a *messiah* (it is not clear that they will; compare John 5:46). As the phrase, *the God of his fathers*, does not include *Jehovah*, it is a lesser term than that generally used for the faith of the Jewish People (though it is used in 1 Chronicles 5:25; 2 Chronicles 20:30; 34:32).

> • And God said moreover unto Moses, Thus shalt thou say unto the children of Israel, the **LORD God of your fathers**, the God of Abraham, the God of Isaac, and the God of Jacob, hath sent me unto you: this is my name for ever, and this is my memorial unto all generations. Go, and gather the elders of Israel together, and say unto them, **The LORD God of your fathers**, the God of Abraham, of Isaac, and of Jacob, appeared unto me, saying, I have surely visited you, and seen that which is done to you in Egypt (Exod 3:15,16).
>
> • That they may believe that **the LORD God of their fathers**, the God of Abraham, the God of Isaac, and the God of Jacob, hath appeared unto thee (Exod 4:5).
>
> • **The LORD God of your fathers** make you a thousand times so many more as ye are, and bless you, as he hath promised you (Deut 1:11)!
>
> • Now therefore hearken, O Israel, unto the statutes and unto the judgments, which I teach you, for to do them, that ye may live, and go in and possess the land which **the LORD God of your fathers** giveth you (Deut 4:1).
>
> • And they forsook **the LORD God of their fathers**, which brought them out of the land of Egypt, and followed other gods, of the gods of the people that were round about them, and bowed themselves unto them, and provoked the LORD to anger (Jdg 2:12).

The question is an open one, but the simple fact that the Antichrist will hate the Jews and seek to destroy them makes it unlikely that he will be fully Jewish. The God of his fathers could just as easily refer to a Roman Catholic or Greek Orthodox background. Large sections of both have been anti-Semitic. As we have previously shown, Daniel seems to point to the origin of Antichrist in the Eastern or Grecian side of the Roman Empire.

DANIEL 11. JERUSALEM'S CONFLICT: ANCIENT DAYS AND LAST DAYS

Daniel Chapters 7/8/9/11 shows a narrowing focus to the origin of Antichrist

THE ANTICHRIST WILL COME FROM AMONG THE TEN (Dan 7:7,8). As the Ten Horns are clearly the same as the Ten *Roman* Toes of the great image (Daniel 2), the Antichrist will come from *among* ten powerful nations that had their origin in the Roman Empire. He does not directly come from one of the Ten, but from *among* one of these Ten.

THE ANTICHRIST WILL COME FROM AMONG FOUR OF THE TEN (Daniel 8:8,9). The Antichrist is seen coming from among the Four divisions of Alexander's Grecian Empire. These four divisions became part of the eastern half of the Roman Empire. He is not said to come directly from one of these four divisions, but rather *out of them* (he could hardly come from *each* of the four); thus the Antichrist has a special association with the Four without necessarily coming from one of them. This could possibly mean that he is Greek Catholic (Orthodox) rather than Roman Catholic.

The four regions taken by Alexander's generals were vast, and the language here indicates that their extent may ultimately be greater. They are *four notable ones toward the four winds of heaven*. In order for the Little Horn to *wax exceeding great, toward the south, and toward the east, and toward the pleasant land* (Dan 8:9), he would have to come either from the northwest of Alexander's Empire or from its north-western edge.

THE ANTICHRIST IS LINKED TO TITUS AND THE LEGIONS WHICH DESTROYED JERUSALEM (Dan 9:26). Titus himself, he was born in Rome. Before leading the onslaught on Jerusalem he served in Britannicus and was a military tribune in Germania. He then joined his father Vespasian in Greece where they drew up plans for the attack on the city. The Legion usually mentioned first in the attack on the city was the Fifth Macedonian. It was based in the Balkan provinces of Macedonia, Moesia (Serbia) and Dacia (Romania). After the fall of Jerusalem it left Judaea and returned to Oescus (Bulgaria). In the 2nd century the Fifth was in Dacia protecting the Danube frontier.

The north western setting of these historical facts lend an interesting parallel to the prophecy that the Little Horn will **wax exceeding great, toward the south, and toward the east, and toward the pleasant land** (Dan 8:9; thus from the northwest). We could speculate and say that the coming Antichrist may be from an Orthodox rather than Catholic background. Three European leaders are currently atheist (2016): Hollande of France, Tsipras of Greece and Milanovic of Croatia.

> • When I have bent Judah for me, filled the bow with Ephraim, and **raised up thy sons, O Zion, against thy sons, O Greece**, and made thee as the sword of a mighty man. And the LORD shall be seen over them, and his arrow shall go forth as the lightning: and the LORD God shall blow the trumpet, and shall go with whirlwinds of the south (Zech 9:13,14).

THE ANTICHRIST IS DISTINGUISHED FROM THE KING OF THE NORTH AND THE KING OF THE SOUTH (Daniel 11:36-45). This brings us to our present considerations. Daniel concludes his prophecy by showing that while the Antichrist does not necessarily originate from the Seleucid or Ptolemaic region, yet it is in this region that the future King of the North and King of the South fight against him, and it is in this area that he has his rise to power (11:40-45).

The Willful King Disregards the Norms of Faith.

Neither shall he regard the God of his fathers, <u>nor the desire of women</u>, nor regard any god (11:37). As the desire of women is the link between two statements dealing with *God*, it must also be a statement dealing with the "religion" of the Antichrist. Therefore it is not likely that it simply means "he will not be *distracted* by women".

Merrill Unger presents another and more common view:

The most plausible explanation, in the light of Daniel's Jewish background and Antichrist's prime persecuting energies that will be spent against the Jews, is that the reference is to the natural desire of Hebrew women to become the mother of the promised Messiah (Gen. 3:15), making the expression a symbol of the Messianic hope in general. The "desire of women" would be a subjective genitive: "that desired by women."

Favoring that interpretation is the contextual position of the phrase sandwiched between references to "the gods of his fathers" and "any god," suggesting that the Antichrist "would disregard the gods of the past as well as the promised Son of God who is to come from heaven" (J. F. Walvoord, *Daniel*, p. 275).

Nevertheless, as Arthur Bloomfield writes, "Jewish women in general today have no such desire or any knowledge of such a possibility; and even if they did, it would have nothing to do with the exaltation of the Antichrist. His interest in himself is so great that he has no time nor thought for women." (*The End of the Days, The Prophecies of Daniel Explained*).

It is likely that this is a reference to homosexuality. The *days of Lot* will characterise the days of the End Times. Those in Lot's time that were involved in this sin went about their daily lives as if life would go on forever. It did not!

• *Likewise also as it was in the days of Lot; they did eat, they drank, they bought, they sold, they planted, they builded; But the same day that Lot went out of Sodom it rained fire and brimstone from heaven, and destroyed them all. Even thus shall it be in the day when the Son of man is revealed (Luke 17:28-30).*

Will the *Huge* Homosexual Agenda of Barak Obama Prepare the Way for the Antichrist?

No international leader *in history* has gone so far as Barak Obama in seeking to bring homosexuality into every facet of American life and around the world. He has brought far more gay appointees into his administration than previous American presidents (by a very large margin!). His gay agenda has been the defining *characteristic* of his eight years in office. The defining *image* was the rainbow emblazoned White House after the passage of the USA gay marriage act. When Obama began his first term in 2009, only two states allowed gay marriage. The Supreme Court legalized gay marriage nationwide in June 2015.

First US President on the Cover of an LGBT Magazine. *Out* November 2015

In a 6 July 2016 article entitled, **Obama pushing pro-homosexual agenda on entire world!** Mathew Staver of *Liberty Counsel Action* reported the following.

"Here are some disturbing excerpts from a Presidential Memorandum signed by Barak Obama last week:

...I declared before heads of state gathered at the United Nations, 'no country should deny people their rights because of who they love, which is why we must stand up for the rights of gays and lesbians everywhere."

"Under my Administration, agencies engaged abroad have already begun taking action to promote the fundamental human rights of LGBT [Lesbian, Gay, Bisexual, Transgender] persons everywhere. Our deep commitment to advancing the human rights of all people is strengthened when we as the United States bring our tools to bear to vigorously advance this goal."

Under the guise of promoting human rights," President Obama has issued a memorandum outlining seven specific actions that the Department of State and other federal agencies will be required to implement on a global scale "to ensure that U.S. diplomacy and foreign assistance promote and protect the human rights of LGBT persons."

Under Obama's mandate, federal agencies are directed to offer moral, legal, and financial support to national and international organizations which support LGBT advancement – while preferential expedition and asylum will be offered to LGBT people allegedly forced to flee persecution in their home countries.

There is already mounting international backlash and disapproval from leaders of countries where sodomy or homosexuality is banned by law, which includes most of the Middle East, Africa, Latin America, and Oceania.

Among Barak Obama's presidential mandates:

• "To combat discrimination, homophobia, and intolerance on the basis of LGBT status or conduct." (Force acceptance of homosexuality whether a country wants to or not)

• "The Federal Government has the ability to identify and expedite resettlement of highly vulnerable [LGBT] persons with urgent protection needs." (Grant preferential asylum to those who claim LGBT status)

• "Ensure the Federal Government's swift and meaningful response to serious incidents that threaten the human rights of LGBT persons abroad." (Presumably, such a "response" could include U.S. military and/or police action)

• "Broaden the number of countries willing to support and defend LGBT issues in the multilateral arena." (Using United States pressure to advance the LGBT agenda by recruiting core "allies" in the community of nations)

All federal agencies involved in Obama's initiative are to file a report within 180 days of the December 6th announcement and submit subsequent annual reports to the Department of State, which will also be reviewed by the President. In short, our President is dictating that government agencies with foreign operations direct their workers to advance the LGBT agenda and then submit regular reports to him on how the effort is progressing. Under President Obama and his pro-homosexual administration, the forced reception of the radical LGBT agenda into our culture (including our military) – and now international society – is happening at unprecedented levels."

(http://www.fourwinds10.net/siterun_data/education/public/news.php?q=1467127070).

Will the *Huge* Homosexual Agenda of the Modern Church Prepare the Way for the Antichrist?

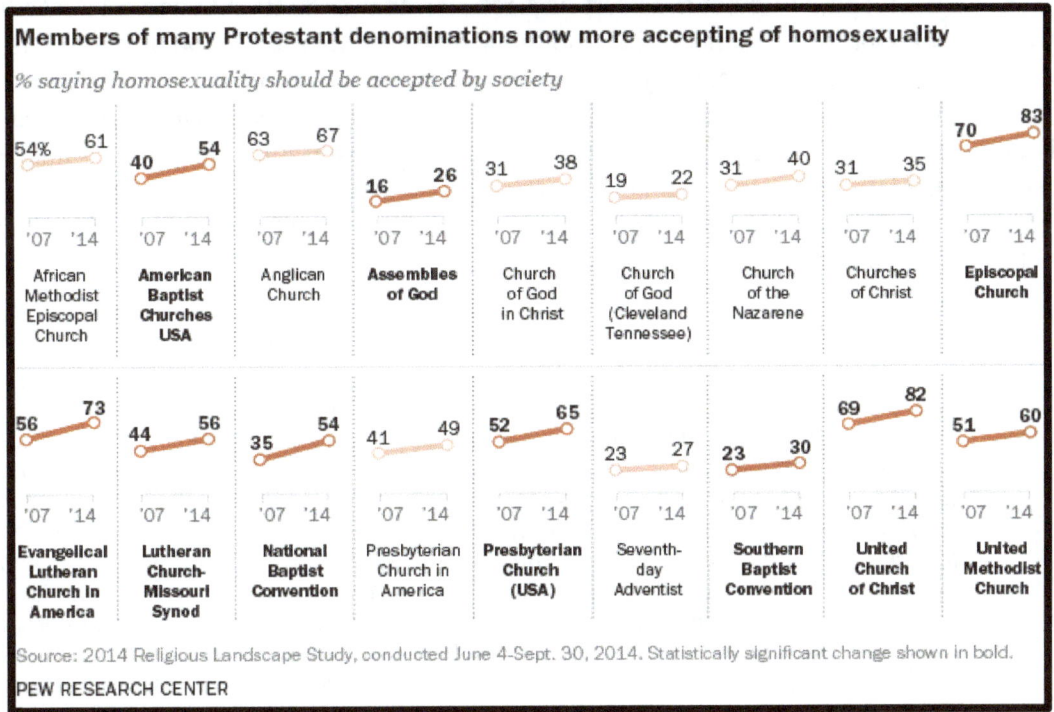

Thus the coming Willful King will disregard his ancestors faith; he will also disregard the norms of faith. That is, in his rise to power he will approve of a religion in which homosexuality plays a part, but ultimately he will not regard any faith – except that which is directed toward him.

The Willful King Will Disregard Any Faith: *nor regard any god: for he shall magnify himself above all.* While there may be debate as to the meaning of his not regarding *the God of his fathers*, nor *the desire of women desire*; yet with this statement, and as a further emphasis upon verse 36, we are left in no doubt as to the depths this man will plumb.

- *he shall exalt himself, and magnify himself above every god (11:36).*

The Antichrist will proclaim himself as being above everyone and every faith on earth (Isa. 14:13; 2 Thess 2:4). Imbued as he will be with the satanic spirit, with even try to imitate Christ's incarnation by being the incarnation of Satan himself (Isa 14:14; Rev 13:2).

The Willful King Will Install a Monstrous Faith.

Its Strength. *But in his estate shall he honour the God of forces: and a god whom his fathers knew not shall he honour with gold, and silver, and with precious stones, and pleasant things* (11:38).

Its Strangeness. *Thus shall he do in the most strong holds with a strange god, whom he shall acknowledge and increase with glory: and he shall cause them to rule over many, and shall divide the land for gain* (11:39).

This is a "Frankenstein" faith! This must certainly refer to the image of the Beast described in Revelation 13.

- *And deceiveth them that dwell on the earth by the means of those miracles which he had power to do in the sight of the beast; saying to them that dwell on the earth, that*

DANIEL 11. JERUSALEM'S CONFLICT: ANCIENT DAYS AND LAST DAYS

*they should **make an image to the beast**, which had the wound by a sword, and did live. And he had **power to give life unto the image of the beast**, that the image of the beast should both speak, and cause that as many as would not worship the image of the beast should be killed (Rev 13:14,15).*

This image will be at the heart of a religion that is STRONG and STRANGE. In the *estate* of *the God of his fathers*, the Antichrist will **honour the God of forces.** This is a god whose worship is not directed by Scripture, but rather by absolute and *brute force*. This is further expressed with the statement: ***Thus shall he do in the most strong holds*** (Dan 11:39). The military might of the entire world will be set up to insure that this god and this god alone is worshipped. It will be like but on a far greater scale than Nebuchadnezzar's ***god of forces*** on the plain of Dura. Note the ***great force*** that was used to coerce the worship of Nebuchadnezzar's god.

> • **Nebuchadnezzar the king made an image of gold**, whose height was **threescore cubits**, and the breadth thereof **six cubits**: he set it up in the plain of Dura, in the province of Babylon, **Then** Nebuchadnezzar the king sent to gather together the princes, the governors, and the captains, the judges, the treasurers, the counsellors, the sheriffs, and all the rulers of the provinces, to come to the dedication of the image which Nebuchadnezzar the king had set up. **Then** the princes, the governors, and captains, the judges, the treasurers, the counsellors, the sheriffs, and all the rulers of the provinces, were gathered together unto the dedication of the image that Nebuchadnezzarthe king had set up; and they stood before the image that Nebuchadnezzar had set up. **Then** an herald cried aloud, To you it is commanded, O people, nations, and languages, That at what time ye hear the sound of the cornet, flute, harp, sackbut, psaltery, dulcimer, and all kinds of musick, ye fall down and worship the golden image that Nebuchadnezzar the king hath set up: And **whoso falleth not down and worshippeth shall the same hour be cast into the midst of a burning fiery furnace** (Dan 3:1-6).

(https://s-media-cache-ak0.pinimg.com/236x/3f/92/8d/3f928dfd7a5391b8b44dcb3b91a19557.jpg)

The *God of Forces* at the Beginning of the Times of the Gentiles

The Times of the Gentiles begins and ends with the ***god of forces***. Worship in that day will be enforced by devastating and worldwide military force. It is the ***god of forces***, but it is also a ***strange god*** (11:39) that is used in concert with the worship of the Antichrist. All false religion and idolatry is *strange*, and *strange* in a wicked sense. But rising out of the plethora of 6000 years of idolatry, the world during the Tribulation will worship the ***strange god***. It will supersede all other gods

Some of what makes it strange is shown in the description of the Image of the Beast in Revelation 13. Unlike all other idols that stood motionless in mute silence, this will be a "living" idol. Something further of its strangeness can be seen in all that is lavished upon it. The Willful King is seen leading the entire world in preparing and adorning this idol.

- *shall he honour it with **gold**, and **silver**, and with **precious stones**, and **pleasant things**…. and increase with **glory** (Dan 11:38,39).*

- *saying to them **that dwell on the earth**, that they should make an image to the beast (Rev 13:14).*

This monstrous, strange, Frankenstein faith of the Wilful King concludes with a twofold statement: ***and he shall cause them to rule over many, and shall divide the land for gain*** (11:39). As this statement immediately follows the lavishing of the Antichrist's image, and as that image will be set up on the Temple Mount in Jerusalem, the ***them*** whom he ***causes to rule***, are very likely apostate Jews who directly support the transition that takes place at the midpoint of the Tribulation (Dan 9:27). "Those who honour him will he honour."

It will be the same as with those apostate Jews who aided Antiochus Epiphanes.

- *he shall even return, and have intelligence with them that forsake the holy covenant (11:30).*

As a further reward to those in Israel who aid him in the breaking of the covenant (Dan 9:27), he will parcel out parts of the Land of Israel. He ***shall divide the land for gain*** (11:39). Thus while he betrays the nation at large he will still among many Jewish people retain his power base in Israel. Christ promised the apostles that they would *sit upon twelve thrones judging the twelve tribes of Israel* (Matt 19:28); therefore, the Antichrist (who would also know this Scripture) may try to do the same and appoint governors over twelve divisions of Israel.

It is inferred also that when the Antichrist kills the two witnesses, many of the important people of his government will gather in Jerusalem for a big celebration, and seven thousand will be killed in an earthquake (Rev 11:13). *Hutchings*.

The Warfare of the Willful King 11:40-45.

And at the time of the end shall the king of the south push at him: and the king of the north shall come against him like a whirlwind, with chariots, and with horsemen, and with many ships; and he shall enter into the countries, and shall overflow and pass over. (11:41) He shall enter also into the glorious land, and many countries shall be overthrown: but these shall escape out of his hand, even Edom, and Moab, and the chief of the children of Ammon. (11:42) He shall stretch forth his hand also upon the countries: and the land of Egypt shall not escape. (11:43) But he shall have power over the treasures of gold and of silver, and over all the precious things of Egypt: and the Libyans and the Ethiopians shall be at his steps. (11:44) But tidings out of the east and out of the north shall trouble him: therefore he shall go forth with great fury to destroy, and utterly to make away many. (11:45) And he shall plant the tabernacles of his palace between the seas in the glorious holy mountain; yet he shall come to his end, and none shall help him.

The end of Chapter 11 describes a devastating war. It will likely take place near the middle of the seven year Tribulation. It will take place in the Middle East. There are three protagonists. The Willful King, to whom we were introduced in verse 36, continues to be the primary subject in these concluding verses of Chapter 11. He is the Antichrist, the Roman *Prince that shall come* (Dan 9:26). Fighting against him is the King of South, a pan Arab/African coalition; and the King of the North, Russia with other nations from the north and the far flung reaches of the old Seleucid Empire.

The Daniel 11:40-45 war coincides with Ezekiel 38,39, the Gog and Magog invasion of Israel. Russia's centuries-old dream has been to dominate the Middle East in order to secure the land bridge of Israel and Egypt, enabling them to have warm, year-round harbours and (with the Suez Canal) ready access to the oceans of the world.

The Daniel 11:40-45 / Ezekiel 38,39 war will likely also coincide with Satan being cast out of Heaven at the mid-point of the Tribulation (Rev 12:6-9), and the Antichrist breaking his covenant with Israel (Dan 9:27). At this time the Antichrist will rise to totally dominant power in the world (Rev 13:4,5).

Russia will feel that she can move against Israel because that though the Antichrist has made a covenant with Israel, he does not have a military presence there sufficient to thwart an attack by Russia. It is only after this that the Antichrist is able to become militarily dominant in the Middle East.

Warfare in the Middle of the Tribulation: Daniel 11:40-45 and Ezekiel 38, 39.

We have previously looked at the likelihood that another war; that described in Psalm 83, will take place near the beginning of the Tribulation. It will be fought by Israel against her immediate neighbours and remove the threat posed by them. The relative peace she then enjoys will make it easier for the Antichrist to enter into a seven year covenant with her (Dan 9:26,27). Both the Antichrist and Russia will move their armies into Israel at the midpoint of the Tribulation. This will be triggered by the casting out of Satan upon the earth (Rev 12:6-9). This will be Satan's two-pronged attempt to destroy Israel and thus destroy the Messianic expectancy.

We consider first the King of the North and his invasion as described in Ezekiel 38,39 and Daniel 11. It becomes apparent this can only take place at the midpoint of the Tribulation; not its end or beginning.

THE INVASION OF RUSSIA AND HER ALLIES

And at the time of the end shall the king of the south push at him: and the king of the north shall come against him like a whirlwind, with chariots, and with horsemen, and with many ships; and he shall enter into the countries, and shall overflow and pass over (11:40).

The King of the South in the *fulfilled* section of Daniel 11 is Egypt and the Ptolemaic Empire. As we come to the *unfulfilled* section, the question arises as to whether it is still Egypt, or an Arab/African coalition in which Egypt does not have a central role (or any role at all). The answer is not directly given.

Looking at the King of the North, there is little doubt that this is Russia. The Seleucid Empire extended into southern Russia and the descriptions in Ezekiel 38,39 points strongly to Russia. But, as the King of the South and King of the North are assumed to move in concert against the Willful King, it is noteworthy that Ezekiel does not mention Egypt as one of Russia's allies, instead it is Ethiopia and Libya.

*● **Persia, Ethiopia, and Libya** with them; all of them with shield and helmet: Gomer, and all his bands; the house of Togarmah of the north quarters, and all his bands: and many people with thee (Ezek 38:5,6).*

After the Russian invader is destroyed by God, the Willful King (Antichrist) will move his armies against Ethiopia, Libya and also Egypt.

(11:43) But he shall have power over the treasures of gold and of silver, and over all the precious things of Egypt: and the Libyans and the Ethiopians shall be at his steps.

1. The Russian Invasion will Cause Both Israel and the Nations to *Know* the Lord

The fact that seven years will be needed to clear the rubble in in the Israel after the Ezekiel 38,39 war has led many to believer that Russia as the King of the North would invade Israel at the beginning of the Tribulation.

> • And they that dwell in the cities of Israel shall go forth, and shall set on fire and burn the weapons, both the shields and the bucklers, the bows and the arrows, and the handstaves, and the spears, and they shall burn them with fire **seven years**: So that they shall take no wood out of the field, neither cut down any out of the forests; for they shall burn the weapons with fire: and they shall spoil those that spoiled them, and rob those that robbed them, saith the Lord GOD (Ezek 39:9,10).

However, from the day that Russia is defeated on the *mountains of Israel*, that Nation will begin to *know* the Lord. It will be an event that will catapult them into the knowledge of true Messianic faith. Such could not be the case at the beginning of the Tribulation; for then they will be following Antichrist for the next three and one half years. And, as there are too many differences to make this battle the same as Armageddon at the end of the Tribulation (for example, a northern confederation rather than the entire world; Rev 16:13,14); the mid- point is the only likely place that it can occur. Therefore this seven year cleaning up of the battlefield will extend into the Millennial Reign.

Note the ***might know*** passages in Ezekiel 38,39:

> • And thou shalt come up against my people of Israel, as a cloud to cover the land; it shall be in the latter days, and I will bring thee against my land, that the heathen **may know me**, when I shall be sanctified in thee, O Gog, before their eyes (38:16).

> • Thus will I magnify myself, and sanctify myself; and **I will be known** in the eyes of many nations, and **they shall know** that I am the LORD (38:23).

> • And I will send a fire on Magog, and among them that dwell carelessly in the isles: and **they shall know** that I am the LORD. So will I make my holy name known in the midst of my people Israel; and I will not let them pollute my holy name any more: and **the heathen shall know** that I am the LORD, the Holy One in Israel (38:6,7).

> • Yea, all the people of the land shall bury them; and **it shall be to them a renown** the day that I shall be glorified, saith the Lord GOD (38:13).

> • And I will set my glory among the heathen, and **all the heathen shall see my judgment** that I have executed, and my hand that I have laid upon them. So the house of Israel **shall know** that I am the LORD their God from that day and forward (38:21,22).

> • Thus will I magnify myself, and sanctify myself; and **I will be known in the eyes of many nations, and they shall know that I am the LORD** (38:23).

> • And I will set my glory among the heathen, and **all the heathen shall see my judgment** that I have executed, and my hand that I have laid upon them (39:21).

> • Then shall they know that I am the LORD their God, which caused them to be led into captivity among the heathen: but I have gathered them unto their own land, and have left none of them any more there. Neither will I hide my face any more from them: for I have **poured out my spirit** upon the house of Israel, saith the Lord GOD (39:28,29).

"In Revelation 7:4-17 there is a description of a multitude of Jews and of Gentiles who are saved during the tribulation period. One wonders, in the face of the intense persecution against any believer, how any come to a knowledge of God in that time. In Ezekiel 38:23 it is revealed that the destruction of the armies of Gog is used as a sign to the nations and in 39:21 reference is made to this same fact again. In 39:22 the same event is a great sign to Israel. Since the book of Revelation pictures many people saved during the tribulation, and not just at the end of it, and since this event of Ezekiel's prophecy is used as a sign to bring many to the Lord, this event must have taken place before the end of the tribulation and at some time within that period. This destruction, so obviously by the hand of the Lord, is an event used by the Lord to remove some of the blindness to bring many to a knowledge of the Lord." (Dwight Pentecost, *Things to Come*, p. 353).

During the last three and one half years of the Tribulation, and with the Antichrist at the height of his power, both Israel and the nations will have this battle to think about! It will be a sign that as God has intervened so powerfully in the middle of the Tribulation, He will do so again, and much more so, at its end.

2. The Russian Invasion Occurs When Israel is at Peace

Israel will not only have defeated her immediate neighbours (near the beginning of the Tribulation), but she will also be experiencing the false peace of the Antichrist's covenant (Dan 9:26; Isa 28:15). Her dwelling in peace is a repeated point in Ezekiel 38,39; thus the invasion cannot occur at the end of the Tribulation.

> • *After many days thou shalt be visited: in the latter years thou shalt come into the land that is brought back from the sword, and is gathered out of many people, against the mountains of Israel, which have been always waste: but it is brought forth out of the nations, and* **they shall dwell safely** *all of them (Ezek 38:8).*

> • *And thou shalt say, I will go up to* **the land of unwalled villages**; *I will go to them that are* **at rest**, *that* **dwell safely**, *all of them* **dwelling without walls**, *and having* **neither bars nor gates** *(Ezek 38:11).*

> • *Therefore, son of man, prophesy and say unto Gog, Thus saith the Lord GOD; In that day when my people of Israel* **dwelleth safely**, *shalt thou not know it (Ezek 38:14)?*

"Those who believe that this invasion takes place at the beginning of the millennium interpret this peace as the peace promised by the Messiah. There is nothing in the text here to indicate that this is the true Messianic peace. It rather seems to be the false peace that has been guaranteed Israel by the covenant, which is called *your agreement with hell* in (Isa 28:18). Israel, as yet, is in unbelief, for the nation will not be a believing nation until after the Second Advent of Christ. This regathering is described in Ezekiel 37 and the lifeless condition of the nation is clearly indicated in 37:8. Israel could not be said to be at peace at the end of the Tribulation period, for the land has been destroyed by invasion (Zech 14:1-3) and the people scattered (Zech 13:8,9). Yet, the nation could be dwelling in relative peace in the land in the first half of the week. It is altogether possible that the first judgments of the tribulation may not affect Israel so as to destroy the beauty and prosperity of the land." (Pentecost, p. 351).

3. The Casting Out of Satan Will Trigger the Russian Invasion and Corresponding Events

"The event that causes the Beast to move in is the invasion of Israel from the north by the King of the North (Dan 11:40). The covenant made by the Beast (Dan 9:27) has evidently guaranteed Israel an inviolate right to the Land. Some event must be necessary to cause the Beast to abrogate his covenant. Since the covenant is said to be broken in the middle of the week (Dan 9:27) and the invasion from the north is seen to be the cause of the breaking of the covenant (Dan. 11:41) it may be concluded that this invasion takes place in the middle of the week.

It is recognized that the events of the last half of the week are occasioned by the casting of Satan out of heaven (Rev 12:7-13). Evidently Satan's first act in opposition to Israel is to move the King of the North to this invasion...In Isaiah 30:31-33; 31:8,9, and Micah 5:5 this invader from the north is called "the Assyrian." As Assyria was a rod in the hand of the Lord previously to punish Israel for their iniquity, so the Lord will take up a rod again for the same purpose. This coming scourge will bear the same name because of the identity of his mission, to chasten Israel. Isaiah 28:18 speaks of *the covenant with death* and *the agreement with hell* for which God will punish Israel. This must refer to the covenant of Daniel 9:27, when Israel seeks peace from the hands of men rather than from the hand of the Lord. For this covenant, Isaiah says, they will be punished *when the overflowing scourge shall pass through, then ye shall be trodden down by it* (Isa 28:18). This scourge could hardly be the occupation by the Beast, for he was a party to the covenant, but must refer to the invasion by the "Assyrian" who will be used by the Lord to chasten Israel. The destruction of the Assyrian in the passages referred to seems to parallel the destruction of the armies of Gog in Ezekiel 38—39, and thus, are considered parallel references. God could not punish Israel for this false covenant until after the covenant had been made. This seems to give further cause to believe that the invasion takes place sometime in the middle of the week." (Pentecost, pp. 352,353).

4. Russia's Defeat Makes Possible Antichrist's Three and One Half Year Control of the Earth

"In Revelation 13:7 the Beast is pictured as having a world-wide power. This is true at the time of his manifestation as a world ruler in the middle of the Tribulation. The question arises: How could the Beast have world-wide power if the power of the northern confederation has not been broken? The fact that the Beast is in authority over the earth at the middle of the week lends support to the thesis that the King of the North has been destroyed. This destruction would produce a chaos in the world conditions, which would bring the nations together as is seen in Psalm 2, at which time the government would be formed over which the Beast is the head. Since there could be no unity of nations as long as the King of the North is operative, this unity must be brought about after his destruction." (pp. 353,354).

"The chronology of several important passages dealing with these events seems to support the thesis. In Isaiah 30 and 31 there is a description of the destruction of the King of the North. This is followed in Isaiah 33 and 34 with the destruction of all the nations, and then follows a description of the millennium in Isaiah 35. In the book of Joel we find the same chronology. In Joel 2 there is the description of the invasion by the northern army (v. 20), followed by a description of the destruction of the nations in Joel 3 and then the millennium is described in 3:17-21. In both of these passages the chronology is the same. The armies of the north are destroyed at a separate time, in a distinct movement, prior to the destruction of the armies of the nations, which will be followed by the millennium. To place the events in the middle of the week is the only position consistent with the chronology of these extended passages." (Pentecost, p. 354).

II. THE INVASION BY THE ARMIES OF THE WILLFUL KING

(11:40) And at the time of the end shall the king of the south push at him: and the king of the north shall come against him like a whirlwind, with chariots, and with horsemen, and with many ships; and he shall enter into the countries, and shall overflow and pass over. (11:41) He shall enter also into the glorious land, and many countries shall be overthrown: but these shall escape out of his hand, even Edom, and Moab, and the chief of the children of Ammon. (11:42) He shall stretch forth his hand also upon the countries: and the land of Egypt shall not escape. (11:43) But he shall have power over the treasures of gold and of silver, and over all the precious things of Egypt: and the Libyans and the Ethiopians shall be at his steps. (11:44) But tidings out of the east and out of the north shall trouble him: therefore he shall go forth with great fury to destroy, and utterly to make away many. (11:45) And he shall plant the tabernacles of his palace between the seas in the glorious holy mountain; yet he shall come to his end, and none shall help him.

Note again the pronouns: Beginning at verse 36 and here in verses 41-45, *all* the pronouns apply to the Willful King, none to the King of the North. Though the King of the South and the King of the North *come against him*, it is still the Willful King who is the primary subject and the antecedent of the pronouns. This is the view of two of the three widely read prophecy teachers from the *old* Dallas Theological Seminary. John Walvoord and J. Dwight Pentecost believed that all the pronouns beginning from verse 36 and to the end of the chapter refer to the Willful King; whereas Merrill Unger believed that with the first *he* in verse 40 (and to the end of the chapter) it is referring to Russia.

Pentecost says:

> Verses 40-45 can hardly describe the activities of the combined forces of the Kings of the North and the South, for the pronoun "they" would have been used. Since "he" is used, the passage must describe further the activities of the Wilful King (p. 356).

The great victories described in verses 40-44 could hardly refer to Russia, for Russia will be destroyed as soon as soon as her armies attack Israel (Ezek 38,39). Any remaining doubt is removed in verse 45, a statement that could only refer to Antichrist, not Russia.

> • And *he* shall plant the tabernacles of *his* palace between the seas in the glorious holy mountain.

The Antichrist is not mentioned in Ezekiel 38,39 (cp. Ezek 38:13), and that likely for the reason that he has absolutely nothing to do with the destruction of the Russian armies; this is entirely the work of God. Further, the Antichrist in the first half of the Tribulation and the months leading up to the midpoint is not seen as having massive armies stationed in Israel, but rather he is the *guarantor* of the covenant with Israel. It is his authority rather than his resident military might that is at issue.

Ezekiel 38:12 states that Russia will come against Israel for *spoil*; but now in Daniel 9:26,27 and 11:40 the further motive is inferred that Russia invades to challenge the Antichrist's influence in Israel. With Israel at ease in its unwalled cities (Ezek 38:11), and not protected by a "boots on the ground" foreign army, Russia army views this invasion as "easy pickings". The opposite of what she expects takes place.

> *(38:19) For in **my jealousy** and in the fire of **my wrath** have I spoken, Surely in that day there shall be a great shaking in the land of Israel; (38:20) So that the fishes of the sea, and the fowls of the heaven, and the beasts of the field, and all creeping things that creep upon the earth, and all the men that are upon the face of the earth, shall shake at my presence, and the mountains shall be thrown down, and the steep places shall fall, and every wall shall fall to the ground. (38:21) And **I will call for a sword** against him throughout all my mountains, saith the Lord GOD: every man's sword shall be against his brother. (38:22) And **I will plead** against him with pestilence and with blood; and **I will rain** upon him, and upon his bands, and upon the many people that are with him, an overflowing rain, and great hailstones, fire, and brimstone. (38:23) **Thus will I magnify myself**, and sanctify myself; and **I will be known** in the eyes of many nations, and they shall know that I am the LORD. (39:1) Therefore, thou son of man, prophesy against Gog, and say, Thus saith the Lord GOD; Behold, **I am against thee, O Gog**, the chief prince of Meshech and Tubal: (39:2) And **I will turn thee back**, and leave but the sixth part of thee, and will cause thee to come up from the north parts, and will bring thee upon the mountains of Israel: (39:3) And **I will smite** thy bow out of thy left hand, and will cause thine arrows to fall out of thy right hand. (39:4) Thou shalt fall upon the mountains of Israel, thou, and all thy bands, and the people that is with thee: **I will give thee** unto the ravenous birds of every sort, and to the beasts of the field to be devoured. (39:5) Thou shalt fall upon the open field: for **I have spoken it**, saith the Lord GOD. (39:6) And **I will send a fire** on Magog, and among them that dwell carelessly in the isles: and they shall know that I am the LORD. (39:7) **So will I make** my holy name known in the midst of my people Israel; and I will not let them pollute my holy name any more: and the heathen shall know that I am the LORD, the Holy One in Israel.*

The *I wills* show that this is entirely the work of God. Though the world is amazed and shaken at the catastrophic defeat of Russia, the Antichrist will refuse to recognize it as Divine intervention and will see it instead as an opportunity to break his covenant with Israel and move his own armies into the Middle East.

Six Steps of Antichrist to World Dominion and Utter Dissolution

Shortly after the midpoint of the Tribulation, the Antichrist will achieve military dominance over the entire world.

> • And they worshipped the dragon which gave power unto the beast: and they worshipped the beast, saying, Who is like unto the beast? **who is able to make war with him** (Rev 13:4)?
>
> • And it was given unto him to make war with the saints, and to overcome them: and **power was given him over all kindreds, and tongues, and nations**. And all that dwell upon the earth shall worship him, whose names are not written in the book of life of the Lamb slain from the foundation of the world (Rev 13:7,8).

Beginning with the first *he* in Daniel 11:40 we see six steps that the Antichrist will take on the road to world dominion and then (!) utter and ignominious defeat.

ONE: *he shall enter into the countries, and shall overflow and pass over* (11:40). Dominion for good or bad begins in Israel and the Middle East. It is the land bridge between three continents. *This is Jerusalem, I have set it in the midst of the nations* (Ezek 5:5). The Antichrist knows this also, and at the beginning of his path to the military domination of the world, the starting point is Israel and the surrounding nations. It will also be that way when Christ returns:

> • Consume them in wrath, consume them, that they may not be: and let them know that **God ruleth in Jacob unto the ends of the earth**. Selah (Psalm 59:13).

TWO: ***He shall enter also into the glorious land, and many countries shall be overthrown: but these shall escape out of his hand, even Edom, and Moab, and the chief of the children of Ammon*** (11:41). In addition to the surrounding nations, and likely the very nations Israel defeated in the Psalm 83 war at the beginning of the Tribulation, the Antichrist enters Israel itself. It is called the *glorious land*, for it is *Immanuel's Land* (Isa 8:8), and there Immanuel walked among men, and to it Immanuel will return. The area that escapes the Antichrist's onslaught, present day Jordan, may be the *wilderness* to which Israel flees.

> • When ye therefore shall see the abomination of desolation, spoken of by Daniel the prophet, stand in the holy place, (whoso readeth, let him understand:) Then let them which be in Judaea **flee into the mountains**....For then shall be great tribulation, such as was not since the beginning of the world to this time, no, nor ever shall be (Matt 24:15,16,21).
>
> • And the woman **fled into the wilderness**, where she hath a place prepared of God, that they should feed her there a thousand two hundred and threescore days (Rev 12:6).

THREE: ***He shall stretch forth his hand also upon the countries: and the land of Egypt shall not escape* (11:42)**. *But he shall have power over the treasures of gold and of silver, and over all the precious things of Egypt: and the Libyans and the Ethiopians shall be at his steps* (11:42,43). Egypt in the past had been a refuge for the children of Israel, but the fact that Egypt will not escape the Antichrist's invasion means that Israel will not be able to find refuge there during the Tribulation. By controlling Egypt, the Antichrist will control the Suez Canal and the huge sums Egypt has amassed from that crucial waterway.

Note again that here Libya and Ethiopia are objects of the Willful King's aggression, whereas in Ezekiel they are allies of Russia (38:5), therefore the Willful King and the King of the North are not the same. Libya's oil fields would be prized acquisition; especially if the fields to the north (*Persia*, Ezek 38:5) were destroyed in Russia's invasion.

FOUR: ***But tidings out of the east and out of the north shall trouble him: therefore he shall go forth with great fury to destroy, and utterly to make away many*** (11:44). The Antichrist will receive word of the westward march of the 200,000,000 man Chinese army. This massive army begins to march at the blowing of the sixth trumpet during the midpoint period of the Tribulation. It will leave in its wake the death of one third of the world's population. Nevertheless, the passage here indicates that it will be neutralized by the armies of the Willful King. Note that this is not the same as the *Kings of the East* army that moves toward Israel and Armageddon at the end of the Tribulation (Rev 16:12-16).

> • And the number of the army of the horsemen were **two hundred thousand thousand**: and I heard the number of them. And thus I saw the horses in the vision, and them that sat on them, having breastplates of fire, and of jacinth, and brimstone: and the heads of the horses were as the heads of lions; and out of their mouths issued fire and smoke and brimstone. **By these three was the third part of men killed**, by the fire, and by the smoke, and by the brimstone, which issued out of their mouths (Rev 9:16-18).

The Antichrist is also troubled by reports *out of the north*. This may refer to the "home guard" of Russia's army which did not take part in the Ezekiel 38,39 invasion. The following passages may or may not be a reference to this.

> • Gomer, and all his bands; **the house of Togarmah of the north quarters**, and all his bands: and many people with thee (Ezek 38:6).

> • And I will turn thee back, and **leave but the sixth part of thee**, and will cause thee to come up from the north parts, and will bring thee upon the mountains of Israel (39:2).

> • And **I will send a fire on Magog**, and among them that dwell carelessly in the isles: and they shall know that I am the LORD (Ezek 39:6).

FIVE: ***And he shall plant the tabernacles of his palace between the seas in the glorious holy mountain*** (11:45).. This event is in addition to all the other things the Antichrist will do in the Jewish Temple and on the Temple Mount. As we have seen in Chapter 8, Antichrist's activities in the Tribulation Temple will last for 2300 days (8:13,14). It is comprised of two proceedings: **(1)** *the daily sacrifice,* and **(2)** *the transgression of desolation*, The *daily sacrifice* will last for three and one half years or 1260 days. The Antichrist having made the Covenant with Israel and allowing them to resume their sacrifices will make certain that he himself receives maximum publicity for this action. A daily world-wide telecast, every morning and every evening, will extol the *great man of peace* (Dan 8:25) on the Temple Mount. For these 1260 days he will appear as Israel's benefactor and will give warm "lip service" to the God of Israel. But all will change. He will unexpectedly be *seen* in this telecast in an altogether different light; and for the remaining 1040 days (2300 − 1260 = 1040 days) he will *appear* as the object of the world's worship.

> • Who opposeth and exalteth himself above all that is called God, or that is worshipped; so that he as God sitteth in the temple of God, **shewing himself** that he is God (2 Thess 2:4).

Less than five months (140 days) before the Return of Christ (1260 + 1260 − 2300 = 220 days; 360 − 220 = 140 days), the "lights will go out" on this worldwide telecast.

> • And the fifth angel poured out his vial upon the seat of the beast; and **his kingdom was full of darkness**; and they gnawed their tongues for pain (Rev 16:10).

We now discover, and amidst all else that is happening on the Temple Mount, that another structure will be erected. Like Solomon with his palace that he spent *thirteen years building* (1 Kng 7:1), the Antichrist will **plant the tabernacles of his palace…in the glorious holy mountain.** With this grand palace he will, rather than Rome or any other city, declare Jerusalem as his world capital. In Jerusalem where Jehovah has placed His Name (2 Chron 6:6), the Beast has reached the pinnacle of his power, but in a short time *the lights will go out!*

SIX: ***yet he shall come to his end, and none shall help him*** (11:45). "When the nations of the earth are gathered together around Jerusalem (Zech 14:1-3) and the valley of Jehoshaphat (Joel 3:2), the Lord will return to destroy all Gentile world powers so that He might rule the nations Himself. This is further described in Zechariah 12:1-9; 14:1-4; Isaiah 33:1—34:17; 63:1-6; 66:15-16; Jeremiah 25:27-33; Revelation 20:7-10" (*Pentecost*). The world *wondered* at him and *worshipped* him but at the *end, none shall help him* (Rev 13:3-8).

- *And I saw the beast, and the kings of the earth, and their armies, gathered together to make war against him that sat on the horse, and against his army. And the beast was taken, and with him the false prophet that wrought miracles before him, with which he deceived them that had received the mark of the beast, and them that worshipped his image. These both were cast alive into a lake of fire burning with brimstone. And the remnant were slain with the sword of him that sat upon the horse, which sword proceeded out of his mouth: and all the fowls were filled with their flesh (Rev 19:19-21).*

- *Therefore wait ye upon me, saith the LORD, until the day that I rise up to the prey: for my determination is to gather the nations, that I may assemble the kingdoms, to pour upon them mine indignation, even all my fierce anger: for all the earth shall be devoured with the fire of my jealousy (Zeph 3:8).*

II THE TIMES OF THE GENTILES REGARDING JERUSALEM 8-12

C. The Desolations and Final Blessing of Jerusalem 10-12

    1. Desolations and The Glory of Christ 10

    2. Desolations: Future to Daniel 11:1-35

    3. Desolations and Glory: Future to Us 11:36-12:13

DANIEL 12. THE CHARACTER AND TIMES OF THE GREAT TRIBULATION

Chapter 12 now concludes the prophecy which began in Chapter 10, and with Chapter 12 we have the conclusion of the Old Testament's foundational Book on Bible Prophecy. The final chapter has two main sections. Both deal with the second half of the Tribulation. As bad as the first half of the Tribulation is, the second half becomes the *Great* Tribulation.

    1. The Character of the Great Tribulation 12:1-4

    2. The Times of the Great Tribulation 12:5-13

The Character of the Great Tribulation 12:1-4.

And at that time shall Michael stand up, the great prince which standeth for the children of thy people: and there shall be a time of trouble, such as never was since there was a nation even to that same time: and at that time thy people shall be delivered, every one that shall be found written in the book.

(12:2) And many of them that sleep in the dust of the earth shall awake, some to everlasting life, and some to shame and everlasting contempt.

(12:3) And they that be wise shall shine as the brightness of the firmament; and they that turn many to righteousness as the stars for ever and ever. (12:4) But thou, O Daniel, shut up the words, and seal the book, even to the time of the end: many shall run to and fro, and knowledge shall be increased.

This final Chapter of Daniel begins abruptly with the words, And at that time. There is no time for introduction. All niceties in preparing the reader are suspended. This time is stated starkly and ominously in the last verse of Chapter 11.

    • *And he shall plant the tabernacles of his palace between the seas in the glorious holy mountain (11:45).*

This is a summary statement concerning the abomination of desolation. Chapter 12 begins **at that time**. That time is called the Great Tribulation. By what authority do we call this period the Great Tribulation? It is by the authority of the Lord Jesus Christ. That is what He called it (Matt 24:21). And that is what the Spirt of Christ speaking in Daniel (1 Pet 1:11) calls it here. In these opening verses of Daniel 12 we have the darkest picture imaginable and yet rising from it we have the brightest light possible.

<u>The Satanic Horror and Angelic Victory During the Great Tribulation</u>. ***And at that time shall Michael stand up, the great prince which standeth for the children of thy people: and***

there shall be a time of trouble, such as never was since there was a nation even to that same time (12:1). The opening phrase of the chapter, *At that time*, marks out a time of infamy far beyond anything the world has seen. It will take place on the Temple Mount in Jerusalem. This is the one place in all the earth which to the LORD is *His Hill*, where he has placed His *Name* and will shortly set *His King*.

- *But I have chosen Jerusalem, that **my name** might be there (2 Chron 2:6).*

- *Yet have I set **my king** upon **my holy hill** of Zion (Psalm 2:6).*

At that time and when in that place the Antichrist **will plant** the tabernacles of his palace, **shall Michael stand up** (cp. Dan 10:21). At the time the Antichrist commits the abomination of desolation; *at the time* he receives and recovers from a deadly wound (Rev 13:3); at the time the forty two months of the Great Tribulation begin (Rev 14:5); *at the time* Israel flees into the wilderness; **at that time shall Michael stand up**. This *standing up* by the Archangel Michael is described in Revelation 12 when he casts Satan to the earth.

- *And there was war in heaven: **Michael and his angels fought against the dragon**; and the dragon fought and his angels, And prevailed not; neither was their place found any more in heaven. And **the great dragon was cast out**, that old serpent, called the Devil, and Satan, which deceiveth the whole world: **he was cast out into the earth**, and his angels were cast out with him (Rev 12:7-9).*

This may well be the event to which Christ referred when He said: *I beheld Satan as lightning fall from heaven* (Lk 10:18). And (!) as Noah Hutchings explains, it may ultimately be to this angelic warfare during the Tribulation that the famous passage in Isaiah 14 refers.

When Michael and his army of angels go to help Israel, the devil and all his angels stand in the way to prevent it. It is then that the battle that began when Lucifer, the bright and shining one, who left his estate to oppose God, will be finally joined. The issue can be delayed no longer — one must be the ultimate victor and one must be the final loser. Those who worship the devil in Satan's churches believe that the devil will win this war, but the Bible says that God's forces under the leadership of Michael will win it.

Michael's army will rout the army of Satan and he and all his fallen angels will be cast out of the heavens unto the earth...From Ezekiel 28:18 it is evident that the devil and his angels hold strong and well-fortified sanctuaries in outer space.

- *Thou hast defiled thy sanctuaries by the multitude of thine iniquities, by the iniquity of thy traffick; therefore will I bring forth a fire from the midst of thee, it shall devour thee, and I will bring thee to ashes upon the earth in the sight of all them that behold thee (Ezek 28:18).*

- *And it shall come to pass in that day, that the LORD shall punish **the host of the high ones** that are on high, and the kings of the earth upon the earth (Isa 24:21).*

- *For we wrestle not against flesh and blood, but against principalities, against powers, against the rulers of the darkness of this world, against **spiritual wickedness in high places** (Eph 6:12).*

Once the Devil is cast down to earth, he will enter into the body of Antichrist and the man of sin will become Satan incarnate. In conjunction with this event, let us consider Isaiah chapter fourteen:

- *How art thou fallen from heaven, O Lucifer, son of the morning! how art thou cut down to the ground, which didst weaken the nations! (Isa 14:12).*

This refers prophetically to the casting of Satan and his angels out of the heavens down to the earth by Michael [Note the mention of nations. There were no nations is past eternity. Thus Isaiah 14 must ultimately be referring to the future].

DANIEL 12. THE CHARACTER AND TIMES OF THE GREAT TRIBULATION

> • *For thou hast said in thine heart, I will ascend into heaven, I will exalt my throne above the stars of God: I will sit also upon the mount of the congregation, in the sides of the north: I will ascend above the heights of the clouds; I will be like the most High (Isa 14:13,14).*

These two verses describe Satan's ambition from the very beginning of his rebellion against God's sovereign authority. During the Tribulation, he will make his supreme effort to take over the universe and rule over God. Satan worshippers today believe that he will succeed.

> • *Yet thou shalt be brought down to hell, to the sides of the pit. They that see thee shall narrowly look upon thee, and consider thee, saying, Is this the man that made the earth to tremble, that did shake kingdoms (Isa 14:15,16).*

This scene describes Satan's estate as he takes the form of man, and those who have been deceived by him and worshipped him as their god consider his fallen and lowly condition. Nevertheless, he will not be robbed of all his power. Like a wounded snake, he will still be dangerous and vengeful. We read in Revelation 12:12:

> • *Therefore rejoice, ye heavens, and ye that dwell in them. Woe to the inhabiters of the earth and of the sea! for the devil is come down unto you, having great wrath, because he knoweth that he hath but a short time (Rev 12:12).*

We read the corresponding warning given in Daniel 12:1: and there shall be a time of trouble, such as never was since there was a nation even to that same time. And the Lord Jesus Christ said of this last three and a half years of the Tribulation in Matthew 24:21: For then shall be great tribulation, such as was not since the beginning of the world to this time, no, nor ever shall be. (pp. 281 - 285).

This will be the first judgement since the Flood that will be world-wide. This will be one sense in which it will be as it was in the days of Noah (Lk 17:26).

> • *Fear, and the pit, and the snare, are upon thee, **O inhabitant of the earth**. And it shall come to pass, that he who fleeth from the noise of the fear shall fall into the pit; and he that cometh up out of the midst of the pit shall be taken in the snare: for the windows from on high are open, and the foundations of **the earth** do shake. **The earth** is utterly broken down, **the earth** is clean dissolved, **the earth** is moved exceedingly. **The earth** shall reel to and fro like a drunkard, and shall be removed like a cottage; and the transgression thereof shall be heavy upon it; and it shall fall, and not rise again (Isa 24:17-20).*

Five Distinguishing Marks of the Remnant During the Great Tribulation

ONE. The Distinguishing Deliverance: ***and at that time thy people shall be delivered, every one that shall be found written in the book*** (12:1). There are a number of contrasting statements concerning the deliverance and salvation of the Jewish People during the Tribulation. These ultimately focus upon the believing remnant.

> • *For I would not, brethren, that ye should be ignorant of this mystery, lest ye should be wise in your own conceits; that **blindness in part is happened to Israel**, until the fulness of the Gentiles be come in. And so **all Israel shall be saved**: as it is written, There shall come out of Sion the Deliverer, and shall turn away ungodliness from Jacob (Rom 11:25,26).*

> • *And it shall come to pass, that in all the land, saith the LORD, **two parts therein shall be cut off and die; but the third shall be left therein**. And **I will bring the third part through the fire**, and will refine them as silver is refined, and will try them as gold is tried: they shall call on my name, and I will hear them: I will say, It is my people: and they shall say, The LORD is my God (Zech 13:8,9).*

> • *For I will gather all nations against Jerusalem to battle; and the city shall be taken, and the houses rifled, and the women ravished; and **half of the city shall go forth into captivity**, and **the residue of the people shall not be cut off** from the city (Zech 14:2).*

> • And I will bring you into the wilderness of the people, and there will I plead with you face to face. Like as I pleaded with your fathers in the wilderness of the land of Egypt, so will I plead with you, saith the Lord GOD. And **I will cause you to pass under the rod**, and I will bring you into the bond of the covenant: And **I will purge out from among you the rebels**, and them that transgress against me: I will bring them forth out of the country where they sojourn, and they shall not enter into the land of Israel: and ye shall know that I am the LORD (Ezek 20:35-38).

Note especially the Prophet Malachi's mention of *the Book of Remembrance* for the remnant of Israel and then the immediately following description of the Great Tribulation.

> • Then they that feared the LORD spake often one to another: and the LORD hearkened, and heard it, and **a book of remembrance was written before him for them that feared the LORD**, and that thought upon his name. And they shall be mine, saith the LORD of hosts, in that day when I make up my jewels; and I will spare them, as a man spareth his own son that serveth him. Then shall ye return, and discern between the righteous and the wicked, between him that serveth God and him that serveth him not (Mal 3:16-18).

> • For, behold, **the day cometh, that shall burn as an oven**; and all the proud, yea, and all that do wickedly, shall be stubble: and the day that cometh shall burn them up, saith the LORD of hosts, that it shall leave them neither root nor branch. **But unto you that fear my name shall the Sun of righteousness arise with healing in his wings**; and ye shall go forth, and grow up as calves of the stall (Mal 4:1,2).

TWO. The Distinguishing Resurrection. *And many of them that sleep in the dust of the earth shall awake, some to everlasting life, and some to shame and everlasting contempt* (12:2). Hutchings writes:

> "The resurrection of the Church is not in view here, because the Rapture of the church will have already occurred. There is no evidence that the Church will go through the Tribulation. Every saved person of the dispensation of grace will be resurrected before the Tribulation begins. Daniel was not concerned about the Gentiles; he was concerned only about his people. The resurrection described by the Lord in this scripture relates only to Israel. It in no way teaches a general resurrection. Some of Israel will be raised to everlasting life, and some of Israel will be raised to everlasting shame and contempt.

> The resurrection of the redeemed of Israel is always associated with the appearance of the Messiah to bring in the Kingdom. Israel's impotent plight back in their own land, their flight into the wilderness from Antichrist, the coming of the Lord, and the resurrection of the righteous are put in proper perspective in Isaiah 26.

> • We have been with child, we have been in pain, we have as it were brought forth wind; we have not wrought any deliverance in the earth; neither have the inhabitants of the world fallen. Thy dead men shall live, together with my dead body shall they arise. Awake and sing, ye that dwell in dust .for thy dew is as the dew of herbs, and the earth shall cast out the dead. Come, my people, enter thou into thy chambers, and shut thy doors about thee: hide thyself as it were for a little moment, until the indignation be overpast. For, behold, the LORD cometh out of his place to punish the inhabitants of the earth for their iniquity…(26:18-21).

> Some believe that both the saved and lost of Israel will be raised at this time; however, this would be in contradiction of Revelation 20:5-6: But the rest of the dead lived not again until the thousand years were finished. This is the first resurrection. Blessed and holy is he that hath part in the first resurrection: on such the second death hath no power. . . Some contend that the resurrection of Daniel 12:2 pertains only to a spiritual resurrection of Israel, but we believe there are too many scriptures connecting the hope of resurrection of redeemed Israel to the coming of the Lord to believe that it relates only to a spiritual rebirth. Certainly, there will be a spiritual rebirth of Israel at this time, but there will also be a literal resurrection." (pp. 285-287).

This resurrection of Israel (Hos 13:14-16) will constitute one of the orders, or stages, of the first resurrection to life (1 Cor 15:23). Those orders, or stages, of the first resurrection

DANIEL 12. THE CHARACTER AND TIMES OF THE GREAT TRIBULATION

are Christ's resurrection (1 Cor 15:20), followed by a token resurrection (Matt 27:52-53), then the still future resurrection of the church prior to the Tribulation (1 Cor 15:24), and of Old Testament saints and Tribulation martyrs after the Tribulation period (referred to in this passage and in Rev 20:4-6). (see *Unger's OT Commentary*).

THREE. The Distinguishing Brightness. *And they that be wise shall shine as the brightness of the firmament; and they that turn many to righteousness as the stars for ever and ever* (12:3). Hutchings continues:

> "This wonderful promise has often been applied to soul-winning Christians, and it does apply to them indirectly, because all who win souls to Jesus Christ are wise and they will receive the most cherished of all rewards. However, this promise is made directly to those who wins souls during the Tribulation, and particularly to the 144,000 witnesses of God. We read in Revelation 7:1-8 that twelve thousand out of each of the twelve tribes of Israel will be called to be soul winners during the Tribulation. Their ministry will be the most difficult of all of God's servants who preceded them. They will witness children dying by the thousands of famine; they will witness sin and abominations on earth the likes of which men have never committed; and they will witness millions beheaded by the guillotine because they refuse to worship the Beast and receive his mark. Yet they will go throughout the world testifying that Jesus is the Christ and calling sinners to have their sins washed in His blood. After describing the 144,000 in Revelation 7:1-8, we read of their converts in verses 9-17."

> • *After this I beheld, and, lo, a great multitude, which no man could number, of all nations, and kindreds, and people, and tongues, stood before the throne, and before the Lamb, clothed with white robes, and palms in their hands; And cried with a loud voice, saying, Salvation to our God which sitteth upon the throne, and unto the Lamb (Rev 7:9,10).*

> • *And one of the elders answered, saying unto me, What are these which are arrayed in white robes? and whence came they? And I said unto him, Sir, thou knowest. And he said to me, These are they which came out of great tribulation, and have washed their robes, and made them white in the blood of the Lamb (Rev 7:13,14).*

FOUR. The Distinguishing Preservation. *But thou, O Daniel, shut up the words, and seal the book, even to the time of the end: many shall run to and fro, and knowledge shall be increased* (12:4). This *shutting up* and *sealing* refers to the preservation of the Book of Daniel. True believers will recognize this. All of Scripture is given verbally by inspiration, and all of Scripture is verbally preserved across the centuries (2 Kng 10:10; Psa 12:6,7; 100:5;119:89; 119: 140; 119:152; 119:160; Prov 30:5; Isa 40:8; 55:11; Matt 5:18; 24:35; Lk 16:17; Jhn 10:35; I Pet 1:23;1:25). The Book of Daniel has been a special object of Satan's attack. Thus there is the special emphasis that Daniel must *shut up the words, and seal the book, even to the time of the end.* He must put it in a place of *safe keeping*.

To *seal* the words can, depending on the context, also mean to "not understand", or to "keep from being understood" (Rev 20:10). Here it is clearly that Daniel is being told to make certain that the Book is kept in a safe place, rather than to "make certain that no one understands the Book"!

To say that the Book of Daniel will be sealed in the sense of not being understood until the time of the end, misses the point of the basic message of the Book. The primary message of both Daniel and Revelation is that the Messiah will come to reign on the earth (2:31-35; 7:9-14; 8:25; 9:24-27). The message further describes the tumultuous events that will accompany Christ's coming to earth. There is nothing "sealed" about this; it could and can be understood in any generation. As Hutchings says,

> "Christ did not consider it a sealed book and He referred to a portion of Daniel's prophecy in the Olivet Discourse. The Jewish historian Josephus had no difficulty in interpreting the prophecies of Daniel which had been fulfilled up to the time of the

> destruction of the Temple in 70 AD. Therefore, when our Lord instructed Daniel to seal up the book to the time of the end, it is evident that He did not mean that... no one could understand it until the last half of the Tribulation."

The fact that so many did not understand Daniel across the centuries was not that it could not be understood, but rather the intrusion and acceptance of three blatantly false beliefs:

(1) Bible prophecy is not to be interpreted literally.

(2) Christ will not literally and visibly reign on the earth.

(3) There is no national future for Israel. The many promises that state that there will be are fulfilled in a spiritual and symbolical sense by the Church or individual Christians.

<u>FIVE. The Distinguishing Perseverance</u>. ***But thou, O Daniel, shut up the words, and seal the book, even to the time of the end: many shall run to and fro, and knowledge shall be increased*** (12:4). Taken at face value, the passage states plainly that at the *time of the end* (at which time the words of the Book of Daniel will maintain their preservation) *many shall run to and fro, and knowledge shall be increased*. Both of these statements have a negative connotation. To **run to and fro** speaks of restlessness, agitation, a lack of direction and purpose in the life. It is the opposite of: *Be still and know that I am God* (Psa 46:10). It is also likened to -

> • *Behold, the days come, saith the Lord GOD, that I will send a famine in the land, not a famine of bread, nor a thirst for water, but of hearing the words of the LORD: And they shall wander from sea to sea, and from the north even to the east, they shall run to and fro to seek the word of the LORD, and shall not find it (Amos 8:11,12).*

Related to this is an ***increase in knowledge***. Glaringly obvious in this phrase is the absence of *the LORD*! It is an increase in *knowledge* where God is not *acknowledged*.

> • *The fear of the LORD is the beginning of wisdom: and the knowledge of the holy is understanding (Prov 9:10).*

> • *The wicked, through the pride of his countenance, will not seek after God: God is not in all his thoughts (Psa 10:4).*

It is a worldly wise, God ignoring, God denying kind of knowledge. It is a plugged into everything but the LORD kind of knowledge. The righteous will not be distracted or drawn off course by the world's restless quest after broken cisterns that can hold no water (Jer 2:13). There will be a distinguishing perseverance that *presses toward the mark for the prize of the high calling of God in Christ Jesus* (Phil 3:14).

The first four verses of this concluding chapter of Daniel deal with the character of the Great Tribulation and the character of those who stand during that terrible time. The last nine verses deal with the time that is involved for those terrible days to reach their conclusion. These final nine verses are divided between two questions that are asked.

1. The Question of the Angels: *How long shall it be to the end of these wonders?* 12:5-7

2. The Question of Daniel: What shall the end be of these things? 12:8-13

The Question of the Angels: ***How long shall it be to the end of these wonders?*** **12:5-7**

> *Then I Daniel looked, and, behold, there stood other two, the one on this side of the bank of the river, and the other on that side of the bank of the river. (12:6) And one said to the man clothed in linen, which was upon the waters of the river, How long shall it be to the end of these wonders? (12:7) And I heard the man clothed in linen, which was*

DANIEL 12. THE CHARACTER AND TIMES OF THE GREAT TRIBULATION

> *upon the waters of the river, when he held up his right hand and his left hand unto heaven, and sware by him that liveth for ever that it shall be for a time, times, and an half; and when he shall have accomplished to scatter the power of the holy people, all these things shall be finished.*

<u>The Angels and the River</u>. ***Then I Daniel looked, and, behold, there stood other two, the one on this side of the bank of the river, and the other on that side of the bank of the river*** (12:5). The final prophecy and vision closes as it began. It is a vision of the Messiah and attending angels (10:4,16). He then saw two celestial persons, one on one bank and the other on the other bank of the river, Hiddekel (Tigris). Significantly, Daniel employed the word for ***river*** (*ye'or*), the common designation of the Nile River. This would call to mind the Egyptian bondage and deliverance and that the same Lord stands ready to rescue His people once again from wicked world power.

<u>The Messiah and the Question</u>. ***And one said to the man clothed in linen, which was upon the waters of the river, How long shall it be to the end of these wonders*** (12:6)? One of the persons (8:16) said to *the man clothed in linen* (10:5; Ezek. 9:2) is the preincarnate Christ. His glorious Deity was described in Chapter 10 and here further indicated by central position upon the waters.

> • *Then I lifted up mine eyes, and looked, and behold a certain man clothed in linen, whose loins were girded with fine gold of Uphaz: His body also was like the beryl, and his face as the appearance of lightning, and his eyes as lamps of fire, and his arms and his feet like in colour to polished brass, and the voice of his words like the voice of a multitude (10:5,6).*

To the Messiah one of the angels calls out: *How long shall it be to the end of these wonders?* This is a question a *saint talking to another saint* asked (Dan 8:13); and Daniel asked (12:8); and the Disciples asked (Matt 24:3; Mk 13:4).

<u>The Affirmation and the Answer</u>.

<u>The Affirmation</u>. ***And I heard the man clothed in linen, which was upon the waters of the river, when he held up his right hand and his left hand unto heaven, and sware by him that liveth for ever*** (12:7). "The preincarnate Christ, in theophanic manifestation as an angel, raised his right hand and his left toward heaven, and swore by Him who lives forever (Ezek 20:5; cp. Rev 10:5,6). Here God swears by Himself (Gen 22:16), because He could swear by no greater (Heb 6:13), a most solemn oath, the solemnity of which is emphasized by both hands being raised, whereas normally only one hand was raised (cf. Gen 14:22; Deut 32:40)." (Unger).

<u>The Answer</u>: ***that it shall be for a time, times, and an half; and when he shall have accomplished to scatter the power of the holy people, all these things shall be finished***. (Dan 7:25; Rev 12:14; a year, two years and a half; i.e. three and a half years. This oath of such an extremely solemn nature is directed against the Antichrist during the last and most terrible of Israel's sufferings, and limits his God-allowed power for the period of three and one-half years duration (Dan 7:25; Rev 11:2,3; 12:6,14; 13:5).

These time periods do not indicate in any way the duration from Daniel's day to the Return of Christ; they are limited solely the Great Tribulation. Note also that while the Tribulation will last for seven years and be divided into two halves (Dan 9:26,27), these time periods (1260 days; 42 months; time, times, half a time) all relate to the second half. As will be shown in our notes on Revelation, it will be during this second half that we have the ministry of the 144,000 and Two Witnesses.

<u>The Question of Daniel: *What shall the end be of these things*? 12:8-13.</u>

And I heard, but I understood not: then said I, O my Lord, what shall be the end of these things? (12:9) And he said, Go thy way, Daniel: for the words are closed up and sealed till the time of the end. (12:10) Many shall be purified, and made white, and tried; but the wicked shall do wickedly: and none of the wicked shall understand; but the wise shall understand. (12:11) And from the time that the daily sacrifice shall be taken away, and the abomination that maketh desolate set up, there shall be a thousand two hundred and ninety days. (12:12) Blessed is he that waiteth, and cometh to the thousand three hundred and five and thirty days. (12:13) But go thou thy way till the end be: for thou shalt rest, and stand in thy lot at the end of the days.

The Enquiry. ***And I heard, but I understood not: then said I, O my Lord, what shall be the end of these things*** (12:8)? **At the beginning of the prophecy in Chapter 10 Daniel pleaded** to be excused from further revelations, because he was terrified at those things which were to come upon his nation. But at the conclusion of the revelation, he greatly desired to be shown more. Daniel's questions are an example of what we read in First Peter of how the OT prophets sought further light concerning the prophecies given them.

> • *Of which salvation the prophets have **enquired and searched diligently**, who prophesied of the grace that should come unto you: Searching what, or what manner of time the Spirit of Christ which was in them did signify, when it testified beforehand the sufferings of Christ, and the glory that should follow (1 Pet 1:10,11).*

The First: *Go thy way*.

Concerning the Words. ***And he said, Go thy way, Daniel: for the words are closed up and sealed till the time of the end*** (12:9). We may be assured that the two, *Go thy ways,* of this closing section are to let Daniel know that he is *homeward bound*. This final prophetic section given in the third year of the reign of Cyrus (10:1) brings us not only to the end of the Book of Daniel but to the long earthly sojourn of Daniel's life. Though the Prophet is leaving, the Prophecy will remain and be ***sealed*** (preserved) unto the time of the Great Tribulation. It may be read and understood across the ages, but as for its fulfilment it is ***shut up*** until the end of the age. Any attempt to "manufacture" a fulfilment before the events attending Christ's Return are doomed to failure. Compare the following.

> • *And in those times there shall many stand up against the king of the south: also **the robbers of thy people shall exalt themselves to establish the vision; but they shall fall** (Dan 11:14).*

Concerning the Righteous and the Wicked. ***Many shall be purified, and made white, and tried; but the wicked shall do wickedly: and none of the wicked shall understand; but the wise shall understand*** (12:10). The last three and one half years of the Tribulation will bring out the very best and the worst in people. The contrast could not be greater.

> • ***I will make a man more precious than fine gold***; *even a man than the golden wedge of Ophir* (Isa 13:12).

> • *And **men were scorched with great heat, and blasphemed the name of God**, which hath power over these plagues: and they repented not to give him glory* (Rev 16:9).

> • ***Why do the heathen rage***, *and the people imagine a vain thing? The kings of the earth set themselves, and the rulers take counsel together, against the LORD, and against his anointed, saying, Let us break their bands asunder, and cast away their cords from us* (Psa 2:1-3).

Concerning the Time Durations. ***And from the time that the daily sacrifice shall be taken away, and the abomination that maketh desolate set up, there shall be a thousand two hundred and ninety days. Blessed is he that waiteth, and cometh to the thousand three hundred and five and thirty days*** (12:11,12). In verses 11 and 12 further revelations are given,

DANIEL 12. THE CHARACTER AND TIMES OF THE GREAT TRIBULATION

especially for the benefit of the Jewish remnant, which in that future time will be passing through the Great Tribulation and awaiting the Kingdom, to clarify for them the duration of *the time of the end* (12:8,9). Here to the usually stated period of 1260 days for the second half of the Tribulation are added periods of 30 and 45 days (cp. Dan 7:25; Rev 11:2,3; 12:6,14; 13:5).

The 1,260 days (42 months of 30 days each) is the period from the time when the Antichrist breaks His covenant with Israel unto Christ's Second Advent and the conclusion of Daniel's Seventieth Week (of years. That climactic event will be followed by divine judgments purging out the wicked beast-worshipers, both of Israel (Ezek 20:34-38; Matt. 25:1-13) and the nations (Joel 3:1-16; Zech. 6:1-8; Matt 25:31-46).

Those judgments will take time. It may be surmised that by the time 1,335 days have passed (75 days after the Second Coming), those great judgments will have been completed and the Millennial Kingdom formally set up. Those who attain to that period (Matt 24:13) are plainly those who have been termed blessed, because they have been judged worthy to enter the Kingdom. They will manifest their saving faith in that they will keep waiting for the Lord (Isa 30:18) and reach the end of the period of suffering and persecution (Rev 11:2; 12:6; 13:5) and enter full Kingdom blessing.

Note, that as no man knoweth the day or the hour of the Lord's Return, Christ must come before the Tribulation, for during the Tribulation believers will be able to determine the time of the Lord's Return

* *Watch therefore, for ye know neither the day nor the hour wherein the Son of man cometh (Matt 25:13).*

The Second: *Go thy way*. **But go thou thy way till the end be: for thou shalt rest, and stand in thy lot at the end of the days** (12:13). Like his fellow Israelites, Daniel was patiently and confidently to await the ultimate blessing in the Kingdom, to which all his prophecies pointed in their ultimate purview. He was to set his vision beyond the persecution and suffering of his people, Israel, which was looming like a dark cloud and reaching over many centuries, and lift up his eyes to behold the bright millennial day that would dawn after the fiercest and blackest storm of the Great Tribulation was over.

Daniel would have to wait until the church saints would be brought in, at the first resurrection, *God having provided some better thing for us*, that he and other Old Testament believers, *without us should not be made perfect* (Heb 11:39,40). He would then **stand in his lot**, rise in resurrection (12:2) and participate in the glorious triumph of the Messiah-Christ as the Kingdom is set up.

This concluding revelation of Daniel's prophecy, acting as a capstone on all the preceding revelations, establishes the book of Daniel as the greatest and most comprehensive prophetic revelation of the Old Testament. The book forms an indispensable introduction to its New Testament counterpart, the Book of the Revelation, and is the key to its interpretation.

Little wonder the book of Daniel, being of such vast importance in revealing God's sovereign plans for Israel and the nations, as well as the sinister working of evil supernatural forces behind the scenes to thwart that plan (Dan. 10:13), has been the target of satanic attack and the battleground between faith and unbelief during the ages. (from Unger, and quoting Walvoord p. 1697).

We will let Noah Hutchings in his usual thought provoking way have a final word in this commentary. Regarding the extra days mentioned above and with which the Book of Daniel ends he writes:

> We assume the extra days will be required to regather the Jews. The angels are to go into all the nations of the world and bring back all the twelve tribes to the Land. There will not be an Israelite left in any Gentile nation. We read in Mark 13:26,27: And then shall they see the Son of man coming in the clouds with great power and glory. And then shall he send his angels, and shall gather together his elect from the four winds, from the uttermost part of the earth to the uttermost part of heaven. And we read in other Scriptures that the Lord will bring them back from all nations. In verse ten is it indicated that regardless of their spiritual states, both righteous and wicked will be gathered back into the Land [as Ezekiel 20:33-44 describes]. (pp. 295,296).

But as great and comprehensive as the Book of Daniel is, it is incomplete without its New Testament counterpart ...*The Book of Revelation.*

ABOUT THE AUTHOR

Dr. J. A. Moorman and his wife, Dot. 2017

Jack A. Moorman studied for a while at the Indianapolis campus of Purdue University, attended briefly Indiana Bible College, and graduated from Tennessee Temple Bible School. He has been with Baptist International Missions Inc. (BIMI) since 1967 and has been involved in church planting, Bible Institute teaching and extensive distribution of Scriptures and gospel tracts in Johannesburg, South Africa from 1968 – 1988, and in England and London since 1988. He married his wife, Dot, on November 22 1963.

J.A. Moorman has written the following scholarly books defending the King James Bible and the Hebrew, Aramaic and Greek words that underlie it:

1. When the KJV Departs from the "Majority Text".
2. Early Manuscripts, Church Fathers, and the Authorized Version.
3. Forever Settled
4. Missing in Modern Bibles—The Old Heresy Revived.
5. Samuel P. Tregelles—The Man Who Made the Critical Text Acceptable to Bible Believers.
6. 8,000 Differences Between the Textus Receptus and the Critical Text.
7. Bible Chronology: The Two Great Divides.
8. The Biblical and Observational Case for Geocentricity.

These well-documented works and are replete with evidence which he has gleaned from his own resources as well as references found in the British Museum, British Library and other libraries in South Africa and the United Kingdom.

He has been the pastor of Bethel Baptist Church in London, England since 1993. A great deal of his time, and on a nearly daily basis, is spent in distributing Gospel Literature on the crowded streets of London and beyond. May God bless his unfailing service to the Lord Jesus Christ.

www.ingramcontent.com/pod-product-compliance
Lightning Source LLC
Chambersburg PA
CBHW080916230426

43668CB00014B/2137